Annual R(
of Irish Law 2001

Raymond Byrne
B.C.L., LL.M., Barrister-at-Law
Lecturer in Law, Dublin City University

William Binchy
B.A., B.C.L., LL.M., F.T.C.D., Barrister-at-Law
Regius Professor of Laws, Trinity College, Dublin

Thomson Round Hall
2002

Published in 2002 by
Round Hall Sweet & Maxwell
43 Fitzwilliam Place,
Dublin 2, Ireland.

Typeset by
Gough Typesetting Services, Dublin.

Printed by
MPG Cornwall.

ISBN 1-85800-315-6

A catalogue record for this book
is available from the British Library.

Table of Contents

Preface

In this fifteenth volume in the Annual Review series, our purpose continues to be to provide a review of legal developments, judicial and statutory, that occurred in 2001. In terms of case law, this includes those judgments which were delivered in 2001, regardless of whether they have been (or will be) reported and which were circulated up to the date of this preface. In terms of legislation, we endeavour to discuss those Acts and statutory instruments enacted and made during the year. Once again it is a pleasure to thank those who made the task of completing this volume less onerous.

For this fifteenth volume of the Annual Review series, the authors are delighted to have had the benefit of specialist contributions on Agriculture and Food Law, Contract Law, Defence Forces, Environmental Law, Equity, Evidence, Human Rights, Information Law, Planning Law, Practice and Procedure, Restitution and Social Welfare included in this volume. The authors continue to take final responsibility for the overall text as in the past, but are especially grateful for the contributions of Raymond O'Rourke in Agriculture and Food Law, Eoin O'Dell in Contract Law and Restitution, Ciaran Craven and Gerard Humphries in Defence Forces, Yvonne Scannell in Environmental Law, Hilary Delany in Equity and Practice and Procedure, Declan McGrath in Evidence, Rosemary Byrne in Human Rights, Estelle Feldman in Information Law and Gerry Whyte in Social Welfare.

Finally, we are very grateful to Round Hall Sweet & Maxwell, in particular David McCartney, and to Gilbert Gough, whose professionalism ensures the continued production of this series.

Raymond Byrne and William Binchy,
Dublin

October 2002

Preface

Table of Cases

IRELAND

ENGLISH AND COMMONWEALTH CASES

EUROPEAN CASES AND DECISIONS

UNITED STATES OF AMERICA

Table of Legislation

STATUTORY INSTRUMENTS

EUROPEAN CONVENTIONS AND TREATIES

ENGLAND

Administrative Law

APPROPRIATION

The Appropriation Act 2001 provided as follows. For the year ended December 31, 2001, the amount of supply grants in accordance with the Central Fund (Permanent Provisions) Act 1965 was £20,362,692,000. Under the Public Accounts and Charges Act 1891, the sum for appropriations-in-aid was £1,802,444,000. The 2001 Act also provided that the financial resolutions passed by Dáil Éireann on December 5, 2001 (after the 2001 Budget), which dealt with changes in the taxation of life assurance policyholders, excise duties on fuels, tobacco and in VAT, would have legal effect provided that, in accordance with section 4 of the Provisional Collection of Taxes Act 1927, legislation was enacted in 2002 (in the Finance Act 2002) to give full effect to the resolutions. The 2001 Act came into effect on its signature by the President on December 20, 2001.

JUDICIAL REVIEW

The case law under Order 84 of the Rules of the Superior Courts 1986 is discussed in the various chapters in the Annual Review where the substantive subjects arising are detailed, notably in the Planning Law chapter. Further reference may also be obtained through the Table of Statutory Instruments under the entry for the Rules of the Superior Courts 1986.

OIREACHTAS AND OTHER PUBLIC OFFICES

Allowances and salaries: general   The Ministerial, Parliamentary and Judicial Offices and Oireachtas Members (Miscellaneous Provisions) Act 2001 amended the Ministerial and Parliamentary Offices Acts 1938 to 1998 and the Oireachtas (Allowances to Members) Act 1938. Its purpose was to amend the arrangements for remuneration, allowances and superannuation payable to and in respect of certain holders and former holders of ministerial, parliamentary and judicial offices. It also provided for the transfer of previous pensionable service of persons who hold such offices. The Members of the Oireachtas and Ministerial and Parliamentary Offices (Allowances And Salaries) (No.2) Order

2001 (S.I. No. 333 of 2001) increased the salaries of members of the Oireachtas and ministerial and parliamentary office holders with effect from July 1, 2001.

Party leader allowances   The Oireachtas (Ministerial and Parliamentary Offices) (Amendment) Act 2001 amended the Ministerial and Parliamentary Offices Act 1938 for the purposes of altering the payment of allowances to parliamentary leaders of qualifying parties within the Oireachtas.

Standards in Public Office Commission   The Standards in Public Office Act 2001 provides for the establishment of the Standards in Public Office Commission. Against the background of revelations in recent tribunals of inquiry concerning some politicians, the purpose of the Commission is to oversee ethical standards for members of the Oireachtas and other persons in senior public office. The Act provides for the furnishing of tax clearance certificates to that Commission by persons upon election to either House of the Oireachtas or upon appointment to judicial office or senior office.

RECORDS AND STATISTICS

Census of population   The Statistics (Census of Population) Order 2001 (S.I. No. 491 of 2001), made under the Statistics Act 1993 (*Annual Review of Irish Law 1993*, p.10), specified the information to be provided by householders and adult members of private households on census night, April 28, 2002. It also provided that the manager or person in charge of a communal establishment and the master or other person in charge of a vessel within the jurisdiction of the State are also required to provide the information specified. It also revoked the Statistics (Census of Population) Order 2000 (S.I. No. 395 of 2000), which had proposed to conduct a census in 2001, but which had to be postponed owing to the Foot and Mouth crisis (discussed in the Agriculture and Food chapter, 4, below).

Winter time   The Winter Time Order 2001 (S.I. No. 506 of 2001), made under the Standard Time (Amendment) Act 1971, gave effect to Directive 2000/84/EC. It varies, for 2002 onwards, the periods of winter-time and summer-time provided for in the 1971 Act.

STATE BODIES

ACC Bank   The ACC Bank Act 2001 provided for the privatisation of the ACC Bank plc: see the Commercial Law chapter, 22, below.

ESB   The Electricity (Supply) (Amendment) Act 2001 provided for the privatisation of the State electricity body, the Electricity Supply Board (ESB): see the Electricity and Energy Chapter, 242, below.

INPC The Irish National Petroleum Corporation Limited Act 2001 provided for the privatisation of the Irish National Petroleum Corporation Ltd (INPC): see the Electricity and Energy Chapter, 242, below.

Nítrigin Éireann Teoranta (NET) The Nítrigin Éireann Teoranta Act 2001 enables the Minister for Finance to discharge certain obligations of Nítrigin Éireann Teoranta. The 2001 Act repeals the Nítrigin Éireann Teoranta Acts 1963 to 1993. At the time of writing the Commencement Order required to bring the Act into effect had not been made.

TRIBUNAL OF INQUIRY

Obstruction of Tribunal of Inquiry The decision of Smyth J. in *Flood v. Lawlor*, High Court, January 15, 2001, in which the respondent, a member of Dail Éireann, was found guilty of contempt, is discussed in the Criminal law chapter, 180, below.

Agriculture and Food Law

RAYMOND O' ROURKE, Mason Hayes & Curran

AGRICULTURAL APPEALS

Agricultural Appeals Act 2001   The Act gives the Minister of Agriculture powers to appoint a Director of Agricultural Appeals and as many appeals officers as he/she sees fit. The functions of such officers shall be to consider and make determinations on appeals made by affected persons against decisions taken by Department of Agriculture officials in respect of various monetary entitlement schemes. The various entitlement schemes covered by the Act are set out in a Schedule and include the Beef Cow Scheme, Headage Payments, Ewe Premiums, Extensification Premiums, Suckler Cow Premiums, the Farm Improvement Programme, the Rural Environment Protection Scheme (REPs), the Early Retirement Scheme and Sheep Headage Scheme.

Appeal officers shall be independent in the performance of their functions. The Act gives persons powers to appeal any decision of the Department of Agriculture/Minister of Agriculture in relation to such payment schemes. An appeal officer, shall if requested by an appellant hold an oral hearing for the purposes of ascertaining the fullest amount of information about the particular case under appeal. The decision of the appeal officer and the reasons for making it shall be notified in writing to the appellant and will be final. Decisions may be revised in light of new evidence or new facts. Any person dissatisfied by the decision of an appeals officer may appeal the decision to the High Court on any question of law.

DISEASES OF ANIMALS

Diseases of Animal (Amendment) Act 2001   Section 3 of the 2001 Act amends section 29 of the Diseases of Animal Act 1966 regarding the position of cattle "dealers". "Dealers" are defined as persons who purchase an animal or poultry and sell/supply the animal or poultry to another person within 45 days. Under a sub-clause of section 3, the Minister is given powers to regulate the possession, purchase, sale or supply of animals and poultry for the purpose of preventing the outbreak or spread of an animal disease. It also gives the Minister powers to introduce an approval and registration system for "dealers" and "dealers" premises. The Act specifies that dealers purchasing live animals are not permitted to sell or supply the animal to another person for a period of 30 days and during this period they must hold the animal on their own land. In emergency situations, the Minister may relax these rules in order to move animals by means of a "permit to sell" system.

The courts are given powers under section 7 of the 2001 Act to forfeiture to the Minister any land, premises, vehicle, aircraft or container involved in the commission of an offence under section 4 of the 1966 Act. Additionally, section 8 of the 2001 Act specifies that any person convicted under section 4 of the 1966 Act may be disqualified from keeping, dealing, having charge or control of any animal or classes of animals. They can also be disqualified from the slaughter, manufacture, importation, preparation, handling, storage, transport, export, distribution, sale or supply of food intended for human consumption. Such a disqualification may be varied or discharged upon application to the Courts.

The Act amends section 17 of the 1966 Act by specifying that an "authorised officer" under the Act means:

"(a) an inspector of the Minister,
(b) any other officer of the Minister authorised for purposes of section 25(3),
(c) authorised officers under section 10 of Animal Remedies Act 1993 (S.I. No. 23 of 1993),
(d) any other officer appointed by the Minister."

Section 8(a) of the 2001 Act gives an "authorised officer" powers to enter and search a premises if he/she has reasonable grounds to suspect that an animal, poultry, a product, fodder or litter may be infected with a disease or come from an area infected with a disease. Any person who obstructs an "authorised officer" fulfilling duties under section 8(a) is guilty of an offence on summary conviction to a fine not exceeding £1,500 or imprisonment for six months or both and on indictment to a fine not exceeding £100,000 or imprisonment for five years or both.

Finally, section 10 of the 2001 Act introduces a new inference in relation to ear-tagging (if it has been tampered with) and animal identification (if the document has been forged or replaced with another form of identification). If either ear tags or animal identifications have been tampered with, then a person can infer in court that the animal in question was unlawfully brought into the State and should be destroyed.

Diseases of Animal Act   The Diseases of Animal Act 1966 (Approval and Registration of Dealers) Order 2001 (S.I. No. 79 of 2001) provides for the approval and registration of dealers in animals and poultry and their premises and it makes it illegal for a dealer to operate without such approval and registration. It regulates the operations of dealers and lays down their obligations and responsibilities in relation to the keeping of records and provision of information relating to their operations. It provides for the revocation or suspension of approval and registration of a dealer and/or his/her premises and also for refusal to approve or register a dealer or his/her premises. It makes it illegal for any person to buy from or sell to a dealer any animals or poultry unless the dealer is approved, registered and in possession of current approval numbers, i.e. a dealer approval number and a premises approval number. It also transposes into Irish Law Council Directive 97/12/EC, amending and updating Directive 64/432/EEC on health problems affecting intra-community trade, in so far as it relates to dealers in bovine animals and swine.

Foot and Mouth Disease   An outbreak of foot and mouth disease in the United Kingdom in February 2001 led to a raft of protective measures being introduced by the Irish Government as a means of maintaining Ireland's "disease-free" status. The following Regulations were introduced and included specific measures relating to the Cooley Peninsula, Co. Louth where a limited number of foot and mouth cases were detected in late February 2001.

The Foot and Mouth Disease (Hay, Straw and Peat and Moss Litter) Order 2001 (S.I. No. 49 of 2001) continues the prohibition on the importation of Hay, Straw and Peat Moss Litter (except for material of Northern Ireland origin imported across the land frontier) save under licence from the Minister of Agriculture, Food and Rural Development. The Foot and Mouth Disease (Prohibition of Exhibition and Sale of Animals) Order 2001 (S.I. No. 50 of 2001) prohibits the presentation of bovine, ovine, caprine or animals for exhibition or sale at livestock marts licensed under the Livestock Marts Act 1967, in order to prevent the spreading of foot and mouth disease. The Foot and Mouth Disease (Restriction of Import of Vehicles, Machinery and other equipment) Order 2001 (S.I. No. 51 of 2001) prohibits, except under licence, the importation of used agricultural or horticultural machinery which has been in Great Britain, The Channel Islands or The Isle or Man and any vehicle or container which has been used to transport or contain any animal and which has been in Great Britain, The Channel Islands or The Isle or Man to prevent the spreading of Foot and Mouth Disease. The Foot and Mouth Disease (Restriction of Import of Horses and Greyhounds) Order 2001 (S.I. No. 52 of 2001) restricts the importation of horses or greyhounds from Great Britain, The Channel Islands or the Isle of Man to prevent the spreading of Foot and Mouth Disease.

The European Communities (Import Restrictions (Foot and Mouth Disease)) Regulations 2001 (S.I. No. 55 of 2001) implement restrictions on imports from the United Kingdom of certain animals and animal products in accordance with Commission Decision 2001/145/EC concerning certain protection measures with regard to foot and mouth disease in the United Kingdom. The Diseases of Animals (Restriction of Movement of Animals) Order 2001 (S.I. No. 56 of 2001) prohibits the transport by road of any cattle, sheep, swine or pigs or any other cloven-footed animals except under permit. Animals, while in transit, must be accompanied by the permit. The Foot and Mouth (Restriction on Movement) Order 2001 (S.I. No. 59 of 2001) restricts the movement of animals in a controlled area (Cooley Peninsula, Co. Louth). The Foot and Mouth (Restriction on Movement) (No.2) Order 2001 (S.I. No. 60 of 2001) restricts the movement of poultry in a controlled area. The Diseases of Animals (Restriction of Movement of Animals) (Amendment) Order 2001 (S.I. No. 61 of 2001) amends the Diseases of Animals (Restriction of Movement of Animals) Order 2001. The effect of the amendment is (a) to delete the commencing date of March 6, 2001 in relation to the movement of animals directly to slaughter only by permit issued by the Minister for Agriculture, Food and Rural Development under the Diseases of Animals Act 1966, and (b) to enable an animal-movement permit issued under the Act other than that issued under (S.I. No. 56 to be used for the movement of animals to slaughter or any other destination. The Foot and Mouth (Restriction on Movement) (No.3) Order 2001 (S.I. No. 62 of 2001) restricts movement of animals and produce in a controlled area. The Foot and Mouth (Restriction on Movement of Horses) Order 2001 (S.I. No. 68 of 2001) restricts the transport of horses save under permit to prevent the spreading of foot and mouth diseases. The Foot and Mouth Disease (Restriction of Import of Horses and Greyhounds) (Amendment) Order 2001 (S.I. No. 70 of 2001) amends the Foot and Mouth Disease (Restriction of Import of Horses and Greyhounds) Order 2001 (S.I. No. 52 of 2001) by extending the restriction on the importation of horses or greyhounds from the United Kingdom, the Channel Islands or the Isle of Man to prevent the spreading of foot and mouth disease. The Diseases of Animal Act 1966 (Prohibition in respect of certain Imported Horses, Greyhounds, Machinery, Vehicles and Equipment) Order 2001 (S.I. No. 81 of 2001) makes the possession of illegally imported horses, greyhounds, machinery, vehicles and equipment an offence. The Diseases of Animal Act 1966 (Foot and Mouth Disease) (Import Restrictions) Order 2001 (S.I. No. 82 of 2001) implements the previsions of Commission Decisions 2001\172\EC and 2001\190\EEC concerning certain protection measures with regard to foot and mouth disease in the UK. The Diseases of Animal Act 1966 (Foot and Mouth Disease) (Import restrictions) Order 2001 (S.I. No. 83 of 2001) implements the previsions of Commissions Decision 2001\208\EC concerning certain protection measures with regard to foot and mouth disease in France. The Diseases of Animals Act 1966 (Foot and Mouth Disease) (Import Restrictions) Orders 2001 (S.I. Nos. 108, 110, 502 of 2001) implement the provisions of Commission Decisions concerning certain protection measures with regard to foot and mouth disease in Netherlands, Ireland, Spain.

The Foot and Mouth Disease (Prohibition on the Use of Swill) Order 2001 (S.I. No. 104 of 2001) prohibits the feeding of swill to cattle, pigs, goats, deer, sheep other cloven hoofed animals or poultry. The Order remains in force until December 31, 2001. The Diseases of Animal Act 1966 (Foot and Mouth

Disease) (Import Restrictions) (No.2) (Amendment) Order 2001 (S.I. No. 107 of 2001) provides for the certification of horses being imported or exported to another Member State. The Foot and Mouth Disease (Restriction of Import of Horses and Greyhounds) (No.2) (Amendment) Order 2001 (S.I. No. 109 of 2001) extends the prohibition on import of horses and greyhounds without a licence, to horses and greyhounds from the Netherlands. The European Communities (Import Restrictions) (Foot and Mouth Disease) (Revocation) Regulations 2001 (S.I. No. 120 of 2001) prohibit the movement of bovine; ovine, caprine or any biungulates save under licence. These also revoke the Diseases of Animals (Restriction on Movement of Animals) Order 2001 (S.I. No. 56 of 2001), and the Diseases of Animals (Restriction of Movement of Animals) Order 2001 (S.I. No. 61 of 2001). The Diseases of Animal Act 1966 (Section 29A(4)) (No. 2) Order 2001 (S.I. No. 149 of 2001) prohibits for a period of two months from April 14, 2001 the movement of animals within 30 days of purchase save under permit. The Foot and Mouth (Temporary Restriction of Imports from Netherlands) Order 2001 (S.I. No. 151 of 2001) prohibits until April 19, 2001 the import of animals or produce from Northern Ireland except under and in accordance with a licence.

The Diseases of Animal Act 1966 (Miscellaneous Amendments and Revocations) Order 2001 (S.I. No. 152 of 2001) (a) removes restriction on certain imports from France imposed due to the foot and mouth disease situation; (b) removes the "protection zone" around Proleek, Co. Louth while retaining the wider "surveillance area"; (c) amends rules relating to movement of certain animals within the State; (d) amends rules relating to imports from the United Kingdom and the Netherlands. The Diseases of Animal Act 1966 (Foot and Mouth Disease) (Restriction on Movement of Persons) (S.I. No. 160 of 2001) Order 2001, came into operation on April 21, 2001; it prevents a person entering the State who, in the previous 21 days, has been in an agriculture related place or premises in either the United Kingdom or the Netherlands from entering onto such a place or premises and other places relating to processing of food animal origin for 21 days after arrival. The Diseases of Animal Act 1966 (Foot and Mouth Disease) (Restriction on Artificial Insemination) (Amendment) Order 2001 (S.I. No. 161 of 2001) prohibits artificial insemination until April 23, 2001 and from that date, permits artificial insemination only under licence. The Diseases of Animal Act 1966 (Foot and Mouth Disease) (Export and Movement Restrictions) (Revocation) Order 2001 (S.I. No. 166 of 2001) revokes The Diseases of Animal Act 1966 (Foot and Mouth Disease) Order 2001 (S.I. No. 110 of 2001). This order gives effect to Commission Decision No. 2001/234/EC of 22 March 2001 concerning certain protection measures with regard to Foot and Mouth Disease in Ireland. The Diseases of Animal Act 1966 (Foot and Mouth Disease) (Temporary Restriction on Sheep Shearing) Order 2001 (S.I. No. 196 of 2001) places restriction on sheep shearing until May 21, 2001.

The Diseases of Animal Act 1966 (Foot and Mouth Disease) (Export and

Import of Horses) (Amendment) Order 2001 (S.I. No. 197 of 2001) amends Diseases of Animals Act 1966 (Foot and Mouth Disease) (Export and Import of Horses) Order 2001 (S.I. No. 105 of 2001) (This Order provides for the certification of horses being imported from or exported to another Member State) to take account of the evolving foot and mouth disease situation in France. The Diseases of Animal Act 1966 (Foot and Mouth Disease) (Restriction on Movement of Horses) (Amendment) Order 2001 (S.I. No. 216 of 2001) bans the movement of horses imported from either the United Kingdom or the Netherlands save under licence. The Diseases of Animal Act 1966 (Foot and Mouth Disease) (Temporary Restriction on Sheep Shearing) (Amendment) Order 2001 (S.I. No. 217 of 2001) restricts sheep shearing until May 28, 2001. The Foot and Mouth Disease (Prohibition on the Use of Swill) (Amendment) Order 2001 (S.I. No. 227 of 2001) amends Foot and Mouth Disease (Prohibition on the Use of Swill) Order 2001 (S.I. No. 104 of 2001), to permit the feeding of swill containing certain non-animal products, to animals under stringent conditions. The Diseases of Animal Act 1966 (Foot and Mouth Disease) (Restriction on Imports from the Netherlands) (Amendment) Order 2001 (S.I. No. 233 of 2001) amends The Diseases of Animal Act 1966 (Foot and Mouth Disease) (Restriction on Imports from the Netherlands) Order 2001 (S.I. No. 210 of 2001) (This Order provides for restriction on imports from the Netherlands due to Foot and Mouth Situation in that country), to take account of the new Commission Decision regarding the Netherlands.

The Diseases of Animal Act 1966 (Foot and Mouth Disease) (Removal of Certain Import Restrictions) Order 2001 (S.I. No. 239 of 2001) removes the restriction on the import of (a) agricultural vehicles registered in Northern Ireland and (b) equipment, hay straw or peat moss litter of Northern Ireland origin imported into the State across the land frontier with Northern Ireland. The Foot and Mouth Disease (Prohibition of Exhibition and Sale of Animals) (Amendment) Order 2001 (S.I. No. 275 of 2001) permits the presentation of bovine animals for exhibition or sale at livestock marts licensed under the Livestock Marts Act 1967 from June 18, 2001. The Diseases of Animal Act 1966 (Foot and Mouth Disease) (Control on Artificial Insemination and Embryo Transfer in Sheep) Order 2001 (S.I. No. 381 of 2001) provides for licensing of Artificial Insemination and Embryo Transfer in sheep on the same basis as for cattle. The Diseases of Animal Act 1966 (Classical Swine Fever) (Restriction on Imports from Spain) (No.2) (Second Amendment) Order 2001 (S.I. No. 574 of 2001) implements restrictions on certain imports from designated areas of Spain due to the presence of Classical Swine Fever in that country.

Brucellosis in cattle   The Brucellosis in Cattle (General Provisions) (Amendment) Order (S.I. No. 229 of 2001) restricts the movement of bovine animals into or out of a holding restricted for Brucellosis except under and in accordance with the terms of a movement permit or in accordance with conditions laid down by a veterinary inspector. It requires a keeper ("Keeper" has the meaning assigned to it by the European Communities (Identification and Registration of Bovine Animals) Regulations, 1999 (S.I. No. 276 of 1999), whose holding has been declared a restricted holding, to display and maintain a health warning notice at or near each entrance to or exit from the holding for as long as the holding remains restricted. It also makes it illegal for a keeper to be in possession of or have under his control an animal whose ear tag has been interfered with or altered in any way except in accordance with the Order.

Examination of pig meat for trichinae upon importation from Third World countries The European Communities (Examination of Pig meat for Trichinae upon Importation from Third World Countries) Regulations 2001 (S.I. No. 464 of 2001) give effect to Directive 77/96/EEC which requires that pig meat imported from Third World countries be tested or appropriately treated to ensure that it is not contaminated with trichinae.

FEEDING STUFFS

Disposal, processing and placing on the market of animal by products The European Communities (Disposal, Processing and Placing on the Market of Animal By products) (Amendment) Regulations 2001 (S.I. No. 77 of 2001) amend the European Communities (Disposal, Processing and Placing on the Market of Animal by-products) Regulations 1994 (S.I. No. 257 of 1994) by setting out a revised list of animals excluded from entering the animal feed chain.

Putting into circulation of feed materials The European Communities (Putting into Circulation of Feed Materials) (Amendment) Regulations 2001 (S.I. No 170 of 2001) cover the putting into circulation and use of feed materials and give effect to European Parliament and Council Directive No. 2000/16/ EC (before: Council Directive No 96/25/EC of 29 April, 1996; Commission Directive 98/67/EC of 7 September 1998; Commission Directive 99/61/EC of 18 June 1999).

Marketing of compound feeding-stuffs The European Communities (Marketing of Compound Feeding-stuffs) (Amendment) Regulations 2001 (S.I. No. 171 of 2001) amend the European Communities (Marketing of Compound Feeding-stuffs) Regulations 2000 (S.I. No. 148 of 2000) so as to give effect to Council Directive 2000/16/EC.

Processed animal products The European Communities (Processed Animal Products) (Amendment) Regulations 2001 (S.I. No. 553 of 2001) amend the European Communities (Processed Animal Products) Regulations 2000 (S.I. No. 486 of 2000) so as to give effect to Commission Decision 2001/165/EC.

They also clarify certain provisions in the original Regulations in relation to eligibility for a licence. "Commission Decision" means Commission Decision 2001/9/EC of December, 29, 2000 providing for control measures required for the implementation of Council Decision 2000/766/EC concerning certain protection measures with regard to transmissible spongiform encephalopathies and the feeding of animal protein, as amended by Commission Decision 2001/165/EC of February 27, 2001.

Additives in animal nutrition   The European Communities (Guidelines for the Assessment of Additives in Animal Nutrition) (Amendment) Regulations 2001 (S.I. No. 556 of 2001) implement Council Directive 1990/90/EC of November 15, 1999 amending Council Directive 90/539/EEC, as amended by Council Directive 93/120/EEC of December 22, 1993 on animal health conditions governing intra-Community trade in and imports from Third World countries of poultry and hatching eggs.

Animal Nutrition Inspections   The European Communities (Animal Nutrition Inspections) (Amendment) Regulations 2001 (S.I. No. 655 of 2001) amend the European Communities (Animal Nutrition Inspections) Regulations 2000 (S.I No. 4 of 2000) so as to give effect to European Parliament and Council Directive 2000\77\EC. These establish a reliable harmonised procedure for the system of official inspections in the field of animal nutrition and improve the protective measures, which may be introduced.

FOODSTUFFS

Genetically modified organisms   The Genetically Modified Organisms (Contained Use) Regulations 2001 (S.I. No. 73 of 2001) give effect to Council Directive 90/219/EEC, as amended by Directive 98/81/EC, on the contained use of genetically modified micro-organisms. They replace Part II of the Genetically Modified Organisms Regulations 1994 (S.I. No. 345 of 1994) and all other provisions and Schedules of those Regulations which relate to contained use activities. The Environmental Protection Agency (EPA) is the competent authority for the purposes of the Regulations and it may consult the Advisory Committee on Genetically Modified Organisms (provided for in Part VI of the 1994 Regulations) on any aspect of its functions. Member States were given a delay of grace until October 23, 1991 "to bring into force the laws, regulations and administrative provisions necessary to comply into" with the Deliberate Release Directive (90/220/EEC). The first steps were not taken until the adoption of the Environmental Protection Agency Act 1992.The fundamental objective of the Regulations is to protect people and the environment from any adverse effect arising from the contained use of genetically modified organisms (GMOs). In this regard they provide for the application of various procedural matters to contained use activities. Part II provides specifically for regulation of the contained use of genetically modified micro-organisms (GMMs) and gives full effect to the EU Directives. Part III provides an updated framework for the regulation of all contained uses involving GMOs other than GMMs covered under Part II. Subject to limited exclusions in Parts II and III, all contained uses must comply with the Regulations. Proposed uses must be subjected to an environmental risk assessment, which must be submitted, or otherwise made available, to the EPA for evaluation. Proposed contained uses of GMMs, which fall into the moderate and high classes of risk, may not proceed without explicit consent from the Agency. As well as applying specific containment measures in each case, users of GMMs are required to apply principles of good microbiological practice, and good occupational safety hygiene, and users of GMOs are required, as appropriate, to apply good greenhouse, growth room or animal house practice. All users are required to keep appropriate records and to submit them, or otherwise make them available, to the EPA. Subject to limited confidentiality requirements, a register of all contained uses must be maintained by the EPA and made available to the general public. The Regulations include provisions for their enforcement by the EPA, including powers in Part V to prosecute offences, to obtain a High Court Order to prohibit or restrict an activity involving a contained use, or to serve a notice requiring a user to take specific measures which it regards as necessary for the protection of people and the environment. The Regulations came into effect on March 15, 2001.

Additives, colours and sweeteners   In the past, differences between national laws relating to food additives and the conditions for their use caused barriers to trade between Member States. A true single market could not exist without harmonised rules for the authorisation and the conditions for use of additives. With that in mind, in the late 1980s the European Union began the task of harmonising rules on the use of food additives, which can be seen as one of the major achievements of EU Food Law. The European Communities (Additives, Colours and Sweeteners in Foodstuffs) (Amendment) Regulations 2001 (S.I. No. 342 of 2001) amend the European Communities (Additives, Colours and Sweeteners in Foodstuffs) Regulations 2000 (S.I. No. 437 of 2000). These Regulations implement Commission Directive 2000/51/EC of July 26, 2000 amending Directive 95/31/EC laying down specific criteria of purity concerning sweeteners for use in foodstuffs. Purity criteria concern the specifications and analytical techniques for all approved additives. The European Communities (Purity Criteria on Food Additives other than Colours and Sweeteners) (Amendment) Regulations 2001 (S.I. No. 343 of 2001) amend the European Communities (Purity Criteria on Food Additives other than Colours and Sweeteners) (Amendment) Regulations 1998 (S.I. No. 541 of 1998). These Regulations implement Commission Directive 2000/63/EC which amends Commission Directive 96/77/EC laying down specific purity criteria on food additives other than colours and sweeteners as set out in Council Directive 95/2/EC. European Parliament and Council Directive 95/2/EC is the final part of the European Union's attempt to harmonise EU Food Law in relation to food additives. The Directive covers preservatives, antioxidants and other additives where national rules regarding their authorisation prevents the free movement of foodstuffs and affects the smooth functioning of the Internal Market.The Regulations replace the purity criteria already laid down for E320 (butylated hydroxyanisole) and establish new purity criteria for some categories of additives listed in Council Directive 95/2/EC in addition to those purity criteria already established in the Annex to Commission Directive 96/77/EC and Directive 98/86/EC.

Contaminants in foodstuffs The European Communities (Certain Contaminants in Foodstuffs) Regulations 2001 (S.I. No. 400 of 2001) give effect to European Commission Regulation 194/97 and Corrigenda, Commission Regulation 1525/98 of July 16, 1998, Commission Regulation 864/1999 of April 26, 1999, Commission Regulation 1566/1999 of July 16, 1999 and, with effect from April 5, 2002, Commission Regulation (EC) No. 466/2001 of March 8, 2001. The principal effect of these Regulations is to set maximum levels for certain contaminants in foodstuffs. The European Communities (Sampling Methods and the Methods of Analysis for the Official Control of the Levels of Certain Contaminants in Foodstuffs) Regulations 2001 (S.I. No. 401 of 2001) give effect to Commission Directive 98/53/EC of July 16, 1998 laying down the sampling methods of analysis for the official control of the levels of contaminants in foodstuffs and Commission Directive 2001/22/EC laying down the sampling methods and the methods of analysis for the official control of the levels of lead, cadmium, mercury and 3-MCPD in foodstuffs. The principal effect of these Regulations is to provide for the methods of sampling criteria and methods of analysis used for the official control of the levels of certain contaminants in foodstuffs in accordance with the criteria described in the Annexes of various Council and Commission Directives and Regulations cited.

Dietary Foods The European Communities (Dietary Foods for Special Medical Purposes) Regulations 2001 (S.I. No. 64 of 2001) give effect to Council Directive 89/398/EEC on the approximation of the laws of the Member States relating to foodstuffs intended for particular nutritional uses as amended by Directive 96/84/EC of the European Parliament and Council of June 7, 1999, and for the purposes of giving effect to Commission Directive 1999/21/EC of March 25, 1999 on dietary foods for special medical purposes, as amended by Corrigendum of January 5, 2000. The effect of these Regulations is to lay down compositional and labelling requirements, and general provisions for the sale in Ireland of dietary foods for special medical purposes. The 1985 White Paper on the Completion of the Internal Market indicated that national laws relating to foodstuffs for particular nutritional uses should be fully harmonised. Council Directive 77/94/EEC had approximated laws in this area but there were still problems in relation to the free movement of such foodstuffs throughout the Internal Market. This Directive presupposed that at a later stage the European Union would draw up a common definition for such foodstuffs in order to inform and protect the consumer better. The Commission therefore prepared a draft Directive in 1989, the framework Directive 89/398/EEC regarding these particular foodstuffs. The 1989 Directive covers foodstuffs the composition and preparation of which must be specially designed to meet the particular nutritional needs of the persons for whom they are mainly intended.

Case Law in relation to foodstuffs

Kelly v. Minister for Agriculture, **High Court, Butler J., May 1, 2001**   The plaintiff had been employed as a line supervisor in the boning hall at the Anglo Irish Beef Processors factory at Rathkeale, Co. Limerick. As part of the requirements of beef processing the signature of the plaintiff was required on various documents relating to the deboning of intervention beef on the premises. The plaintiff was instructed by Anglo Irish Beef Processors to desist from signing any intervention beef documents as of April 1990. Between July 1990 and October 1991 wrongful description and quantification of intervention beef coming from the Rathkeale plant took place. When investigated by the authorities, the signature of the Plaintiff appeared on forms, which recorded the particulars of the deboning of intervention beef for all of the relevant period. The plaintiff claimed that his signature had been wrongfully affixed to documentation by officers of the Minister and therefore initiated proceedings. On December 4, 2000 directions were made in the High Court for the trail of a number of points for determination as preliminary issues of law. Barry J. ruled that on the facts as pleaded that a clear breach of duty could be inferred. As the wrongful use of the plaintiffs signature led to his arrest and prosecution which subsequently led to a breach of the duty of care by the defendant, this contributed to the alleged loss or damage suffered by the plaintiff.

Minister for Agriculture v. Alte Leipziger, **Supreme Court, February 23, 2001**   This is one of a series of cases which has arisen out of a fire at the United Packers Plant at Ballaghaderreen, Co. Roscommon on January 7, 1992. As a result of the fire, meat worth £22M is alleged to have been destroyed. The plaintiff had delivered the meat to the plant in his capacity as intervention agent on behalf of the European Communities. The plaintiff (the Minister) claimed to have a valid contract of insurance with the company *Alte Leipziger.* The insurance company agreed that the insurance policy was valid but contested the Irish High Court's jurisdiction to hear and determine the Minister's insurance claim, citing an article in the contract that all disputes between the parties must be heard in the Tribunal de Commerce in Paris. In a written judgement in the High Court (March 6, 1997), the High Court refuted *Alte Leipzeiger's* claim, ruling that the High Court did have the jurisdiction to hear the case. The insurance company appealed that decision to the Supreme Court, which dismissed the appeal and affirmed the original order of the High Court.

HORSE AND GREYHOUND RACING

Horse and Greyhound Racing Act 2001 The Act establishes the Government body – Horse Racing Ireland – while dissolving the existing Irish Horseracing Authority which was established via the Irish Horseracing Industry Act 1994. The general functions of Horse Racing Ireland shall be: registry office functions relating to horses, racehorse owners, horserace entries, prizes and the racing calendar; provision of mobile track equipment, photo finish and camera patrol equipment at racecourses; representing the Irish horseracing industry internationally; negotiating media rights in relation televised race meetings and financial/other support to the Irish thoroughbred horse industry. Horse Racing Ireland will also include a *Racegoers Consultative Forum* aimed at liaising with racegoers regarding existing and future developments in the Irish Horseracing industry.

Finally, a *Horse & Greyhound Racing Fund* will be established by means of the Act and the fund will be managed and controlled by the Minister for Agriculture. The amount of money in the fund will be equivalent to the revenue that was paid into Exchequer in the year 2000 from excise-duty on off-course betting. The amount of money in the fund should not exceed IR £200m and it should be distributed in the ratio of 80% to the Horse Racing Ireland and 20% to Bord na gCon.

Horse Racing Ireland (Membership) Act 2001 The Act specifies that the Horse Racing Ireland body shall consist of a chairman and 13 ordinary members to be appointed by the Minister of Agriculture. Five members shall be nominated by the Racing Regulatory Body, one from each of the following interests:

(a) Authorised racecourses,
(b) racecourse owners,
(c) racecourse trainers,
(d) racecourse breeders,
(e) authorised bookmakers,

one from persons representing those employed in the horseracing industry, one from persons employed directly in the horseracing industry and one from persons representing the horseracing industry in Northern Ireland

The term of office for the chairman of Horse Racing Ireland shall be five years and for an ordinary member of Horse Racing Ireland it shall be four years. A member of Horse Racing Ireland shall not serve more than two consecutive terms.

Horse and greyhound racing The Greyhound Race Track (Totalisator) (Operating) Amendment Regulations 2001 (S.I. No. 3 of 2001) (these Regulations came into operation on January 8, 2001) amend the Greyhound Race Track (Totalisator) (Operating) Regulations 1971 (S.I. No. 47 of 1971) to allow for the minimum unit on the win and place pool to be increased to £1 and for the minimum stake on all other pools to be increased to £1. The Horse and Greyhound Racing Act 2001 (Section 19) (Commencement) Order 2001 (S.I. No. 363 of 2001) states that the zero rating of turnover charge on off-course betting commences on July 29, 2001. The Greyhound Race Track (Totalisator) (Operating) Amendment Regulations 2001 (S.I. No. 425 of 2001 (these Regulations came into operation January 1, 2002) amend the Greyhound Race Track (Totalisator) (Operating) Regulations, 1971 to allow for the minimum unit on all totalisator pools to be one euro. The Horse and Greyhound Racing Act 2001 (Establishment Day) Order 2001 (S.I. No. 630 of 2001) sets the establishment day provided for in section 3 of the Horse Greyhound Racing Act 2001 for the commencement of most of the main provisions of the Act.

PLANT HEALTH

Plant protection products The European Communities (Authorisation, Placing on The Market, Use and Control of Plant Protection Products) (Amendment) Regulations 2001 (S.I. No. 33 of 2001) give effect to Commission Directive 2000/66/EC of October 23, 2000, Commission Directive 2000/67/EC of October 23, 2000 and Commission Directive 2000/68/EC of October 23, 2000 which provide for the inclusion of the active substances: Triasulfuron, Esfenvalerate and Bentazone respectively in Annex 1 to Council Directive 91/414/EEC. The European Communities (Authorisation, Placing on The Market, Use and Control of Plant Protection Products) (Amendment) Regulations 2001 (S.I. No. 141 of 2001) amend the European Communities (Authorization, Placing on the Market, Use and Control of Plant Protection Products) Regulations 1994 to 2001 (S.I. No. 139 of 1994, S.I. No. 200 of 1995, S.I. No. 159 of 1996, S.I. No. 290 of 1997, S.I. No. 466 of 1997, S.I. No. 182 of 1999, S.I. No. 198 of 1999, S.I. No. 356 of 1999, S.I. No. 461 of 1999, S.I. No. 366 of 2000 and S.I. No. 33 of 2001). The amendments specify revisions to certain application fees payable and specify that annual fees due be provided in a single payment.

The European Communities (Authorisation, Placing on The Market, Use and Control of Plant Protection Products) (Amendment) Regulations 2001 (S.I. No. 623 of 2001) give effect to Commission Directive 2000/80/EC of

December 4, 2000, Commission Directive 2001/28/EC of April 20, 2001, Commission Directive 2001/47/EC of June 25, 2001, Commission Directive 2001/49/EC of June 28, 2001, Commission Directive 2001/87/EC of October 12, 2001 and Commission Directive 2001/99/EC of November 21, 2001. These Regulations, which amend Council Directive 91/414/EEC concerning the placing of plant protection products on the market, consolidate Annex I of that Directive and provide for the inclusion of the active substances: Lambda, Cyhalothrim, Amitrole. Diquat, Prydate, KBR 2738, respectively in Annex I to Council Directive. The European Communities (Authorisation, Placing on The Market, Use and Control of Plant Protection Products) (Amendment) Regulations 2001 (S.I. No. 359 of 2001) give effect to Commission Directive 2001/28/EC of April 20, 2001 and Commission Directive 2001/49/EC of June 28, 2001 which provide for the inclusion of the active substance KBR 2738 (fenhexamid) and DPX KE 459 (flupyrsulfuron-methyl) respectively, in Annex 1 to Council Directive 91/414/EEC.

Classification, packaging and labelling of pesticides   The European Communities (Classification, Packaging and Labelling of Pesticides) (Amendment) Regulations 2001 (S.I. No. 140 of 2001) amend the European Communities (Classification, Packaging and Labelling of Pesticides) Regulations 1994 (S.I. No. 138 of 1994) and 1999 (S.I. No. 463 of 1999). The amendment specifies that annual fees due be provided in a single payment.

Beet seed   The European Communities (Beet Seed) Regulations 2001 (S.I. No. 142 of 2001) consolidate existing Regulations, relating to such seeds and provide a framework to introduce detailed rules in respect of genetically modified plant varieties and plant genetic resources.

Vegetable seeds   The European Communities (Vegetable seeds) Regulations 2001 (S.I. No. 306 of 2001) consolidate existing Regulations, relating to such seeds and provide a framework to introduce detailed rules in respect of genetically modified plant varieties and plant genetic resources.

Organisms harmful to plant health   The European Communities (Introduction of Organisms Harmful to Plants or Plant Products) (Prohibition) (Amendment) Regulations 2001 (S.I. No. 414 of 2001) implement the provisions of Commission Directives 2001/32/EC and 2001/33/EC extending the period of recognition of EU protected zones, modifying the current description of certain protected zones, and amending provisions to take into account the present distribution of certain harmful organisms.

Pesticide residues   Pesticide residue levels in treated crops are regulated through the establishment of Maximum Residue Levels (MRLs). When MRLs are exceeded, officers of the Pesticide Control Service can remove the produce concerned from the market and destroy it at the owner's expense. Prosecutions may also be taken by the Minister. Where warranted, a Rapid Alert can be issued by the FSAI. A Rapid Alert is issued when the residues detected in food are considered to be harmful to the consumer. The European Communities (Pesticide Residues) (Foodstuffs of Animal Origin) (Amendment) Regulations 2001 (S.I. No. 137 of 2001) insert an additional pesticide residue "kresoxim methyl" to Annex II and also a provisional maximum residue level for this substance. The European Communities (Pesticide Residues) (Foodstuffs of Animal Origin) (Amendment) (No. 2) Regulations 2001 (S.I. No. 249 of 2001) amend existing Regulations on the fixing of maximum residue levels for pesticides in and on foodstuffs of animal origin.

The European Communities (Pesticide Residues) (Cereals) (Amendment) Regulations 2001 (S.I. No. 250 of 2001) amend existing Regulations on the fixing of maximum residue levels for pesticides in and on cereals. The European Communities (Pesticide Residues) (Cereals) (Amendment) Regulations 2001 (S.I. No. 620 of 2001) amend existing Regulations on the fixing of maximum residue levels for pesticides in and on foodstuffs of animal origin. The European Communities (Pesticide Residue) (Product of Plant Origin, Including Fruit and Vegetables) (Amendment) Regulations 2001 (S.I. No. 621 of 2001) amend or add to existing regulations on the fixing of maximum residue levels for pesticide residues in and on products of plant origin, including fruit and vegetables.

Potato growers and potato packers   The Registration of Potato Growers and Potato Packers Regulations 2001 (S.I. No. 637 of 2001) replace the Registration of Potato Growers and Potato Packers Regulations 1985 (S.I. No. 336 of 1985) and prescribe certain additional information, relating to seed potatoes acquired for planting, which must be included in records kept by registered potato growers.

Cereal Seed   The European Communities (Cereal Seed) Regulations 2001 (S.I. No. 640 of 2001) implement the provisions of Council Directive No. 98/95/EC of December 14, 1998 with regard to the definition of marketing, removal of the national derogation with regard to the marketing of second generation cereal seed with effect from April 1, 2004 and set out provisions for the placing of small quantities of genetically modified cereal seed on to the market for trial purposes. The Regulations implement the appropriate provisions of Council Directives No. 98/96/EC, 99/8/EC and 99/54/EC in relation to cereal seed. Finally the Regulations provide a framework to introduce detailed rules in respect of chemically treated cereal seed, genetically modified cereal varieties, varieties suitable for organic production and conservation of plant genetic resources.

TRADE IN ANIMALS

National Beef Assurance Scheme Act 2000   The National Beef Assurance Scheme Act 2000 (First Schedule) (Amendment) Order 2001 (S.I. No. 393 of 2001) extends the application of the National Beef Assurance Scheme Act 2000 to persons to whom the Diseases of Animals Acts 1966 to 2001 (Approval and Registration of Dealers and Dealers Premises) Order 2001 (S.I. No. 79 of 2001) applies who deal in bovine animals. The National Beef Assurance Scheme Act 2000 (Commencement) Order 2001 (S.I. No. 394 of 2001) brings into operation Part I, sections of Part II not already commenced, Part III and Part IV of the National Beef Assurance Scheme Act 2000 regarding the implementation of the National Beef Assurance Scheme.

Livestock marts   The Livestock Marts Regulations 1968 (Amendment) Regulations 2001 (S.I. No. 462 of 2001) revoke Regulation 15 of the Livestock Marts Regulations 1968 (S.I. No. 251 of 1968) requiring *inter alia* that the licensee of a mart deposit a guarantee bond with the Minister.

Fresh poultry meat   The European Communities (Fresh Poultry Meat) (Amendment) Regulations 2001 (S.I. No. 25 of 2001) implement Council Directive No. 1999/89 of December 15, 1999 which amends Council Directive No. 91/494/EEC of June 26, 1991 as amended by Council Directive No.93/121/EEC of December 22, 1993 on animal health conditions governing intra-community trade in and imports from third countries of fresh poultry meat.

Live poultry and hatching eggs   The European Communities (Live Poultry and Hatching Eggs) (Amendment) Regulations 2001 (S.I. No. 26 of 2001), implement Council Directive No.1999/90/EC amending Council Directive 90/539/EEC, as amended by Council Directive 93/120/EEC on animal health conditions governing intra-community trade in and imports from third countries of poultry and hatching eggs.

BSE and specified risk materials   The European Communities (Specified Risk Material) Regulations 2001 (S.I. No. 24 of 2001) amend the European Communities (Specified Risk Material) Regulations 2000 (S.I. No. 332 of 2000) by setting out a revised definition of specified risk material, which includes the entire bovine intestine. The Diseases of Animals (Bovine Spongiform Encephalopathy) (Specified Risk Material) Order 2001 (S.I. No. 31 of 2001) amends the Diseases of Animals (Bovine Spongiform Encephalopathy) (Specified Risk Material) Order 2000 (S.I. No. 331 of 2000) by setting out a revised definition of specified risk material, which includes the entire bovine intestine.

Slaughter of bovine animals   The European Communities (Slaughter of

Bovine Animals Aged Over 30 Months) Regulations 2001 (S.I. No. 48 of 2001) limit the slaughter of bovine animals aged 30 months or over to premises approved under the European Communities (Fresh Meat) Regulations 1997 (S.I. No. 434 of 1997). A person who fails to comply with or contravenes these Regulations is guilty of an offence and shall be liable on summary conviction to a fine not exceeding £ 1,500 or to imprisonment for a term not exceeding 6 months, or to both. Where an offence under these Regulations is committed by a body corporate and is proved to have been so committed with the consent or connivance of or to be attributable to any neglect on the part of any person, being a director, manager, secretary or other officer of the body corporate, or a person who was purporting to act in any such capacity, that person, as well as the body corporate, is guilty of an offence and shell be liable to be proceeded against and punished as if he or she were guilty of the first-mentioned offence. An offence under these Regulations may be prosecuted by the Minister or by a local authority in whose functional area the offence has been committed.

WILDLIFE

The Wildlife (Wild Birds) (Open Seasons) (Amendment) Order 2001 (S.I. No. 428 of 2001) amends the Open Seasons list of huntable species of wild birds by the inclusion of the Ruddy Duck from September 1, in each year to January 1 in the year immediately following that year on a countrywide basis.

Commercial Law

ARBITRATION

Remittal: discretion In *McCarrick v. Gaiety (Sligo) Ltd*, High Court, April 2, 2001, Herbert J. remitted a case to an arbitrator under section 36(1) of the Arbitration Act 1954 in the following circumstances. The arbitration was to determine, on a rent review, the current market rent of certain properties held by the applicant, as lessee, from the respondent. As a result of an error or oversight on the part of the applicant's advisers, certain submissions had not been furnished to the arbitrator within the time stipulated; as a result, the arbitrator made his final award. The applicant sought to have the matter remitted and, as indicated, Herbert J. granted the relief sought, subject to the payment by the applicant of the costs associated with the failure to file the relevant submissions within the time specified.

He held that there was no imperative of policy, reason or justice which would cause him to set any permanent inflexible and immutable limits to the exercise of the wide power conferred on it in section 36(1) of the 1954 Act for the obvious purpose of ensuring justice and fairness between the parties within the arbitration framework. He was of the view that the occasions on which the Court would exercise its discretion to remit matters referred or any of them to the reconsideration of the arbitrator remained open, but very limited. This, of course, is entirely consistent with a long line of authority on the matter, including the leading Supreme Court decision in *Keenan v. Shield Insurance Ltd* [1988] I.R. 89 (*Annual Review of Irish Law 1988*, pp.43-6). In the present case, Herbert J. held that the possible injustice which the applicant would suffer, now and in the future, should the award not be remitted for the reconsideration of the arbitrator exceeded any risk of detriment to the respondent as lessor. In particular he considered that the determination of the review rent obviously impacted on the viability of the applicant's business, could be a basis for future rent reviews, and was clearly relevant to such matters as leasehold enfranchisement and the sale value of the applicant's interest in the property.

CASUAL TRADING

Designation of casual trading area In *Byrne v. Tracey*, High Court, February 7, 2001, Morris P. declined to grant judicial review in respect of a designation of a casual trading area under section 6 of the Casual Trading Act 1995 (*Annual*

Review of Irish Law 1995, pp.21-22). The applicant was a casual trader and held a casual trader's licence in Blessington, Co Wicklow. Wicklow County Council had adopted a bye-law pursuant to the Casual Trading Act 1995 in which it had designated certain parts of Blessington as a casual trading area, but not including 'The Square', Blessington. The applicant considered that the place designated for casual trading was unsuitable and that 'The Square' was a more appropriate area. He applied for an order quashing the designation bye-law, but Morris P. refused the relief sought.

He noted that there had been strict compliance by the Council with the provisions of the Casual Trading Act 1995 and thus the adoption of the bye-law was in accordance with section 6 of the 1995 Act. Indeed, the applicant's arguments on the unsuitability of the place designated for casual trading and the suitability of 'The Square' were more appropriately matters which should have been made before the District Court on appeal under section 6 of the 1995 Act. The applicant had also argued that his previous activity as a casual trader had given rise to a legitimate expectation, in effect, of a licence to trade in 'The Square', Blessington. But Morris P. rejected this claim also, since nothing in the way of conduct on the part of the respondent had been identified as giving rise to any expectation such as might have entitled the applicant to relief.

The applicant had also argued the existence of a market right, defined in the 1995 Act as 'a right conferred by franchise or statute to hold a fair or market.' While the Supreme Court in *DPP (Long) v. McDonald* [1983] I.L.R.M. 223 held that there were circumstances in which a market right could be presumed to exist from immemorial usage, the onus was on the applicant to establish the existence of such a right and he had failed to do so. Morris P. commented that there was insufficient evidence which would lead him to believe that a market right existed It is worth noting that, in the *Long* case, Henchy J. (speaking for the Supreme Court) had acknowledged that a market right was a property right protected by Article 40.3 of the Constitution. In *Byrne*, the applicant had argued that another constitutional right, the right to work or earn a livelihood (an unenumerated right under Article 40.3), had been curtailed by the bye-law. But, echoing the views of McCracken J. in *Shanley v. Galway Corporation* [1995] 1 I.R. 369 (*Annual Review 1995*, p.24), Morris P. held that the right was not unqualified and was limited by considerations of the common good. As McCracken J. had held in *Shanley*, Morris P. concluded that a restriction of casual trading based on the factors contained in the 1995 Act was consistent with the constitution limitation on the right.

Casual trading and markets   In *Bridgeman v. Limerick Corporation*, Supreme Court, June 14, 2001, the Court considered the relationship between the Casual Trading Act 1995 and legislation relating to markets. The circumstances were that, pursuant to section 6 of the 1995 Act, the respondent, Limerick Corporation, made bye-laws that provided for the designation of a casual trading area in the same location as a market at which the applicant had operated as a casual trader for more than 30 years. The division of the area into smaller allotments would not accommodate the vehicle from which the applicant had been trading and the designation would, it was claimed, seriously affect his ability to earn a livelihood. He contended that the bye-laws constituted the establishment of a market within the municipal boundaries of the County Borough of Limerick and accordingly contravened the provisions of the Limerick Markets Act 1852, as amended. The High Court and, on appeal, the Supreme Court, declined to quash the bye-laws on judicial review.

The Supreme Court took account of the legislative history of the 1995 Act, namely that the legislature had, *inter alia*, replaced in a different form the statutory regime controlling the activities of hawkers that existed at the time of the 1852 Act. The 1852 Act had ultimately been consolidated in the Hawkers Act 1888, which had been repealed by section 19(1) of the Casual Trading Act 1980, which, in turn, had been repealed by the 1995 Act. Thus, the bye-laws made by the respondent under the 1995 Act did no more than give effect to the form of statutory regime intended to regulate the activities of persons previously controlled by the legislation relating to hawkers. It was clear, the Court concluded that it had not been the intention of the Oireachtas, in enacting the 1995 Act and enabling bye-laws to be made, to create a market as commonly understood in law. The distinction between hawkers (casual trading) and markets was, indeed, underlined by the wording of sections 7 and 8 of the 1995 Act, which expressly empower a local authority to acquire and extinguish a 'market right', defined as 'a right conferred by franchise or statute to hold a fair or market, that is to say, a concourse of buyers and sellers to dispose of commodities.

COMPETITION LAW

Abuse of dominant position: dominance   In *Meridian Communications Ltd v. Eircell*, High Court, April 5, 2001, O'Higgins J. considered whether dominance had been established within the meaning of section 5 of the Competition Act 1991. He also dealt with other common law issues concerning the contracts between the parties involved in the litigation. The background was that the plaintiff was a company whose principal business was in selling mobile phone time, principally to businesses. It did not have a licence to operate a mobile phone service. As a result, it could only operate as a business through purchasing mobile phone time from a licensed operator. It entered into a Volume Discount Agreement (VDA) with the defendant, a licensed mobile phone operator, under which the defendant agreed to supply mobile phone time at discounts of up to 40% to the plaintiff. The terms of the VDA did not preclude the plaintiff from passing this discount on to its customers; it appears that substantial discounts were passed on. Where the plaintiff successfully signed up a customer, the VDA provided that the defendant would make a 'transfer of subscriber' as soon as possible. Under the 'transfer of subscriber' arrangement, the customer formally remained a customer of Eircell, as required by the terms of its mobile phone licence, but its phone charges were paid to the plaintiff who then paid the defendant. In the course of dealings between the parties, the defendant became concerned that the plaintiff was using the VDA to undercut the defendant's business and, ultimately, it sought to terminate the VDA. Pending the proceedings, the defendant suspended all 'transfer of subscriber' arrangements and wrote to the plaintiff's customers a 'process letter' explaining that it intended to terminate the VDA. The plaintiff then instituted these proceedings, claiming that the defendant was engaging in an abuse of a dominant position within the meaning of section 5 of the Competition Act 1991, as well as for alleging breaches of contract and/or alleged torts arising out of the conduct and operation of the agreement. It was agreed between the parties that the court could proceed on the basis that the relevant market was that of mobile telephony services within the State. In a detailed judgment, O'Higgins held that the defendant had breached certain terms of the VDA but had not been in a dominant position in the relevant market.

In relation to that market, a key point was that the defendant had, until 1999, been part of a State body, Bord Telecom Éireann (BTE) (it was privatised, as Eircom plc, in 1999 in a public flotation). BTE had, in effect, been the monopoly provider of all telephone services, including mobile phone services in the State (under the Eircell name), until the mid-1990s. In the mid-1990s, a second mobile phone licence had been awarded to another company operating under the name Digifone. O'Higgins J. had to consider, *inter alia*, the effect of Digifone's arrival in terms of the defendant's dominance in the market. Obviously, prior to Digifone, the defendant was dominant, holding 100% of the relevant market.

In terms of dominance, O'Higgins J. cited the leading decision of the Court of Justice in *United Brands v. Commission* [1978] E.C.R. 207, to the effect that dominance relates to a position of economic strength enjoyed by an undertaking that enables it to prevent effective competition being maintained on the relevant market by affording it the power profitably to behave independently of its competitors, customers and ultimately its consumers to an appreciable extent.

Applying this test, O'Higgins J. stated that, although the defendant retained a majority of the mobile telephone market at the time of the case, this had dramatically declined in a relatively short period since the arrival of Digifone. This greatly diminished the significance of the defendant's remaining large market share. In addition, Digifone's strengths were relevant in the assessment of the defendant's capacity to act to an appreciable extent independently of it. Thus, he concluded that the significance of the low number of competitors to the defendant was diminished by the fact that Digifone was a strong company well placed to exploit any laxity on the part of the defendant. On a related issue, he held that the significance of high barriers to entry in the market to the defendant's capacity to act to an appreciable extent independently of its rivals was vastly reduced by the fact that barriers to expansion, for a company such as Digifone, were so low. Finally, there was considerable pricing evidence strongly suggesting that the defendant was not dominant and that its behaviour in pricing decisions was strongly constrained by competition from Digifone. On this basis, he concluded that the plaintiffs had failed to prove, on the balance of probabilities, that the defendant was dominant, and accordingly it followed that any claims based on abuse of a dominant position under section 5 of the Competition Act 1991 were moot.

Turning to the common law contract and tort issues raised by the plaintiff, O'Higgins J. accepted that the suspension of transfers of subscribers constituted a breach of contract, in particular the term of the VDA that required transfers to the plaintiff to be effected as soon as possible. In addition, the defendant's failure to tell the plaintiff on demand or at least shortly after whether a transfer had been effected to it constituted a breach of an implied term in the VDA, applying the officious bystander test. However, other than in cases where the defendant chose to delay effecting the transfers in order to send out a 'process letter', O'Higgins J. was not convinced that the defendant was in breach of the terms of the VDA that required the transfer requests to be processed as soon as possible. He held that the failure of the defendant to supply the plaintiff with transfer books, containing the names of customers actually transferred amounted to a breach of another implied term that either party would not deliberately seek to frustrate the VDA. But he held that the provision of electronic billing information was not an implied term of the VDA, since it was not necessary to give business efficacy to the contract.

On the tort side, he considered that the 'process letters' did not constitute an inducement or procurement of a breach of contract: he held that the letters were true and accurate, reasonably expressed, and did not go beyond what could be considered advice, and the persons to whom they were addressed were told in them that they were obliged to honour their contractual commitments. He also expressed the view (strictly *obiter* but with an eye to a possible appeal) that if, contrary to his finding that the 'process letter' did constitute an inducement, it was an inducement lawfully to terminate the contract between the plaintiff and its customers, and not an inducement to breach it.

In conclusion, while the plaintiff was successful on a number of the contract law issues it raised, it failed on the dominant position argument under the Competition Act 1991. The result was that, subject to complying with the implied terms of the VDA as found by the Court, the defendant was entitled to terminate the VDA with the plaintiff.

Non-compete clause: reasonableness In *Lennon and Pakatak Ltd v. Doran*, High Court, February 20, 2001, Carroll J. examined the enforceability of a non-compete clause. The first plaintiff, a shareholder of the second plaintiff, entered into an agreement to buy out the first and second defendant's interests in the second plaintiff. The buy-out contract contained a two-year non-compete clause, restricting the defendants from competing with the plaintiffs. The plaintiffs instituted these proceedings for damages claiming that the defendants had breached the non-compete clause. The defendants argued that the non-compete clause was an unreasonable restraint of trade and/or was in breach of the Competition Act 1991. Carroll J. found substantially in the plaintiffs' favour but limited the reach of the non-compete clause.

In terms of general principles, she applied the test in *Reuters v. BASF AG* [1976] C.M.L.R. 244 that the non-compete clause must be examined to see how far the clause is essential to the preservation of the transferred worth of the undertaking and whether it exceeds what is necessary for such preservation. In the present case, she noted that the non-compete clause referred to the defendants not competing in the 'territory' of the second plaintiff. In order to give this clause business efficacy (as discussed in cases such as *Cadbury Ltd v. Kerry Co-Op Ltd* [1982] I.L.R.M. 77), she held that it should be interpreted as the area in which the business was being carried on at the time of the share transfer. In relation to the reasonableness of the time, Carroll J. held that two years was excessive within the meaning of the *Reuters* case. The issue then was whether this made the clause unenforceable under the 'blue pencil' test. Crucially, Carroll J. did not apply the 'blue pencil' test, but the more flexible approach taken, for example, by Lord Denning MR in *Littlewoods Organisation v. Harris* [1978] 1 All E.R. 1026, and discussed with apparent approval by McWilliam J. in *European Chemical Industries Ltd v. Bell* [1981] I.L.R.M. 345. Thus, she read the non-compete clause as being limited to one year, which she held would be sufficient for the purposes of protecting the first plaintiff's investment. Carroll J. also rejected an argument by the defendants that this was an agreement between undertakings which had as its object the prevention restriction or distortion of competition in trade in any goods, within the meaning of the Competition Act 1991. Rather, it was a buyout between shareholders where, for the protection of the goodwill of the business, a limit on competition by the vendors was necessary. But, as set out in *Reuters*, this may only be to the extent required to protect the investment of the purchaser, or as Carroll J. put in it, to let the company get off the ground. Having considered the evidence on the impact on the second plaintiff of the defendants' breach of the non-compete clause (limited to the one year she found was reasonable), Carroll J. held that damages of £10,000 would be adequate in the circumstances.

CONSUMER PROTECTION

Distance selling   The European Communities (Protection of Consumers in Respect of Contracts Made by Means of Distance Communication) Regulations

2001 (S.I. No.207 of 2001) are discussed separately, 28, below.

Injunctive relief: consumer organisations The European Communities (Protection of Consumers' Collective Interests) Regulations 2001 (S.I. No. 449 of 2001) implemented Directive 98/27/EC, which entitle qualified entities, such as the Director of Consumer Affairs and consumer organisations, to apply to the Circuit Court for injunctions requiring the cessation or prohibition of certain infringements of relevant Directives which have been made in the area of consumer protection. These include: Directive 84/450/EEC on misleading advertising; Directive 87/102/EEC on consumer credit; Directive 90/314/EEC on package travel, package holidays and package tours; Directive 92/28/EEC on advertising medicinal products for human use; Directive 93/13/EEC on unfair terms in consumer contracts; Directive 94/47/EC on timeshare purchases; and Directive 97/7/EC on distance contracts (see above).

Product prices The European Communities (Requirements to Indicate Product Prices) Regulations 2001 (S.I. No. 422 of 2001) implemented Directive 98/6/EC, which imposes obligations on sellers to indicate the selling price (including VAT and all other taxes) of a product offered for sale to consumers as well as the unit price of the product, that is, the selling price per kilo, litre, metre, square metre or cubic metre of the product, as appropriate. Certain exclusions are possible from this general requirement. The Regulations came into effect on October 1, 2001.

CURRENCY: EURO CHANGEOVER

Euro Changeover (Amounts) Act 2001 The Euro Changeover (Amounts) Act 2001 provided for the substitution of convenient amounts of euro and cent for amounts expressed in Irish pounds and pence in various Acts and Regulations. It came into effect on January 1, 2002.

Euro coinage and withdrawal of Irish currency Various Orders were made in 2001 under the Economic and Monetary Union Act 1998 (*Annual Review 1998*, p.334) for the purpose of bringing into being the euro currency and providing for the withdrawal of the Irish pound as legal tender. These were as follows. The Economic and Monetary Union Act 1998 (Section 11(2)) (Commencement) Order 2001 (S.I. No. 310 of 2001) brought section 11(2) of the Economic and Monetary Union Act 1998, which deals with the provision and issuance of euro and cent coins, into force on January 1, 2002. The Economic and Monetary Union Act 1998 (Design of Coins) (No.2) Order 2001 (S.I. No. 347 of 2001), made under section 11(1) of the 1998 Act, revoked the Economic And Monetary Union Act 1998 (Design of Coins) Order 2001 (S.I. No. 312 of 2001), and set out the Irish design of the national face of the euro and cent coins, with effect from July 26, 2001. The Irish Pound Notes and Coins (Cessation of Legal Tender Status) Order 2001 (S.I. No. 313 of 2001) made under section 9(1) of the 1998 Act provided that February 9, 2002 would be the "earlier operative date" for the purposes of Chapter III of the Economic and Monetary Union Act 1998, which relates to legal tender and legal tender amounts; in effect providing that dual circulation of the Irish and euro currencies would cease on that date. The Irish Pound Coinage (Calling In) (No.2) Order 2001 (S.I. No. 348 of 2001), made under section 15(1) of the 1998 Act, revoked the Irish Pound Coinage (Calling In) Order 2001 (S.I. No. 311 of 2001) and provided for the calling-in of coins denominated in Irish pounds, pence and shillings, with effect from February 10, 2002.

DISTANCE SELLING

Introduction   The European Communities (Protection of Consumers in Respect of Contracts Made by Means of Distance Communication) Regulations 2001 (S.I. No.207 of 2001), which came into effect on May 14, 2001, implemented Directive 97/7/EC, the Distance Selling Directive. For the general background to the Directive, see McMahon, "Contracts Negotiated Away From Business Premises And The 1997 Distance Selling Directive" (1999) 17 I.L.T. 139.

Scope   The 2001 Regulations apply to contracts for goods or services to consumers where the contract is made *exclusively* by a 'means of distance communication.' The phrase 'means of distance communication' is defined in Reg.2 as 'any method which, without the simultaneous physical presence of the supplier and the consumer, may be used for making a contract between those parties, including any method referred to in... Schedule 1.' Schedule 1 of the 2001 Regulations includes the following examples: addressed and unaddressed printed matter; press advertising with order form; catalogue; telephone with or without human intervention; radio and television (teleshopping); and electronic mail (e-mail). Given that this list is non-exhaustive, the more recent explosion in Internet shopping is also clearly within the scope of the general definition of 'means of distance communication' in the 2001 Regulations. Certain contracts are excluded from the scope of the 2001 Regulations. These are: contracts relating to financial services, including investment services, insurance and reinsurance services, banking services and operations relating to dealings in futures or options; contracts made by automatic vending machines; contracts made with telecommunications operators through public payphones; contracts for the construction and sale of real property (other than rental of property); and contracts made at an auction. In addition, the 2001 Regulations exempt two categories of contracts from the provisions on advance information, written confirmation and the right to cancellation. These are: contracts for the supply of foodstuffs, beverages or other goods for everyday consumption supplied to the home, residence or workplace of the consumer by regular 'roundsmen' (a title which it must be assumed is difficult to gender proof); and contracts for the provision of accommodation, transport, catering or leisure services where the supplier undertakes, when the contract is made, to provide those services on a specific date or within a specific period. Subject to these exclusions, the 2001 Regulations apply to most consumer sale of goods and services contracts.

Information to consumer   The Regulations impose requirements on the supplier both before and after a contract has been concluded. Before the contract is concluded, regulation 4 of the 2001 Regulations provides that a distance contract is not enforceable unless the supplier has provided the consumer with the information listed in Schedule 3. This includes: the identity and address of the supplier; the main characteristics of the goods or services; the price, including all taxes; delivery costs, where appropriate; arrangements for payment, delivery or performance; the existence of a right of cancellation; the period for which the offer or the price remains valid; where appropriate, the minimum duration of the contract where the contract is to be performed permanently or recurrently. In addition, the information must be given in a clear and comprehensible manner appropriate to the means of communication used, with due regard to any requirement of good faith in commercial transactions or governing protection of those who are unable to give their consent, such as minors. The Regulations also require that the commercial purpose of the contract and the information supplied is clear to the consumer. Regulation 4 of the 2001 Regulations also impose an obligation on the supplier to confirm these details in writing 'in good time during the performance of the contract.'

'Cooling off' cancellation right   After the contract has been concluded, regulation 6 of the 2001 Regulations provide that it is an implied condition of a distance contract that the consumer has seven days after receipt to cancel the contract without giving a reason. Where this 'cooling-off' right of cancellation is exercised, the consumer cannot be charged anything other than the direct cost of returning goods, where appropriate. The right of cancellation does not apply to certain specified contracts, namely: contracts that have begun, with the consumer's agreement, before the end of the seven day 'cooling off' period; contracts for goods or services whose price is dependent on fluctuations in the financial market which cannot be controlled by the supplier; contracts for the supply of goods made to the consumer's specifications or clearly personalised or which, by their nature, cannot be returned or are liable to deteriorate or expire rapidly; contracts for the supply of audio or video recordings which have been unsealed by the consumer; contracts for the supply of newspapers, periodicals and magazines; contracts for gaming and lottery services.

Performance of contract   Regulation 9 of the 2001 Regulations also provides that, unless otherwise agreed, the contract must be performed within 30 days from the day following that on which the consumer forwarded his or her order to the supplier. There are limited circumstances in which equivalent goods or services may be provided by the supplier if the original goods or services are unavailable.

Fraudulent use of credit card   Regulation 10 entitles a consumer to request immediate cancellation of any payment made where a credit card or equivalent charge card has been used to purchase the goods or service if there has been any fraudulent use of the card.

Inertia selling and 'cold calling'   The 2001 Regulations also deal with inertia selling, or unsolicited sales, already largely dealt with in the Sale of Goods and Supply of Services Act 1980. They prohibit the supply of goods or services to a consumer without their being ordered by the consumer beforehand, where such supply involves a demand for payment. The 1997 Directive which was implemented by the 2001 Regulations also stated that the absence of a response to unsolicited selling by the consumer does not constitute acceptance of the contract; since this was already included in the 1980 Act, this provision is not explicitly included in the 2001 Regulations. Similarly, regulation 12 of the 2001 Regulations deal with 'cold calling', in particular the use of automatic dialling and fax machines. The Regulations prohibit the use of any such means of telecommunication unless there has been no clear objection from the consumer.

Exclusion clauses and choice of law restrictions   Regulation 18 prohibits any waiver by the consumer of the rights conferred by them, thus rendering unlawful the use of any exclusion or limitation clauses in this area. Similarly, regulation 19 prohibits any purported attempt to apply the law of a non-EU or non-EEA State to a distance contract if the contract has a 'close connection' with a Member State. This clearly places some limitations on choice of law contracts.

Enforcement   Finally, the 2001 Regulations contain enforcement mechanisms, by which the Director of Consumer Affairs or consumer organisations may apply to the District Court for injunctive and other relief in respect of activities in breach of the Regulations. In addition, failure t comply with many provisions of the Regulations are criminal offences carrying a maximum penalty on summary conviction of €3,000 (£2,362.69).

FINANCIAL SERVICES

ACC Bank Act 2001   The ACC Bank Act 2001 provided for the sale of the publicly owned ACC Bank plc. It increased the authorised share capital of the bank; provided for the issue of shares in the bank in connection with an employee share ownership trust for the benefit of its employees; allowed for the disposal by the Minister for Finance of his shares in the bank; provided for certain guarantees of the bank's borrowing; and repealed in large part the ACC Bank Acts 1978 to 1999. The Act came into effect on June 15, 2001: ACC Bank Act, 2001 (Commencement) Order 2001 (S.I. No. 278 of 2001).

Dormant Accounts Act 2001   The Dormant Accounts Act 2001 provides for the transfer of moneys from dormant accounts (that is, accounts in which there have been no transactions for 20 years) and the Intestate Estates Fund Deposit Account to the newly-established Dormant Accounts Fund. The Fund is under the control and management of the National Treasury Management Agency (NTMA). The Act also provides for the disbursement of moneys from the fund through the Dormant Accounts Fund Disbursements Board.

Credit unions   The Credit Union Act 1997 (Commencement) Order 2001 (S.I. No. 378 of 2001) brought sections 46 to 52 of the Credit Union Act 1997 (*Annual Review of Irish Law*, 1997, p.64), which deal with savings protection schemes, insurance against fraud of officers, and the provision of additional services to members, into effect on August 1, 2001. The Credit Union Act 1997 (Alteration Of Financial Limit) Regulations 2001 (S.I. No. 476 of 2001) amended section 27(1)(b) of the 1997 Act for the purpose of altering the value of shares a member must hold for a credit union to raise funds by accepting a deposit from that member. They took effect on October 25, 2001.

Trustee Savings Banks (Amendment) Act 2001   The Trustee Savings Banks Act (Amendment) Act 2001 amended the Trustee Savings Banks Act 1989 for the purposes of providing for the sale of the TSB Bank. While the TSB Bank was not formally in public ownership, its savings were guaranteed by the Minister for Finance and the 2001 Act provided for the arrangements for its sale to private owners. This was effected in 2001: see the Trustee Savings Banks Act 1989 (Section 57) (TSB Bank) Order 2001 (S.I. No. 175 of 2001), which authorised the reorganisation of the TSB with effect from April 20, 2001.

INSURANCE

Life assurance: information   The Life Assurance (Provision of Information) Regulations 2001 (S.I. No. 15 of 2001), made under section 43 of the Insurance

Act 1989, belatedly require suppliers of life assurance to provide information to clients resident in Ireland before they sign a proposal or an application form in respect of life assurance and also throughout the term of the policy. They came into effect on February 1, 2001.

INTELLECTUAL PROPERTY

Data protection   The Data Protection (Registration) Regulations 2001 (S.I. No.2 of 2001) made under the Data Protection Act 1988, provide for the registration, under section 16 of the 1988 Act, of persons who provide telecommunications services and internet services, and who keep personal data in relation to users of those services. They came into effect on January 10, 2001. The European Communities (Data Protection) Regulations 2001 (S.I. No.626 of 2001) amended in significant respects the Data Protection Act 1988 in order to implement those provisions of Directive 95/46/EC on Data Protection which prohibit the transfer of data to non-EU/EEA States unless appropriate protections are in place. The Regulations came into effect on April 1, 2002. At the time of writing, the Data Protection Bill 2002, which proposes to implement in full the 1995 Directive, has not yet been enacted.

Trade Marks: Community marks   The Trade Marks Act 1996 (Section 66) Regulations 2001 (S.I. No. 9 of 2001) enable certain details regarding the seniority of Community trade marks to be recorded in the Register of Trade Marks. They came into effect on January 29, 2001.

Trademark registration: confusion   In *Montex Holdings Ltd v. Controller of Patents, Designs and Trademarks and Diesel Spa* [2000] 1 I.L.R.M. 481 (HC); Supreme Court, April 5, 2001, the Court upheld the decision of O'Sullivan J. (*Annual Review of Irish Law 2000*, pp.38-9) who had refused the plaintiff's application for registration of the word 'Diesel' as a trademark for use in connection with clothing. The plaintiff had applied to the Controller to register the word on the ground that ownership of the mark and goodwill vested in the plaintiff. The second defendant had filed a notice of opposition, claiming that it had the ownership of the mark and goodwill attached to it. Registration of the mark was refused by the Controller and the plaintiff appealed by way of special summons. The plaintiff submitted that the wrong test had been applied by the Controller in interpreting section 19 of the Trade Marks Act 1963, which prohibited, *inter alia*, any registration which would, by reason of its being likely to deceive or cause confusion or otherwise, be disentitled to protection in a court of law (see now section 8 of the Trade Marks Act 1996: *Annual Review of Irish Law 1996*, pp.68-9). O'Sullivan J. had held that the plaintiff had established a sufficient user prior to the date of application to entitle it, *prima facie*, to be registered as owner, but the second defendant had also established a sufficient user prior to that date to entitle it to *locus standi*. On the competing interests of the two parties, therefore, he was not satisfied on the evidence before it that the plaintiff's proposed user of the mark was *bona fide*. He noted that the clear and unambiguous meaning of the words of section 19 of the 1963 Act (and section 8 of the 1996 Act) excluded registration where it was established that use of the mark would have involved confusion, deception or otherwise, thereby disentitling such use to protection in a court of law. The Supreme Court, on further appeal, upheld the essential elements of O'Sullivan J's decision, but it also emphasised that there was no justification for introducing an element of blameworthy conduct such as passing off into the test contained in section 19 of the 1963 Act. It did not accept that section 19 had to be interpreted as imposing a prohibition on the registration of a trade mark only in cases where there was blameworthy conduct; the sole issue was the likelihood of confusion and, in this respect, the Court held there had been ample evidence before the High Court to justify the finding of a likelihood of confusion sufficient to satisfy the test in section 19. The Court also added that, if an element of blameworthiness was to arise at all, it could only be in relation to an application for expungement, and not in an application for registration of a trade mark.

Trade Marks: WIPO Madrid Protocol   The Trade Marks (Madrid Protocol) Regulations 2001 (S.I. No. 346 of 2001), made under the Trade Marks Act 1996 (*Annual Review of Irish Law 1996*, pp.68-9) set out the procedures to be followed in connection with international trade marks under the World International Property Organisation's (WIPO) Madrid Protocol. They took effect on October 19, 2001.

INTERNATIONAL TRADE

Trade sanctions: former Yugoslavia   The European Communities (Prohibition of the Sale and Supply of Petroleum and Certain Petroleum Products to the Federal Republic of Yugoslavia) Regulations 2001 (S.I. No. 97 of 2001), which came into effect on March 22, 2001, revoked previous Regulations which had provided for penalties for breaches of the EU prohibition on the sale and supply of petroleum and certain petroleum products to the Federal Republic of Yugoslavia (Serbia and Montenegro). In effect, this also marked the overthrow of former Yugoslav President Milosevic.

Trade sanctions: Liberia   The European Communities (Introduction of Certain Restrictive Measures in Respect of Liberia) Regulations 2001 (S.I. No. 416 of 2001) provide for penalties for infringement of Regulation (EC) No.1146/2001 in regard to the export and import of certain goods and services to and from Liberia. They came into effect on September 10, 2001.

Trade sanctions: Afghanistan   A number of Orders and Regulations made in respect of Afghanistan in 2001 reflected the move from limited restrictions on the former Taliban regime in March 2001 to more extensive restrictions focused on that regime in the aftermath of the September 11, 2001 attack on New York. The more extensive provisions were in the European Communities (Prohibition of the Export of Certain Goods and Services to Afghanistan and Strengthening of the Flight Ban) Regulations 2001 (S.I. No. 417 of 2001) and the European Communities (Prohibition of the Export of Certain Goods and Services to Afghanistan and Strengthening of the Flight Ban) (Amendment) Regulations 2001 (S.I. No. 467 of 2001), which provided for penalties for breaching Regulation (EC) No.467/2001 (which came into effect on September 10, 2001) and Regulation (EC) No.1354/2001 (which came into effect on October 11, 2001), respectively. The Financial Transfers (Taliban of Afghanistan) (Prohibition) Order 2001 (S.I. No. 447 of 2001), made under the Financial Transfers Act 1992, provided for financial sanctions against the Taliban by prohibiting financial transfers relating to funds in respect of persons and bodies specified in and funds frozen by Regulation (EC) No.467/2001 prohibiting the export of certain goods and services to Afghanistan, strengthening the flight ban and extending the freeze of funds and other financial resources in respect of the Taliban. This Order came into effect on October 3, 2001. The European Communities (Taliban of Afghanistan) (Sanctions) Regulations 2001 (S.I. No. 496 of 2001) provided for penalties for breaching financial sanctions against the Taliban imposed by Regulation (EC) No.467/2001, as amended and they came into effect on November 2, 2001.

MEASUREMENTS AND METROLOGY

Units of measurement   The European Communities (Units of Measurement) (Amendment) Regulations 2001 (S.I. No. 283 of 2001) further amended the 1992 Regulations (*Annual Review of Irish Law 1992*, p.46), as last amended in 2000 (*Annual Review of Irish Law 2000*, p.40), to provide for a further extension of the period during which conversion of road distance and speed measurement signs to the metric system may be carried out. They came into effect on June 21, 2001.

PUBLIC WORKS CONTRACTS

On the regulation of public supply contracts generally, see the *Annual Review of Irish Law 1992*, p.46; *Annual Review of Irish Law 1993*, p. 66; *Annual Review of Irish Law 1994*, p.44; *Annual Review of Irish Law 1995*, p.55, and the *Annual Review of Irish Law 1998*, p.36. In 2001, the judicial review procedure provided for in the relevant Regulations was used to an increasing extent: see below.

Public service contracts   The European Communities (Award of Public Service Contracts) (Amendment) Regulations 2001 (S.I. No.334 of 2001) gave further effect to Directives 92/50/EEC and 97/52/EC on the award of public service contracts in relation to the designation of contracts. They came into effect on July 17, 2001.

Pre-selection criteria: public works   In *Whelan Group (Ennis) Ltd v. Clare County Council*, High Court, March 9, 2001, Kelly J. dismissed a claim that the pre-selection criteria for a public works contract was discriminatory and in breach of Directive 93/37/EC. The applicant claimed that some of the technical specifications of the pre-selection criteria in the restricted procedure contained discriminatory requirements, in particular the requirement that a contractor had to have completed an individual road works project to the value of at least £10 million. The applicant claimed that such a requirement was discriminatory and lacked proportionality. As indicated, Kelly J. disagreed and dismissed the proceedings. He held that the pre-qualification criterion impugned in the proceedings was made on the advice of an expert standing committee; it had been taken in accordance with the practice determined by the National Roads Authority, which took into account its experience nationally in relation to the use of the restricted tendering procedure. In addition, the criterion applied to all potential contractors and could not be said to be discriminatory. Kelly J. held that it was an objective criterion in that it was capable of objective assessment and application. Specifically in relation to Directive 93/37/EC, he noted that the criterion manifestly related to economic and technical conditions and that the 1993 Directive did not attempt to set out the technical or economic criteria that were to be applied. Rather, it indicated the references or methods of proof by which technical and economic criteria were to be judged. Nor did he accept the argument that the criterion specified in this case suffocated genuine competition. Once it was proportionate and a rational basis existed for it and it was applied objectively it did not offend the requirements of EC law.

Appropriate respondent: public supply contract   In *Kayfoam Woolfson v. Healthcare Materials Management Board*, High Court, June 29, 2001, Finnegan J. (as he then was) rejected an argument by the respondent that it was not the appropriate respondent in a judicial review of a public supply contract. The applicant sought judicial review of the respondent's award of a public supply contract, arguing that it had breached Directive 93/36/EC. The respondent issued a motion to have the application dismissed on the grounds that it was not a contracting authority within the definition of the 1993 Directive; rather, the contracting authorities were the bodies on whose behalf the respondent sought tenders for services, and that consequently those bodies in turn were the appropriate respondents to the action. In refusing to strike out the applicant's claim, Finnegan J. referred to the case law on abuse of process, such as *Sun Fat Chan v. Osseous Ltd* [1992] 1 I.R. 425 (*Annual Review of Irish Law 1991*, pp.325-6) and noted that the jurisdiction to strike out cases arose not just when the facts were admitted, but also where those facts were clear and showed that the claim was unsustainable. In the instant case, he noted that the arrangement between the applicant and the respondent, whatever the respondent's precise status under the 1993 Directive, could amount to a contract, and the performance of that contract by the respondent could be subject to judicial review, since the respondent was a public body. Moreover, he held that there was no bar to the applicant instituting proceedings against the respondent in its own name. Indeed, he felt that it was clear that the respondent acted as more than a mere agent for the other bodies, and that it appropriated to itself many functions appropriate to a contracting party rather than an agent. On this basis, since at least one part of the applicant's case against the respondent survived the examination of the court under Order 84 of the Rules of the Superior Courts 1986, Finnegan J. concluded that its application for judicial review ought to be allowed to proceed.

Conflicts of Law

DIVORCE AND PARENTAL RESPONSIBILITY

The Brussels II Regulation   The Brussels II Regulation on divorce, other matrimonial matters and parental responsibility introduces changes to the rules for the recognition of divorce which are truly of seismic proportions.

The background to the Regulation   Before examining the Regulation it may be helpful to provide a brief summary of its background. Irish private international law on matrimonial proceedings and parental responsibility was largely a creature of common law developments, supplemented by recent statutory initiatives. Jurisdiction for proceedings for nullity of marriage, divorce and judicial separation was grounded on either domicile or one year's ordinary residence in the State immediately prior to the proceedings. The recognition and enforcement of foreign annulments is still governed by common law principles, with a dearth of Irish decisions: see Binchy, *Irish Conflicts of Law* (Butterworths, Dublin, 1988), pp. 255-265. A similar lack of judicial authorities is apparent in relation to the recognition of foreign legal separations.

The long saga on the recognition of foreign divorces and legal separations need not be revisited here. Suffice it to mention that the obscurely drafted terms of Article 41.3.3 of the Constitution, in conjunction with the constitutional prohibition on divorce legislation prior to 1995, led to a complex judicial policy in this area. The Domicile and Recognition of Foreign Divorces Act 1986 changed the rules for recognition of foreign divorces prospectively. In summary, a foreign divorce will be recognised here if *obtained* in the state of the domicile of one of the spouses or *recognised* in the state (or states) of domicile of both spouses.

Let us now turn to the European context. The Brussels Convention of 1968 on jurisdiction and the enforcement of judgments in civil and commercial matters excluded matters relating to family status from its purview. This was in part "because of their complexity and the fact that they did not directly affect economic integration. Moreover, there were significant differences as to the substantive law and rules for recognition among Member States." (*Explanatory Report on the 1998 Convention*, prepared by Dr. Alegria Borras, para. 3 (OJ 1998 C221/27)), para. 5.

Over the following decades, with the increasing mobility of people throughout the Community, as well as the tendency to greater similarity in the grounds for divorce among Member States, there was a growing feeling that a new Convention should be drawn up. Some Member States considered that the Hague Convention of 1970 on the Recognition of Divorces and Legal Separation provided a sufficient basis for the future, but others disagreed. The arguments in favour of drawing up a new Convention were threefold:

> "(a) the desire to introduce uniform standards for jurisdiction in matrimonial matters;
> (b) the need to introduce modern rules for the recognition and enforcement of judgments on annulment, divorce and separation among the Member States of the European Union, establishing a uniform procedure;
> (c) the avoidance of parallel procedures on matrimonial matters in different Member States, establishing rules on *lis pendens*, an innovation that on its own would be justification for the Convention and would contribute to the prevention of contradictory rulings." *Id.*

It was decided to draft a new Convention largely modelled on the 1968 Brussels Convention. The new Convention was drawn up on May 28, 1998: Council Act of May 28, 1998 drawing up, on basis of Article K.3 of the Treaty on European Union, the Convention on Jurisdiction and the Regulation and Enforcement of Judgments in Matrimonial Matters (98/C221/01).

This Convention was later translated into a Regulation, with some important modifications. The Regulation, generally referred to simply as "Brussels II", came into force on March 1, 2001. The title to the regulation is Council Regulation (EC) No. 1347/2000 of May 29, 2000 on jurisdiction and the recognition and enforcement of judgments in matrimonial matters and in matters of parental responsibility for children of both spouses. For analysis, see McEleavy, "The Brussels II Regulation: How the European Community Has Moved into Family Law" (2002) 51 I.C.L.Q. 883; Ancel & Muir Watt, "La désunion européenne: Le Reglement dit 'Bruxelles II'" [2001] Rev. Crit. de dr. internet. privé 403; Shannon & Kennedy, "Jurisdictional and Recognition and Enforcement Issues in Proceedings Concerning Parental Responsibility under the Brussels II Convention" [2000] I.F.L. 111; Treux, "Brussels II – Beware!" [2001] Fam. L. 233; Woelke, "Practice Checklist to EU Matrimonial Regulation", [2001] Fam. L. 138; Mostyn, "Brussels II – The Impact on Forum Disputes", [2001] Fam. L. 359; Karsten, "Brussels II – An English Perspective" [1998] I.F.L. 75; Hodson, "*White* and Forum – The International Implications", [2001] I.F.L. 4; Barker & Smith, "A Response to Brussels II – A View from Scotland" [2002] I.F.L. 44.

Brussels II Regulation summarised The Regulation has many echoes of the Brussels Convention of 1968. It deals with jurisdiction, recognition and enforcement but not choice-of-law. It places the emphasis on setting out clear rules for jurisdiction, letting recognition and enforcement follow more or less automatically. It prescribes limited grounds for non-recognition, giving very little scope to public policy. Even judgments based on fraudulent assertions as to jurisdiction have to be recognised. It does not bind Denmark.

The Regulation deals with matrimonial judgments affecting status and with decisions as to parental responsibility in the context of these proceedings. The relatively limited scope of the Regulation creates anomalies and invites questions as to where particular lines should be drawn. Let us now examine certain particular aspects of the Regulation.

Matrimonial proceedings   Article 2 prescribes the rules for jurisdictional competence in respect of divorce, legal separation and "marriage annulment": Article 2, paragraph 1. The latter concept requires some specific consideration under Irish law. There are two types of proceedings which could plausibly be described as marriage annulment. One concerns a voidable marriage, the validity of which can be challenged only by one of the parties to the purported marriage, and only during the lifetime of the other party. Unless and until a decree of nullity of marriage is made in respect of the purported marriage, the marriage is presumed to be valid, regardless of what evidence may be available to third parties which casts doubt on its validity. The legal process for the decree of annulment of a voidable marriage unquestionably falls within the definition of "marriage annulment" under Article 2, in spite of the fact that the language of the decree declares that the marriage was "void", from the start.

The other kind of decree of nullity of marriage in Irish law relates to a *void* marriage. Void marriages are truly, and unambiguously, void *ab initio*. They may be treated as such, not only by the parties themselves but also by third parties. A decree of nullity of a void marriage may be granted to either party or to a third party with a legitimate interest even after one or both of the parties is dead. Can a decree of nullity of this kind of marriage be characterised as a "marriage annulment", in all cases or even in some cases (as, for example, where the petitioner is himself or herself a party to the purported marriage and the other party is still alive)? The answer is not entirely clear. Certainly, the jurisdictional grounds specified in Article 2 appear premised on the assumption that the litigation is between the parties to the purported marriage and does not extend to nullity proceedings initiated by third parties. If this is the case, then Article 2 can be interpreted either as completely excluding proceedings for a decree of nullity of a void marriage or as restricting the remit of the Article to cases where one party to the purported marriage is petitioner and the other is respondent. Of these options, the second seems much more sensible. The idea that a large swathe of nullity litigation should be excluded because (in theory more than in practice) a third party could take the proceedings would create a range of anomalies and frustrate the purpose of the Regulation.

It has to be acknowledged, nonetheless, that an interpretation which brings proceedings in respect of void marriages within the scope of Article 2 but which excludes petitions taken by third parties creates its own substantial anomalies. For example, what is to be the position where a third party takes nullity proceedings in England in respect of an allegedly void marriage and two months later, one of the parties to the purported marriage launches similar proceedings in the Irish courts? Are the *lis pendens* provisions in Article 12 simply to be ignored because the first proceedings, on this assumed interpretation, fall outside the scope of Article 2? And is Ireland free, or required, to prescribe distinctive rules of jurisdiction and recognition to cover third party petitions in respect of void marriages? If so, is it open to Ireland to integrate these distinctive rules with those under the Regulation? An immediate difficulty here would result from the fact that constitutional issues might arise in respect of certain of these rules once the cover of necessity *qua* membership of the Community is removed.

Let us now look in more detail at the jurisdictional rules prescribed in Article 2. In paragraph (a), jurisdiction lies with the courts of the Member State in whose territory:

— the spouses are habitually resident, or

— the spouses were last habitually resident, in so far as one of them still resides there, or

— the respondent is habitually resident, or

— in the event of a joint application, either of the spouses is habitually resident, or

— the applicant is habitually resident if he or she resided there for at least a year immediately before the application was made, or

— the applicant is habitually resident if he or she resided there for at least six months immediately before the application was made and is either a national of the Member State in question or, in the case of the United Kingdom and Ireland, has his 'domicile' there. (Article 2, paragraph 2 provides that, for the purposes of the Regulation, 'domicile' is to have 'the same meaning as it has under the legal systems of the United Kingdom and Ireland'.)

In paragraph (b), jurisdiction lies with the courts of the Member State of the nationality of both spouses or, in the case of the United Kingdom and Ireland, of the 'domicile' of both spouses.

Habitual residence is thus the crucial basis for jurisdiction, with only a limited extension to cover cases of joint nationality or domicile. Broadly speaking, the Regulation proceeds on the basis that joint habitual residence, if ongoing, should constitute a good jurisdictional ground and, once it has formerly been established, that former state should be the basis of jurisdiction if one of the parties still "resides" there. It seems that the party's mere residence rather than habitual residence will suffice, provided the parties had formerly both habitually resided there.

The Regulation does not define 'habitual residence'. Dr. Alegria Borras explains ((*Explanatory Report on the 1998 Convention*, (OJ 1998 C221/27)), para. 32) that:

> "[a]lthough the possibility of including a provision determining habitual residence similar to the one in Article 52 of the 1968 Brussels Convention was discussed, in the end it was decided not to insert any particular provision on the matter. However, although not applicable under the Brussels Convention, particular account was taken of the definition given on numerous occasions by the Court of Justice, i.e. 'the place where the person had established, on a fixed basis, his permanent or habitual centre of interests, with all the relevant facts being taken into account for the purpose of determining such residence'."

So far as a single party's habitual residence is concerned, the Regulation regards the *respondent's* habitual residence as constituting an adequate jurisdictional ground. Certainly the respondent can have little complaint regarding it. Whether from a social standpoint the nexus of one party's habitual residence is sufficient may give rise to differing views. Since our present law prescribes jurisdictional competence based on the ordinary residence of either spouse, it would seem hard for us to complain.

When one moves away from the habitual residence of the respondent to consider the circumstances in which the habitual residence of the applicant should constitute a good jurisdictional ground, the social concerns change somewhat. The desire to discourage forum shopping becomes prominent. A further concern may be to protect the expectations of the respondent spouse so far as the security against being exposed to an unduly liberal divorce regime is concerned. If we assume that State A has a more conservative divorce regime, or one more protective of the interests of respondent spouses, than State B, it could perhaps be argued that spouses who have no connection with State B should be protected from easy resort to it by their partners.

Article 2 provides that the habitual residence of either spouse affords a good jurisdictional basis in the event of a joint application. This could arise, of course, in cases where the habitual residence in question is that of the respondent but that category has already been prescribed in the third indent, regardless of whether the application is by one of the parties or is made jointly. So the case that is really captured here arises where the habitual residence is that of the applicant. Clearly, if the respondent participates in a joint application, he or she can scarcely complain about the ill effects of forum shopping.

In the two other cases based on the applicant's habitual residence it is adjudged necessary to establish further elements of connection with the Member

State to which jurisdiction is ascribed. The first is that the applicant should have resided there for at least a year immediately before the application was made. This residence need not have been of a habitual character. The second is that the applicant should have resided there for at least six months and either be a national of the Member State or, in the case of the United Kingdom and Ireland, have his or her 'domicile' there.

This means that a combination of six months' residence combined with proof of habitual residence, of however short duration, is sufficient to provide a basis for jurisdiction. Thus, to take a practical example, an Irishman domiciled in Ireland, with his habitual residence, ordinary residence and residence in Ireland, could gain an entitlement to a divorce in another state based on residence of six months' duration combined with a more recent acquisition of the status of habitual residence, possibly over a period of (say) three or four months. He would not have to go through any pretence of changing his domicile. (It should be borne in mind that it is quite possible to be held to reside in more than one place at the same time, in contrast to the position in relation to one's domicile.) Whatever may be the merits of this change in the law, it is of potentially radical character.

It is worth noting that neither the domicile of the applicant spouse nor that of the respondent spouse constitutes a good basis, on its own, for jurisdiction. The domicile of the applicant spouse, in conjunction with six months' habitual residence, will do so. The domicile of the respondent spouse, in conjunction with six months' habitual residence, will *not* do so, though of course the habitual residence of the respondent spouse *will* do so, regardless of its duration and of any requirement as to domicile.

The domicile of *both* spouses will constitute a good basis for jurisdiction under paragraph (b). So, for example, if two English domiciliaries have lived for twenty years in Ireland after their marriage, while not changing their domicile, either is free to divorce the other in England on the basis of their combined domiciliary connection.

This brings us to a crucial question. 'Domicile' for the purposes of the Regulation, has "the same meaning as it has under the legal system of the United Kingdom and Ireland": Article 2, para. 2. The Regulation does not contain within itself as express provision whereby these Member States are to prescribe the meaning of domicile *for the purposes of the Regulation*. So what, therefore, is the meaning of domicile under Article 2? On one view, the meaning is to be found under the law of either Member State at the time of the promulgation of the Regulation: in Ireland, therefore, one would look to the common law, as modified by the Domicile and Recognition of Foreign Divorces Act 1986 and subject, of course, to the Constitution. Cf. *W. v. W.* [1993] 2 I.R. 96. On another view, the meaning is indeed to be found under the law of either Member State but that meaning is not frozen in time and is susceptible to change by way of judicial development and legislative intervention. Whether there are any limits to the power of courts or legislature to change the meaning of domicile for the purpose of the Regulation is not clear. For example, if the Oireachtas were in the future to define domicile as meaning four week's residence in a state, this would have the result that a connection deemed too tenuous to warrant acceptance under paragraph (a) would reappear under paragraph (b). This might seem to give an impermissible power to our legislature. As against this, paragraph (b) can be seen in a different light. It affords a basis for jurisdiction entirely separate from paragraph (a). It does not seek to justify that basis on the same rationale as underlies paragraph (a). On the contrary, it locates it in the distinctive legal cultures of the civil law system and the common law system. It may seem mistaken to attempt to freeze the development of the latter legal culture. One suspects, at the end of the day, that any liberalisation of the concept which equiparated domicile with a connection more tenuous than habitual residence would not be tolerated.

Parental responsibility proceedings: Scope of application of the Regulation
The Regulation also applies to civil proceedings relating to parental responsibility for the children of both spouses on the occasion of proceedings relating to divorce, legal separation or marriage annulment: Article 1, paragraph 1. It is important to note what the Regulation does *not* embrace. It is not concerned with proceedings involving non-marital parents, or proceedings involving parents who are indeed married to each other but which are not one of the three categories of matrimonial proceedings just mentioned. So, for example, straightforward custody or access disputes under the Guardianship of Infants Act 1964 will not fall within the terms of the Regulation save where they occur "on the occasion of" one of these matrimonial proceedings.

Jurisdictional rules relating to parental responsibility Let us now turn to consider the jurisdictional rules relating to parental responsibility. The courts of a Member State exercising jurisdiction of virtue of Article 2 on an application for divorce, legal separation or marriage annulment have jurisdiction in a matter relating to parental responsibility over a child of both spouses where the child is habitually resident in the Member State: Article 3, paragraph 1. Where the child is not habitually resident in the Member State dealing with the matrimonial matter, the courts of that Member State nonetheless will have jurisdiction over the parental responsibility matter if the child is habitually resident in one of the Member States and two further elements are established: first that at least one of the spouses has parental responsibility in relation to the child and secondly that the jurisdiction of the courts of the Member State in question has been accepted by the spouses and is in the best interests of the child: Article 3, paragraph 2.

This latter ground for jurisdiction is largely similar to Article 10 (1) of the 1996 Hague Convention but less demanding in that it does not require that one of the parties should habitually reside in the Member State at the time of the commencement of the proceedings. Dr. Alegria Borras (writing before the

Convention was translated into a Regulation) explains this difference as:

> "deriv[ing] from the differing subject matters of the two Conventions: the Hague Convention deals with protection of children, whereas the Convention to which this report relates deals with matrimonial matters and for that reason the parents' connection with the courts of a State for the purposes of determining jurisdiction in matrimonial matters is determined by the grounds set out in Article 2. Article 3 (2) is designed to cover one particular situation in which the best solution is to use the same grounds as in the Hague Convention." (Para 38 of *Explanatory Report on the 1998 Convention*, (OJ 1998 C221/27).

The parental responsibility jurisdiction conferred by paragraphs 1 and 2 is finite. It ceases in three circumstances:

> First, as soon as the judgment allowing or refusing the application for divorce, legal separation or marriage annulment has become final;
>
> secondly, in those cases where proceedings in relation to parental responsibility are still pending at the time the judgment in the matrimonial proceedings has become final, as soon as a judgment in the parental responsibility proceedings becomes final; and
>
> thirdly, as soon as either the matrimonial proceedings or the parental responsibility proceedings have come to an end for some other reason: Article 3, para. 3.

Examples include cases where a divorce application is withdrawn or one of the spouses dies. (*Alegria Borras Report*, para. 39.)

These rules for cesser echo Article 10 (2) of the Hague Convention of 1996 and are designed to avoid any contradiction between the two texts.

A few points about when proceedings 'become final' may be appropriate. Divorce and annulment proceedings do not present a problem. Proceedings for legal separation are not really problematic in spite of the theoretical possibility that the order for separation may be rescinded at some later time. If finality of proceedings means merely that the judgment 'cannot be the subject of any sort of appeal', then a decree for judicial separation under Irish domestic legislation is indeed final in spite of the possibility of its subsequent rescission. But is this test the proper one to apply to proceedings relating to parental responsibility? The essence of proceedings of this character is their non-finality, in that issues relating to the welfare of the child, including custody and access, can always be revisited throughout his or her minority. At what point, therefore, may proceedings of this kind be considered to have become final? Dr. Alegria Borras's analysis (para. 39) does not give the clearest of answers:

"[S]ubparagraph (b) adds [to subparagraph (a)] another situation where, on the date on which the judgment cannot be the subject or any sort of appeal, proceedings in relation to parental responsibility are still pending and provides that jurisdiction will not cease until a judgment in the responsibility proceedings has become final; in any event in this situation jurisdiction on parental responsibility may be exercised even if the judgment allowing or refusing the application for divorce, legal separation or marriage annulment has become final. It was necessary to insert this provision .... because it is conceivable that when different authorities within the same country are involved or in cases before the same authorities, the judgment on the matrimonial proceedings may be final at a time when the proceedings on parental responsibility have not yet come to an end. Jurisdiction on the parental responsibility therefore ceases on whichever of those two dates applies. It is therefore understood that proceedings on parental responsibility, once initiated, must continue until a final judgment is reached. The fact that the application relating to the marriage has been resolved may not prejudice the expectations created both for the parents and for the child that the parental responsibility proceedings will terminate in the Member State in which they began. Although not expressly stated, the intention is that there should be no *perpetuatio jurisdictionis* but that proceedings on parental responsibility initiated in connection with matrimonial proceedings should not be interrupted."

The import of this analysis appears to be that proceedings relating to parental responsibility, even if entirely limited in their intended temporal scope, will be deemed to have become final once the time for appeal has expired.

Article 4 confronts a crucial issue of policy. This concerns the relationship between the Regulation and the Hague Child Abduction Convention of 1980. The 1980 Convention, which was incorporated into Irish law by the Child Abduction and Enforcement of Custody Orders Act 1991, seeks to provide a robust solution to the problem of child abduction by requiring the courts of the state to which the child has been abducted to return the child to the state from which the child was abducted. This is a general rule subject only to limited exceptions. The Convention was necessary because of several factors: the increased breakdown of parental relationships, the reduction in the cost of international travel, the tendency of courts to be over-sympathetic to parents who return to their home state and the fact that the delay involved in plenary proceedings favours the abducting parent because disturbing the child's new environment may be detrimental to his or her welfare. We have seen many cases under the 1980 Convention coming before the Irish courts over the past decade.

It would clearly be unacceptable if all the benefits achieved by the 1980 Convention could be imperilled, or even compromised, by the Regulation.

Accordingly Article 4 of the Regulation concedes the right of way to the 1980 Convention in areas of potential conflict. It provides that:

> "[t]he courts with jurisdiction within the meaning of Article 3 shall exercise their jurisdiction in conformity with the Hague Convention of 25 October 1980 on the Civil Aspects of International Child Abduction, and in particular Articles 3 and 16 thereof."

Integration of jurisdictional rules with wider international framework We now must consider how the jurisdictional rules prescribed by Articles 2 to 6 are integrated with the wider international context of matrimonial and parental responsibility proceedings. The first and most obvious point to note is that proceedings other than those specified in the Regulation continue to be governed by the pre-existing private international law rules. So, for example, parental responsibility proceedings relating to children of unmarried parents or of married parents outside the context of divorce, legal separation or marriage annulment proceedings will be subject to these pre-existing rules.

The second issue concerns the question of the exclusive nature of the jurisdiction under these five Articles. This is dealt with by Article 7, which provides that a spouse who (a) is habitually resident in the territory of a Member State or (b) is a national of a Member State or, in the case of the United Kingdom and Ireland, has his or her 'domicile' in the territory of one of the latter Member States, may be sued in another Member State only in accordance with the five Articles.

So it is not possible for Ireland to prescribe ancillary bases for jurisdiction which will impact on a spouse who is habitually resident in another Member State, or is a national of another Member State or, in the case of the United Kingdom, domiciled there. Articles 2 to 6 represent the total range of jurisdictional options in relation to such a spouse. Accordingly, Ireland could not prescribe a jurisdictional base more liberal than indents five and six of Article 2, para 1 so far as it might affect a spouse who comes within the scope of Article 7. A jurisdictional ground based on the mere habitual residence of the applicant here, or his or her habitual residence coupled with only *three* months' residence immediately before the application was made, would accordingly be exorbitant and impermissible to the extent that it affects a respondent spouse who is embraced by Article 7. Equally all the other Member States are prohibited from taking such a step.

A few questions may be addressed about the detail of Article 7. First, on the question of exorbitant jurisdictional grounds, it would seem that neither Ireland nor the United Kingdom is permitted to introduce nationality as a basis on which a spouse would be entitled to apply for a divorce, separation or annulment in Ireland or the United Kingdom, whether as an unqualified ground or one that is in conjunction with the requirement of six months' residence on the part of the applicant immediately before the application.

Secondly, we can return to the issue of whether Ireland (or the United Kingdom) is permitted to change its rules of domicile so, for example, as to render the concept equivalent to that of habitual residence, with the effect that the habitual residence of the applicant, combined with six months' residence immediately before the making of the application, would suffice for the purposes of indent six of Article 2, paragraph 1. If this were permitted, there would be a significant dissonance between the law here (or in the United Kingdom) and the law in other Member States. Perhaps it could be argued that there is a similar potential for elasticity in the concept of nationality. A practical difference, however, is that the concept of nationality has a considerably greater role to play in the legal systems of Member States in areas other than private international law than does the concept of domicile, which extends beyond private international law only in the context of taxation policy.

Let us now consider Article 8, which deals with what it calls 'residual jurisdiction'. It provides as follows:

1. Where no court of a Member State has jurisdiction pursuant to Articles 2 to 6, jurisdiction shall be determined in each Member State, by the laws of that State.

2. As against a respondent who is not habitually resident and is not either a national of a Member State or, in the case of the United Kingdom and Ireland, does not have his 'domicile' within the territory of one of the latter Member States, any national of a Member State who is habitually resident within the territory of another Member State may, like the nationals of the State, avail himself of the rules of jurisdiction applicable in that State.

Under existing law in Ireland, there are grounds for jurisdiction which fall outside the jurisdictional grounds prescribed by Articles 2 to 6. Our courts have jurisdiction in divorce (Family Law (Divorce) Act 1996, section 39), legal separation (Family Law Reform Act 1989, section 31), and annulment (Family Law Act 1995, section 39), where either of the spouses is domiciled in the State on the date of the proceedings or has had his or her ordinary residence here for one year immediately preceding the proceedings.

So far as Article 8, paragraph 2 is concerned, a practical example may be of help. If a French national habitually resident in Ireland were to marry a Canadian citizen with a domicile in British Columbia, the Canadian citizen not being habitually resident in Ireland at the time of an application by the French national for a divorce here, the rules of jurisdiction under Irish law – which can be broader than those prescribed in Articles 2 to 6 – can be availed of by the French national.

Examination as to jurisdiction and admissibility   Section 2 of the Regulation deals with examination as to jurisdiction and admissibility. Article 9 imposes on the court of a Member State seised of a case over which it has no jurisdiction under the Regulation and over which the court of another Member State has jurisdiction by virtue of the Regulation, to declare of its own motion that it has no jurisdiction. Article 10, paragraph 1 deals with the situation where a respondent habitually resident in a State other than the Member State where the action was brought does not enter an appearance. The court with jurisdiction must stay the proceedings so long as it is not shown that the respondent has been able to receive the document instituting the proceedings or an equivalent document in sufficient time to enable him or her to arrange for his or her defence, or that all necessary steps have been taken to this end. Article 10, paragraph 2 provides that Article 19 of Council Regulation (EC) No. 1348/ 2000 of May 29, 2000 on the service in the Member States of judicial and extra judicial documents in civil or commercial matters is to apply instead of the provisions of paragraph 1 if the document instituting the proceedings or an equivalent document had to be transmitted from one Member State to another pursuant to that Regulation. In cases where the provisions of that Regulation are not applicable, Paragraph 3 provides that Article 15 of the Hague Convention of November 15, 1965 on the service abroad of judicial and extra judicial documents in civil or commercial matters is to apply if the document instituting the proceedings or an equivalent document had to be transmitted abroad pursuant to that Convention.

Lis pendens *and dependent actions*   Let us now consider Article 11 of the Regulation, which is the source of considerable controversy. Its rationale might, at first sight, seem an obviously sensible one. Further reflection reveals the more problematic implications of its provisions. Article 11 may be quoted in full:

> "1. Where proceedings involving the same cause of action and between the same parties are brought before courts of different Member States, the court second seised shall of its own motion stay its proceedings until such time as the jurisdiction of the court first seised is established.
>
> 2. Where proceedings for divorce, legal separation or marriage annulment not involving the same cause of action and between the same parties are brought before courts of different Member States, the court second seised shall of its own motion stay its proceedings until such time as the jurisdiction of the court first seised is established.
>
> 3. Where the jurisdiction of the court first seised is established, the court second seised shall decline jurisdiction in favour of that court.
>
>   In that case, the party who brought the relevant action before the court second seised may bring that action before the court first seised.

4.　For the purposes of this Article, a court shall be deemed to be seised:

(a) at the time when the document instituting the proceedings or an equivalent document is lodged with the court, provided that the applicant has not subsequently failed to take the steps he was required to take to have service effected on the respondent;

or

(b) if the document has to be served before being lodged with the court, at the time when it is received by the authority responsible for service, provided that the applicant has not subsequently failed to take the steps he was required to take to have the document lodged with the court."

The impact of these provisions is considerable. Paragraph 1 contains a clear rule: where proceedings involving the *same cause of action and between the same parties* are brought before courts of different Member States, the court second seised is *obliged*, of its own motion, to stay the proceedings until such time as the jurisdiction of the court first seised is established. So, for example, divorce proceedings taken in Ireland must concede the right of way to divorce proceedings in France where the French courts were seised before the Irish courts. This is so, regardless of the practical implications for either spouse, having regard to the differences in the grounds for divorce and the ancillary provisions in the legal systems of the two States. British legal commentators have strongly criticised the abrogation of *forum non conveniens* jurisprudence in this context. See McEleavy, "The Brussels II Regulation: How the European Community Has Moved into Family Law" (2002) 51 I.C.L.Q. 883 at 887; Barker & Smith, "A Response to Brussels II – A View from Scotland" [2002] I.F.L. 44 at 44.

Paragraph 2 deserves a closer look. First, one should note that, in contrast to paragraph 1, it does not apply to *all* the kinds of proceedings that fall within the scope of the Regulation. Only matrimonial proceedings and not parental responsibility proceedings fall within its scope. The effect of the paragraph is that if (say) divorce proceedings are initiated in one Member State before annulment proceedings are initiated in another Member State, the annulment proceedings must be stayed, even though the logic of the situation might be thought to be that if a marriage is or may be null and void under the law of the second Member State, the courts of the second Member State should not have to concede jurisdiction to proceedings in the first Member State which are likely to result in a decree that is incompatible with the view that the marriage was null and void. Whether this criticism would find such support around Europe today is doubtful, however, since marriage annulment is generally regarded as a species of remedy for spouses rather than truly involving a matter of determining the status of an alleged marriage *ab initio*. In any event, paragraph 3 enables the spouse who brought the annulment proceedings to initiate annulment proceedings before the court first seised. In this context one should contrast the effect of this paragraph with Article 5, which provides that the court in which proceedings are pending on the basis of Articles 2 to 4 has also jurisdiction to examine a counterclaim, in so far as the latter comes within the scope of the Regulation. Dr. Alegria Borras observes (para. 55) that:

> "it needs to be noted that the rule in paragraph 3 of ...... Article [11] differs from the one in Article 5 ...... The rule in Article 5 is a rule of jurisdiction whereas the one in Article 10 is a provision applying the rules of jurisdiction in dependent actions. We must remember that it will operate differently since there will be cases in which no counterclaim would be possible (for instance because the time is not right), but it would still be possible to apply the rule in Article 11 (3)."

Provisional, including protective, measures   Article 12 provides that:

> "[i]n urgent cases, the provisions of this Regulation shall not prevent the courts of a Member State from taking such provisional, including protective, measures in respect of persons or assets in that State as may be available under the law of that Member State, even if, under this Regulation, the court of another Member State has jurisdiction as to the substance of the matter."

Dr. Alegria Borras notes (para. 55) that nothing is said about the type of measures or their connection with the matrimonial proceedings:

> "These measures, accordingly, affect even matters that do not come within the scope of the Convention. This is a rule which enshrines matrimonial law jurisdiction, thereby derogating from the rules laid down in the first part of the Convention."

Dr Alegria Borras was of course writing before the Convention was translated into the Regulation. The Regulation contains a provision identical to that in the Convention.

Recognition and enforcement   The provisions in the Regulation relating to recognition and enforcement are of crucial importance and have provoked some controversy. The basic rule as to recognition is set out in Article 14, para. 1:

> "A judgment given in a Member State shall be recognised in the other Member States without any special procedure being required."

Four grounds for *non-recognition* of a judgment relating to a divorce, legal separation or marriage annulment are set out in Article 15, paragraph 1. They are as follows:

> "(a) where recognition would be contrary to the public policy of the Member State where recognition is sought;
> (b) where, in cases of judgment in default of appearance, the respondent was not properly served;
> (c) where the judgment is irreconcilable with a judgment given in proceedings between the same parties in the Member State in which recognition is sought; and
> (d) where the judgment is irreconcilable with an earlier judgment given in another Member State or in a non-Member State between the same parties, provided that the earlier judgment fulfils the conditions necessary for its recognition in the Member State in which recognition is sought."

The potential impact of the first of these grounds for non-recognition – that of public policy – is significantly weakened by Article 17, which provides that:

> "[t]he jurisdiction of the court of the Member State of origin may not be reviewed. The test of public policy referred to in Article 15 (1)(a) and (2)(a) may not be applied to the rules relating to jurisdiction set out in Articles 2 to 8."

In practice, this means that if an Irish-domiciled couple are living in Ireland, and a divorce is obtained based on a fraudulent assertion of an habitual residence on the part of one or both of them in England, that divorce has to be recognised in Ireland even where the fraud can later be shown. This is a radical transformation from the previous legal position and differs from what the Convention had contained in order to assuage concerns of this kind. Whether Article 6 of the European Convention on Human Rights may be called in aid by the spouse who is the victim of such fraud remais to be seen: cf. Mole, "From Rome to Brussels via Strasbourg – Pellegrini v. Italy and Brussels II" [2002] I.F.L. 9.

The grounds for non-recognition of a judgment relating to parental responsibility, set out in Article 15(2), are modelled largely on Article 23 of the 1996 Hague Convention. They include the grounds that the child was not given an opportunity to be heard and that a person whose parental responsibility was infringed was not given an opportunity to be heard.

Article 21, paragraph 1 provides that a judgment on the exercise of parental responsibility in respect of a child of both parties given in a Member State which is enforceable in that State and has been served is to be enforced in another Member State when, on the application of "any interested party", it has been declared enforceable there.

Future developments Let us now consider briefly the future developments that are likely to take place. In July 2000, France produced a fairly modest proposal, OJ 2000 C234/07 to provide automatic enforcement of rights of access for children under the age of sixteen. This already looks somewhat passé. The Council and the Commission have a much broader agenda: cf. the Commission Working Document, *Mutual Recognition of Decisions on Parental Responsibility* Com/2001/0166; Karsten, "The Draft EC Regulation on Parental Responsibility", [2001] Fam. L. 885. The Commission has issued a Proposal for the Council Regulation on jurisdiction and the recognition and enforcement of judgments in matters of parental responsibility (OJ 2001 C332E/269). On May 3, 2002 it adopted a Proposal which incorporated the provisions of the previous Proposal; on July 6, 2002, in the light of this development, the Commission formally withdrew its previous Proposal. Among the matters under consideration are extending the scope of relationships covered by the Regulation to include families outside marriage, addressing issues of choice-of-law and enhancing the substantive rights of children, reflecting the values of the United Nations Convention on the Rights of the Child. In truth the journey is in the direction of a unified system of family law for all Member States, based on common values. Cf. McGlynn, "Families and the European Union Charter of Fundamental Rights: Progressive Change or Entrenching the *Status Quo*" 26 Eur. L. Rev. 582 (2001). Whether this is the best direction and whether the goal can be achieved in practice are much larger questions. For thoughtful consideration of these trends, see McEleavy, "The Brussels II Regulation: How the European Community Has Moved into Family Law" (2002) 51 I.C.L.Q. 883 at 895–908; Everall & Nicholls, "Brussels I and II – The Impact on Family Law" [2002] Fam. L. 674; Clarkson, Brussels III – Matrimonial Property European Style" [2002] Fam. L. 683.

STATUTORY AND COMMON LAW RULES FOR RECOGNITION OF FOREIGN DIVORCES

In the *Annual Review of Irish Law 1999*, pp.67-9 we analysed *McG v. W* [2000] 1 I.L.R.M. 107, where McGuinness J. held that recognition might be afforded to foreign divorces on the basis of residence as well as domicile. She came to this conclusion because the introduction of a divorce regime in Ireland, with a residence-based jurisdiction, warranted recognition of foreign divorces on the principle of reciprocity, following the inspiration of *Travers v. Holley* [1953] P. 246. Moreover support for this approach could be gleaned from *Indyka v. Indyka* [1969] 1 A.C. 33. McGuinness J. went so far as to hold, albeit *obiter*, that the power of the courts to develop a residence-based ground for recognition operated, not only for the period before the enactment of the Domicile and Recognition of Foreign Divorces Act 1986 but also as a supplement to the grounds for recognition prescribed by section 5 of that Act.

The Attorney General was not represented in *McG v. W.* In *M.E.C. v. JAC* [2001] 2 I.R. 399, the same issue fell for consideration this time with full representation for the Attorney General. The facts, briefly, were that spouses of Irish origin, having married in 1968 in Ireland, lived thereafter together in England until 1979, when the wife returned to Ireland. In 1980, the parties were divorced in England, having asserted an English domicile. Kinlen J. held that neither spouse was domiciled in England at the time of the divorce: see below. Thus, if the divorce was to be recognized, it would have to be on the basis of the husband's residential connections with England.

The Attorney General presented several formidable arguments against the adequacy or correctness of the holding in *McG v. W.* He conceded that it was open to the courts further to develop the rules for recognition of foreign divorces granted before the enactment of the 1986 Act but argued that it would be undesirable for them to do so. He pointed to instances where amending the recognition rules in one case could cause hardship in another case. He gave the following example. A couple were married in Ireland in 1970. Difficulties arose between them and the wife went to England where she obtained a divorce on the basis of her residence in 1977. She returned to Ireland in 1978 and was subsequently reconciled with her former husband. They decided to buy a home and start a family. If they consulted a lawyer then, they would have been told that the 1970 marriage subsisted in Irish law and they were thus still married. It would not be consistent with justice for them now to be deprived of their status under Irish law.

The Attorney General gave a further example of how hardship could result from a retrospective extension of recognition rules to embrace residence as a ground for recognition:

> "A marries B. He moves to England for a few years but intends ultimately to return to Ireland. He obtains a divorce in England in 1975 which is not then entitled to recognition in Ireland. He then marries C in England but they eventually separate. B dies and A marries D in Ireland. (His marriage to C not entitled to recognition in Ireland). If the residence is retroactively adopted as a ground of recognition then:
> (a) The divorce between A and B is entitled to recognition.
> (b) The marriage between A and C 'becomes' entitled to recognition in Irish law even though it was not so when it occurred or when they separated.
> (c) The marriage between A and D ceases to be valid under Irish law even though it was valid when it occurred.
> (d) The marriage between A and D 'becomes' bigamous even though it was not so when it occurred."

The Attorney General pointed out that, in *K.D. (otherwise C) v. N.C.* [1985] I.R. 697, where the Supreme Court had refused the invitation to apply the 'real and substantial connection' test developed by the House of Lords in *Indyka v. Indyka* [1969] 1 A.C. 33, one reason for declining to do so which Finlay C.J. had mentioned was that to apply *Indyka*'s test would be much more likely to lead to 'substantial injustice in the application of any decision of this court to other parties in different cases then it could possibly contribute to any requirements of justice in the instant case before us.' The hazards of judicial development of the law on recognition were well illustrated by the fact that, despite the best efforts of the English courts in *Indyka v. Indyka*, the issue had been soon revisited by legislation.

A further argument in favour of legislative rather than judicial development of the law on recognition was that a convention on jurisdiction and the recognition and enforcement of judgments in matrimonial matters (1998 OJC 221) had recently been formulated. (This had subsequently been transmogrified into a Regulation, which came into force on March 1, 2001: see above 37).

The Attorney General argued that *W. v. W.* [1993] I.L.R.M. 294 was not authority for treating the enactment of the Family Law (Divorce) Act 1996, and in particular its provisions regulating the jurisdiction of the Irish courts to grant a divorce, as a reason to extend further the rules for recognizing foreign divorces. In fact what Blayney J. had said in *W v. W* was that judge-made recognition rules could not leave out of account statutory recognition rules as opposed to statutory jurisdictional rules. So far as the Fifteenth Amendment and the 1996 Act provided any justification for the judicial modification of the recognition rules, such justification was only operative with effect from the date the Act came into force. In the normal course of events a statute operated prospectively. Likewise the Attorney General submitted that an amendment to the Constitution was prospective unless expressly declared to operate retroactively. He relied on J.M. Kelly *The Irish Constitution* (3rd ed by Hogan & Whyte eds., Butterworths, Dublin, 1994), p.13, for this proposition.

The Attorney General argued that McGuinness J. had adopted a mistaken approach in *McG v. W* concerning the entitlement of the courts with regard to divorces obtained subsequent to the coming into force of the 1986 Act to develop the grounds for recognition further than those prescribed in the 1986 Act itself. He contended that the recognition rules were to be found exclusively in the Act. In *W v. W* Egan J. had made it clear that the courts' power to develop these rules was limited to 'the period before' the enactment of the legislation.

Turning to the terms of the legislation, the Attorney General argued that what section 5(1) did was to substitute a 'rule' for a 'rule of law'. While courts could develop rules of law, which were judge-made, this power had been replaced by a legislative rule so far as divorces obtained after the enactment of the legislation were concerned.

If it had been the intention of the Oireachtas to preserve the power of the courts to develop their own rules in regard to recognition of divorces granted after 1986 it could have easily done so. For example, it could have formulated the section in terms such as:-

> "Notwithstanding any rule of law, a divorce shall be recognized if granted in the country where either spouse is domiciled."

To modify the statutory rule applicable to foreign divorces granted after October 2, 1986 would be contrary to Article 15.2 of the Constitution.

Kinlen J. made it clear that he favoured the conclusion advocated by the Attorney General, but his judgment does not clarify exactly which of the arguments put forward by the Attorney General met with his approval. Certainly he accepted the argument based on the negative implications associated with an extension:

> "If the grounds of recognition are retrospectively extended to include the residence of either party then that will have serious implications for the way in which the State and many of its citizens have ordered their affairs. In an affidavit sworn by Ms O'Mahony of the Chief State Solicitor's Office, she avers that the 1991 Census showed that the marital status of 6,103 residents was regulated by foreign divorces; by 1996 that number had increased to nearly 10,000."

Kinlen J. did not appear to accept the argument that judicial changes should be stayed pending radical developments at a European level, since the courts could 'not assume the result of referenda or prospective legislation'. In fact Brussels II had already come into force a few days before Kinlen J. delivered his judgment.

At all events, Kinlen J. held that the divorce obtained in England should not be recognised. He thus adopted a position opposed to that favoured by McGuinness J. in *McG. W.*

Kinlen J's approach may be contrasted with that of Morris P in *D.T. v. F.L.* [2002] 2 I.L.R.M. 152. The divorce with which Morris P. was concerned had been obtained in the Netherlands in 1994 by an Irish husband, who was held not to have been domiciled there at the time.

Morris P. pointed out that the divorce in *McG v. W* had been obtained before the 1986 Act came into effect. He regarded this difference as decisive, against recognition of the 1994 divorce, for three reasons. First, dicta of Egan and Blayney JJ. in *W. v. W.* clearly contemplated that, on the passing of the 1986 Act and thereafter, the recognition of foreign divorces became regulated by statute. Secondly, section 5(1) of the Act by its wording clearly intended to substitute a 'rule', which meant a statutory rule, for a 'rule of law', which meant a judge-made rule. Thirdly, it was apparent that the legislature had intended that all aspects of recognition of foreign divorces would be governed by the 1986 Act since section 5(4) provided for circumstances in which courts should recognize a divorce which was recognized, though not granted, by courts of the spouses' common domicile (or respective domiciles), reflecting the holding in the English decision of *Armitage v. Attorney General* [1906] P. 135. Morris P. observed that this issue:

> "had not been litigated in the courts in this jurisdiction. However, in my view, it is of significance that the legislature by providing for this circumstance in advance of the courts being called upon to consider the issue clearly intended to remove from the common law all matters in relation to recognition."

Morris P. went on to reiterate that he had no doubt that since it had been open to the court in *McG v. W* to bring the common law in line with current policy, it had been correct for it to have done so. He would had done the same in a similar case, but the passing of the 1986 Act had removed this jurisdiction from him so far as divorces obtained after its coming into force were concerned.

Morris P.'s reasons for holding that section 5 of the 1986 Act should not be interpreted as being subject to a common law supplementary jurisdiction to expand grounds for recognition of foreign divorces are convincing. His invocation of 'current policy', which traces its origins to *W. v. W.*, might have been expanded upon. It is surely odd that current policy can prescribe grounds for recognition of a divorce on grounds broader than those provided for in existing legislation provided only that the divorce was obtained before that legislation came into force sixteen years ago. This is a time warp that can be justified neither on principle nor on policy grounds.

It should be noted that in *A.S. (otherwise A.B.) v. R.B.*, Supreme Court, December 18, 2001, the case proceeded on the basis, accepted by the parties, that the principles of *W. v. W.* applied to the recognition of foreign divorces. Thus the Court did not have to address the question whether recognition should be afforded to a foreign divorce granted on the basis of citizenship.

DOMICILE

Retrospective ascriptions of intention, especially where they relate to a failed marriage, inevitably cause difficulty for courts in trying to identify where subjective recollection coincides with objective fact. In *D.T. v. F.L.*, High Court, November 23, 2001, the question whether a divorce obtained by the husband was entitled to recognition, either on the basis of his domicile or residence in the Netherlands at the time. The spouses, both of Irish domicile of origin, married in 1980. They lived in Ireland after the marriage until 1987 when the husband took up employment in the Netherlands as project manager responsible for his new employer's undertakings there. They sold their family home in Dublin and went to live in the Netherlands with their three children.

The employment contract was for five years with the possibility of renewal.

Significant tax advantages attached to employment for this period. The spouses made a conscious decision that the time they would spend in the Netherlands would be a worthwhile experience and that they should become fully integrated into the life and culture of the country. They chose to live in a semi-rural area, becoming fluent in the Dutch language.

Differences arose in the marriage. As a result, the wife and children returned to Ireland. The family home in the Netherlands was sold. As regards the husband's intentions around that time, the husband gave evidence that it had always been his intention to remain on in the Netherlands. His job required his continued attendance there. He pointed to the fact that, when leaving Ireland in 1987, he had cancelled membership of his clubs in Ireland. This, said Morris P. was 'a significant factor' as he was a gifted helmsman sailing to Olympic standards. The husband some time later, after the divorce, did return to live in Ireland where he took up new employment.

Applying the principles stated in *Joyce v. Fagan* [1946] I.R. 277, Morris P. held that the husband had not acquired a domicile in the Netherlands at the time of the divorce. He observed:

> "In this case I would be prepared to accept that the [husband] became fond of living in Holland and that he was content to remain there for the purposes of his work. I would have no difficulty in accepting that if [the company employing him] had renewed and continued to renew his contract in Holland all other things being equal he would have been prepared to remain there. However I am equally sure that, if for any reason his employment was discontinued with [that company] and if he was willing to travel to another country to pursue a job opportunity, I could never foresee the possibility that the [husband] would remain in Holland come what may and even if he were without employment. In my view he has not satisfied the positive element of the test. No more do I consider that he formulated any intention of abandoning Ireland as his domicile of origin. The only evidence which is consistent with his intention was the sale of the family home and the cancelling of his membership of clubs. If one weighs these factors against the evidence that he returned to Ireland for his summer holidays, that he visited his family in Ireland on a number of occasions, that he arranged for his wife to return to Ireland when difficulties arose in the marriage, in my view it is clear beyond doubt that he never abandoned his domicile of origin."

In *A.S. (otherwise A.B.) v. R.B.*, Supreme Court, December 19, 2001, the petitioner, who had gone through a ceremony of marriage with the respondent ('the wife') in 1986, after she had been divorced from the notice party ('the husband') in Germany in 1985, sought the annulment of the marriage on the basis that the German divorce should not be recognised under Irish law. The

Court had little hesitation in denying recognition of the divorce and in upholding Lavan J.'s declaration of nullity. The wife and husband, both of German origin, had been living in Ireland for most of their childhood and adult years. The parents of each of them had come to Ireland from Germany and had lived here continuously. The wife was born in Germany in 1952. Her family came to Ireland when she was ten years old. Her father died in 1968. She married her husband (who was the notice party in the instant proceedings) in 1976. He was born in Germany in 1949. He had come to Ireland when he was six years old with his parents.

There was some factors linking the spouses and their respective parents with Germany. The wife's father had expressed a wish to be buried in the German military cemetery. Her mother would have wished to return to Germany but this was not a practical proposition since her home had been in the German Democratic Republic; moreover financial considerations also made it impossible for her to return. The 1985 divorce had been sought and obtained on the basis of the wife's German citizenship. The husband's parents had never become Irish citizens; his father, though in his eighties, still travelled to Germany at least once a year. The husband had spent all his working life in Ireland, apart from two periods when he worked for about eighteen months in Britain and Germany. He said that he did not regard himself as committed to living permanently in Ireland. He retained a number of connections with Germany and, as a result of a new business venture, was now going there every fortnight for two or three days. His company had plans to expand and he said that he might move to Germany within the next year. Neither he nor his father, when dealing with the revenue authorities, asserted an Irish domicile. Both the wife and the husband spoke German in their homes, preferred to mix socially with other German nationals living in Ireland and kept up German customs, such as celebrating Christmas on Christmas Eve.

The Supreme Court hearing proceeded on the basis that *W. v. W.* [1993] 2 I.R. 477 represented the appropriate law for determining whether the divorce should be recognised. Recognition thus depended on establishing that either party had a German domicile at the time it was obtained. The Supreme Court held that neither party had a German domicile at that time and that both of them had an Irish domicile.

The Chief Justice was satisfied that there had been evidence from which Lavan J. had been entitled to infer that the wife's parents had acquired an Irish domicile when she attained her majority in 1973. There could be little room for doubt that, at some stage prior to the death of her father in 1968, her parents had decided to live in Ireland indefinitely:

> "They had built up a business here, they had brought their children with them, the latter being educated in Ireland and going back to East Germany, where their home originally had been, was out of the question. That was also the position of the wife's mother after her husband died:

while her preference would have been to return to her native country, she accepted that, in practical terms, it was not a realistic option."

Similarly, Lavan J. had been entitled to hold on the evidence that the parents of the husband had at some stage abandoned their domicile of origin and acquired an Irish domicile prior to his reaching majority in 1970. They had built a house in Ireland and had never since then at any stage taken any steps to return to Germany to live there.

Even if it could be said that the parties had retained their dependent domiciles of origin when they reached the age of majority in 1973 and 1970 respectively, the Chief Justice was satisfied that the only inference that could be drawn from the evidence was that by 1985, when the divorce was granted, that domicile had been abandoned:

> "They had both been living in this country since childhood, in the case of the [husband] since he was 6 and in the case of the wife since she was 10 years old. They had been educated in this country, worked here, had bought a house here and had married and started a family here. There is nothing to suggest that at any time they had ever intended to reside permanently in any place other than in Ireland. If the test for establishing whether a person has acquired a domicile of choice in a particular place is whether he has fixed his sole or chief residence there with the intention of continuing to reside there for an unlimited time, to use the words of Lord Westbury in *Udny v. Udny*, then there seems to me to be no reason to doubt that, assuming that they had not lost their domicile of origin when they respectively attained the age of majority, they had undoubtedly acquired a domicile of choice by the time of the divorce proceedings ... The somewhat tentative suggestion in evidence by the notice party that he thought it possible, given the nature of his business, that he might return to live in Germany is of no assistance in determining his domicile [at the time of the divorce].
>
> The fact that all the parties concerned – the wife, the [husband] and their respective parents – treasured their links with their native country, spoke its language whenever they could, had close social relations with other Germans living in Ireland and observed the customs of their land of origin, is, as Budd J. pointed out in *Re Sillar, Hurley v. Wimbush* [1956] I.R. 344, entirely reconcilable with an intention to make Ireland their permanent home. The same can be said of the declarations as to their domicile made on different occasions by the [husband] and his father for tax purposes."

Keane C.J. went on to reject a submission, made only tentatively, that the petitioner, by his conduct at the time in encouraging and facilitating the divorce, was estopped from contesting the validity of his marriage. It was 'clear from the judgment of Walsh J. ... in *Gaffney v. Gaffney*, [1975] I.R. 133 that the doctrine of estoppel cannot operate so as to change a person's status where the status, as a matter of law, has not changed.' See further Binchy, *Irish Conflicts of Law* (Butterworths, Dublin, 1988), pp. 287–9.

It is worth noting that the judgment in the instant case proceeded on the basis that the domicile of a child born within marriage is determined by his or her father during the lifetime of the father. On the facts of the case, nothing turned on whether the child's domicile of dependency should be determined by the father, the mother or both parents and it does not appear that the parties sought to make any argument, whether of a constitutional nature or otherwise, that the common law rules, as partially modified by section 4 of the Domicile and Recognition of Foreign Divorces Act 1986, should no longer represent the law. For an excellent discussion on the subject, see Conor Power, "The Domicile of Children: Towards a New Basis" [2000] 2 Ir. J. of Fam. L. 21.

In *M.E.C. v. J.A.C.* [2001] 2 I.R. 399, Kinlen J. held that, at the time a divorce decree was granted in England in 1980, neither spouse was domiciled there. Both spouses were Irish. They had married in Sligo in 1968. After the marriage, they lived in England where they had three children. The spouses managed a pub in England. They did not purchase any property during the time they were together. They always travelled on an Irish passport. The husband was an active member of the Sligo Men's Association in London and for period was its chairman.

The wife had trained as a nurse in England before the marriage. She returned home to Sligo every year to visit her friends. It was her intention 'to continue nursing in England for a while but eventually to return to Ireland'. In 1965 the wife established a relationship with her future husband, who moved to England.

In 1972 he bought 16 acres of land in Sligo, near his father's farm and put cattle on it. His father looked after the cattle in his absence. He returned home to Ireland at least three times a year, stocking the land and having a family holiday. In 1976 he bought a licensed premises and 30 acres in Sligo. A manager was employed to run the licence premises. The lands were set in conacre.

The wife stated in evidence that it had been the parties' long-term plan to come home and live in Ireland and bring up the children there. In relation to the licensed premises in Sligo, evidence was given that it was their joint intention to run the pub and live on the premises. The wife left her husband in 1979 and returned to her mother's house with her three children. She continued to live in Sligo thereafter.

The husband remained in England until 1993 or 1994. Shortly after the separation in England he starting living with another woman whom he married after the divorce in 1980. He sold the Sligo pub in 1988, having sold the land near his father's farm to finance the divorce settlement. He bought a derelict house on over fifteen acres of land in Sligo in 1986. he moved into it in 1993 with his second wife. He had bought twelve acres of land in Cavan in 1989 which he had given her as a wedding present. He also bought a further fifteen acres of land near his new home, for the purposes of farming.

The husband had a property portfolio in England, owning one house in his own right and two other houses with his second wife. All were rented out. They bought another house in London in 1990 which was intended to be the family home, in which they lived for six months, but which was occupied by their children.

The second wife gave evidence that she never intended to return to stay permanently in Ireland and that her husband still intended to return to England, as she did. She understood that the house bought in Sligo was 'just for the purpose of a holiday home.'

Kinlen J. considered that the issue of domicile was:

> "a simple one. What was the domicile of the parties at the time of the divorce [in] 1980? There is no doubt on the evidence by [the first wife]. She stated that she had the intention of returning to Ireland in the future. In his own evidence the [husband] intended to return to Ireland. He did not waive his domicile of origin. However, the [second wife]'s evidence is in direct conflict with that of the [husband]. She was in a relationship with the [husband] at the time of the divorce, therefore her evidence is of some relevance. However, her evidence does not establish as against the evidence of the [first wife] and the [husband] that at the time of the divorce either of the two parties were domiciled in England. Of course it was wrong to aver to the English court that they were domiciled in England. Any application based on apparent perjury must be suspect. However, this court is quite satisfied as a matter of urgency of probability that both parties were resident in England, but not domiciled there."

The conclusion that the wife's domicile was Irish at the time of the divorce seems easy to reconcile with the facts. Even if she had acquired an English domicile after what appears to have been close to two decades' continuous residence in England, her return to her home county in Ireland after the break-up of her marriage would appear to support an ascription of an Irish domicile of choice. Significantly, Kinlen J., laying emphasis on the wife's testimony, found that she had not acquired an English domicile.

The husband's domicile is less easy to characterise. He lived in England from 1968 to around 1993. His second wife appears to have been English. His children remained there. It is true, however, that he maintained ongoing connections with his home and had business interests in Ireland before the time of the divorce. Moreover, he did return to Ireland to live and work. One can therefore understand the attribution of a continuing Irish domicile to him by Kinlen J.

FOREIGN TRIBUNALS EVIDENCE ACT 1856

In *Novell Inc v. MCB Enterprises* [2002] 1 I.L.R.M. 350; [2001] 1 I.R. 608, the Supreme Court gave an important analysis of the Foreign Tribunals Evidence Act 1856. This legislation provides for a procedure of 'letters of request' whereby witnesses maybe examined in one country in respect of proceedings taking place in another: see Binchy, *Irish Conflicts of Law,* (Butterworths, Dublin1988), pp.634-6. The position where letters of request are received in Ireland from foreign courts is covered by section 1of the Act. It provides as follows:

> "Where, upon any application for this purpose, it is made to appear to any court or judge having authority under this Act that any court or tribunal of competent jurisdiction in a foreign country, before which any civil or commercial matter is pending, is desirous of obtaining the testimony in relation to such matter of any witness or witnesses within the jurisdiction of the first mentioned court, or of the court to which such judge belongs, or of such judge, it shall be lawful for such court or judge to order the examination upon oath, upon interrogatories or otherwise, before any person or persons named in such order, of such witness or witnesses accordingly; and it shall be lawful for the said court or judge, by the same order, or for such court or any other judge having authority under this Act, by any subsequent order, to command the attendance of any person to be named in such order, for the purposes of being examined, or the production of any writings or other documents to be mentioned in such order, and to give all such directions as to the time, place and manner of such examination, and all other matters connected therewith, as many appear reasonable and just; and any such order may be enforced in the like manner as an order made by such court or judge in a cause depending in such court or before such judge."

Section 5 of the Act contains a privilege against self-incrimination, giving anyone examined under any order made under the Act 'the like right to refuse to answer questions tending to incriminate himself, and other questions, which a witness in any cause pending in the court by which or by a judge whereof or before the judge by whom the order for examination was made would be entitled to ...' and affording a similar protection in relation to the production of documents.

In the instant case, the plaintiff company had initiated proceedings in a federal court in the United States in the central district of Utah, against other parties. On its initiative an application was made under the 1856 Act to examine the appellants and require them to produce certain documents relevant to these proceedings, which involved allegations relating to the theft of software. The appellants resisted unsuccessfully in the High Court, arguing that they should not be required to participate in the proceedings in this way as the plaintiff had failed to disclose that there were proceedings in Ireland between the plaintiff and themselves arising form the same subject matter, that a criminal investigation was taking place in Ireland arising from matters common to both proceedings and that their right to fair procedures under the Constitution would be circumvented. On the appeal to the Supreme Court they added the further argument that, since the Utah proceedings were for 'discovery' as that term is understood in the United States, the process did not fall within the terms of the 1856 Act, as it did not involve the giving of 'testimony' for the purposes of that Act.

The essence of the appellants' first argument was that it would be oppressive on them to be examined on an issue in an action pending in the State, that the plaintiff would be in a preferred position for knowing the information and that, as there were allegations of fraud against them, the proposed procedure was particularly oppressive.

Following the lead of the English Court of Appeal in *First American v. Sheikh Zayed Al-Nahyan* [1998] 4 All E.R. 439 and having regard to the constitutional guarantee of fair procedures, Denham J. (Murray and Geoghegan J. concurring) considered that the appellants should not be required to be questioned in the Utah proceedings. She observed that there were:

> "clear allegations of fraud against the appellants in the Irish proceedings. If the plaintiff respondent was permitted to examine the appellants on the very subject of the Irish proceedings (albeit for the purpose of the proceedings in Utah), it would give [it] an advantage and potentially place the appellants in an invidious position with regard to preparing and advancing their own defence to the case of fraud being made against them by the respondent. It would, in all the circumstances, be oppressive to permit the respondent to examine the appellants in advance of the hearing of the fraud action against them in Ireland. If the proceedings in Utah were adjourned until after the Irish proceedings the position would then be quite different."

Denham J. then made some tentative remarks on the question whether the appellants' second argument regarding the nature of discovery proceedings in the United States of America was a valid one. Stressing that it was not necessary to express a formal opinion on the issue as it did not arise in view of the Court's holding on the oppression issue, she observed that it had been explained that in pre-trial procedures in the District Court in Utah the evidence obtained could be used by either side to establish that it had an unlosable case, in which case summary judgment could be obtained. On the other hand, if the case went on for full trial the evidence could be used at the trial. Denham J. stated:

> "On the face of it there would seem to be nothing in the 1856 Act

which would preclude the evidence being used for an application for summary judgment in those circumstances. The evidence in that event would itself be 'testimony' and not information with a view to obtaining evidence analogous to discovery in the Irish sense."

Counsel for the plaintiff had in argument said that, if the documents indicated in the letter of request were too broad, the order could be amended to refer only to the software the subject of the claim as set out in the complaint and limited to the topics and documents which could be proved under Irish rules of evidence. Denham J. observed that:

"[g]iven the[se] limitations . . . which would have the effect that the evidence obtained would be confined to evidence which could be used in an Irish county but that such evidence having been obtained could be used either for the purpose of summary judgment or at the final trial, the members of the court would incline to the view that there would be no legal obstacle in the way of the court approving such an order."

JURISDICTION

Injunction   In *McKenna v. E.H.*, High Court, July 18, 2001, the relationship between the Rules of the Superior Courts 1986, statute and the inherent jurisdiction of the courts fell for consideration in proceedings under the Proceeds of Crime Act 1996. The plaintiff had been given liberty by Finnegan J. to issue an originating plenary summons against the defendant and serve notice of it out of the jurisdiction on the defendant, who was not an Irish citizen. This had been on the basis of Order 11, rule 1(g) which provides that service out of the jurisdiction may be permitted where:

"any injunction is sought as to anything to be done within the jurisdiction, or any nuisance within the jurisdiction is sought to be prevented or removed whether damages are or are not sought in respect thereof."

The defendant entered a qualified appearance for the purposes of challenging jurisdiction and issued a motion seeking to set aside the order granting liberty, on the grounds that the action did not fall within the class set out in rule (g).

The plenary summons had set out in its schedule assets in the jurisdiction consisting of sums standing to the credit of bank accounts and two policies of assurance. The plaintiff was seeking orders pursuant to sections 2 and 3 of the 1996 Act, prohibiting the defendant from disposing of the property described in the schedule, an order pursuant to section 7 appointing a receiver to take possession of the property described in the schedule and an order pursuant to section 9 directing the defendant to file an affidavit in the Central Office of the High Court specifying:

> "the property of which the defendant was in possession or control; and the defendant's income and sources of the income during the past ten years, and an order pursuant to section 5 directing that the said property be transferred to the Minister for Finance."

On the basis of the Supreme Court decision in *Caudron v. Air Zaire*, [1986] I.L.R.M. 10, the defendant argued, first that, there was no jurisdiction to make an order under Order 11, rule 1(g) where the relief sought was ancillary in nature and/secondly that if there was such jurisdiction it could only be exercised where the substantive relief itself fell within one of the sub rules Order 11 Rule 1.

Finnegan J. proceeded on the basis that the following propositions represented the law:

> "1. Under the Rules of the Superior Courts the categories of actions listed in Order II Rule 1 are exhaustive.
> 2. In construing the Rules of the Superior Courts Order 11 Rule 1 the sub clauses thereof should be construed widely.
> 3. If a statute confers jurisdiction upon the courts it is the duty of the courts to give effect to the intention of the Oireachtas and any conflict between the provisions of a statute and the rules of procedural law including the Rules of the Superior Courts must be resolved in favour of the former."

He was satisfied that Order 11, rule 1(g) encompassed statutory injunctions whatever might be the statute in which they had their origin. Even if that were not the case it was the function of procedural law to give effect to the intent of the Oireachtas. Moreover, the courts were obliged to construe the rules widely:

> "If it is the intention of the Oireachtas, and I am satisfied that it is, the persons resident outside the jurisdiction with assets inside the jurisdiction which represent the proceeds of crime should be subject to the procedures of the Act then I am satisfied that it is the duty of the court to give effect to that intention and if necessary have resort to the inherent jurisdiction of the court pending the introduction of appropriate rules of procedure to give effect to the intention."

It was therefore not necessary for Finnegan J. to determine whether the injunctive reliefs provided by sections 2 and 3 of the Proceeds of Crime Act 1996 were in the nature of ancillary relief similar to the Mareva injunction sought in *Caudron v. Air Zaire* or substantive reliefs such as the injunctive relief sought in *Joynt v. M'Crum*, [1899] 1 I.R. 217. While the 1996 Act created a statutory right to an injunction to preserve the assets said to be the proceeds of crime, it was not necessary that it should do so as in the ordinary course of the court would have jurisdiction to grant interim and interlocutory injunctions in aid of the statutory right, created by the Act in section 4, to have a disposal order made. The statute did not regard the orders pursuant to sections 2 and 3 as identical in nature to an ordinary interim or interlocutory injunction in so expressly providing for them and in providing for the evidence which must be adduced in order to obtain the same and in removing them from the ordinary regime laid down in *Campus Oil v. Minister for Industry and Energy (No 2)* [1983] I.R. 88. The fact that section 5 provided for orders ancillary to an interim or interlocutory order under the Act suggested that the orders were not identical to what would ordinarily be regarded as the substantive relief sought such as a permanent injunction or an award of damages. The statutory interim and interlocutory injunction was 'a creature *sui generis*'.

Finnegan J. summarised his holding as follows:

> ".... I am satisfied that an interim injunction under section 2 and an interlocutory injunction under section 3 of the Proceeds of Crime Act, 1996 do not have the characteristics of mere ancillary relief in the sense of the relief sought, in *Caudron v. Air Zaire* but rather are *sui generis* having been created expressly by statute. Statutory injunctions come within the ambit of Order 11 Rule 1(g). Having regard to the clear intention of the Oireachtas in creating these statutory injunctions namely to preserve assets in respect of which an order pursuant to section 4 of the Act may be sought, it is the duty of the Court to give effect to that intention. Orders under the Proceeds of Crime Act section 2 and section 3 having regard to the true construction of the Act do not amount to mere interim or interlocutory relief and so are not affected by the judgment of the Supreme Court in *Caudron & Ors v. Air Zaire*. If I am wrong in this then there is a conflict between the Rules of Court and the Proceeds of Crime Act 1996 on its true construction which confers upon the Court that jurisdiction necessary to give effect to the Act or in the alternative the Court under its inherent jurisdiction may make such an order for the purpose of giving such effect."

Accordingly, Finnegan J. refused to set aside his earlier order giving liberty to the plaintiff to serve notice of the plenary summons out of the jurisdiction.

Insurance contract and exclusive jurisdiction   In the *Annual Review of Irish Law 1998*, pp.84-6, we analysed Laffoy J.'s decision in *Minister for Agriculture v. Leipziger Versicherung Aktiengesellschaft t/a Alte Leipziger*, High Court, March 6, 1998, holding that a particular jurisdiction agreement related to a contract of insurance which covered risks that were not within the ambit of Article 12(a) of the Brussels Convention. The facts of the case were somewhat complicated and involved the interpretation of a number of documents: see the *Annual Review of Irish Law* 1998, p. 85. Laffoy J. went on to hold that, since the agreement on jurisdiction did not fall within the ambit of any of the paragraphs set out in Article 12, it was contrary to that Article. In the circumstances, the court's jurisdiction was not prorogued by virtue of Article 17.

The Supreme Court affirmed, taking the same view of the facts and the law: [2001] 2 I.R. 82. Thus Keane C.J. (Denham, Murray, McGuinness and Hardiman JJ. concurring) adopted the reasoning of Staughton L.J. in the English Court of Appeal decision of *Charman v. W.O.C.* [1993] 2 Lloyd's Rep. 551, to the effect that the court should imply the words 'and no other' at the end of Article 12 (5). In the instant case, moreover, whatever transport element there might have been in the contract of insurance, it was 'clearly of extremely minor significance when compared with the storage element.' The Chief Justice adopted with approval Staughton L.J.'s observation in *Charman* that:

> "the extra risks or interests covered by para. (4) must not be disproportionately large compared with those covered by paras. (1) to (3). They must not be the main or almost the main subject matter of the contract, but a lesser part of it. The tail must not be allowed to wag the dog, or an insurance on land based property ... be converted into an insurance within Article 12a by the inclusion of some trivial marine risk."

Matrimonial proceedings and parental responsibilities Earlier in the Chapter, above, 37, we analyse the Brussels II Regulation on divorce, other matrimonial matters and parental responsibility, which deals *inter alia* with issues of jurisdiction.

Child abduction In the Practice and Procedure Chapter, below, 475, the Rules of the Superior Courts (Child Abduction and Enforcement of Custody Orders Act 1991) 2001 (SI No. 94 of 2001) are noted.

Forum non conveniens In *Jahwar v Owners of the M V. "Betta Livestock"*, High Ct., May 29, 2001, Barr J., applying the principles laid down by the Supreme Court in *Intermetal Group Ltd. v Worslade Trading Ltd.* [1998] 2 I.R. 1, declined to stay proceedings on the basis of the *forum non conveniens* doctrine. The plaintiff, master of the defendant's vessel, made a claim for wages and disbursements. The proceedings came within the scope of the Jurisdiction of the Courts (Maritime Conventions) Act 1989. The ship was released from arrest in October 1999 when the defendant provided security. Section 7(1) of the 1989 Act enables the court to apply the *forum non conveniens doctrine* in appropriate cases to claims for wages where the ship is not Irish.

The plaintiff was domiciled and resident in Syria. The vessel was owned by a Honduran company with a registered address in Greece. It was managed by a Syrian company. The flag state of the vessel was Cambodia.

Arguing that the proceedings should be stayed in favour of the Syrian maritime courts, the defendant pointed to the fortuitous connection of the proceedings with Ireland, the Syrian connections of the plaintiff and the management company, the fact that the contract of service had been made in Syria and the practical difficulties of bringing Syrian witnesses, proving Syrian law and translating documents and evidence. There were, however, factors of some formidable weight to be considered in favour of maintaining the Irish proceedings. There was a major doubt as to whether the Syrian courts actually had jurisdiction: Barr J. was told that, unless the governing law of the contract was Syrian, they would not and there were doubts on how that issue would be determined. Moreover, the plaintiff would have to give security for costs in Syria. Furthermore the defendant had delayed for eleven months before bringing its motion. These factors, in Barr J.'s view, were decisive against granting a stay.

In *In re Tradalco Ltd.; Bluzwed Metals Ltd. v Transworld Metals S.A.*, High Court, May 9, 2001, Lavan J. declined to grant a stay on winding-up proceedings pending "the determination of a Swiss court dealing with totally different causes of actions and a variety of parties including the claimant and respondent." He was satisfied that the proceedings before the Irish court were governed by the Lugano Convention and, that if he were to accede to a postponement, "then the court would be repudiating an international convention, which is a course I decline to take". It was essential that a liquidator should be appointed at the earliest opportunity, who would be the proper person to decide whether any action might have to be taken on behalf of the company to protect its interest in Switzerland and other jurisdictions.

The judgment contains no detailed discussion of the provisions of the Lugano Convention so it seems pointless to speculate on nuanced jurisdictional issues that could arise in relation to that Convention. It seems clear enough, in spite of Lavan J.'s remarks about the suitability of the liquidator to address international aspects of litigation involving the company, that he was declining to postpone proceedings, not in the application of principles relating to the *forum non conveniens* doctrine, but because the Lugano Convention did not permit it. Article 22 gives courts other than the court first seised, the entitlement to stay their proceedings, but only in respect of "related actions", which does not appear to have been the position in the instant case.

In *D.C. v W.O.C.* [2001] 2 I.R. 1, Finnegan J. held that in proceedings where both parties are domiciled in a contracting state under the Brussels Convention, the doctrine of *forum non conveniens* does not have any application. The parties in this case were both domiciled in Ireland. The plaintiff sought damages 'for rape and sexual assault' alleged to have occurred when she and the defendant, a co-employee, were on a visit to Sweden in the course of their employment. Under Article 5.3 of the Convention, which is concerned with matters relating to tort, the plaintiff would have been permitted to sue in the Swedish courts as "courts for the place where the harmful event occurred." She chose, however, to base jurisdiction, under Article 2, on the defendant's Irish domicile.

Finnegan J. was guided by paras. 76 to 78 of the *Schlosser Report (O.LC. 59/72)* and by *Boss Group Ltd. v Boss France* [1997] 1 W.L.R. 351. Having regard to the scheme of the Convention and the terms of its Articles, including Article 21, he was satisfied that 'the doctrine of *forum conveniens* has not survived the incorporation of the Convention into Irish law...' In this regard he noted that the Swedish courts would be obliged under Article 21 to decline jurisdiction. Of course, the existence of Article 21 does not *in itself* determine the question whether a court on which is conferred under the Convention is obliged to exercise that jurisdiction in every case.

Constitutional Law

ACCESS TO THE COURTS

In *Dumitru P v. Governor of the Training Unit*, Supreme Court, 28 November 2001 (*ex tempore*), echoes of the old police practice of spiriting people across the border to frustrate their attempts to vindicate their rights in the courts were adverted to, discreetly, by Keane C.J. (Murphy and Hardiman JJ. concurring). The strong criticism by Ó Dálaigh C.J. of this practice, in *State (Quinn) v. Ryan* [1965] I.R. 70 at 122 still resonate through our constitutional system:

> "It was not the intention of the Constitution in guaranteeing the fundamental rights of the citizen that these rights should be set at nought or circumvented. The intention was that rights of substance were being assured to the individual and that the courts were the custodians of these rights. As a necessary corollary it follows that no one can with impunity set these rights at nought or circumvent them, and that the court's powers in this regard are as ample as the defence of the Constitution requires. Anyone who sets himself such a course is guilty of contempt of the courts and is punishable accordingly."

In *Dumitru P*, the State had been in the process of implementing a deportation order in relation to the applicant to Bucharest, involving a change of flight at Schipol Airport, when Aer Lingus was notified, as it understood it, of court proceedings in relation to the applicant's deportation. Rather than proceed with the second flight the Gardaí who were accompanying the applicant, having been informed by Aer Lingus that this was its understanding of the position, brought the applicant back to Dublin on a flight. Aer Lingus said that it was cancelling the second leg of the flight because of what it had been told about court proceedings. The applicant in the instant proceedings argued that the deportation order was spent as a result of his being returned to Ireland in this fashion. The Supreme Court rejected this argument. Keane C.J. said:

> "[I]t has to be said that the Gardaí acted perfectly properly and the court, in fact, would express their commendation of the Gardaí for so acting because there is an unfortunate history in this jurisdiction, which one hopes is now simply a matter of history, of attempts to circumvent people's rights to apply for orders protecting their right to be at liberty. That one hopes is past history and certainly in the case of the Gardaí in

this situation, whether they were over scrupulous or whether they were over meticulous is certainly not a matter on which I would wish to address any criticism of them. They did what they thought was proper having regard to their information that there were in existence court proceedings.

I would conclude from that, that it would be quite wrong to say that in those circumstances the deportation order was spent. It would be quite wrong to infer [that] the Gardaí having properly acted, or certainly acted at worst with an excess of caution of deference to the position of the courts in this country, ... one should then treat the consequence of their action as in some way retrospectively invalidating the deportation order. The deportation order was an order which meant that the applicant was no longer entitled as a matter of law to remain in this country and was further an order which entitled the State to take any necessary steps to ensure that he did not remain in this country. Those are the twin effects of a deportation order and I have no doubt that it remained in force in both those contexts, notwithstanding the fact that the plaintiff came back to the country in order, as the Gardaí saw it, that he could exhaust whatever legal remedies might be open to him in this country."

In *Mallows v. Governor of Mountjoy Prison*, Supreme Court, July 31, 2001, the Supreme Court held that O'Donovan J. had correctly exercised his discretion under section 53 of the Extradition Act 1965 to order the discharge of a person who had been in prison awaiting extradition for several months after his application for judicial review had been refused by Carney J. A copy of the letter to him from the Registrar of the High Court, informing him of this fact, had been placed on his prison file. Counsel for the respondent argued that O'Donovan J. had been obliged to exercise his discretion against the applicant because the Chief State Solicitor's Office had believed at all relevant times that judicial review proceedings were pending and that the applicant, having failed to disabuse the office, had given no explanation for not having done so.

Murray J. (Murphy and Geoghegan JJ. concurring) described this submission as 'rather audacious'. No enquiry had been made by the Office as to the status of the judicial review period of over six months. There had been no proper basis for assuming in these circumstances that the application to the High Court was still in being. Murray J. went on to observe that:

"an unconvicted person in detention awaiting extradition is effectively dependent on the administrative arm of the State to ensure that he or she is not kept in custody any longer than is necessary to effect surrender to the authorities seeking rendition, or would be, but for section 53. Here the Oireachtas have chosen to protect the right of a person in custody awaiting extradition to be kept in custody for no longer than is necessary or at least no longer than one month unless there is justification for doing so. The Constitution guarantees that no citizen shall be deprived of his personal liberty save in accordance with the law. In my view section 53 requires the State to ensure that persons who are the subject of an order for extradition or rendition are not kept in custody for a period longer than one month unless proceedings have been initiated under section 50 of the 1965 Act or there is other good reason for doing so. Section 53 also has the effect of respecting an individual's right to a speedy trial where he or she is being detained by the State for the purpose of being put on trial even if that trial is to take place outside the jurisdiction. The State has a duty to vindicate those rights....

In my view the learned High Court judge was correct in finding that, as a result of the inaction by the Sate the respondent spent six months in jail in this country which otherwise he would not have had to spend.

The duty of the State to ensure that procedures under the Extradition Acts are carried out properly is not diluted by the fact that a person, in the situation of the respondent, through ignorance or otherwise, does not make an application under section 53 at the earliest possible moment. Accordingly, the submission that the learned High Court judge exercised his discretion wrongly because, as it was put, the instrument by which the respondent might shorten his custody lay in his own hands must be rejected. 1 would simply add that this argument has resonances of the argument made in *State Quinn) v. Ryan* [19651 I.R. 70 that there is a constitutional right of resort to the courts but only if one specifically asks for it and which was roundly rejected by this Court."

The Supreme Court decision of *Murphy v. Minister for Justice, Equality and Law Reform* [2001] 2 I.L.R.M. 144, holding that reasonable charges for court services are not in breach of the constitutional right of access to the courts, is considered in the Practice and Procedure Chapter, below, 475.

COMPOSITION OF THE COURTS

In *Riordan v. an Taoiseach* [2001] 3 I.R. 365, the plaintiff referred to the Supreme Court proceedings of June 29, 2000 rejecting his attempt to have set aside earlier Supreme Court proceedings challenging the constitutional validity of the Nineteenth Amendment of the Constitution Act 1998. He now argued that the Constitution did not permit the proceedings of June 29, 2000 to be heard by a Court of three judges. Keane C.J. (Murphy and Hardiman JJ. concurring) referred to Articles 12.3.1° and 26.2.1° of the Constitution where there is a is a specific requirement that the Supreme Court consist of not less than five judges. He went on to observe:

"Those are the only provisions to be found in the Constitution which require that a decision of the court is to be given by not less than a specified number of the members of the court. Their existence is wholly irreconcilable with any alleged requirement that every matter coming before the court in the existence of its appellate jurisdiction may only de decided by a court consisting of all the members of the court for the time being. No such provision exists either in the Constitution or in statute law and, given the extent of the court's appellate jurisdiction and the necessity to ensure, in the interests of the proper administration of justice, its reasonably expeditious and economic despatch, it would be remarkable if any such provision existed.

The claim made in these proceedings for declarations that specified legislation was invalid having regard to the provisions of the Constitution was heard and determined by a court consisting of not less than five judges of this court as required by s.7(5) of the Courts (Supplemental Provisions) Act 1961. No question as to the validity of any law having regard to the provisions of the Constitution is raised on the present motion."

Accordingly the Court dismissed the motion.

DAMAGES FOR INFRINGEMENT OF A CONSTITUTIONAL RIGHT

In the Torts Chapter, below, 554, we examine two important decisions in dealing with the circumstances in which an award of damages for infringement of constitutional rights is appropriate. These are *Sinnott v. Minister for Education*, [2001] 2 I.R. 545, where the Supreme Court reversed an award by Barr J. in favour of Mrs. Sinnott (as well as her son, the first plaintiff in the proceedings), and *An Blascaod Mór Teoranta v. Commissioners for Public Works* [2001] 1 I.L.R.M. 423, where Budd J. declined to make an award of damages to the plaintiffs whose right to equal treatment under Article 40.1 had been infringed by the enactment of An Blascaod Mór National Historical Parks Act 1989.

Also in the Torts Chapter, below, 554, we examine the Law Reform Commission's *Report on Aggravated, Exemplary and Restitutionary Damages* (LRC 60-2000), which contains a recommendation that would synthesise the criteria for awarding exemplary damages for torts and for breach of constitutional rights, which would have an impact on the approach adopted by the Supreme Court in *Conway v. Irish National Teachers Organisation* [1991] 2 I.R. 305.

DELAY IN CRIMINAL PROSECUTION

In the Criminal Law Chapter, below, 180, we analyse several decisions, including *B.F. v. Director of Public Prosecutions*, Supreme Court, February 22, 2001, *Knowles v. Malone*, High Court, April 6, 2001, *McNamara v. MacGruaire*, Supreme Court, July 5, 2001, and *Marley v. Director of Public Prosecutions*, High Court, June 20, 2001, on the subject of delay in prosecution for criminal offences.

DISCOVERY

In *Controller of Patents Designs & Trademarks v. Ireland*, Supreme Court, November 19, 2001 (*ex tempore*) where the plaintiff claimed that the passage of the Intellectual Property (Miscellaneous Provisions) Act 1998 had unconstitutionally interfered with judicial review proceedings he had taken, in violation of the principles set out in *Buckley v. Attorney General* [[1950] I.R. 67, the plaintiff unsuccessfully sought an order of discovery against the defendants of documentation in relation to the preparation, drafting, advices, amendments and discussions with and briefing of members of the Oireachtas concerning the legislation in Bill form. Affirming Kelly J.'s refusal to make such an order, Keane C.J. (Denham, Murphy, McGuinness and Fennelly JJ. concurring) was:

> "satisfied that the discovery the plaintiff seeks could not in the slightest degree assist or even be in any way relevant to these proceedings. Either the Act as passed by the Oireachtas and as signed by the President is unconstitutional for the reasons being advanced by the plaintiff or it is not. What was said or may have been said or may have been written by the Minister to advisors, to Dáil Deputies, to Senators as to what motives were prompting the initiation of the Bill could not in the slightest degree assist the plaintiff in his claim that the Act was unconstitutional. This court has recently said that it will not even entertain the citation of passages from debates in the Oireachtas with a view to ascertaining what the intention of Government or the executive was in introducing particular legislation. It would indeed be quite remarkable if, notwithstanding that decision, the court was possessed of some power to consider discussions and interviews, all part of the political process, which Ministers may have with Dáil Senators or Deputies before piloting legislation through either house of the Oireachtas. That in my view is a wholly unsustainable claim."

EDUCATION

In *Sinnott v. Minister for Education*, [2001] 2 I.R. 545 the Supreme Court reversed the judgment of Barr J. in the High Court, October 4, 2000 and held that a 23-year old young man with a condition of autism had not a constitutional right for primary education, justifying the award of damages and orders of a specific character against the State in respect of services relating to such matters as occupational therapy and medical care. The Supreme Court also held that there was no basis for an award in favour of his mother, who continued to care for his needs. We consider that aspect of the case in the Torts Chapter, below, 554. The entire subject is comprehensively analysed by Whyte, *Social Inclusion and the Legal System: Public Interest Law in Ireland* (Institute of Public Adninstration, Dublin, 2002), Chapters 1 and 5 and Addendum.

The majority of the seven-judge court (Denham, Murphy, Murray, Hardiman, Geoghegan and Fennelly JJ.) interpreted the State's guarantee under Article 42.4 to provide for free primary education as not extending to adults. Whether a literal, historical or purposive interpretation was adopted none supported the conclusion that it embraced a lifelong guarantee, in the majority's view. Keane C.J. dissented.

Literal approach   As to the literal approach, Denham J. observed:

> "The term 'child' falls to be construed in light of the plain language of Article 42. The word 'child' in general use describes a young person. It is a term used in a context where the focus is on the family, parents and children. The article anticipates the teaching of young children. The article makes reference to schools - of different types. The article specifically refers to children. The article speaks of a certain minimum education. The article addresses the rights of parents. The article stresses education in a context of schools. The article is not addressing issues such as, for example, succession where the term 'child' might be used in a different sense. It would be rewriting the Constitution to construe the term 'child' as meaning a childish person. Consequently, the meaning of the words 'child' and 'children' is clear. There is no ambiguity. The child is described within a family where the parents are the educator. It is addressed to a young person. It is age related."

Hardiman J. considered it:

> "manifest that, whether one reads the Constitution in its Irish or English text, the primary provider of education is seen as the parent, and the recipient as a child of such parent. This appears to me plainly to involve the consequence that the recipient of primary education would be a person who is not an adult and in respect of whom the primary educator,

according to the natural order, is his family.

In making the contrary case, counsel for the plaintiff suggested that the word 'child' where it occurs in Article 42 should be interpreted as meaning merely 'offspring' or 'descendant', terms which, they said, might apply to a person of any age. This view does not appear to me to be tenable. Firstly, it entirely ignores the language and structure of the Article, where the term 'child' is never used in isolation but always with a correlative of 'parent' or 'Family'. Secondly, it is even more difficult to maintain the construction contended for if one has regard to the primary (Irish) text, where that connotation would be expressed in a term such as 'sliocht' rather than 'leanbh'.

The correlatives used for the term 'child' ('leanbh') are 'Family' ('Teaghlach'), and 'parents' ('tuistí'). Moreover, the word 'clann' is used as a synonym for the recipients of education, meaning the children of a family.

Accordingly, I cannot accept the artificial construction advanced on behalf of the plaintiff: that the word 'child' or its equivalent in the national language should be interpreted as extending to a person of any age who has an ongoing need for education. Apart altogether from the analysis of the language and of the structure of the Article offered above, the plaintiff's contention simply does violence to the ordinary meaning of the word."

Neither was Hardiman J. impressed with the argument that, because Article 42 did not specify the age of cesser of the condition of being a child, it should be interpreted as open-ended:

"This appears to me to empty the term 'child' or its equivalent of all meaning and treat it as synonymous with 'person' or 'citizen'. Indeed, counsel for the plaintiff specifically submitted that Article 42.4 should be read 'as though primary education were guaranteed to the citizen'. This is plainly not the intention of the Constitution. Both of these terms are used elsewhere in the text of the Constitution; the use of the term 'child', rather than either of them in Article 42 must therefore be given significance. For example, the term 'citizen' is widely used in Article 40 and, in Article 40.1, emphasis is laid on the status of each 'citizen' as human persons. Article 40.4, in providing a procedure for the challenging of unlawful deprivation of liberty extends its protection to 'persons'...."

Historical approach   As to the historical approach, Murphy J. observed:

"The imposition of an express obligation on the State to provide for primary education might ... seem surprising but it was not revolutionary.

When the Constitution was adopted such an obligation was already in existence as Murnaghan J. explained in *McEneaney v. The Minister for Education* [1941] I.R. 430 at 438....

The nature of that education and the children for whom it was provided is well understood by the people who adopted the Constitution. Its meaning is not found by reference to experts however distinguished. No doubt improvements have been made in the buildings in which such education is provided and hopefully the facilities are better now than they were 60 years ago but these are changes in detail and in style. In my view primary education as identified in the Constitution is education provided for children the age limits of which were determined historically by the Education (Ireland) Act, 1892, which required parents to send their children between the ages of 6 and 14 years to receive certain schooling. Primary education is provided by teachers in classrooms. It was and is a basic scholastic education in the sense that it is a first stepping stone on a career which may lead to secondary level and ideally graduate to a third level. It is distinguishable from secondary level education on the one hand and nursery schools, or any other form of pre-primary education, on the other.

If such needs as toilet training fell within the ambit of 'primary education' at all, it seems to me that they would also necessarily come within the scope of the 'minimum education, moral, intellectual and social' which every child is bound to receive. Having regard to the structure of the Constitution it is extremely unlikely that those who framed it or the people by whom it was adopted would have authorised the State to intervene in such intimate matters."

Purposive approach So far as the purposive approach was concerned, there was support for the view of Walsh J. *McGee v. Attorney General* [1974] I.R. 284 at 319, echoed by O'Higgins C.J. in *The State (Healy) v. Donoghue* [1976] I.R. 325, that constitutional interpretation is dynamic. Thus, Denham J., referring to the special recognition given to the family by Article 41, observed that it was 'not to be construed as representing a norm of a society long changed utterly. Rather it is to be construed in the Ireland of the Celtic Tiger'. Moreover, Murray and Geoghegan JJ. referred to the late Professor John Kelly's text, *The Constitution of Ireland 1937–1987*, which envisaged a contemporaneous interpretation of value-laden concepts. Members of the majority were willing to acknowledge that there had been an increasing societal appreciation of the opportunities for education of disabled people. Nonetheless a purposive interpretation of the concept of education, and more specifically of primary education, did not in the view of the majority translate into a constitutional guarantee of primary education into adulthood.

The problem of "unlearning" educational benefits A particular aspect of the

first named plaintiff's condition troubled Geoghegan J. This was the fact that
the benefits he derived from education were quickly lost in the absence of his
continuing exposure to that education. He observed:

> "would be surprised if this 'unlearning' aspect applied in all forms of
> handicap. For instance I do not think that it would apply in the case of
> a Down Syndrome child. But I accept that it probably does apply in
> other categories of mentally handicapped children. Where it does not
> apply, the constitutional duty would clearly come to an end at probably
> about the age of eighteen as suggested by the State in this case or at the
> end of whatever might in all the circumstances be a reasonable though
> lesser extension over the normal period of primary education. I have
> carefully considered whether the position might be different in cases
> where the 'unlearning' problem arises. It could be argued that even
> though the duty is to a non-adult, it cannot in practice be effectively
> discharged unless there is continuing training into the future. But I have
> reluctantly come to the conclusion that to so hold would amount to an
> excessive straining of the wording of Article 42.4 when read in context."

No claim for educational malpractice In an interesting observation by way of
obiter dictum, Geoghegan J. stated:

> "while it does not fall to be determined in this case, I would be of the
> opinion that in the case of the vast majority of children in this State
> who are non-handicapped the constitutional duty is discharged simply
> by ensuring that there are schools providing the necessary minimum
> education available for every child and that the education therein will
> be provided free of charge. The Constitution must be interpreted in the
> light of the realities of life. One of those realities is that no matter how
> efficient an education system there may be, there cannot be a guarantee
> of high quality teaching. It may well be, therefore, that largely due to
> poor teaching in a particular school a child who has difficulty in learning
> to read and write may never acquire those skills. But apart from possibly
> exceptional circumstances, such a child either at the time of schooling
> or in later life would not be entitled to bring an action based on an
> alleged breach of Article 42.4. Still less would some adult immigrant
> be entitled to invoke the Article, an idea which was mooted at the hearing
> of the appeal."

This passage is important as it appears to shut the door – almost completely –
to claims of a constitutional nature taken against the State by badly educated
children in respect of the deficiencies in their education. It is true that a crack
of light remains in that Geoghegan J. envisages 'possibly exceptional
circumstances' where such a claim could be sustained, but the overall tenor of

his analysis is not receptive to claims of this genus.

One may hope that this question will be revisited. Clearly it is possible for there to be an infringement of the child's right to education warranting compensation by way of an award of damages. The rash of decisions resulting from the Drimoleague dispute so attests: see, *e.g.*, *Crowley v. Ireland* [1980] I.R. 102, *Hayes v. Ireland* [1987] I.L.R.M. 651 and *Conway v. Irish National Teachers Organisation* [1991] 1 I.R. 305. These cases, of course, dealt with intentional wrongdoing rather than institutional neglect or managerial deficiency. But that difference is not necessarily one of principle.

If a plaintiff could establish that the 'poor teaching in a particular school' was not merely some academic happenstance but was attributable to State neglect or discrimination regarding the social environment in which it operated, there surely would be formidable constitutional issues that would need to be addressed. It is true that they could not, and should not, be considered in the context of an isolated analysis of Article 42.4, and thus Geoghegan J. is correct in saying that an action would not (save possibly in exceptional cases) be capable of being 'based on an alleged breach of Article 42.5'; but the claim could plausibly be made in conjunction with Articles 40.1 and 40.3.

Keane C.J.'s dissent Keane C.J. dissented on the age–limit question. Adopting O'Hanlon J.'s approach towards the meaning of primary education in *O'Donoghue v. Minister for Health* [1996] 2 I.R. 20 (as to which see Whyte, *Social Inclusion and the Legal System: Public Interest Law in Ireland* (Institute of Public Administration, Dublin, 2002), pp.199–204), the Chief Justice emphasised that:

> "it was not within the competence of the Oireachtas to subject the plaintiff's constitutional right to … an age limitation [of eighteen years]. … *A fortiori*, it is certainly not the function of the Minister to determine the age at which the constitutional right of a person in the position of the plaintiff ceases. As the whole history of this litigation from beginning to end eloquently demonstrates, that is the function of the courts and the courts alone."

Having reviewed the common law and statutory code, which prescribe different ages for particular purposes, such as criminal responsibility and the minimum ages for consensual sexual intercourse and the right to vote or to marry, Keane C.J. responded:

> "Where in this spectrum can it be said with any semblance of truth that the plaintiff passed from childhood to adulthood? So far as the evidence in this case goes, virtually none of these stages is of any significance in his case. He is one of a relatively small category of people in our society who, because of their mental handicap, can never enjoy life in all its

diversity and richness but to whom at least a measure of happiness may be available. The uncontested evidence in this case is that, to attain even that low plateau, the plaintiff requires continuing access to what, in his case, is education, as defined by Ó Dálaigh C.J. [in *Ryan v. Attorney General* [1965] I.R. 294], albeit often extremely basic in character. No principled basis exists either in law or in the evidence for the contention advanced by the defendants that a person in his position ceases to be in need of primary education at age 18, at age 22 or at any age in the future which can now be identified with any precision."

The Chief Justice was therefore satisfied that the plaintiff was entitled to a declaration that the Minister was obliged by Article 42.4 of the Constitution to provide for free primary education for the plaintiff appropriate to his needs for as long as he was capable of benefiting from it.

The Supreme Court decision in *Sinnott v. Minister for Education* [2001] 2 I.R. 505 clarified the position, however controversially, with regard to persons who have reached full age. Less clear was the power of the courts with respect to persons whose right to education had been infringed, to order the executive to take positive and specific steps to remedy the breach. For incisive critical analysis of *Sinnott*, see Whyte, *op. cit.*, 340–57.

In *Nagle (a minor) v. The South Western Area Health Board et al.*, High Court, October 30, 2001, Herbert J. granted an interlocutory mandatory injunction directed solely against the Minister for Education and Science, requiring that he forthwith provide for appropriate, free education and support services to the plaintiff, a seven-year-old boy with autism and a learning disability. Applying the principles set out by the Supreme Court in *Campus Oil v. Minister for Industry and Energy (No 2)* [1983] I.R. 88, at 107 and in *Sinnott*, Herbert J. was satisfied on the affidavit evidence that there was a real likelihood that at plenary stage the plaintiff would be granted a mandatory injunction or a declaration that the Minister for Education and Science had failed to fulfil his statutory obligation under section 7(1) of the Education Act 1998 and had failed to provide for free primary education for the plaintiff appropriate to his needs, as required by Article 42.4 of the Constitution. Damages would clearly not be an adequate remedy. There would be a much greater risk of serious injustice being done if the court were to refuse the relief sought at interlocutory stage than by granting it. Herbert J. observed:

"I cannot make what I might describe as an 'interim declaration' and I do not believe that I should make a final declaration at this interlocutory stage of the proceeding. In the circumstances I am left with no option but to grant a mandatory injunction..."

Less than two months later, in *T.D. v. Minister for Education*, December 17, 2001, the Supreme Court, in another controversial decision, held that the doctrine of the separation of powers restricted severely the scope of the courts' power to make positive orders in this context. For detailed analysis, see Whyte op. cit., pp.357-363. We examine the decision in the section on the Separation of Powers, below, 109.

EUROPEAN COMMUNITY AND UNION

In *Maher v. Minister for Agriculture* [2001] 2 I.L.R.M. 481 the Supreme Court, affirming Carroll J. in the High Court; [2001] 2 I.R. 139, rejected a triple assault on the constitutional validity of the European Communities (Milk Quota) Regulations 2000 (SI No 94 of 2000). We summarise the effects of the Regulations in the *Annual Review of Irish Law 2000*, pp.15–16 and the facts of *Maher* in *Annual Review of Irish Law 2000*, p.16. The constitutional attacks were (1) that the Regulations were not necessitated by the obligations of membership within the meaning of Article 29.4.7°, (ii) that they were in breach of Article 15.2.1° of the Constitution and (iii) that they infringed the applicants' property rights under Article 40.3.1 and 2 and Article 43 of the Constitution. We consider the latter issue in this Chapter in the section on Property Rights, below, 94. Here we consider the first two points of controversy.

"Necessitated by the obligations of membership ..." The first question requiring the Court's consideration was whether the implementation of the regulations was necessitated by the obligation of membership within the meaning of Article 29.4.7°. All members of the Court were satisfied that it was. Keane C.J. described the result of the passage of the Eleventh Amendment of the Constitution as 'a historic transfer of legislative, executive and judicial sovereignty to the European Communities ...' In particular, the exclusive roles previously enjoyed by the Oireachtas as in the legislative lied and the courts in the administration of justice had been 'significantly abridged'.

Article 7(1) expressly required the making of detailed rules by the member states as to the transfer of quotas with a holding in the case of its sale, lease or transfer by inheritance to purchasers. This could not be achieved simply by administrative decisions.

Equally, members of the Court were agreed that the making of the rules in the form of SI 2000 rather than an Act had not been necessitated by the obligations of membership. The choice of the form of implementation was a matter for each member state.

The Article 15 issue All members of the Court were also agreed that there had not been a breach of Article 15.2.1°. Applying the test set out in *Cityview Press Ltd v. An Chomairle Oiliúna* [1980] I.R. 381 at 399, the Court held that this test had been fulfilled. While the parent statute was the 1972 Act, the relevant principles and policies could not be derived from that Act, having regard to the very general terms in which it was couched. In each case, it was necessary to look at the directive or regulation and, it might be, the Treaties in order to reach a conclusion as to whether the statutory instrument did no more than fill in the details of the principles and policies contained in the EC or EU legislation.

Fennelly J's observations on the matter are worth recording here:

> "The 'principles and policies' test applies *mutatis mutandis* where the delegated legislation represents an exercise of a power or discretion arising from community law secondary legislation. It applies with particular clarity to the case of directives where Article 249 EC leaves the choice of form and methods to the member states. The question will not arise so frequently in the case of regulations since they are directly applicable without the need for nationwide implementing measures. Where a regulation leaves open a range of choice, the test will apply. Each case will have to be decided on its own merits. The mere existence of a community regulation implies some sort of community policy. Article 253 EC obliges the community legislature to state in such acts 'the reasons on which they are based.' Member states implementing measures come inherently within the scope of such a stated policy. However, the principle of the applicability of the test is a recognition of the possibility that the choices left to the member states may be of such significance in their nature or scope or so unconnected with community of policies and aims that they require legislation and that resort to regulations in such cases would infringe Article 15.2.1."

In the instant case, the EC regulations required the member states to adopt detailed rules as to the transfer of quotas with land and they required the authorisation of temporary transfers of quotas which producers who were entitled thereto did not intend to use. In these areas, it was left to the member states to decide whether they elected to pursue specified courses of action.

Fennelly J. provided the most detailed analysis of the question whether this general schema or the provision for special choices at national level required implementation by legislation. Under regulation 5(1) of the 2000 Regulations, the State decided to avail itself of the power given by community law to break the link between land and milk quota, subject to a number of exceptions. It was crucial in this context to discern whether, whether, in making this decision, the State was pursuing a community objective or a purely national one. Fennelly J. considered that the Sixth Recital in the Preamble to the EC regulation and the general scheme of the milk regime:

> "demonstrate that the State is acting as a delegate of the Community in making the choice to separate land and the milk quota. As is shown by the case-law, the fact that community regulations authorise the member

states to exercise discretion does not take action of the latter kind outside the scope of the community regime. Member state discretionary action is circumscribed by the objectives of the scheme authorising it. The milk quota is itself a creature entirely of community law. Member states are bound, by virtue of Article 10 EC (formerly Article 5 of the Treaty), to ensure that community law is implemented; national rules must comply with the general principles of community law and the particular rules which apply. In the instant circumstances, member states are authorised to act only to achieve the aim of ensuring that reference quantities are attributed to producers. Any action by the State in pursuit of an unauthorised objective would be susceptible of challenge, by means of an infringement action pursuant to Article 226 EC (formerly Article 169) in the Court of Justice, as being contrary to the terms of Regulation 1256/99.

Thus applying the principles and policies test on the basis that Regulation 1256/99 stands in the place of an Act of the Oireachtas, I believe that the State, in adopting regulation 5 of the 2000 Regulation, was exercising a power expressly conferred and the purpose for which it was given."

In the light of this conclusion it was probably not necessary to give separate consideration to the exceptions. Nevertheless, Fennelly J. engaged in that process and concluded that they did not warrant distinct legislative choices. If it was correct to say that member states were authorised by community law to restrict or end the rule that milk quotas transferred with land, there was no basis for saying that community law would regard it as impermissible to make an exception for certain defined family transaction. The Court of Justice interpreted provisions of community law so as to favour family transactions. Article 33 EC required account to be taken of 'the social structure of agriculture'. This 'unarguably' included the family basis of farm ownership. The relaxation of the new rule to favour family transactions accorded with that aim.

THE FAMILY

In the Family Law Chapter, below, 315, we examine the important decision of *North-Western Health Board v. W. and W.* [2001] 3 I.R. 622, in which the scope of parental autonomy for decisions affecting the welfare of their children is analysed.

INJUNCTION

In *Gilligan v. Special Criminal Court*, Supreme Court, 7 December 2001 (*ex tempore*), affirming High Court, November 27, 2001, the plaintiff failed to obtain an injunction against the commencement of an inquiry by the Supreme Criminal Court pursuant to section 4 of the Criminal Justice Act 1994 as amended by section 25 of the Criminal Justice Act 1999 as to whether he had benefited from drug trafficking. He had been convicted of offences under the Misuse of Drugs Acts and sentenced to twenty eight years' imprisonment in respect of the supply charges and twelve years' imprisonment in respect of the importation offences, the terms to run concurrently. His appeal against conviction and sentence was pending.

The plaintiff had instituted proceedings challenging the constitutional validity of these statutory provisions. The argument that would be advanced in these proceedings was structured as follows: either the inquiry was a criminal proceeding, not minor in character, which denied him his right to trial by jury, with a presumption of innocence and the requirement of proof beyond reasonable doubt, or it was civil in nature, in which case the Special Criminal Court could have no jurisdiction. Keane C.J. (Geoghegan and Fennelly JJ. concurring) conceded that:

> "[i]t is to be said at once that clearly these are arguable grounds and raise important issues which will have to be determined by the High Court in due course and indeed that is not contested by [counsel for] the Director of Public Prosecutions that an arguable case has been raised. . . ."

The plaintiff relied strongly on the Supreme Court decision in *Pesca Valentia v. The Minister for Fisheries* [1985] IR193. Keane C.J. observed that it 'would need very unusual circumstances' to justify the intervention of the High Court, since it would lead to a lengthy interval of time between the conviction and the holding of an enquiry, which was 'clearly not what was contemplated by the legislation.' The Chief Justice continued:

> "That would be the same in any form of criminal proceedings but it would be particularly so, and arises in a particular and specific way in the case of the Special Criminal Court which . . . is a court which has no necessarily permanent existence, which is brought into being because of special circumstances referred to in the Constitution and which can undoubtedly have its existence terminated if the executive and the Oireachtas reach the conclusion that the circumstances which brought it into being no longer exist. That gives it, as it is put, a more fragile tenure in the whole judicial system than the permanent courts established under the Constitution. It is a court which in this case is sitting in a

division of three judges and clearly untold complications could result if any events occurred during the time that this litigation was proceeding on its way through the High Court and it may be to this Court if it was no longer possible for whatever reason to reconvene that court as originally constituted.

It seems to me there are serious grounds for questioning whether the High Court has any jurisdiction such as was sought to be invoked in this case to intervene to prevent the Special Criminal Court from proceeding with a statutorily mandated inquiry on the ground that the legislation which requires the inquiry to take place is either unconstitutional or if constitutionally interpreted cannot give the Special Criminal Court jurisdiction to conduct the inquiry."

In *Pesca Valentia*, Finlay J. had particularly emphasised that the court undoubtedly must have regard to the public interest in the prosecution of crime and the maintenance of prosecutions. What the court was really concerned with in *Pesca Valentia* was whether, when that was balanced against the consequences in that case if the matter was allowed to proceed, the balance of convenience was in favour of restraining the proceedings rather than allowing them to continue.

It seemed to Keane C.J. that *Pesca Valentia* was:

"entirely different because the plaintiff has been convicted and sentenced to terms of imprisonment and while undoubtedly being subjected to this inquiry may on one view be damaging to him in the sense that he will have in addition to the lengthy criminal trial which he has undergone, he will be implicated in other forms of proceedings which may result in orders being made forfeiting assets which are his and in the proceedings which he has brought he strongly contends that the court has no right to do. One can understand the objection that would be taken to that form of proceeding. But that is not to say that anything that happens in this inquiry is of a irremediable or irretrievable nature that cannot be rectified if it should transpire that the legislation is indeed unconstitutional or is being operated in an unconstitutional manner. It is wholly unlike the *Pesca Valentia* case in my view, where quite clearly the damage that would be done to the plaintiffs by the maintenance of the proceedings against them would clearly be irremediable. I see no reason to suppose that a court which deals with this matter and ultimately finds the legislation, if that be the outcome, to be unconstitutional or to have been operated by the Special Criminal Court in an unconstitutional manner cannot afford the plaintiff such redress as he is entitled to for any damage or loss of a sort he has suffered as a result of, what would then would have been undoubtedly the violation of his constitutional right to the appropriate form of procedure."

Perhaps it can be argued that the fragile continuity of the Special Criminal Court should not be a reason for denying to a person challenging the constitutional validity of a law the protection which would otherwise be his or her due under the *Pesca Valentia* principle. If there is a risk that the Court may, on account of a change in social circumstances, be abolished, it seems unfortunate that the negative consequences associated with that risk should fall on that individual.

IRISH LANGUAGE

The precise legal status of the Irish language has been a matter for discussion over a number of years: see Niamh Nic Shuibhne, 'The Constitution, the Courts and the Irish language' in T. Murphy and P. Twoney eds., *Ireland's Evolving Constitution 1937–1997*, 253 (1998), Niamh Nic Shuibhne, 'State Duty and the Irish Language [1997] Dublin U.L.J. 33. In *Ó Beoláin v. District Judge Mary Fahy* [2001] 2 I.R. 279, sharp differences of interpretation of the constitutional basis of the use of the Irish language in judicial proceedings were apparent in the Supreme Court. The applicant, who had been charged with offences in relation to the drink-driving code under the Road Traffic Act 1994, had sought a number of declarations, including one that he was entitled to Irish translations of the legislation and of the District Court Rules of 1997, as well as an order of prohibition of the continued hearing of the proceedings until he received the latter document. By the time the application was heard by Laffoy J, the translation of the Constitution, but not the Rules, had become available.

The background to this litigation is the fact that, as McGuinness J. observed, 'it is clear that the State is simply unwilling to provide the resources to fulfil its clear constitutional duty'. Article 25.4 provides (in part) as follows:

> "3. Every Bill shall be signed by the President in the text in which it was passed or deemed to have been passed by both Houses of the Oireachtas and if a Bill is so passed or deemed to have been passed in both the official languages, the President shall sign the text of the Bill in each of those languages.
>
> 4. Where the President signs the text of a Bill in one only of the official languages, an official translation shall be issued in the other official language."

Statutes were translated in Irish until 1979. Since then, they have been published only in English, with rare, ad hoc, exceptions.

There has been a considerable volume of litigation in recent years, largely coming before O'Hanlon J., in which the language rights of litigants have been clarified. It is clear that a litigant is entitled to use the Irish language in judicial proceedings but is not entitled to insist that others also do so. He or she is further entitled to have the proceedings translated into Irish. In *Delap v. Minister for Justice* [1980-1998] I.R. (Special Reports) 46, O'Hanlon J. held that a solicitor who used the Irish language in his practice was entitled to an Irish translation of the *Rules of the Supreme Court 1986*. In the instant case, Laffoy J, guided by *Delap*, was of opinion that:

> "the State is obliged, under the accurate interpretation of Article 34.3.1° in conjunction with Article 40.3.1°, in the context of Article 8, to make the official translation of the 1997 rules available within a reasonable length of time after the third named respondent had accepted them in the English version, and that the citizen, under Article 40.3.1°, has a personal right that this publication be fulfilled."

Laffoy J. considered, however, that the State had not yet failed to fulfil its obligation in regard to the District Court Rules of 1997. The Minister had signed the Rules on 24 February 1997 and the document was a very lengthy one consisting of over a thousand pages. It had been sent to the chief translator on 25 March 1997. The applicant's proceedings had been issued on 19 March 1998 and Laffoy J. gave her judgment on June 17, 1999. Accordingly she considered that the State should be given some further time to complete a translation of the rules; she added that it was imperative that the work be undertaken and finished as soon as possible. She declined to make an order for prohibition.

The Supreme Court, by a majority (McGuinness and Hardiman JJ, Geoghegan J. dissenting) held that certain declarations should be made but that an order for prohibition should not be granted.

McGuinness J. acknowledged that Article 25.4.4° did not provide any time frame within which an official translation of the legislative measure was to be made. Article 25 as a whole, however, seemed to envisage 'a fairly rapid procedure'. Where time limits were provided they were short. The pre-1980 system of providing a translation virtually simultaneously with the enactment of the Statute seemed considerably more in accordance with the general tenor of the Article than the present system which, as far as the Court could ascertain, provided a translation only when a special or urgent demand was made for it:

> "The respondent's argument for a reasonable time to be allowed for translation would ring more sincerely were it not for the fact that virtually no official translations of statutes have been provided for the past twenty years. This could not be described as a 'reasonable time'. Indeed it seems probable that the statutes in question in this case – statutes which are used daily in the District Court – would never have been translated were it not for the efforts of the applicant and his legal advisors."

The applicant was entitled to a declaration that the Minister for Justice, Equality and Law Reform and Ireland had a constitutional duty to make available an official Irish language translation of the Acts of the Oireachtas to the public in general when the President signed the text of a Bill in English. It seemed to McGuinness J. that the State had been 'frequently and over a long period of time in breach of this constitutional duty and that it would be desirable for this Court publicly to stress the mandatory nature of the duty set out in Article 25.4.4°.' In doing so, she 'would assume that the State will take steps to remedy the present situation of neglect with a short time frame'. Since more than a year had elapsed after Laffoy J's judgment with, so far as could be ascertained, 'no step whatever' having been taken to conform with the findings of the High Court, a declaration that the appellant was entitled to a translation of the District Court Rules was now appropriate.

Hardiman J.'s judgment was expressed in trenchant terms. He was of the view that:

> "the Irish language which is the national language and, at the same time, the first official language of the State cannot (at least in the absence of a law of the sort envisaged by Article 8.3) be excluded from any part of the public discourse of the nation or the official business of the State or any of its emanations. Nor can it be treated less favourably in these contexts than the second official language. Nor can those who are competent and desirous of using it as a means of expression or communication be precluded from or disadvantages in so doing in any national or official context. . . . [T]he institution by a statutory official, and subsequent adjudication by a Judge, of a criminal charge whether minor or otherwise is part of . . . the public discourse of the nation and the official business of the State.
>
> A citizen summoned under compulsory process (issued in Irish though this point is not essential) to answer a charge in Court, is plainly entitled to make such answer in Irish if he so wishes. Nor can he be disadvantaged in doing so, by reason of his lawful linguistic preference. Furthermore, he is entitled to make his answer in Irish regardless of whether or not he also understands English. See *An Stát (MacFhearraigh) v. MacGamhna* [1984] I.R.S.R. (1980–1998) 38. . . .
>
> It is also clear from the *MacFhearraigh* case that a litigant wishing to conduct his case in Irish cannot be ordered or constrained to do so in English on grounds of convenience, or because of the additional time taken by the necessity to translate his questions or submissions for the benefit of those without competence in Irish.
>
> Having regard to the status of the Irish language it seems to me that persons wishing to use it are absolutely entitled to do so and to be afforded every necessary facility in doing so at least to the extent that such facilities are available to those using the second official language.

...

It appears to me that the effect of [the Supreme Court decision in *Attorney General v. Coyne and Wallace* (1967) 101 ILTR 17] is to confer on a person, whether an official or not, a right to choose which of the official languages he will use for any particular official transaction. This choice relates to his side of the transaction: no-one can dictate another's choice of language. In *Coyne and Wallace*, the evidence was that in a particular part of the country it was usual to serve notices of intention to prosecute and summonses in Irish. This, however, could not exclude the right of a defendant to conduct his case in English if he wished. Similarly, a defendant may conduct his defence in Irish, although proceedings might have been commenced against him in English. In view of the terms of Article 8, and the official policy of bilingualism to which the State is committed, the State must facilitate the use of either language without discrimination. The production of laws in one language only is totally inconsistent with bilingualism, and is not paralleled to my knowledge in any other bilingual country."

The Rules of the District Court were extremely important for the conduct of litigation. In relation to the trial of summary offences, they contained provisions for such vital matters as services, powers of adjournment, powers of amendment and the effect of variations between the offence alleged in the summons and the evidence actually given in Court. Furthermore, they provided the appropriate forms to be used for such basic purposes as the summoning of a witness and the giving of notice of appeal:

"In the absence of an official version of these forms in Irish an unwilling witness served with a summons in Irish might omit to attend and, if it were sought to compel him, object that the summons was not in the prescribed form. A party served with notice of appeal might take a similar point. Again, the document containing the result of the analysis conducted by the Medical Bureau of Road Safety must, if it is to be admissible in evidence, be in the statutorily prescribed form and a non-statutory translation might be the subject of objection. I express no opinion on the validity of any such objections as envisaged above: they are mentioned to illustrate the additional difficulties which may beset either party seeking, in the absence of official translations of Acts and orders, to conduct his or its legal business in the national language."

It was noteworthy that an Irish tradition had been provided for the former Rules of the District Court, made in 1948:

"It would appear that in this regard, as with the Statutes, there has been a grave shortfall in the provision of legal materials in Irish since about the year 1980. This can only be described as a failure to observe the constitutional imperative contained in Article 8, and a failure for which apparent lack of staff in the office of the Chief Translator in the Houses of the Oireachtas is no sort of excuse."

The policy of inertia in relation to translation of statutory measures was 'in clear and obvious breach of the express constitutional requirement contained in Article 25.4.4°'.

Counsel for the State had made the argument that where that State had an obligation to provide a translation of Acts, the Constitution did not say when it was to be provided:

"According to this line of argument, years may elapse, during which the Statute in question is in daily use without any translation being provided, without the State being in breach of its obligation, just so long as the authorities sincerely intend to provide the translation at some future date. It must be obvious that this line of argument is utterly inconsistent with the constitutional status of the national language and with the long standing policy of bilingualism in relation to the business of the Courts, repeated in statutory form as recently as 1998. In my view, there must be implied into the terms of Article 25.4.4° at the very least a requirement that the official translation shall be provided as soon as practicable and there is clearly scope for the contention (not made in this case) that it must be available before the Act is sought to be enforced on a person competent and wishing to conduct his official affairs in Irish."

Hardiman J. went on to refer to:

"the stark reality that an individual who seeks basic legal materials in Irish will more than likely be conscious of causing embarrassment to the officials from whom he seeks them and will certainly become conscious that his business will be more rapidly and efficaciously dealt with if he resorts to English. I can only say that this situation is an offence to the letter and spirit of the Constitution. I am sure that it has not arisen by reason of any deliberate decision by any official person or body. But it has arisen and must be remedied if the law is to be administered as the Constitution intended that it should be.

Bilingualism, or multi-lingualism is a living reality in many countries and of course the European Union daily produces complex documents, many of them of a legal nature, in all official languages. I have no doubt that it is quite possible to produce all relevant legal materials in Irish. I have no doubt that the applicant of this case is entitled to have an Irish version of the Rules of the District Court if he wishes as it is clear that he does. What is lacking is a system which existed for many years: one which routinely produced legal materials in both official languages, as appears to happen in other countries with a policy of bilingualism or multi-lingualism, and the continued failure to provide such a system is inconsistent with the Constitution. In this context the lip service paid to the national language can only be regarded, in the inimitable phrase of the late Professor John M. Kelly, as 'focal scoir don Gaeilge'."

Geoghegan J., dissenting, adopted an approach strikingly different from that formed by Hardiman J. Having interpreted Articles 8.1 and 2 as meaning 'that for all legal and official purposes the Irish language and the English language are in an equal position', he went on to observe:

"A constitution is not simply a piece of legislation. It embodies the aspirations and emotional feelings of the people who have enacted it. Not everything in a constitution therefore is intended to have legal implications. Long before the relevant Article was abolished by Referendum the provision as to the special position of the Roman Catholic Church was not considered by constitutional lawyers to have any legal implication. It was merely reflecting what was perceived to be a fact on the ground at the time of the enactment of the Constitution. I think that the reference to the Irish language as 'the national language' albeit aspirational rather than factual in Article 8 paragraph 1 is similar. The whole purpose of paragraph 2 of Article 8 is to make clear that for official and legal purposes English and Irish are in an identical position."

Geoghegan J. considered that, as a result of the Supreme Court's interpretation of Article 8.3 in *Attorney General v. Coyne and Wallace* (1967) 101 I.L.T.R. 17:

"it would seem to follow that unless there is a statutory provision saying otherwise, official business may always be conducted either in English or Irish in so far as any reliance is being placed upon Article 8. Of course natural justice requirements may, in any given instance, impose an obligation to provide a document or a translation in one particular language."

The nature and extent of the right to conduct a case in Irish had never been fully considered by the Supreme Court and it was not necessary or desirable in the instant case that the Court, being composed of three judges only, should embark on such an analysis. There was *obiter dicta* from the Supreme Court judges which clearly recognised the right of a litigant to conduct a case in Irish and it had always been generally accepted that such a right existed; a final determination on this matter, however, had to await a fully argued case in the Supreme Court

On Geoghegan J.'s analysis, in a prosecution such as in the instant case, the State was entitled to prosecute in English even if the defendant wanted to conduct his or her defence in Irish. Furthermore, even if out of courtesy or for other reasons the Director of Public Prosecutions or other prosecuting authority in such circumstances decided orally to conduct the prosecution in Irish, this did not mean that a document to be relied upon by the prosecution was required in Irish:

> "By document I am including anything put in evidence which would normally be described as a document, and also any statutory instrument including Rules of Court which are being relied on. For this purpose I am not including statutes as there is a separate constitutional provision relating to them...."

Article 25.4.4° did not avail the applicant. Even the State had been in breach of a direct constitutional obligation, Geoghegan J. did not think that it necessarily followed that some corresponding constitutional right was conferred on a litigant in a civil or criminal case involving an Act of the Oireachtas not yet officially translated. A constitutional obligation placed on some organ of the State did not necessarily give rise to some corresponding constitutional right vested in an individual.

Ó Beoláin is an important and helpful decision in forcing a national debate on the issue of the use of the Irish language in the public forum. Those who view with distaste the cynicism and hypocrisy that characterised aspects of state policy in this context over the years will no doubt be drawn to Geoghegan J.'s analysis. Nevertheless, the majority judgements are undoubtedly more convincing: see Niamh Nic Shuibhne, 'The Use of the Irish Language for Official Purposes', (2001) 19 Ir. L. Times (n.s.) 174.

THE JUDICIAL POWER

In *Gorman v. Minister for the Environment and Local Government* [2001] 2 I.R. 414, the scope of the famous Supreme Court judgment in *Buckley (Sinn Féin) v. Attorney General* [1950] I.R. 67 – the 'Sinn Féin Funds' case – fell for consideration. The factual background was an attempt by the Minister to introduce limited deregulation of the taxi industry in Dublin by Regulations had been found by Murphy J. in the High Court to be *ultra vires* in *Humphrey v. Minister for the Environment* [2001] 1 I.R. 263. An appeal had been taken to the Supreme Court but, before it was heard, the Minister had introduced a second set of Regulations repealing the earlier Regulation and completely abolishing the limitations on the number of taxi licences that could be issued.

The applicants, who had been on the losing side in *Humphrey*, argued that the issuing of the new Regulations violated the *Buckley* principle.

Carney J. considered that, notwithstanding the repeal of the earlier Regulations, there was 'a great deal for the Supreme Court to debate and rule upon'. In no sense could it be said that the effect of the repeal was to require the Supreme Court to dismiss the appeal without any hearing and without forming any opinion as the rights of the respective parties to the dispute. Nevertheless, Carney J. held that the introduction of the second set of Regulations had interfered with the litigation because it had prevented the possibility of the earlier Regulations reviving by operation of law if the applicants succeeded in convincing the Supreme Court that the introduction of the earlier Regulations had been *ultra vires*. This was, in his view, 'an unwarrantable interference arising in the unique circumstances of this case in the applicants' appeal'. Accordingly Carney J. held that the provision in the new Regulations which purported to repeal the earlier Regulations was invalid but that this invalid provision could be severed from the remaining provisions in the new Regulations, which were not invalid, surviving a challenge based on the applicants' property rights, as to which, see below, 94.

LIBERTY

In *McConnell v. Governor of Castlerea Prison*, Supreme Court, October 26, 2001, an application under Article 40.4.2° of the Constitution was successful. Under the Circuit Court order, the applicant had been convicted of a number of offences, one of which was described as 'unauthorised firearm', and had been given an sentence on that count which was conceded to be one that was not open to the Circuit Court judge to impose having regard to the fact that the defendant had no previous conviction of the relevant sort. Counsel for the respondent also conceded that the parts of the order recording convictions on other offences and sentences on those offences were not severable from the admittedly impugnable part of the order.

Hardiman J. (McGuinness and Geoghegan JJ. concurring) stated:

> "In terms of the provisions of Article 40.4.2° of the Constitution, what this Court is obliged to consider is whether the detention has been justified and, in the words of the Article, we are to order the release of such person from such detention unless satisfied that he is being detained in accordance with the law. Now it seems impossible to me to be satisfied that he is detained in accordance with the law and therefore the Constitution appears to direct that we order his release."

Hardiman J. did not think it appropriate for the Court to express any view as to what might happen in the event of any further action being taken by the Director of Public Prosecutions. He contented himself with stating the Court was not disposed to order the remittal of the matter to the Circuit Court. Accordingly the Supreme Court simply ordered that the applicant be released from custody.

In *Murray v. Governor of Mountjoy Prison*, Supreme Court, March 9, 2001, the applicant for habeas corpus challenged the legality of his detention as a prisoner. He alleged that he had been assaulted by a fellow prisoner in the prison and that the Governor had 'failed to inform him that this assault was consequent upon a threat and that he had not been informed of this threat'. He claimed that his right to bodily integrity had been violated by such failure. The High Court appears to have treated the application as one by way of judicial review.

Keane C.J. (Murphy and Fennelly JJ. concurring), in a brief judgment, stated that, if the facts were as stated by the applicant, this would clearly not be a matter which went in any way to the legality of the applicant's detention in Mountjoy Prison. That issue was separate from the question whether the applicant could maintain a case for damages arising out the incident.

Two comments appear appropriate. First, the prospects of a successful claim for negligence would not seem great in view of the persistent reluctance on the part of the courts to imposed liability for assaults by fellow prisoners: see P.A. McDermott, *Prison Law* (Round Hall Sweet & Maxwell, Dublin, 2000), paras 7–23ff. Secondly, it is worth noting that in *The State (Gallagher) v. Governor of Portlaoise Prison*, April 25, 1983, McMahon J. did not object to the idea that the remedy of habeas corpus should be available for negligent facilitation of assault. The fact that he held against the applicant on the evidence weakens the impact of this decision, however.

In *Holland v. Governor of Portlaoise Prison*, High Court 8 March 2001, Murphy J. refused an application for an enquiry into the legality of the applicant's detention at Portlaoise Prison. The applicant set out a number of grounds for his application, most of which were considered by Murphy J. to have already been raised, and addressed, in previous proceedings. To the extent that the facts to which he deposed in his grounding affidavit did not appear to have been dealt with in previous proceedings, Murphy J. observed that 'the question of newly discovered evidence is a matter for the Court of Criminal Appeal itself pursuant to the Crim[inal] Procedure Act 1993 rather than ... this Court.'

Murphy J. quoted several passages from earlier decisions which had made it clear that not all defects would warrant release under Article 40.4. Thus, in *State (McDonagh) v. Frawley* [1978] 1 I.R. 131 O'Higgins C.J. had stated:

> "The stipulation in Article 40.4.1° of the Constitution that a citizen may not be deprived of his liberty save 'in accordance with law' does not mean that a convicted person must be released on habeas corpus merely because some defect or illegality attaches to his detention. The phrase means that there must be such a default of fundamental

requirements that the detention may be said to be wanting in due process of law. For habeas corpus purposes, therefore, it is insufficient for the prisoner to show that there has been a legal error or impropriety, or even that jurisdiction has been inadvertently exceeded."

Moreover, in *State (Aherne) v. Cotter* [1982] I.R. 188, Henchy J. had observed:

"Before a convicted person who is serving his sentence may be released under our constitutional provisions relating to habeas corpus it has to be shown not that detention resulted from an illegality or mere lapse from jurisdictional propriety but that it derived from a departure from the fundamental rules of natural justice, according as those rules require to be recognised under the constitution in the fullness of the revolution at a given time and in relation to the particular circumstances of the case. Deviations from legality short of that are outside the range of habeas corpus."

LIMITATION OF ACTIONS

In the Chapter on Limitation of Actions below, 423, we discuss *White v. Dublin Corporation*, High Court, May 25, 2001, in which Ó Caoimh J. held that the applicants had *locus standi* to challenge the constitutional validity of a short limitation period contained in the planning legislation.

LOCUS STANDI

In *Riordan v. Taoiseach*, High Court, May 11, 2001, the plaintiff challenged (*inter alia*) the constitutionality of the appointment of Mr. Robert Molloy TD as Minister of State to the Government. An 'Isaac Wunder' order had earlier been made against him. It fell to Ó Caoimh J. to determine whether to give leave for the institution of these proceedings.

Ó Caoimh J. held that the plaintiff lacked *locus standi*. The plaintiff had contended that the law did not permit the appointment of any individual as a Minister of State to the Government as opposed to a Minister of State at a Department. Mr. Molloy had purportedly been appointed to both positions. The plaintiff did not seek to impugn the latter appointment. Ó Caoimh J. observed that the plaintiff had:

"not indicated any possible good that can stem from this proposed action and furthermore he has not indicated to this Court any basis upon which he would have *locus standi* to impugn the appointment in question. Aside from this there may be an arguable case to be made in relation to the contention put forward by [the plaintiff] but I am satisfied that I should refuse him the leave which he seeks on the basis indicated that this amount[s] to the bringing of a claim which can only be described as vexatious in the circumstances, where [the plaintiff] has shown no *locus standi*."

In the Chapter on Limitation of Actions below, 423, we discuss *White v. Dublin Corporation*, High Court, May 25, 2001, in which Ó Caoimh J. held that the applicants had *locus standi* to challenge the constitutional validity of a short limitation period contained in the planning legislation.

PROPERTY RIGHTS

In *Maher v. Minister for Agriculture* [2001] 2 I.L.R.M. 48; [2001] 2 I.R. 139, the Supreme Court upheld the constitutional validity of the European Communities (Milk Quotas) Regulations 2000 (S.I. No. 94 of 2000). We set out the facts of the case and address other aspects of the legal issues that fell for consideration, earlier in this Chapter, in the section on the European community and Union, above, 79. Here we note the Court's disposition of the argument that the Regulations violated the applicants' right to property under the Constitution. The plaintiffs conceded that, in *R. v. Minister for Agriculture, Fisheries and Food, ex p. Bostock* (Case C–2/92) [1994] E.C.R. I–955, the Court of Justice had taken the view that milk quotas did not generally constitute property rights under community law but they sought to limit that decision to situations involving the right to dispose of a quota for profit. They argued that the instant case involved what was effectively a form of compulsory acquisition by the State of a quota at a price substantially less than prevailing market value. They invoked the opinion of the Advocate General in *Demand v. Hauptzollamt Trier* (Case C–186/96) [1998] E.C.R. I–8529 in their aid. They sought a declaration that the purported abolition by the Minister of a milk quota holder's right to sell or lease a milk quota with land on the open market was an unjust attack on their property rights guaranteed by Article 40.3.1° and 2° and Article 43 of the Constitution.

The Supreme Court rejected these arguments, adhering to what the Court of Justice had held in *Demand* so far as community law was concerned, rather than adopting the Advocate General's view. Nor had there been any violation of the applicants' constitutional rights. Their entitlement with respect to the milk quota scheme was simply not a property right. Keane C.J. had:

"no doubt that the regulations do not violate any property rights within the meaning of the relevant articles of the Constitution. Even if one were to adopt the most expansive view of what is meant by a right of property within the meaning of those articles and extend it beyond the

> well accepted species of property under our law – real and personal property, including, under the latter category, choses in action – it could still in no sense be equated to a right of property."

It seemed unnecessary in this context to consider whether rights in the nature of licences conferred by the law in relation to particular property, such as planning permissions or licences for the sale of alcohol, constituted property rights. The quotas to which the applicants were entitled in the instant case were not licences or permits which might enhance the value of property which they owned or occupied. The applicants might produce as much milk as they pleased and require no licence from any authority to do so.

The fact that a right might effectively be disposed of for cash did not mean that it was a property right: those in a queue to buy a particular commodity might well sell their place in the queue but 'most assuredly' they were not disposing of a property right. No parallel could be drawn with intellectual property rights as systems of law in developed societies invariably protected those who produced such intangible assets in the expectation of reward by creating a discrete structure of legal protection for them. They were not 'remotely comparable' to the opportunities for profit presented by a regulatory scheme designed for the benefit of subsidised producers.

Denham J., treating the applicants' entitlement as analogous to a licence in Irish law, referred to previous decisions, including *Hempenstall v. Minister for the Environment* [1994] 2 I.R. 20 and *State (Pheasantry Ltd) v. Donnelly* [1982] I.L.R.M. 512. She observed:

> "The nature of a domestic right such as a licence is dependent on the law, usually statutory, which creates and develops the specific scheme. Behind the stated scheme is a policy being implemented through the legislation by the legislature. Such a scheme is in the public interest. It may be viewed through the concepts of the exigencies of the common good and proportionality.
>
> The milk quota scheme at community level is based on policy related to the market and to the aims of the community ... Policy changes and develops. Conditions and terms of the milk quota scheme change from year to year ... It is a policy with the general aim of the common good. The applicants have an advantage, a right, as a consequence of this policy. It is a right created in the public interest and subject to the public interest. It is a right to which the applicants know the terms and conditions and know of their variability. On this analysis the scheme is constitutionally permissible."

Murray J. stressed that the 2000 Regulations applied to all persons who were holders of a milk quota in accordance with objective criteria. These regulations entitled all such holders to retain the quotas attributed to them on resuming production of milk. It was for reasons wholly personal to them that they would not do so. Their quota were not being forfeited. The Regulations were internally rational to the objectives to be achieved by the regulatory regime. There was 'no interference with a substantive right, such as a property right.' Murray J. thus did not take the position of the Chief Justice in holding that the applicants' rights in respect of the milk quotas were simply not property rights. Nor did he favour Denham J.'s characterisation of them as analogous to a licence. Murray J. preferred to resolve the issue of constitutionality under Article 40.1 and 3 and Article 43 by reference to the internal rationality of the objectives to be achieved by the regulatory scheme which meant that there could be no interference with a property right, if such was the status of the applicants' entitlement, a matter not needing definitive clarification. Fennelly J. agreed with Murray J's analysis of this question.

In *Gorman v. The Minister for the Environment and Local Government* [2001] 2 I.R. 414, Carney J. held that Regulations deregulating the taxi industry in Dublin did not infringe the applicants' property rights. He applied the principle stated by Costello J. in *Hempenstall v. The Minister for the Environment* [1994] 2 I.R. 20, to the effect that property rights arising in licences created by law (enacted or delegated) 'are subject to the conditions created by law and to an implied condition that the law may change those conditions'. A change in the law which had the effect of reducing property values could not in itself amount to an infringement of the constitutionally protected property rights.

In the *Planning and Development Bill 1999* [2000] 2 I.R. 321, the Supreme Court had accepted that a person compulsorily deprived of property in the interest of the common good should normally be fully compensated. In the instant case there had been a 'minimal', justified interference with property rights 'implemented by means of an implied condition of which the applicants were fully aware and one which [was] envisaged by the very terms and conditions under which [the] licence was held ...' Carney J. considered that in such circumstances it would be incongruous to oblige the State to introduce a concomitant scheme of compensation. Accordingly he rejected the argument that compensation should be paid. Perhaps another way of regarding the impact of the Regulations on the applcant's property rights was that they did not compulsorily *deprive* them of any rights since the possibility of the introduction of regulations of this character was inherent in the terms on which the licences were granted: on this view, the Regulations did not *deprive* the applicants of property rights but rather impacted on those rights in a way that had been anticipated in their creation.

REFERENDA

In *Fizgibbon v. Ireland*, Supreme Court, June 8, 2001, the traditional deference afforded by the courts to the process of legislation and of putting issues to the People for resolution by referenda was apparent. The plaintiff sought an injunction to defer the holding of referenda on the Treaty of Nice, the jurisdiction of the International Court and the abolition of the death penalty, or in default, a deferral of the counting of the votes cast. His application was heard, and rejected, by Murphy J. in the High Court, June 6, 2001, the day before voting took place on the mainland, and his appeal was dismissed two days later by the Supreme Court.

The plaintiff sought the postponement until a case was made to the courts to declare the referenda null and void on account of the gross inadequacy of the procedures used to ensure a fair and balanced debate leading to the likelihood of a decision based on adequate information presented in a fair manner.

Keane C.J. (with which Denham and Murphy JJ. concurred) found that the law had been helpfully stated by Professor James Casey in *Constitutional Law in Ireland* (3rd ed, Round Hall Ltd, Dublin 2000). The earlier Supreme Court decision of *Slattery v. An Taoiseach* [1993] 1 I.R. 286 (analysed in *Annual Review of Irish Law 1992*, pp.218-9), had made it plain that the courts should not, as a general principle, intervene in the legislative and constitutional process.

Keane C.J. was of the view that all the considerations mentioned in *Slattery* were fully applicable to the instant case:

> "It is unnecessary to consider, as the learned author in that book goes on to point out, whether there are indeed exceptional circumstances in which the court might be satisfied that the provisions of the Constitution itself were not being complied with in relation to the holding of a referendum to amend the Constitution. All that need be said this morning in relation to that is that those cases, if indeed there is more than one case, and the learned author only indicates one possible exception, would be so rare and so exceptional that it is difficult to conceive of them arising in practice. It is sufficient anyway for the purposes of this case this morning to say that no ground has been put forward whatever which goes beyond what the court found to be wholly unjustifiable as a ground of interference in *Slattery's* case and indeed in earlier cases and it is only necessary again to refer to a further observation of Mr. Justice Hederman where he said in the same case that a proposal to amend the Constitution cannot per se be unconstitutional and the procedure adopted for so doing cannot be unconstitutional if it complies with the requirements of the Constitution. Nothing in this case has demonstrated any such failure to comply."

Professor Casey, *op. cit.*, 717–718, mentions the hypothetical instances of the Oireachtas including other proposals in a Bill to amend the Constitution or submitting the Bill to the people and, through, inadvertence, failing to ensure that it is expressed to be 'An Act to amend the Constitution', contrary to Article 46.3.

Denham J., concurring, observed that, on the facts alleged, the plaintiff had not met the test for granting an interlocutory injunction set out by the Supreme Court. She went on to state in *Campus Oil Limited v. The Minister for Industry and Energy (No. 2)* [1983] I.R. 83:

> "However, this application is not a commercial matter, it seeks to restrain the counting of the votes of the referenda. The order sought is to restrain an exercise in direct democracy, to intervene on the basis of the alleged actions of the executive. In all the circumstance it is not apparent that the court has jurisdiction in this application."

In the section on the Right to Vote, below, we note the decision of *O'Doherty v. Attorney General*, Supreme Court, June 6, 1991, in which the Court declined to grant an interlocutory injunction against the holding of the Nice Treaty referendum and other referenda on June 7, 2001.

THE RIGHT TO VOTE

In the *Annual Review of Irish Law 2000*, pp. 85–6, we recorded that, in *Breathnach v. Ireland* [2000] 3 I.R. 467, Quirke J. had held that denying prisoners the right to vote violated their right to equal treatment under Article 40.1 but that the Supreme Court, on July 11, 2001, had reversed on appeal: [2001] 3 I.R. 230. We now examine the Supreme Court's analysis of the issue in *Breathnach*.

It will be recalled that Irish constitutional jurisprudence on the separate issues of the right to vote and the rights of prisoners is somewhat passive. It is not perhaps surprising that a factual situation involving a coalescence of these two issues should generate still greater passivity.

The Supreme Court's unwillingness in *Draper v. Attorney General* [1984] I.R. 277 to treat the effective denial of the right to vote to disabled electors as a matter of urgency was disconcerting to many who read its judgment at the time, still more so today when the right of the disabled to equal treatment is more widely acknowledged. O'Higgins C.J., delivering the judgment of the Court in *Draper* said:

> "In the opinion of the court, the present law, contained in the Electoral Act, provides a reasonable regulation of elections to Dáil Éireann, having regard to the obligation of secrecy, the need to prevent abuses and other requirements of the common good. The fact that some voters are unable to comply with its provisions does not of itself oblige the state to tailor that law to suit their special needs. The State may well regard the cost

and risk involved in providing special facilities for particular groups as not justified, having regard to the numbers involved, their wide dispersal throughout the country and the risks of electoral buses. The case made by the plaintiff in this action rests entirely on the failure of the State to provide special facilities for her and for those similarly situated. In the opinion of the court, such failure does not amount to an interference by the State in the exercise of the right to vote under Article 16, section 1, subs. 2 of the Constitution. Nor is it, in the opinion of the court, a breach by the State of the provisions of section 1 of Article 40. While under this Article the State could, because of the plaintiff's incapacity, have made particular provisions for the exercise by her of her voting rights, the fact that it did not do so does not mean that the provisions actually made are necessarily unreasonable, unjust or arbitrary. For the reasons already stated, the court could not so find."

In *Breathnach*, Keane C.J. quoted this passage from *Draper*, and commented:

"It may be ... that the considerations referred to by [O'Higgins C.J.] are not necessarily applicable to the same extent in the case for the prison population. But it is also pointed out in that passage that the fact that some voters were unable to comply with the provisions of the then electoral law did not of itself oblige the State to tailor that law to suit their special needs. That seems to me to be equally applicable in the case of persons such as the applicant who are in lawful detention. Indeed, given that their incapacity to vote is the result of their own voluntary actions, it has to be said that the restriction thus imposed on their right to exercise to vote is at least as reasonable as the restriction on the disabled which existed until the enactment of the 1986 Act."

The other stream of judicial authority against the applicant's claim was that encapsulated by *Murray v. Ireland* [1991] I.L.R.M. 465, where the Supreme Court, affirming Costello J., held that a married couple serving life sentences for murder had no constitutionally-based entitlement to be given the opportunity to exercise conjugal rights in order to beget a child. Costello J. stated:

"Those rights which may be exercised by a prisoner are those:
  (a) which do not depend on the continuance of his personal liberty (so a prisoner cannot exercise his constitutional right to earn a livelihood), or
  (b) which are compatible with the reasonable requirements of the place in which he is imprisoned or, to put it another way, do not impose unreasonable demands on it."

Costello J. held that to permit the plaintiffs to leave prison from time to time to exercise these rights was clearly incompatible with the restriction on their liberty brought about by their imprisonment; to permit them to exercise these rights within the prison would place unreasonable demands on the prison service.

In the Supreme Court, McCarthy J., having said that the right to procreate children could be lost temporarily as a result of any form of detention or imprisonment, added:

> "The suspension or abeyance of the right does not depend upon practical considerations but because of the nature of a constitutional right. If a person is deprived of liberty in accordance with law, then that person loses, for instance, the express right to vote (Article 16); the person loses the non-expressed or unenumerated right to travel, to earn a livelihood, the right to be let alone, to give some examples."

In *Breathnach*, Keane C.J. was satisfied that McCarthy J. had correctly stated the law:

> "I do not read this passage as suggesting that the right to vote is 'lost' in the full sense in consequence of the imprisonment: rather that it cannot be exercised unless, for example, the prisoner is on temporary release. The learned judge did not speak of the right as being permanently 'lost', but as being in suspension or abeyance. That, as was found in that case, is a necessary consequence of the voluntary acts of the applicant/respondent, resulting in the loss of his liberty. No doubt the provision of facilities to enable the applicant to exercise [his] rights by post or in the precincts of the prison would not be wholly impractical, although it would undoubtedly require legislation. For the reasons stated, however, there is no obligation on the State to provide the machinery, since the right remains in suspension or abeyance during the period of the applicant's imprisonment."

The Chief Justice gave short shrift to the applicant's argument based on Article 40.1 of the Constitution:

> "As has so often been pointed out, this Article does not forbid discrimination: on the contrary, to legislate is on occasions necessarily to discriminate. The State must have regard to differences of capacity, physical and moral, and that such differences exist between persons detained because they have broken the law and other citizens is beyond argument."

Keane C.J. acknowledged that a distinction might be drawn in relation to prisoners on remand, since, they were presumed to be innocent of the criminal offences with which they had been charged. What they had in common, however, with convicted prisoners was that they were being detained in accordance with law and, accordingly, for as long as they were so detained, some of their constitutional rights, including the right to exercise the franchise, were necessarily in suspension or abeyance.

Denham J. in her judgment also referred to *Draper* and *Murray*. As to *Draper*, she observed that:

> "[t]he law providing for voting by people who suffer from disability has developed since that case. However, the recognition of the special role of the legislature is a fundamental constitutional principle which is still relevant and applicable. At issue then was whether the law was unreasonable, unjust or arbitrary – did it breach the principle of equality stated in the Constitution [?] That test remains applicable."

With regard to the applicant's claim based on Article 40.1, Denham J. stated:

> "All citizens as human persons are held equal before the law. However, that does not mean uniformity. The State may have regard to differences of capacity, physical and moral, and of social function.
>
> No legislation in Ireland prohibits or excludes the applicant or any prisoner from voting. Indeed, the legislation is enabling of the applicant.
> . . .
> The applicant is in a special category of person – he is in lawful custody. His rights are consequently affected. The applicant is in the same situation as all prisoners: there is no provision enabling any prisoners to vote. Consequently there is no inequality as between prisoners. The inequality as between a free person and a person lawfully in prison arises as a matter of law. It is a consequence of lawful custody that certain rights of the prisoner are curtailed, lawfully. Many constitutional rights are suspended as a result of the lawful deprivation of liberty. It is a consequence of a lawful order not an arbitrary decision.
>
> The applicant has no absolute right to vote under the Constitution. As a consequence of lawful custody many of his constitutional rights are suspended. The lack of facilities to enable the applicant vote is not an arbitrary or unreasonable situation. The absence of such provisions does not amount to a breach by the State of the applicant's right to equality.
>
> The words of McCarthy J., cited previously, in *Murray v. Ireland* correctly state the law. If a person is lawfully deprived of their liberty and is in prison then that person loses certain constitutional rights including the right to vote. That does not exclude the legislature from deciding in the future to legislate for a scheme whereby prisoners could vote."

Whether one is convinced by the Supreme Court's analysis in *Breathnach* will depend on two factors, both in the realm of values. The first is the worth one attaches to the right to vote. Viewed from a utilitarian perspective, one person's vote may not seem to have a great deal of value since it is but a drop in the ocean so far as its power to direct national policy is concerned. Viewed from the standpoint of democratic norms, however, the right to vote is of very great value and importance since it represents the link between the individual citizen and his or her society; it acknowledges the unique and equal value of every citizen's understanding of how best his or her society should construct its political philosophy and implement it in practice. From this standpoint, the right to vote is something that has a great value, and should not be denied to any citizen save for grave reason.

To offend against the criminal law leads to a sanction, and that sanction includes imprisonment. Imprisonment involves the denial of the liberty of the convicted person. That is its legitimate purpose. The denial of the right to vote would not be a legitimate purpose and arguably would be unconstitutional. If this is so, a question arises as to what response the courts should have to the effective denial of that right, not as an express part of the sanction but rather as a consequence. This brings us to the central criterion of practicality and administrative demands, which formed the basis for the plaintiffs' claim in *Draper* and *Murray*. If that which is in peril of being lost as a consequence of imprisonment is a right of very great value, then surely the courts should be anxious to set a high test before excusing the loss of the right on the basis of practicality. It is not enough for the executive to make a bald claim of impractibility: the courts should examine that claim critically. *Draper* looks particularly bad in view of the ease with which legislation was enacted a couple of years later remedying the position and going a good distance towards respecting the voting entitlement of disabled citizens.

It is true that cases can arise where the administrative difficulties, in the absence of remedial legislation, are indeed formidable but capable of easy resolution by a reforming statute. In the instant case the applicant did not challenge the constitutional validity of the legislative machinery which had the effect of denying him the right to vote without imposing significant administrative burdens. If the court were to come to the conclusion that the administrative burdens could have been removed by legislation, is it simply to wring its hands, note the denial of the constitutional right and let the Oireachtas continue to do nothing about it?

It is unfortunate that the Supreme Court did not consider developments in other countries on this issue. A comparative study could well have encouraged the Court to take a broader view: cf. P. McDermott, *Prison Laws* (Round Hall Sweet & Maxwell, 2000), Chapter 10; Gallagher, 'The Captive Vote: Prisoner's Suffrage in Ireland' (2001) 1 University College Dublin L. Rev. 1; Mbodla, 'Should Prisoners Have a Right to Vote?' (2002) 46 J. of African L. 92; Demleitner, 'Continuing Payment on One's Debt to Society: The German

Model of Felon Disen-franchisement as an Alternative' (2000) 84 Minnesota L. Rev. 753. Even on the Court's own rationale, troublesome constitutional issues remain, equally in relation to remand prisoners, who are merely suspected of having committed an offence. Where bail is denied on account of an apprehension of what the accused may do in the future (cf. the Bail Act 1997, section 2(1)), the rationale is at breaking point.

In *Redmond v. Minister for the Environment*, High Court, 31 July 2001, Herbert J. appears to have attached greater weight to the democratic values underlying the electoral process, albeit in the context of eligibility to be a candidate rather than of eligibility to vote. The plaintiff challenged the constitutional validity of the statutory requirements for deposits, which would not be returned in certain circumstances, on the basis that they offended (*inter alia*) Articles 16 and 40.1. He was a man with limited financial resources, who could not afford the amounts in question.

Herbert J. held that section 47 of the Electoral Act 1992 was unconstitutional as being *ultra vires* the powers of the Oireachtas under Article 16 and that this section, section 48 of the 1992 Act and section 13 and rules 8 and 9 of the Second Schedule of the European Parliament Elections Act 1997 conflicted with Article 40.1. Guided by the Supreme Court judgment of *In re Article 26 of the Constitution and the Electoral (Amendment) Bill 1983* [1984] I.R. 268, Herbert J. identified the right of citizens to be electable for membership of Dáil Éireann as 'deriving from and constituting an essential feature of th[e] Article 16 code and not from any regulatory laws authorised by Article 16, section 7.' Herbert J. went on to observe that:

> "The fundamental entitlement of citizens to participate in government as a right must follow from the declaration in Article 5 of the Constitution that "Ireland is a . . . democratic State". Article 6 of the Constitution additionally proclaims the right of the Irish people to designate the rulers of the State. The right of all adult citizens to stand for election to the national legislature is an essential feature of a democratic State. The power therefore granted to the Oireachtas by the Constitution to place citizens under disability or incapacity for eligibility for membership of Dáil Éireann must be limited in its application.
>
> In my judgment this power conferred on the Oireachtas is only to be exercised for objective and weighty reasons, for example to maintain in changing circumstances the tripartite division of the powers of government upon which our democratic system is based and perhaps to safeguard the security of the State. I am satisfied that the Oireachtas does not have power under Article 16 Section 1 subsection 1 to create impediments to, or impose conditions on, eligibility for membership of Dáil Éireann in the nature of deposit requirements....
>
> Power to render citizens ineligible for election to Dáil Éireann is expressly conferred upon the Oireachtas by Article 16, Section 1

subsection 1 of the Constitution. It is therefore totally unlikely that the framers of the Constitution intended to confer the self-same powers by Article 16 Section 7. That this is so is clearly observable by a consideration of the provisions of Article 16 Section 7 itself. It is first stated to be 'subject to the foregoing provisions of this Article', and then it confers nothing more than a right to regulate *elections*. The Oireachtas is empowered to establish by law procedural and administrative rules and measures for the proper and orderly conduct of elections. The requirement of a deposit is not just a matter or rules and procedures. Such a requirement involves the imposition of an impediment to participation in the election and is not, as was clearly intended by Article 16 Section 7, nothing more than the ordering of such participation.

I am driven therefore to the conclusion that as contended by the Plaintiff the provisions of Section 47 of the Electoral Act, 1992, are *ultra vires* the powers of the Oireachtas and are unconstitutional."

Herbert J. gave a thorough analysis of the argument based on Article 40.1. He observed at the outset that:

"[t]his right to stand for election to Dáil Éireann, though it is subject to certain limitations, remains a most basic and important right guaranteed to all citizens over the age of 21 years by Article 16 Section 1 subsection 1 of the Constitution and is an essential aspect of the nature of the State, which is proclaimed by Article 5 of the Constitution to be a democratic State (as to the characteristics of which see *McKenna v. An Taoiseach and Others* [1995] 2 I.R. 10 at 52 *per* Denham J.)"

In a crucial passage, Herbert J. stated:

"In my judgment a law which has the effect, even if totally unintended, of discriminating between human persons on the basis of money is an attack upon the dignity of those persons as human beings who do not have money. This is far removed for instance from issues such as alleged rights to wage parity or increases or issues of the uneven impact of taxation upon citizens in various marital or non-marital relationships or on farmers or householders or occupiers. The history of poverty and of social deprivation in Ireland, but by no means exclusively in Ireland, demonstrates overwhelmingly the extent to which the essential dignity of persons as human beings is involved. In my judgment this is exactly the type of discrimination for which the framers of the first sentence of Article 40.1 of the Constitution were providing."

It was clear from the second sentence of Article 40 section 1 that the State in its enactments might discriminate between citizens in the interest of the common good, but there was a limit to such discrimination. In the Supreme Court decision of *O'B. v. S.* [1984] I.R. 316, Walsh J. had stated:

> "Thus, it may be seen from the decisions of this Court referred to above that the object and the nature of the legislation concerned must be taken into account, and that the distinctions or discriminations which the legislation creates must not be unjust, unreasonable or arbitrary and must, of course, be relevant to the legislation in question. Legislation which differentiates citizens or which discriminates between them does not need to be justified under the proviso if justification for it can be found in other provisions of the Constitution. Legislation which is unjust, unreasonable or arbitrary cannot be justified under any provision of the Constitution. Conversely if legislation can be justified under one or more Articles of the Constitution, when read with all the others, it cannot be held to be unjust within the meaning of any Article. . . ."

Herbert J. commented:

> "Such unjust, unreasonable or arbitrary distinctions or discriminations are commonly referred to in reported cases as, 'invidious'. In my judgment the terms unjust, unreasonable or arbitrary are used disjunctively by Walsh J. so that the existence of any one of these circumstances would be sufficient to render the particular discrimination or distinction unconstitutional."

The Supreme Court decision of *de Burca v. Attorney General* [1976] I.R. 38 was an important precedent as it had held that Article 40.1 was offended by a statutory provision which made eligibility of jury service depend on satisfying a requirement as to owning property with a particular rateable value. Walsh J. had observed:

> "The property qualification in the Act of 1927 has been impugned as being inconsistent with the provisions of Article 40. It is true that for a long time before the foundation of the State and since then, jury service was based upon a property qualification. So also was the franchise in other periods. Up to comparatively recent times, the franchise in local government elections in this State was based upon a property qualification. The fact of the existence of property qualifications in such circumstances, now or in the past, is not a valid argument to rebut a claim of inconsistency with the provisions of Article 40 of the Constitution. The property qualification undoubtedly discriminates between those citizens who have the qualification and those who have not and does so solely upon the basis on the amount of the poor-law

valuation of property in a particular district. This property qualification could not conceivably be said to refer to the physical or moral capacity of a prospective juror. Can it seriously be suggested that a person who is not the rate occupier of any property, or who is not the rated occupier of property of a certain value, is less intelligent or less honest or less impartial than one who is so rated? The answer can only be in the negative. Can such a discrimination be based on social function? Just as a man's intelligence and honesty is not directly or at all proportionate to the poor-law valuation of his houses or lands, which seems to be the underlying assumption of the property qualification, so it cannot be said that such a qualification marks him out as having a social function which makes him more fitted for jury service than another – if, indeed it does in any way constitute a social function within the meaning of Article 40, section 1, of the Constitution."

Herbert J. considered that this passage disposed of what he termed 'the long pedigree argument' advanced by the defendants in support of the impugned sections.

Article 16, section 7 of the Constitution admittedly conferred on the Oireachtas a power to regulate elections by law and that this had the effect of placing on the Oireachtas a corresponding duty so to do. On an integrated construction of the Constitution, however, such a power could not entitle the Oireachtas to impose on prospective candidates for membership of Dáil Éireann conditions of entry to the poll which were repugnant to Article 40, section 1 of the Constitution.

Herbert J. proceeded to examine the argument that the deposit requirement was necessary to protect the electoral system from abuse by frivolous or vexatious persons, and from commercial or other improper exploitation. He concluded on the evidence adduced that these concerns did not afford a justification:

"It is altogether improbable that the percentage of poor adult citizens likely to offer themselves for election to these institutions would be any greater than has been the case with respect to their more fortunate fellow citizens in the same period. In my judgment all the arguments which postulate the emergence, but for these deposit requirements, of 'excessively large' numbers of candidates or suggest that but for these requirements there would be, 'major' increases in the numbers of adult citizens wishing to stand for election to Dáil Éireann or the European Parliament appear to be based upon surmise and no evidential link has been shown to exist between the number of persons in fact standing for election and these requirements.

Likewise, I find no evidence to support the proposition that individual voters would be confused or confounded by an increase in the number of candidates on a ballot paper. It was accepted by the defendants that Irish voters have shown a high degree of sophistication in making political decisions within what some political theorists consider to be a very complex system of voting. I see no reason why I should accept that such an electorate would suddenly become bereft of this capacity of discernment in the face of a larger choice of candidates on a ballot paper. In the absence of some compelling evidence I simply could not accept such an argument.

No evidence has been adduced that an increase in numbers of candidates for membership of Dáil Éireann or the European Parliament would result in insoluble problems in the management of elections or unacceptably long delays in the checking and counting of votes. In any event, in my judgment, it behoves the Oireachtas which has the power and the corresponding duty under Article 16, section 17 of the Constitution to regulate elections, to adapt the regulatory and administrative system to accommodate this supposed increase in the number of candidates and not to seek to restrict the number of candidates by reference to the capacity of the existing system. The electoral system must be the servant of democracy not its master."

Five days before the Supreme Court handed down its judgment in *Breathnach*, the Supreme Court, in *O'Doherty v. Attorney General*, June 6, 2001, had given short shrift to an appeal by a prisoner from a judgment of Murphy J. in the High Court refusing his application for an injunction and an order of mandamus compelling the respondents to enable him to exercise his vote in the three referenda. The applicant had been sentenced to a term of two years' imprisonment on October 3, 2000. On May 30, 2001 – eight days before the holding of the referenda – he was given leave to serve short notice of motion on the respondents for an injunction. He explained his delay on the basis that he had been believed until May 24 that voting facilities would be available to him in the prison. The applicant's case was based on the High Court decision in *Breathnach*.

Denham J. (Murphy and Hardiman JJ. concurring) referred to *Draper* and *Murray*. She also noted that, in *Holland v. Ireland*, High Court, November 18, 1993, where the applicant had sought an order of *mandamus* by way of judicial review directing a postal vote to be granted to a prisoner, Geoghegan J. had observed:

"The applicant admits that there is no satisfactory provision permitting postal votes for prisoners. Accordingly, I must refuse the application. If the applicant considers that he can mount a constitutional challenge to the relevant enactments in the electoral Acts, he should do so by plenary proceedings. In the circumstances judicial review would not be appropriate."

On appeal this decision had been upheld by the Supreme Court on January 28, 1994. Echoing Geoghegan J.'s remarks in *Holland*, Denham J. stated:

> "In this case the procedure used – judicial review and interlocutory relief - is not the appropriate tool to achieve a decision in relation to the constitutionality of Acts of the Oireachtas. Further, the applicant has not made out a case that there is a strong likelihood that his ultimate action will succeed. The case law is to the contrary. In an interlocutory application the severe consequences for the prison system of such an order cannot be ignored. Further, while conscious of the right and duty of the courts to consider the constitutionality of Acts of the Oireachtas, this approach is taken from the basis of the presumption of constitutionality. Further, as the applicant is in lawful custody due regard must be had to the duty of the executive in that regard.
>
> The power of this Court to direct the relief sought has not been established. The applicant has not made out a case to the standard required by *Campus Oil v. Minister for Industry* [1983] I.R. 88."

The applicant was also held to have been 'in gross and obvious delay'. Hardiman J. observed that:

> "[n]o serious claim of a constitutional nature can properly be met at a few days' notice. The effect of this delay, therefore, tends to deprive the constitutional institutions involved of the opportunity to meet the applicant's claim in a proper and orderly manner."

RIGHT TO A GOOD NAME

The question of the scope of constitutional protection to the good name of a deceased person was touched on in *McDonnell v. Brady* [2001] 3 I.R. 588, but must await further analysis. The applicant, the widow of the group chief executive of Corás Iompair Éireann, obtained a right of representation on her own behalf and on behalf of her children at the proceedings of the Oireachtas Sub-Committee on the Mini-CTC Signalling Project established by the Dáil and Seanad.

Kelly J. in the High Court gave the applicant leave to apply by way of judicial review for a number of reliefs arising out of the conduct by the sub-committee of its proceedings. In addition, his order provided that the proceedings of the sub-committee be stayed until the determination of the application for judicial review.

Ó Caoimh J. discharged the stay. He referred to doubts as to whether the applicant's constitutional rights had been infringed, having regard to the sections 6 and 7 of the Civil Liability Act 1961 and the decision of Gannon J. in *Hilliard v. Penfield Enterprises Ltd* [1990] 1 I.R. 138, from which it could be inferred that the constitutional guarantee of a person's good name was confined to living persons. The Supreme Court affirmed Ó Caoimh J. Keane C.J. (Murphy and Murray JJ. concurring) observed that it was:

> "beyond doubt that the applicant has been afforded important safeguards which will be of assistance to her in defending her late husband's reputation against unjust attack. The sub-committee allowed her to be legally represented, although she is clearly in a significant different position from those persons still alive who have an admitted and indisputable constitutional right to the vindication of their good name. Her legal representatives are entitled to cross examine any witnesses whose testimony may be in any way damaging to the interests she seeks to protect and, while it is doubtless always preferable to be able to mount an immediate challenge by way of cross examination to such evidence, it is at least arguably a matter for the sub-committee to determine the time at which such cross examination should be conducted. That is an issue which will have to be resolved in the High Court during the course of the present proceedings, but it certainly does not, of itself, constitute a denial of constitutional and natural justice such as to demand the intervention by the High Court in the form of so drastic a weapon as an indefinite stay of the sub-committee's proceedings."

In the Torts Chapter, below, 554, we note that the decision of *Hill v. Cork Examiner Publications Ltd*, Supreme Court, December 14, 2001, in which little movement of thought from the principles laid down in *De Rossa v. Independent Newspapers* [1999] 4 I.R. 432 and *O'Brien v. Mirror Group Newspapers Ltd.* [2001] 1 I.R. 1 is discernible.

SEPARATION OF POWERS

2001 was, par excellence, the year for the most considered analysis by the Supreme Court of the nature, purpose and scope of the doctrine of the separation of powers under the Constitution. Whether what emerges represents the last word may be doubted. Far from resolving the questions that surround this subject, the Court has left the law in an unsatisfactory and unfinished state. This area of the law is subjected to comprehensive, incisive analysis in Gerry Whyte's *Social Inclusion and the Legal System: Public Interest Law in Ireland* (Institute of Public Administration, Dublin, 2002), especially, Chapter 1 and the Addendum.

That there has to be some element of separation between the judicial, executive and legislative powers is beyond argument in civil society, which has millennia of recorded instances of the tyranny that can result from their integration. Equally it is not in dispute, but no constitutional order can segregate these powers to such a degree of isolation that they do not encounter each other at crucial meeting points. The executive has to act within the parameters of legislative controls; the legislature must heed and respect the executive function; and the courts must have powers to control legislative and executive excesses and neglects, with due regard for their respective functions.

No particular difficulty arises in the exercise of the judicial function in striking down unconstitutional legislation. The powers of the courts are unambiguously stated in the Constitution. Where a problem is perceived to arise is in respect of positive orders by the court, directed at either the executive or the legislature.

There is no principled objection to the courts' making a positive order that binds the executive. Article 40.4 prescribes one such instance and the Supreme Court, in *State (Quinn) v. Ryan* [1965] I.R. 70, recognised a broad jurisdiction to protect the constitutional rights of citizens from being 'set at nought or circumvented', by acts of the executive or others. Ó Dálaigh C.J. observed that:

> "no one can with impunity set these rights at nought or circumvent them, and . . . the courts' powers in this regard are as ample as the defence of the Constitution requires. Anyone who sets himself such a course is guilty of contempt of the courts and is punishable accordingly."

While Ó Dálaigh C.J. referred to the courts' powers of criminal contempt, it may be considered that their jurisdiction in respect of civil contempt applies *a fortiori*. (Hardiman J., in *Sinnott*, took a very narrow interpretation of Ó Dálaigh C.J.'s statement. Reading this passage again in the light of Hardiman J.'s suggested interpretation it is hard to see how it should be thus limited.)

So far as unconstitutional conduct by the legislature is concerned, the Article 26 procedure represents one way in which the courts can, in effect, render a legislative initiative nugatory before it becomes law. It is true that the courts have shown themselves very reluctant to intervene in the legislative process outside that context, preferring to limit their functions to reviewing the constitutionality of measures that have become law rather than policing their progress through the Oireachtas. Nevertheless, the *Pesca Valentia* line of jurisprudence constitutes, in substance if not form, a significant level of judicial control on legislation over which there is a constitutional question mark.

The really troubling area is where the court is called on to make an order against the State or its legislative or executive organ which carries with it financial implications. This was the position in *Sinnott v. Minister for Education* [2001] 2 I.R. 545. The case concerned a young adult with a condition of autism, whose needs had been neglected by the State over many years. Barr J. awarded him damages for infringement of his constitutional rights, notably under Article 42.5, and made several orders against the State of both a general and specific character: to provide for free primary education for the plaintiff appropriate to his needs for as long as he was capable of benefiting from it and to provide the necessary funding for a behavioural analysis home-based programme for sufferers from autism and for home-based ancillary services, speech, physiotherapy, occupational and music therapies and medical care.

The Supreme Court held that Article 42.4 should not be interpreted as entitling adults to the provision for primary education. We analyse this aspect of the decision above at 73. The Court also held that it was not appropriate for courts to make orders of this character directed against the State. That is the issue that falls for discussion here.

Central to the Court's analysis was the decision by Costello J. in *O'Reilly v. Limerick Corporation* [1989] I.L.R.M. 181 in which members of the Traveller community living on unofficial sites in circumstances of great poverty and deprivation unsuccessfully sought damages for the infringement of their constitutional rights, as well as a mandatory injunction directing the local authority to provide them with accommodation in accordance with its statutory duty.

In a memorable phrase, Costello J. observed that the plaintiffs' claim for damages 'should, to comply with the Constitution, be advanced in Leinster House rather than in the Four Courts.' Costello J. posed the central question as follows:

"Can the courts with constitutional propriety adjudicate on an allegation that the organs of government responsible for the distribution of the Nation's wealth have improperly exercised their powers? Or would such an adjudication be an infringement by the courts of the role which the Constitution has conferred on them?"

Costello J. went on to analyse juridical the basis of the constitutional separation of powers. He traced it to the distinction, acknowledged since the time of Aristotle, between distributive justice and commutative justice:

"There is an important distinction to be made between the relationship which arises in dealings between individuals . . . and the relationship which arises between the individual and those in authority in a political community (which for convenience I will call the Government) when goods held in common for the benefit of the entire community (which would nowadays include wealth raised by taxation) fall to be distributed and allocated. . . .

An obligation in distributive justice is placed on those administering the common stock of goods, the common resource and the wealth held in common which has been raised by taxation, to distribute them and the common wealth fairly and to determine what is due to each individual. But that distribution can only be made by reference to the common good and by those charged with furthering the common good (the Government); it cannot be made by any individual who may claim a share in the common stock and no independent arbitrator, such as a court, can adjudicate on a claim by an individual that he has been deprived of what is his due. This situation is very different in the case of commutative justice. What is due to an individual from another individual (including a public authority) from a relationship arising from their mutual dealings can be ascertained and is due to him exclusively and the precepts of commutative justice will enable an arbitrator such as a court to decide what is properly due should the matter be disputed. This distinction explains why the Court has jurisdiction to award damages against the State when a servant of the State for whose activity is vicariously liable commits a wrong and why it may not get jurisdiction in cases where the claim is for damages based on a failure to distribute adequately in the plaintiff's favour a portion of the community's wealth."

Costello J. went on to observe:

"The State (against whom damages were sought) is the legal embodiment of the political community whose affairs are regulated by the Constitution. The powers of government of the State are to be exercised by the organs of State established by it. The sole and exclusive power of making laws for the State is vested in the Oireachtas; the executive power of the State is exercised by or on the authority of the Government; and justice is to be administered in court established by law. In relation to raising of a common fund to pay for the many services which the State provides by law, the Government is constitutionally responsible to Dáil Éireann for preparing annual estimates of proposed expenditure and estimates of proposed receipts from taxation. Approval for plans for expenditure, and the raising of taxes, is given in the first instance by Dáil Éireann and later by the Oireachtas by the enactment of the annual Appropriation Act and the annual Finance Act. This means that questions relating to raising common funds by taxation and the mode of distribution of common funds are determined by the Oireachtas, although laws enacted by the Oireachtas may give wide discretionary powers to public authorities and public officials (including Ministers) as to their distribution in individual cases."

Costello J. considered that:

"[t]he Courts' constitutional function is to administer justice but I do not think that by exercising the suggested supervisory role it could be said that a court was administering justice as contemplated in the Constitution. What could be involved in the exercise of the suggested jurisdiction would be the imposition by the Court of its view that there had been an unfair distribution of national resources. To arrive at such a conclusion it would have to make an assessment of the validity of the many competing claims on those resources the correct priority to be given to them and the financial implications of the plaintiff's claim ... In exercising this function the Court would not be administering justice as it does when determining an issue relating to commutative justice but it would be engaged in an entirely different exercise namely an adjudication on the fairness or otherwise of the manner in which other organs of state had administered public resources."

Costello J's analysis in *O'Reilly* received strong support in *Sinnott*. Hardiman J. observed:

"In my view all of the considerations mentioned by Costello J. are of prime importance in dealing with the present case. In particular, the constitutionally mandated separation of powers is a vital constituent of the sovereign independent republican and democratic State envisaged by the Constitution. It is not a mere administrative arrangement: it is itself a high constitutional value. It exists to prevent the accumulation of excessive power in any one of the organs of government or its members, and to allow each to check and balance the others. It is an essential part of the democratic procedures of the State, not inferior in importance to any Article of the Constitution."

Hardiman J. went on to state:

"In *Buckley v. Attorney General* [1950] I.R. 67, the High Court and the Supreme Court affirmed in strong terms the courts' independence of the other branches of government, and specifically the unconstitutionality of a legislative measure purporting to determine the disposal of funds when the courts were seized of the issue. . . . It appears to me that the courts must be equally concerned not to infringe upon the proper prerogatives and area of operations of the other branches of government. The functions of these branches, like those of the courts, are themselves of constitutional origin and constitutionally defined.

In my view, the foregoing principles underlie the essential distinction drawn by Mr. Justice Costello between the issues which can be pursued in the Four Courts and issues which, to comply with the Constitution, must be pursued in Leinster House. It is easy to imagine a particular case in which a party might think, and might convince a judge, that a particular act or omission of the legislature or executive was clearly wrong and that another course of action (outlined perhaps in considerable detail in uncontradicted evidence) clearly right or at least preferable. That indeed was what happened in *O'Reilly's* case. But even if a court were quite satisfied that this situation existed, that fact alone would not justify it in purporting to take a decision properly within the remit of the legislature or the executive. I reiterate that it is an independent constitutional value, essential to the maintenance of parliamentary democracy, that the legislature and the executive retain their proper independence in their respective spheres of action. In these spheres, the executive is answerable to Dáil Éireann and the members of the legislature are answerable to the electorate."

Moreover, the Constitution 'imperatively required' that the independence of these organs of government within their spheres had to be real and not merely nominal.

Hardiman J. adopted a contextualised and highly restrictive interpretation of Ó Dálaigh C.J.'s famous observations in *State (Quinn) v. Ryan* [1965] I.R. 70 at 122, that:

"no one can with impunity set these rights at nought or circumvent them, and that the courts' powers in this regard are as ample as the defence of the Constitution requires."

In Hardiman J.'s view, reading this passage in context, it was clear that it was not an assertion of an unrestricted general power in the judicial arm of government but rather 'a strong and entirely appropriate statement that a pettyfogging, legalistic response to an order in the terms of Article 40.4 of the Constitution will not be permitted to obscure the realities of the case, or to preclude appropriate action by the courts.'

Hardiman J. acknowledged that the courts retained "powers and duties" intervene in extreme cases where a government ignored a constitutional imperative, such as by making no provision whatever for primary education. The Supreme Court had made a similar acknowledgment in *MacMathúna v. Ireland* [1995] 1 I.R. 484. Hardiman J. went on to say, however, that:

"the fact that the powers to deal with extreme circumstances must be retained cannot be a basis for the exercise of such powers in any other circumstances. Firstly, to do so would offend the constitutional separation of powers. Secondly, it would lead the courts into the taking of decisions in areas in which they have no special qualification or experience. Thirdly, it would permit the courts to take such decisions even though they are not, and cannot be, democratically responsible for them as the legislature and the executive are. Fourthly, the evidence-based adversarial procedures of the court, which are excellently adapted for the administration of commutative justice, are too technical, too expensive, too focused on the individual issue to be an appropriate method for deciding on issues of policy."

Hardiman J. observed that this view of the separation of powers had for many years been implicitly accepted by lawyers and jurists. It could be found in most if not all of the great constitutional documents and in the writings of such commanding figures as Aristotle, Locke, Montesquieu and the founding fathers of the United States of America. Hardiman J. went on to say:

"In the last quarter century, there has arisen another point of view whose major manifestation in a quasi legal context is found it the works of the American academic John Rawls. It subordinates politics to a theory of justice, seeming to view political philosophy as a branch of jurisprudence. Theorists of this view consider that they can provide a body of principles which can be interpreted and applied by courts, to the virtual exclusion or marginalisation of the political process. Preferably, but not essentially, the mechanism of this process is to enshrine the selected principles in some form of code or charter. Failing this, one can try to imply them into older texts. The political process thus avoided or marginalized is regarded as too diverse, clamorous, and populist in values to be worth preserving as more than an inferior organ of government.

In my view, conflicts or priorities, values, modes of administration or sentiments cannot be avoided or ignored by adopting an agreed or imposed exclusive theory of justice. And if judges were to become involved in such an enterprise, designing the details of policy in individual cases or in general, and ranking some areas of policy in priority to others, they would step beyond their appointed role. The views of aspirants to judicial office on such social and economic questions are not canvassed for the good reason that they are thought to be irrelevant. They have no mandate in these areas. And the legislature and the executive, possessed of a democratic mandate, are liable to recall by the withdrawal of that mandate. That is the most fundamental, but by no means the only, basis of the absolute necessity for judicial restraint in these areas. To abandon this restraint would be unacceptably and I believe unconstitutionally to limit the proper freedom of action of the legislature and the executive branch of government."

Hardiman J. emphasised that the instant case was not one in which the law had no remedy for the plaintiff. In particular, recent statutory provisions had effected 'a revolution in educational legislation'. Similarly, the court retained its wide jurisdiction to ascertain and enforce the rights of individuals, whatever their origin in law or in the Constitution. The rejection of the very specific and unique claim advanced by the plaintiff did not alter the fact that the courts would continue to develop the jurisprudence of individual rights and enforce those rights on all appropriate occasions.

Keane C.J. 'entirely agree[d]' with Hardiman J's analysis of the doctrine of the separation of powers and the exclusive role of the legislature and the executive in the distribution of the nation's wealth.

Geoghegan J. expressed agreement with Costello J.'s approach in *O'Reilly v. Limerick Corporation*. Whilst reserving his position on what would have been appropriate had Mr. Sinnott established the existence and breach of a continuing constitutional duty to him, he did think that 'in very exceptional circumstances' it might be open to a court to order allocation of funds where a constitutional right had been 'flouted without justification or reasonable excuse of any kind.' He admitted, however, to having great doubts that the courts should ever involve themselves in making the detailed kind of orders made in some American decisions in relation to education.

Before commentating on *Sinnott*, we must refer to *T.D. v. The Minister for Education*, Supreme Court, December 17, 2001, where the Supreme Court carried further its analysis of the separation of powers doctrine. In this case, Kelly J. had made a mandatory order against the Ministers for Education and Health and Children requiring them to take all steps necessary to facilitate the building and opening of secure 'high support' units in ten locations providing special care for minors with special needs. The intended effect of the injunction was that the developments had to be completed within the time scales specified in evidence given on behalf of the Minister in a previous hearing. If there was to be any change, it would have to be by way of variation of the injunction, warranted by objectively justifiable reasons. Kelly J. had reached the end of his judicial tether, following a saga of undertakings made and broken.

The Supreme Court reversed Kelly J, holding that it was not within the competence of the court to make orders of this character and more generally that the separation of powers doctrine did not support it. As regards the specific question of the nature of the order, Murray J. stated the objection succinctly:

> "It seems to me that, in incorporating the policy programme as part of a High Court order, the policy is taken out of the hands of the executive which is left with no discretionary powers of its own. It becomes the policy and programme of the court which cannot be varied or any decision taken which might involve delay (or an adjustment of policy) without the permission and order of the court. A judicial imperative is substituted for executive policy. The judge becomes the final decision maker. In short he is administrator of that discrete policy. That is not a judicial function within the ambit of the Constitution.
>
> Another inevitable consequence of the High Court order would be to undermine the answerability of the Executive to Dáil Éireann and thus impinge on core constitutional functions of both those organs of

State. Article 28.4.1 provides 'The Government shall be responsible to Dáil Éireann'."

Keane C.J. expanded on this objection:

"The difficulty created by the order of the High Court in this case is not simply that it offends in principle against the doctrine of the separation of powers, though I have no doubt that it does. It also involves the High Court in effectively determining the policy which the executive are to follow in dealing with a particular social problem. This difficulty is not met by the contention advanced on behalf of the applicants that the Ministers are being asked to do no more than carry into effect a programme prepared by them and which they assert it is their intention to implement. The evidence in this case establishes clearly that, in what is unarguably an extremely difficult area, approaches which at one time seemed appropriate may have to be reconsidered: in particular, officials are naturally concerned with how equivalent problems are being dealt with in other countries. There is no reason in principle why the executive should not adopt a flexible and open minded approach to the problems of children with special needs while at the same time ensuring that their constitutional right to have those needs met is respected. The making of the High Court order in this form, as the judgment of the trial judge emphasises, will make it necessary for the Minister to return to the High Court to obtain its sanction to any change in policy which necessitates a departure from the precise terms of the order. It cannot be right that the executive power of the Government can only be exercised in a particular manner, even though so to do would not contravene any person's constitutional rights, without the sanction of the High Court. . . .

I find the conclusion inescapable that, since the High Court first began the difficult task of grappling with this problem, a Rubicon has been crossed, clearly from the best of motives, in which it is moving to undertake a role which is conferred by the Constitution on the other organs of State, who are also entitled with the resources necessary to discharge that role in the interests of the common good."

On the wider aspects of the separation of powers doctrine, Hardiman J. gave a formidable analysis, which merits extensive quotation:

"If a judge considers that there has been a 'failure of the legislature and the executive' (to use a phrase of the learned trial judge in this case) in some particular area of constitutionally significant policy, can he or she on that account 'attempt to fill the vacuum' by ordering either of those bodies to implement a particular policy? If this is possible, it may gratify those who agree with the judge that there has been a failure, and who find the solution which he or she imposes acceptable. But it would represent an enormous increase in the power of an unelected judiciary at the expense of the politically accountable branches of government. It would attribute to the judiciary a paramountcy over the other branches in the form of a residual supervisory governmental power which, once asserted and exercised, would certainly be appealed to again and again. This paramountcy might develop in a context of widespread popular approval in a particular case, but it would be equally available in all such cases, regardless of public opinion. It would represent a very significant change in our constitutional order, not easily reversed."

Hardiman J. was of the view that:

"if the courts (or either of the other organs of government) expand their powers beyond their constitutional remit, this expansion will necessarily be at the expense of the other organs of government. It will also be progressive. If citizens are taught to look to the courts for remedies for matters within the legislative or executive remit, they will progressively seek further remedies there, and progressively cease to look to the political arms of government. Such a development would certainly downgrade the political arms of government and, just as significantly, it would tend to involve the courts, progressively, in political matters. This cannot be permitted to occur. The mandatory procedures whereby the courts give judgment only on legal evidence, almost always heard in public, and legal submissions, necessarily often technical, do not remotely equip them to evolve and to alter policy. Their necessary immunity from election and from popular approbation or the reverse make them quite unfitted to direct the expenditure of public funds."

Hardiman J.'s analysis conflates the issue of the separation of powers with that of the justiciability of rights with a social or economic element to their content. Of course important questions of political philosophy can arise in this context. Thus one must heed the observations of Dr. Gerard Hogan, quoted with approval by Hardiman J., that, if an amendment is passed by the People giving specific constitutional protection to socio-economic rights, this:

"will mean a further significant transfer of power from the elected branches of government to an unelected judiciary which is already by the standards of most western democracies extremely powerful."

Murphy J.'s close analysis of the relationship between the Constitution and socio-economic rights is worth recording:

"With the exception of the provisions dealing with education, the personal rights identified in the Constitution all lie in the civil and political rather than the economic sphere. These are indeed important rights which were won for citizens in different societies over a period of centuries often in the face of bitter opposition. Whilst limited poor law relief or workhouse accommodation has existed in this and neighbouring jurisdictions for many years the demand for a coherent system of socio-economic rights, and more particularly the acceptance of that demand, does not appear to have emerged until the widespread acceptance of socialist doctrines following the Second World War resulting in the now generally accepted concept of the Welfare State.

The absence of any express reference to accommodation, medical treatment or social welfare of any description as a constitutional right in the Constitution as enacted is a matter of significance. The failure to correct that omission in any of the twenty-four referenda which have taken place since then would suggest a conscious decision to withhold from rights which are now widely conferred by appropriate legislation the status of constitutionality in the sense of being rights conferred or recognised by the Constitution.

The reluctance to elevate social welfare legislation to a higher plane may reflect a moral or political opposition to such change or it may be a recognition of the difficulty of regulating rights of such complexity by fundamental legislation which cannot be altered readily to meet changing social needs. Alternatively it may have been anticipated that the existence of a constitutional right enforceable by the courts would involve – as the present case so clearly demonstrates – a radical departure from the principle requiring the separation of the powers of the courts from those of the legislature and the executive. The inclusion in the Constitution of Article 45 setting out directive principles of social policy for the general guidance of the Oireachtas – and then subject to the express provision that they should not be cognisable by any court – might be regarded as in ingenious method of ensuring that social justice should be achieved while excluding the judiciary from any role in the attainment of that objective."

Murphy J. noted that a similar approach had been adopted in the Constitution of India 1949, which, having provided in Part IV for certain 'Directive Principles of State Policy', went on to provide in Article 37 that:

"The provisions contained in this Part shall not be enforceable by any court, but the principles therein laid down are nevertheless fundamental in the governance of the country and it shall be the duty of the State to apply these principles in making laws."

Murphy J. observed that the status the status of socio economic rights in the Constitution and the detailed provisions in relation to education had been explained by Professor Gerard Quinn in his essay "Rethinking the Nature of Economic, Social and Cultural Rights in the Irish Legal Order" in Cathryn Costello ed., *Fundamental Social Rights* (Irish Centre for European Law, Dublin, 2001), 49 'in the following colourful terms':

> "De Valera cleverly genuflected before socio economic rights but made sure to insert them into a part of the Constitution that is unenforceable by the courts (Article 45 on Directive Principles of Social Policy). One socio economic right escaped into the hard text: Article 42 on the right to education. Its presence in the text has more to do with history than with logic. The intention of the British in the 1830s was to set up and fund a network of free primary schools on a purely non denominational basis. This was fiercely resisted by all Churches. In the compromise that ensued, the State agreed to pay for the education and the religious bodies agreed to provide it. The main intention of Article 42 seems to have been to copper fasten this historic arrangement between Church and State."

Murphy J. concluded his judgment as follows:

> "It is, of course, entirely understandable, and desirable politically and morally, that a society should, through its laws, devise appropriate schemes and by means of taxation raise the necessary finance to fund such schemes as will enable the sick, the poor and the underprivileged in our society to make the best use of the limited resources nature may have bestowed on them. It is my belief that this entirely desirable goal must be achieved and can only be achieved by legislation and not by any unrealistic extension of the provisions originally incorporated in Bunreacht na hÉireann. I believe that Costello J. was entirely correct when in *O'Reilly v. Limerick Corporation* [1989] I.L.R.M. 181 he concluded that the courts were singularly unsuited to the task of asserting the validity of competing claims on national resources and that this was essentially the role of the Oireachtas. It is only fair to add, as I have already pointed out, that those who framed the Constitution seem to have anticipated this problem and provided a solution for it."

Denham J. in her dissent, quoted from the powerful words of Barak C.J. in the Israeli Supreme Court decision of *United MizRahi Bank Ltd v. Migdol Village* (1995) 49 (4) P.D. 221:

> "Judicial review of constitutionality is the very essence of democracy, for democracy does not only connote the rule of the majority. Democracy

also means the rule of basic values and human rights as expressed in the constitution. Democracy is a delicate balance between majority rule and the basic values of society. Indeed democracy does not mean formal democracy alone, which is concerned with the electoral process in which the majority rules. Democracy also means substantive democracy, which is concerned with the defence of human rights in particular. . . . Judicial review of constitutionality therefore prevails over what is known as the 'counter-majoritarian dilemma'. One way to accomplish this is by emphasising that when judges interpret the constitution and invalidate contradictory laws they give expression to the fundamental values of society that have developed over time. Thus the court safeguards constitutional democracy and maintains the delicate balance upon which it is based. Remove majority rule from constitutional democracy and its essence is harmed. Remove the sovereignty of fundamental values from constitutional democracy and its very existence is called into question. Judicial review of constitutionality enables the society to be true to itself and to honour its basic conception. This is the basis for the substantive legitimacy of judicial review. This is also the true basis for the principle of constitutionality itself. We are bound by the constitution that was enacted in the past because it expresses the fundamental outlook of modern society. It may therefore be said that each generation enacts the constitution anew. By means of judicial review we are loyal to the fundamental values that we took upon ourselves in the past, that reflect our essence in the present, and that will direct our national development as a society in the future. . . . It may be said that whoever argues that judicial review is undemocratic is in effect arguing that the constitution itself is undemocratic. To maintain that judicial review is undemocratic is to maintain that safeguarding human rights is undemocratic. To maintain that judicial review is undemocratic is to maintain that defending the rights of the individual against the majority is undemocratic. The democratic nature of the state is not determined by the representative nature of each of its branches but rather by the democratic nature of the government as a whole. . . ."

The decisions of *Sinnott* and *T.D.* call for the following comments. First, to a large extent, the majority judgments set up, and then refute, arguments that are far too general in their thrust. The Court was not being called on to hold that the Constitution has incorporated the philosophy of John Rawls, though there is little doubt that the search for ensuring justice which inspires the work of that scholar may be considered to underlie much constitutional analysis. A legal system that does not seek to place the value of justice at its core or, worse still, is indifferent to the relationship between constitutional norms and justice runs the risk of losing sight of one of the great Aristotelian virtues recognised by Walsh J. as being the pillars on which our Constitution is built.

It need hardly be said that concern for the value of justice, including distributive justice, is not the same as presenting the argument that the courts must seek to effectuate distributive justice outside the parameters of the constitutional system of the protection and vindication of rights. In *T.D.*, Denham J. was right to point out that *O'Reilly v. Limerick Corporation* could be distinguished from the instant case on the basis that:

> "Costello J. in *O'Reilly* did not determine that there was a breach of a constitutional right. Rather he analysed the concept of distributive justice. I agree with his analysis of distributive justice and the fact that such a concept does not apply to the justice rendered by the courts. The distribution of the nation's wealth is a matter for the executive and the legislature. In this case the applicants are not making a case that the nation's wealth be justly distributed. Their cases have been brought to protect constitutional rights which had been recognised and acknowledged."

This brings us to the second criticism of *Sinnott* and *T.D.*: somewhat similar to the first: the failure of the majority in both cases to distinguish between a claim based on a theory of socio-economic rights as opposed to one based on the rights identified expressly or protected and vindicated implicitly by the Constitution. Again the error lies in the notion that the plaintiffs' case sought recognition for some new constitutional right or theory never previously identified by the courts. On the contrary, in both cases, the plaintiffs argued that the right to education, and not some new, previously unacknowledged, right, required the court to translate fine words into real protection.

The third difficulty with the majority judgments in the two decisions concerns the mantra of interference with the common wealth. The majority proceeds on the basis that the national cake is beyond the remit of the courts and that the legislature, which determines the size of the cake, should have final responsibility for slicing it into such portions as it, and not the courts, should decide. Such a political philosophy – for that is what it is – is quite at variance with the philosophy underlying the Constitution. Of course the courts should not take over the function of generating the national cake and deciding how it is to be sliced: for the courts to do so would clearly trespass on the legislative power. But, equally clearly, the courts must scrutinise both the size of that cake and the portions of the slices in order to protect a range of constitutional rights.

If the rights to life, to health, to bodily integrity and to equality and the rights of the family are to have substantial reality, the courts must scrutinise the distribution of the common wealth. A policy that distributed national resources in a discriminatory way, so as to harm the economic viability of members of a particular religious denomination or ethnic group, for example, would clearly offend against the Constitution. The neglect by the State of the health or bodily integrity of a particular group in society must equally be monitored by the courts. If the courts find that the State's guarantee in respect of primary education is simply not being given practical effect, not only are they entitled, they are surely obliged, to take whatever steps are necessary to vindicate the rights of the victims of that breach.

It should also be noted that the expansion by the judiciary of some rights that are emphatically not socio-economic in character, may have far more radically limiting implications for the executive and legislature than does the judicial of certain socio economic rights, whether in their own right or as integral aspects of 'traditional' civil and political rights.. The expansion of the individual-centred right of privacy, for example in the United States of America, has had significant effects in restricting the powers of state legislatures in wide areas of criminal law and family law.

This brings us to the final comment on the two decisions. One can sympathise with the majority's reluctance to convert the judicial function into an executive policy, where judges become administrators of a detailed agenda for education, housing or health. The objection here is not that the courts are limited to operating on an adversarial model: their wardship jurisdiction (which has its own constitutional difficulties) involves an inquisitorial function which can extend over a long period of time. The true objection is that the effectuation of detailed programmes in these areas is clearly a matter for the executive and legislative. Courts should be very reluctant to go any distance down that path.

But what are the courts to do when the executive, in breach of undertakings made to them, simply neglects to adopt any policy that will vindicate the constitutional rights of a citizen which it has already breached? Declarations, which have proven conclusively to be ineffective, cannot be the solution. At this point, courts reach a defining moment. They can surrender the judicial function to the might of the executive or they can assert the judicial function in the vindication of the constitutional rights which have been violated. If the courts adopt the former course, everything may appear at the surface to continue as before, but the judicial function has been sacrificed at the unconstitutional insistence of the other organs of the State. If the courts adopt the latter course, there can of course be no guarantee that the executive will comply with the courts orders. The experience under the Constitution up to now has been that the executive fully respects the exercise by the courts of their judicial function. If in the future the executive elects to defy a court order, it, rather than the court, will precipitate a constitutional crisis and the court will have been faithful to its duty of vindicating constitutional rights.

For analysis of *Sinnott* and *T.D.*, see Blathna Ruane, 'The Separation of Powers: The Granting of Mandatory Orders to Enforce Constitutional Rights' (2002) 7 Bar Rev. 11.

TEMPORARY RELEASE

In *Lynch v. The Minister for Justice*, Equality and Law Reform, High Court, March 26, 2001, Herbert J. rejected the argument that the failure to grant a prisoner temporary release was a denial of a fundamental right guaranteed to him by Articles 34, 38.1 and 40 to 44 of the Constitution. He also rejected an argument based on recourse to the Universal Declaration of Human Rights and the European Convention on Human Rights and Fundamental Freedoms, as neither of these instruments was part of the domestic law of the State and was therefore not justiciable in the courts of the State.

Herbert J. was of the view that 'a prisoner has no constitutional or inherent right to early release from prison or temporary release'. This was clear from the decisions of Murphy J. in *Ryan v. Governor of Limerick Prison* [1988] I.R. 198 and Johnson J. in *Sherlock v. Governor of Mountjoy Prison* [1991] 1 I.R. 451 as well as the United States Supreme Court in *Greeholtz v. Nebraska Penal Inmates* (1979) 442 US 1 and *Ohio Adult Parole Authority v. Woodard* (1998) 523 U.S. 272. Herbert J. went on to state:

> "After conviction the powers of comminution and of temporary release are vested in Executive and are administrative matters in which the Courts have no function and in respect of which the relevant authorities have a wide discretion. This discretion was recognised by the European Court of Human Rights in the case of *Boyle & Rice v. The United Kingdom* (1988) 10 EHRR 425."

In the instant case there was no evidence that the authorities were dealing with the applicant's applications for transfer and temporary release on a category basis, such as had been the position in *Cornish v. Minister for Justice*, High Court, January 13, 2000, where O'Neill J. had held that such a practice was *ultra vires* the powers of the Minister under the provisions of section 2 of the Criminal Justice Act 1960. In *McHugh v. Minister for Justice* [1997] I.R. 245 the Supreme Court had reiterated that the granting or withholding of temporary release was a matter exclusively within the discretion of the Minister and that the Court had no jurisdiction to intervene in the process. In that case, as in the instant case, the applicant had relied on the fact that temporary release had been granted to other prisoners but had been withheld from him.

In the Prisons Chapter, below, 495, we consider another decision dealing with temporary release: *Kinahan v. The Minister for Justice, Equality and Law Reform*, Supreme Court, February 21, 2001. The subject is well analysed by P.A. McDermott, *Prison Law* (2000) Chapter 12.

Contract Law

EOIN O'DELL, Trinity College, Dublin

BREACH

Effect of breach   Breach of contract does not of itself discharge a contract; it merely gives rise to a right to damages and/or specific performance for the innocent party; and, if the breach is sufficiently serious, it will give the innocent party the right to elect to terminate, which right of election must be exercised promptly. The breach will be sufficiently serious if it is a breach of a condition or a serious breach of an innominate term (*Annual Review of Irish Law 1995*, p.201; *Annual Review of Irish Law 1998*, pp.138-153), or if before performance is due, a party either renounces the contract or disables himself from performing it (this may be termed an anticipatory or repudiatory breach).

If the innocent party elects to keep the contract on foot, both parties can rely on it, so that, for example, the party now in breach can later rely on a term of the contract to discharge it (*Fercometal v. Mediterranean Shipping (The Simona)* [1989] A.C. 788 (HL)). Again for so long as the contract, such as a contract of employment, subsists, the mutual obligations of the parties, such as the employer and employee, continue. In particular, the employer's duty to pay the employee's wages continues, even through the employee's illness, unless and until the contract is terminated. Hence, in *Morrison v. Bell* [1939] 2 K.B. 187, 198 Scott L.J. held that under a contract of service, wages continue through sickness and through incapacity from sickness to do the work contracted for, until the contract is terminated by a notice by the employer in accordance with the terms of the contract (see also *Boyle v. An Post* [1992] 2 I.R. 437). Consequently, non-payment of wages amounts to a breach of contract, for which specific performance will lie. Hence in *Rooney v. Kilkenny*, High Court, March 9, 2001, Kinlen J. made an interlocutory order (by analogy with *Charlton v. Aga Khan*, High Court, Laffoy J., December 22, 1998) that the defendant continue to pay the plaintiff's wages.

On the other hand, if the innocent party elects to terminate the contract, all future obligations under the contract are discharged, though this does not undo all that has gone before (*Johnson v. Agnew* [1980] A.C. 367 (HL)); the parties are relieved of the duty to perform their primary obligations, but the contract's former existence helps to determine secondary obligations such as the level of damages, or the continuance of clauses such as exclusion, arbitration and restraint of trade clauses (*Photo Productions v. Securicor* [1980] A.C. 827 (HL)). Finally, whether or not the innocent party elects to terminate the contract, the right to damages and/or specific performance for the breach persists.

Breach and repudiation   In *Superwood v. Sun Alliance*, High Court, April 4-7, 2001, the defendants had purported to repudiate their liability under a contract of insurance, but this repudiation was not accepted by the plaintiffs. Following a marathon hearing before O'Hanlon J. who held in favour of the insurer, the Supreme Court held that the repudiation was invalid on the ground advanced ([1995] 3 I.R. 303 (SC)), and the matter returned to the High Court for a second marathon hearing before Smyth J. It took him four days to read his judgment, during the course of which he held that it "is settled law that a party who elects to disregard a repudiation by his co-contractor cannot afterwards recover damages at law for breach of contract. If a contract is still in being, it has not been broken. Asquith L.J. in *Howard v. Pickford Tool Company* [1951] 1 K.B. 417, 421 remarked that '[a]n unaccepted repudiation is a thing writ in water and of no value to anybody; it affords no legal rights of any sort or kind'. . . . There is no question here of the Plaintiffs having elected to treat the contract as discharged and having communicated that unequivocally to the Defendants, the effect of which would have been to terminate the contract as from the moment of acceptance is communicated to the party in default" (at pp. 261–262 of the transcript of day 4 of the judgment; April 7, 2001). As a consequence, he dismissed the plaintiffs' action for damages for breach of contract against the defendants.

The word repudiation in this context has at least four shades of meaning (*Annual Review of Irish Law 1998*, pp.138–150). First, a repudiation in the sense of a repudiatory or anticipatory breach occurs where a party either renounces the contract or disables himself from performing it. Second, where one party has committed a breach sufficient to allow the other to terminate the contract, it is often said that the party in breach has repudiated the contract. Third, conversely and confusingly, where one party commits a breach of contract, it is often said that the other party's right to terminate for that breach is a right to repudiate the contract. Fourth (in what might be a special case of the third), contracts often provide for circumstances in which one party may treat the contract as at an end as a consequence of the actions of another party, and often describe that as a right to repudiate the contract (this usage is common in the insurance industry; see *Superwood* [1995] 3 I.R. 303 (SC); see *Annual Review of Irish Law 1995*, pp.228–232); *Doyle v. Irish National Insurance Co.* [1998] 1 I.R. 89, 91; [1998] 1 I.L.R.M. 502, 503 (HC), Kelly J.; see *Annual Review of Irish Law 1998*, pp.143–146). This instability of the word repudiation makes precise analysis difficult; in particular, considerations appropriate to one usage would not necessarily be appropriate to another.

Where the word "repudiation" is used in either the first or second senses, it simply amounts to a breach which gives the other party a right to elect to terminate the contract; until that right to elect has been exercised, the contract continues; the breach, the repudiation in these two senses, does not automatically terminate the contract (cf. *Hearn v. Collins*, High Court O'Sullivan J., February 3, 1998; see *Annual Review of Irish Law 1998*, pp.146–150). If the *dictum* of Asquith L.J. in *Howard v. Pickford* is placed in the context of these first two senses, then it amounts a strong statement of these basic principles. Where the word "repudiation" is used in either the third or fourth senses, it simply amounts to one party seeking to rely on the other's breach of contract to bring the contract to an end, either according to the general law or according to the terms of the contract itself. It would be rare for repudiation or an attempt to repudiate, in either of these two senses, to constitute a breach; and even if it did, it would still have to be accepted by the other party before it would bring the contract to an end. If the *dictum* of Asquith L.J. in *Howard v. Pickford* is placed in the context of these last two senses, then it stresses that very point. Given the insurance context of the case, is more than likely that this is the sense in which the word repudiation is being used by Smyth J. in *Superwood*, so that the insurer's unaccepted repudiation would have meant that the contract had not in fact been discharged. However, this is not an end of the analysis, since, if the attempt by the insurer to repudiate itself constituted a breach of contract, even if the insured did not terminate for that breach, the insured's right to damages for the breach would still have subsisted. The dismissal of the damages claim must be taken to amount to a finding that the attempted repudiation did not constitute a breach of contract, because if it had, damages would have necessarily followed.

Finally, although as a matter of principle, breach of itself will not terminate a contract, the contract itself may expressly provide for this. A rare example of such automatic termination according to the terms of the contract is provided by the decision of Murphy J. in *Phelan v. Goodman and El Taher*, High Court, September 11, 2001. In 1986, Mr Phelan and Mr El Taher entered into a joint venture agreement and related agreements, one of which provided that neither party would sell shares held by him personally or through any company, without first offering such shares to the other; the Articles of Association of the joint venture companies provided likewise; and the joint venture agreement provided that it would terminate upon any such sale of shares or if either party ceased to hold or control at least 10% of the equity. In 1987, without Mr Phelan's knowledge, Mr Goodman purchased from Mr El Taher 80% of the vehicle through which Mr El Taher held his interest in the joint venture, with an option over Mr El Taher's remaining 20%. In 1988, Mr Goodman through the joint venture company was later able to invoke the terms of the agreement to purchase Mr Phelan's interest. Murphy J. held that the 1987 agreement involved the disposal of Mr El Taher's beneficial interest in the shares, which amounted to a breach of the Articles of Association and of the side agreement. Although Mr El Taher held 20% of his former holding, he held it subject to an option for Mr Goodman, and since "a share is of no value to anyone without the benefits it confers then, after . . . 1987, Mr El Taher [held] nothing" (7). Consequently, by virtue of its terms, the 1986 joint venture was terminated automatically by the 1987 sale.

Breach of conditions and conditions precedent   On the one hand, breach of a condition of a contract will not of itself terminate a contract, but it will give the party not in breach the right to elect to terminate for the breach. On the other hand, the parties might make the contract subject to a condition precedent, by which the contract would not be binding unless an agreed specified event occurs. Hence, there is an important practical difference between a breach of condition and a breach of a condition precedent; in the former case, contractual obligations subsist and continue until discharged; in the latter, they simply never arise. In *Blackall v. Blackall* [2000] 3 I.R. 456 (HC) (see *Annual Review of Irish Law 2000*, pp.88–9), Finnegan J. held that a clause in a contract for the sale of land requiring the payment of a deposit is usually a condition of the contract breach of which would entitle the vendors to elect to terminate, rather than a condition precedent to the existence of the contract itself.

Had the condition been a condition precedent, it would have had to have been reasonably strictly observed. For example, in the context of options to purchase land, Kenny J. in *Cassidy v. Baker* (1969) 103 I.L.T.R. 40 held that it is "a general rule that any matters which by the terms of an option are made conditions precedent to its exercise, must be reasonably strictly observed". On the basis of this standard, in *Terry v. Albion Enterprises*, High Court, November 14, 2001, McCracken J. held that the terms of an option to purchase had been satisfied and ordered specific performance (cp. *O'Hara v. Flint* [1979] I.L.R.M. 156). The plaintiff was a tenant of the defendant under a lease, which gave the plaintiff "the option to purchase the premises from the landlord ... on or before the 31 January 1988". The plaintiff purported to exercise the option on January 9, 1998, but a dispute arose between the parties, not least because the landlord had failed in his contractual obligation to furnish within six months evidence of his title to the premises, and the sale was not completed by January 31 or at any other time. McCracken J. held that it would have been understandable that time would have been of the essence of option if the defendant had already satisfied the plaintiff of title; but that, since it was the defendant's default which meant in effect that the plaintiff could not complete, the defendant could not hold the plaintiff to the January 31 deadline.

CERTAINTY

A contract may be uncertain because it is simply too vague, or because it is incomplete. As to contracts potentially uncertain on the grounds of vagueness, where a phrase is capable of too many meanings, and the intended meaning is not specified or capable of specification by the court, the contract will be void for vagueness. As to contracts potentially uncertain on the grounds of incompleteness, a contract may be incomplete due to the absence of an important term or terms: "unless all the material terms of the contract are agreed there is no binding obligation . . . nor is there a contract if a material term is neither settled nor implied by law and the document contains no machinery for ascertaining it" (*Foley v. Classique Coaches* [1934] 2 K.B. 1, 12 per Maugham L.J.). However, simply because a term or terms remain to be agreed, the contract is not necessarily incomplete (*Pagnan SpA v. Feed Products* [1987] 2 Lloyd's Rep. 601 (CA)). There is, however, a fine line between a contract uncertain for incompleteness and a contract sufficiently certain to be enforceable on its own terms, even if other terms remain to be agreed. For example, if a price is not agreed, courts will often conclude that the contract is uncertain for incompleteness (*Peter Lind v. Mersey Docks and Harbour Board* [1972] 2 Lloyd's Rep. 234 (CA)), though the performance of a contract on both sides can result in the implication of such a term (*British Bank for Foreign Trade v. Novinex* [1949] 1 K.B. 623 (CA)) and in the context of contracts for the sale of goods, section 8(3) of the Sale of Goods Act 1893 allows the court to imply a term as to a reasonable price if there is a concluded contract for the sale of goods but no agreement on price. Hence, in some cases at least, if the contract is sufficiently certain apart from the issue of the price, then the court can imply a term as to a reasonable price. More generally, uncertainty by incompleteness can often be avoided by the implication of terms (Coote "Contract Formation and the Implication of Terms" (1993) 6 J.C.L. 51). This was acknowledged by Barron J. in the Supreme Court in *Mackey v. Wilde* [1998] 1 I.L.R.M. 449 (SC) 455: "There have been many cases in which the full terms of the contract are not set out precisely, but which have been found to be valid binding agreements. Examples ... [include] where a term is implied ...". However, on the facts, he held that the word "few" in a clause by which each party to a joint fishery would grant only 25 annual tickets and a few day tickets was void was too uncertain, and hence the contract was void for uncertainty (see *Annual Review of Irish Law 1997*, pp.202–208).

Mackey was an example vagueness rather than incompleteness; the decision of the Supreme Court this year in *Lawlor v. Ross*, Supreme Court, November 22, 2001, Keane C.J., Fennelly and Geoghegan JJ.) provides an example of incompleteness. The plaintiff alleged that the parties had agreed, as a joint venture, to form a company to purchase and develop certain lands, and that the defendants' subsequent acquisition of the lands without him was a breach of that contract. The Supreme Court struck out the plaintiff's claim on the grounds that the contract as pleaded by the plaintiff was incomplete and therefore void for uncertainty. As Keane C.J. put it, certain aspects of the arrangement between the parties "remain[ed] remarkably vague" (4). In particular, because finance had yet to be agreed, "the contract relied on could not possibly constitute a concluded contract between the parties which would give rise to any action at law" (4). For Fennelly J., the fatal defect in the plaintiff's claim was

"the clear evidence ... that an integral part of the agreement ... was that how the entire joint venture was to be financed was left over for discussion at a later date. ... The agreement in this case was for the formation of a company. The parties did not address the question of the capital of that company at all. Most crucially, they agreed in the terms, which the plaintiff was so careful to formalise that this issue would be discussed at a later date. ... The parties may well have reached an agreement in principle to enter into a joint venture and on their respective shares. However, they remained in negotiation so long as they had not agreed on finance. Hence, there was no concluded contract" (10-11).

In *Mackey*, for Barron J., the essential question had been whether "the parties have left over some matter to be determined which can only be determined by themselves" ([1998] 1 I.L.R.M. 449, 455); if they had, in his view, then the contract would be incomplete and uncertain. However, this will not always be the case. Although some if not many agreements to agree a specific matter at a later date may not be enforceable (*May & Butcher v. R.* [1934] 2 K.B. 17n (HL)), this is not an invariable conclusion (e.g., *Foley v. Classique Coaches* [1934] 2 K.B. 1). As Lloyd L.J. observed in *Pagnan SpA v. Feed Products* [1987] 2 Lloyd's Rep. 601, there are many situations in which "parties intend to be bound forthwith even though there are further terms still to be agreed ... there is no legal obstacle which stands in the way of the parties agreeing to be bound now while deferring important matters to be agreed later. It happens every day when parties enter into so-called 'heads of agreement'." ([1987] 2 Lloyd's Rep. 601, 619). The parties had agreed "the cardinal terms" of a contract for the purchase and sale of corn feed pellets: the "product, price, quantity, period of shipment, range of loading ports and governing contract terms" ([1987] 2 Lloyd's Rep. 601, 611); but they had not agreed a specific loading port, the rate of loading, and other matters. However, the Court of Appeal, having decided that the cardinal terms were agreed, held that the contract was not uncertain as incomplete. On the other hand, in *Mackey v. Wilde* itself, Barron J. held that "what the parties have left over, what is meant by the word 'few', is something which only they can settle. It follows that there was no concluded agreement" ([1998] 1 I.L.R.M. 449, 455). In *Lawlor*, unlike *Pagnan,* the parties had not agreed all of the "cardinal" terms; in *Lawlor*, like *Mackey*, what was left over was something which only the parties could have settled; hence *Lawlor* fell on the same side of the line as *Mackey*. There being no contract at all, there was nothing into which a term could have been implied.

DAMAGES

Damages for mental distress for breach of contract   The aim of damages for breach of contract is to place the party not in breach, so far as money can do it, in as good a situation as if the contract had been performed (*Robinson v.*

Harman (1848) 1 Ex 850; *British Westinghouse v. Underground Electric Rlys of London* [1912] A.C. 673; *Murphy v. Wexford County Council* [1921] 2 I.R. 230). However, a plaintiff is not entitled to recover "damages for the disappointment of mind occasioned by the breach of contract" (*Hamlin v. Great Northern Rly* (1856) 1 H&N 408, 411; 156 E.R. 1261, 1262 *per* Pollock CB; *Addis v. Gramophone Co. Ltd* [1909] A.C. 488 (HL); *Kinlen v. Ulster Bank* [1928] I.R. 171 (SC)). Hence, in *Addis*, the House of Lords held that a plaintiff cannot recover damages for damage to the plaintiff's reputation or injury to the plaintiff's feelings arising from the manner of the breach of contract (see, generally, Jackson "Injured Feelings Resulting From Breach of Contract" (1977) 26 I.C.L.Q. 502; Macdonald "Contractual Damages for Mental Distress" (1994) 7 J.C.L. 134; Palmer and Hudson "Damages for Distress and Loss of Enjoyment in Claims Involving Chattels", in Palmer and McKendrick (eds.), *Interests in Goods* (2nd ed., LLP, London, 1998), p. 867).

To this general rule, however, there had always been exceptions. Hence, damages for mental distress would be available in, for example, the case of disastrous holiday (*Jarvis v. Swans Tours* [1973] 1 All E.R. 71 (CA); *Jackson v. Horizon Holidays* [1975] 3 All E.R. 92 (CA); *The Mikhail Lermontov*). The exceptions were often expansively applied (*Heywood v. Wellers* [1976] 1 All E.R. 300 (CA); *Cox v. Philips Industries* [1976] 3 All E.R. 161; *Perry v. Sidney Philips* [1982] 3 All E.R. 705 (CA)) especially in Ireland (*Johnson v. Longleat Property*, High Court, MacMahon J., May 19, 1976; *Murphy v. Quality Homes*, High Court, McWilliam J, June 22, 1976; Clark "Damages for Loss of Enjoyment and Inconvenience Resulting From Breach of Contract" (1978) XIII Ir. Jur. (ns) 186).

However, a retrenchment in England from this expansive view (*Bliss v. South East Thames Regional Health Authority* [1987] ICR 700 (CA); *Hayes v. Dodd* [1990] 2 All E.R. 815 (CA); and the very important *Watts v. Morrow* [1991] 4 All E.R. 937 (CA) presaged in Ireland in *Garvey v. Ireland* (High Court, unreported, 19 December 1979, McWilliam J.) has recently in its turn been the subject of a counter-retrenchment. *Addis* did not fare well in *Malik v. BCCI* [1998] A.C. 20 (HL) where it came under a sustained attack on many levels. Lord Steyn held that the decision in *Addis* was simply that the loss of reputation in that particular case could not be compensated because it was not caused by a breach of contract; so that, if a loss of reputation was caused by a breach of contract, it could be compensated. By the same reasoning, *Addis* ought not to preclude compensation for mental distress caused by a breach of contract (see *Annual Review of Irish Law 1997*, pp.229–256). Whilst the House of Lords seems to have drawn back from reaching that radical conclusion (*BCCI v. Ali* [2001] 1 All E.R. 961 (HL) (noted Wheat (2002) 65 M.L.R. 425); *Johnson v. Gore Wood* [2001] 2 W.L.R. 72 (HL); *Johnson v. Unisys* [2001] 2 W.L.R. 1076 (HL)) nevertheless the exceptions have recently been decisively expanded in *Farley v. Skinner* [2000] Lloyd's Rep. PN 516 (CA) (noted Capper (2000) 116 LQR 553); [2001] 3 E.L.R. 988 (HL) (noted Capper (2002) 118

L.Q.R. 193; Carey "Breach, Distress and Damages" (2002) 9 (1) C.L.P. 3; McKendrick and Graham "The Sky's The Limit: Contractual Damages for Non-Pecuniary Loss" [2002] L.M.C.L.Q. 161; Pearce "*Farley v. Skinner*: Right or Wrong" [2002] C.L.J. 24). The Court of Appeal in the earlier *Watts v. Morrow* had identified two categories of case in which damages for distress from breach of contract would exceptionally be available, (i) where the very object of the contract is to provide pleasure, relaxation, peace of mind or freedom from molestation, or (ii) where the plaintiff has suffered mental distress directly related to physical inconvenience and discomfort for which damages are available. In *Farley v. Skinner*, the House of Lord significantly broadened these two categories and held that the case came within both. Unlike in the earlier *Watts v. Morrow*, which concerned merely an ordinary surveyor's contract, the present case concerned a plaintiff who had specifically requested the defendant surveyor to consider possible inconvenience from overflights and so on from a nearby airport, which was an important term of the contract. All of the members House of Lords refused to take a narrow approach to the first exception, and held that since the specific request in the survey was an important term of the contract, this was sufficient to bring it within a flexible understanding of the object of the contract. Furthermore, Lords Clyde and Scott, taking an expansive view of the second exception, held that the plaintiff suffered physical inconvenience from the defendant's breach of contract, and suffered mental distress directly related to this physical inconvenience; the language of Lords Steyn and Hutton is slightly narrower on this point, but they also reach the same conclusion.

In New Zealand, Canada, and Australia, the general rule has only reluctantly been accepted, the exceptions have been interpreted widely, and there is a discernible movement to abandon the general rule altogether. There is a limited degree of support for a rigid application of *Addis* and a small number of narrow exceptions, often expressed for policy reasons (*Bloxham v. Robinson* [1996] 2 N.Z.L.R. 664n (NZ CA); Brennan J. in *Baltic Shipping v. Dillon (The Mikhail Lermontov)* (1992–1993) 176 C.L.R. 344 (HCA)). But a common position is a wide view of the exceptions (the majority in *Vorvis v. Insurance Corpn of British Columbia* (1989) 58 D.L.R. (4th) 193 (SCC); Deane and Dawson JJ in *The Mikhail Lermontov*) often as the second best solution of those who would prefer to abolish the rule in *Addis* altogether (Mason C.J. and McHugh J. in *The Mikhail Lermontov*). Another common position among the critics of *Addis* is to confine it to commercial cases, allowing the recovery of damages for mental distress in non-commercial cases (the approach of Cooke P. in *Horsburgh v. New Zealand Meat Processors Industrial Union of Workers* [1988] 1 N.Z.L.R. 698; *Hetherington v. Faudet* [1989] 2 N.Z.L.R. 224; *Watson v. Dolmark Industries* [1992] 3 N.Z.L.R. 311). And there are the critics who would have no truck with such half-way houses, and would simply apply the rules of causation and remoteness to the issue of the availability of damages for mental distress (Gallen J. in *Rowlands v. Callow*; Wilson J. in *Vorvis*).

Little of this debate seems to have detained the Irish courts in recent years. Thus, for example, the availability of damages for mental distress for breach of contract (often described, following the position in tort, as general damages) has often simply been assumed (see, for example, *Smith v. Custom House Docks Development Authority*, High Court, McGuinness J., March 20, 1997, discussed in *Annual Review of Irish Law 1997*, pp.230–231, 247-250); *Sullivan v. Southern Health Board* [1997] 3 I.R. 123 (SC); *Bolger v. Osborne* [2000] 1 I.L.R.M. 250 (HC; Macken J.)). There may have been some element of this in Carroll J.'s approach in *Coonan v. Attorney General* High Court, January 31, 2001, discussed in the Estoppel section, immediately below). Furthermore, in this year's *Dooley v. Great Southern Hotels Ltd*, High Court, July 27, 2001, McCracken J, having found a breach of the plaintiff's contract of employment by the defendants' failure to follow proper procedures in terminating the contract, held that this caused the plaintiff some short-term depression. As a consequence, McCracken J. awarded the plaintiff a further £2,000 in "general damages" (14).

The best position is the sweeping away of the rule in *Addis* and its exceptions in favour simply of the application of the general remoteness rules. That, in fact, seems to have been the position assumed by McGuinness J. in *Smith*, by Murphy J. in *Sullivan*, by Macken J. in *Bolger*, and now by McCracken J. in *Dooley*. Indeed, *Addis* must no longer even on its own facts be good law in Ireland: it concerned a denial of damages for distress arising from the manner of dismissal (followed on this point in *Bliss v. South East Thames Regional Health Authority* [1987] I.C.R. 700 (CA)); on the other hand, *Smith* and *Dooley* both allowed a claim for damages for distress in just such circumstances. All that remains is for this sweeping away of *Addis* to be admitted explicitly.

ESTOPPEL

In many ways, the modern law of equitable estoppel begins with the decision of Denning J. in *Central London Property Trust v. High Trees House* [1947] K.B. 130 (see Breen "Dusting Down Equity's Armour. High Trees (1947) in Perspective" in O'Dell (ed.), *Leading Cases of the Twentieth Century* (Round Hall Sweet & Maxwell, Dublin, 2000), p.164; see generally Cooke, *The Modern law of Estoppel* (OUP, 2000)) which was approved in Ireland by Kenny J. in *Cullen v. Cullen* [1962] I.R. 268, 291-292 and in *Revenue Commissioners v. Moroney* [1972] I.R. 372, 381. Estoppel featured in the Supreme Court in *Doran v. Thompson* [1978] I.R. 222; see also *O'Reilly v. Granville* [1971] I.R. 90 (SC)) and again in *Webb v. Ireland* [1988] I.R. 353 (SC). There, referring to Lord Denning MR's decision in *Amalgamated Property Co Ltd v. Texas Bank* [1982] Q.B. 84 (CA), Finlay C.J. – in an unfortunate but widely quoted passage – held that the doctrine of legitimate expectations was "but an aspect of the well recognised equitable concept of promissory estoppel" ([1988] I.R. 353,

384). This is a pernicious equation from which Irish law has yet to recover. Subsequent Supreme Court decisions on legitimate expectations have done little to sort this issue out (for example, *Wiley v. Revenue Commissioners* [1993] I.L.R.M. 482 (SC) did clarify the essentially procedural nature of legitimate expectations but did not disentangle that doctrine from estoppel, while *Duff v. Minister for Agriculture (No. 2)* [1997] I.R. 22 (SC) is quite frankly a mess). Unsurprisingly, therefore, the conflation has often simply been replicated in subsequent decisions (e.g., *Kenny v. Kelly* [1988] I.R. 457 (HC); *Eogan v. University College Dublin* [1996] 1 I.R. 390; [1996] 2 I.L.R.M. 302 (HC; Shanley J.)). Nevertheless, some High Court decisions did begin to appreciate that promissory estoppel protects the reliance interest at private law, whilst legitimate expectation protects the reliance interest at public law; (e.g., *Tara Prospecting v. Minister for Energy* [1993] I.L.R.M. 771 (HC; Costello J.) and *Abrahamson v. Law Society* [1996] 1 I.R. 403; [1996] 2 I.L.R.M. 481 (HC; McCracken J.)); and three Supreme Court decisions this year have accelerated the important and necessary process of the separation of the two doctrines.

In *Coonan v. Attorney General*, Supreme Court, May 29, 2001, the Supreme Court by a majority (Geoghegan and Fennelly JJ., Murphy J. dissenting) held that the Attorney General's refusal to extend the plaintiff's appointment as State Solicitor amounted to a breach of contract. The plaintiff had also argued that the Attorney General was precluded from refusing to extend the contract on the basis either of promissory estoppel or of legitimate expectation. Without clearly distinguishing between them, Carroll J. seemed to have acceded to this argument in the court below (High Court, January 31, 2001). On appeal, Geoghegan J. for the majority, having held in the plaintiff's favour on the breach of contract point, did not feel the need to reach this issue, though he seemed to appreciate that estoppel is a private law doctrine, whereas legitimate expectation is a matter of public law; as did Murphy J. dissenting. In the subsequent *Glencar Exploration v. Mayo Co. Co.*, Supreme Court, July 19, 2001) the applicants' claim for damages for breach of their legitimate expectations was dismissed for lack of any meaningful legitimate expectation. Both Keane C.J. (Denham, Murray and McGuinness JJ. concurring) and Fennelly J. emphasised the European law origins and public law nature of the doctrine of legitimate expectations. Whilst Fennelly J., in a considered obiter, provided the first thorough Supreme Court assessment of the doctrine in public law terms since *Wiley*, he could not prevent some language appropriate to estoppel seeping through (he observed that if "the official position is altered, the Court may have to furnish 'such remedy as the equity of the case demands'" (29), referring to the decision of Lord Denning MR in *Amalgamated Property*, the estoppel case relied upon by Finlay C.J. in *Webb*, for a proposition that is clearly tied to estoppel; see, e.g., *Revenue Commissioners v. Moroney* [1972] I.R. 372, 381 per Kenny J.; *Crabb v. Arun DC* [1976] Ch. 179 (CA); *Waltons v. Maher* (1988) 164 C.L.R. 387 (HCA)). Keane C.J., on the other hand, was more terse in his treatment of legitimate expectation, but he did point out (as he had previously done in *Truck and Machinery Sales v. Marubeni Komatsu* [1996] 1 I.R. 12, 29) that the judgment of Finlay C.J. in *Webb* "proceeded on the basis that the facts in that case gave rise to a sustainable claim based on promissory estoppel, rather than on the doctrine of legitimate expectations" (42). Finally, in *Daly v. Minister for the Marine*, Supreme Court, 4 October 4, 2001, they were properly pleaded and treated as entirely separate doctrines, but both failed since the applicant had not acted on foot of the letter on which both pleas were constructed. In the process, Fennelly J. (Keane C.J., Denham, Murphy and Geoghegan J.J concurring) expressly held that the doctrines are not co-extensive (23), and – though without reference to the judgment of Keane C.J. in *Glencar* – treated *Webb* as an estoppel case (23-24).

This year disclosed the usual crop of public law legitimate expectations cases (see, e.g., *Casey v. Minister for Arts, Heritage, Gaeltacht and the Islands*, High Court, Murphy J., May 31, 2001) (14-15); *Gulyas v. Minister for Justice*, High Court, Carroll J., June 25, 2001 (refusal of leave to land in Ireland was unreasonable, mistaken, breached fair procedures and the plaintiff's "legitimate expectation that any decision based on accurate facts would have resulted in permission to land" (7)); *Kayfoam Woolfson v. Healthcare Materials Management Board* (High Court, Finnegan J., June 29, 2001); *CAB v. P. McS.*, High Court, Kearns J., November 16, 2001) (13-14, 30-31; holding that issue of statutory requirements for a notice of appeal "a fair procedures point, rather than a legitimate expectation point, or an estoppel point ..." (31)); these cases are discussed in the Administrative Law chapter, above). And with the crop came the usual batch of cases beginning their legitimate expectation analysis with a citation of Finlay C.J.'s judgment in *Webb* (see for example not only Carroll J. in the High Court in *Coonan* (10-11) but also *Kavanagh v. Governor of Mountjoy Prison*, High Court, Finnegan J., June 29, 2001) a decision which was affirmed on appeal (Supreme Court, March 1, 2002), where Fennelly J. (Keane C.J., Denham, Hardiman and Geoghegan JJ. concurring) referred to his own decision in *Daly* rather than to *Webb*; on the legitimate expectation alleged by the applicant, cp. *Lynch v. Minister for Justice*, High Court, Herbert J., March 26, 2001; appeal adjourned generally: Supreme Court, June 26, 2001; Keane C.J. *ex tempore*, Murray and Fennelly JJ. concurring); *Kinahan v. Minister for Justice*, Supreme Court, February 21, 2001; Hardiman J., Geoghegan and Fennelly JJ. concurring)).

The first step in disentangling legitimate expectation and estoppel is to sort out *Webb*. It would have been better for the development of both doctrines had Finlay C.J. never uttered his fateful words. But since he did, the fairest way to treat them is as concerned with estoppel, as their treatment by Keane C.J. in *Glencar* and by Fennelly J. in *Daly* makes clear. *Webb* should be therefore cited for that doctrine only, and not for legitimate expectation. In that context, *Webb* has much to say. There, the Director of the National Museum was held to his representation that the plaintiffs would be "honourably treated" when they handed over the Derrynaflan Hoard to him. In enforcing this representation.

Finlay C.J. allowed estoppel to be used as a cause of action in a non-contractual situation, transcending the traditional limitations associated with *Combe v. Combe* [1951] 2 K.B. 215 and still enforced in England (see *First National Bank v. Thompson* [1996] Ch. 231 (CA); *Republic of India v. India Steamship Co. Ltd. (The Indian Endurance) (No. 2)* [1998] A.C. 878 (HL); *Johnson v. Gorewood* [2001] 1 All E.R. 481 (HL); *Nat West v. Somer* [2002] 1 All E.R. 198 (CA); see also Treitel, *Some Landmarks of Twentiety Century Contract Law* (Clarendon Press, Oxford, 2002), 29–41) thereby anticipating the approach to estoppel now being taken in the High Court of Australia (*Legione v. Hately* (1983) 152 C.L.R. 406 (HCA); *Waltons v. Maher* (1987-88) 167 C.L.R. 387 (HCA); *Foran v. Wight* (1989-90) 168 C.L.R. 385 (HCA); *Commonwealth v. Verwayen* (1990) 170 C.L.R. 394 (HCA); *Giumelli v. Giumelli* (1999) 196 C.L.R. 101 (HCA); see generally Spence, *Protecting Reliance* (Hart Publishing, Oxford, 1999); Hence, in *Daly*, although the appellant's argument amounted to a representee seeking to assert an estoppel as a cause of action, Fennelly J. was absolutely correct to consider the substance of the argument: the traditional limitation upon estoppel which sought to confine it to defensive duties (as a shield but not a sword, as Birkett L.J. had it in *Combe*, adopting the metaphor of counsel) was transcended in *Webb*, and the combination of that case with *Daly* now conclusively demonstrates that estoppel can be relied upon as a sword as well a shield (and perhaps it might not be too much to hope to do without the shield and sword metaphor in the future).

The second step in disentangling legitimate expectation and estoppel is then to assess the current state of the doctrines independently. Much private law learning has seeped into the public law field of legitimate expectation; it must be excised and the doctrine reconceptualised in exclusively public law terms; and Fennelly J.'s judgments in *Glencar* and *Daly* are important contributions to that process. Furthermore, the private law doctrine of estoppel is then free to develop consistently with its equitable origins (on the Irish development of estoppel, see Mee "Lost in the Big House: Where Stands Irish Law on Equitable Estoppel" (1988) XXVIII *Irish Jurist* (ns) 187) and, in particular, to develop independently of the public law doctrine of legitimate expectation. The judgments in *Coonan* and *Daly* are important contributions to that process.

In *Coonan v. Attorney General*, the plaintiff was appointed State Solicitor, and signed a document accepting the conditions of his employment, including the provision that he would be entitled to hold office until he attained "the age of sixty-five years but, provided that he is then in good health, the age of retirement may be extended by the Attorney General, with the concurrence of the Minister for Finance, to any age not exceeding seventy years". In the past, such extensions had routinely (Geoghegan J., 5) invariably (Murphy J., 2) and without exception (Carroll J., 2, 8) been granted, but, on foot of a new policy, the plaintiff's application for an extension was refused. He was the first person to be refused on his first application for an extension, he had received no formal notice of the new policy (Carroll J., 9-10), and he had not anticipated it (Carroll J., 6). He argued either that this amounted to a breach of contract, or that the Attorney General was precluded from refusing to extend the contract by virtue of either promissory estoppel or legitimate expectation. (This strategy of pleading contract and estoppel in the alternative was also evident in *Aer Rianta v. Ryanair*, High Court, December 5, 2000; Supreme Court, November 13, 2001). Kelly J. had granted summary judgment to the plaintiffs in the amount of £433,740 in respect of landing charges for the defendant's use of the plaintiff's facilities at Dublin airport, recoverable as a simple contract debt by virtue of section 39 of the Air Navigation and Transport (Amendment) Act 1998. The defendant argued that negotiations between the parties had either resulted in a contract varying the landing charges or had raised an estoppel against the defendants, and, on appeal (Supreme Court, November 13, 2001) McGuinness and Hardiman JJ. reversing Kelly J. (in judgments in which Denham J. concurred) held that summary judgment was inappropriate. Although there were considerable weaknesses in the defendant's defence, nevertheless, the probability remained open that the defendant had a real or bona fide defence (applying the *First National Commercial Bank v. Anglin* [1996] 1 I.R. 75 (SC) line of authority); there was, as Hardiman J. observed, "a conflict of evidence of a much more radical and downright sort than is usual in commercial actions"; and matters were so acutely at issue between the parties that they could only be resolved at full hearing). In the High Court in *Coonan*, Carroll J. held in the plaintiff's favour on the basis of estoppel, and awarded damages of £100,000:

> "This case seems to me to fit four square within the doctrine expressed by Lord Denning MR in *Amalgamated Property Co Ltd v. Texas Bank* [1982] Q.B. 84 and referred to by Finlay C.J. in *Webb* ... I consider that the treatment that Mr Coonan received was indefensible. ... I am not saying that the Attorney General could not change the policy of renewal on request, heath permitting. But I do say that he was not entitled to change this long standing custom, rule or policy, by whatever name it is called, and relied on by Mr Coonan, without giving adequate notice to enable him to arrange his affairs to cope with this alteration to his life plan. ... This is an appropriate case to give Mr Coonan such remedy as the equity of the case demands (11)."

The State appealed, and the Supreme Court by majority upheld, though on a different ground. For the majority, Geoghegan J. (Fennelly J. concurring) held that whilst the Attorney General had a contractual discretion to refuse to extend the contract he was not contractually entitled to introduce a blanket policy fettering that discretion. It would never have occurred to the plaintiff, while he was State Solicitor that the "discretion in the Attorney General for which he had been guaranteed in the contract would be at the relevant time effectively removed. In order to construe [the contract] in this way, I do not think that it is necessary to imply any term. This would seem to be the natural interpretation of the express term but if it is necessary to imply a term, I would have no hesitation in doing so" (8). Finally, he held that for the breach of this term, the remedy of damages in the amount of £100,000 was reasonable, and he therefore upheld Carroll J. in the result though not in the reasoning. He considered that her judgment went more on the basis of estoppel than legitimate expectation (6-7); counsel for the Attorney General had sought to distinguish the two doctrines – an argument which might have met with a sympathetic hearing since he commented that the *Amalgamated Property* case was "a private law case and not a public law case" (6) – but he did not address it since he held in favour of the plaintiff on the breach of contract point.

Murphy J. forcefully dissented, holding that it was difficult to reconcile the conclusion of Carroll J. with the discretion expressly conferred by the contract upon the Attorney General, and that there was no basis "on which the ill defined and inadequately explored doctrine of legitimate expectations could be invoked so as to prevent successive Attorneys General exercising or declining to exercise the discretion expressly reserved to them simply because a practice or pattern could be identified which indicated that for many years the discretion had in fact been exercised one way rather than another" (7). This begs the question, as it comes perilously close to saying that the exercise of contractual discretion could never be subject to judicial control, whether for contractual reasons of on the basis of the doctrine of legitimate expectation. As to contractual reasons, it is well settled that "[w]here A. and B. contract with each other to confer a discretion on A., that does not render B. subject to A.'s unhibited whim ... not only must the discretion be exercised honestly and in good faith, but, having regard to the provisions of the contract by which it is conferred, it must not be exercised arbitrarily, capriciously or unreasonably" (*Abu Dhabi National Tanker Co. v. Product Star Shipping (The Product Star)* [1993] 1 Lloyd's Rep. 397 (CA) 404 *per* Leggatt L.J.; see also *Gan Insurance v. Tai Ping Insurance* [2001] 2 All E.R. (Comm.) 299 (CA); *Nash v. Paragon Finance* [2002] 1 W.L.R. 685 (CA)). As to legitimate expectation, whatever else it may stand for, *Duff* at least demonstrates that the doctrine can indeed be relied upon to control the exercise of discretion. Furthermore, it is unfortunate that he did not go on to make a separate finding that no estoppel had arisen. This may be implicit in the tenor of his judgment; since he cites *Webb* but doesn't distinguish the two doctrines, it may even be bound up with his findings in respect of legitimate expectation; but it would have been better to have been explicit, as Fennelly J. would be in the subsequent *Daly v. Minister for the Marine*.

In *Daly*, the applicant sought judicial review of the Minister's decision to withdraw an offer contained in a letter to the applicant. He failed both before O'Sullivan J. (High Court, February 25, 1999) and on appeal. Fennelly J. (Keane C.J., Denham, Murphy and Geoghegan JJ. concurring) rejected the applicant's submission by reference to *Webb* that he did not have to demonstrate any reliance on this letter to found an estoppel. He commented that it would not be "unfair to characterise that as a daring submission, striking, as it does, at the root of the concept of equitable estoppel" (23) and treated *Webb* as an estoppel decision, which, on the basis of the decision of Lord Denning MR in *Amalgamated Property*,

> "proceeded precisely from the fact that the parties had 'conducted the dealings between them' on foot of an underlying assumption. *It is the fact that it would be unconscionable for one party to be permitted to depart from a position, statement or representation, upon which the other party has acted to his detriment, that justifies the courts in intervening to restrain him from doing so.* If the recipient of a promise or representation, is to be dispensed from any obligation to demonstrate reliance, the doctrine would be more than exceptionally generous. It would be a virtually ungovernable new force affecting potentially not only equity but the law of contract and property and, as here, the exercise of administrative power" (23; emphasis added).

This is an important passage, confirming the orthodoxy that estoppel is directed to preventing unconscionability (see O'Dell "Estoppel and Ultra Vires Contracts" (1992) 14 D.U.L.J. (ns) 123; *McMahon v. Kerry Co. Co.* [1981] I.L.R.M. 419, 421-423 per Finlay P.; noted Brady "Judicial Pragmatism and the Search for Justice Inter Partes" (1986) XXI Ir. Jur. (ns) 47; *Giumelli v. Giumelli* (1999) 196 C.L.R. 101 (HCA)) where one party has relied upon the representations of another. This is made clear in the earlier judgment of Griffin J. in the Supreme Court in *Doran v. Thompson* [1978] I.R. 222, 230:

> "Where one party has, by his words or conduct, made to the other a clear and unambiguous promise or assurance which was intended to affect the legal relations between then and to be acted on accordingly, and the other party has acted on by altering his position to his detriment, it is well settled that the one who gave the promise or assurance cannot afterwards be allowed to revert to their previous legal relations as if no such promise or assurance had been made by him, and that he may be restrained in equity from acting inconsistently with such promise or assurance" [1978] I.R. 222, 230, to like effect, see [1978] I.R. 222, 233 *per* Kenny J.).

In *Ryan v. Connolly*, Supreme Court, January 31, 2001, Keane C.J. (Murphy and McGuinness JJ. concurring) cited the judgment of Griffin J. in *Doran* with approval as an example of the application of the general principles of estoppel to the category of cases in which the defendant may be held to be precluded from relying on the Statute of Limitations, 1957 (see also *O'Reilly v. Granville* [1971] I.R. 90 (SC); *Traynor v. Fegan* [1985] I.R. 586 (HC; Barrington J.); *Tate v. The Minister for Social Welfare* [1995] 1 I.R. 418 (HC; Carroll J.); cp *Commonwealth v. Verwayen* (1990) 170 C.L.R. 394 (HCA)) and held that, on the facts, the defendants' representations did not estop them from raising a limitation issue. Similarly, in *Daly*, Fennelly J. also cited *Doran* as an example of the application of the general principles of estoppel (24), and held that since the applicant had never relied upon the Minister's letter, it was not inequitable for the Minister to withdraw the offer contained in it (24-25).

However, there is in the submission of counsel and the judgment of Fennelly J. responding to it, a failure to distinguish detriment and reliance. The notion of detriment is notoriously tricky though almost automatically assumed in many Irish judgments to be a necessary element of the doctrine of estoppel (see, e.g., *McCambridge v. Winters*, High Court, Murphy J., August 28, 1984; *Industrial Yarns v. Greene* [1984] I.L.R.M. 15 (HC; Costello J.); *Incorporated Law Society of Ireland v. O'Connor*, Supreme Court, November 25, 1994; at p.8 of the judgment of Blayney J.)). However, if the doctrine of estoppel is properly concerned with the protection of the reliance interest, then proof of detriment is not an essential element of the doctrine. Three related points arise here. First, it is not so much that the reliance on the representation has resulted in detriment to the representee as that if the representation were gone back upon the representee would then suffer detriment – the protection of the representee's reliance upon the representation therefore prevents the detriment from arising. This is the pattern of *In re J.R., a Ward of Court* [1993] I.L.R.M. 657 (HC; Costello J.; noted Coughlan "Swords, Shields and Estoppel Licences" (1993) 15 D.U.L.J. (ns) 188); it was recognised many years ago in Australia (in *Grundt v. Great Boulder Pty Gold Mines Ltd* (1937) 59 C.L.R. 641 (HCA), Dixon held that the "basal purpose" of estoppel is "to avoid or prevent a detriment" ((1937) 59 C.L.R. 641, 674); and it reflects the flexible approach to detriment properly taken in the context of proprietary estoppel (*Gillett v. Holt* [2000] 2 All E.R. 289 (CA)). Hence, if the representee has relied upon the representation, the reliance will raise an equity, and to satisfy it, estoppel should remedy any detriment already suffered or prevent detriment flowing from any change to the position as represented. Second, and more generally, detriment, whether already suffered or apprehended, is often the index of reliance; but the latter and not the former is the proper focus of the doctrine. As a consequence, Lord Denning MR frequently asserted that detriment is not necessary to generate an estoppel (see, e.g., *Alan v. El Nasr* [1972] 2 Q.B. 189; *Brikom v. Carr* [1979] Q.B. 467; see also *Société Italo-Belge pur le Commerce et l'Industrie v. Palm and Vegetable Oils (Malaysia) Sdn Bdh* [1982] 1 All E.R. 19, 27). Third, if the proper analysis asks whether, in the detriment suffered or apprehended by one party in reliance upon the representation of another, an equity has been raised, then there is nothing in the nature of that enquiry which mandates detriment as the sole or exclusive means of raising such an equity.

Hence, there was substance in the applicant's argument that detriment is not necessary to found an estoppel. However, rather than an actual or apprehended detriment, it is reliance which is of the essence of estoppel, and there was no substance whatsoever in the applicant's argument that reliance is not necessary to found an estoppel. Consequently, Fennelly J. was quite right to reject this second submission, which he did in the colourful and apocalyptic language already set out. And having held that the applicant must at least demonstrate reliance on the Minister's letter, his failure to do so was fatal to his estoppel claim.

ILLEGALITY

Ex turpi causa non oritur actio From a claim (cause) that is the tainted (turpis) no action can arise. Thus a plaintiff cannot rely on an illegal contract, and to that extent illegality may be pleaded as a defence to a claim to enforce the contract (*Holman v. Johnson* (1775) 1 Cowp. 341; 98 E.R. 1120; *Scott v. Brown, Doering, McNab & Co.* [1892] 2 Q.B. 724; *Furnivall v. O'Neill* [1902] 2 I.R. 422; *McIlvenna v. Ferris* [1955] I.R. 318; *Tinsley v. Milligan* [1994] 1 A.C. 340 (HL)). Thus, in *Holman v. Johnson*, Lord Mansfield set out the underlying policy:

> "The objection that the contract is immoral or illegal as between the plaintiff and defendant sounds at all times very ill in the mouth of the defendant. It is not for his sake however that the objection is ever allowed, but it is favoured in general principles of policy, which the defendant has the advantage of, contrary to real justice as between himself and the plaintiff, by accident if I may say so. ... No court will lend its aid to a man who founds his cause of action upon an immoral or an illegal act. If from the plaintiff's own stating or otherwise the cause of action appears to arise ex turpi causa or the transgression of a positive law of this country, then the court says he has no right to be assisted. It is upon this ground that the court goes, not for the sake of the defendant, but because they will not lend their aid to such a plaintiff. So if the plaintiff and the defendant were to change sides, and the defendant was to bring an action against the plaintiff, the latter would not then have the advantage of it ..."

And this policy was reaffirmed by Lindley L.J. in *Scott v. Brown, Doering, McNab*:

> "*Ex turpi causa non oritur actio* ... No court ought to enforce an illegal contract or allow itself to be made the instrument of enforcing obligations alleged to arise out of a contract or transaction which is

illegal if the illegality is duly brought to the notice of the court and if the person invoking the aid of the court is himself implicated in the illegality

On the one hand, these policies are alive and well in the Irish courts, especially where the illegality consists in champerty (*McElroy v. Flynn* [1991] IRM 294 (HC; Blayney J.); *Fraser v. Buckle* [1994] 1 I.R. 1; [1994] 1 I.L.R.M. 276 (HC; Costello J.); [1996] 1 I.R. 1; [1996] 2 I.L.R.M. 34 (SC); (1996) 14 ILT (ns) 85; Capper (1997) 113 LQR 49; cf. *O'Keeffe v. Scales* [1998] 1 I.L.R.M. 393 (SC)) or fraud upon the revenue (*Hayden v. Quinn* [1994] E.L.R. 45 (HC; Barron J.); Barry (1994) 12 I.L.T. (ns) 32; cf. the same judge's flexibility in the context of illegality pleaded against a reference to arbitration in *Vogelaar v. Callaghan* [1996] 1 I.R. 88 (HC; Barron J.)). And the House of Lords in *Tinsley v. Milligan* [1994] 1 A.C. 340 (HL) has rejected a flexible approach outright and reaffirmed the *Holman v. Johnson* approach to the issue of illegality.

On the other hand, there have recently been signs of a change towards a more rationally graded response, with the Irish courts taking a relatively flexible approach to the effect of illegality upon plaintiffs' claims. In many cases, where a defendant pleads illegality, the court will now look beyond the fact of the illegality to the quality of the illegality relied upon and the proximity of the illegal conduct to the plaintiff's claim, to determine whether there was an illegality of which the court should take notice, and if there was, whether by affording the plaintiff the relief sought, it would affront the public conscience more than by refusing it. For example, in *Webb v. Ireland* [1988] I.R. 353 (SC) the illegality of the trespass upon which the plaintiffs' claim was founded did not preclude a successful action in estoppel; it could be said that the underlying trespass was too remote from the museum governor's assertion, which founded the estoppel. In *Hortensius v. Bishop* [1989] I.L.R.M. 294 (see the *Annual Review of Irish Law 1989*, pp.129-130) Costello J. pointed out that "public policy has never required that trustees should be deprived of their right to enforce proprietary claims over property obtained in breach of trust" ([1989] I.L.R.M. 294, 302), in the process he approving the flexible approach to illegality taken by Kerr L.J. in *Euro-Diam Euro v. Bathurst* [1988] 2 All E.R. 23 (CA). Furthermore, in the later *Shield Life Insurance v. Ulster Bank* [1995] 3 I.R. 225 (HC) the same judge again approved a flexible approach to illegality, this time in *Thackwell v. Barclays Bank* [1986] 1 All E.R. 676 (Hutchinson J.). A similar flexibility is evident in the High Court of Australia (*Nelson v. Nelson* (1995) 184 C.L.R. 538 (HCA); *Fitzgerald v. F.J. Leonhardt* (1997) 189 C.L.R. 215 (HCA)).

Cases this year fall mainly the flexible side of the line. For example, in *Holman v. Johnson*, Lord Mansfield said that the court had to give effect to the illegality, however it came to light, whether it emerged "from the plaintiff's own stating or otherwise" (emphasis added). Consequently, in *Hayden v. Quinn*,

Barron J. took the question of illegality of his own motion. The policy underlying the strict view of illegality would favour this approach. On the other hand, the policy underlying the flexible approach to illegality would require the defendant to plead and prove it with particularity, and this approach was taken by Herbert J. in *Whelan v. Kavanagh*, High Court, January 29, 2001, and by Murphy J. in two related applications, *Phelan v. Goodman and El Taher*, High Court, December 4, 2001 and *Mastertrade v. Phelan*, High Court, December 4, 2001).

In *Whelan v. Kavanagh*, the plaintiff purchaser sought specific performance of a contract for the sale of land; the defendant vendor resisted on the grounds that the contract fraudulently overstated the purchase price (and apologised to the court for his collusion in the fraud). However, Herbert J. rejected the defendant's evidence in this regard, and held:

> "... a party who has executed a contract required by Law to be evidenced in writing and which is regular and lawful on its face, and whose execution of that contract has been witnessed by his or her solicitor should not lightly be permitted to impugn that contract, particularly to his or her own advantage, by pleading illegality as a defence to a claim for specific performance. The onus of proving such alleged illegality lies firmly with the party raising it and the burden of proof is the same as in all civil actions. Extrinsic evidence, i.e., statements, facts or circumstances outside the document, is admissible despite some older authorities to the contrary, to prove a smaller 'real' consideration inconsistent with that expressed in the agreement (*Turner v. Forwood* [1951] 1 All E.R. 746; *Woods v. Wise* [1955] 2 Q.B. 29; *Peffer v. Rigg* [1977] 1 W.L.R. 285, 293) ... there is no proof placed before the Court in this regard other than the parole evidence of the Defendant himself, unsupported by any documentation, or by an reliable corroborative evidence" (11–12).

Consequently, Herbert J. affirmed the order of specific performance, which had been granted in the Circuit Court. A similar approach to the question of proof of illegality was taken by Murphy J. in two applications arising out of his decision (above) in *Phelan v. Goodman and El Taher*, High Court, September 11, 2001, to the effect that a joint venture agreement between Mr Phelan and Mr El Taher was breached by Mr El Taher and terminated automatically according to its terms when Mr El Taher sold 80% of the vehicle through which he held his interest to Mr Goodman. In *Phelan v. Goodman and El Taher*, High Court, December 4, 2001, Mr Phelan then sought to have various notices of indemnity and contribution which had been served in the proceedings struck out, arguing that they were affected *inter alia* by various illegalities which emerged in the first proceedings. Relying on *Tinsley v. Milligan*, he argued that where "A puts property in the name of B. intending to conceal his (A.'s) interest in the property for a fraudulent or illegal purpose, neither law or equity will allow A to recover the property, and equity will not assist in asserting an equitable interest in it" (23). Murphy J. refused that motion, holding that the illegality issue has to await oral evidence as it concerned matters not ready for adjudication (27–28). He continued that the

> "... question of illegality, which is, as yet, merely an allegation, has to be inferred from the intention of the transferee. See *Bowmakers v. Barnett* [1945] K.B. 65. Once it does come to the attention of a court of equity that a claimant has not come to court with clean hands, the Court can refuse to assist such claimant, even though the claimant can *prima facie* establish his claim *without recourse to the fraudulent or illegal purpose*. This issue requires a finding of *an intention to conceal* which requires further evidence. .... The Court cannot say at this juncture, that the claims, made by way of Notice of indemnity and contribution, should be struck out. ... further evidence is necessary to prove intention and to resolve conflicts" (30–31, emphasis in original).

Whilst Murphy J.'s attitude to requiring further evidence on the question of illegality is welcome, his assertion in reaching that conclusion that the "the Court can refuse to assist such claimant, even though the claimant can *prima facie* establish his claim without recourse to *the fraudulent or illegal purpose*" is, at the very least, open to question. In fact, *Bowmakers v. Barnett* and *Tinsley v. Milligan* are authorities for the precisely opposite proposition that if the plaintiff can establish a proprietary claim without reference to the illegality, the court will enforce the plaintiff's claim (see also *Singh v. Ali* [1960] A.C. 167 (PC); *Tribe v. Tribe* [1996] Ch. 107 (CA); Wade "Legal Status of Property Transferred Under An Illegal Transaction" 41 Ill L.R. 487 (1946); Hamson "Illegal Contracts and Limited Interests" (1949) 10 C.L.J. 248; Gooderson "Turpitude and Title in England and India" (1958) 19 C.L.J. 199; Higgins "The Transfer of Property under Illegal Transactions" (1962) 25 M.L.R. 149; Coote "Another Look at *Bowmakers v. Barnet Instruments*" (1972) 35 M.L.R. 38; Stewart "Contractual Illegality and the Recognition of Proprietary Interests" (1988) 1 J.C.L. 134; Enonchong "Title Claims and Illegal Transactions" (1995) 111 L.Q.R. 135). Be that as it may, it does not undercut Murphy J.'s ultimate conclusion that further evidence was necessary on the illegality issue. He took a similar approach on another application in which Mr Phelan sought to strike out various related proceedings being taken against him (*Mastertrade v. Phelan*, High Court, December 4, 2001) alleging that they were affected *inter alia* by various illegalities which emerged in the first proceedings, so that the plaintiffs should not be heard at all (relying in particular on *Scott v. Brown, Doering, McNab*, a case which concerned a conspiracy to purchase shares artificially to sustain the price). Murphy J. observed that for public policy reasons the court will not assist a party whose claim is founded in illegality but held that there was no evidence before the court that the object of the concealment of Mr El Taher's sale of his shares to Mr Goodman was "to cheat the public" as had been the case in *Scott v. Brown, Doering, McNab* (17), and dismissed the application to strike out the proceedings.

Rather than taking an illegality point however it emerges, the policy underlying the flexible approach to illegality would require the defendant to plead and prove it with particularity, as Herbert J. insisted in *Whelan v. Kavanagh* and as Murphy J. insisted in *Phelan v. Goodman and El Taher* and *Mastertrade v. Phelan.* These welcome developments form part of a process which has been charted in recent Reviews (see *Annual Review of Irish Law 1993*, pp.184–189; *Annual Review of Irish Law 1995*, pp.204–209; *Annual Review of Irish Law 1996*, pp.180–182; *Annual Review of Irish Law 1997*, pp.208–209) by which the Irish courts have, by and large, tended to ameliorate the negative consequences of potential illegality upon the enforceability of contracts or at least upon the availability of contractual and related remedies.

MISREPRESENTATION

In any claim for misrepresentation, the plaintiffs must demonstrate that there was a representation of fact that that representation was untrue and that the plaintiffs were induced to enter into the settlement by reason of the representation. Whilst a misrepresentation will of itself be sufficient to set a contract aside, if it is either fraudulent or negligent it will also sound in damages (for the torts respectively of deceit or negligent misrepresentation).

As to the tort of deceit, it was again made clear by Kinlen J. in *Jobling-Purser v. Jackman*, High Court, November 27, 2001, that in "an action of deceit the plaintiff must prove actual fraud. Fraud is proved when it is shown that a false representation has been made knowingly or without belief in its truth or recklessly without caring whether it be true or false" (33; referring to *Derry v. Peek* (1889) 14 App. Cas. 337). He also affirmed that a person alleging such fraud must plead it and prove it with particularity (49; citing *Superwood v. Sun Alliance* [1995] 3 I.R. 303 (SC; Denham J.)) and that any inference of fraud must not be lightly drawn without due regard to all the relevant circumstances of the case (*ibid.*; and also 34; citing *Banco Ambrosia v. Ansbacher* [1987] I.L.R.M. 668, 672 *per* Henchy J.).

As to the tort of negligent misrepresentation, in *Wildgust v. Bank of Ireland*, High Court, August 17, 2001, the plaintiff and his wife had a life assurance policy with the Norwich Union, the premia for which were paid monthly by direct debit. However, due to a breakdown in the direct debit system, one debit was unpaid and the policy lapsed, and the Norwich Union refused to pay out on the death of the plaintiff's wife. The policy was a security for a loan made by Hill Samuel Merchant Bankers, and the plaintiff claimed that the defendant had negligently misrepresented to Mr O'Hanlon of Hill Samuel that the policy had been reinstated. Having already been before Morris P. (July 28, 1988; see *Annual Review of Irish Law 1999*, pp.173–174) and the Supreme Court (April 3, 2000; see the 2000 Review, 94-95) on a pleading point, Morris P. now held that even if the Norwich Union had made the alleged misrepresentations, the plaintiff was at no stage aware of the assurances to Mr O'Hanlon of Hill Samuel, let alone relied on them, and had not been misled by them. Consequently, he held that Mr O'Hanlon's representations "in no way influenced or contributed towards the conduct of the plaintiff. It did not influence him or cause him to act to his detriment" (17) and he dismissed the plaintiff's claim. On this view of the facts (for another view, see the Tort chapter, below) this is entirely unexceptionable. In *Peek v. Gurney* (1873) L.R. 6 HL 377 (applied in *Al Nakib Investments v. Longcroft* [1990] 1 W.L.R. 1390) the plaintiff had purchased shares from shareholders who had purchased the shares from the promoters of the company on foot of the promoters' prospectus. That prospectus had contained false statements, on the faith of which the plaintiff had purchased the shares. However, the House of Lords held that the prospectus was only addressed to the first applicants for shares. Since the representation was not addressed to the plaintiffs, they could not rely on it as against the defendants. It is *a fortiori* where the representation was not only not addressed to the plaintiffs but the plaintiffs did not know even about it, as in *Wildgust*. It would be otherwise if the representor had intended that the representation be passed on (*Commercial Banking Co. of Sydney Ltd v. Brown* [1972] 2 Lloyd's Rep. 360) but this was not the case in *Wildgust*.

OFFER AND ACCEPTANCE

Subject to contract In *Boyle v. Lee* [1992] 1 I.R. 555; [1992] I.L.R.M. 65 (SC) the Supreme Court affirmed that the use of the phrase "subject to contract" in correspondence precluded agreement and prevented the correspondence from being used as evidence of agreement for the purposes of section 2 of the Statute of Frauds (Irl) 1695 (see *Annual Review of Irish Law 1991*, pp.112–113, 125-127; and Dwyer "'Subject to Contract' – A Controversy Resolved?" (1991) 1 I.S.L.R. 26). But the contrary view had been persistent, and subsequent *dicta* threaten to revive it (see *Embourg v. Tyler [1996]* 3 I.R. 480 (SC) discussed in *Annual Review of Irish Law 1996*, pp.211–212, 426-427; *Shirley Engineering v. Irish Telecommunications Investments*, High Court, Geoghegan J., December 2, 1999, discussed in *Annual Review of Irish Law 1999*, pp.105–108; *Jodifern v. Fitzgerald* [2000] 3 I.R. 321 (SC); *Supermac's v. Katesan (Naas) Ltd* [2001] 1 I.L.R.M. 410 (SC); and *Moran v. Oakley Park Developments*, High Court, O'Donovan J., March 31, 2000 all discussed in *Annual Review of Irish Law 2000*, pp.103–108). This unwelcome process continued indirectly in *Dekra Erin Teo v. Minister for the Environment*, High Court, November 2, 2001, where O'Neill J. held that in a tendering process, where the unsuccessful parties had been informed by letter the tender of the successful party would be accepted subject to contract, time to challenge that decision under Order 84 would run from the date of the letter. While the inclusion of the phrase "subject to contract"

> "... may have given rise to some reflection as to what it precisely meant in the context in which it was used, its inclusion, in this letter does not in my view, at all diminish the clear intent expressed in the letter namely to award the contract to [the successful party] and does not negate the knowledge that a decision to that effect had been made by the respondents. ... the most obvious meaning of the phrase in the context in which it was used was, that the decision to award, was subject only to the formal execution of the contract itself, ... [Even if the phrase could be equated] with 'the existence of the contract being denied', that of course could not amount to a negation of the facts that 'the decision to award' the contract had been made. Thus while the phrase 'subject to contract' could be said to have conveyed to Dekra that the contract was not yet formally awarded to [the successful party], it could not have conveyed to them and understanding that a decision to award the contract to [the successful party] had not been made" (29–30).

This is very similar to the kind of reasoning which undercut the subject to contract rubric by making it a matter of construction in each case as to what the phrase meant (see, in particular *Tiverton v. Wearwell* [1975] Ch. 146 (CA): *Kelly v. Park Hall School* [1979] I.R. 340 (SC); *Casey v. Irish Intercontinental Bank* [1979] I.R. 364 (SC)). Indeed, it is this very reasoning which was displaced by the Supreme Court in *Boyle v. Lee*, which held that the phrase necessarily denies the existence of a contract and necessarily precludes any document bearing it from amounting to a note or memorandum in writing for the purposes of s2 of the Statute of Frauds (see also *Mulhall v. Haren* [1981] I.R. 364 (HC; Keane J.)). If the policy of the approach to subject to contract announced by the Supreme Court in *Boyle v. Lee* applies to the contract between the successful tenderer and the respondent, then, in any litigation between them, a court would be driven to the conclusion that the use of the phrase prevented a contract from coming into existence between them. No contract would have come into existence until the subsequent formal execution of the contract it, even if no terms remained to be negotiated. At any stage before that formal execution, the effect of the phrase would have been to allow either party to walk away from the arrangement. It would therefore only be when the respondents decided on the formal execution of the contract that they would have made a decision to award the contract. Because they could have walked away at any earlier stage, the best that could be said of their decision is that they had decided not so much to award the contract as merely to intend to award it.

However, O'Neill J. held that, although the respondent's decision to award the contract to the successful tenderer was a decision to award it subject to contract, the fact remained that the decision to award had been taken and notified to the applicant. Since it is this decision to award which it was sought to review judicially, time to challenge that decision ran from the date of the letter, which informed the applicant of the decision.

PRACTICE AND PROCEDURE

Improperly commencing a private law claim at public law   In recent years, there has been a rising tide of cases seeking to litigate breach of contract issues against public bodies by means of the judicial review procedure. It is but one aspect of the increasing pressure to expand the ambit of judicial review well beyond its public core. The advantages of the judicial review procedure over the plenary summons procedure (see *O'Leary v. Minister for Transport* [2000] 1 IRLM 389 (HC) 397-398 *per* Kelly J.; rvsd [2001] 1 I.L.R.M. 132 (SC)) have made it very attractive to plaintiffs, but it is inappropriate for the private law context. It has therefore been a theme of recent Reviews (see *Annual Review of Irish Law 1998*, pp.178–182; *Annual Review of Irish Law 1999*, pp.116–120; *Annual Review of Irish Law 2000*, pp.95–99) that this development must be resisted. In particular, it is inappropriate that what is essentially a breach of contract action be ventilated by way of judicial review. Public bodies can still make contracts, and sue and be sued on them; such actions are private law actions, attracting private law procedures; and this conclusion should not change simply because the defendant is a creature of public law (e.g., *Zockoll v. Telecom Éireann* [1998] 3 I.R. 287 (HC; Kelly J.); *Howberry Lane Ltd v. Telecom Éireann* [1999] 2 I.L.R.M. 232 (HC; Morris P.)). Since actions upon contracts are private law actions attracting private law procedures, it would have been more appropriate for the applicants in cases like *O'Leary v. Minister for Finance* [1998] 2 I.L.R.M. 321 (HC, Quirke J.) and *Moran v. Minister for Health and Children* (High Court, Morris P., December 15, 1998), to have sought specific performance of their contracts with their respective respondents, rather than seeking to compel the respondents by means of judicial review to perform the contracts.

There may be some sets of facts which raise issues both of public and of private law, and the plaintiff should be able to pursue all of the issues on the more appropriate procedure. In both *Glencar Exploration v. Mayo County Council,* Supreme Court, July 19, 2001 and *Daly v. Minister for the Marine*, Supreme Court, October 4, 2001, the matters proceeded by way of judicial review even though there were some important private law issues as well. Similarly, for this reason or another, there may be uncertainty as to whether judicial review or plenary summons is the appropriate procedure in the circumstances, and again the plaintiff should be able to choose the more appropriate procedure. For example, claims against schools often seem to fall along the disputed borderline – some issues of school discipline have been held amenable to judicial review (e.g. *Murtagh v. Board of Governors of St Emer's School* [1991] 1 I.R. 482 (HC: Barron J. and SC); *Student A and Student B v. Dublin Secondary School*, High Court, Kearns J., November 25, 1999; *Tobin v. Cashell*, High Court, Kearns J., March 21, 2000), but most such matters are better pursued by plenary summons (see *O'hUallachain v. Burke* [1988] I.L.R.M. 693 (HC) 702 *per* Murphy J.; and consider *Wright v. Board of Management of Gorey Community School*, High Court, March 28, 2000).

However, where it is clear that an issue is purely a matter of contract, then the private law plenary summons procedure is the appropriate one, even if the defendant is in some sense a public body. An excellent example is provided by *Coonan v. Attorney General*. An action in contract and estoppel was quite properly commenced by plenary summons even though the defendant was a public officer and contract related to the public office of State Solicitor. Hence, at first instance (High Court, January 31, 2001) whilst Carroll J. perceived connotations of public law in the case, she quickly held that the case concerned the exercise not of a statutory discretion but of a discretion in a private contract to which the Attorney General was party, and the case was properly taken not by way of judicial review but by means of a plenary summons. On appeal (Supreme Court, May 29, 2001) Geoghegan J. (Fennelly J. concurring) for the majority declined to "consider the exact legal nature of the office of State Solicitor. Even if, for some purposes, his office might be regarded as being governed by public law (and I am expressing no opinion whatsoever on this matter) it is the contractual terms of his appointment and matters arising there from which are in issue in this case, which was an ordinary action commenced by plenary summons ..." (2) and concerned with private law matters such as estoppel rather than public law matters such as legitimate expectation (6-7). Equally, Murphy J. (dissenting) was alive to the same issues. The lesson of *Coonan*, then, is that if the elements of an estoppel are made out, there is every reason why the case should proceed on that basis at private law on foot of a plenary summons (cp *Lever (Finance) v. Westminster Corp* [1971] 1 B.Q. 222; *Crabb v. Arun DC* [1976] Ch. 179; *Western Fish Products Ltd v. Penwith DC* [1981] 2 All E.R. 204) and no reason for it to proceed at public law by way of judicial review.

The most common such private law cases involve allegations on the part of the applicants that the respondents have failed to follow fair procedures. In some cases, the real complaint will be with an administrative decision or procedure prior to or independent of the contract, and judicial review will properly lie in respect of that decision or procedure (see *Kayfoam Woolfson v. Healthcare Materials Management Board*, High Court, Finnegan J., June 29, 2001; judicial review of a decision to award a contract on the grounds that it had not followed the relevant regulations and in breach of legitimate expectations). For example, in *Dekra Erin Teo v. Minister for the Environment*, High Court, O'Neill J., November 2, 2001, the gravamen of the applicant's complaint concerned the respondent's decision-making procedure in offering a contract to another party. The three-party structure makes the distinction between the statutory and contractual issues very clear, but it would have been the same in a two party situation both in respect of a decision by the respondent to give a contract to the applicant and in respect of the exercise of other statutory powers in the contractual context. Thus, in *Carr v. Minister for Education* [2000] E.L.R. 78 (HC; Morris P) affd. [2001] 2 I.L.R.M. 272 (SC) the real question was whether section 7 of the Vocational Education (Amendment) Act 1944 provided the Minister with the power he purported to exercise. Thus, the real issue was the exercise of a public law power, which was successfully challenged by way of judicial review. Again, in *O'Donoghue v. South Eastern Health Board*, High Court, November 27, 2001, the applicant hospital consultant was employed by the respondent under the Consultants' Common Contract which provided that he held his appointment under Part II of the Health Act, 1970; of which section 22 concerned suspension, section 23 concerned removal, and section 24 concerned the setting up by the Minister of a committee for removal. The applicant sought judicial review of a decision of the CEO of the respondent to set up a team to investigate allegations of bullying against the applicant. Kelly J. (July 28, 2000) directed a preliminary issue as to whether there was a sufficient public element to justify the judicial review procedure; and Carroll J. held that there was. As in *Carr*, notwithstanding the contractual overlay, the applicant's real focus was upon a statutory procedure: since the Common Contract "is nationally negotiated and invokes statutory provisions in its disciplinary procedures, this provides sufficient public law content to make the matter justiciable under Judicial Review proceedings" (at 5 *per* Carroll J, referring to *Beirne v. Commissioner of An Garda Síochána* [1993] I.L.R.M. 1 and *Rafferty v. Bus Éireann* [1997] 2 I.R. 424; emphasis added). Similarly, claims against the Commissioner of An Garda Síochána by probationers and Gardaí raises such similar mixed statutory and contractual claims. In *McGrath v. Minister for Justice* [2000] E.L.R. 15 (HC; Morris P.) the plaintiff's successful claim arising out of his suspension from his employment as a Garda was taken by way of plenary summons. On the other hand, in *McMahon v. Commissioner of An Garda Síochána* High Court, 19 October 2001, Ó Caoimh J, the applicant's unsuccessful claim that the commissioner had failed to follow fair procedures in deciding to dispense with a probationer garda's services at the end of his period of probation (*Duffy v. Commissioner of An Garda Síochána* High Court, 10 July 1998, McGuinness J.; *McAuley v. Commissioner of An Garda Síochána* [1996] 3 I.R. 208; *Healy v. Commissioner of An Garda Síochána* High Court, 7 November 2000, Herbert J.; considered and applied) was taken by way of judicial review. Likewise, in *Whelan v. Commissioner of An Garda Síochána* (High Court, 21 December 2001, O'Sullivan J.) the applicants' successful claim that the commissioner had failed to follow fair procedures in not dealing with the applicants' complaints under the agreed grievance procedure and confining them to indoor duties was also taken by way of judicial review.

However, in the vast majority of such cases, the allegation is that the respondent failed to observe fair procedures in pursuing a contractual procedure, as for example a claim against a representative or sports body that it had failed to follow its contractual procedures (*McEvoy v. Prison Officers Association* [1999] 1 I.L.R.M. 445 (SC) 451 *per* O'Flaherty J.; *Moloney v. Bolger* [2000] 1 I.L.R.M. 250 (HC)) or a claim by a disciplined or dismissed employee (see e.g. *Sherriff v. Corrigan* (1999) 10 E.L.R. 146; *Lonegan v. Salter-Townshend* (2000) 11 E.L.R. 15). It is clear that a term that an employer must follow fair procedures in suspending or dismissing an employee, if not expressed in contracts of employment, is implied into them (see *Glover v. BLN* [1973] I.R. 388 (SC); *Tierney v. An Post* [2000] 2 I.L.R.M. 214 (SC)). An action against an employer to restrain a suspension or for wrongful dismissal is an action for breach of that (express, or more often, implied) term; it is a breach of contract action, and as such attracts not a judicial review but private law procedures (see, e.g. *O'Donnell v. An Post* (High Court, unreported, 18 June 1999); *Howard v. UCC* [2000] ELR 8 (HC; O'Donovan J.)). For example, in *Dooley v. Great Southern Hotels Ltd*, High Court, July 27, 2001, McCracken J. held that there "is no doubt that some at least of the principles of natural justice must apply to a situation where an employee is being dismissed for misconduct" (9). Where the contract is silent on the conduct of any disciplinary procedures against an employee, Barrington J. in *Mooney v. An Post* [1998] ELR 238 (SC) held that the employee is entitled at a minimum "is to be informed of the charge against him and to be given an opportunity to answer it and to make submissions". This not having happened in *Dooley,* the defendants were in breach of contract and liable in damages. This conclusion would not alter if the employer were a public authority.

The courts have become increasingly astute to ensure that the arteries of the judicial review procedure are not clogged with private law claims. In *Tierney v. An Post* [2000] 2 I.L.R.M. 214 (SC) 217, Keane C.J. chose to reserve for another day the issue as to whether such breach of contract actions are maintainable by way of judicial review. Echoing the sentiments of the law three years, this other day cannot come soon enough to sort out the procedural muddle in which many of the cases are currently mired.

PRINCIPLES OF INTERPRETATION

Intention In any case in which "the parties are in disagreement as to what a particular provision of the contract means, the task of the court is to decide what the intention of the parties was, having regard to the language used in the contract and the surrounding circumstances" (*Kramer v. Arnold* [1997] 3 I.R. 43, 55 *per* Keane J.; see the 1997 Review, 22–229; see generally Carey, "Contractual Interpretation: Recent Developments" (2001) 19 ILT 250). The search is for the parties' intentions; but it is not a search for elusive motive or subjective intention; rather it is a more objective (see *BCCI v. Ali* [2001] 2 W.L.R. 735 (HL) 739 *per* Lord Bingham; 762 *per* Lord Clyde) search for their intentions as expressed in the contract. Hence, as Lord Shaw made clear in *Great Western Railway v. Bristol Corporation* [1918] 87 L.J. Ch 414 in a passage cited with approval by Murphy J. in *Igote v. Badsey* (Supreme Court, 18 July 2001, at 3):

> "... courts of law when on the work of interpretation are not engaged upon the task or study of what parties intended to do, but of what the language they employed showed that they did; in other words, they are not constructing a contract on the lines of what may be thought to have been what the parties intended, but they are construing the words and expressions used by the parties themselves. What do these mean? That, when ascertained, is the meaning to be given effect to, the meaning of the contract by which the parties are bound. The suggestion of an intention of parties different from the meaning conveyed by the words employed is no part of interpretation, but is mere confusion ."

In the end, therefore, "interpretation is the quest to discover what a reasonable man would have understood ... [the] parties to have meant ..." (*BCCI v. Ali* [2001] 2 W.L.R. 735 (HL) 752 *per* Lord Hoffman; cp. *Investors Compensation Scheme v. West Bromwich BC* [1998] 1 W.L.R. 896 (HL) 913).

The factual matrix   In the search for that intention, most rules of construction focus on the language used (Staughton [1999] CLJ 303). Indeed, by virtue of the parol evidence rule, evidence cannot be admitted to add to, vary or contradict a written instrument, and neither party can rely on evidence extrinsic to it (*Jacobs v. Batavia and General Plantations Trust* [1924] 1 Ch. 297, 295). In particular, the conduct of the parties subsequent to the making of the contract is inadmissible as a guide to the interpretation of the contract (*In re Wogan's (Drogheda) (No. 1)* [1993] 1 I.R. 157; see the 1992 Review, 53-56). Nevertheless, the words used must be understood in their context (*Mannai Investments v. Eagle Star* [1997] 3 All E.R. 352 (HL)) and "set in the landscape of the instrument as a whole" (*Charter Reinsurance v. Fagan* [1996] 3 All E.R. 46 (HL) 51 per Lord Mustill). Furthermore, to achieve commercially sensible constructions of contracts, the courts have in recent years also begun to focus not only upon the parties' language but also on the circumstances – the factual matrix – in which it was used (Steyn (1988) 41 CLP 23; *Deutsche Genossenschaftsbank v. Burnhope* [1995] 1 W.L.R. 1580 (HL) 1589; *Napier and Ettrick v. Kensow* [1999] 1 W.L.R. 756 (HL) 763; cf. Staughton above)). A "deed or an agreement in writing is to be construed as a whole to give effect to the intention of the parties and ... the relevant time to ascertain that intention is the date of the instrument" (*Lillington v. Doyle's Stores* (Supreme Court, 14

April 1995) per O'Flaherty J.). Although direct evidence of the parties' subjective intentions is inadmissible (*Plumb Bros v. Dolmac (Agriculture) Ltd* (1984} 271 EG 373 (CA) 354 *per* May LJ), nevertheless, as Lord Wilberforce put it in *Prenn v. Simmonds* [1971] 1 W.L.R. 1381 (HL) 1383 a court should be able to consider "the factual background known to the parties at or before the date of the contract, including evidence of the 'genesis' and objectively the 'aim' of the transaction". He returned to this theme in the subsequent *Reardon Smith Line v. Yngvar Hansen-Tagen*:

> "No contracts are made in a vacuum: there is always a setting in which they have to be placed. The nature of what is legitimate to have regard to is usually described as 'the surrounding circumstances' but this phrase is imprecise; it can be illustrated but hardly defined. In a commercial context it is certainly right that the court should know the commercial purpose of the contract and this in turn presupposes a knowledge of the genesis of the transaction, the background, the contract, the market in which the parties are operating ([1976] 1 W.L.R. 989, 995; and see also *Investors Compensation Scheme v. West Bromwich BS* [1998] 1 W.L.R. 896 (HL) 913 *per* Lord Hoffmann; *BCCI v. Ali* [2001] 2 W.L.R. 735 (HL) 749 *per* Lord Hoffman)."

This approach has been expressly adopted in Ireland by Griffin J. in *Rohan Construction v. ICI* [1988] I.L.R.M. 373 (SC) 380 and was followed by Keane J. in *LAC Minerals v. Chevron* (High Court, 6 August 1993). In *Dillon v. McGovern* (High Court, 16 March 1993), Geoghegan J. held that parol evidence would be admissible to show the circumstances under which the parties contracted and the general context within which the contract was entered into, especially where the clause under construction was ambiguous (cp *Schuler v. Wickman* [1974] A.C. 235 (HL) 261). Similarly, Flood J. in *Bank of Ireland v. McCabe*, High Court, March 25, 1993; see *Annual Review of Irish Law 1993*, pp.189–191, 193–194) was prepared to take a broad view of evidence admissible to explain the context in which the contract was made. Following the speech of Lord Wilberforce in the *Reardon Smith Line* case, he had admitted evidence of the circumstances under which a written guarantee had come into existence, but had nonetheless held that since the guarantee was expressed to cover present and future liabilities, it covered both the initial loan in respect of which it was executed and also a subsequent loan to which the bank had sought to apply it. On appeal (Supreme Court, December 19, 1994; see *Annual Review of Irish Law 1995*, pp.218–219) Egan J. focused more on the evidence admitted by Flood J. as to the surrounding circumstances. He found that the guarantee had been "entered into to cover a specific transaction but the bank are attempting to use it for another purpose i.e. to cover a later transaction. ... The parties in this case agreed that once a specific transaction had been completed the guarantee was at an end. They did not qualify this in any way so it meant that there was to be so irrespective of the contents of the agreement itself" (9). He therefore allowed the appeal.

Igote v. Badsey is a similar case concerning the surrounding circumstances, the factual matrix in which the contract was signed. A share subscription agreement between the parties provided that "in respect of any financial period of the company of twelve months duration, the [defendant] Company shall distribute at least Ir£40,000" (Article 4.3) to the plaintiff. Butler J. (High Court, July 12, 2000, *ex tempore*) held that this was a contractual commitment to make an annual payment rather than one to pay a dividend out of available profits, and that the defendant was in breach. On appeal, (Supreme Court, July 18, 2001), Murphy J. (Keane C.J. and Denham J. concurring) allowed the appeal. He accepted the *Prenn v. Simmonds* and *Reardon Smith Line v. Yngvar Hansen-Tagen* approach as adopted in *Rohan Construction*, but tempered it with the observations of May L.J. in *Plumb Bros v. Dolmac* that the search is not for subjective intention but is instead an examination of the general circumstances surrounding the making of the document and in which it was made to deduce the intention of the parties from the actual words of the document itself. In the High Court, Butler J. had held that the annual payment in Article 4.3 was in the nature of a fixed royalty for a patent licence, and ordered that it be paid. However, on appeal, Murphy J. held that Butler J. had

> "... erred in ascertaining the intentions of the parties from the evidence heard by him as well as the alterations aforesaid and documents prepared in the course of negotiations. The intention of the parties may be gleaned only from the document ultimately concluded by them albeit construing it in the light of surrounding circumstances but not ascertaining their intentions from such circumstances. Such a process would be justified only where one or other of the parties claimed rectification of the document executed by him: that is not the present case (11)."

Focusing then first on the words used in Article 4.3, he concluded that the obligation on the defendant was to distribute the sum of £40,000 by way of dividend rather than royalty (11) not least because "the use of the word 'distribute' suggests the payment of a dividend rather than the discharge of a particular commercial indebtedness" (12). As Lord Mustill put it in *Charter Reinsurance v. Fagan* [1996] 3 All E.R. 46 (HL) 50 "most expressions do have a natural meaning, in the sense of their primary meaning in ordinary speech ... [Hence] the inquiry will start, and usually finish, by asking what is the ordinary meaning of the words used". Here, for Murphy J., the ordinary meaning of the word "distribute" was more consistent with a dividend than a royalty, a conclusion as reasonable on the facts as the contractual description of a transaction as an "annuity" in *McCabe v. South City and County Investment Co.* [1997] 3 I.R. 300; [1998] 1 I.L.R.M. 264 (SC) (see *Annual Review of Irish Law 1997*, pp.228–229).

In the end, therefore, for Murphy J. in *Igote*, the proper approach was to start from the words used, and then to consider them in their surrounding circumstances; that being so, Butler J. had fallen into error by first considering the surrounding circumstances and asking whether the words reflected them. For Murphy J., Butler J.'s effort to place the Agreement in the context in which it had been made went beyond what was permissible and had instead evolved "into an impermissible investigation of the subjective intentions of the parties in entering into the Agreement" (13). This must be right. The "parties cannot give direct evidence to show that their real intentions were at variance with the provisions of the document and the task of the Court is to construe the contractual term without any preconception as to what the parties intended" (Beatson, *Anson's Law of Contract* (28th ed., OUP, Oxford, 2002), 160; citing *Prenn v. Simmonds* [1971] 1 WLR, 1385; *Hyundai Merchant Marine v. Gesuri Chartering Co. Ltd* [1991] 1 Lloyd's Rep 100, 102; *British Movietonews Ltd v. London & District Cinemas Ltd* [1952] A.C. 166; *Zoan v. Rouamba* [2000] 1 W.L.R. 1509, 1523; *Pagnan SpA v. Tradax* [1987] 1 All E.R. 81, 88; affd [1987] 3 All E.R. 565). Hence, the law "excludes from the admissible background the previous negotiations of the parties and their declarations of subjective intent" (*Investors Compensation* (above) *per* Lord Hoffman).

However, if *Igote* is correct on this issue, then it raises questions about the correctness of the decision of the Supreme Court in the earlier *Bank of Ireland v. McCabe*. There, Flood J. in the High Court had admitted evidence of the circumstances surrounding the execution of the guarantee, but had commenced his construction from the terms of the guarantee itself; on the other hand, Egan J. in the Supreme Court had set out from the surrounding circumstances and he had read down an otherwise clear and unambiguous clause accordingly. Egan J.'s approach in *McCabe* is very like that of Butler J. in *Igote*, whereas Flood J.'s approach is much closer to that of Murphy J.; if so, then this calls Egan J.'s judgment into serious question. It is not permissible to cross the line between interpreting the clause and taking into account such admissible evidence as will aid in that interpretation, on the one hand, and, on the other, admitting direct evidence of intention and then asking whether the words used achieved it. Although it is hard to see how Egan J. in *McCabe* did not cross that line, it is clear that Murphy J. in *Igote* did not. Neither did O'Higgins J. in *Meridian v. Eircell*, High Court, April 5, 2001. The defendant had agreed to supply mobile telecommunications to the plaintiff at a discount; the plaintiff attracted customers by offering them some of that discount; and when the plaintiff's customer numbers began a substantial increase, Eircell sent a letter (called the "process letter" by the parties) to customers wishing to transfer to Meridian, explaining in particular that Meridian's low rates flowed from the VDA which Eircell intended not to renew. O'Higgins J. held that Eircom's delays in transferring customers to Meridian occasioned by the sending of the process letter were unnecessary and avoidable. The VDA provided that "any instructions regarding additions to or removals of nominated Eircell numbers from the Eircell Volume Discount shall be implemented as soon as possible". On the evidence, transfer requests were running at sixteen per day, which the person looking after the Meridian transfers could have done in half a day if that was the only work on which they were engaged. The fact that the clause was in a standard form agreement of which many other customers were availing, and was also to be found in other of Eircom's standard agreements, constituted part of the factual matrix in the light of which O'Higgins J. construed the obligation to transfer "as soon as possible". Although it had to be "interpreted in the light of what is reasonable. Otherwise Eircell might be faced with the absurd – although engaging – prospect of the entire workforce from Chief Executive to cleaning staff abandoning all other tasks to ensure that the transfers were effected as soon as possible", nevertheless he held that the obligation to effect transfer "as soon as possible" meant "something more urgent" than merely to transfer within a reasonable time. As a consequence, he held that there was a failure to process the transfer requests as soon as possible in the cases where a process letter was sent, but not in other cases where, viewed in the light of all the surrounding circumstances, the transfers were effected as soon as possible.

The *contra proferentem* rule   *Verba chartarum forius accipiuntur contra proferentem*; the words of written documents are construed more forcibly against the party putting forward the document (Beatson, *Anson*, 162). Hence, if a party to a contract chooses "to adopt ambiguous words it seems to me good sense, as well as established law, that those words should be interpreted in the sense which is adverse to the persons who chose and introduced them. ..." (*In re Sweeney and Kennedy's Arbitration* [1950] I.R. 85, 98 *per* Kingsmill-Moore J.). This rule is especially strictly applied in the context of exclusion clauses (e.g. *Lee (John) & Son (Grantham) Ltd v. Railway Executive* [1949] 2 All E.R. 581 (CA); *Photo Productions v. Securicor* [1980] A.C. 827 (HL); *Ailsa Craig v. Malvern Fishing* [1983] 1 All E.R. 101 (HL); *Lynch v. Lynch* [1996] 1 I.L.R.M. 311 (HC; Costello P.); though a well-drafted exclusion clause will operate to exclude such personal liability; (e.g. *Regan v. RIAC* [1990] 1 I.R. 278 (HC); see, generally, Beatson, *Anson*, pp.170–171), but it is nonetheless of general application across the entire of the law of contract (see, e.g. Geoghegan J. in *Dillon v. McGovern* (High Court, 16 March 1993, Geoghegan J.); *Cuffe v. CIE and An Post* (Supreme Court, 22 October 1996); *Bolger v. Osborne* [2000] 1 I.L.R.M. 250 (HC; Macken J.); *Blackall v. Blackall* [2000] 3 I.R. 456 (HC; Finnegan J.); *Sunreed Investment Ltd v. Gill*, High Court, Finnegan J., June 3, 2000). Even then, however, the *contra proferentem* principle may be displaced if the circumstances of the case so require; for example, in *Browne v. Mariena Properties* [1998] 1 I.R. 568, the court was "dealing with a general condition in a standard contract of sale approved by the ... Law Society on the basis, presumably, that it preserves a fair balance between vendor and purchaser. In these circumstances, ... the Court should approach the question of interpretation with an open mind and examine the wording of the clause itself" ([1998] 1 I.R. 568, 593 *per* Barrington J.).

This year, the *contra proferentem* rule arose the context not of a contract but of a planning permission. In *Cork Co. Co. v. Cliftonhall Ltd*, High Court, April 6, 2001, Finnegan J. held that "... insofar as the planning permission is ambiguous it should be construed *contra proferentem* ..." against the body which granted the permission, in this case the applicant. On the one hand, the same kinds of policies apply in both cases: the party who drafts the clause and seeks to enforce it should be compelled to ensure that the clause achieves its intended end by construing strictly against such a party. On the other hand, it would probably have been more appropriate to have arrived at the same conclusion on the basis of the planning and environmental policies underlying the legislation being enforced by the applicant body.

RESTRAINT OF TRADE

Contracts on the sale of a business often contain clauses restraining the vendor from re-entering that business. Distribution contracts often contain clauses preventing the shop from dealing with the distributor's competitors. Employment contracts often contain clauses restraining employees from working with competitors or preventing them setting up in opposition after that employment ceases. In such cases, the restraint of trade clause must be reasonable as between the parties and in the public interest (*Nordenfelt v. Maxim Nordenfelt* [1894] A.C. 535 (HL); *McEllistrim v. Ballymacelligott Co-op* [1919] A.C. 548 (HL); *Kerry Co-Op and Avonmore v. An Bord Bainne* [1990] I.L.R.M. 664 (HC; Costello J.); [1991] I.L.R.M. 851 (SC)). To help determine such reasonableness as between the parties, the term must be reasonable in time, space and subject matter. Carroll J. conducted this exercise in *Lennon and Pakatak v. Doran and Corrigan*, High Court, February 20, 2001.

Mr Lennon bought into Pakatak, a business owned by Mr Doran and Mr Corrigan, and then agreed to buy Mr Doran and Mr Corrigan out. Having found that, to ensure to Mr Lennon the full benefit and goodwill of the company, the buy out contract contained a clause retraining Mr Doran and Mr Corrigan from competing with Pakatak for two years, Carroll J. proceeded to consider whether the non-compete clause was reasonably necessary to protect the business sold (referring to *John Orr Limited v. Orr* [1987] I.L.R.M. 703). As to reasonableness in time, Carroll J. held that for the purpose of protecting Mr Lennon's investment, two years was excessive, one year would have been sufficient, and concluded that "Mr Lennon's investment in the goodwill of the company ... [would] be adequately protected by one year non competition period". As to reasonableness in space, the clause referred to "Territory"; this remained undefined; but Carroll J. held that "in order to give the clause business efficacy, territory should be interpreted as the area in which the business was being carried on at the time of the share transfer".

Historically, the courts leaned against restraint of trade clauses entirely, and even in the modern law, a clause in restraint of trade is void unless reasonable as between the parties and in the public interest. Where a clause would on this test be void, however, it is possible to sever the offending clause and leave the remainder of the contract untouched, and it is possible even to sever words from the restraint of trade clause so as to render it reasonable (e.g. *Attwood v. Lamont* [1920] 3 K.B. 571; *Skerry v. Moles* (1907) 42 I.L.T.R. 46; *John Orr Limited v. Orr* [1987] I.L.R.M. 703; Beatson, *Anson*, 413–417). Hence, it is only to the extent that restraint of clauses are reasonable that they will be enforced; if not reasonable, and not severeable, they should fall. Against this backdrop, Carroll J.'s approach – which went well beyond severance to the wholesale rewriting of a clause which she should have regarded with suspicion – was very benign.

There are obvious similarities between the enquiries mandated by the restraint of trade doctrine and those undertaken pursuant to the terms of section 4 of the Competition Act 1991. The consequences of these similarities have been raised but not resolved in *RGDATA v. Tara Publishing* [1995] 1 I.R. 89; [1995] 1 I.L.R.M. 453 (HC; Murphy J.) (see the *1994 Review*, 151–157) and *Sibra Building v. Ladgrove* [1998] 2 I.R. 589 (SC) (see *Annual Review of Irish Law 1998*, pp.183–184). In *Lennon and Pakatak v. Doran and Corrigan*, Carroll J. sidestepped the issue in the (puzzling) finding that the Act did not apply:

> "this is not an agreement between undertakings which has as its object or effect the prevention, restriction or distortion of competition in trade in any goods. It is a buyout between shareholders where for the protection of the goodwill of the business a limit on competition by the vendors, who were the founders of the company, is necessary. But this may only be to the extent required to protect the investment of the purchaser, or in other words to let the company get off the ground" (8).

Admittedly, because the policies served by the common law doctrine of restraint of trade and by section 4 of the Act are similar, the results will be the same in many instances (*RGDATA*; *Sibra Building*); but since the policies are not in fact the same, there will inevitably be situations – of which *Lennon* may be an example, if its interpretation of the Act is correct – in which the common law policy pulls one way and the statutory policy the other, and the results will be different.

SPECIFIC PERFORMANCE

A plaintiff who seeks specific performance must be ready, willing and able to perform that contract; otherwise a court will not make the order sought. Specific performance was refused on this ground by McCracken J. in *Forbes v. Tobin*, High Court, March 8, 2001. The plaintiff had agreed to purchase from the defendant premises comprising a filling station, shop and workshop and paid a deposit. The contract of sale provided that the plaintiff was to pay any exigible value added tax but the plaintiff disputed that any such tax was payable. The defendant also required that the plaintiff take over its agreements with its oil suppliers, but the plaintiff refused. The defendant then purported to serve two completion notices and sought to forfeit the deposit, and the plaintiff in turn sought specific performance. McCracken J. found that value added tax was indeed payable on the sale, and held that as a consequence the plaintiff was not ready willing and able to close and was therefore not entitled to an order for specific performance. However, he went on to hold that the defendants were not entitled to require the plaintiffs to take over the oil supply contracts, and that, as a consequence, they were also not ready willing and able to close when they served their completion notices, so that the contract for sale was not properly rescinded and the deposit was not properly forfeit. He therefore made an order requiring the return of the deposit plus interest.

On the other hand, in *Griffin v. Madden*, High Court, May 11, 2001, O'Donovan J. ordered specific performance of an agreement to compromise proceedings relating to a boundary dispute. In the course of trial, the defendant contended for the invalidity of the agreement on grounds, *inter alia*, of misrepresentation and coercion, but O'Donovan J. rejected these grounds as without factual foundation. The agreement had not been carried out because the parties had not been able to agree a disputed boundary in particular because the defendant – who "appears to have been totally intransigent" (10) – refused to accept the boundary determined by engineers appointed under the terms of the agreement.

TERMS

Implied terms   Terms may be implied into contracts either as a matter of fact (because the term was, or would be presumed to have been, intended by the parties) or as a matter of law (because they are necessarily required by the nature of the contract; a term may also be implied by statute. Nevertheless, "[i]t is for the parties to make their own contract and the Courts must be careful not to impose on parties terms which they would never have accepted if such terms were suggested in the pre-contract bargaining" (*Fagan v. General Accident Fire and Life Assurance Corporation* (Supreme Court, October 14, 1998, Lynch J.); see also his judgment in *Carna Foods v. Eagle Star Insurance Co.* [1997] 2 I.R. 193; [1997] 2 I.R. 499 (SC); cp *Tradax v. Irish Grain Board* [1984] I.R. 1 (SC) 14 *per* O'Higgins C.J. (Hederman J. concurring); 26 *per* McCarthy J. (dissenting on the application of an agreed principle to the facts); *Grehan v. NEHB* [1989] I.R. 422 (HC) 425 *per* Costello J.).

When a term is implied as a matter of fact, it may be done for one of two related but separate reasons (*Tradax v. Irish Grain Board* [1984] I.R. 1 (SC)). First, it may have been the intention of the parties that the term be included, but for them, it was "so obvious that it [went] without saying; so that, if while the parties making their bargain, an officious bystander were to suggest some express provision for it in the agreement, they would testily suppress him with a common 'Oh, of course'." (*Shirlaw v. Southern Foundries* [1939] 2 K.B. 206 (CA) 227 *per* MacKinnon LJ; affd [1940] A.C. 701 (HL); [1997] 2 I.L.R.M. 211 (SC); *Carna Foods v. Eagle Star Insurance Co.* [1997] 2 I.R. 193; [1997] 2 I.R. 499 (SC); *Sullivan v. Southern Health Board* [1997] 3 I.R. 123 (SC)). Any term implied on the basis of this test might be said to reflect the actual intentions of the parties (as did the term implied by Morris P. in *Moran v. Minister for Health and Children*, High Court, December 15, 1998); and if that intention cannot be demonstrated, no such term will be implied. This emerges from *Terry v. Albion Enterprises*, High Court, November 14, 2001 McCracken J. ordered specific performance of an option to purchase. The plaintiff may have been in technical breach of contract by arrears of rent, but it seems there was an explanation for the plaintiff's arrears and when the error was pointed out, the amount outstanding was tendered reasonably quickly. Furthermore, McCracken J. observed that the option agreement did not contain any express provision making it a condition precedent to the exercise of that option that there be no breach of covenant and he was "not prepared to imply such a condition precedent in the absence of any evidence that this might have been the intention of the parties" (10; cp *Wildgust v. Bank of Ireland and Norwich Union Life Assurance Society*, High Court, Morris P., July 28, 1998).

The officious bystander put in a very brief appearance this year in *Coonan v. Attorney General*, High Court, January 31, 2001; Supreme Court, May 29, 2001; discussed in the Estoppel section, above). In the Supreme Court, Geoghegan J. (Fennelly J. concurring) held that the Attorney General was in breach of his contract with the plaintiff by declining to exercise his discretion to renew the plaintiff's appointment as State Solicitor. It was not necessary to imply a term to construe the contract in this way. "This would seem to be the natural interpretation of the express term but if it is necessary to imply a term, I would have no hesitation in doing so" (8). Murphy J. dissented:

> "It is difficult to reconcile that conclusion with the discretion expressly and admitted[ly] conferred on the Attorney General by the conditions of his appointment. It seems to me that this decision necessarily involves the substitution of an obligation for a discretion subject to the qualification that the discretion could be restored to the Attorney General on his giving reasonable, but undefined, notice to Mr Coonan and presumably all other State Solicitors. I cannot envisage the officious bystander postulated in *Shirlaw* ... (and more recently by this Court in *Carna Foods* ...) suggesting a provision to that effect. Less still could I

envisage either party testily suppressing his intervention with a common 'Oh of course'. At the very least such a suggestion would give rise to a debate and the very existence of debate would preclude the implication of the suggested term" (6-7).

Second, the courts presume that the parties intend that their contract will in fact be operable, and so will imply terms into it necessary to give it effect; thus a term may be implied "from the presumed intention of the parties with the object of giving the transaction such efficacy as both parties must have intended that at all events it should have" (*The Moorcock* (1889) 14 P.D. 64, 68 *per* Bowen LJ; cp *Luxor (Eastbourne) v. Cooper* [1941] A.C. 108, 137 *per* Lord Wright; *Equitable Life v. Hyman* [2000] 3 W.L.R. 529 (HL); *Ward v. Spivack Limited* [1957] I.R. 40 (SC); *Sweeney v. Duggan* [1997] 2 I.R. 531; [1997] 2 I.L.R.M. 211 (SC)). Any term implied on the basis of this test might be said to reflect the courts' presumption that the parties intended that the contract be operative. Any such term must be not only reasonable but also necessary, it must not be inconsistent with the express wording of the contract, and it must be capable of formulation with reasonable precision.

Whether an implied term met this standard was the issue before Lavan J. in *Jestdale v. Millennium Theatre Co.*, High Court, July 31, 2001. It was an express term that the defendant would transfer the property to the plaintiff upon completion of certain works carried out in accordance with a planning permission already acquired by the defendant; further express term that the defendant would have the right to rescind the contract (without compensation for any work done) if the relevant works had not been completed by the due date. The works were not completed on time and the defendant refused to extend the completion date. The plaintiff argued that there was implied into the contract a term that the defendant would if necessary extend the completion date if the plaintiff could not complete by virtue of acts or omissions of the defendant and a term that in such circumstances the defendant would not unreasonably withhold its consent to the extension of the completion date. Lavan J. was satisfied that the plaintiff's claim must fail and therefore struck it out:

> "The express terms of the contract with regard to rescission and the relatively short time scale specified for completion of the works can have left the plaintiff in little doubt as to its obligations to act expeditiously in seeking to complete the works on time if it hoped to reap the benefits of the agreement from its perspective. ... the plaintiff failed to honour its commitments under the agreement, and now seeks to frustrate the defendant's attempts extricate itself from the ensuing imbroglio. I accept that the Court ought not to imply a provision into a contract, which would have the consequence of contradicting the express terms of the contract agreed between the parties. I also find it difficult

to infer the implied terms relied upon by the plaintiff on the grounds
that they cannot be formulated with reasonable precision" (10–11).

The officious bystander and business efficacy tests are related in that each
may be said to reflect the parties' intentions; but they are separate because the
officious bystander test reflects their actual intentions whilst the business
efficacy test reflects their presumed intentions. The two tests ask different
questions, and therefore can come up with different answers on the same facts.
For example, in *Associated Japanese Bank v. Crédit du Nord* [1988] 3 All
E.R. 912, Steyn J. declined to imply a term on the basis of the business efficacy
test, but did so on the basis of the officious bystander test. Conversely, on the
latter test a term may be implied "independently of the intention of the parties
where it is necessary as a matter of law or logic to enable the provisions of the
agreement to have operative effect" (*Sweeney v. Duggan* [1997] 2 I.R. 531
(SC) 545; [1997] 2 I.L.R.M. 211, 222 *per* Murphy J.). These are two of the
important structural differences between the two tests; they have separate
historical sources and are in the modern law separate, parallel, tests (Phang,
"Implied Terms Revisited" [1990] J.B.L. 394; Phang, "Implied Terms in English
Law – Some Recent Developments" [1993] J.B.L. 242; Phang, "Implied Terms,
Business Efficacy and the Officious Bystander" [1998] J.B.L. 1).

Both tests featured in the judgment of O'Higgins J. in *Meridian v. Eircell*,
High Court, April 5, 2001, which concerned an agreement between a
telecommunications company and a customer by which the company provided
discounts due to the customer's volume of calls (a Volume Discount Agreement,
or VDA). In 1997, the defendant mobile telecommunications company Eircell
agreed to provide the plaintiff with a VDA. Meridian attracted customers by
offering them some of the discount available under the VDA. It initially ran
from August 1997 to August 1998; it was continued in operation until
November 1998, when it was formally renewed for a further year. Thereupon
Meridian began significantly to expand its operations and customer base. Eircell
declined to renew that agreement when it expired, and in April 1999, Eircell
sent a letter (called the "process letter" by the parties) to customers wishing to
transfer to Meridian, explaining in particular that Meridian's low rates flowed
from the VDA, which Eircell intended not to renew.

In earlier judgments, O'Higgins J. held that Eircell were entitled to decline
to renew the VDA and were not estopped by their conduct from doing so
(High Court, April 4, 2000) and that there was prima facie evidence that Eircell
was dominant in the relevant market (High Court, October 4, 2000). In the
present judgment, he held that the plaintiffs had failed to prove on the balance
of probabilities that Eircell are dominant, and any claims based on abuse of
dominance and hence breach of section 5 of the Competition Act 1991 failed
(on this aspect of the case, see Dodd, "Abuse of Dominance in Meridian v.
Eircell" (2001) 7 (1) Bar Rev. 12). However, the plaintiffs also alleged that the
defendants were in breach of various terms implied into the VDA, which

O'Higgins J. considered on the basis of the following principles:

> "Before a term will be implied in a contract it must be necessary to do so, and not merely reasonable.
>
> The term must be necessary to give business efficacy to the agreement.
>
> It must be a term, which both parties must have intended, that is, a term based on the presumed common intention of the parties.
>
> The Court will approach the implication of terms into a contract with caution.
>
> There is a presumption against importing terms into a contract in writing and the more detailed the terms agreed in writing the stronger is the presumption against the implication of terms.
>
> If the term sought to be implied cannot be stated with reasonable precision, it will not be implied. ...."

O'Higgins J. held the sending of the process letter did not of itself constitute a breach of contract, but he did find various other breaches of the VDA by Eircell. For example, he that held that there was no justification for Eircell's failure to tell Meridian upon enquiry or at least shortly after whether or not a transfer had been effected to them: in particular when "one takes into account that an administration fee of £16 is paid for transfer, the failure to tell the customer borders on the absurd". He held that this conduct amounted to a breach of an implied term in the VDA:

> "Under the VDA there is an express term to process transfer requests as soon as possible. A necessary implication of such term in a commercial contract is that the party be told on demand, or at least within a reasonable time thereafter that such a transfer has been effected. It must have been agreed between the parties, and in my view is so obvious as not that it was not necessary to state it. The necessity to wait until the receipt of the first bill which could be weeks later is a clear breach of such an obligation."

Furthermore, Meridian claimed that for a period the defendant either refused to supply or only fitfully and inadequately supplied books of transfer forms to them. O'Higgins J. held that the excuses given by the defendants for failing to supply the necessary transfer books were varied and singularly unconvincing, that their behaviour in so refusing was obstructive, obdurate and arrogant, and that was no valid financial, logistical or security justification for such conduct. As a consequence, he held that this it amounted to a breach of a term implied into the contract that either party would not deliberately seek to frustrate the operation of the contract (referring to *Royal Trust Company of Canada v. Kelly*, High Court, Barron J., February 27, 1989; *Sweeney v. Duggan* (above)). Such a term is akin to the mutual duty of fidelity implied into employment contracts, but such terms are implied either for business efficacy reasons or because the nature of the contract necessarily requires it (cp *Liverpool City Council v. Irwin* [1977] A.C. 239 (HL). However, here, O'Higgins J. held that:

> "Such a term is not only reasonable (which would not be sufficient), it was agreed but unexpressed. It would pass the officious bystander test."

Hence, here, the term was implied neither for business efficacy reasons nor arising out of the nature of the contract but because the separate officious bystander test required it. On the other hand, he rejected most of the implied terms contended for by the plaintiff. For example, the plaintiff had earlier argued that there was a term implied into the contract that Eircell had a duty to supply books of transfer forms to Meridian, but O'Higgins J. rejected this contention for two reasons. First:

> "It is quite clear that a clause such as was contended for by the plaintiffs is not required to give business efficacy to the contract. This is evident from the fact that other users of the VDA have been operating without such a clause. In the case of other customers the transfer forms are sent directly from Eircell to the person wishing to transfer. Such a clause is thus not necessary to give business efficacy to the Agreement. If the term cannot be implied to give business efficacy to the standard form agreement in respect of other users, it cannot be implied in the same standard form agreement merely because of the use which Meridian makes of it."

Second, most of the implied terms contended for by the plaintiffs were put forward by them and considered by O'Higgins J. on the basis of the business efficacy test. Indeed, his statement of principle amounts to an extended statement of that test. However, he also rejected this proposed implied term on the basis of the officious bystander test:

> "A term cannot be implied in the VDA providing for the granting of transfer forms to Meridian, on the basis that their provision is something that was obviously agreed between the parties but unexpressed. If the officious bystander had inquired of the Eircell representative whether there was an agreement concerning the supply of transfer books to Meridian he would probably been met with the response "What ever for?" from a baffled [Eircell representative]."

This could amount either to a restatement of the initial rejection of the term as not fulfilling the business efficacy test or to a separate reason for rejecting it as not fulfilling the alternative officious bystander test. Given that the business efficacy and officious bystander tests are separate tests, any reading of these reasons as eliding the two tests should be resisted, and this second reason should therefore be treated as a separate reason rejecting the term on a separate ground.

Furthermore, Meridian had also argued that the process letter was a breach of a confidentiality term implied into the VDA, but O'Higgins J. held that there was no need to imply a confidentiality term into the contract in order to give it business efficacy. Again, Meridian argued that such a confidentiality obligation arose under an implied term in the contract not to frustrate it, but O'Higgins J. also held that any such term would not render it impermissible for Eircell communicate the contents of the process letter to its then customers.

Similarly, Meridian argued that there should be implied into the contract a term that Eircell would provide customer-billing information to Meridian in electronic format. However, O'Higgins J. held that if the officious bystander had been asked about such a term it was most unlikely that the answer would have been a testy – "oh, of course"; rather, he held that it was much more probable that Eircell would have replied that it would be necessary to discuss the matter further. Furthermore, he held that as such information was not supplied to other similar customers in electronic format, it was not reasonable to expect that such a term would be implied into this VDA. This amounts to a holding that it was not necessary to give efficacy to the contract to imply the term into it; and if so, as before, the question arises as to whether these are the same reason restated, or whether they amount to separate rejections of the proposed terms on the basis of separate tests. As before, this second reading is to be preferred. Even if the various tests for the implication of terms represent different points on a continuous spectrum (*Liverpool City Council v. Irwin* [1977] A.C. 239 (HL) 254 *per* Lord Wilberforce; *Sweeney v. Duggan* [1997] 2 I.R. 531 (SC) 538; [1997] 2 I.L.R.M. 211, 216 *per* Murphy J.), as colours on a spectrum are different, so too are the various tests for the implication of terms different tests. Clarity of analysis is not served by eliding them, and O'Higgins J.'s careful judgment in *Meridian v. Eircell* should not be read as having done so.

In a subsequent procedural skirmish which was appealed (Supreme Court, May 10, 2001), an appeal by the plaintiffs was envisaged, but in the meantime, the Court McGuinness J. (Hardiman and Fennelly JJ. concurring) made orders to allow Meridian to sell on its customer base and otherwise wind up in an orderly fashion.

Implied terms and employment contracts If a contract – especially a contract of employment – is silent on termination, a term allowing for termination upon reasonable notice will readily be implied (*Royal Trust Company of Canada v. Kelly*, High Court, Barron J., February 27, 1989; *Clarke* *v. Kilternan Motor Co.*, High Court, McCracken J., December 10, 1996); but if the contract contains detailed provisions dealing with termination (*NEHB v. Grehan* [1989] I.R. 422 (HC; Costello J.)), or if it is clearly for a fixed term or for indefinite duration (*Walsh v. Dublin Health Authority* (1964) 98 I.L.T.R. 82 (HC; Budd J.)), a further term allowing for termination upon reasonable notice will not so readily be implied, in particular because the courts will not countenance the introduction of an implied term which would run counter to an express term. (*Tradax v. Irish Grain* [1984] I.R. 1 (SC) 17 *per* Henchy J.; *Carroll v. An Post National Lottery Company* [1996] 1 I.R. 443 (HC; Costello P.)). Finally, in most contracts of employment, there is an implied term that the contract may be determined without notice for serious misconduct.

The contract of employment facing McCracken J. in *Dooley v. Great Southern Hotels Ltd*, High Court, July 27, 2001, provided that "it [was] intended that this employment should extend up to normal retiring date, i.e., age 65 in present circumstances" and that if "either party should wish, for good and sufficient reason, to terminate the employment, then the applicable period of notice would be six months". On the face of it, therefore, the contract both contained a provision dealing with termination (cp *Grehan*) and was otherwise clearly to continue until retirement (cp *Walsh*), and there would seem to be little room for the implication of another term dealing with termination. Interpreting these provisions, McCracken J. held:

> "I do not think that this was ever intended to be a contractually binding contract of employment until the Plaintiff reached the age of 65, particularly in the light of the commencement of the relevant clause with the words 'it is intended that'. In my view this was a contract, which could be terminated on reasonable notice by either party at any time. The contract then provides that it may be determined on six months notice 'for good and sufficient reason'. I think this phrase is of considerable importance, as it does not in my view either expressly or impliedly limit the right to give notices to cases where the has been some form of misconduct. I think, had that been intended, it would have been very clearly stated. Accordingly, in my view this contract may be determined by six months notice for any good and sufficient reason, whether it is related to the plaintiff's misconduct or to the general relationship between the parties. I also am quite satisfied that, like most contracts of employment, there is an implied term that the contract may be determined without notice for serious misconduct."

The defendant had purported summarily to dismiss the plaintiff. On the facts, McCracken J. held that although the plaintiff had not carried out the instructions of his superior in respect of which there was either a specific order from the superior or at least an agreement between himself and his superior, and had then lied about it, this was undoubtedly misconduct but not sufficiently serious in the circumstances to justify instant dismissal (distinguishing *Pepper v. Webb* [1969] 2 All E.R. 216; *Brewster v. Burke*, High Court, Hamilton J., February 8, 1978). The defendant had not sought to imply an additional term allowing summary dismissal on another ground; any such argument would almost certainly have failed, because the contract in fact contained a termination clause. On the basis of that clause, McCracken J. held that the totality of the plaintiff's conduct did constitute good and sufficient reason to terminate his employment by giving him six months' notice. It was a breach of his contract not to give him such notice but to purport to dismiss him summarily, which entitled him to damages amounting to six months gross salary.

Removing terms   Not only are terms added by the law but also terms are often removed from a contract by the common law, by statutory instrument, or by statute. *APH Manufacturing v. DHL* [2001] 1 I.L.R.M. 224 (HC; Finnegan J.); (Supreme Court, July 20, 2001; Denham, Murphy, Murray, Hardiman and Fennelly JJ.) is a good example of this last category. Property of the plaintiffs was damaged whilst being transported by air by the defendants. The carriage was subject to the terms of the Warsaw Convention (implemented into Irish law by the Air Navigation and Transport Act 1936, as amended). Article 23 of the Convention rendered null and void any term, which purported to relieve a carrier of liability or to fix a limit on liability lower than that provided by the Convention. As this was the purport of certain terms in the contract, Finnegan J. in the High Court applied Article 23 and held them ineffective. On appeal, the appellants did not challenge this conclusion. Instead, they focused on section 7 of the Air Navigation and Transport Act, 1959 which provides that the limits on the carrier's liability in Article 22(2) of the Convention shall not apply "if it is proved that the damage resulted from an act or omission of the carrier, his servants or agents, done with intent to cause damage or recklessly and with knowledge that damage probably result ...". In the High Court, Finnegan J. had found that the terms of section 7 had been made out, but on appeal, Fennelly J. (Denham, Murphy, Murray and Hardiman JJ. concurring) held that the facts as proven did not rise to the level of recklessness required by section 7, and allowed the appeal.

Incorporation   The contract between the parties in *APH Manufacturing v. DHL* was partly oral and partly in writing, incorporating various documents, including the defendants' standard terms and conditions, an airway bill relating to the specific carriage, and faxes between the parties. "Important Notes" (wichtige Hinweise) printed on the German version of the airway bill provided that where the Convention applied, liability of the carrier would be limited by the Convention, except in cases of "gross negligence" (grobe Fahrlassigkeit). All of the discussions between the parties were in English; the English language version of the airway bill contained no reference to "gross negligence", and the German language version was never given to the respondent. Fennelly J.

held that all of these points:

> "tend[ed] to the contrary of the "Important Notes" as a contractual document. The Appellants have, of course, acknowledged in oral argument that a carrier may, in principle, ... assume obligations and thus liability greater than the terms of the Convention. Nonetheless, that liability must be based on the terms of the contract. I do not believe that the "Important Notes" formed part of the contract between the respondent and the Appellants. ... Accordingly, the Appellants could not be held liable for gross negligence. I would allow the appeal on this ground also."

A contract may contain terms set out on its face, or it may incorporate additional terms in many ways. For example, a clause or clauses may be incorporated by means of a course of dealing between the parties (*Henry Kendall & Sons v. William Lillico & Sons Ltd* [1969] 2 A.C. 31 (HL); *Spurling v. Bradshaw* [1956] 1 W.L.R. 461; *Lynch Roofing Systems (Ballaghadereen) Ltd v. Bennett,* High Court, June 26, 1998, Morris P.; see *Annual Review of Irish Law 1998,* pp.163–168). Again, they may be incorporated by reference to other documents (as in *Sweeney v. Mulcahy* [1993] I.L.R.M. 289 (HC; O'Hanlon J.), *Carroll v. An Post National Lottery Company* [1996] 1 I.R. 443 (HC: Costello J.; see *Annual Review of Irish Law 1996,* pp.168–178) or *Tierney v. An Post* [2000] 2 I.L.R.M. 214 (SC)) provided that steps taken by the party seeking to rely on the clause to bring the clause to the attention of the other party were reasonable in the circumstances (as in the early and leading English case of *Parker v. South East Railway* (1877) 2 C.P.D. 416); in such cases, where a term to be incorporated is particularly onerous or unusual, it must be brought specifically to the attention of the other party before it can be said that the party seeking to rely on it has taken reasonable steps (*Spurling v. Bradshaw; Thornton v. Shoe Lane Parking* [1971] 2 Q.B. 163; *Interfoto Picture Library v. Stilletto Visual Programmes* [1989] Q.B. 433; *Carroll v. An Post National Lottery Company*). Even though the contract in *APH Manufacturing v. DHL* incorporated many documents, nevertheless, because the German language "Important Notes" were never brought to the notice of the respondents, they were never incorporated into the contract, and thus never bound the respondents.

UNDUE INFLUENCE

Since a contract is based upon the consent of the parties, if the consent of one or both parties is vitiated, then the contract is invalid. Thus, if one party coerces another into entering into the contract, the consent of that other will be vitiated. At common law, the remedy for such coercion is supplied by the doctrine of duress. In equity, a similar remedy is supplied by the doctrine of actual undue influence. Equity also goes further, providing a similar remedy not only where undue influence has actually occurred but also where, for policy reasons, it is presumed.

The principles relating to undue influence were at issue this year in the judgment of O'Donovan J. in the High Court in *Ulster Bank Ireland Ltd v. Fitzgerald*, High Court, November 9, 2001, in the judgment of Keane C.J. *ex tempore* (Murphy and Murray JJ. concurring) in *Johnson v. Church of Scientology* (Supreme Court, November 7, 2001) and in the decision of the House of Lords in *Scotland v. Etridge (No. 2)* [2001] U.K.H.L. 44; [2001] 4 All E.R. 448 (HL) (on Etridge, see Bigwood, "Undue Influence in the House of Lords: Principles and Proof" (2002) 65 M.L.R. 435; Breslin, "Undue Influence: Guarantor's Equitable right or Creditor's Contractual Obligation" (2002) 9 (2) C.L.P. 35; Oldham "If at first ... Undue Influence and the House of Lords" [2002] C.L.J. 29; O'Sullivan, "Developing O'Brien" (2002) 118 L.Q.R. 337; Phang and Tijo, "The Uncertain Boundaries of Undue Influence" [2002] L.M.C.L.Q. 231; White, "Undue Influence and Suretyship" (2002) 20 I.L.T. (ns) 70).

Actual Undue Influence   "Undue influence is one of the grounds of relief developed by the courts of equity as a court of conscience. The objective is to ensure that the influence of one person over another is not abused. ... To this end the common law developed a principle of duress ... [but] equity extended the reach of the law to other unacceptable forms of behaviour ... [including] overt acts of improper pressure or coercion" *Royal Bank of Scotland v. Etridge (No. 2)* [2001] U.K.H.L. 44, para. 44; [2001] 4 All E.R. 448 (HL) 457 *per* Lord Nicholls. "In the eye of the law, undue influence means influence that has been misused" (*ibid.*, para. 32).

With the evolution of the rules at common law this category is now less important than it was formerly. There are very few cases in which it can unequivocally be said that actual undue influence was the ground upon which equity set the contract aside, though it has often featured as one ground (in tandem with others; see e.g.: *Re Craig* [1971] Ch. 95 (Ungoed-Thomas J.); *O'Flanagan v. Ray-Ger* (1963–1993) Ir. Co.L. Rep. 289 (High Court, Costello J., April 28, 1983); *Cheese v. Thomas* [1994] 1 All E.R. 35 (CA)).

It used to be thought that a plaintiff seeking to plead actual undue influence had to demonstrate that the transaction was manifestly disadvantageous (from *BCCI v. Aboody* [1990] 1 Q.B. 923 (CA)) but this requirement of manifest disadvantage was overruled in *CIBC v. Pitt* [1994] 1 A.C. 200 (HL) and *Pitt* was approved on this point by Lord Nicholls in *Etridge* (para 12). The matter was not resolved as a matter of Irish law either in *Carroll v. Carroll* (HC; Shanley J.); [1999] 4 I.R. 241; [2000] 1 I.L.R.M. 210 (SC) (discussed in *Annual Review of Irish Law 1998*, pp.186–189 and *Annual Review of Irish Law 1999*, pp.121–125) or in this year's cases, but it is to be hoped that the requirement will be repudiated at the first opportunity.

However, although actual undue influence represents the direct equitable analogue of illegitimate pressure, there are two important extensions, relating to the absence of the plaintiff's will and to the abuse of the relationship between the parties.

First, as to absence of will, "[i]importunity and pressure, if carried to the point at which the complainant can no longer exercise a will of her own, amounts to undue influence, but pressure is neither always necessary nor always sufficient. In *Bank of Montreal v. Stuart* [1911] A.C. 120 [before the Privy Council] the wife succeeded in establishing that she was the victim of actual undue influence even though no pressure was exerted on her by her husband because none was needed: 'She had no will of her own. Nor had she any means of forming an independent judgment even if she had desired to do so ...'. ([1911] A.C. 120, 136)" (*Royal Bank of Scotland v. Etridge (No. 2)* [1998] 4 All E.R. 705 (CA) 712). Second, as to abuse of relationship, in the House of Lords in *Etridge*, Lord Nicholls held that undue influence can arise not only in cases of overt acts of improper pressure but also in cases of "a relationship between two persons where one has acquired over another a measure of influence, or ascendancy, of which the ascendant person then takes unfair advantage" (para. 8). In such cases, "the influence one person has over another provides scope for misuse without any specific acts of persuasion" (para. 9). "Proof that the complainant placed trust and confidence in the other party in relation to the management of the complainants financial affairs, coupled with a transaction which calls for explanation, will normally be sufficient" for the plaintiff to discharge the burden of proving undue influence; the evidential burden then shifts to the defendant to produce evidence to counter the inference of undue influence thereby arising (para. 14). Though this has been described as a presumption of undue influence, nevertheless, when "a plaintiff succeeds by this route he does so because he has succeeded in establishing a case of undue influence", i.e. a case of actual undue influence (para 16; see also para. 161 *per* Lord Scott). This is an important development: it emphasises that cases which were once thought to be examples of presumed undue influence are in fact cases where an inference of actual undue influence arises on the facts, and that this inference arises from the combination of the relationship and a transaction calling for explanation.

Whether there is such a relationship (see paras. 10-11) is a question of fact arising from the circumstances of the relationship and especially the transaction between the particular parties. This seems to be especially so in the context of elderly people reposing trust in younger family members or advisors (see, e.g., *Gregg v. Kidd* [1956] I.R. 183 (HC; Budd J.); *McGonigle v. Black*, High Court, Barr J., November 14, 1988; *Carroll v. Carroll*); it can be so, but is unlikely, in the case of bank manager and customer (*Lloyds Bank v. Bundy* [1975] Q.B. 326 (HL); *Nat West v. Morgan* [1986] A.C. 686 (HL)); it can also be so, but is even more unlikely, in the case of husband and wife (*Bank of Montreal v. Stuart* [1911] A.C. 120; *Barclays Bank v. O'Brien* [1994] 1 A.C.

180 (HL)). Since it is a question of fact arising from the circumstances of the relationship and the transaction, the categories are not closed.

In *Nat West v. Morgan* [1985] A.C. 686 (HL) Lord Scarman seemed to require the proof manifest disadvantage to establish this species of undue influence by abuse of relationship. By analogy, the Court of Appeal in *Aboody* required it for improper pressure cases, but *Aboody* was overruled on this point in *Pitt* (above) in language which was wide enough to cast doubt on *Morgan*. Later Court of Appeal decisions therefore sought to read the requirement down; for example, in *Royal Bank of Scotland v. Etridge (No. 2)* [1998] 4 All E.R. 705 the Court of Appeal explained that "the presence of manifest disadvantage is obviously a powerful evidential factor ... [which] assists the complainant in establishing her claim against the [defendant] in a case of presumed undue influence..." ([1998] 4 All E.R. 705, 714), and in *Barclays Bank v. Coleman* [2001] Q.B. 20 (CA) 30–32 Nourse L.J. doubted its utility. However, in *Etridge* in the House of Lords, Lord Nicholls equated Lord Scarman's requirement of "manifest disadvantage" in this context with the factor which gives rise to the need for the explanation of the transaction, and dispensed with the label of "manifest disadvantage" for it, thereby in effect getting rid of it (see para. 21-31). As to Irish law, there is no case on manifest disadvantage in this context, and as with the context of undue influence by improper pressure, the matter was resolved neither in *Carroll v. Carroll* [1999] 4 I.R. 241; [2000] 1 I.L.R.M. 210 (SC) (discussed in Annual Review of Irish Law 1998, pp.186-189 and *Annual Review of Irish Law 1999*, pp.121–125) nor in this year's cases but it is to be hoped that the requirement will be repudiated at the first opportunity.

Presumed undue influence   In cases of duress and actual undue influence, the remedy given respectively at law and in equity is a remedy for real pressure, for compulsion or coercion. Equity's remedies are not, however, confined to remedies for actual pressure; equity sees a similar vice where a contract is concluded between unequal parties, and therefore provides remedies for the weaker party, for example, by presuming that such undue influence was exercised by the stronger party over the weaker (presumed undue influence), or by focussing on the loss made by the weaker party (improvidence) or simply on the unfairness of the transaction (unconscionability).

In cases where undue influence is presumed, the court intervenes "on the ground of public policy and to prevent the relations which existed between the parties and the influence arising therefrom being abused" (*O'Flanagan v. Ray-Ger* (1963–1993) Ir. Co. L. Rep. 289, 299–300 *per* Costello J.). The focus is on the presumption, rather than on the undue influence, and to that extent, by presuming the pressure rather than by requiring it to be established directly or by inference, equity is providing a policy-motivated remedy for contracts entered into due to the weakness of one party. In the language of the older cases, such undue influence is presumed to prevent the "victimisation" of the weaker party. The leading common law case is probably the Irish case of *Kirwan v. Cullen* (1854) Ir. Ch. Rep. 322 but the later English case of *Allcard v. Skinner* (1887) 36 Ch. D 145 gets all the glory. For example, it is cited with approval by Denham J. in the Supreme Court in *Carroll v. Carroll* [2000] 1 I.L.R.M. 210, 222, 226 who therefore held that the reason for such equitable protection "is one of public policy – to protect a frail person".

Certain relationships "as a matter of law raise the presumption that undue influence has been exercised" (*Barclays Bank v. O'Brien* [1994] 1 A.C. 180 (HL) approving *Aboody*). Again, these are "relationships which are by presumption of law irrebuttably treated as relationships of trust and confidence" (*Royal Bank of Scotland v. Etridge (No. 2)* [1998] 4 All E.R. 705 (CA) 711). "The law has adopted a sternly protective attitude towards certain types of relationship in which one party acquires influence over another who is vulnerable and dependent and where, moreover, substantial gifts by the influenced or vulnerable person are not normally to be expected. Examples of relationship within this special class are parent and child, guardian and ward, trustee and beneficiary, solicitor and client, and medical advisor and patient. In these cases the law presumes, irrebuttably, that one party had influence over the other. The complainant need not prove he actually reposed trust and confidence in the other party. It is sufficient for him to prove the existence of the type of relationship" (*Etridge*, para. 18). The classic examples include the relationships of religious advisor and disciple (*Huguenin v. Baseley* (1807) 14 Ves. Jun. 273; *Kirwan v. Cullen* (1854) 2 Ir. Ch. Rep. 322; *Allcard v. Skinner* (1887) 36 Ch. D. 145 (CA)), of parent and (dependent) child, of doctor and patient, and of solicitor and client. The relationship of bank manager and client or husband and wife are not of this nature (as O'Donovan J. put it in this year's *Ulster Bank Ireland Ltd v. Fitzgerald* (High Court, November 9, 2001; – discussed below in the section on Surety Wives, Third Parties, and Undue Influence – where they are parties to the same contract, the relationship of husband and wife does not give rise to a presumption of undue influence), though actual undue influence by abuse of relationship may be established in those cases. Lord Nicholls' folding of manifest disadvantage in *Etridge* into the matter calling for explanation was intended to apply also to this species of undue influence. Again, there is no Irish case on manifest disadvantage in this context, and the matter was resolved neither in *Carroll v. Carroll* nor in this year's cases but it is to be hoped that the requirement will be repudiated at the first opportunity.

Rebutting the presumption   "Where the presumption exists, it can be rebutted by evidence which establishes on the balance of probability that the transaction was the consequence of the exercise by the donor of his own free will and not the result of undue influence" (*Carroll v. Carroll* [1998] 2 I.L.R.M. 218 (HC) 229 *per* Shanley J.; compare: the recipient must prove that the contract resulted from the "free exercise of the donor's will" (per Cotton L.J. in *Allcard* *v. Skinner*)). The evidence must establish that the contract was "the independent and well-understood act of a man in a position to exercise a free judgment based on information as full as that of the donee" (*Johnson v. Butress* (1936) 56 C.L.R. 113 (HCA) 134-135 *per* Dixon J. approved *Carroll v. Carroll* [2000] 1 I.L.R.M. 210 (SC) 223 *per* Denham J.).

The facts of the case may establish such a free exercise of the donor's will: *McCormack v. Bennett*, High Court, Finlay J., July 2, 1973. But the courts have become fixated with looking for independent legal advice as a proxy for establishing the free exercise of the donor's will. For example, the Court of Appeal in *Etridge* held that "[a]s between the complainant and the alleged wrongdoer, the presumption cannot be rebutted merely by evidence that the complainant understood what he or she was doing or intended to do it, but only by showing that she was either free form the influence of the alleged wrongdoer or had been placed by the receipt of independent legal advice in an equivalent position ... the problem is not lack of understanding but lack of independence ... The question is ... how the intention was produced" ([1998] 4 All E.R. 705, 714). The leading case on this role of independent legal advice is *Inche Noriah v. Shaik Allie Bin Amar* [1929] A.C. 127 (PC); followed in Ireland in *Gregg v. Kidd* [1956] 1 I.R. 183 (Budd J.) and *Carroll v. Carroll* [2000] 1 I.L.R.M. 210 (SC) 223 *per* Denham J. However, in the House of Lords in *Etridge*, Lord Nicholls said that although such advice may often lead to the donor's consent, nevertheless "a person may understand fully the implications of a proposed transaction ... and yet still be acting under the undue influence of another. Proof of outside advice does not, of itself, necessarily show that the subsequent completion of the transaction was free from the exercise of undue influence" (para 20). In principle, the matters which go to rebutting this species of presumed undue influence may also go to rebutting the inference of undue influence in the cases above where an inference of actual undue influence is raised by a combination of a relationship of influence and a transaction within it calling for explanation.

Alternative structures   Under the traditional view of undue influence, the "cases where a plaintiff seeks to set aside a gift or other transaction on the ground that it was procured by undue influence have been divided into two classes; firstly, those in which it can be expressly proved that undue influence was exercised ...; secondly, those in which the relations between donor and donee have at or shortly before the execution of a gift been such as to raise a presumption that the donor had influence over the donee" (*O'Flanagan v. Ray Ger* (1963–1993) Ir. Co. L. Rep. 289, 299 (Costello J., April 28, 1983); followed by Shanley J. in the High Court in *Carroll v. Carroll* [1998] 2 I.L.R.M. 218, 228-230). This traditional view was repackaged by the Court of Appeal in *BCCI v. Aboody* [1990] 1 Q.B. 923 (CA) and approved by the House of Lords in *Barclays Bank v. O'Brien* [1994] 1 A.C. 180, so that actual undue influence (class 1 undue influence) comprised of improper pressure, whilst there were two species of presumed undue influence (class 2 undue influence), undue influence arising in a relationship irrebuttably presumed to be one of trust and confidence (class 2(a)) and undue influence presumed because a relationship of trust and confidence existed on the facts (class 2(b)). This mechanical structure was a strong form of the traditional understanding of undue influence at least since *Kirwan v. Cullen* (1854) Ir. Ch. Rep. 322 and *Allcard v. Skinner* (1887) 36 Ch. D. 145.

The *Aboody* structure did not commend itself to Lord Clyde in *Etridge* who "question[ed] the wisdom of the practice which has grown up, particularly since *Aboody* of attempting to make classifications of cases of undue influence ... [which] to my mind add mystery rather than illumination" (para. 92; compare Lord Hobhouse at para. 98). The *Aboody* structure was a mechanical classification which owed more to jurisdictional history (the fact that the two classes of undue influence were creatures of equity rather than the common law) than to substance (ignoring the fact that duress at law and class 1 undue influence were substantively similar doctrines aimed at providing remedies for the exercise of improper pressure, whilst the very different class 2 undue influence cases and unconscionability were substantively similar doctrines motivated by underlying policy concerns). Consequently, much to be preferred is a structure which combines the analysis of duress with actual undue influence, and combines the analysis of both species of presumed undue influence with unconscionability.

Lord Nicholls' approach in *Etridge* is much more fluid than, and vastly superior to, the mechanical *Aboody/O'Brien* classification, the language of which he quite properly eschewed in his speech (cp Lord Clyde and Lord Hobhouse above; cf Lord Scott at paras. 151–152). But, he took what on the latter classification was class 2(b) presumed undue influence and transformed it into a species of actual undue influence. This move is explicit in the speech of Lord Hobhouse (see paras. 103–107, where he distinguishes between actual and presumed undue influence, adopts the *Aboody* language only to disparage it, and pours cold water over treating the 2(b) cases as cases of presumption rather than of actual undue influence; see also para 161 *per* Lord Scott). This appears to be a radical move which may come under fire in future commentary and authority. Nevertheless, it has to be admitted that there are some affinities between actual undue influence by improper pressure and undue influence arising from the abuse of a relationship. This may be seen in the judgment of Keane C.J. *ex tempore* (Murphy and Murray JJ. concurring) in *Johnson v. Church of Scientology*, Supreme Court, November 7, 2001, reversing the High Court made an order for further and better particulars in respect of the plaintiff's allegations of pressure against the defendant, and upholding the High Court, refused to strike out the plaintiff's claim for failure to comply with an extraordinarily wide order of discovery with which she had in any event attempted to comply. Keane C.J. said of the plaintiff's claim that:

"... she seeks a declaration that the payments made to her ought to be set aside as having been procured by the undue influence of the first named defendant and an order to repay that. That of course is a plea and raises as a cause of action which is well known to the law and established for many centuries indeed that person who can be shown to have paid over money or transferred property because of undue influence exerted upon them by persons who occupy a particular relationship such as a person in a religious capacity can be ordered to repay the money or property to the plaintiff if indeed it has been shown to have been procured by the undue influence of the person occupying a particular relationship to the person concerned which in the view of the law would give rise to a presumption of undue influence. So far as that is concerned, whether it succeeds or not of course is entirely a different matter, but that is a plea and it raises a cause of action which is known to the law" (6–7).

On the basis of these principles, he held that the defendants were entitled to further particulars at that stage as to what precisely is being alleged against them and especially to particulars indicating what form this pressure is alleged to have taken. The plaintiff may be alleging that the defendant had exercised actual undue influence either by the imposition of improper pressure, or by abusing the relationship of trust and confidence between them; either way, the defendant is entitled to particulars of the pressure or of the abuse of the relationship; although if the relationship is established, the mere fact of the payments will be sufficient indicia of the abuse of the relationship, and particulars of the payments would therefore be sufficient to call for an explanation by the defendant. Or the plaintiff may be alleging that undue influence should be irrebutably presumed because the relationship was functionally that of religious advisor and disciple (by analogy with the great cases of *Huguenin v. Baseley*, *Kirwan v. Cullen* and *Allcard v. Skinner*); in which case again, all that will have to be established for the presumption to be raised and to cast on the defendant the onus of rebuttal are the facts of the relationship and the payment.

Although much of what was achieved in *Etridge* is to be welcomed, some aspects of the approach give some pause. In particular, Lord Nicholls almost seemed to smuggle the cases of a relationship irrebutably presumed to be one of trust and confidence into the abuse of relationship cases (that is to say that he seemed to coat-tail the former class 2(a) cases with the former class 2(b) cases into his expanded category of actual undue influence; see e.g., para. 18; Lord Scott's treatment is similar: see, e.g., para. 153). However, if there is, as argued above, a difference in substance between intervention to remedy improper pressure and intervention for policy reasons, then abuse of relationship cases are very different from cases of a relationship irrebutably presumed to be one of trust and confidence because the former are examples of a remedy for improper pressure whilst the latter are examples of intervention for policy reasons. Hence, the treatment here has followed Etridge in accommodating the abuse of relationship cases within the rubric of actual undue influence, but has not followed it by treating cases of a relationship irrebuttably presumed to be one of trust and confidence as analytically distinct (cp. Beatson, *Anson*, pp.287–288). Consequently, much to be preferred is the structure followed here which combines the analysis of duress with actual undue influence as examples of remedies for coercion, and combines the analysis of both species of presumed undue influence with unconscionability as examples of intervention for policy reasons.

Surety wives, third parties, and undue influence   In a contract between P. and D., which D. entered because of the undue influence exercised upon D. by a third party T., English and Irish courts have decided that D can only avoid the contract as against P., if P. had (constructive) notice of T.'s undue influence, and did not take reasonable steps to ensure that D. freely consented to the transaction. According to Lord Browne-Wilkinson in *Barclays Bank v. O'Brien*:

> "[Where D.] has been induced to stand as surety for [T.]'s debts by his undue influence ... [then D.] has an equity against T. to set aside that transaction. Under the ordinary principles of equity, D.'s right to set aside that transaction will be enforceable against ... [P.] if P. had actual or constructive notice of the facts giving rise to D.'s equity. ... Therefore, where D. has agreed to stand as surety for T.'s debts as a result of T.'s undue influence ... P. will take subject to D.'s equity to set aside the transaction if the circumstances are such as to put P. on inquiry as to the circumstances in which D. agreed to stand surety. . . .
>
> It follows that unless P. who is put on inquiry takes reasonable steps to satisfy himself that D's agreement to stand surety has been properly obtained, P. will have constructive notice of D's rights ... [the requirement of such reasonable steps will be satisfied if P] insists that D attend a private meeting (in the absence of T) with a representative of P. at which D is told of the extent of the liability as surety, warned of the risk D is running, and urged to take independent legal advice...."

Note that in such three-party cases, the function of the legal advice is simply to protect the bank; this function is fundamentally different from the function it is thought to have in rebutting the inference or presumption of undue influence in two-party cases. In the three-party cases, the proof of adequate independent advice is enough to allow the bank to enforce the transaction; whereas, in the two-party cases, even if there is independent advice, the inference or presumption might not be rebutted.

This analysis seems to have been adopted by the Irish Supreme Court in *Bank of Nova Scotia v. Hogan* [1996] 3 I.R. 239; [1997] 2 I.L.R.M. 407 (SC) (see *Annual Review of Irish Law 1996*, pp. 219–227). After *O'Brien*, banking practice in England had been not to hold a private meeting but instead to require that the wife seek legal advice, and many of the huge number of subsequent cases which gave rise to *Etridge* involved deficiencies in the quality of the legal advice given to the wives and in the system of such independent advice (see *Etridge*, paras. 51-53).

Lord Nicholls stressed that "quite simply, a bank is put on inquiry whenever a wife offers to stand surety for her husband's debts" (para. 44, emphasis added), and he concluded that a bank must insist "that the wife attend a private meeting with a representative of the bank at which she is told of the extent of her liability as surety, warned of the risk she is running and urged to take independent legal advice. In exceptional cases the bank, to be safe, has to insist that the wife is separately advised" (para. 50). If the bank insists instead that she take independent legal advice, then, since:

> "... the bank is looking for its protection to legal advice given to the wife by a solicitor who, in this respect, is acting solely for her, I consider the bank should take steps to check directly with the wife the name of the solicitor she wishes to act for her. To this end, in future the bank should communicate directly with the wife, informing her that for its own protection it will require written confirmation from a solicitor, acting for her, to the effect that the solicitor has fully explained to her the nature of the documents and the practical implications they will have for her. She should be told that the purpose of this requirement is that thereafter she should not be able to dispute she is legally bound by the documents once she has signed them. She should be asked to nominate a solicitor whom she is willing to instruct to advise her, separately from her husband, and act for her in giving the necessary confirmation to the bank. She should be told that, if she wishes, the solicitor may be the same solicitor as is acting for her husband in the transaction. If a solicitor is already acting for the husband and the wife, she should be asked whether she would prefer that a different solicitor should act for her regarding the bank's requirement for confirmation from a solicitor."

This has been widely welcomed as an important development of the *O'Brien* principle; (for example, Oldham [2002] C.L.J. 29 said that it "builds upon" (30) and "constitutes a very welcome further development of the principles expounded in" *O'Brien* (32), while for O'Sullivan (2002) 118 L.Q.R. 337 it clarifies and develops *O'Brien*, anchors it more firmly in orthodoxy, and irons out a range of uncertainties (338)), and since *Hogan* largely adopted *O'Brien*, one might expect that Irish courts will soon follow the path beaten by Lord Nicholls (Breslin (2002) 9 (2) C.L.P. 35; White (2002) 20 I.L.T. (ns) 70).

Unfortunately, the issue was not considered by O'Donovan J. in *Ulster*

Bank Ireland Ltd v. Fitzgerald, High Court, November 9, 2001. The plaintiff had recovered judgment against the first defendant in respect of a debt which his wife, the second defendant, had guaranteed, and in these proceedings the plaintiff sought to enforce the guarantee against her. She sought to resist on the grounds that of "undue and wrongful influence exercised over her by the First Named Defendant who is her husband; a wrongful influence of which the plaintiffs were aware, or are deemed to have been aware" (3).

O'Donovan J. accepted that she signed the guarantees because her husband prevailed upon her to do so and that had she not done so it would have compounded their existing marital problems (6). He had also accepted the bank manager's evidence that each defendant had signed the guarantees in the bank manager's presence in his office, they were not present together, and prior to their signatures, he had explained to each of them the meaning and effect of the guarantees, and he had advised the second defendant to seek legal advice. Nevertheless, she signed them 'on the spot' (3, 6). And these facts were fatal to the second defendant's claim:

> "I am prepared to accept that [her husband] ... may, indeed, have exercised inordinate pressure on his wife to execute the guarantees ... and I am prepared to accepted that she believed that she had little option but to sign them. Moreover, while I do not think it necessary for the purposes of this judgment to determine whether or not the influence in that regard exercised by [him] over his wife was unlawful, I think that it may well have been so. However, whether or not it was, I heard no evidence whatsoever to suggest that [the bank manager], or, indeed, any other representative of the plaintiff bank had even an inkling that there were difficulties in the [defendants'] marriage ... or that there was any other reason by [the second defendant] might not have been a free agent; in the sense that she did not do so of her own free will, when she executed the ... guarantees. ... where they are parties to the same contract, the relationship of husband and wife does not give rise to a presumption of undue influence and, accordingly, the burden of proving undue influence is on the party alleging it, I am not persuaded that the plaintiffs had constructive notice that the [second defendant] executed the ... guarantees as a result of undue influence exercised over her by her husband; if that be the case" (7; see also 9).

On the *O'Brien/Hogan* formulation, this is an entirely orthodox holding, as Lord Browne-Wilkinson's approach requires that there be facts to put the bank manager on enquiry. In the absence of such facts, and having been advised to consult a solicitor, the guarantee executed by the second defendant was valid and enforceable. The *Etridge* formulation strengthened the position of the surety wife in many ways, but in particular, Lord Nicholls took the view that the bank should always be put on notice of the possibility of undue influence by the husband by the mere fact of the wife's suretyship; indeed, he went further, and held his modified *O'Brien* approach applied "in every case where the relationship between the surety and debtor is non-commercial"; in such cases, he held that the creditor-bank "must always take reasonable steps to bring home to the individual guarantor the risks he is running by standing as surety" (para 87). In *Ulster Bank Ireland Ltd v. Fitzgerald*, in effect applying the *O'Brien* standard (though without direct reference to it), O'Donovan J. held that the bank was not put on notice of the husband's undue influence on his wife, but even if it had been, the steps the bank manager had taken would have counted as reasonable, thereby allowing the bank to enforce its guarantee for two reasons. However, had the *Etridge* standard applied, whether or not the bank actually had notice of the husband's undue influence would have been irrelevant; the mere fact that it was a non-commercial guarantee would have been sufficient to put the bank on notice; nevertheless the fact that the bank manager had taken reasonable steps would still have allowed the bank to enforce its guarantee.

Criminal Law

ABOLITION OF COMMON LAW OFFENCES

In *Grealis and Corbett v. Director of Public Prosecutions* [2002] 1 I.L.R.M. 241 (SC), the Supreme Court held that where a common law offence was repealed by statute, it ceased to exist for all purposes. Thus, in the absence of any transitional saving provision in the repealing legislation, no prosecution could be maintained in respect of the abolished offence after the repealing statute had taken effect. The background was as follows. The first applicant had been charged with three counts of assault, two contrary to common law and one contrary to section 47 of the Offences against the Person Act 1861. These incidents were alleged to have occurred in May 1997. The second applicant had been charged with assault contrary to common law and section 47 of the 1861 Act, as amended by section 10 of the Criminal Justice (Public Order) Act 1994. He was alleged to have committed the assault in February 1997. The common law offence of assault had been abolished by the Non-Fatal Offences Against the Person Act 1997 (see the 1997 Annual Review, 304-313) which came into effect in August 1997. The 1997 Act had not been in force on the dates that the two applicants were alleged to have committed the offences nor on the date that the second applicant's summons was issued; but it had come into force when the first applicant's three summonses were issued.

Shortly after the Non-Fatal Offences Against the Person Act 1997 had come into force, a number of cases arose which challenged the continued validity of prosecutions under the pre-1997 law which were pending when the 1997 Act came into effect. In light of these cases, the Oireachtas enacted the Interpretation (Amendment) Act 1997, which provided that, subject to the Constitution, the repeals effected by the Non-Fatal Offences Against the Person Act 1997 were to operate prospectively only. The intention of the 1997 Act appeared to be to attempt to provide that pending prosecutions under the pre-1997 law could proceed notwithstanding the repeal of the relevant common law offences by the 1997 Act. In the immediate wake of the passing of the Interpretation (Amendment) Act 1997, there had been conflicting views expressed about whether this intended result could be achieved in light of the relevant constitutional provisions (see *Annual Review of Irish Law 1997*, pp.284-5). The decision in *Grealis and Corbett v. Director of Public Prosecutions* [2002] 1 I.L.R.M. 241 (SC) confirmed, in effect, that the absence of a transitional provision in the Non-Fatal Offences Against the Person Act

1997 itself precluded pending cases from proceeding.

Delivering one of the leading judgments, Keane C.J. referred to the extensive case law on the effect of the repeal by statute of a common law offence. This included *Miller's case* (1764) 1 Black W. 451, *R v. MacKenzie* (1820) Russ & Ry 429 and *Massey v. United States*, 291 US 608 (1934). The Chief Justice held that the effect was that the repealed offence ceased to exist for all purposes and no prosecution could be maintained in respect of it after the repealing statute had taken effect. On the specific issue that arose in the cases, he noted that section 28(1) of the Non-Fatal Offences against the Person Act 1997 (which had repealed the common law offence of assault) was clear and unambiguous, and the only construction of which it was capable was that the common law offences to which it applied were abolished from the coming into force of the section.

Thus, in the absence of any saving provision, the repeal prevented any prosecution of the offences alleged against the applicants. As there were no transitional provision contained in the Non-Fatal Offences against the Person Act 1997 itself, he concluded that no proceedings could be instituted in respect of the abolished offences once the Act had come into force. As to whether such a transitional arrangement could be implied, he was of the view that the doctrine of the separation of powers meant that the courts could not infer or imply transitional provisions into a statute where the Oireachtas had failed to include them. The approach thus taken by the Supreme Court rejected contrary views expressed by McGuinness J. in *Quinlivan v. Governor of Portlaoise Prison* [1998] 2 I.R. 112 (*Annual Review of Irish Law 1997*, pp.284-5), which had been followed by O'Higgins J. in *Mullins v. Harnett* [1998] 4 I.R. 426 (*Annual Review of Irish Law 1998*, p.205).

On the effect of the Interpretation (Amendment) Act 1997, the Court noted that it provided, in general, that the repeal of common law offences was to be deemed to apply prospectively only. In so far as this applied to such offences repealed after November 1997, there was no difficulty. But the issue in *Grealis and Corbett* was whether this could apply to a repeal effected prior to November 1997, such as the repeals effected by the Non-Fatal Offences against the Person Act 1997. The Interpretation (Amendment) Act 1997 provided that (a) it should apply to pre-November 1997 repeals but (b) only in so far as this retrospective application was constitutionally permissible. In *Grealis and Corbett* the Supreme Court unanimously found that such retrospective application was not constitutionally permissible, thus concluding that the Interpretation (Amendment) Act 1997 applied prospectively only. In a concurring judgment, Denham J. took the view that a purported validation retrospectively of the law would conflict with the accused's right to a trial in due course of law in Article 38.1 of the Constitution because the actions involved in the offence 'had ceased to be an offence [in August 1997] and remained so at the time of the issuing of the summonses.'

The effect of the *Grealis and Corbett* case is that no further trials of assaults committed prior to the 1997 Act came into effect in August 1997were permissible after that date; this lacuna would apply to a large number of cases, though obviously its impact would lessen as the years progress. Because, even were complaints of pre- August 1997 assaults to be made, say, in 2001 there would be other difficulties arising from possible prejudicial delay which might become applicable at that remove. As for future repeals of common law offences, the provisions of the Interpretation (Amendment) Act 1997 would prevent the type of difficulty which was identified in the *Grealis and Corbett* case. It is notable, indeed, that in another major amending statute enacted in 2001, the Criminal Justice (Theft and Fraud Offences) Act 2001, a specific transitional and saving provision was included: see 219, below.

In conclusion, we should note that not all assaults at common law or dealt with by statute were affected by the Non-Fatal Offences against the Person Act 1997. Thus, in *S.O.C. v. Governor of Curragh Prison*, Supreme Court, July 13, 2001, the applicant had been convicted of indecent assault and sentenced to prison. He appealed his conviction on the grounds that the proper description of the offence had been altered to "sexual assault" by virtue of section 2 of the Criminal Law (Rape) (Amendment) Act 1990 and that the offence of indecent assault had been abolished by section 22(1)(a) of the Non-Fatal Offences against the Person Act 1997. The claims was rejected in the High Court and, on appeal, by the Supreme Court. In dismissing the claim, the Court held that the effect of section 2 of the Criminal Law (Rape) (Amendment) Act 1990 had been to change the name of the offence while leaving its nature and constituents unaltered. While the Court accepted that indecent assault is a common law offence, the Non- Fatal Offences against the Person Act 1997 did not have the effect of abolishing the offence of indecent assault nor was it intended to do so. In that respect, the Court's decision in *Grealis and Corbett* did not apply to the circumstances of the instant case. It seems likely that a similar conclusion would be made in respect of other sexual assault cases, including older child abuse cases. In such cases, the main argument advanced for prohibiting trial will continue to be the effect of delay.

APPEALS

Miscarriage of justice   In *The People (DPP) v. Meleady and Grogan (No.2)*, Court of Criminal Appeal, March 20, 2001, the issue arose as to whether a certificate of a miscarriage of justice pursuant to section 9 of the Criminal Procedure Act 1993 should issue. The applicants had, in a *cause celebre* of the 1980s and 1990s, been twice tried and convicted of, *inter alia,* theft of a car: see the background discussed in *Annual Review of Irish Law 1997*, p.263. On appeal from their second conviction, the Court of Criminal Appeal had quashed the convictions but refused to grant a section 9 certificate. On further appeal, the Supreme Court held that the Court had erred in law in refusing to grant the certificate by reason only of the fact that the guilt or innocence of the applicants had not been determined by a jury at the trial where non-disclosed material had been available to the accused. The Supreme Court held that a refusal might still be made and thus remitted the case to a differently composed Court of Criminal Appeal: see *The People (DPP) v. Meleady and Grogan*, Supreme Court, March 4 1997 (*Annual Review of Irish Law 1997*, pp.263-4).

In this second application for a section 9 certificate, the Court of Criminal Appeal permitted a number of witnesses, including the applicants and another accused, to give evidence. It ultimately concluded that a section 9 certificate should issue. The Court accepted that the mere possibility, however reasonable, that had the matter gone to a retrial a jury would have had a reasonable doubt on foot of the newly discovered facts is not a ground for granting the certificate under section 9 of the Criminal Procedure Act 1993. The Court held that, in that situation the applicants would not have established, as a matter of probability as distinct from possibility, that the newly discovered facts would have led to an acquittal.

Applying the principles laid down by the Supreme Court in *The People (DPP) v. Pringle (No. 2)* [1997] 2 I.R. 225 (*Annual Review of Irish Law 1997*, pp.262-3), the Court in *Meleady and Grogan (No.2)* held that a miscarriage of justice need not necessarily be certified in every case where, had the possibility of a new trial been open, it would not have been appropriate to apply the proviso leading to a dismissal of the appeal and refusal of a new trial. To do so, the Court held, would interpret the rights under section 9 far too broadly and conflict with the concept of a civil onus of proving miscarriage of justice as a matter of probability. As to the instant case, the Court noted that one of the newly discovered facts was that the trial judge would have excluded the only evidence implicating the applicants and which would therefore have meant that there was no evidence against the applicants that could have gone to a jury. This showed that there had, in fact, been a miscarriage of justice and a section 9 certificate should issue.

Finally, in coming to this conclusion, the Court noted that it was not making a finding as to whether the applicants were in fact innocent of actual involvement in the events surrounding the offences in question. This comment might be regarded as being superfluous since the concept of finding a person 'innocent' plays no part in a criminal trial; to that extent it is curious and clearly *obiter*. Moreover, while it is notable that the phrase 'miscarriage of justice' is not defined in the 1993 Act, it must be assumed that a trial which falls into this category is one which has failed to meet the ends of justice, a concept which is central to the role of the courts under Article 34. To that extent, the courts role under the 1993 Act is to determine whether that central concept has been applied. Where a finding has been made that the essence of justice has not been applied in a trial, that is where it has been miscarried, the courts have no further function. It would seem to be equally fatuous to add that they might apologise for such a miscarriage as it would be for them to make some irrelevant comment about whether this relates to the innocence of the persons involved.

BAIL

Pending appeal In *The People v. Quinn*, Court of Criminal Appeal, February 15, 2001, the Court applied the principles set out by the Supreme Court in *The People v. Corbally* [2001] 2 I.L.R.M. 102 (SC) (*Annual Review of Irish Law 2000*, p.116) in rejecting the applicant's claim for bail pending appeal. Following a plea of guilty, the applicant was convicted of the offence of larceny and sentenced to nine months' imprisonment. The applicant sought bail, pending an application for leave to appeal against the severity of his sentence. The application was on two grounds: that the sentence would expire before the hearing of the appeal; and that there were good arguable grounds that no sentence of imprisonment ought to have been imposed. Applying the *Corbally* case, the Court held that the mere fact that a sentence will have been served before an appeal is heard is not a ground upon which bail should be granted: the applicant for bail in this situation is a convicted person and the court should therefore exercise its discretion to grant bail sparingly. Moreover, the issue of the expiry of the sentence prior to the hearing of an appeal should not be considered in isolation and the Court should be satisfied that there is a reasonable prospect of the sentence being reduced on the appeal before it would grant bail on the ground that the sentence will expire before the appeal date. In the instant case, the offence in question was a serious offence for which a sentence of imprisonment would seem appropriate; since it carried a maximum penalty of 10 years' imprisonment, a sentence of nine months was at the lower end of the sentencing band. In addition, since all matters in mitigation were opened before the trial judge, the Court of Criminal Appeal was satisfied neither that there was a reasonable prospect of the sentence being reduced on appeal nor that the applicant had established a strong chance of success on appeal.

CONTEMPT OF COURT

Obstruction of Tribunal of Inquiry In *Flood v. Lawlor*, High Court, January 15, 2001, Smyth J. found the respondent, a member of Dáil Éireann, guilty of contempt of court. The contempt arose from the respondent's failure to comply with a number of orders, made by Smyth J. and upheld by the Supreme Court on appeal, which had been sought by the applicant, who was the sole member of a Tribunal of Inquiry into Certain Planning Matters and Payments and which had been established by resolution of Dáil Éireann. The orders had sought production by the respondent of various documents, in particular bank and other financial records. The circumstances in which a member of Dáil Éireann was found in contempt in connection with a tribunal established by Dáil Éireann itself and the imposition of a prison sentence on the respondent attracted enormous publicity at the time.

In a lengthy judgment, Smyth J. held that he was satisfied beyond all reasonable doubt there had been substantial non-compliance with the orders on all the material placed before the Tribunal. He described the non-compliance as 'blatant defiance' of the orders made. He also held that the respondent's actions could not be described as unintentional. Turning to the penalties to be imposed, he first imposed a fine of £10,000, commenting that in imposing a fine he had considered, *inter alia*, the serious nature of the contempt and all pleas of mitigation, the nature and extent and the volume of the transactions, and the defendant's disclosed income and earning capacities. As to whether a term of imprisonment should be imposed, he accepted (citing *Thorpe v. Thorpe* [1998] 2 F.L.R. 127) that it was not a matter of automatic consequence of the breach of a court order that imprisonment should follow and equally, there was no principle that there should be no imprisonment for a 'first offence.' In the instant case, Smyth J. held that by his failure to make full and proper discovery and his omissions in that regard, the respondent could be viewed in material fact and to a serious degree to have obstructed and hindered the Tribunal in the performance of its function by non-compliance with the orders. In structuring the punitive element of the sanction of the Court for past contempt, he stated that he was mindful that not only was imprisonment a most intrusive sanction interfering with the liberty of the person affected, but also his whole personal and family life, his financial position and his reputation. Against this background, he imposed a three month sentence of imprisonment, suspending all but seven days of the prison term until November 2001. The effect was that the respondent was required to serve seven days imprisonment in January 2001. In a further contempt application in the High Court in July 2001 which was later appealed unsuccessfully to the Supreme Court, *Flood v. Lawlor (No.2)* Supreme Court, 12 December 2001 (see *The Irish Times,* December 13, 2001), Smyth J. found the respondent in further contempt, imposed a further fine of £5,000 and ordered that he serve a further seven days in prison, to be served in November 2001. On appeal, the Supreme Court, in an *ex tempore* judgment, upheld the decision of the High Court but postponed execution of the term of imprisonment until January 2002 to facilitate the respondent travelling to the United States over the Christmas 2001 period. In postponing the sentence, the Supreme Court took into account that the respondent had already made preparations to visit his son and daughter-in-law, who was pregnant at the time. Again, this decision received a great deal of publicity at the time.

CORRUPTION AND FRAUD

The Prevention of Corruption (Amendment) Act 2001 amended the Prevention of Corruption Act 1906 for the purpose of ratifying three Conventions, each of which aimed at preventing corruption with an international dimension. These Conventions were drawn up by: the European Union, the OECD and the Council of Europe. The 2001 Act also extended the scope of existing corruption legislation with a purely domestic element. The three Conventions ratified by the 2001 Act were: the 1997 EU Convention on the Fight against Corruption involving Officials of the European Communities or Officials of Member States of the European Union; the 1997 OECD Convention on Bribery of Foreign Public Officials in International Business Transactions; and the 1999 Council of Europe Criminal Law Convention on Corruption.

Corruption of or by an agent Section 2 of the 2001 Act inserts a new section 1 into the 1906 Act, which deals with corruption of or by an agent. Three changes were made to the original offence in the 1906 Act. First, the 1906 Act only applied to corruption of an agent, whereas the revised section 1 offence now applies to corruption of a third party, for example a spouse of the agent, with a view to influencing the conduct of the agent. Second, the definition of 'agent' was extended to cover categories of office holders and officials, both national and foreign, not covered by the original 1906 Act. Third, the maximum penalty for the offence was being increased from seven years imprisonment and/or a fine of £50,000 to 10 years imprisonment and/or an unlimited fine.

Corruption occurring partially in State Section 3 of the 2001 Act provides that a person may be tried in the State for the offence of corruption if any element of the offence occurred in the jurisdiction, for example, where an offer of a bribe is made abroad but received in Ireland. This implemented the elements of the three Conventions referred to which require the national law of participating states to apply to corrupt acts which occur wholly or partly on their territories.

Corruption occurring outside State Section 4 involves an express intention to apply certain elements of the corruption offences in the 2001 Act extra-territorially, overcoming the normal presumption against extra-territoriality: see Byrne and McCutcheon, *The Irish Legal System*, 4th ed. (Butterworths, Dublin, 2001), p.508. Section 4 provides that it applies to corruption abroad involving Irish office holders or officials. Prior to the 2001 Act it could be argued that, if the offence were limited to the national territory, an Irish office holder or official could evade the Prevention of Corruption Acts by accepting a bribe while outside Ireland.

Corruption in office Section 5 of the 2001 Act created a new offence of corruption in office. It applies to Irish office holders and officials and seeks to deal with a situation not covered by the offence of corruption. The offence of corruption deals only with situations where an office holder or official seeks or accepts a bribe from someone in return for doing or not doing some act. Section 5 of the 2001 Act makes it an offence for an Irish office holder or official to engage in any act or omission with the intention of corruptly obtaining a gift, consideration or advantage for that office holder or official or any other person. This was intended to deal with a situation where an office holder or official acts corruptly without the involvement of any other person, for example by making a biased decision in order corruptly to benefit a member of his or her family.

Liability of directors and officers for offences by corporate bodies Section 6 of the 2001 Act is a standard provision which provides that where any offences dealt with by the Act are committed by a corporate body and can be attributed to the acts or omissions of any director, manager, secretary or other officer, those individuals as well as the corporate body can be prosecuted as well as the corporate body. This can indeed be described as a standard provision, though until recently it was normally only to be found in 'regulatory' legislation, such as environmental or consumer protection legislation. But a similar provision can also now be found in a comparable piece of criminal legislation, the Criminal Justice (Theft and Fraud Offences) Act 2001: see 219, below.

DEATH PENALTY ABOLITION

The Twenty First Amendment of the Constitution Act 2001, which was approved by a referendum held in June 2001, provided for the deletion of all references to the death penalty in the Constitution. It gave effect to recommendations made in the *Report of the Constitution Review Group* (1996) and in the *Third Progress Report of the All-party Oireachtas Committee on the Constitution* (1999).

Prior to 1964, the death penalty was applicable to murder, though no execution had been carried out since 1954. The Criminal Justice Act 1964 abolished the death penalty for offences other than treason, capital murder and certain military offences. The death penalty was abolished in statute law for these remaining offences by the Criminal Justice Act 1990 (see *Annual Review of Irish Law 1990*, p.195). The Twenty First Amendment of the Constitution Act 2001 completed the process by deleting all references to the death penalty from the Constitution.

The two references to the death penalty in the Constitution prior to the 21st Amendment were to be found in Articles 13.6 and 40.4.5°. Article 13.6 provided:

"The right of pardon and the power to commute or remit punishment imposed by any court exercising criminal jurisdiction are hereby vested in the President, but such power of commutation or remission may, except in capital cases, also be conferred by law on other authorities."

Article 40.4.5°, which is part of the *habeas corpus* provisions of the Constitution, provided:

"Where an order is made under this section by the High Court or a judge thereof for the production of the body of a person who is under sentence of death, the High Court or such judge thereof shall further order that the execution of the said sentence of death shall be deferred until after the body of such person has been produced before the High Court and the lawfulness of his detention has been determined and if, after such deferment, the detention of such person is determined to be lawful, the High Court shall appoint a day for the execution of the said sentence of death and that sentence shall have effect with the substitution of the day so appointed for the day originally fixed for the execution thereof."

The changes effected by the 21st Amendment relate to four Articles of the Constitution, Articles 13, 15, 28 and 40. They were: a new Article 15.5.2° to the effect that the Oireachtas shall not enact any law providing for the imposition of the death penalty; the deletion of the reference to the death penalty in Article 13.6; the deletion of Article 40.4.5°; and the amendment of Article 28.3.3°, which deals with times of war and armed rebellion, to exclude the new Article 15.5.2° from the override provisions of that Article so that the prohibition on the reintroduction of the death penalty will apply even in time of war or armed rebellion.

As was pointed out during the Oireachtas debate on the amendment proposal, without a constitutional prohibition the death penalty could have been reintroduced again by statute, though it must be admitted that this would have been extremely in light of the State's international commitments. Thus, Article 1 of the Sixth Protocol to the European Convention on Human Rights, which the State ratified in 1994, prohibits use of the death penalty in peace time, but allows for a derogation in time of war or imminent threat of war. In addition, the Second Optional Protocol to the UN International Covenant on Civil and Political Rights, ratified by the State in 1993, also abolishes the death penalty but allowed for the possibility of a reservation in time of war. This reservation was not availed of by the State on ratification in 1993. During the Oireachtas debate, the Minister for Justice also noted that Sweden has proposed an additional protocol to the European Convention on Human Rights to abolish the death penalty completely and that the Irish Government had been supportive of this proposal.

DEFENCES

Provocation   In *The People v. McDonagh*, Court of Criminal Appeal, May 31, 2001, the Court of Criminal Appeal again considered the subjective nature of the defence of provocation in Irish law. The defendant in this case had been found guilty of murder in the Central Criminal Court. The evidence was that he had stabbed his wife after separating her and another women who were fighting. The applicant submitted that the trial judge failed to direct the jury adequately on the question of intent to kill or cause serious injury, in particular to have regard to his attitude after the stabbing as evidence of an absence on his part of an intention to kill or cause serious bodily harm. The Court of Criminal Appeal dismissed the defendant's appeal against conviction. The Court (whose judgment was delivered by Murray J.) applied the purely subjective test in relation to the issue of provocation in a murder trial, as laid down in *The People v. MacEoin* [1978] I.R. 34 and affirmed in *The People v. Kelly* [2000] 2 I.R. 1 and *The People v. Davis* [2001] 2 I.L.R.M. 651 (see *Annual Review of Irish Law 2000*, pp.120-23). The Court considered that it was for the trial judge in the first instance to decide whether there is any evidence on which provocation could properly be allowed to be considered by a jury. In this respect, a trial judge must decide whether, on the state of the evidence, it would be open to a jury to conclude that it was reasonably possible that the accused had been the subject of provocation that triggered off a total loss of self-control, having regard to the particular accused, given his state of mind, his personality and all the circumstances. In the instant case, as the evidence established the presumption that a deliberate stabbing of the deceased in the manner alleged was intended to do her serious injury, and as that evidence had not been rebutted, the trial judge was correct in telling the jury that if they decided that the death was caused by non-accidental stabbing they should regard the homicide as murder;

DELAY

Assault   A number of assault cases raised the issue whether delay in proceeding with the prosecution were sufficiently long or prejudicial to justify granting an order of prohibition. In *Knowles v. Malone*, High Court, April 6, 2001, McKechnie J. applied well-established principles in concluding that, although there had been delay in proceeding with a prosecution of the applicant for assault, no prejudice had arisen. The applicant had been charged with assault causing harm contrary to section 3 of the Non-Fatal Offences against the Person Act 1997. The charge arose from an alleged assault of a man in January 1999, who subsequently died from his injuries. The Director of Public Prosecutions did not proceed with the preliminary examination of the charge until April 2000. The applicant contended that this amounted to excessive, unexplainable and inexcusable delay in the prosecution of his case. As already indicated, McKechnie J. refused to prohibit the prosecution. He held that, given the Gardaí had been involved in a murder enquiry, the initial periods of delay had not been excessive and were reasonable. While the applicant was entitled to feel aggrieved at the delay in presentation of the book of evidence at the preliminary examination, no specific prejudice had been alleged by the applicant, and he was not impaired in any way from mounting a full defence to the prosecution. Moreover, he concluded that the overall time lapse did not constitute excessive delay that would breach the applicant's constitutional right to a trial in due course of law and with reasonable expedition.

In *McNamara v. MacGruairc*, Supreme Court, July 5, 2001, a similar conclusion was reached in connection with an assault charge involving greater delay but no prejudice. The applicant was charged with being involved (along with a number of others) in an assault alleged to have occurred in August 1992. He was interviewed by Gardaí a short time after the incident and while the Garda inquiry had been completed by the end of August 1992, it was not until November 1994 that the applicant was arrested and charged with the offence in question. The book of evidence was served on him in December 1994. In January 1995 the applicant applied for an order of prohibition to prevent the prosecution proceeding on the grounds of delay. In 1996, the High Court refused the relief sought and, on further appeal, the Supreme Court affirmed this conclusion. In light of the extensive case law in this area, the Court accepted that over and above the right of an accused to have a fair trial, with the full panoply of rights that entails, there is an additional and sometimes overlapping unenumerated constitutional right to a speedy trial under Article 40.3 of the Constitution. The Court acknowledged that in the circumstances of the present case the applicant had made out a strong *prima facie* case of delay; but while the delay had been excessive and had not been adequately explained or justified by the prosecuting authorities, it had not prejudiced the applicant and accordingly the relief sought was refused. While the application of the principles in this case are unremarkable in one respect, it is notable that the Court was delivering judgment in the case five years after the appeal to the Court had been formally lodged. While there may clearly be an appropriate explanation for this further delay in the case, it seems an ironic situation to have arisen in the context of the issue being raised in the case. It clearly points to the need for greater judicial case management in these and other cases, a point mentioned in a different context by Keane C.J. in *Orange Communications Ltd v. Director of Telecommunications Regulation* [2000] 4 I.R. 159.

In a third case, *Marley v. Director of Public Prosecutions*, High Court, June 20, 2001, the delays had been more excessive and, on the circumstances, Kelly J. held that the delay had been prejudicial. The applicant is this case had been charged with assault occasioning actual bodily harm on a date unknown between 1970 and 1972, and assault on a date unknown in 1973. The two complainants were at the time residents at an industrial school where the applicant had been a member of staff. The offences charged were not sexual in nature, which is regarded as a relevant factor in whether dominion might have been exercised over the victims and whether this would in turn explain delay in making a complaint. No complaint was made concerning the alleged offences until 1997 and 1998 respectively. The applicant sought to prohibit the further prosecution of both offences on the grounds of delay. As indicated, Kelly J. granted the relief sought and granted a perpetual injunction restraining the respondent from proceeding further with the charges pending against the applicant in the Circuit Criminal Court.

Kelly J. accepted, applying the decision in *B v. Director of Public Prosecutions* [1997] 3 I.R. 140 (*Annual Review of Irish Law 1997*, pp.289-90) that the delay of the magnitude involved in the present case between the alleged offences and the complaint to the police was inordinate. He noted that in cases of non-sexual offences, much shorter times than that involved in the present case had been regarded as inordinate, with a delay of three years described as 'extreme' in the leading decision of the Supreme Court in *The State (O'Connell) v. Fawsitt* [1986] I.R. 362. In the instant case, no form of psychological or psychiatric impairment to the complainants had been established to justify the delay, and there was no evidence from the testimony or the literature that physical abuse alone could give rise to a reaction that would justify a complaint not being made for many years. Nor had it been suggested that the applicant himself was responsible for the delay in making complaint concerning the alleged assaults. Kelly J. was not persuaded that he should apply what he described as the 'separate and quite exceptional standard' established in sex offence cases involving delay to a case such as this where there was no allegation of sexual abuse of any form levelled against the applicant. But, even with the application of the special approach, the delay was so excessive as to give rise to a presumption of prejudice, and he was satisfied on the evidence that there was actual prejudice. Kelly J. concluded that it would be only in the rarest of circumstances that a court should allow a prosecution for sexual offences against children or young children that had occurred a very long time ago to proceed in the absence of an element of dominion exercised by the applicant over the complainant and its psychological continuance, and there was no dominion in the present case;

Extradition While the general principles involved in extradition cases involving delay largely reflect the case law in other cases, they also require the application of the specific provision in section 50(2)(bbb) of the Extradition Act 1965, as amended by the Extradition (Amendment) Act 1987, which provides that extradition may be refused where there has been such a lapse of time or other exceptional circumstances that would render it unjust or oppressive for the extradition to proceed. This provision was considered in two cases in 2001.

In *M.B. v. Conroy*, High Court, March 5 1999; [2001] 2 I.L.R.M. 311 (SC), the Supreme Court refused to order the plaintiff's extradition to England to face an indecent assault charge dating from 1992. He had pleaded guilty to the charge in 1992, but stated that he had done so solely on the advice of his lawyers, and that he in fact denied the charge. His case had been remanded for the preparation of a probation report but he had failed to show up on the remand date. He had returned to Ireland, where he was from originally, as he did not want to go to prison. He contended that he had lived openly in Ireland since his return in 1992 and that he had not attempted to conceal his whereabouts. At the time of the application for release, the plaintiff was very ill, and evidence was tendered that, if he were to be extradited from Ireland, there would be grave implications for his health. He had returned to Ireland. In 1995, the English courts had issued a warrant for the plaintiff's arrest, and the District Court had ordered that he be delivered into the custody of the English authorities under section 47(1) of the Extradition Act 1965. The plaintiff then applied for his release pursuant to section 50 of the 1965 Act. The application was not heard for nearly three years owing to his ill health. In the High Court, McCracken J. held that the delay in the case was of such a length as to justify refusing his extradition and that the plaintiff's health was a very serious matter, and was an exceptional circumstance under section 50 of the 1965 Act: see *Annual Review of Irish Law 19999*, pp.135-6. The Director appealed against this decision, but the Supreme Court affirmed.

In dismissing the appeal, Keane C.J. (with whom Murray and Geoghegan JJ agreed) accepted that it was not sufficient for a plaintiff whose extradition would otherwise be justified to show that there had been a significant lapse of time in his case. Applying the Court's own decision in *Fusco v. O'Dea (No. 2)* [1998] 3 I.R. 470 (*Annual Review of Irish Law 1998*, pp.199-200), the Chief Justice stated that he also must satisfy the Court that there were other exceptional circumstances which would render it unjust for the extradition to proceed. In the instant case, he held that the length of the lapse of time was of such an order as to allow the High Court to consider whether there were other exceptional circumstances such as would make it unjust to extradite the plaintiff. Specifically, the three year delay by the relevant English police in securing the whereabouts of the plaintiff in Ireland was an exceptional circumstance which could be taken into account by the court. And he also agreed that subjecting the plaintiff to further legal process in England would be invidious or oppressive, given the state of his health.

The same argument arose in *Martin v. Malone*, High Court, May 1, 2001. Here, the extradition application was made in March 1998 in respect of offences of conspiracy to cause explosions and possession of explosive substances allegedly committed by the applicant in England in 1988. It emerged that warrants in relation to the applicant were prepared in 1991 but not served until 1998. In that context, the applicant argued that extradition would be unjust, oppressive or invidious under section 50(2)(bbb) of the Extradition Act 1965. Herbert J. agreed.

He held that, whereas a lapse of time entirely or substantially occasioned by the deliberate and voluntary actions of a person in seeking to evade discovery should always be discounted, some regard may be had to a lapse of time referable to that person serving a term of imprisonment in looking at the overall lapse of time. Where there was in addition a specific and separate particular lapse of time to be taken into account for which the accused was in no manner to blame or which was due to some unnecessary or blameworthy delay on the part of the relevant authorities in the requesting State or in this State, then this would fall within section 50(2)(bbb) of the 1965 Act. In the instant case, he considered that the wholly unexplained lapse of seven years in issuing the warrants was the sort of lapse of time envisaged by section 50(2)(bbb) and such delay was a negation of the applicant's right to a trial with reasonable expedition. Alluding expressly to the general case law on delay, Herbert J. stated that after such an unexplained delay and in the absence of the sort of special circumstances that arose in cases concerning sexual offences against minors, the Court was entitled to infer from the excessive length of time itself that the risk of an unfair trial had been established as a reality.

Sexual offences: young person In *B.F. v. Director of Public Prosecutions*, Supreme Court, February 22, 2001, the Supreme Court considered the issue of delay in the context of an offence alleged to have been committed by the applicant when he was 14 years of age. The charges alleged were sexual offences that occurred in 1995 involving two young girls. No charges were proffered against the applicant in 1995, and the applicant had contended that he had not coerced the young girls. He had returned to England with his parents shortly afterwards and this return to England had, it appeared, not been discouraged by the Gardaí. In November 1996, the applicant learned that the Gardaí were considering making an application to have him extradited back to Ireland. He was arrested in England in February 1998. He voluntarily agreed to return to Ireland, and he did so after he had finished a course which he had been attending. He argued that any examination of the delay in this case had to take account of the special circumstances of this case and the age of the alleged offender. The High Court dismissed the application to prohibit the trial but, on appeal, the Supreme Court reversed and granted the relief sought.

The Court noted that it would not be a proper exercise of the powers of the prosecuting authorities to proceed with the prosecution of a child or young person where other more suitable courses of action might be open to it merely because the parents of the victims were insisting on it. It also noted that this was a case where the decision whether or not to prosecute at all had been marginal and that it was possible that there was no serious criminal intent on the applicant's part. It also was of the view that even if the applicant was convicted after a trial, it was possible that no custodial sentence would be imposed. The Court held that, once the Director had decided to prosecute, that prosecution ought to have been proceeded without delay, while memories were still fresh in the minds of the parties. As to the extradition application, the Court held that the delay in extraditing the applicant had been inexplicable.

Applying the views of Geoghegan J. in *P.P. v. Director of Public Prosecutions* [2000] 1 I.R. 403 (*Annual Review of Irish Law 1999*, pp.130-1), the Court held that where it was proved that there had been culpable delay on the part of the Garda authorities in the prosecution of sexual offences which had occurred a long time previously, the trial ought to be prohibited even if prejudice were not proved. Moreover, in the case of a criminal offence alleged to have been committed by a child, there was a special duty on the State authorities over and above the normal duty of expedition to ensure a speedy trial.

EXTRADITION (EUROPEAN UNION CONVENTIONS) ACT 2001

Introduction   The Extradition (European Union Conventions) Act 2001 made a number of significant amendments to the Extradition Act 1965. It gave effect to two European Union Conventions on Extradition, the 1995 Convention on simplified extradition procedures between the Member States of the European Union and the 1996 Convention relating to extradition between Member States of the European Union. Both Conventions were made under Article K3 of the Treaty on European Union. The 2001 Act also made other substantive and procedural changes to extradition arrangements, including transfer of all extradition applications to the High Court, thus removing the preliminary jurisdiction of the District Court in this area. The 2001 Act will come into effect on the making of relevant Commencement Orders.

The 1995 EU Extradition Convention   The 1995 Convention on simplified extradition procedures between the Member States of the European Union provides for a simplified procedure only where the person sought consents to his or her surrender. The 2001 Act provides that such consent must be given before the High Court and it must be satisfied that the consent is given voluntarily and in full awareness of the consequences. Once consent is given and, where the person claimed is a citizen of Ireland, the Minister for Justice, Equality and Law Reform agrees, the person will be extradited. A person who has consented to his or her surrender may also renounce his or her right to the Specialty Rule (the rule whereby a person extradited for one offence may not be tried for other offences committed before his or her extradition). Again, any such renunciation must be recorded before the High Court and the consent of the Minister for Justice, Equality and Law Reform is also required. The 1995 Convention provides that consent or renunciation may not be revoked but allows parties to opt out of this requirement by making a declaration to that effect on ratification. During the passage of the 2001 Act, it was stated that Ireland will make such a declaration, and the 2001 Act allows for revocation.

The 1996 EU Extradition Convention The 1996 Convention relating to extradition between the Member States of the European Union provides for the improvement and simplification of extradition procedures generally in a number of respects. As implemented by the 2001 Act, extradition requests, documents and correspondence may be sent by facsimile transmission provided the facsimile machine is fitted with a cryptographic device to ensure authenticity and confidentiality. Changes are also implemented in relation to the authentication and certification of documents. The Convention also requires all states to designate a Central Authority to be responsible for transmitting and receiving extradition requests and supporting documentation; the 2001 Act provides that the Minister for Justice, Equality and Law Reform is the Central Authority for Ireland. Section 11 of the 2001 Act amends section 10 of the 1965 Act to give effect to the reduction in the threshold for extradition as between contracting states provided for in Article 2(1) of the 1996 Convention which provides that offences will be extraditable if they are punishable by six months imprisonment in the requested Member State and 12 months in the requesting Member State. In addition, the 1996 Convention extends the range of extraditable offences to include, for example, revenue offences. Under the 1965 Act, revenue offences were not extraditable and the 2001 Act now deletes this for Convention countries as well as providing that revenue offences will in future be extraditable in extradition treaties with non-Convention states, such as the United States of America.

Extradition procedure generally The 2001 Act also involves general changes in extradition law. Section 20 of the 2001 Act provides that all extradition proceedings are to be held in the High Court. Prior to the 2001 Act, the 1965 Act provided that the initial application for the extradition of persons from the State is made to the District Court. The justification for consolidating all proceedings in the High Court was that 'nearly all' extradition cases end up in the High Court on a special summons procedure, so that the change would provide for a more efficient and expeditious hearing of such cases. It was also pointed out that, since 1994, all bail applications in extradition cases must be taken in the High Court. In addition to this change, the 2001 Act amended the Criminal Justice Act 1992 to provide that evidence in any extradition proceedings may be given by a witness outside the State through a television link or by affidavit. Finally, in relation to the backing of warrants procedure in Part III of the 1965 Act, for extradition to the United Kingdom, the 2001 Act contains a new definition of 'corresponding offence' to deal with difficulties that may arise because acts that constitute offences by the law of both States may be designated differently. The 2001 Act provides that the offence in the State need not be in the same category or of the same description as the offence in the United Kingdom; rather, offences will be regarded as corresponding where the acts of the person sought would constitute an indictable offence if committed in Ireland or are punishable on summary conviction by at least six months imprisonment.

FIREARMS AND OFFENSIVE WEAPONS

Firearms certificates: directive requiring firearms cabinet   In *Dunne v. Donohoe*, High Court, July 27, 2001, Ó Caoimh J. held that a requirement to install a firearms cabinet when issuing or renewing firearms certificates under the Firearms Acts 1925 to 2001 was *ultra vires*. The case concerned a directive or circular issued by the Garda authorities directing superintendents of the Garda Síochána to require the installation of such a firearms cabinet. It also provided that the cabinet facilities were to be inspected by the Garda Síochána prior to issue or renewal of the certificate. No such requirement was contained in the Firearms Acts 1925 to 2001. The applicant submitted that the directive was invalid and void in that its effect was that superintendents were acting under the direction of a third party in the exercise of a judicial discretion and was, accordingly, an unlawful fettering of their discretion. Ó Caoimh J. agreed. He held that the impugned directive was invalid and void insofar as it had the effect of fettering the discretion of a superintendent in the exercise of the functions conferred by sections 3 and 4 of the 1925 Act. He considered that it was not permissible to impose a fixed precondition of the nature applied in this case by the impugned directive to an application for a firearms certificate such as would preclude a superintendent from considering a case on its merits where something of equivalent safety was provided by the certificate holder or applicant for a certificate.

INTERNATIONAL CRIMINAL COURT

The Twenty Third Amendment of the Constitution Act 2001, which was approved by a referendum held in June 2001, provided for the ratification by the State of the 1998 Rome Statute of the International Criminal Court. It provides for an additional paragraph in Article 29 to the effect that: 'The State may ratify the Rome Statute of the International Criminal Court done at Rome on the 17th day of July, 1998.' During the Oireachtas debate on the amendment proposal, it was noted that a draft statute for an international criminal court was prepared by the International Law Commission in the early 1950s but work was not resumed on it until 1989. Events in the former Yugoslavia and in Rwanda in the 1990s prompted the United Nations Security Council to establish ad hoc tribunals to bring to justice those responsible for the atrocities committed in those places. The establishment of such tribunals for the first time since the

Second World War focused minds on the need to establish a permanent international criminal court with the power to deal with such crimes in the future. In 1994 the International Law Commission submitted its draft statute to the General Assembly and from then on progress was swift. The General Assembly established the Ad Hoc Committee on the Establishment of an International Criminal Court to consider major substantive issues arising from the draft and this committee met twice in 1995. After considering the committee's report, the General Assembly created the Preparatory Committee on the Establishment of an International Criminal Court to draw up a draft text for submission to a diplomatic conference. That committee held its final session and completed the drafting of the text in March and April of 1998.

The 1998 Rome Statute provides for the establishment of a permanent international criminal court, related to the United Nations system, with jurisdiction over persons in respect of genocide, crimes against humanity, war crimes and the crime of aggression. The statute of the court is an international agreement which entered into force approximately two months after 60 States became party to it. This occurred in 2002, when Ireland was one of a number of States who ratified the Statute.

The statute deals with the establishment of the court, its jurisdiction and the general principles of criminal law to be applied. It sets out the composition of the court, its administration, the procedures for investigation, prosecution and trial, the penalties which can be imposed on conviction and provides for appeals. States parties are under obligation to co-operate with the court and provision is made for the enforcement of judgments and the carrying out of sentences. The statute further provides for an assembly of states parties and for the financing of the court. The court will sit at the Hague in the Netherlands. The assembly will consist of one representative from each state and elect 18 full-time judges who will be persons of high moral character, impartiality and integrity possessing the qualifications required in their respective states for appointment to the highest judicial offices. There may not be more than one judge of the same nationality and in selecting judges the states parties will take into account the need for the membership of the court to represent the principal legal systems of the world, equitable geographical representation and a fair representation of female and male judges. There will also be an independent Office of the Prosecutor and the prosecutor, like the judges, will be elected by the Assembly of States Parties by secret ballot. A situation in which a crime appears to have been committed may be referred to the prosecutor of the court by a state party or the Security Council of the United Nations acting under Chapter VII of the UN charter, or the prosecutor may initiate an investigation. Where a state party has referred a situation to the prosecutor or the prosecutor has initiated the investigation, the court may exercise its jurisdiction if the state on the territory of which the alleged crime was committed is a party to the statute or if the person accused of the crime is a national of a state party. States parties are obliged to co-operate fully with the court in its investigation and prosecution of crimes within its jurisdiction. The statute contains numerous provisions governing the conduct of a trial and the rights of an accused.

The court will be complementary to national legal systems. The primary obligation to investigate crimes covered by the statute and prosecute the perpetrators will remain with the states parties. Only where the state party in question is unwilling or unable genuinely to investigate the crimes alleged or prosecute the accused person may the court exercise its jurisdiction. In this way, the court provides an additional means of administering justice, where serious international crimes are committed, without in any way detracting from existing domestic structures which states may have put in place. In addition to its function in electing judges and the prosecutor, the Assembly of States Parties will also be responsible for the budget of the court and provide management oversight to the president of the court, the prosecutor and the registrar regarding the administration of the court. Draft rules of procedure and evidence were adopted by the preparatory commission for the court in 2000. These provide further detail on the way in which the court will function. It is envisaged that the assembly will adopt these rules and the financial rules and regulations. The court will be funded by contributions from states parties and the United Nations and may also accept voluntary contributions.

Under Article 5 of the Statute the court's jurisdiction is limited to the most serious crimes of concern to the international community as a whole, namely, the crime of genocide, crimes against humanity, war crimes and the crime of aggression. The court will exercise jurisdiction over the crime of genocide, crimes against humanity and war crimes committed after the statute enters into force in 2002. The court will not, however, exercise jurisdiction over the crime of aggression until the provision is adopted by the states parties defining the crime and setting out the conditions under which the court shall exercise jurisdiction with respect to this crime. A review conference is to be held seven years after the entry into force of the statute, that is in 2009, and a provision governing the crime of aggression may be adopted at that conference. The definitions of genocide, crimes against humanity and war crimes contained in the statute codify existing international law.

The 1948 Convention on the Prevention and Punishment of the Crime of Genocide provides that genocide means any of the following acts committed with intent to destroy in whole or in part a national, ethical, racial or religious group such as killing members of the group; causing serious bodily or mental harm to members of the group; deliberately inflicting on the group conditions of life calculated to bring about its physical destruction in whole or in part; imposing measures intended to prevent births within the group; and forcibly transferring children of the group to another group. This definition of genocide has been incorporated in the Rome statute. Like genocide, crimes against humanity can be committed both in time of war and peace. Particularly serious violations of human rights such as murder, extermination, slavery, forcible transfer of population, unlawful imprisonment, torture, sexual violence, persecution of a group, enforced disappearance and apartheid constitute crimes against humanity when committed as part of a widespread or systematic attack directed against the civilian population. War crimes, for the purpose of the 1998 statute, include grave breaches of the Geneva Convention of 1949 as well as attacks during armed conflict against civilians and humanitarian and peacekeeping missions, attacks directed against religious, educational and cultural buildings, pillaging, rape, sexual slavery and enforced prostitution and the use of child soldiers. For a critical analysis of the Court's jurisdiction, see Murphy, 'The International Criminal Court – solving the missing link in the international legal system? (2000) 18 I.L.T. 319.

MURDER

In its *Consultation Paper on Homicide: The Mental Element in Murder* (LRC – CP17-2001), the Law Reform Commission provisionally recommends that the fault element for murder be broadened to embrace reckless killing manifesting an extreme indifference to human life. The Commission, in a closely-reasoned analysis, takes the view that the present law, contained in section 4 of the Criminal Justice Act 1964, is not sufficiently broad to capture certain kinds of wrongdoing resulting in death which warrant, in its view, the ascription of the offence of murder. Under section 4, the mental element for murder is an intention to kill or to cause serious injury. The Commission is concerned that people such as arsonists, terrorists and reckless users of guns or of motor vehicles fall outside the offence of murder in circumstances where this would be an appropriate characterisation of their conduct.

The concept of intention has troubled the courts. The Commission summarises the position, in England and Ireland, respectively, as follows (paras. 2.19-2.20):

> "As a result of the decision in *R v. Woollin*, the law in England (at least in cases where it is not the defendant's purpose to kill) is that a jury is not entitled to *find* the necessary intention, unless they feel sure that death or serious bodily harm was a virtual certainty and the defendant appreciated that such was the case."

In Ireland the law would appear to be set out the Court of Criminal Appeal in *People v. Douglas & Hayes* [1985] I.L.R.M. 25. Foresight of death as a natural and probable consequence of one's actions does not amount to intention *per se*, although it may be evidence from which intention can be inferred.

The Commission acknowledged that it does not necessarily follow that intention bears the same meaning in Irish law as it does in English law. It stated (para. 4.005):

"It may well be that intention in Irish law bears a much wider meaning than that ascribed to it in England. Conceivably the meaning of the term 'intention' in the context of murder could range from purposeful killings on the one hand, to killings committed with foresight of a risk of death on the other. In view of the relative scarcity of reported Irish authority on the meaning of intention it is difficult to express and firm view on this question."

The Commission considers (paras 4.006-8) that confining the *mens rea* of murder to 'intention':

"runs the risk of excluding from the definition of murder many killings which ought to be properly punishable as murder. A defendant who, while not intending to kill, is prepared to act with reckless disregard for the loss of human life, and consciously ignores even a high probability that death will result, would not be guilty of murder if death did in fact result under the current English rule. To take the much quoted example, a terrorist who plants a bomb in a public building, not intending to kill but merely to damage property, but who is nonetheless aware of a high probability of death resulting, would not be guilty of murder if death resulted on a *Woollin*-type definition of intention. Such a result seems unsatisfactory…"

There are other examples of such inexcusable risk-taking where, for example, the defendant does not intend to kill, but nevertheless foresees a socially unacceptable level of risk of death resulting. Thus, the arsonist who sets fire to an occupied building, the defendant who discharges a firearm into an occupied house or moving automobile, or the defendant who drives a heavy trust into a bar having been thrown off the premises, would probably all escape liability for murder if the mental element runs no further than foresight of a virtual certainty.

These examples illustrate that some reckless killings may be no less heinous than intentional ones, and accordingly deserve to be treated as murder rather than manslaughter. At some point a person's preparedness to run a known risk of killing another is so culpable as to be equivalent to that of an intentional killer.

The Commission is impressed by the approach adopted by the American *Model Penal Code* under section 202.2(c) of which criminal homicide constitutes murder when 'it is committed recklessly under circumstances manifesting extreme indifference to the value of human life'. It accepts that its inherent flexibility 'carries the risk of inconsistent jury verdicts or verdicts based on irrelevant or discriminatory factors, such as the defendant's background, allegiance or other activities': para 4.046. it is confident, however, that it would withstand an attack on its constitutional validity under Article

38.1. Several decisions in the United States of America have upheld the formulation against due process and equal protection attacks based on its lack of specificity.

It has to be said that some of the examples mentioned by the Commission give pause for thought. Drunken drivers, dangerous drivers and reckless gun users (including those who shoot over a person's head in order to scare) are all highly antisocial people who may deserve to be convicted of manslaughter in appropriate cases and murder where the likelihood of death or serious injury is virtually certain but it is far from self-evident that they should be characterised as murderers. Society must protect itself and its citizens through a criminal justice system that guarantees condign punishment for those who take unwarranted and callous risks with the lives of their fellow-citizens but this goal can be achieved through an appropriate categorisation of their conduct and an appropriate sentence on conviction. In the current climate, the civilising, restraining, liberal values of the criminal justice system are tending to be displaced by a rush to vengeance, accompanied by an impatience about examining the subjective components of the guilt of the accused. As a society we do not need to expand the scope of the definition of murder in order to satisfy the emotion that seriously wrongful conduct must be recognised as such. Just as monetary inflation devalues the currency similarly an inflation of the term 'murder', which has traditionally carried with it an awesome quality, may weaken that important value in the scaffolding of societal norms.

The Commission goes on to recommend provisionally that an intent to cause serious injury should continue to ground a murder conviction, even where the accused does not actually intend to kill. It considers that a defendant who deliberately inflicts serious injury 'must be taken to know that he is risking life in view of the inherent vulnerability of the human body and mind'. para. 4.097. It discusses possible definitions of 'serious injury' designed to ensure that a conviction will not occur in cases where injuries of a relatively minor nature have been intended by the accused. The Commission recommends provisionally against incorporating any express reference to recklessness as to serious injury. Instead, such killings would fall within the more general head of reckless killings manifesting extreme indifference to the value of human life: para. 4.109. The Commission argues (paras. 4(07-8) that:

> "[s]uch an approach would have the advantage of providing a filtering device by which more serious homicides could be punishable as murder, while leaving less serious killings, as appropriate, to be punished as manslaughter. Thus, where the risk of injury was relatively slight, or the projected serious injury would not be regarded as life threatening, then it would be open for a verdict of manslaughter, rather than murder, to be returned."

A possible weakness of this approach is that it may exclude reckless infliction of serious injury which falls short of 'extreme indifference' to human life, but his is theoretical criticism: a clear and simple formula is to be preferred to a longer provision which tries specifically to cover every eventuality in detail. Examples in practice of cases where an accused is reckless as to serious injury, but not death, would be likely to be rare.

Perhaps it would be better for the legislation to provide expressly what it intends to be the conceptual basis of the offence of murder rather than leave matters unresolved in the hope – even the confident hope – that juries will be able to come to satisfactory verdicts unguided by conceptual clarity. The notion of more serious homicides being capable of being distinguished in this context from 'less serious killings' seems opaque. When one is speaking in moral terms, the degree of risk of injury or the degree of seriousness of the risk of the injury are but two (incidentally, separate) factors: such other matters as the age and personal circumstances of the accused and the victim and the motive of the accused will obviously come into consideration.

PROCEDURE

Bias: juror with experience of offence charged   In *The People v. Tobin*, Court of Criminal Appeal, June 22, 2001, the Court of Criminal Appeal allowed an appeal against the defendant's conviction on various counts of rape and indecent assault. The appeal was on the ground that the trial court had failed to discharge a juror when it was brought to the attention of the court that that juror had a prior experience of sexual abuse. In quashing the conviction and directing a retrial, the Court held that the right of an accused person to be tried by a jury free from any suspicion or taint of bias was one of the cornerstones of the criminal justice system. In the special circumstances of this case a reasonable and fair-minded observer would consider that there was a danger, in the sense of a possibility, that the juror might have been unconsciously influenced by his or her personal experience and that for that reason the appellant might not have received a fair trial. But, with a view to future such cases, the Court did not accept that discharge of the jury would be an invariable result in such a case. The Court commented, arguably *obiter* that it would not discount the possibility that a judge, by a considered and carefully worded special direction to the jury, might sufficiently counteract those dangers as to render it unnecessary to discharge the jury.

Decision to prosecute: internal review procedure   In *Eviston v. Director of Public Prosecutions* [2002] 1 I.L.R.M. 134 (HC), the applicant, who had been involved as a driver in a fatal traffic accident, successfully challenged the decision of the Director to prosecute her for dangerous driving causing death. The Director had initially decided not to prosecute the applicant, but later initiated charges after the victim's family had written to the Director seeking an internal review. Such an internal review is part of the *Victims'* *Charter* introduced by the Department of Justice in 1999: see Byrne and McCutcheon, *The Irish Legal System*, 4th ed. (Butterworths, Dublin 2001), para.6.107. In *Eviston*, Kearns J. acknowledged that the scope to review the prosecutorial discretion of the Director was almost uniquely limited and that there was no general obligation on the Director to give reasons for a decision to prosecute or not. Nonetheless, where the review in this instance had not revealed any new material on which the original decision not to prosecute could have been challenged, the High Court quashed the revised decision to prosecute, largely on the basis that the Director's own guidelines on reviews had not been applied (referring to *R v. DPP ex parte C* (1995) 1 Cr. App. Rep. 136 in this respect). Kearns J. also accepted that the leading authorities which limit the scope of review of the Director's decision to prosecute, such as *H v. Director of Public Prosecutions* [1994] 2 I.R. 589 (*Annual Review of Irish Law 1994*, p.208), were not in any way affected by the unusual nature of the instant case.

Indictments: consolidation   In *Conlon v. Kelly* [2001] 2 I.L.R.M. 198 (SC), the Supreme Court, held that section 6(1) of the Criminal Justice (Administration) Act 1924 provided no basis for the consolidation of two separate indictments. The applicant had been returned for trial in respect of two separate indictments, both alleging that he was guilty of fraudulent conversion, though against different persons. He sought judicial review of the trial judge's order to consolidate the two indictments, contending that the Circuit Court had no such power to consolidate indictments or, if it did, that it had not been fairly exercised in his case. The applicant contended that the Criminal Justice (Administration) Act 1924 only allowed for charges to be joined in the same indictment, not consolidated. The respondent contended that order 49, rule 6 of the Rules of the Superior Courts 1986 permitted the consolidation of actions and that this should be applied in the Circuit Court in the absence of a specific rule in the Rules of the Circuit Court 1950. The High Court refused judicial review, but on appeal the Supreme Court reversed and granted the relief sought. Delivering the main judgment for the Court, Fennelly J. held that the provisions cited by the respondent dealt with the indictment as originally framed by the prosecution, and they did not deal with its amendment. Moreover, the relevant provisions of the 1924 Act did not confer any power on the court to permit amendment, whether by adding counts or otherwise. Specifically, section 6(1) of the 1924 Act did not permit amendment by combining counts from separate indictments based on separate returns for trial and so there was no statutory authority for the consolidation of two indictments of the sort which occurred in the present case. Fennelly J. also held that Order 49, rule 6 of Rules of the Superior Courts 1986 was not intended to apply to criminal proceedings. Since the Circuit Court did not have the jurisdiction to consolidate the two indictments, the Supreme Court consequently held that the orders of the respondent were void.

Legal representation for complainants in sexual assault trials   Part 6 of the Sex Offenders Act 2001 (the remainder of the Acts is discussed below, 214), which came into effect in September 2001, provides for separate legal representation for complainants in rape and serious sexual assault cases when application is made to the trial court by the defence seeking leave to adduce evidence or cross-examine about the complainant's past sexual experience with any person. Against the background of the adversarial and accusatorial nature of the criminal trial, Part 6 of the 2001 Act has introduced a novel arrangement, dispensing at least in part with the long-standing model in which prosecution and defence only are legally represented, the complainant being accorded the position of witness only. In 1988, the Law Reform Commission, in its *Report on Rape and Allied Offences* (LRC 24-1988), had expressed doubts as to the constitutionality of separate legal representation for complainants in rape and other serious sexual assault cases, on the ground that it would alter the balance of the criminal process and deprive the accused of a trial in due course of law. But because the sexual history of a complainant may only be introduced into a trial by leave of the trial judge and since such applications are made in the absence of the jury, the government was advised (it was stated in the Oireachtas debate of the 2001 Act) that the limited form of representation provided for in the 2001 Act does not present constitutional difficulties. Section 33 of the 2001 Act amends the Criminal Law (Rape) Act 1981 by providing for separate legal representation for complainants in rape and serious sexual assault cases when application is made to the court by the defence under sections 3 or 4 of the 1981 Act, seeking leave to adduce evidence or cross-examine about the complainant's past sexual experience with any person. The trial judge is obliged to ensure that before the hearing of the application he or she is satisfied that (i) the complainant is aware of his or her entitlement to be heard during the application and to be legally represented for that purpose and (ii) the complainant has been given a reasonable time within which to arrange for such representation. Section 34 amends the Civil Legal Aid Act 1995 by entitling complainants referred to in section 33 to legal aid under the 1995 Act automatically and free of any financial contribution.

Plea bargaining   In *The People v. Heeney*, Supreme Court, April 5, 2001 the Supreme Court criticised the practice of 'private' plea bargaining while also accepting that, where it occurred the prosecution could not later appeal the leniency of any sentence imposed after such discussions. The defendant had pleaded guilty to certain sexual offences and was sentenced to concurrent sentences of six years. It emerged that discussions had taken place prior to the trial between the trial judge and counsel for the prosecution and defence, which in effect amounted to plea bargaining. After sentence was imposed, the Director had then applied to the Court of Criminal Appeal pursuant to section 2 of the

Criminal Justice Act 1993 seeking to have the sentences increased on the ground that they were unduly lenient. The Court of Criminal Appeal upheld the appeal and substituted in each case a sentence of 10 years to run concurrently. On a further appeal on a point of law of exceptional public importance, the Supreme Court reversed.

The Court reiterated the formal view in Irish law against plea bargaining that there could be no question of any form of bargain being entered into in private which would determine in advance the sentence to be imposed by a Court. As noted in *Annual Review of Irish Law 1998*, p.213, a direction was issued by the Director of Public Prosecutions in 1999 discontinuing any practice of having meetings in chambers with the trial judge to discuss sentencing issues prior to trial.

In the present case, however, the Supreme Court was of the view that the Court of Criminal Appeal had erred in law in declining to have regard to the discussions which had actually taken place prior to the trial between the trial judge and counsel for the prosecution and defence. In the circumstances, even if the Director were in a position to satisfy the Court of Criminal Appeal that the sentences were unduly lenient that Court was required to have regard to the chain of circumstances in which the Director participated and which had led to the defendant pleading guilty and to the imposition of the particular sentence as a result.

Preliminary examination: abolition   The Criminal Justice Act 1999 (Part III) (Commencement) Order 2001 (S.I. No.193 of 2001) brought Part III of the Criminal Justice Act 1999 into effect on October 1, 2001. Part III of the 1999 Act abolished the preliminary examination and replaced it with a truncated procedure for sending forward for trial in indictable matters: see *Annual Review of Irish Law 1999*, pp.139–42.

Remittal after judicial review   In *Gilmartin v. Murphy*, High Court, February 23, 2001, Kearns J. considered the circumstances in which remittal is appropriate after a conviction has been quashed on judicial review. The applicant had been charged with the drink driving offence under section 49 of the Road Traffic Act 1961, as amended. He did not have legal representation but indicated that he wished to plead guilty in the District Court. He was thereupon convicted without the opportunity to seek legal advice. In the course of the applicant's judicial review, the respondent accepted that the quashing of the convictions could not be opposed. Thus, the only issue to be determined was whether the matter should be remitted back to the District Court. Applying the leading recent decision on this matter, *Sweeney v. Brophy* [1993] 2 I.R. 203 (*Annual Review of Irish Law 1992*, pp.268-70), Kearns J. accepted that where a conviction is quashed because of a fundamental breach of the requirements of natural justice in the course of the hearing, a defendant is entitled to plead *autrefois convict* or *autrefois acquit*. As had been pointed out by Hederman J. in the *Sweeney* case, it is considered unfair to subject an accused person, who had already undergone the ordeal of a trial, perhaps accompanied following conviction by a period of detention, to endure all that again. The key point, then, was whether the applicant fell into this category. Kearns J. acknowledged that the applicant did not contribute in any way to the situation that occurred where he was convicted without the benefit of legal representation. Equally, he felt that the prosecution had to be held partly to blame for what went wrong, as in *Nevin v. Crowley,* Supreme Court, February 17, 2000 (*Annual Review of Irish Law 2000*, p.136). On the other side, however, the void nature of the sentences imposed in this case permitted the court to hold that the accused was never in peril of the sentence and qualification imposed; he had not actually spent any time in prison; and finally, he had not established any prejudice that would outweigh the public interest in seeing that the prosecution against him would now proceed in due course of law.

ROAD TRAFFIC

Drunk in charge In *Director of Public Prosecutions v. Byrne* [2002] 2 I.L.R.M. 68 (SC), the Supreme Court held that a person found asleep at the wheel of a car with the keys in the ignition was 'in charge' of the vehicle and had an 'intent to drive' within the meaning of section 50 of the Road Traffic Act 1961, as amended by the Road Traffic Act 1994. The defendant had been observed by a Garda asleep in the driver's seat at night with the car lights on, the car being parked on the hard shoulder of a road. The keys were in the ignition and were turned two clicks to the 'ready' position. The Garda woke the defendant, noticed his eyes were bloodshot and bleary, that there was a smell of alcohol and that he was unsteady on his feet. The defendant was arrested and charged with being in charge of a vehicle with intent to drive at a time when he had an excess of alcohol, contrary to section 50 of the Road Traffic Act 1961, as amended by the Road Traffic Act 1994. On a case stated from the Circuit Court, the Supreme Court held that the circumstances were such that a conviction could arise. Delivering the Court's main judgment, Murray J. noted that this appeared to be the first decided case in the State when the phrases 'in charge' and 'intent to drive' had been considered by the superior courts.

As to being 'in charge', while acknowledging that comparable legislation in England differed from the structure of section 50 of the 1961 Act, as amended, Murray J. cited with approval the general views expressed in *Director of Public Prosecutions v. Watkins* [1969] Q.B. 821 that being in charge had connotations of control and possession. On the facts in this case, he concluded that the trial judge was entitled to conclude that the defendant was in charge of the vehicle. As to the second issue, Murray J. held that the intentions of the defendant before he went to sleep could be taken into account, since they were part of the *res gestae*, that is, an intrinsic part of the circumstances being investigated and thus admissible evidence (citing in this respect *Halsbury's Laws of England*, 4th ed, vol. 17, para. 6). Specifically on the issue of intent, Murray J. opined that '[i]ntention is a sense of purpose as to future action. The mere fact that a person fell asleep, even involuntarily, did not therefore mean that the intention has ceased to exist. He gave as an analogy the situation where a person pulls into a lay-by for a rest during a long journey; if the driver falls asleep during that rest, voluntarily or otherwise, Murray J. held that this does not mean that he has abandoned his intention to drive or that it has ceased to exist. Nor did he consider that there was anything in section 50 of the 1961 Act to indicate a legislative intention that there must be an 'immediate' intention to drive; indeed a comparison of the text of section 50 as originally enacted with section 50 as amended by the Road Traffic Act 1994 appeared to show a contrary intention, leading him to conclude that a stricter liability offence (though not necessarily one of strict liability) was being created. He did, however, consider that there might be some circumstances in which a person could be 'in charge' but not having an intent to drive, such as where a person, being in excess of the permissible alcohol level, went to retrieve something from the boot of the car at night but did not 'intend' to drive until the next day. Assuming the person would be under the permissible level the next day, Murray J. considered that the retrieval of something from the boot in those circumstances would be too remote from the driving act that no offence would be committed under section 50 of the 1961 Act. But the circumstances of the instant case were far from that hypothetical scenario.

Intoxilyser *Director of Public Prosecutions v. Syron*, High Court, March 7, 2001 was an unsuccessful challenge to the intoxilyser test introduced as part of the procedure to prosecute the drink driving offence under section 49 of the Road Traffic Act 1961, as amended by the Road Traffic Act 1994 (*Annual Review of Irish Law 1994*, pp.217-22). The respondent had been charged with the drink driving offence and his alcohol level had been checked with an intoxilyser at the time of his arrest. The respondent contended that the prosecution had failed to show the relevant formula to the court by which the concentration of alcohol in the respondent's breath was calculated for the purposes of the prosecution. In the absence of such a formula, the respondent contended that he was unable properly to defend himself. In particular, the respondent noted that the intoxilyser had given a reading of 89 microgrammes of alcohol per 100 millilitres of breath, but that the summons for the purpose of the prosecution showed a figure of 73 microgrammes. The respondent argued that the basis on which the figure of 73 microgrammes was calculated was not identifiable in any Road Traffic Act passed by the Oireachtas or in any Regulations made under such Act. In the absence of any Regulations governing the matter, the respondent contended that the court was obliged to dismiss the summons against him. The prosecution's argument in reply was that the Road

Traffic Act 1994 stated that the certificate from the intoxilyser was to be prima facie evidence of the offence and also of compliance with the 1994 Act. On a case stated, O'Higgins J. held in the prosecution's favour and remitted the matter back to the District Court. He held that the respondent had not been deprived of any of his rights to fair procedure, as identified in *The State (Healy) v. Donoghue* [1976] I.R. 235. In particular, there was no denial of the respondent's right to challenge the certificate in whatever manner he saw fit. He accepted that, while there were no Regulations which set out the scientific formulation by which the quantity of alcohol in the breath was to be calculated, the absence of this did not preclude the certificate emanating from the intoxyliser from being the *prima facie* evidence it purported to be. Pursuant to the 1994 Act, the certificate in relation to the breath sample had the same validity as certificates in respect of blood and urine samples. Thus, the certificate was evidence of the facts stated on it until the contrary was proved. On this basis, he remitted the case.

Samples: omission to state year of Road Traffic Act when sample demanded   In *Director of Public Prosecutions v. Mangan*, Supreme Court, April 6, 2001, the Supreme Court held that the omission by a Garda to state the year of the Road Traffic Act 1994 after a demand for a blood sample was immaterial to the validity of a subsequent charge. The defendant had been charged in the District Court with certain offences contrary to the Road Traffic Acts, in particular, that he had refused to permit a doctor to take a sample of his blood contrary to section 13 (3) of the Road Traffic Act 1994. Having being convicted in the District Court, he appealed to the Circuit Court. On a case stated, the Supreme Court was asked to determine whether the reference to 'the Road Traffic Act' made to the defendant by the Garda when she asked him to provide a urine sample could be taken to mean the Road Traffic Act 1994. The defendant argued that for a request to provide a sample to be valid the defendant had to be informed of the specific section of the relevant statute, namely section 13 of the 1994 Act. In addition, it was argued that when, after the defendant had been unable to provide a urine sample, the Garda had made a further request to provide a blood sample, the Garda had again failed to refer to section 13 of the 1994 Act, thus making the prosecution fatally flawed. The Supreme Court found that the omission of the date "1994" after Road Traffic Act was immaterial. So far as being informed of the legal basis for the demand was concerned, the Court applied its decision in *Director of Public Prosecutions v. McGarrigle* [1996] 1 I.L.R.M. 267 in holding that the defendant was in as good a position as he would have been if the Garda had used the correct formula of words. In the instant case, therefore, the Court concluded that the Circuit Court was entitled to reach the conclusion in this case that the requirements laid down by the Supreme Court in the *McGarrigle* case had been met. The Court also held that once a period of time to allow the defendant to provide a sample of urine himself had elapsed, the duty on the defendant to provide a blood sample to a doctor revived. Thus, when the Garda made a further requirement for the defendant to provide a blood sample, she was doing no more that drawing his attention to the fact that the obligation to provide a specimen of his blood had now revived.

SEARCH WARRANTS

Absence of reference to area of responsibility of Peace Commissioner *The People v. Edgeworth*, Supreme Court, March 29, 2001 was a 'without prejudice' appeal by the Director under section 34 of the Criminal Procedure Act 1967. The defendant had been tried in the Circuit Criminal Court with offences under the Misuse of Drugs Act 1977. At the trial, a preliminary point was argued on the validity of a search warrant which had been issued in the case, to the effect that the warrant had not stated that the Peace Commissioner who issued the warrant was for the County of Dublin and further that the warrant was headed the District Court. The trial judge found that these errors invalidated the warrant. The defendant was subsequently found not guilty. The Director referred the question as to whether the search warrant was, indeed, bad in law in the circumstances which had arisen. The Supreme Court held that the warrant was not invalid.

The Court held that while the warrant was not in itself in a statutorily prescribed form, it complied with section 26(2) of the Misuse of Drugs Act 1977. Indeed, while no special form was provided by the authorities for use when the application for a warrant was made to a Peace Commissioner and not to a judge of the District Court, this did not invalidate the warrant. Although the Court acknowledged that the warrant featured an inappropriate statement on its face whose effect was to associate the document with the District Court whereas it was issued without any application to a judicial personage, it was not calculated to mislead and there was no evidence before the trial judge that any person was in fact misled. The status of the person actually issuing the warrant appeared clearly on its face. In this respect, the defects were not in the same category which had led to the invalidation of the search warrant in *Director of Public Prosecutions v. Dunne* [1994] 2 I.R. 537 (*Annual Review of Irish Law 1994*, p.233), which concerned a search of a private dwelling. Finally, the Court noted that the uncontradicted evidence at the trial was that the appointment of the Peace Commissioner was in respect of the relevant county. A warrant issued under the provisions of section 26 of the 1977 Act was not required either by the terms of that section or by any general enactment or rule to carry on its face a statement of the counties to which a Peace Commissioner's warrant of appointment related. The omission to do so did not, therefore, constitute a breach of any condition laid down by law for the issue of a warrant.

SENTENCING

Community service: adjournment for probation   In *Scully v. Crowley*,
Supreme Court, May 3, 2001, the Supreme Court dealt with some procedural
aspects of the imposition of community service orders under the Criminal
Justice (Community Service) Act 1983. The case arose against the background
of the applicant having been convicted by the respondent judge of the District
Court of certain offences under the Road Traffic Acts, including a charge of
dangerous driving. A conflict arose as to the precise orders made by the
respondent on conviction, which gave rise to the present judicial review. The
solicitor representing the applicant deposed that the respondent had actually
imposed community service orders on the respondent in respect of each of the
charges under the Road Traffic Acts, with various prison terms to be served in
default, and had also imposed disqualification orders on the applicant. It was
argued that the orders were *ultra vires* because: (a) the respondent had not
sought the applicant's consent to the making of a community service order, as
required by the 1983 Act and (b) such an order could only be made following
on a report of a Probation and Welfare Officer, and no such report had been
before the court. The Garda appearing in the District Court deposed, on the
other hand, that the respondent had simply indicated that he was merely
indicating his intentions as to the sentence he was likely to impose; and that
since he had adjourned the matter pending the compilation of a probation and
welfare report, the correct interpretation of what had occurred was that no
sentence had actually been imposed at the hearing to which the applicant took
objection. Of some interest is that the deposing Garda stated that it was common
practice where the 1983 Act was to be invoked for the trial judge to give an
initial indication that he or she was prepared to invoke the 1983 Act, pending
the outcome of a favourable probation and welfare report and subject to the
consent of the defendant as required by the 1983 Act.

In effect, the Supreme Court concurred with the view given by the
prosecuting Garda. It agreed with the views of Murphy J. in the High Court
that the only rational view of the evidence was that the respondent had adjourned
the case in order to allow for the compilation of a probation and welfare report.
It followed from this that he could not possibly have been intending there and
then to impose a community service order. The Court thus agreed that, whatever
ambiguity might have arisen during the actual trial and hearing in the District
Court, the correct view was that the respondent was merely indicating his
intention, subject to obtaining a probation and welfare report. Although the
Court accepted that the order made, which included reference to community
service, also included the imposition of an immediate disqualification from
driving, the Court considered that this did not assist the applicant in his
contentions, as the respondent had also stated that he wanted to impose a
disqualification and not to have it suspended pending the completion of the
probation and welfare report. Finally, the Court noted that there might be some

difficulty for the prosecution because the respondent had retired by the time of the appeal hearing (the High Court hearing had been in 1995), but it did not offer any final view on whether this might be an insuperable difficulty. It confined itself to commenting that the applicant could ventilate any such arguments as might be open to him in another judicial review in respect of the imposition of any sentence in the District Court before a different judge; it also commented that the applicant could also still appeal against the driving disqualification to the Circuit Court.

Not guilty plea not an aggravating factor In *The People v. Connaughton*, Court of Criminal Appeal, April 5, 2001, the issue arose as to whether a plea of not guilty should be regarded as an aggravating factor in sentencing. The issue arose in this way. The defendant had pleaded not guilty to various charges, including dangerous driving causing serious bodily harm. He was found guilty and was then sentenced to two years' imprisonment and disqualified from driving for eight years. He sought leave to appeal and was granted bail pending his application. A number of issues were raised concerning the conviction itself, but these were rejected by the Court of Criminal Appeal (he submitted, for example, that worn tyres on his car constituted a hidden danger, which ought to have been pointed out to the jury: the Court of Criminal Appeal gave short shrift to this, noting that as the applicant ought to have ensured that his own car was roadworthy, the state of his own tyres was not a hidden danger). On sentencing, he argued that the trial judge had viewed his decision to fight the case as an aggravating factor when imposing the two year sentence. The Court of Criminal Appeal (which had granted bail pending the appeal) affirming the sentence of two years, but suspended the final six months. It held that the trial judge had been correct when he viewed the offence as coming in the medium range of offences. It accepted that while a plea of guilty might be a mitigating factor when deciding on sentence, the fact that a defendant invoked his constitutional right to a trial could not be viewed as an aggravating factor; thus, the reference in sentencing to the applicant's not guilty plea was in error. While the Court concluded that the sentence imposed was appropriate in the serious circumstances of this case, it was appropriate to suspend the last six months of it.

Robbery: suspension on condition of compensation In *The People v. Kennedy*, Court of Criminal Appeal, February 27 2001, the prosecution applied successfully to review the sentences imposed on the two defendants pursuant to section 2 of the Criminal Justice Act 1993. The defendants had pleaded guilty to charges of robbery contrary to section 23 of the Larceny Act 1916. They had been sentenced to five years' imprisonment, with the entire sentence suspended, subject to a review after one year, with the trial judge indicating that the defendants were also to compensate their victim. The defendants subsequently paid £2,000 to him. The prosecution argued that the sentence had been unduly lenient and did not reflect the gravity of the offences and that the condition of paying compensation to the victim had been inappropriate.

In approaching the issue whether the sentence had been unduly lenient under the 1993 Act, the Court applied the test in *The People v. Byrne, sub nom Director of Public Prosecutions v. Byrne* [1995] 1 I.L.R.M. 279 (*Annual Review of Irish Law 1994*, pp.224-6) that the onus was on the Director to prove that the sentence was unduly lenient, and that the Court had to balance conflicting matters in order to achieve a just sentence, which had to be proportionate to the crime, to the circumstances of the defendants, and to the impact on the victim. In the instant case, the Court was satisfied that a five year prison sentence was appropriate, but that the suspension of the entire sentence was inappropriate as the type of offence warranted an immediate custodial sentence. In particular, the Court held that the trial judge erred in adjourning sentence for a year for the purpose of allowing the defendants to collect adequate compensation: it emphasised that there should be no sense of purchasing a way out of a sentence. While the Court also accepted that the lapse of time was a factor to be taken into account on the appeal, it nonetheless concluded that the suspension of the entirety of the five year sentence had been unduly lenient. It substituted a suspension of the final four and a half years of the sentence, thus requiring the defendants to serve six months' imprisonment.

Sentence review by trial judge: desirability   In *The People (DPP) v. Finn* [2001] 2 I.L.R.M. 211 (SC), the Supreme Court once again appeared to disapprove the use of sentencing reviews by trial judges while at the same time affirming orders in which they had been used in the particular circumstances which arose. The background was that the defendant had pleaded guilty in the Central Criminal Court to rape. In December 1996, the trial judge (Lavan J) had imposed a sentence of seven years imprisonment, but subject to a review of the sentence to be made in 1998 having regard to the defendant's behaviour in the meantime. In October 1998, having heard evidence of the defendant's behaviour in prison, the trial judge suspended the sentence on certain conditions. At a further hearing in April 1999, the trial judge noted that the conditions referred to in October 1998 had been met and he affirmed the order made.

The Director of Public Prosecutions appealed, pursuant to section 2 of the Criminal Justice Act 1993, against the sentence on the grounds of being unduly lenient. The defendant argued that the time limit of 28 days for making such an appeal in the 1993 Act ran from the date at which the sentence was originally imposed in December 1996. The Court of Criminal Appeal rejected this argument in an *ex tempore* judgment and substituted a sentence of six years with no suspension in respect of the rape offence. The Court certified that the case involved a point of law of exceptional public importance. On further appeal, the Supreme Court held that the time limit for appeals under the 1993

Act did indeed run from the time of the original sentence in 1996 and that the Director was thus out of time. Delivering the only judgment, Keane C.J. applied conventional principles of statutory interpretation in noting that the facility afforded to the State to challenge a sentence as being 'unduly lenient' constituted a significant encroachment upon the finality of a judicial decision in favour of a convicted person which, at least in the case of sentences imposed on persons convicted on indictment, was without precedent. Hence the importance of the time limit of 28 days for making such an application prescribed by section 2(2) of the 1993 Act and the absence of any power in the court to extend that time. Not having applied to the Court of Criminal Appeal within the 28 days, Keane C.J. held that the Director was precluded from making an application to the court in respect of the orders subsequently made by the trial judge in October 1998 and April 1999. Thus, the Court of Criminal Appeal was wrong in law in substituting a sentence of six years with no suspension. In the circumstances, the Court in effect held that it too was without jurisdiction and concluded that the orders made by Lavan J. in October 1998 and April 1999 should stand.

Notwithstanding that the Supreme Court was thus *functus officio* and that, as Keane C.J. himself acknowledged, any comments on the use of the review procedure would be *obiter*, the Court went on to discuss *in extenso* the desirability of such sentencing procedure. The Court concluded, in effect, that the sentence review procedure usurped the role of the Oireachtas in connection with remission of sentences. In the stark words of the Chief Justice 'it should be discontinued.' In coming to this conclusion, the Court firmly agreed with similar comments made by Henchy J, delivering the judgment of the Court of Criminal Appeal in *The People (DPP) v. Cahill* [1980] I.R. 8.

The judgment of Keane C.J. in *Finn* contains a lengthy analysis of the position of the sentencing judge at the conclusion of a criminal trial. He noted that the trial judge is required to impose a sentence on the convicted person, and that when he or she has done so he or she is, as a general rule, *functus officio* and cannot thereafter impose a further sentence. If, the Chief Justice opined, the review procedure availed of by the trial court in this case were to be regarded as the imposition by the trial judge of a different sentence at a later stage, its invalidity would be beyond argument. But, because the trial judge was entitled to reserve to himself a power, when imposing sentence, to consider at a later date whether it should be suspended in whole or in part having regard to the behaviour of the applicant in the interim period, to that extent and that extent alone, the trial judge was not *functus officio*, and the order made by him at the review procedure was no more than the carrying into effect of the sentence already imposed upon him. In this respect, Keane C.J. acknowledged that there had been no binding decision of the courts considering whether such a practice was invalid as opposed to being 'merely' undesirable (indeed, he expressly noted that judicial views were clearly divided on this).

Nonetheless, having considered the *Cahill* case in particular, Keane C.J.

stated that the making of such review orders was not merely inconsistent with the provisions on remission of sentence in section 23 of the Criminal Justice Act 1951 Act. It also offended, he considered, the separation of powers in this area mandated by Article 13.6 of the Constitution, which expressly vests the power of commutation or remission in the President but provides that the power may also be conferred by law on other authorities. Since under Article 15.2.1 the sole and exclusive power of making laws is vested in the Oireachtas, it was for the legislative arm alone to determine which authorities other than the President should exercise that power. It was on that basis, albeit accepting that his comments were *obiter* (and thus ironically exceeding the boundaries of the *functus officio* prescript), that Keane C.J. concluded for the Court that the practice of sentence reviews be discontinued. Whether because of the questionable precedental value of the decision in *Finn* or because of the peculiar nature of the sentencing function, it must be acknowledged that the practice of sentence review has continued since the decision in *Finn*. We may thus have to wait until the recommendations on this area by the Law Reform Commission's *Report on Sentencing* (LRC 53-1996) (referred to by the Chief Justice in *Finn*) are implemented by appropriate legislation. Until then, the views of the Supreme Court in *Finn* seem destined to be ignored.

SEX OFFENDERS AT 2001

Introduction The Sex Offenders Act 2001 provides, *inter alia*, for a register of certain sex offenders. The Act came into effect on September 27, 2001: Sex Offenders Act, 2001 (Commencement) Order 2001 (S.I. No. 426 of 2001). The Act imposes a requirement on certain sex offenders to notify the Garda Síochána of their name and address and any changes to those details in order to ensure that the information in that respect contained within the Garda Síochána national computer is kept fully up to date. The Act also creates a new civil court order against sex offenders whose behaviour in the community gives the Garda Síochána reasonable cause for concern that the order is necessary to protect the public from serious harm from him or her. It creates a new offence for sex offenders who seek or accept work involving unsupervised contact with children without informing the employer of their conviction. It also provides for the post-release supervision of sex offenders by the Probation and Welfare Service. Part 6 of the 2001 Act deals with quite a separate issue: it introduces separate legal representation for complainants in rape and other serious sexual assault cases during applications to adduce evidence or cross-examine on the complainant's past sexual experience: this element is discussed above.

Register of offenders Part 2 of the 2001 Act (sections 3 to 12) deals with the register of sex offenders. Section 3 of the 2001 Act is a key provision, which defines sexual offences for the purposes of the Act. It provides that, subject to certain exceptions discussed below, the offences referred to in the Schedule to the Act will be the sexual offences to which the Act will apply, namely those which will trigger the notification requirement and other provisions concerning the register of offenders and related offences. The list in the Schedule is extensive, and includes rape, aggravated sexual assault, sexual assault and other sexual offences which involve children. During the Oireachtas debate on the legislation, it was stated that the aim of the Act was to target the child sex abuser and the serious sex offender. Because of this, a number of offences that would otherwise attract the notification obligation are exempted. The offences of sexual assault and incest in cases where the victim was 17 years of age or more and the convicted person was not sentenced to imprisonment for the offence are exempted. Consensual teenage sexual activity where the victim is between 15 and 17 years of age and the other party to the offence is no more than three years older than the victim is also exempted.

Section 8 of the 2001 Act sets out the notification periods which apply under the Act. These are a minimum five year period for those convicted and sentenced to a non-custodial sentence or a fully suspended sentence; a seven year period for those sentenced to a custodial sentence of six months or less; a 10 year period for those sentenced to a custodial sentence of between six months and two years; and a lifetime notification obligation for those sentenced to more than two years. In the case of consecutive terms for two or more qualifying offences, the period will be the aggregate of those terms. In the case of concurrent terms, it will be the aggregate of those terms less any deduction necessary to ensure that no period is counted more than once. The periods that would otherwise be applicable are halved for offenders under 18 years of age at the time of sentence.

Section 9 of the 2001 Act defines the nature of the notification requirements. Initially an offender must, either by personal attendance at a major Garda station or by written notice, notify his or her name and home address to the Garda Síochána within 10 days of becoming subject to the requirement. Thereafter he or she must, again within 10 days of the event, notify the Garda Síochána of any subsequent changes to his or her name or address and any other address at which he or she spends a qualifying period (defined as 10 days or 2 or more periods which taken together amount to 10 days or more) in any 12 month period. Persons who leave the State for an intended continuous period of 10 days or more at a time must inform the Gardaí in advance of their leaving. If the person, when leaving, did not intend to remain outside the State for a continuous period of 10 days, but does, he or she must so inform the Gardaí within a further 10 days.

Section 10 of the 2001 Act provides that a person who is subject to the lifetime notification requirement may apply to the Circuit Court for an order discharging him or her from the obligation to comply with those requirements on the ground that the interests of the common good are no longer served by his or her continuing to be subject to them. Such an application may be made after 10 years have elapsed from the applicant's date of release from prison and the applicant is required to notify the Garda Síochána of his or her intention to make such an application. The Garda Síochána are entitled to appear and be heard at the hearing of the application and will in the event of the court making an order discharging the applicant from the obligation, be notified by the Court of the discharge.

Section 11 makes failure to comply with the notification requirements or the provision of false or misleading information a summary offence (for which there is provision for a defence of reasonable excuse for failure to so comply).

Section 12 of the 2001 Act brings under the terms of the Act persons who have been convicted of sex offences abroad who, at the time of the conviction or thereafter, become resident for a qualifying period in Ireland. There must be comparability between the offence to which the foreign conviction applies and offences covered by the Act.

Section 13 of the 2001 Act provides that the court in which a person is convicted of an offence to which the Act applies, will immediately on conviction notify the Garda Síochána that the offender is subject to the notification requirements by issuing a certificate to this effect. The minimum five year notification period will apply until the sentence is determined. Once sentence is determined, the court will notify the Garda Síochána of the precise notification period applicable in the individual case by way of the issue of a second certificate. Copies of the certificate(s) will also be issued by the court to the convicted person and to the person in charge of the place where the convicted person is detained and the Probation and Welfare Service, as appropriate.

Sex offenders orders   Part 3 of the 2001 Act (sections 14 to 23) provides for a new civil court order (called the sex offender order) against sex offenders whose behaviour gives cause for concern that they pose a risk of serious harm to the public. Section 15 enables a Garda superintendent to apply to the Circuit Court for a sex offender order against any sex offender whose behaviour in the community gives the Garda Síochána reasonable cause for concern that an order is necessary to protect the public from serious harm from him or her. Section 15 defines "serious harm" as the risk of death or serious personal injury, either physical or psychological, which would be occasioned if the respondent were to commit a sexual offence subsequent to the making of an application under section 15. Two criteria must be satisfied before an order can be applied for and made. First, the offender must have been convicted of, or found guilty but insane for, a sexual offence as defined in section 3 of the 2001 Act. Such a conviction can have occurred either before or after the commencement of Part 3 of the 2001 Act. Where the offender was convicted abroad, the court will also need to satisfy itself that the offence corresponds with a sexual offence as defined in section 3. Second, the respondent must have acted, since the commencement of Part 3, in such a way as to give the court reasonable grounds for believing that an order is necessary to protect the public from serious harm from him or her. Section 15 also provides that the prohibitions contained in the order must be limited to those which are necessary for the purpose of protecting the public from serious harm from the respondent. The order will be in negative or prohibitive terms; the court will not be able to compel a person to do anything, only *not* to do certain things. Section 15 provides that the order may be granted for a minimum of five years or such longer period as the court may provide. Finally, section 15 also provides that one of the consequences of the making of a sex offender order will be to bring the respondent within the notification requirements of Part 2 of the 2001 Act. Section 20 provides that a court, in hearing applications for the making, varying, discharge, or appeal from a sex offender order, will act in its civil capacity and that the civil standard of proof, the balance of probabilities, will apply. It also provides that proceedings under Part 3 (except under section 21) will the heard otherwise than in public. Section 21 provides for a maximum penalty of £1,500 and/or 12 months imprisonment on summary conviction and for a maximum penalty of 5 years imprisonment and/or a fine on conviction on indictment in respect of a contravention of a sex offender order.

Information to prospective employers   Part 4 of the 2001 Act (sections 24 and 25) places an onus on convicted sex offenders to inform prospective employers of the fact and nature of their conviction when applying for a position involving unsupervised access to children. Section 25 makes it an offence for a convicted sex offender to apply for or to accept work or to offer services, a necessary and regular part of which consists mainly of unsupervised access to, or contact with, children without informing the employer of his or her conviction for a sexual offence, as referred to in the Schedule.

Post-release supervision for sex offenders   Part 5 of the 2001 Act (sections 26 to 32) applies to convicted sex offenders for whom the sentencing court considers the appropriate sentence to be one of deprivation of liberty. Section 27 places an obligation on the court, in sentencing a sex offender, to consider whether or not to impose a "sentence involving post-release supervision". In so doing, the court must take into account the need (a) for a period of post-release supervision of the offender, (b) to protect the public from serious harm from the offender, (c) to prevent the commission of further sexual offences by the offender and (d) the need to rehabilitate or further rehabilitate the offender. In order to assist it in deciding whether or not to impose a sentence involving post-release supervision, the court may hear evidence or submissions from any concerned person. Persons sentenced to life imprisonment are excluded because on release from prison they are always placed under lifelong Probation and Welfare Service supervision in the community as a condition of temporary release. Section 28 provides that a sentence involving post-release supervision will be made up of (a) the custodial period that the court would have imposed in any event and (b) a "supervision period" of such duration as the court considers necessary, and during which the offender will be subject to post-release supervision by the Probation and Welfare Service. The supervision period commences on the date the offender is released from prison. The combined custodial sentence and period of post-release supervision cannot exceed the maximum term of imprisonment available for the offence concerned. Section 29 enables the court, when imposing post-release supervision, to impose additional requirements, including the requirement to receive psychological counselling or other appropriate treatment programmes run by the Probation and Welfare Service or other bodies or a requirement prohibiting a sex offender from doing things which the court considers necessary for the purpose of protecting the public from serious harm from the offender. Section 32 provides that non-compliance with any of the post-release supervision conditions will be a summary offence. Provision is made for a defence of reasonable excuse.

SEXUAL OFFENCES

Extra-territoriality   *Hatchell v. Director of Public Prosecutions*, High Court, April 6, 2001 concerned a challenge to a charge under the Sexual Offences (Jurisdiction) Act 1996 (*Annual Review of Irish Law 1996*, pp.273-4). The applicant had been charged with sexually assaulting a child in England, the indictment specifying that this was 'contrary to section 2(1) of the Sexual Offences (Jurisdiction) Act 1996.' It was in respect of this single offence that the District Court returned the applicant for trial to the Circuit Criminal Court. The applicant contended that the return for trial was invalid on the basis that section 2(1) of the 1996 Act did not disclose an offence known to law. The trial judge rejected this submission, but granted an adjournment to enable judicial review proceedings be taken. McKechnie J. granted the relief sought, namely an order quashing the return for trial.

The crucial provision to be considered was section 2(1) of the 1996 Act, which states:

> "Where a person, being a citizen of the State or being ordinarily resident in the State, does an act, in a place other than the State ('the place'), against or involving a child which—
>
> (a) constitutes an offence under the law of the place, and
> (b) if done within the State, would constitute an offence under, or referred to in, an enactment specified in the Schedule to this Act,
>
> he or she shall be guilty of the second-mentioned offence."

The enactments specified in the Schedule include, for example, the Criminal Justice (Rape) Act 1981. McKechnie J. held that there was one net point for consideration, namely whether section 2 of the 1996 Act created a new separate and distinct offence from any of those mentioned in the enactments specified in the Schedule to the 1996 Act. If it did the return for trial was clearly valid and the Circuit Criminal Court had jurisdiction to hear and determine the prosecution. If it did not then the single matter in respect of which the return for trial was made failed to disclose any criminal offence known to law. As such the return for trial would be invalid and inoperative. He held that the reference to 'the second-mentioned offence' in section 2(1) of the 1996 Act could only mean that the accused person would be guilty of at least one of the offences specified in the Scheduled enactments. To hold otherwise would be a serious and impermissible rewriting of the plain and unambiguous wording of the subsection itself. Accordingly the phrase 'second mentioned offence' could only be referable to one or more of the offences identified in the enactments mentioned in the Schedule thereto. Consequently, he rejected the submission that a new offence had been created. On this basis, he concluded that the return for trial was invalid, and the accused person was not legally before the Circuit Court. That Court therefore had no jurisdiction to embark upon or proceed with the prosecution.

The prosecution had also argued that the Court should, in its discretion, refuse relief on the basis of the applicant's failure to comply with the time limits in Order 84, rule 21 of the Rules of the Superior Courts 1986. But McKechnie J. rejected this argument also. He held that if the court was to refuse to grant an order of *certiorari*, the applicant would have to submit himself to the Circuit Criminal Court for further prosecution of a criminal charge in circumstances where it had no jurisdiction to do so and he could not under any such circumstances facilitate that. To do so would be in clear violation of the applicant's right to a trial in due course of law under Article 38.1.

THEFT AND FRAUD OFFENCES ACT 2001

Introduction   The Criminal Justice (Theft and Fraud Offences) Act 2001 is an enormously significant legislative enactment. It updated and consolidated the law relating to dishonesty and fraud, repealing and replacing previous legislation on larceny and forgery. It also abolished the common law offences of larceny, burglary, robbery, cheating, extortion under colour of office and forgery. The 2001 Act implements many of the recommendations in the Law Reform Commission's *Report on The Law Relating to Dishonesty* (LRC 43-1992) (*Annual Review of Irish Law 1992*, pp.275-85) and the *Report of the Government Advisory Committee on Fraud* (1993). In effect, the 2001 Act replaced the law on dishonesty found to a limited extent in the common law but more significantly in the Larceny Act 1861, the Larceny Act 1916 and the Larceny Act 1990 (see *Annual Review of Irish Law 1990*, pp.229-35), the 1990 Act largely updating the offences surrounding receiving and handling stolen property. As acknowledged during the Oireachtas debates, the previous legislation covered the more serious offences of dishonesty, but there had been difficulties caused by the fact that a number of different offences existed to describe similar dishonest behaviour. Equally, the previous law does not always deal adequately with some forms of dishonesty, such as false statements as to future intentions. The 2001 Act also deals with offences of forgery and counterfeiting, replacing the Forgery Acts 1861 and 1913. It also provided for amendments concerning the investigation of such offences and to trial procedures. Finally, the 2001 Act also includes measures designed for the protection of the European Union's financial interests from fraud and corruption and the protection of the euro currency.

Commencement   Most provisions of the 2001 Act will come into effect on the making of Commencement Orders, but the following came into effect on the passing of the Act on December 19 2001: section 23 (designation of States under the Criminal Justice Act 1994), section 53 (summary trial of indictable offences), section 58 (liability for offences by corporate bodies), section 60(1) (use of foreign evidence), Part 5 (counterfeiting) and Part 7 (investigation of offences). At the time of writing (July 2002), no Commencement Orders have been made under the 2001 Act.

Overview of Act   In brief, Part 2 of the 2001 Act (sections 4 to 15) sets out the main offences of theft and dishonesty. These include: stealing, deceiving another person or using a computer unlawfully such that one makes a gain or receives a benefit or causes another to suffer a loss, failing to pay for goods or services, false accounting, burglary, robbery and possessing articles for use in committing certain offences. Part 3 of the 2001 Act (sections 16 to 23) relates mainly to offences of handling or possessing stolen property and withholding information regarding stolen property. Part 4 (sections 24 to 31) amends the law on forgery and replaces the offences contained in the Forgery Acts 1861 and 1913. It sets out the various offences relating to forgery and the copying and use of false instruments for the purpose of inducing a person to accept these as genuine with consequent prejudice to that person. Part 5 of the 2001 Act (sections 32 to 39) contains provisions against counterfeiting of currency notes and coins, including euro notes and coins. Part 6 (sections 40 to 47) contains measures to counter fraud affecting the European Union's financial interests as well as corruption of or by officials. Part 7 of the 2001 Act (sections 48 to 52) deals with the investigation of offences covered by the Act, including the granting of search warrants, forfeiture of property and orders to produce evidential material. Part 8 (sections 53 to 57), relating to the trial of offences, provides for summary trial of offences under the Act and for alternative verdicts concerning offences of stealing, handling or possessing stolen or unlawfully obtained property. It also provides for the restitution of property to the true owner and for the provision of documents to juries to assist them in their deliberations. Part 9 (sections 58 to 66) deals with miscellaneous matters, including the liability of corporate bodies, the reporting of offences by auditors and the admissibility of certain documents as evidence. It is not possible in the current context to provide a comprehensive discussion of the 2001 Act. What follows, therefore, is a brief outline of the main provisions.

Theft   Section 4(1) of the 2001 Act provides that a person will be guilty of the offence of theft where he or she dishonestly (that is, without a claim of right made in good faith) appropriates property with the intention of depriving the owner of it. The word appropriates is defined as usurping or adversely interfering with the owner's proprietary rights and 'depriving' may be temporary or permanent for the purposes of the section. This is in line with the recommendations of the Law Reform Commission) and can be described as similar to the main elements contained in the UK's Theft Act 1968, while taking into account the difficulties encountered in some elements of the 1968 Act (see the discussion in the Annual Review 1992, 276). Under section 4(2) no appropriation without consent occurs where the person believes he or she had consent (excluding consent obtained by deception) or where he or she believes the true owner could not reasonably be discovered. The maximum penalty which the court may impose on a person found guilty of theft is an unlimited fine and/or up to 10 years in prison. Section 5 of the 2001 Act list a number of exceptions to the offence of theft. Thus, a transfer of property will not amount to theft in circumstances where a person has obtained the property for value and in good faith but it subsequently transpires that the property had been stolen. Other exceptions include land or things forming part of land and severed from it or the picking of wild flowers and fruit and the taking of wild creatures not already in another's possession.

Deception offences   Section 6 of the 2001 Act provides it is an offence for any person dishonestly to induce another person to do or not to do some act with the intention of making a gain for oneself or some other person or causing a loss to another. The maximum penalty for conviction on indictment is an unlimited fine and/or five years in prison. Section 7 provides it is an offence for a person, by any deception, to dishonestly obtain services (including a loan) with the intention of making a gain, either personally or for another, or causing loss to any person. The maximum penalty for conviction on indictment is an unlimited fine and/or five years in prison. Section 8 provides it is an offence for a person, knowing that payment on the spot is required or expected, dishonestly to make off without paying for the goods or services with the intention of avoiding payment on the spot, except in such circumstances where the payment would not be legally enforceable. The maximum penalty for conviction on indictment is a fine of £3,000 and/or 2 years in prison. Thus, while the offences under sections 6 and 7 are arrestable offences (carrying maximum penalties of five years), the offence under section 8 is not. For this reason, section 8 makes specific provision for arrest powers.

Unlawful use of computer   Section 9 makes it an offence dishonestly to operate or cause to be operated (whether the act occurs within the State or outside the State) a computer within the State with the intention of making a gain for oneself or for another or causing a loss to another. The maximum penalty for conviction on indictment is an unlimited fine and/or 10 years in prison.

False accounting   In line with the *Report of the Government Advisory Committee on Fraud* (1993), section 10 of the 2001 Act introduces the offence of false accounting. This is committed where a person, intending to make a gain for oneself or another or to cause loss to another, does any one of the following: destroys or otherwise falsifies accounts or documents for accounts; fails to complete accounts or documents; furnishes false or misleading accounts or documents. Falsifying accounts or documents arises where misleading or false entries are made or where relevant particulars are omitted. The maximum penalty for conviction on indictment is an unlimited fine and/or 10 years in prison.

Falsification of valuable documents   In a similar vein, section 11 provides that it is an offence dishonestly to procure the execution of valuable documents, such as conveyances, securities or wills, or to procure their destruction, defacement or concealment, with the intention of making a gain for oneself or another or causing a loss to another. The maximum penalty for conviction on indictment is an unlimited fine and/or 10 years in prison.

Burglary and aggravated burglary   Section 12 provides that a person will be guilty of burglary if he or she enters a building (which includes inhabited vehicles or vessels or other structures) as a trespasser intending to commit an arrestable offence (that is, an offence carrying a penalty of at least five years in prison upon conviction) or, being present as a trespasser, commits or attempts to commits such an offence. The maximum penalty on conviction on indictment is an unlimited fine and/or 14 years in prison. Section 13 provides that aggravated burglary consists of burglary committed in circumstances where the perpetrator has with him or her at the time a firearm, imitation firearm, weapon of offence or explosive. The maximum penalty upon conviction on indictment is life imprisonment.

Robbery   Section 14 provides that a person who steals will be guilty of robbery if, at the time or immediately before the stealing and in order to do so, he or she uses force or threatens force on any person. The maximum penalty on conviction on indictment is life imprisonment.

Possession of certain articles Section 15 provides that it is an offence for a person to have in his or her possession, when not at his or her own residence, any article intending to use it in connection with certain offences, for example theft, burglary, certain offences involving deception, blackmail, extortion and the unauthorised taking of a vehicle. The maximum penalty on conviction on indictment is an unlimited fine and/or five years in prison.

Handling and receiving stolen property and other proceeds of crime   Part 3 of the 2001 Act (sections 16 to 23) deal with handling and receiving stolen property and largely replicates, with some amendments, the provisions introduced by the Larceny Act 1990 (see *Annual Review of Irish Law 1990*, pp.229-35). Thus, section provides that the offence of handling stolen property consists of doing any of the following other than in the course of stealing: dishonestly receiving, arranging to receive, undertaking or assisting in, its retention or removal, knowing it was stolen or being reckless as to whether it was stolen. The maximum penalty on conviction on indictment is an unlimited fine and/or 10 years in prison. Section 18 provides it is an offence for a person without lawful authority or excuse to possess stolen property, other than in the course of stealing, knowing, or being reckless as to whether, it was stolen. The maximum penalty on conviction on indictment is an unlimited fine and/or five years in prison. Section 19 provides that the Gardaí are empowered to require any person to account for property in his or her possession where there are reasonable grounds for believing that an offence of theft or handling stolen property has been committed and where the person is found in possession of such property and the Gardaí inform the person of their belief concerning the property. Failure or refusal, without reasonable excuse, to give such an account is an offence carrying a maximum penalty on summary conviction of a fine of €1,900 and/ or 12 months in prison or both, but this will only apply where the person was told in ordinary language of the consequences of failure to provide the account. Section 20 provides that the provisions of Part 3 of the Act apply whether the stealing occurred before or after the Act commences and to stealing outside the State.

Money laundering   Section 21 of the 2001 Act inserts a new section 31 of the Criminal Justice Act 1994, which deals with money laundering. The new section 31 makes it an offence for a person to do any of a number of things in relation to the property knowing or believing, or being reckless as to whether, that property is or represents the proceeds of criminal conduct. These include: converting, transferring, handling or removing the property from the State intending to conceal its true nature, assisting another to avoid prosecution for criminal conduct or avoiding the making of a confiscation order. Other offences in section 31 of the 1994 Act, as amended, include concealing or disguising its true nature, or acquiring or possessing the property, and also deal with knowledge or recklessness as to the source of the property and also assumptions about the intention of persons with regard to the property. The maximum penalty on conviction on indictment is an unlimited fine and/or 14 years in prison.

Forgery   Part 4 of the 2001 Act (sections 24 to 31) deals with forgery offences and replace the offences previously dealt with in the Forgery Acts 1861 and 1913. Section 25 provides that a person who makes a false instrument intending it to be accepted as genuine resulting in prejudice to the person accepting it will be guilty of forgery. The maximum penalty on conviction on indictment is an unlimited fine and/or 10 years in prison. Section 26 provides it is an offence to use a false instrument, knowing or believing it to be false, intending to induce a person to accept it as genuine and thereby cause that person to suffer some loss. The maximum penalty on conviction on indictment is an unlimited fine and/or 10 years in prison. Section 27 makes it an offence for a person to make a copy of an instrument, knowing or believing it to be a false instrument, intending that it should pass as genuine and thereby cause loss to any person accepting it as genuine. The maximum penalty on conviction on indictment is an unlimited fine and/or 10 years in prison. Section 28 makes it an offence for a person to use a copy of a false instrument, knowing or believing it to be false, intending to pass it as genuine and thereby cause loss to another. The maximum penalty on conviction on indictment is an unlimited fine and/or 10 years in prison. Section 29 provides it is an offence to have custody or control of certain false instruments intending to pass them as genuine thereby causing loss to another. These include money and postal orders, postage stamps, revenue stamps and licences, cheques, cheque cards, credit cards, share certificates, birth certificates, passports, social services cards and admission tickets. The maximum penalty on conviction on indictment is an unlimited fine and/or five years in prison for some offences, with others carrying a maximum of 10 years in prison.

Counterfeiting of currency   Part 5 of the 2001 Act (sections 32 to 39) deals with counterfeiting offences concerning currency. Section 32 defines currency note and coin to mean those lawfully issued or customarily used as money in the State or any other state, including euro notes and coins, whether issued or not. A counterfeit includes things which resemble currency notes and coins. Section 33 provides it is an offence to make a counterfeit currency note or coin intending that it pass as genuine. It is also an offence for a person outside the State to make a counterfeit note or coin with the intention that it pass as genuine in any EU Member State. The maximum penalty for conviction on indictment is an unlimited fine and/or 10 years in prison. Section 35 provides it is an offence to make or have in one's custody or control anything intending to use it or to permit another to use it to make a counterfeit of a currency note or coin intending it to be passed as genuine. Section 37 provides it is an offence for a person, without lawful authority or excuse, to import into or export from an EU Member State a counterfeit of a currency note or coin.

Protection of EU's Financial Interests Part 6 of the 2001 Act (sections 40 to 47) implements the Convention on the Protection of the European Communities' Financial Interests. Section 42 is the key section, which provides that it is an offence to commit, participate in or obtain benefit or advantage from a fraud affecting the Communities' financial interests. The maximum penalty on conviction on indictment is an unlimited fine and/or five years in prison. Section 45 makes it an offence to commit, participate in or instigate any fraud affecting the Communities' financial interests or an offence of money laundering outside the State where a benefit is obtained by a person in the State, or where assistance in their commission is rendered by a person within the State or where the offender is an Irish citizen or a national or EU official.

Investigation of offences Part 7 of the 2001 Act (sections 48 to 52) deals with a number of aspects of the investigation of offences under the Act. Thus, section 48 provides that search warrants will only be granted in the case of offences under the Act which carry a penalty of at least five years in prison. A judge of the District Court may grant a search warrant where evidence is given on oath by a Garda that there are reasonable grounds to suspect that evidence relating to such an offence is to be found in any place. Such a warrant will authorise the Gardaí to enter, within 7 days of its issue, to search the place and any persons found there and to examine or seize anything reasonably believed to be evidence relating to the offence. It also authorises the copying of documents or records, the seizure of computers containing records and the operation of a computer by the Gardaí including the provision to the Gardaí of passwords and copies of records. However, items subject to legal privilege may not be seized. Section 49 provides that it is an offence for a person to obstruct a Garda executing a search warrant, to refuse to identify oneself to the Garda if found on premises being searched or to fail to provide computer passwords or computer records when requested. Section 50 provides for the forfeiture and destruction by order of the District Court of property seized by the Gardaí which they suspect is being used in connection with forgery or counterfeiting. Where a person has been convicted of an offence of forgery or counterfeiting the court may order the forfeiture and destruction of property used in the commission of the offence. Before making an order for the forfeiture of property under this section the judge may hear submissions from the owner of the property.

Trial of offences Part 8 of the 2001 Act (sections 53 to 57) deals with the trial of offences covered by the Act. Section 53 provides that any of the indictable offences under the Act may be tried summarily by the District Court where the Court considers that the facts disclose a minor offence fit to be tried summarily, the accused agrees to summary disposal and the Director of Public Prosecutions consents. Section 54(1) provides that in proceedings for offences under sections 6, 7, 9, 10 and 11 it is sufficient for the prosecution to prove that the accused acted dishonestly with the intention of causing loss or making a gain. Section 54(2) provides that any number of persons may be charged in the same indictment with handling or possessing stolen property either at the same or at different times. Section 54(5) provides that stealing, handling or possession may be included in separate counts on the same indictment but may be tried together, while section 54(6) provides that any person or persons charged in the same indictment with separate counts of stealing may be found guilty of stealing, handling or possession. Section 55 deals with alternative verdicts and provides that a person charged with theft may be found guilty of handling or possession if the facts prove the latter and if charged with handling or possession, may be found guilty of theft if the facts prove theft. Section 57 provides that where a person is charged on indictment with an offence under the Act, the trial judge may order that the jury be provided with certain documents including any document admitted in evidence, transcripts of statements or evidence, charts, diagrams and any other document which the judge considers would be of assistance to the jury in its deliberations.

Restitution orders for stolen property; sale of goods   Section 56 of the 2001 Act (also included in Part 8 of the Act) provides that where a person is convicted of an offence related to the theft of property the court may order restoration of the stolen property to the rightful owner or the delivery to the person of property representing the proceeds of the stolen property or the payment of a sum representing the value of the stolen property. Where a person has bought the stolen property in good faith or has lent money on the security of it in good faith the court may order that the purchaser or lender shall be entitled to recover the sums paid or lent. An order under this section will only be made where the court is of the opinion that the evidence at the trial warrants it. This replaces the provisions on restoration of stolen property in section 24 of the Sale of Goods Act 1893, which is repealed by the 2001 Act (the UK Theft Act 1968 had also made a similar repeal).

Offences by corporate and other bodies   Section 58 includes what is now a standard provision (see also the Prevention of Corruption (Amendment) Act 2001, 186, above) that where an offence under the Act is committed by a body corporate or unincorporated body, with the consent or connivance of a director, manager or other similar officer of the body, that person as well as the corporate body is guilty of the offence.

Reporting of offences   Section 59 of the 2001 Act, which was inserted into the Act during its passage through the Oireachtas is an important provision in terms of the general corporate governance debate. It provides that where the accounts of a company or partnership indicate that an offence under the Act (other than sections 8, 12 to 15, 49(1) and 52(8)) may have been committed by the a company or partnership or by a partner in the firm or by a director, manager, secretary or other employee, then an auditor must, notwithstanding any professional obligations of privilege or confidentiality, report that fact to a member of the Garda Síochána. A person who fails, without reasonable excuse, to comply with this duty is guilty of an offence and is liable on summary conviction to a fine not exceeding €1,900 and/or 12 months imprisonment.

Military law   Section 63 of the Act inserts a new section 156 into the Defence Act 1954, which deals with larceny and similar offences by persons subject to military law. The new section 156 provides that it is an offence, triable before court-martial, for such a person to steal or handle or possess stolen property belonging to another such person or any public service property.

Transitional provisions   Section 65 of the 2001 Act is an important provision on transitional arrangements. It provides that it will only apply to offences committed wholly or partly after the appropriate provisions are commenced and that proceedings in being before such commencement will be unaffected by that commencement. It also provides that where an indictment charges, in the alternative, offences under the law existing before the Act's provisions are commenced and offences under the Act after commencement, the person may be convicted of the first mentioned offence. This provision is intended to deal with the difficulties identified in *Grealis and Corbett v. Director of Public Prosecutions* [2002] 1 I.L.R.M. 241 (see 180, above) with the repeal of offences by the Non-Fatal Offences against the Person Act 1997.

Defence Forces

CIARAN CRAVEN and GERARD HUMPHREYS, Barristers-at-Law

OVERSEAS MISSIONS

United Nations Mission in Ethiopia and Eritrea (UNMEE) The dispatch of a further armed contingent of the Permanent Defence Force for service with the United Nations Mission in Ethiopia and Eritrea (UNMEE) established under UN Security Council Resolutions 1312 and 1320 (of July 31, 2000 and September 15, 2000, respectively) was approved by motion of Dáil Éireann on October 25, 2001 (*Dáil Debates* Vol. 543(1) Col. 18). The contingent, which comprises 209 personnel left for service in November 2001.

All Overseas Service In 2001, there were 870 members of the Permanent Defence Force serving overseas in 10 different areas as follows:

1. UN Missions

(i)	UNIFIL (United Nations Interim Force in Lebanon)*	608
(ii)	UNTSO (United Nations Truce Supervision Organisation) – Israel, Syria and Lebanon	11
(iii)	UNFICYP (United Nations Peacekeeping Force in Cyprus)	5
(iv)	UNIKOM (United Nations Iraq Kuwait Observer Mission)	7
(v)	MINURSO (United Nations Mission for the Referendum in Western Sahara)	3
(vi)	UNMIK (United Nations Interim Administration Mission in Kosovo)	3
(vii)	UNMOP (United Nations Mission of Observers in Prevlaka)	1
(viii)	UNTAET (United Nations Transitional Administration in East Timor) UN Mandated Missions**	44
(ix)	SFOR Stabilisation Force in Bosnia and Herzegovina SFOR HQ Sarajevo	48
(x)	KFOR International Security Presence in Kosovo	103

Total number of personnel serving with UN missions   **833**

2. UN HQ (New York)
Department of Peacekeeping Operations (DPKO)   1

3. EU Missions
European Union Monitor Mission (EUMM) to the former Yugoslavia   10

4. Organisation for Security and Co-operation in Europe (OSCE)

(i)	OSCE Mission to Bosnia & Herzegovina	7
(ii)	OSCE Mission in Croatia	4
(iii)	OSCE Mission in Kosovo	1
(iv)	OSCE Presence in Albania	1
(v)	Staff Officer, Higher Level Planning Group, Vienna	1

5. Head of Military Staff (Brussels) 1

6. Western European Union HQ (Brussels)
Western European Union Military Staff 2

7. EU Council Secretariat (Brussels) 1

8. Liaison Office of Ireland, PfP (Brussels) 2

9. Representative to EU Interim Military Body (Brussels) 1

10. Military Representatives/ Advisers (on secondment to Dept of Foreign Affairs)

(i)	Military Adviser, Permanent Mission to UNHQ, New York	1
(ii)	Assistant Military Adviser, Permanent Mission to UNHQ, New York	1
(iii)	Military Adviser, Irish Delegation to OSCE, Vienna	1
(iv)	Military Representative to Ireland's EU/WEU Delegations, Brussels	1
(v)	Military Representative to Partnership Co-ordination Cell/Supreme Headquarters Allied Powers Europe (SHAPE), Mons, Belgium	1

Total Number of Defence Forces Personnel serving overseas*** **870**

Table adopted from *Dáil Debates* Vol. 530(6) Col. 1331 20/02/2001

* Permanent Defence Force involvement in UNIFIL ceased in November 2001.

** Dáil Éireann approved the placing of the contingent of the Permanent Defence Force serving with INTERFET (see, Annual Review 1999, 170) under the authority of the United Nations Transitional Administration in East Timor (UNTAET) on February 24, 2000 (*Dáil Debates* Vol. 515(2) Col. 307)

*** at February 16, 2001. UNMEE participation is not included in this table.

Only the dispatch of armed contingents of the Permanent Defence Force exceeding ten in number require prior Dáil approval (see, *Annual Review of Irish Law 1999*, p.169)

COURTS-MARTIAL APPEALS

Conduct to the prejudice of good order and discipline In *Re Berigan*, Courts-Martial Appeal Court, November 1, 2001 (Fennelly, Barr and O'Sullivan JJ.) the appellant, who was a company sergeant in the military police, had been convicted by limited court-martial in March 1999 on three charges of conduct to the prejudice of good order and discipline contrary to section 168(1) of the Defence Act 1954. He was acquitted on three other charges. Two of the charges on which he was convicted related to the opening and operating without authority of a cash account with a local supplier for the purchase of duty free goods for the Military Police mess of the United Nations Peacekeeping Force in Cyprus (UNFICYP) in Nicosia, where he was serving, at the relevant time. The third charge alleged that he had failed to account for duty free goods to a total value of CY£14,897.21 which he had purchased on the cash account. He appealed conviction and sentence (of a severe reprimand and a fine of IR£450) to the Courts-Martial Appeal Court.

There was no suggestion of dishonesty on the part of the appellant. The essence of the charges against him was the operating of a cash account, without authority, when a credit account – equipped with a bank account and associated record keeping – already existed. At the time, the appellant was a crime reader with the Military Police Corps under the command of the Force Provost Marshal. He was also the president of the committee for the Military Police mess and was *de facto* the day-to-day manager with responsibility for the ordering of supplies including supplies of duty free goods, in particular, alcohol and tobacco. The rules governing the mess required that he was to ensure that all purchases were made from the approved creditors' list and authorised by him. Initially, there was only one account - a credit account – with one supplier, payments being made by cheque drawn on the mess's account with a local bank and for which the signature of the Force Provost Marshal was required. Concern by the then Force Provost Marshal at excessive use of the duty free facility and the possibility that it was being abused by unentitled persons caused him to restrict access solely to persons entitled to use it. The evidence was that the appellant approached the supplier and asked whether the existing account could be split as he wished to be able to have better control of the duty free goods he was buying. A cash account accordingly was created and it was operated by the appellant for a number of months and was paid off when he left Cyprus. Concern by the Force Provost Marshal that the figures for sale of duty free goods were disproportionate led to an investigation and the charges against the appellant.

The evidence that his authority was required, but not sought, for the opening of the cash account and, accordingly, he had been unaware of its existence was, essentially, uncontroverted. Coupled with the other evidence available to the trial court-martial - including the fact that the appellant closed the account before he left and that his successor was unaware of its existence – the appeal court rejected the assertion that the appellant's conviction on the first two charges had been perverse. It also rejected all allegations of unfairness at the hearing – in respect of the absence of an original statement of one prosecution witness and the conduct of the hearing and of the judge-advocate. No unfairness was found to arise from the admission of the witness's evidence without an original statement. His evidence was in relation to opening and operating of the cash account and was tested very fully in cross-examination. In addition, the court found that the court-martial "was conducted with complete fairness and impartiality" and that the allegations against the judge-advocate were "entirely unmeritorious".

Another ground of appeal that was advanced was that certain documents had been admitted into evidence without proper formal proof and without regard to the need to identify them as originals emerging from proper custody, identified by those responsible for their creation, and that they were maintained carefully before being produced at the Court-Martial. As the essence of the first two charges against the appellant was that a separate cash account was opened and operated – and independent non-documentary evidence was available in that regard - the court considered that it was unnecessary for the prosecution to rely on proof of the impugned documents.

In respect of the third charge, the appellant relied on the Criminal Evidence Act, 1992 section 5 (which applies to courts-martial by virtue of section 2 of that Act). As to whether or not the documents relied on to prove the amount set out in this charge had been properly proved, however, the court did not consider that it had to express a view in light of the allowing of the appeal on this charge on the next ground.

On this charge, the court considered that the charge of failure to account was more serious than the others and that it did not arise directly from section 168. "It has to be treated, if anything, as an aspect of conduct prejudicial to good order and discipline." As a general proposition, however, as to whether 'conduct' prejudicial to good order and discipline could be proved by an omission or failure, the Courts-Martial Appeal Court rejected the contention that there was a distinction between neglect and conduct, insofar as the charge relating to the failure to account for the operations of the cash account was concerned. It did not consider that there was "any meaningful distinction between acts of commission and of omission so far as conduct is concerned. Either can constitute conduct." In this regard it might be noted that section 168, in any event, provides that an offence is committed by "any act, conduct, disorder *or neglect* to the prejudice of good order and discipline . . . ." (*emphasis* added). But, the court continued,

> " . . . a failure to account is a potentially confusing and even misleading charge. It is suggestive of an element of dishonesty. It can either mean that a person has kept for his own benefit monies for which he is bound to account or that he has failed to keep proper books and records."

The judge-advocate did not specify in what respect the appellant was bound to account and advised the trial court-martial that the charge could mean that the appellant had failed to disclose the existence of the account and to record sales. The appellant had, in fact, maintained a duty free sales book for this account. In the view of the court, this demonstrated the "unsatisfactory nature of this charge." As the goods were, in fact paid for, and since at least some written record of their purchase appears to have been maintained, it was arguable that, on one meaning, the goods were accounted for. If the essence of the charge was the failure to disclose the existence of the account, it was indistinguishable from the first charge. Essentially, the charge was void for vagueness and, in the circumstances, the appeal against conviction on this charge was allowed. In the circumstances, it was unnecessary to consider whether or not the trial court-martial had sufficient regard to the need for proof of *mens rea* beyond a reasonable doubt on this charge.

Accordingly, the appeal was allowed in respect of the third charge only, i.e. the failure to account for the goods purchased, and the conviction on the first two charges was affirmed. Insofar as penalty was concerned, the court considered that the failure to account for the monies received was the more serious of the three charges on which the appellant had been convicted and noted that the goods were always paid for, "and accounted for to at least some extent." It concluded:

> "However, some penalty must be imposed for a breach of military law. In view of the previous good character of the appellant throughout the entire of his military career, the court will impose the least sanction it can, namely a simple reprimand."

That, by the time of the appeal, the appellant was no longer a serving member of the Defence Forces was irrelevant to a determination of the issues that arose. He was subject to military law at the relevant time. The fact that the offences were alleged to have been committed outside the State was also irrelevant. Indeed, it is not even commented on in the course of the judgment, jurisdiction to deal with the matter being assumed. A soldier of the Permanent Defence Force is always subject to military law, irrespective of his place of service. (See, Humphreys & Craven, *Military Law in Ireland*, (Round Hall Sweet & Maxwell, Dublin, 1997, p.99).

It might be observed that in the imposition of a penalty, the court had regard to the sentence that had been imposed by the trial court-martial and the fact that the appeal against conviction on the most serious of the charges had been allowed. In this there was no departure from the principles set out by Finlay P. in *Re Connolly* 3 Frewen 1.

TERMINATION OF SERVICE

The service of an officer of the Defence Forces may be terminated in accordance with the provisions of the Defence Act, 1954. This provides that (s)he may resign his or her commission, retire voluntarily with permission or on grounds of age or be retired or dismissed by the President. (see, generally, Humphreys

& Craven *Military Law in Ireland*, pp.53 - 7). In particular, section 47(2) of the Act provides that an officer may, for any prescribed reason, be retired by the President. The reasons are prescribed by the Defence Forces Regulations, A.15 and include *inter alia* at paragraph 18(1)(f) retirement "in the interests of the service."

Such was the fate of the applicant in *De Róiste v Minister for Defence & ors* [2001] 1 I.R. 190. Here, the applicant was an officer of the Permanent Defence Force who was retired by the President "in the interests of the service" in June 1969. His case was that, when he was a lieutenant, in April 1969 some four years after he had been commissioned, he was placed in close service custody having been arrested by his superior officer without warning and without having been given a reason. Having been taken to Army Headquarters he was placed in a locked room and interrogated by officers of the intelligence section in an oppressive and intimidating manner and, Kafkaesque-like, was refused any information as to why he was being interrogated, other than that its cause was very serious. He was not furnished with the names of any persons making allegations against him. The questions centred, in particular, on his attendance at traditional music events usually in public bars around the country and on those who were known to attend these events in particular, one named individual. The interrogation, which went on for a number of days, was conducted by relays of army personnel, all of whom were armed, under the command of an officer of the rank of commandant who, at the time of the proceedings, was still alive. He accused the applicant of associating with known subversive elements.

The applicant maintained that he was shouted at, threatened and physically intimidated and feared for his personal safety. He became confused and disorientated and lost all sense of time. Following the interrogation, he was returned to his home station, but no charge was proffered against him. He was not told whether he was being placed in service custody. Being in doubt about his situation, he consulted a solicitor who advised him to request a court-martial if there was any charge or allegation against him, which request was refused. The applicant was questioned less oppressively, again at Army Headquarters, on a number of other occasions, over a period of months. No specific allegations were put to him. He asked to be allowed to have his solicitor present, but this was refused. In response to his repeated requests he was told that a court-martial was not an option at that time. Next he was posted to a Reserve Defence Force unit. Again he was unsuccessful in seeking redress under section 114 of the Act of 1954. (For a description of the redress procedure, see, Humphreys & Craven, *Military Law in Ireland*, pp. 237–9).

In June 1969, he was notified that he was being retired from the Defence Forces "in the interests of the service" and was given only twelve hours to leave the barracks. He was given neither any other reason for his purported "retirement" nor an opportunity to make any representations. In addition, he was given no military conduct assessment in the record of his service. The decision to retire him was published in Iris Oifigiúil, the same day. As Fennelly J. observed (at pp.212-3), although the reason for the applicant's dismissal

" . . . was ostensibly neutral, it was abundantly clear from the surrounding circumstances and above all from the absence of any record of conduct from his discharge record that he was being discharged for discreditable reasons."

There was independent evidence of the traumatic effect on the applicant of his dismissal. Family rejection compounded his distress. His solicitor subsequently discontinued practice and left the country. The applicant did not institute any proceedings at the time. Because of the circumstances of his dismissal, he was unable to obtain work in Ireland and, in 1971, he emigrated, obtaining only temporary manual labour positions in Britain and the United States. He was married but the marriage broke down. He returned to Ireland occasionally before doing so permanently in December 1987. Since that time he had been working on a part-time basis on a limited wage. Some media reports in 1997, when his sister was a candidate in the Presidential election, stated that he had been forced to resign from the Defence Forces because he was a Republican sympathiser. Following this he underwent therapy. It was then that he sought assistance and support and sought to institute his proceedings. He maintained that the trauma of his retirement had long term psychological consequences for him and that it was only within the twelve months preceding his application to the High Court that he had been able, with the assistance of a counsellor, to address the whole episode and its effect on his life. In this general contention he was supported by the evidence of a counsellor and a consultant psychiatrist.

In 1998 he sought and was granted leave to apply, by way of judicial review, for declarations that the actions of the respondents in 1969 were in breach of natural and constitutional justice and *ultra vires* and orders of certiorari quashing the respondents' decisions as there was an absence of fair procedures from the decision-making process and a refusal to accord him the benefit of the redress of wrongs procedure under the Defence Act, 1954. In addition, the applicant maintained that the DFR A. 15 paragraph 18(f) was unconstitutional. As Fennelly J. observed (at 213) this case bore a striking resemblance to that of the prosecutor, in *State (Gleeson) v. Minister for Defence* [1976] I.R. 280, who had been discharged from the Defence Forces under an analogous provision, Defence Force Regulation A. 10, paragraph 58(r) on the grounds of "his services being no longer required." (For a more general discussion of this case in the military law context, see Humphreys & Craven *Military Law in Ireland*, pp. 33-37.)

The respondents' preliminary objection to the granting of leave was that there had been inordinate and inexcusable delay on the part of the applicant and that they were prejudiced in their in their capacity to defend the claim: three of the officers who were directly involved in the investigation of the applicant and in making the decision which subsequently led to his being retired in 1969 had died, i.e. the then Deputy Judge Advocate General, the Director of Intelligence and the Chief of Staff of the Defence Forces. Accordingly, the respondents alleged, it was impossible adequately to respond to the applicant's claims. However, the officer who had supervised the applicant's interrogation was still alive and it was contended by the applicant that it would be unusual for the Deputy Judge Advocate General to be involved in such an investigation. On the trial of this preliminary issue McCracken J. (June 29, 1999) upheld the respondents' contention and dismissed the application. The applicant's appeal was dismissed by a unanimous Supreme Court (Keane C.J., Denham and Fennelly JJ.).

There was no dispute as to the principles of law to be applied in determining whether or not proceedings should be struck out on grounds of delay. These are set out *Rainsford v. Corporation of Limerick,* High Court July 31, 1979; *O'Domhnaill v. Merrick* [1984] I.R. 151; *Toal v. Duignan & ors (No. 1)* [1991] 1 I.L.R.M. 135; *State (Cussen) v Brennan* [1981] I.R. 181; *State (Furey) v. Minister for Defence* [1988] I.L.R.M. 89; *O'Flynn v. Mid-Western Health Board* [1991] 2 I.R. 223 and *Primor Plc v. Stokes Kennedy Crowley & ors,* Supreme Court December 19, 1995). Of those cases, however, the *dictum* of McCarthy J. in *Furey* was the subject of most judicial scrutiny. There, he stated (at 100) he could see:

> " . . . no logical reason why delay, however long, should, of itself, disentitle to *certiorari* any applicant for that remedy who can demonstrate that a public wrong has been done to him - that, for instance, a conviction was obtained without jurisdiction, or that, otherwise, the State has wronged him and that the wrong continues to mark or mar his life."

This was held to be strictly *obiter* both in the High Court, and by a unanimous Supreme Court. Keane C.J. pointed out (at p.197) that: "this passage cannot be regarded as a correct statement of the law." Denham J. (at p.207) stated:

> "These words were *obiter dicta.* Further, they appear in a judgment where the delay was one of four years. That is of an entirely different magnitude to the delay in this case of 29 years."

Fennelly J. also considered the passage as *obiter* and, in his consideration, he examined the decisions of the Supreme Court in *State (Kelly) v. District Justice for Bandon* [1947] I.R. 258 and *State (Vozza) v. Ó Floinn* [1957] I.R. 227 and noted that the court in each case considered, although the applicant was entitled to the order sought *ex debito justitiae,* whether delay and lack of candour would bar relief. Neither ground was established on the facts. In addition, he considered the decision of Henchy J. in *State (Gleeson) v. Minister for Defence*

[1976] I.R. 280 where he suggested (at p.297) that an entitlement to relief might be lost by "delay, acquiescence or other conduct . . . ." He, too, pointed out that the delay in *Furey*, which, it will be recalled, arose out of the same set of circumstances as *Gleeson*, was only 4½ years whereas in the instant case it was 29 years.

As to whether the court's discretion should be exercised in favour of the applicant, having cited *State (Hunt) v Circuit Judge, Midland Circuit* [1934] IR 196 and *State (Vozza) v. Ó Floinn* [1957] I.R. 227, Denham J. stated (at p.208):

> "In analysing the facts of a case to determine if there is a good reason to extend time or to allow judicial review, the court may take into account factors such as:
> (i)   the nature of the order or actions the subject of the application;
> (ii) the conduct of the applicant;
> (iii) the conduct of the respondents;
> (iv) the effect of the order under review on the parties subsequent to the order being made and any steps taken by the parties subsequent to the order to be reviewed;
> (v)   any effect which may have taken place on third parties by the order to be reviewed;
> (vi) public policy that proceedings relating to the public law domain take place promptly except when good reason is furnished. Such list is not exclusive."

She recognised that it would be difficult "to imagine conduct on the part of an applicant for certiorari which would disentitle him to an order of *certiorari* in regard to a conviction of a crime of any sort, where it is established that it was made without jurisdiction", *per* Maguire C.J. in *State (Vozza) v. Ó Floinn* [1957] I.R. 227 at p.244. In addition, Denham J. was satisfied (at p.209) that the actions the applicant sought to have reviewed were "serious, they did affect his life". Fennelly J., for his part (at p.213) conceded that on the applicant's own account of the facts, there could be "no doubt that he had a compelling case." Having reviewed the authorities and being satisfied that the applicant's complaint, if established in a timely fashion, would (if not successfully controverted by the respondent) have entitled the applicant to relief *ex debito justitiae* he held (at 221) that he was "bound . . . to apply 'promptly'".

In the final analysis, a delay of 29 years was found to be inordinate. It was also inexcusable. For Keane CJ, the evidence offered by the applicant was not sufficient to justify his taking no action for nearly thirty years. He had consulted a solicitor initially, and in respect of his not taking any further steps to seek legal redress, he was of the view (at 197) that:

> "[I]t cannot have been the effect of his dismissal and the surrounding

circumstances on him, since that did not prevent him from going to a solicitor in the first place."

Although, in the case of a criminal conviction without jurisdiction the justice of the case might be very clear, Denham J. affirmed the finding of McCracken J. that the applicant had made a choice – to leave the country. She stated (at p.206):

"The onus is on the applicant to prove a good reason [for delay]. This he has not done. The evidence of his conduct in 1969 and subsequent years indicates a choice, not an incapacity or inability or other good reason."

There were circumstances from which the court could hold that the applicant had not shown good reason for extending the period within which the application could be made. The grounds were not delay "of itself" but involved the exercise of discretion in considering the whole circumstances of the case. Denham J. continued (at pp.208-9):

"His conduct is one of the factors to consider. There has been considerable delay since the events in issue. Relevant witnesses upon which the respondents might rely in any such application are dead. The applicant's medical evidence has not met the onus of proof required."

Fennelly J. agreed with Keane C.J. that the delay was both inordinate and inexcusable and with his analysis of the prejudice to the respondent. He also agreed with Denham J.'s analysis of the applicable principles. In a robust dismissal of the applicant's appeal, which is worth setting out, he stated (at pp.221-2):

" . . . a short delay might require only slight explanation. The judicial review time limit is not a limitation period. Prompt pursuit of a remedy is, however, a requirement of a judicial review application.
    A longer delay will require a more cogent explanation. Explicable delays have usually been a matter of months and very rarely years. . . . In my view, extremely long delay, without cogent explanation and justification may in itself constitute a ground for refusing relief. The respondent does not have to establish that he has been prejudiced though prejudice will usually be relevant. . . . It is, of course, conceivable that in exceptional circumstances even very long delay might be explained and even justified. The respondent might, for example, be responsible for concealment or for exercising control over relevant information or even the applicant's own freedom of action. . . .
    The applicant has not, in my opinion, either explained or justified

his failure to commence proceedings to challenge the decision over such a long period of time. . . . He has come nowhere near establishing 'good reason' for his delay."

In conclusion, and having regard to the difficulties the respondents maintained they faced in defending the applicant's claim "this was not a case in which the balance of justice required that the applicant's claim should be allowed to proceed" (*per* Keane C.J. at p.198).

Although the effects on the applicant's life were admittedly serious and the allegations in respect of his enforced retirement in 1969, if uncontroverted, would have entitled him to the relief claimed, the applicant's own actions and the subsequent delay barred him from proceeding by way of judicial review. The evidence, as marshalled, was insufficient to justify the delays that had arisen. From the whole court's hostile approach to the dictum of McCarthy J. in *Furey* that is traditionally relied upon to ground an application for an extension of time within which to apply for leave to apply for judicial review it must now be considered that relatively strict adherence to time limits for such applications - whether in the Rules or in statute – will be the order of the day, absent very compelling reasons to the contrary. This conclusion is re-enforced by the decision of the Supreme Court in *In re Illegal Immigrants (Trafficking) Bill 1999* [2000] 2 I.R. 360 in relation to the (much shorter) time limits within which applications for leave to apply for judicial review of various decisions under the Act of 2000 must be brought (*Annual Review of Irish Law 2000*, pp.82–85). The prospects of success of another *Furey*-type case – let alone one in the nature of *De Róiste* – must be considered questionable.

Although the Supreme Court was careful not to stress the possibility of prejudice to the respondents in this case, it appears that the deaths of three officers who were involved in the decision to have the applicant retired from service was a significant factor in the final determination. But, as is clear from the judgment, the officer who supervised the applicant's interrogation was still alive and the documents leading to the decision to retire the applicant were still extant. Although there is an admitted difference between judicial review proceedings and those commenced by way of plenary summons, the absence of witnesses or faulty or dimmed memories has not always disentitled plaintiffs in, for example, medical negligence actions from continuing those actions where the contemporaneous clinical and other notes were still available (see, for example, *Reidy v. National Maternity Hospital*, High Court, July 31, 1997, Barr J. where proceedings were sought to be continued some 21 years after the events complained of).

It might also be observed that the provision pursuant to which the applicant was retired in this case, and the procedure adopted in relation thereto, was manifestly unconstitutional – as was the procedure adopted and the regulation relied upon in *Gleeson*. In this regard it might be noted that DFR A. 15 paragraph 18(2) was subsequently amended to provide that a recommendation for the retirement of an officer of the Permanent Defence Force for non-medical reasons must not be made unless and until the reasons for the proposed retirement have been communicated to the officer concerned and he has been given a reasonable opportunity to make representations on his own behalf. Following the decision in *Motherway v. Minister for Defence* (High Court, Lardner J., May 26, 1989) such provisions must also be considered to apply to retirement for medical reasons too (see, generally, Humphreys & Craven, *Military Law in Ireland*, 1997, pp.53–54 and 78–82). But, because the printing and notice of publication of Defence Force Regulations was dispensed with by direction of the Attorney General under the provisions of the Statutory Instruments Act, 1947, section 2(3), it is virtually impossible for a civilian practitioner to confirm the precise date of the introduction of that amendment. Suffice it to say, however, it was after 1969.

Fennelly J. noted in his judgment that, in 1969, *Gleeson* was still in the future – as was *Furey*. Although there is nothing in the judgment to suggest that unconstitutionality is time-dependant, that observation seems impliedly to concede that consideration of challenging an apparently accepted way of doing things is. With this in mind, it is, perhaps, unfortunate that the social and political milieu in Ireland in 1969 – more particularly in light of events that came to prominence over the following two years – was not more obviously considered as a factor that informed the applicant's reason for the choice he was found to have made in the aftermath of his retirement from the Defence Forces. The impediment presented by our social history to the institution of many proceedings in negligence and trespass was, after all, recognised by the passing of the Statute of Limitations (Amendment) Act 2000 in respect of sexual abuse claims and the establishment of the Laffoy Commission. When coupled with the evidence that he was shunned by fellow officers and family alike, it might be considered surprising that the applicant's delay was found to have been inexcusable, notwithstanding that he had sought and obtained legal advice early in his case. On the evidence adduced, however, the Supreme Court was not so satisfied.

Education

FREEDOM OF INFORMATION

League tables of examination results In *Minister for Education and Science v. Information Commissioner*, High Court, July 31, 2001, Ó Caoimh J. held that the Freedom of Information Act 1997 did not confer a right of access to examination results from individual schools, which would have formed the basis for 'league tables' of results: see the discussion in the Information Law chapter, 391, below. The application concerned examination results in 1998, after the 1997 Act had come into effect but before s.53 of the Education Act 1998 (which curtails the right of access) had been brought into effect.

NATIONAL COUNCIL FOR CURRICULUM AND ASSESSMENT

The Education Act 1998 (National Council for Curriculum and Assessment) (Establishment Day) Order 2001 (S.I. No. 246 of 2001) appointed July 12, 2001, as the establishment day for the purposes of Part VII of the Education Act 1998, which relates to the National Council for Curriculum and Assessment (NCCA). The Education Act 1998 (Composition of National Council for Curriculum and Assessment) Order 2001 (S.I. No. 247 of 2001) specifies the composition of the NCCA.

PRIMARY EDUCATION

The landmark decision of the Supreme Court in *Sinnott v. Minister for Education*, Supreme Court, July 12, 2001, is discussed in the Constitutional Law chapter, 69, above.

QUALIFICATIONS (EDUCATION AND TRAINING)

The Qualifications (Education and Training) Act 1999 (Commencement) Order 2001 (S.I. No. 57 of 2001) and the Qualifications (Education and Training) Act 1999 (Commencement) (No.2) Order 2001 (S.I. No. 418 of 2001) brought the main provisions of the Qualifications (Education and Training) Act 1999

(Annual Review 1999, 190) into effect on February 26, 2001 and June 11, 2001, respectively. The effect was to bring into being the National Qualifications Authority of Ireland and the Further Education and Training Awards Council and to dissolve the National Council for Education Awards (NCEA).

TEACHING COUNCIL

The Teaching Council Act 2001 provides for the establishment of the Teaching Council, whose role is to promote teaching as a profession. It is empowered to make provision for: the education, training and professional development of national and post-primary teachers; to maintain and improve the quality of teaching in the State; and to provide for the registration and regulation of teachers. The 2001 Act also provides for the repeal of the Intermediate Education (Ireland) Act 1914. At the time of writing, the Act had not been brought into force by a Commencement Order.

VOCATIONAL EDUCATION

General   The Vocational Education (Amendment) Act 2001, which amended the Vocational Education Act 1930, provided for a major recasting of the membership, functions and expenditure of Vocational Educational Committees. At the time of writing, the Act had not been brought into force by a Commencement Order.

Grants to Vocational Education Committees   The Vocational Education (Grants for Annual Schemes of Committees) Regulations 2001 (S.I. No. 279 of 2001), made under the Vocational Education Act 1930, provide for the payment of additional and supplemental and special grants to the Vocational Education Committees for the 2000 financial year.

Electricity and Energy

ELECTRICITY

Deregulation of market   The Electricity Regulation Act 1999 implemented certain elements of Directive 96/92/EC concerning the internal market in electricity. The 1999 Act implemented those provisions requiring the establishment of a regulator for the sector and to facilitate 28% of the Irish market will be opened to competition in 2000, increasing to about 33% by 2003. The Act came into force on July 14, 1999: Electricity Regulation Act 1999 (Commencement) Order 1999 (S.I. No. 213 of 1999). The remaining elements of the 1996 Directive require further legislation involving the establishment of the Electricity Supply Board, currently a commercial State body, as a public limited company under the Companies Acts: see the Electricity (Supply) (Amendment) Act 2001, 246, below.

Commission for electricity generation   Sections 8 to 10 of the 1999 Act provide for the establishment of the Commission for Electricity Regulation and the assignment to the commission of its functions, powers and duties. The Commission came into effect on July 14, 1999: Electricity Regulation Act 1999 (Establishment Day) Order 1999 (S.I. No. 214 of 1999). Detailed provisions relating to the commission are contained in the First Schedule to the Act. These include the functions, powers and duties of the Commission and the basic terms and conditions of employment for members. It provides that the costs of running the Commission shall be recovered by a levy on the electricity industry. See the Electricity Regulation Act 1999 (Schedule, Paragraph 16) Levy Order 1999 (S.I. No. 382 of 1999). It also states that the Commission will be accountable to the Minister, a Joint Committee of the Oireachtas and the Comptroller and Auditor General. Section 10 gave the Minister for Public Enterprise the power to give directions to the commission until the scheduled implementation date of the 1996 Directive on February 19, 2000. Sections 11 and 12 provide for the appointment by the Commission of authorised officers to assist it in the exercise of its functions, and for the obtaining of search warrants. Section 13 provides for a prohibition on unauthorised disclosure of information obtained by any person while performing his or her duties for the Commission. It is also provided that this should not conflict with the operation of the Freedom of Information Act 1997, which applies to the Commission.

Licensing by Commission for electricity generation Section 14 provides for the Commission to grant licences to electricity undertakings, which can include the Electricity Supply Board, to generate or supply electricity to eligible customers. In addition, any generator using renewable, sustainable or alternative sources of energy can supply any customer, no matter how big or small. It was stated by the Minister during the passage of the legislation in the Oireachtas that section 14 effectively introduces competition to 28% of the electricity market. Section 16 provides for the granting of plant authorisations by the commission. An undertaking is not permitted to build a generating station without such authorisation. Section 17 makes provision for applications for authorisations.

Section 18 gives the Minister the power to specify the criteria for the granting of authorisations. These criteria may relate to the safety and security of the electricity system, protection of the environment, public service obligations, energy efficiency and other matters. Thus, the Electricity Regulation Act 1999 (Criteria for Determination of Authorisation) Order 1999 (S.I .No.309 of 1999) provides that an application for an authorisation may be determined by the Commission on the basis that it is satisfied that:

> "(a) if it grants the authorisation, no activity carried out under it will adversely affect the safety and security of the electricity system;
>
> (b) if it grants the authorisation, energy will be used efficiently in the course of any activities carried out under the authorisation;
>
> (c) the applicant will comply with any grid code or distribution code in so far as it is applicable to the applicant and, at the relevant times, will have the capability of doing so;
>
> (d) the applicant has commenced, or will at the appropriate time commence, to apply for all applicable statutory consents related to the matters referred to in section 18 necessary for the construction of the plant to which the application relates;
>
> (e) the generating station to which the application relates will be constructed and commissioned within a period which the Commission shall specify in relation to each application;
>
> (f) the generating station to which the application relates will be capable of providing an appropriate level of ancillary services being the services necessary to ensure the stable and secure operation of the electricity system, including the provision of spinning reserve, reactive power, frequency control or black start capability, as specified by the Commission in the authorisation;
>
> (g) the generating station to which the application relates will be capable of generating electricity for any minimum continuous period which is specified by the Commission in the authorisation using a primary fuel source of a nature other than that proposed to be used predominantly;

    (h) the applicant is a fit and proper person to be granted an authorisation and has the financial capacity and technical skills to carry out the activities to which the application relates and to comply with the authorisation, if granted;

    (i) the applicant will be capable of complying with any order made by the Minister under section 39 of the 1999 Act."

Sections 19 and 20 allow the Commission to modify any licences or plant authorisations it has granted. Where such modifications are not agreed but are still considered necessary by the commission, the modifications may be imposed, subject to minimum notice and certain conditions. The Commission may decide to hold a public hearing before reaching its decision. There is also recourse to an appeals procedure for the parties concerned which is set out in sections 29 to 32.

Sections 21 and 22 set out the way in which the Commission may hold public hearings where it considers that representations or objections to proposed modifications to licences or authorisations raise matters of sufficient public interest. They also define the terms under which reports of such hearings will be prepared and how the concerned companies or individuals will be informed of the outcome of the hearing. Sections 23 to 26 give the Commission powers to enforce by direction the conditions of licences or authorisations it has granted and to take immediate action, if necessary, to protect public health, safety or the environment. The Commission may apply to the High Court for an order to ensure compliance with any direction it has issued, if necessary.

Sections 27 and 28 define those customers who will be eligible to choose their supplier of electricity from February 19, 2000. Those customers are defined by the level of their electricity usage. This level was set to introduce competition to 28% of the market initially, and this is scheduled to increase to 33% by 2003. See the Electricity Regulation Act 1999 (Trading Arrangements in Electricity) Regulations 2000 (S.I. No. 49 of 2000).

In line with a Government decision of April 1996, all electricity customers will be entitled to purchase electricity, which is produced using a renewable or alternative form of energy as its primary source.

Sections 29 to 32 provide for the appeals mechanism in cases where applications for licences or authorisations are refused by the Commission, or where modifications to them are not agreed in the discourse between the commission and an applicant. Appeal panels may be established to hear and determine appeals regarding applications and modifications to licences or authorisations and they will have the powers, rights and privileges vested in the High Court or a High Court judge. The Minister shall, by Order, determine the membership of appeal panels.

Role of Electricity Supply Board   Section 33 of the 1999 Act provides that the Electricity Supply Board (ESB) shall prepare a grid code and a distribution code for the operation of the electricity transmission and distribution systems for the approval of the commission. These codes will set out the technical aspects relating to connection to and operation of the transmission and distribution systems for use by licence or authorisation holders. Section 34 provides that the ESB shall offer to enter into agreement with any licence or authorisation holder or eligible customer regarding connection to and use of the transmission or distribution systems. The Commission may give directions to the ESB as to the matters to be covered by the contents of such agreements.

Section 35 provides that the ESB shall prepare a statement setting out the basis for the level of system charges for connection to and use of the transmission or distribution systems. That statement will be available so that prospective market entrants may estimate and plan for the charges to which they would be liable. Section 36 provides for the approval by the Commission of the statement of charges prepared under section 35.

Section 37 provides that the Commission may grant permission for the construction of direct lines for the transmission or distribution of electricity from licence or authorisation holders to eligible customers, where access is refused on the basis of a lack of capacity in the existing transmission or distribution system. Section 38 provides that the ESB will prepare a statement for the approval of the commission, setting out estimates of future generation and transmission requirements. This statement will be revised annually and will be available to licence and authorisation holders. It will also include a statement on the demand for electricity generated from renewable, sustainable and alternative sources generally.

Public Service Obligations (PSOs)   Section 39 of the 1999 Act provides that the Minister for Public Enterprise, following consultation with the Minister for the Environment and Local Government, shall make an Order directing the commission to impose public service obligations on the board or other licence or authorisation holders in the general economic interest. These obligations may relate to security of supply, regularity, quality and price of supplies, environmental protection, and use of indigenous energy sources. The cost of these obligations would be recovered from all electricity users. It as explained during the passage of the legislation that PSOs will ensure the cost of ensuring the supply of electricity to remote and peripheral areas will be shared equally. Section 40 provides that the Minister shall by Order, subject to the approval of the European Commission, provide for the recovery from consumers of electricity of specified costs or revenue relating to generating stations constructed or under construction before 19 February 1997, which the ESB may be unable to recover as a result of the implementation of the 1996 Directive. It appears that the imposition of a transitional levy will be a part of the implementation of the 1996 Directive as a whole. It has been indicated that this may be for a period of five years.

Repeals and transfer of functions   Sections 41 to 46 contain repeals and amendments of the Electricity (Supply) Act 1927, and an amendment to the Freedom of Information Act, 1997, to include the Commission in its terms. The principal repeals are those of sections 37 and 38 of the Electricity (Supply) Act 1927, which gave the ESB power to authorise and permit the generation, distribution and supply of electricity by other electricity undertakings. This power is now vested in the Commission. Section 47 provides that the power to make a special order to compulsorily acquire land for the purposes of constructing or reconstructing a power station is transferred from the ESB to the Commission and that the Commission may then confer the functions of such an order on any plant authorisation holder or applicant. Sections 48 to 51 provide that certain powers relating to the laying and use of electric lines, previously resting with the ESB, may, with the consent of the Commission, also be exercised by holders of plant authorisations. Sections 52 to 54 provide that certain regulations already made by the ESB shall also apply to other electricity undertakings and eligible customers. Certain further regulations made by the ESB shall be subject to the consent of the Commission for Electricity Regulation.

ESB privatisation   Against the general background of the market deregulation implemented by the Electricity Regulation Act 1999, above, the Electricity (Supply) (Amendment) Act 2001 was aimed primarily at paving the way for the flotation or privatisation of the State electricity body, the Electricity Supply Board (ESB). In formal terms, the 2001 Act provides for amendments to the Electricity (Supply) Acts 1927 to 1995 and for the issue of capital stock by the ESB. The 2001 Act had not been brought into force by Commencement Order at the time of writing and so the ESB remains a State body until the Act has come into force.

GAS

Gas pipelines   The European Communities (Internal Market in Natural Gas) (Compulsory Acquisition) Regulations 2001 (S.I. No. 517 of 2001) amended section 32(1A) of the Gas Act 1976, as inserted by the Gas (Amendment) Act 2000, in order to enable a person to make simultaneous applications for consent to construct a gas pipeline and for compulsory acquisition orders in relation thereto. They took effect on November 15, 2001.

PETROLEUM

INPC privatisation   The Irish National Petroleum Corporation Limited Act 2001 provided for the sale of shares in the Irish National Petroleum Corporation

Ltd (INPC), in effect for its privatisation. The Act came into effect on July 16, 2001: Irish National Petroleum Corporation Limited Act 2001 (Commencement) Order 2001 (S.I. No. 328 of 2001). This paved the way for the completion of the sale of the INPC, in particular its principal asset, the Whitegate oil refinery.

Environmental Law

PROFESSOR YVONNE SCANNELL, Trinity College Dublin

LEGISLATION

Most environmental legislation was enacted to ensure compliance with EU Environmental law and policy. Commentary on the legislation will be restricted to particularly noteworthy features or developments.

Air   The Air Pollution Act 1987 (Sulphur Content of Heavy Fuel Oil and Gas Oil) Regulations 2001 (S.I. No. 13 of 2001) prohibit the use in the State of heavy fuel oils with a sulphur content exceeding 1% by mass and repeal earlier Regulations.

Dangerous Substances   The Chemical Weapons (Licensing of Scheduled Toxic Chemicals and Precursors) Regulations 2001 (S.I. No. 54 of 2001) set up a licensing system for the production, use, acquisition or possession of a toxic chemical or precursor listed in the First Schedule to the Chemicals Weapons Act 1997. The European Communities (Authorisation, Placing on the Market, Use and Control of Plant Protection Products (Amendment) (No.3) Regulations 2001 (S.I. No. 359 of 2001) add KBR 2738 (fenhexamid and DPX KE 459 (flupyrsulfuron-methyl) to the list of active substances authorised for plant protection products.

Environmental Impact Assessment   The European Communities (Environmental Impact Assessment) (Amendment) Regulations 2001(S.I. No. 538 of 2001) were enacted after Ireland lost a case brought by the EC Commission (*Commission v. Ireland* [1999] E.C.R. I–5901) for failure to transpose the EIA Directive properly in relation to, *inter alia*, initial afforestation and peat extraction. The Commission successfully argued that the State exceeded its discretion under the EIA Directive by not taking account of the nature, location or cumulative effect of projects below specified thresholds when considering if EIA should be required.

Development consisting of the thinning, felling and replanting of trees, forest and woodlands, the construction, maintenance and improvement of non-pubic roads serving forests and woodlands, and works ancillary to that development, not including the replacement of broadleaf high forest by conifer species is exempted from planning control under section 4(1)(i) of the 2000 Act. Replacement of broadleaf high forest by conifer species provided the area involved is less than 10 hectares and peat extraction in a new or extended area of less than 10 hectares and peat extraction in a new or extended area of 10 hectares or more, where the drainage of the bogland commence prior to December 19, 2001 is exempted development under the Planning and Development Regulations 2001 (S.I. No. 600 of 2001). The European Communities (Environmental Impact Assessment) (Amendment) Regulations, 2001 (S.I. No. 538 of 2001) introduced a new statutory consent system, involving EIA where required, administered by the Minister for Communications and Natural Resources for forestry developments. The mandatory EIA threshold for forestry development is 50 hectares. The mandatory EIA threshold is 30 hectares for peat extractions. Amendments have been introduced to the Wildlife (Amendment) Act 2000 and the European Communities (Natural Habitats) Regulations 1997 to require EIA for below threshold developments where a project is likely to have significant effects on the environment on specified environmentally sensitive locations including those designated under the Habitats Regulations. The procedures applicable are similar to those that apply under planning legislation.

Waste The Waste Management (Amendment) Act, 2001 was passed largely to resolve the political difficulties experienced in getting elected members of local authorities to exercise their statutory duties in relation to waste management. The Preamble to the Act frankly states that it was being passed "so that obstacles to the State being able to comply fully with the provisions of certain acts adopted by the institutions of the European Communities" by reason of the "failure of local authorities" to make waste management plans.

It has proved extraordinarily difficult to get the elected members of local authorities to adopt waste management plans despite the fact that the European Commission has been relentlessly pursuing the State for its continued failures to implement EU waste management legislation. In theory, waste management plans, since they can have profound implications for property and other rights, should be adopted by a democratic procedure but when this did not work, the solution adopted in the Act was to vest the powers to adopt waste management plans in County and City Managers. (The better solution for democracy and the rule of law would have been to dismiss the elected members of the recalcitrant local authorities) Unelected city and county managers are now empowered to adopt waste management plans when their elected members refuse to do so.

The Act also empowers local authorities to co-ordinate waste collection permitting and to appoint one of their number to do so on behalf of several authorities. This saves waste collection contractors having to get a separate waste collection permit from every local authority where they operate although a national waste collector may still have to get up to 11 permits to operate nationwide. The Act also empowers to Minister for the Environment to impose environmental levies on plastic bags and other articles, to impose a landfill levy for waste disposal and to set up an Environmental Fund which can only be used for specified activities. Section 13(3) of the Act, which purports to deal with the jurisdiction of the Environmental Protection Agency in respect of licensing waste, is a textbook example of bad draftmanship.

The European Communities (Specified Risk Material) Regulations, 2001 (S.I. No. 24 of 2001) amend the European Communities (Specified Risk Material) Regulations, 2000 (S.I. No. 332 of 2000) by revising the definition of specified risk material, which includes the entire bovine intestine. Specified risk material is essentially a waste from the agricultural sector, which must be specially treated, in approved facilities before disposal. The European Communities (Use of Sewage Sludge in Agriculture)(Amendment) Regulations 2001 prescribe more stringent standards and controls for the use of sewage sludge in agriculture. The Waste Management (Farm Plastics) Regulations 2001 (S.I. No. 341 of 2001) oblige producers and suppliers of certain farm plastics to improve recovery of farm plastics. The Waste Management (Licensing)(Amendment) Regulations 2001 (S.I. No. 397 of 2001) provide that an application for a grant or review of a waste licence may be withdrawn only where the said application concerns a proposed waste activity.

Water   New standards and controls for waters intended for human consumption will come into force on January 1, 2004 under the European Community (Drinking Water) Regulations 2000 (S.I. No. 439 of 2000) which give effect to Directive 98/83/EC. The regulations prescribe standards for water intended for human consumption provided by public and most private water supplies. Sanitary authorities must have regard to any Ministerial recommendations in relation to carrying out their duties under the Regulations. They have a duty under Article 4 of the 2000 Regulations to take the necessary measures to ensure that water intended for human consumption is "wholesome and clean" and that it meets the requirements of the Regulations, except when a departure is granted by the EPA under Article 5. Action programmes must be prepared and implemented to *improve* the water quality to ensure compliance with the Regulations within given time frames. Private water suppliers may be served with notices to prepare and implement action programmes. If there is a non- compliance with parametic values of specifications in Table C, Part 1 of the Schedule and there is a risk to public health, action programmes as must be adopted to secure compliance and the sanitary authority, or (in the case of a private water supply) the person/s responsible must take remedial action to *restore* the water quality within the timeframe specified. It appears from the wording of Article 9(2)(c) that sanitary authorities need only take remedial action in this case where "it is necessary to protect public health" whereas private suppliers must take action to restore the water quality *simpliciter.*

Measures taken by sanitary authorities and private water suppliers to implement the Regulations are never allowed to directly or indirectly cause a deterioration in existing water intended for human consumption in so far as this is relevant for protecting human health or to increase pollution of waters used for producing drinking water. Private water suppliers are liable to maximum fines of £1500 and/or six months imprisonment plus £200 for every day the offence is continued after conviction if they fail to prepare or implement a required action programme. A sanitary authority will not be in breach of its obligations under Article 4, 6(a) or 9(2)(a) where the breach of the parametric value is caused by a domestic distribution system over which it has no charge or control in its capacity as a water supplier or where the breach is caused by the maintenance of that system unless the premises is one where water is supplied to the public, including schools, hospitals and food outlets. But it must take action to protect public health in this case. The Regulations also prescribe quality standards for drinking water, monitoring requirements and methods of analysis and requirements to notify consumers on drinking water quality.

Most pollution of private water supplies comes from the agricultural sector. The *National Development Plan* has allocated £533 million to upgrade group water schemes between 2002-2006 in order to meet the standards and targets set in the Regulations. It would have been much cheaper and more consistent with EU environmental policy to prevent the pollution at source in the first place than to spend £533 million providing treatment systems to remove pollutants. But this is an Irish solution to an Irish problem.

The Quality of Bathing Waters (Amendment) Regulations 2001 designates the beach at Stove as a bathing area. The Urban Wastewater Treatment Regulations 2001 (S.I. No. 254 of 2001) give effect to Directives 91/271/EEC and 2000/60/EC on urban wastewater treatment and are part of an on-going programme to upgrade and provide sewage treatment facilities, which will ensure compliance with the Directives.

CASE LAW

Litigation on the Habitats Directive 92/43/EEC on the conservation of natural habitats and wild flora and fauna is likely to increase if the multiplicity of newspaper reports concerning difficulties with the way it is implemented is indicative. In *Waddington v. An Bord Pleanála,* High Court, November 29, 2000 an applicant for leave to apply for judicial review of a planning decision alleged that a planning permission to construct a 60 metre quay extension was invalid because, *inter alia*, of failure to comply with Article 27 of the European Communities (Natural Habitats) Regulations 1997 (S.I. No. 94 of 1997) which requires that an "appropriate assessment" of the implications for the site in view of the site's conservation objectives" must be carried out before certain development is permitted. In refusing leave, the High Court held that Article 27 applied only when the proposed development was likely to have significant effects on a European site. An appropriate assessment was the carrying out of an EIS, which had been done in this case. The applicant could not show that there would be an increase of traffic due to the proposed development and consequently likely significant effects.

An attempt by the Minister for Arts, Heritage, Gaeltacht and the Islands to enforce the Directive failed in *Minister for Arts, Heritage, Gaeltacht and the Islands v. Kennedy,* High Court, December 20, 2001) The lands involved in this case, in Inch, County Kerry, were located in a proposed Special Conservation Area (a Candidate List site) containing habitats listed in Annex 1 and flora and fauna listed in Annex 11 of the Directive 92/42/EEC on the conservation of natural habitats and wild fauna and flora. The defendants proposed developing a golf course on the site. Construction began before the adoption of the Local Government (Planning and Development) Regulations 1994, at a time when the construction of golf courses in rural areas was generally exempted development. No works had been carried out on site since then but the Minister had had some communications from concerned individuals that the landowner was contemplating recommencing the development. She accordingly applied for, and obtained, interim and interlocutory injunctions under Regulation 17 of the European Communities (Habitats) Regulations 1997 which implemented the Directive in 1997.

Article 17(1) obliges the Minister, where she considers that an operation or activity is being or may be carried out on, *inter alia,* a site placed on the list referred to in Article 4(2), paragraph 3 of the Habitats Directive which is likely to have a significant effect thereon, to ensure that an appropriate assessment of the implication for the site in view of the site's conservation objectives is undertaken. Regulation 17(3) obliges the Minister where, having regard to the conclusions of the assessment carried out under Regulation 17(1), she is of the opinion that the operation or activity will adversely affect the integrity of the site concerned, to seek a court order prohibiting "the continuance" of the operation of operation and activity.

At the trial of the Minister's application for a permanent injunctions, the defendants submitted that before the plaintiff could apply for relief under the regulation and in order for the court to have jurisdiction to grant any relief sought, a number of conditions laid down in regulation had to be satisfied, and that the Minister had failed to do this. They also was submitted that, if any one of the conditions precedent was not satisfied, then, in accordance with the decision of the Supreme Court in *Mahon v. Butler* [1998] 1 I.L.R.M. 284, the plaintiff could not apply for any relief pursuant to Regulation 17. It was further submitted that the court could only grant relief under Regulation 17 where the operation or activity in question has commenced and is continuing, not when it is anticipated.

The High Court (Murphy J.) considered the nature and extent of the Minister's powers under Regulation 17 and identified three conditions which were required to be satisfied before the Minister could make an application under the regulation: (a) the site must have been placed on a list in accordance with chapter I of Part II of the Regulations; (b) the Minister must consider that an operation or activity is being carried out or may be carried out which is likely to have a significant effect on the site, and (c) an appropriate assessment of the implications for the site in view of the sites conservation objectives must be undertaken. If the Minister, having regard to the conclusions of the assessment undertaken, was of the opinion that the operation or activity would adversely affect the integrity of the site, then she was obliged to make an application to a Court of competent jurisdiction to prohibit the continuance of the operation or activity.

Murphy J. held (without much reasoned justification) that the Inch site had been appropriately listed at the time of the application for an injunction although the "list" consisted of a mere database, which was capable of being altered daily. He also held that, at all material times, the site was regarded by the Minister as an area of conservation and that this was made known to the defendants. The decision of the European Court of Justice in *R. v. Secretary of State for the Environment, Ex Parte First Corporate Shipping Limited* [2000] E.C.R. 1-9235 at paragraph 22 was relied on, although it is hard to see how the passage in that judgment supported the court's reasoning.

The learned judge was also satisfied that the second condition was satisfied and that the Minister had grounds for considering that an operation or activity was being carried out or might be carried out which was likely to have a significant effect on the site. However, he concluded that the Minister had not carried out the required appropriate assessment of the implications for the site in light of the site's conservation objectives. Regulation 17(2) of the Habitats' Regulations instanced an environmental impact assessment as an example of an appropriate assessment and the court considered that a mere opinion from one of the Minister's staff, however expert, did not fulfill this requirement.

Murphy J., somewhat hesitantly, rejected the defendants' arguments that Regulations 17(3) merely permits the Minister to make an application to prohibit the *continuance* of the operation or activity where the operation or activity in question has commenced and is continuing. Referring to the State's obligations under Articles 6(1) and 6(2) of the Directive, he held that the proper interpretation of Regulation 17(3) is to construe it with Regulation 17 (1) so as to entitle and, indeed, oblige, the Minister to apply for injunctive relief even thought the activity is not being carried out but may be carried out in the future. This is what is termed a purposive interpretation of national legislation although it was not strictly necessary to do this in this case because the Minister was going to lose the case anyway.

Ultimately, the court rejected the application for the permanent injunction because there was not a reasonable, well-grounded, apprehension that any work would be carried out, and because of the Minister's failure to establish the necessary conservation measures and the appropriate management plan for the site at the time of her application.

This decision raises concerns about the manner in which the Department of Arts, Heritage, Gaeltacht and the Islands in implementing the Habitats Directive. The basis on which the site was selected does not appear to have been adequately justified. The "list" sent to the Commission should surely be more than a mere database although the court accepted that this was adequate, presumably to give effect to the objectives of the directive. The Minister decided to apply for the order under Regulation 17(3) without fulfilling the mandatory requirements in Regulation 17(1) to carry out the appropriate assessment and under Regulation 17(3) to have regard to the conclusions of the assessment before initiating legal proceedings. Indeed, the basis for the Minister's application appears to have been an opinion formed by one of her employees and some complaints from individuals. One wonders why a State body choose to fight this case at all given its obvious failures to comply with the required procedures. Fortunately, the defendant had the resources to resist the Minister's application.

Environmental Impact Assessment   Directive 75/337/EEC continues to be a fertile source of litigation. Interesting questions concerning the scope of Directive 85/337/EEC on environmental impact assessment arose in *O'Connell v. O'Connell* [2001] I.E.H.C. 69 (High Court, March 29, 2001).

This case arose in the context of an inquiry into the making of a scheme by a road authority under the Roads Act 1993. Section 49 of the Act requires the road authority to submit a scheme to the Minister for the Environment for his approval when it proposes carrying out road development prescribed in section 47. An environmental impact statement (EIS) must be prepared for road developments specified in section 50. The Minister has power under section 49(3) to approve the scheme with or without modifications or to refuse to approve it. He is obliged under section 49(1) to cause a public local inquiry into all matters relating to the scheme to be held before deciding on the application for approval. In this case, Louth County Council made a road scheme and submitted it and an accompanying EIS to the Minister for his approval. A public local inquiry was held. On the last day of the inquiry, Louth County Council in its closing submissions submitted drawings to the inspector conducting the inquiry omitting a portion of the proposed road from the scheme. This and 12 other maps, which were variations of the alternative proposal, had been put on public display in January 2001 during an adjournment of the inquiry from November 24, 2000 to February 6, 2001. The effect of the amendment was to omit a section of the proposed road and a roundabout for a distance of approximately one kilometre from the scheme.

The respondent, whose lands would be affected by the proposed scheme, if approved, sought leave to amend his original application for judicial review under Order 84 Rule 23(2) by adding thereto-additional reliefs and grounds. He had three main submissions.

The first was that the Minister's warrant was *ultra vires* in that it limited the inquiry to the scheme and failed to require the inspector to inquire, in addition, into "all matters" relating to the scheme including a possible future extension of the road as required by section 49(2)(a). Leave to amend on this ground was refused, the court holding that an inquiry into a scheme necessarily requires an inquiry into all matters relating to the scheme but that it does not require an inquiry into a road which will be the subject matter of a future scheme. That would be the subject of a separate inquiry.

The second ground was that the inspector conducting the inquiry had not taken into account the fact that the alternative proposal constituted a different scheme for which an EIS and public notice was required by section 50 of the Roads Act 1993. This ground failed because the court held that the omission of a section of the scheme is a modification and not a new scheme. The amended scheme, if recommended and approved, was entirety covered by the Environmental Impact Statement. The court held that:

"To construe Section 50 of the Act in the manner contended for by the Respondent fails to acknowledge the scheme of the Act as it appears from Section 49 thereof that is that there is always the possibility of the scheme being approved with modifications."

While this must have been the case in *O'Connell,* it is possible to envisage situations, and indeed the High Court accepted this, where modifications omitting parts of a road could have a significant adverse environmental impacts e.g. if the omission of a particular road from the scheme resulted in much increased traffic on another road.

Annex 11 of Directive 85/337/EEC as amended by Directive 97/11/EC requires EIA for modifications of projects if they will have significant *adverse* environmental impacts. The is transposed by section 50 of the Roads Act 1993 as amended by article 14(2)(b) and (3) of the European Communities (Environmental Impact Assessment) (Amendment) Regulations 1999 but section 50 does not address the problem of modifications to a proposed scheme. This complicates Ministerial powers (now transferred to An Bord Pleanala under section 215 of the Planning and Development Act 2000) to approve road schemes with modifications. Obviouly the Minister (Bord Pleanala) should be empowered to require modifications of a proposed scheme because one of the objectives of EIA is to improve proposals for developments in the light of comments by the public and prescribed authorities on a developer's proposals. Requiring modifications is the normal method of achieving improvements and responding to public participation in the EIA process. But where the modifications are likely to have significant *adverse* environmental impacts, logic suggests and the Directive probably requires that these should also be considered before consent is given for the project. Finnegan J. appeared to have this in mind when he stated "It is possible to envisage circumstances where the modification is such that the scheme as modified goes outside the ambit of the Environmental Impact Statement." Requiring EIA of all impacts, good and bad, as is the normal requirement under Irish planning legislation (see *O'Nuallain v. Dublin Corporation* [1999] 4 I.R. 137) may appear to be imposing stricter standards than required by the Directive, but it could have the inconvenient and possibly detrimental effect of deterring road authorities from proposing modifications which improve road schemes because of the delay and inconvenience of preparing or amplifying an EIS for the modifications. This could prevent them from responding positively to representations suggesting improvements to their proposals and defeat the underlying rationale of the EIA procedure.

This question of whether it is permissible to permit modifications of developments when the modifications have not been subjected to environmental impact assessment has arisen in England. There, the courts, while expressing reservations about outline planning permissions being granted for large projects subject to EIA *(R v. Rochdale Borough Council ex party Tew* [1999] P.L.R. 74) nonetheless accepted that there was no principle of law that an EIA could not be properly made on the basis of an outline application. *(R v. Rochdale Borough Council ex party Milne* (2001) J.P.L. 470) But the scope for so doing is constrained by the provisions of Directive 85/337/EEC as amended by Directive 97/11/EC which envisages that a "consent" for a project subject to environmental impact assessment under the Directive ought to be made in "full knowledge" of the likely significant environmental effects. This would not be possible if the likely significant environmental effects of a modification were not described in the EIS (if only on the hypothesis of a worst case scenario) or if the consent given did not deal with deficiencies in knowledge of likely significant environmental effects by appropriate conditions. In *Tew* Sullivan J. held that "the development which is described and assessed in the Environmental Statement must be the development which is proposed to be carried out and therefore the development which is a subject of the development consent and not some other development".

The respondent's third ground succeeded. He argued that the multiplicity of maps put on public display, the failure to describe the environmental impacts of alternative proposals and the fact that only one of many proposals was chosen introduced such uncertainty to the inquiry that it could not fairly carry out its purpose i.e. to inquire into all matters relating to the scheme. It also deprived him of a fair hearing of the issues relating to the scheme and the alternative proposal. Leave to amend was granted because the inspector had not given the respondent an opportunity to consider and make recommendations in respect of the modified scheme. The problem appeared to be that the multiplicity of modifications proposed placed an unfair burden on the respondent. It is not clear that the decision would have been the same if the modifications proposed had been less numerous and therefore easier to understand and respond to.

Directive 85/337/EEC arose again in *Kenny v. An Bord Pleanala* [2001] 1IR 568, where the applicant for leave to apply for judicial review of a decision granting planning permission for a student housing complex in Rathgar alleged that the EIS was defective because it had not addressed the implications of decentralised boiler house facilities in the complex. While stating that the court should not concern itself with the "qualitive" nature of the EIS, and thereby endorsing previous decisions to the effect that the adequacy of an EIS was a matter of fact for the planning authority, McKechnie J. nonetheless analysed in detail whether the location, nature and extent of boiler house facilities were adequately described and ruled that they were. Leave to apply was refused.

It is respectfully submitted that this question should not have been considered at all because this was not an issue capable of having significant effects on the *environment,* although it might possibly have affected the amenities of a very small number of neighbouring residences, though not Mr Kenny's. (The writer has inspected the site). There is a qualitive difference between effects on the environment and effects on residential amenities This was illustrated in *R (on the application of Malster) v. Ipswich Borough Council* [2001] E.W.C.A. Civ. 1715, a case where the essential question was whether EIA was required for the construction of a football stand at Ipswich, an effect of which was to cast a shadow upon a residential area near it. Relatively few residences could be affected although the planning authority considered that effects on some of them were significant from the occupiers' viewpoint. The Court of Appeal unanimously held that it was an entirely tenable proposition that the effect on a particular property or a particular piece of land may be severe without the threshold contemplated by article 2 of the Directive being met i.e. without there being significant effects on the environment. Likewise, in *R v. Rochdale Borough Council ex party Milne* [2001] J.P.L. 470 Sullivan J. in the English High Court stated that while details of landscaping in application for an outline planning submission may be 'significant' from the point of view of neighbouring householders and thus subject to reserved matters of approval, they are not likely to have 'a significant effect on the environment' in the context of the assessment regulations. Effects on neighbouring amenities can be dealt with by planning conditions if this is necessary and appropriate.

Waste Management   In *de Burca v Wicklow County Council,* High Court, May 24, 2000; [2000] I.E.H.C. 182, a local authority's decision to privatise the collection of household waste under section 33 of the Waste Management Act 1996 was challenged. In that case, the applicant, an elected member of the local authority, applied for judicial review and interlocutory relief to compel the council to collect household waste. Section 32 (1) of the Waste Management Act 1996 obliges local authorities to collect or arrange for the collection of household waste but section 32(2) excuses them from the obligation to provided the conditions in section 33(3) are satisfied. One of the relevant conditions is that the local authority need not collect waste in a part of its area if satisfied that an adequate waste collection service is available in the part of its area concerned. Applicant alleged, *inter alia,* numerous breaches of Directive 75/

442/EEC, as amended by Directive 91/156/EEC, that all but one of the private waste collectors in the county were not legally permitted to collect the waste, that environmental pollution was resulting from the council's failure to collect waste and that the council took into account irrelevant matters and failed to take account of relevant matters in deciding to stop collecting waste. O'Caoimh J. refused interlocutory relief because the applicant was not personally affected by the council's decision but he observed that, in deciding to stop collecting household waste, the council was not entitled for the purposes of availing of the exemption from its statutory obligation in section 33(1) of the Act to collect, or arrange to collect, household waste to conclude that an adequate waste collection service waste "could be" available in the area. The section, he said, required that an adequate waste collection service *is available* in fact.

The dilemma facing local authorities collecting waste when waste generators have not paid for this service is illustrated in *O'Connell v. Cork Corporation,* November 8, 2001, (2001) I.E.S.C. 71. Section 35 of the Waste Management Act, 1996 empowers a local authority to make byelaws controlling the *presentation* of household and commercial wastes for collection and provides that they shall be construed as if made under the Local Government Act, 1994. Matters considered suitable for prescription in the bye-laws are specified in section 35(3) and include requirements relating to waste receptacles, segregation of waste, precautions to be taken, locations and times for collecting waste. A majority of the Supreme Court confirmed in *O'Connell* that the obligation to collect waste does not oblige a local authority to collect wastes, which do not comply with the byelaws. But it also held that a byelaw, which entitled the local authority to refuse to collect waste in receptacles that did not have a sticker, attached indicating that payment for collection had been made or waived, was *ultra vires* because it did not relate to the *presentation* of waste. Geoghegan J. held that:

> "It was never intended that the power to make bye-laws, the breach of which would exempt the corporation could include a so-called presentation type bye-law the substantive purpose of which was to facilitate the collection of charges. Failure to comply with the sticker system therefore does not exempt the corporation from its general obligation under section 33(1)(a). This does not mean, of course, that the householder is not obliged to make the required payment. But if he defaults, the ordinary debt collection remedies are available to the defendant".

This judgment reinforces the obligation on local authorities to act within their statutory powers when making byelaws. They have ample powers to make byelaws enabling them to refuse to collect waste when the generator has not paid for this service but are probably deterred from doing this by public resistance to waste charges. Byelaws have to be democratically adopted and it is sometimes difficult to persuade elected members of local authorities to exercise their statutory powers properly, especially in matters concerning waste and taxation.

Judicial Review   It is astonishing that matters of procedure should generate such litigation but this is the case in Planning and Environmental law. *O'Connell v. Environmental Protection Agency* [2002] 2 I.L.R.M. 1 is another case dealing with issues, which really ought to be clearly laid out in the relevant legislation. This case concerned an application by a notice party, Dungarvan Energy Ltd., in a case to strike out proceedings brought by Ms O'Connell seeking judicial review of a decision made by the EPA on an application for an integrated pollution control licence for an electricity power generating plant. The issues raised were largely procedural and dealt with the conditions under which the High Court would exercise its discretion to strike out proceedings. The court held that:

(1) An application for conventional judicial review is instituted as soon as a motion *ex parte* for leave to apply for judicial review is moved before the court. The two month period for instituting proceedings challenging decisions by the EPA to grant or refuse an IPC licence prescribed by section 85(8) of the Environmental Protection Agency Act 1992 dates from the date that the decision is given so that, in this case, the proceedings were instituted in time. Dungarvan Energy had contended that proceedings are only instituted after leave to apply for judicial review has first been granted and an application for judicial review must be made by originating notice of motion or, if directed by the court, by plenary summons.

(2) Notwithstanding the statutory two-month period prescribed by section 85(8), an application for judicial review must still be made promptly within that two-month period as required by O.84, r.21 (1) of the Rules of the Superior Courts 1986. The applicant had done this.

(3) The discretion to strike out proceedings for frivolity or vexatiousness should only be exercised when the court is confident that the claim must fail. Unless the High court order granting leave to apply for judicial review was obtained by fraud, misrepresentation or material non-disclosure, the discretion to strike would not be exercised. That was not the case here. Moreover, the notice party was not entitled to make the case on behalf of the respondent EPA that the application was frivolous or vexatious.

(4) There were no public law considerations justifying the High Court in refusing to require an undertaking as to damages to a mere notice party. The real substance of the judicial review application was the protection of private property rights and the public law aspects of the challenge were subsidiary though important issues. But a fortified undertaking for damages would not be required. There is a real difference between a limited liability

company without assets and capital and an individual resident in the state of full legal capacity with a legal interest in property in the State. The fact that the potential loss to Dungarvan Energy might exceed the applicant's capacity to meet costs was not a basis for regarding her undertaking as to costs as worthless or an abuse of process.

Damages for passing of unconstitutional legislation   In *An Blascaod Mor Teoranta v. Commissioners of Public Works* [2001] 1 I.L.R.M. 423, the plaintiffs claimed damages for breaches of their constitutional rights caused by the enactment of the An Blascaod Mor National Historic Park Act 1989. The High Court and the Supreme Court had declared the Act unconstitutional in earlier litigation (High Court, February 27, 1998 available on the *Balii* website; Supreme Court [2000] 1 I.L.R.M. 401). Section 4 of the An Blascaod Mor National Historic Park Act 1989, enabled the Commissioners of Public Works to compulsorily acquire the Great Blasket Island for the purpose of creating a Historic Park on the island but it specifically provided that the lands of landowners and their relatives (including their lineal descendants for all time) who were ordinarily resident on the island in 1953 (when it was vacated) could not be compulsorily acquired. The plaintiffs' lands were not exempted because they were not related to the original inhabitants of the islands. They had however a long and honourable association with the island and had probably done more to preserve it than the descendants of the pre-1953 inhabitants, most of whom are now resident in the United States. The effect of section 4 was that plaintiffs were the only persons whose lands could be compulsorily acquired. Essentially section 4 constituted discrimination on the basis of ancestral lineage and for this reason both the High Court and Supreme Court declared that the Act was unconstitutional. The plaintiffs now claimed damages for the losses that they had incurred because of the invalid legislation including loss of opportunities and the increased costs of restoration caused by the delay. The claim was two pronged. Firstly, the plaintiffs claimed damages for misfeasance in public office by the Minster for Arts, Culture, Gaeltacht and the Islands from the manner in which the Oireachtas passed the Act. Secondly, they claimed that the Oireachtas should award damages for the effects of the passing of an unconstitutional Act. This was a novel claim because it was the first time the State was sued for damages for passing unconstitutional legislation. The arguments made were by analogy to the rights of individuals against a State for breach of Community law.

The grounds for the first claim were that the Oireachtas was led to believe (i) that the plaintiffs were not willing to negotiate with the Office of Public Works on the sale of the lands whereas the facts of the case showed that this was not the case, (ii) that the Oireachtas was not appraised of the serious constitutional frailties and defects in the Bill and (iii) that the Oireachtas was not told that the Bill had been drafted by private parties and not in the conventional manner. The High Court (Budd J.) held that the claim was statute barred and that, in any case, action would not lie against a Minister in respect of his utterances in Parliament as such utterances were protected by Article 15.12 of the Constitution which provides that utterances in either Houses of the Oireachtas are privileged and by Article 15.13 which provides that members of the Oireachtas are not amenable to any court, but only to the House itself, for such utterances.

On the second claim, the Court less convincingly distinguished between the principles of law governing State liability for breach of Community law and State liability for legislative action in domestic law, expressed doubts about the causal links between the breach of constitutional guarantees and damages allegedly suffered and distinguished the French case *Societe Anonyme des Produits Laitiers "La Fleurette"* (1938) *Recueil le Bon* 25) holding France liable for damages for discriminatory legislation. The court considered that the since the French court had no power to invalidate unconstitutional legislation, it had to provide an alternative remedy by way of damages. (One suspects that most litigants would prefer the money) The court held, by analogy with earlier cases on Ministerial liability for exercises of statutory powers, that only in exceptional cases should the State be liable for damages in respect of invalid legislation where the legislature is involved in balancing private property rights against other obligations arising from the proper good. In this case, the court considered that, for public policy reasons, the Oireachtas must be given a margin of discretion in balancing various rights and that the plaintiffs' rights had largely been vindicated by the declaration that the Act was invalid.

There may, or may not, be good policy reasons for not making the State liable for damages when it has passed invalid legislation except in exceptional circumstances but the circumstances were surely exceptional in this case. The plaintiffs had been treated very shabbily by the State in this instance. (Some of this is chronicled in the excellent High Court judgment in the earlier case) Such treatment might have merited punitive damages in some jurisdictions. The State must have known, or at least suspected, that there could be constitutional infirmities in such discriminatory legislation affecting property rights. There were very few plaintiffs involved. They had been forced to pursue an unduly long and expensive case in the High Court. Their victory there was appealed by the State with its infinite resources – and still they won. The costs of compensating them would not have been unbearable. How exceptional must exceptional be?

Equity

HILARY DELANY, Trinity College, Dublin

TRUSTS

Constructive trusts   The 'new model' constructive trust, first established by Lord Denning in a series of decisions in England in the 1970s; has resurfaced in this jurisdiction this year in a decision which illustrates that our courts are willing to utilize the constructive trust in a manner which will give effect to "justice and good conscience". In *Kelly v. Cahill* [2001] 1 I.R. 56; [2001] 2 I.L.R.M 205 the deceased informed his solicitor that he wanted to alter his will since he no longer wished to benefit his nephew, the second named defendant, but intended to leave all his property to his wife, the first named defendant. His solicitor advised him to execute a deed transferring his property into the joint names of himself and his wife to avoid a charge to probate tax subsequently arising and the parties believed that the deed executed included all of the lands owned by the deceased. However, through the inadvertence of the solicitor, the lands comprised in a numbered folio had not been transferred and would pass on the deceased's death to the first named defendant for life with remainder to the second named defendant, subject to her legal right to half of the lands concerned. Barr J. stated that the net issue in the case before him was whether a constructive trust arose in relation to the lands, which were not transferred into joint ownership as intended by the testator. This raised the question of whether a 'new model' constructive trust had been established, and if so whether such a trust had a place in Irish law. Barr J. adopted the explanation of the concept of a new model constructive trust set out in Keane, *Equity and the Law of Trusts in the Republic of Ireland,* (Butterworths, Dublin, 1988), p. 186 and said that the kernel of the question was whether the evidence established a clear, positive intention on the part of the testator that his wife should inherit all his property, that he took appropriate steps to bring this about and that he could not reasonably have known that through his solicitor's error, the deed of transfer which had been duly executed did not include all his lands. Barr J. concluded that it had been established that the deceased had expressed the necessary intention to his solicitor and that he had good reason for believing that the deed of transfer had achieved this intention. Barr J. said that it was irrelevant that the second named defendant was neither aware of nor had any responsibility for the error which had been made. The essential element was that the testator had changed his mind about the disposition of his property and that he had taken appropriate steps to give effect to his revised intention. In these circumstances "justice and good conscience" required that the second named defendant should not be allowed to inherit the property and the interest in remainder under the will should be deemed to be subject to a constructive trust in favour of the first named defendant. Barr J. expressed the view that a new model constructive trust was an equitable concept which deserved recognition in Irish law and stated that it accorded with the observations of Costello J in *HKN Invest Oy v. Incotrade Pvt Ltd* [1993] 3 I.R. 152. Barr J. therefore concluded that the second named defendant held the lands as a constructive trustee for the first named defendant and directed that he should execute an assurance as might be necessary to vest the lands in the latter.

EQUITABLE REMEDIES

Interlocutory injunctions A number of decisions concerning the grant of interlocutory injunctions have been handed down this year and the well established principles laid down in *Campus Oil Ltd v. Minister for Industry and Commerce (No.2)* [1983] I.R. 88 have been applied. In *Harkins v. Shannon Foynes Port Company* High Court, January 29, 2001 the plaintiff sought to restrain the defendant from advertising the position of operations manager, which he claimed had effectively been his job (although it had been designated as harbour engineer) with the defendant for several years. O'Sullivan J. considered that there was a degree of overlap between the plaintiff's present responsibilities and those of the new operations manager and that the plaintiff had made out a case for trial to the effect that the defendant's proposal would entail him having to accept less beneficial conditions of service. He also expressed the opinion having regard to the balance of convenience, that if the defendant were permitted to continue with making the appointment, the plaintiff's position at trial would be devalued, possibly irretrievably and in a manner which money could not compensate. O'Sullivan J. therefore made an order prohibiting the defendant from advertising the position of operations manager unless the advertisement made it clear that the position involved no overlap with the functions of the position held by the plaintiff.

In *Ó Murchu v. Eircell Ltd* High Court, February 21, 2001 the appellant appealed against an order of the High Court refusing a number of interlocutory injunctions, the effect of which would have been to compel the respondent to continue supplying or permitting the supply of mobile phones to the appellant and to treat the appellant as an authorised agent for this purpose. Geoghegan J. had to address the argument put forward that what was being sought were mandatory interlocutory injunctions, which on well established principles, the court should be very slow to grant. However, he was satisfied that although the injunctions might arguably be classified as mandatory, they were not really of that type and were directed simply towards retaining the status quo pending the outcome of the action, which is the purpose of a prohibitory injunction. He stated that it was therefore necessary to consider whether there was a serious issue to be tried, whether damages were an adequate remedy, and whether the balance of convenience favoured the granting or the refusal of relief. He held that the appellant had an arguable case and that there was a serious issue to be tried on the breach of contract issue. However, he was satisfied that damages would be an adequate remedy and for that reason decided to affirm the order of the High Court. Geoghegan J. added that even if he had doubts about whether damages were an adequate remedy, he was satisfied that the balance of convenience favoured refusing the injunction. He referred to the well-known principle that in general the courts will not grant an injunction which would involve ongoing supervision, and that they will therefore be very slow to grant injunctions in either service contracts or trading contracts because it will be difficult to assess whether such injunctions are being obeyed. In addition, it will usually be impracticable and undesirable that two parties be compelled to trade with one another when one does not want to carry on such trading. Geoghegan J concluded that on this ground also he would dismiss the appeal.

Similar issues arose in *Meridian Communications Ltd v. Eircell Ltd* Supreme Court, May 10, 2001 in which the plaintiffs appealed against the refusal of the High Court to grant them interlocutory relief relating to the provision of mobile phone services. McGuinness J. stated that Lavan J. had rejected the plaintiffs' application for an interlocutory injunction on equitable grounds, on the basis that the plaintiffs had not come to court with clean hands. However, she concluded that neither party had been entirely free of fault and that in the circumstances the Supreme Court would not refuse the relief sought on the grounds relied on by Lavan J. She stated that the court must therefore approach the matter in the light of the well known principles set out in *Campus Oil Ltd v. Minister for Industry and Commerce (No.2)* [1983] I.R. 88, and referred to in the judgment of Geoghegan J. in *Ó Murchu v. Eircell Ltd* noted above. Effectively what the court was being asked to do was to the preserve the plaintiffs' right to appeal a decision made by the High Court and McGuinness J. accepted the submission of counsel for the plaintiffs that serious and substantive issues arose in that appeal. However, she also felt that there was substance in the contention that damages would be an adequate remedy for the plaintiffs and she stated that should they succeed in their appeal, there would be no insuperable difficulty in calculating an award of damages. While the Supreme Court had been willing to grant a temporary injunction for a period of two weeks, McGuinness J. said that there could be no question of granting a further or continuing injunction. She concluded that the balance of convenience would be served by permitting the orderly winding up of the plaintiffs' affairs by the company itself and by the proper payment of its creditors, including the defendant.

In *Irish Sugar Ltd v. Parlon* High Court, November 29, 2001 O'Donovan J. again applied the *Campus Oil* principles to a dispute in which the plaintiff claimed that the defendants were in breach of section 4 of the Competition Act 1991 and were guilty of inducing breaches of contract between the plaintiff and growers of sugar beet. The plaintiff sought an interlocutory injunction restraining the defendants from taking any steps to organise or participate in the withdrawal of supplies of sugar beet from the plaintiff and from taking any further steps to intimidate or persuade growers of beet not to supply it to the plaintiff. O'Donovan J. was satisfied that the plaintiff had established that there was a fair question to be decided at the trial of the action. In relation to the balance of convenience, he said that he could not envisage what additional harm would befall the defendants in the event that they were required to desist from the behaviour of which the plaintiff complained, whereas if the growers of beet persisted in refusing to deliver supplies to the plaintiff it seemed that there was a high probability of irreparable harm being caused to it. Accordingly, O'Donovan J. was satisfied that the balance of convenience favoured the granting of the injunctive relief sought. In addition, he stated that he was not persuaded that in the event that he refused the relief sought and plaintiff was ultimately successful that it would be reasonably possible to assess the amount of damages which would adequately compensate it for the loss which would flow from the defendants' wrong doing. Consequently, O'Donovan J. held that he would grant an interlocutory junction in the terms sought by the plaintiff.

The conclusions reached by the Supreme Court in both *Bayzana Ltd v. Galligan* [1987] I.R. 238 and *Westman Holdings Ltd v. McCormack* [1992] 1 I.R. 151 made it clear that the common law position clearly favoured the employer where proceedings were brought seeking to restrain picketing by means of an interlocutory injunction. An employer could usually establish that the balance of convenience favoured the preservation of the status quo pending the trial of the action and the courts were often influenced by the potential inability on the part of some of the defendants to pay damages. Attempts were made to redress this imbalance by means of legislation and section 19(2) of the Industrial Relations Act 1990 now provides that once a plaintiff establishes an entitlement to an interlocutory injunction by showing that there is a fair question to be tried, the court must consider whether the defendants can establish a fair case that they were acting in furtherance or contemplation of a trade dispute. If they can, the injunction will not be granted; if they cannot, the court will go on to consider as it does at common law, whether the balance of convenience favours the grant of an injunction. However, this statutory provision can only be availed of by defendants where they have complied with the formalities laid down in the statute in relation to such matters as the holding of secret ballots and the giving of adequate strike notice and the consequence of failing to abide by such procedures is that the new restrictions on an employer's ability to obtain an interlocutory injunction do not apply. As the decisions in *Nolan Transport (Oaklands) Ltd v. Halligan,* High Court (Keane J.) March 22, 1994 and *G. & T. Crampton Ltd v. Building and Allied Trades Union* [1998] 1 I.L.R.M. 431 illustrate, a strict approach has been taken by the courts towards the interpretation of section 19(2) so that a defendant is often deprived of the benefit of the protection of the legislation and this is borne out by the recent decision of McCracken J. in *Malincross Ltd v. Building and Allied Trades Union* High Court, November 30, 2001. The plaintiff sought an interlocutory injunction to restrain picketing by the defendants at a building site, in circumstances where the employer with whom the defendants were in dispute no longer carried on business at the site. McCracken J. was satisfied that the was a fair case to be tried in relation to the construction of section 11 of the Industrial Relations Act 1990, which provides that it is lawful in contemplation or furtherance of a trade dispute to attend at a place where an employer 'works or carries on business,' although he suggested that the construction contended for by the defendant was a very strained use of the present tense as used in the section. In relation to the question of whether the defendants might rely on the provisions of section 19(2) of the Act of 1990, McCracken J. stated that he was satisfied that the union had held a secret ballot in accordance with its rules and that it has given the appropriate notice to the employer of its intention to take industrial action. However, an issue arose as to the extent to which the proposals in the ballot had to identify the nature of the industrial action, and specifically a question remained whether the ballot authorised the placing of pickets at a site when it ceased to be the company site of the employer. A similar question had also arisen in *G. & T. Crampton Ltd v. Building and Allied Trades Union* but had never been determined, as the case had not proceeded to a full hearing. McCracken J. reiterated that the sufficiency of the secret ballot is clearly a condition precedent to the right of the defendants to resist an interlocutory injunction under section 19(2). In his view the purpose of the Act appeared to be to ensure that if a union is to be entitled to the protection of section 19 it must have the clear support of its members. He concluded that a serious issue remained as to whether the picketing of the plaintiff's premises, once the employer had left those premises, was authorised by the ballot and that until that question had been determined, a condition precedent to section 19(2) had not been established by the defendants. As McCracken J. was satisfied that as there was a *bona fide* dispute as to whether the preconditions of section 19(2) had been complied with, the defendant was not entitled to rely on the subsection to prevent the grant of an interlocutory injunction. Accordingly, he proceeded to apply the ordinary *Campus Oil* principles. McCracken J. stated that if he refused an injunction and it was ultimately held that the plaintiff should succeed, he was quite satisfied that it would suffer irreparable loss and damage and that its reputation as a developer could be seriously affected. On the other hand, if an injunction was granted and the defendants succeeded at the trial, he thought the damage to them would be minimal. Certainly any loss or disadvantage which might be incurred by the defendants would be far outweighed by the enormous damage which would be caused to the plaintiff should the injunction be wrongly refused and he was satisfied that the balance of convenience strongly favoured the plaintiff. McCracken J. therefore concluded that on the terms that the plaintiff give an undertaking as to damages he would grant the interlocutory injunction sought.

Given that it is almost inevitable that a defendant will succeed in resisting the grant of an injunction where the provisions of section 19(2) of the Industrial Relation Act 1990 can be relied upon, it is in some respects understandable that a strict approach is being taken by the courts towards the application of the legislation. However, given the obvious advantage from the point of view of a defendant of being able to rely on the provisions of section 19(2), it is surprising that greater care is not being taken to ensure that the necessary statutory requirements have been complied with.

An interesting decision, which also involved consideration of the principles governing the grant of quia timet injunctions, is *Ryanair Ltd v. Aer Rianta Cpt.*, High Court, January 25, 2001. The applicant sought two injunctions restraining the respondent from imposing certain monetary charges relating to activities at Dublin Airport and from operating rules of conduct, which it had introduced. Kinlen J. had granted interim injunctions but the application for interlocutory injunctions was refused by Kelly J. Counsel for the applicant submitted that the strength of the applicant's case in law warranted a departure from the well-established principles applicable to the grant of interlocutory injunctions. Kelly J. rejected this argument on the ground that it ran contrary to authoritative statements of the law in Ireland and England and stated that even if there were a principle which enabled him to depart from the normal rules governing the grant of interlocutory relief, he was not satisfied that the applicant's case was so clear as to be unanswerable by the respondent. On the basis of established principles, Kelly J. concluded that the applicant had demonstrated a serious issue to be tried in respect of each of the complaints. However, in relation to the question of the adequacy of damages, he concluded that damages would provide a complete remedy to the applicant, there being no doubt that the respondent could repay any monies with interest. In addition, he said that the fact that in the affidavit evidence before the court damages had actually been quantified was fatal to the applicant's claim. Kelly J. therefore refused the injunction sought concerning the imposition of charges by the respondent. In relation to the second injunction, which he concluded on the facts was of a *quia timet* nature, Kelly J. referred to the principles set out by Geoghegan J. in *Szabo v. Esat Digiphone Ltd* [1999] 2 I.L.R.M. 102 in which he had stated that there was no difference between the principles applicable to an interlocutory *quia timet* injunction and any other kind of interlocutory injunction. However, the fact that no breach of the plaintiff's rights had taken place as of the date of the hearing was of relevance in that it might be more difficult to establish as a matter of evidence that a sufficient risk of future injury existed to justify the grant of an injunction. In such cases the court must balance the magnitude of the evil against the chances of its occurrence and in order to grant a *quia timet* injunction there would have to be a proven substantial risk of danger. Kelly J. concluded that in the case before him he was not satisfied that there was a sufficient risk of future injury to the applicant to justify the immediate grant of an injunction. He added that even if he was wrong in the view he had expressed concerning the injunction relating to the rules of conduct, he would in any event refuse the injunction on the balance of convenience.

The applicant's appeal from the decision of Kelly J., which was solely concerned with the order for costs made against them, was dismissed by the Supreme Court in a decision delivered on October 26, 2001. Keane C.J. reiterated that it is clear that an interlocutory injunction will only issue where damages are not an adequate remedy and that in the case before the court the applicant's claim was clearly capable of being remedied by an award of damages. While counsel for the applicant had advanced the argument that established principles on this issue should be modified, Keane C.J. stated that the trial judge had quite rightly taken the view that it would need a decision of the Supreme Court to set aside such a well-established principle. Keane C.J. concluded that the order made was plainly one for the discretion of the trial judge and was satisfied that no case had been made out for interfering with this discretion.

Evidence

DECLAN MCGRATH, Trinity College Dublin

BURDEN OF PROOF

The application of the presumption of intention contained in section 50(8) of the Road Traffic Act 1961 (as inserted by section 11 of the Road Traffic Act 1964) was considering in passing by Murray J. in *DPP v. Byrne*, Supreme Court, December 6, 2001. That sub-section provides that "in a prosecution for an offence under this section it shall be presumed that the defendant intended to drive or attempt to drive the vehicle concerned unless he shows the contrary". Commenting on the effect of the sub-section, Murray J. stated that:

> "I conclude, therefore, that if the court is satisfied that the defendant was in charge of the motor vehicle as charged, the presumption of intention to drive pursuant to sub-section 8 of section 50 arises. It is then for the defendant to show to the contrary so as to raise a reasonable doubt in the mind of the trial judge."

This *dictum* is interesting because, at first glance, section 50(8) by using the words "unless he shows the contrary", appears to place a legal burden on the defendant to prove that he did not have the requisite intention to drive i.e. he or she would have to prove this on a balance of probability. The learned judge, however, seems to have assumed that the effect of the section was merely to place an evidential burden on the defendant i.e. it sufficed if he or she raised a reasonable doubt in the mind of the trial judge. This *dictum*, therefore, seems to provide some further limited support for an approach, evident in *Hardy v. Ireland* [1994] 2 I.R. 550 (*Annual Review of Irish Law 1995*, p.182) that, whatever the wording used, all burdens placed on an accused will be construed as being evidential in character only.

In *People (DPP) v. C* [2001] 3 I.R. 345, one of the grounds of appeal advanced by the applicant against his conviction on a charge of rape was that the trial judge failed to charge the jury properly in relation to the facts of the case and, in particular, failed to charge them correctly in relation to the conflict between the evidence given by the complainant in evidence in chief and the concessions made by her under cross-examination. However, Murray J., delivering the judgment of the Court of Criminal Appeal, held that the trial judge had not erred by not directing the jury to accept the version of events which was more favourable to the applicant:

"The fact that there is a conflict in evidence between what a witness said in evidence and what he or she may have said on another occasion does not of itself require the trial judge to direct that a jury should accept one version, even the most favourable version, over another. To direct the jury to rely on one version rather than another would be to usurp its function."

He was satisfied that the jury had, instead, been properly directed that where such a conflict arose, they should accept the version most favourable to the accused unless the other version had been proved beyond a reasonable doubt.

Proceeds of Crime Act 1996   The decision in *FJM v. TH*, High Court, O'Sullivan J., June 29, 2001, is the latest in a series of unsuccessful attempts by respondents to challenge the constitutionality of the Proceeds of Crime Act 1996 on the basis of the civil standard of proof prescribed therein (see also *Gilligan v. Criminal Assets Bureau* [1998] 3 I.R. 185 (*Annual Review of Irish Law 1997*, p.388) and *Murphy v. GM PB PC Ltd*, High Court. O'Higgins J., June 4, 1999 (*Annual Review of Irish Law 1999*, p.224)). At issue in *FJM*, was section 3(1) of the Act, which provides that:

"Where, on application to it in that behalf by the applicant, it appears to the court, on evidence tendered by the applicant, that a person is in possession of proceeds of crime then the court shall make an order ... prohibiting the respondent or any other specified person ... from disposing of or otherwise dealing with the whole or, as appropriate, a specified part of the property ... unless, it is shown to the satisfaction of the court, on evidence tendered by the respondent or any other person ... that the property does not constitute the proceeds of crime."

It was contended that the onus cast upon a respondent to show "to the satisfaction of the court" that the property was not the proceeds of crime was a higher onus than that cast on the applicant who was merely required to make it appear to the court that the property was the proceeds of crime. It was, thus, argued that the Act had not cast an equal burden on the parties and had thereby denied the respondent constitutionally guaranteed fair procedures.

Rejecting this contention, O'Sullivan J. referred to section 8(2) of the Act, which stipulates that the standard of proof required to determine any question arising under the Act is that applicable to civil proceedings, i.e. proof on a balance of probabilities. In his opinion, this sub-section governed any question which might arise in relation to the standard of proof cast upon the parties and he was satisfied that there was no appreciable difference between the standard of proof required of an applicant and that required of a respondent under section 3(1).

Summing up   In *People (DPP) v. Kiely,* Court of Criminal Appeal, March 21, 2001, the applicant had been convicted on charges of assault causing harm and possession of an offensive weapon. One of the grounds of appeal concerned the charge of the trial judge to the jury in relation to the burden and standard of proof and his failure to accede to a requisition made by counsel for the applicant that he should expand upon his charge to make specific references to the principle that where there were two versions of events, the jury should adopt the accused's version unless the prosecution's version had been proven beyond reasonable doubt. Reliance was placed on the decision of Court of Criminal Appeal in *People (AG) v. Byrne* [1974] I.R. 1, 9, where Kenny J. stated that:

> "The correct charge to a jury is that they must be satisfied beyond reasonable doubt as to the guilt of the accused, and it is helpful if that degree of proof is contrasted with that in a civil case. It is also essential, however, that the jury should be told that the accused is entitled to the benefit of the doubt and that when two views on any part of the case are possible on the evidence, they should adopt that which is favourable to the accused unless the State has established the other beyond reasonable doubt."

Having analysed the judgment of Kenny J. in *Byrne*, McGuinness J. identified the main issue before the court in *Byrne* as being whether it was sufficient for the judge in his charge to tell the jury that they had to be "satisfied" of the guilt of the accused. It followed that the *ratio* of the judgment was that the correct standard to be adopted was that of proof "beyond reasonable doubt" which standard had to be clearly explained to the jury.

According to the learned judge, the authorities including the decisions in *AG v. O'Connor* [1935] Ir. Jur. Rep. 1 and *AG v. Berber* [1944] I.R. 405, provided ample authority establishing the necessity for the trial judge to instruct a jury that they must be convinced beyond reasonable doubt on the basis of all the evidence before them as to the guilt of the accused before proceeding to a conviction. However, *Byrne* was the only authority, which specified as an essential ingredient of the judge's charge that he or she explain the necessity to give the benefit of the doubt to the accused. Thus, notwithstanding that this explanation was commonly given, she did not regard its omission as fatal:

> "As a matter of practice this explanation concerning "the benefit of the doubt", or some very similar explanation, is included in the charge to the jury in very many trials. However, it should be borne in mind that in *Byrne's* case...it is the judge's charge as a whole, which is being considered by the appellate court. The issue in each case is whether in his charge as a whole the trial judge has correctly instructed the jury as to the burden and standard of proof."

Therefore, although it would have been preferable for the trial judge to have included an explanation of the benefit of the doubt along the lines indicated by Kenny J., he had emphasised the concepts of the presumption of innocence and proof beyond a reasonable doubt and she was satisfied that the jury had been properly and sufficiently instructed as to the burden and standard of proof to be applied by them in reaching their decision.

Although the Court of Criminal Appeal has, on many occasions, signalled its preference that juries should be instructed in accordance with the guidelines laid down by Kenny J. in *Byrne* (see *People (DPP) v. Cotter*, Court of Criminal Appeal, June 28, 1999 (*Annual Review of Irish Law 1999*, p.206) and *People (DPP) v. Cahill*, Court of Criminal Appeal, July 31, 2001 (below)) it has also sought to preserve a degree of flexibility and avoid any calcification of that charge into ritualised formula. Thus, in *People (DPP) v. Shortt*, Court of Criminal Appeal, July 23, 1996 (*Annual Review of Irish Law 1996*, p.307), it was held that, although it was common for trial judges to do so, there was no obligation to contrast the civil and criminal standards of proof. Indeed, the conclusion of the Court in *Kiely* was clearly signalled by its earlier decision in *People (DPP) v. Rawley* [1997] 2 I.R. 265 (*Annual Review of Irish Law 1997*, p.389) and it is surprising that this case was not referred to. In *Rawley*, it was submitted that the charge was inadequate in that the trial judge ought to have told the jury that if they had any reasonable doubt as to the truth of the accused's explanation they should have given him the benefit of that doubt and acquitted him. However, the Court took the view that the jury had been properly charged and they had not been left in any doubt that they could not convict if taking all the evidence as a whole they were left with any reasonable doubt as to the accused's innocence.

The decision in *Kiely* is also of interest because of the ringing endorsement by the Court of the direction given by the trial judge as to the standard of proof. In the course of his charge the trial judge explained the difference between the civil and criminal standards of proof and the standard of proof beyond a reasonable doubt as follows:

> "You will have a decision to make and an important decision and you will have to weigh it up. I must refer you to that, during your whole life, you are making decision after decision and they are in various categories. There is one category of decision which I will call of a passing or trivial nature. Will I go to the cinema tonight? Will I buy a lottery ticket? Will I look at the Late Late Show?....All these things are little decisions that we make. They are not life changing decisions. ... There is another kind of decision which is much more fundamental which we all again make. Are we going to get married or if we are already married are we going to leave our marriage partner and go with someone else? Are we going to sell our house in the rising property market? ... They are all decisions which we all have to make from time

to time, not very often, but we have to make them, but you make those decisions in a much more fundamental and careful way than the kind of decisions that you are going to watch the Late Late Show or you are going to buy a lottery ticket. They are totally different kinds of decisions. Now the civil standard of proof that I spoke about, the traffic case, injury at work, that kind of thing, you can equate that to the trivial kind of decision and the much more serious decision is equated with the criminal case, so, the difference between the trivial decision and the serious decision gives you some idea of the difference between the civil standards of proof which is lower and the criminal standard of proof which is, much higher. I do not think I can explain it much better than that to you. It is very serious and you have to be satisfied beyond reasonable doubt, that is not mathematical doubt, but beyond reasonable doubt."

In the opinion of McGuinness J., "no possible criticism" could be made of this charge and she regarded his explanation to the jury as "admirably clear and comprehensive as well as being geared to the understanding of the ordinary man and woman in the street". It might be noted that the summing up was in terms not similar to that used by the trial judge in *R v. Ching* (1976) 63 Cr. App. Rep. 7 who defined a reasonable doubt as:

"a doubt to which you can give a reason as opposed to a mere fanciful sort of speculation such as 'Well, nothing in this world is certain, nothing in this world can be proved'...It is sometimes said the sort of matter which might influence you if you were to consider some business matter. A matter, for example, of a mortgage concerning your house, or something of that nature."

This direction was approved by the Court of Appeal, which took the view that the judge's direction could not have been clearer or more accurate.

The summing up of the trial judge in relation to the burden of proof was also considered in *People (DPP) v. Cahill*, Court of Criminal Appeal, July 31, 2001, where issue was taken with statements by the trial judge to the effect that, where there were two interpretations in relation to any particular matter and they were evenly balanced, the benefit of the doubt should be given to the accused. It was argued that the references to interpretations of the evidence being "evenly balanced" might well have left the jury under the impression that, where two such interpretations were open, they could determine the issue on the balance of probabilities. While the court accepted that the direction of the trial judge could have been "more happily phrased", the court was satisfied that the trial judge had made it emphatically clear to the jury that they were to determine the issues before them in accordance with the appropriate criminal standard of proof. The court, however, took the opportunity of stressing the desirability of trial judges charging juries in accordance with the judgment of Kenny J. in *People (AG) v. Byrne* [1974] I.R. 1, 9.

WITNESSES

Calling of Witnesses In general, in criminal proceedings, an accused is free to call any witnesses he or she wishes and the trial judge may not interfere in that decision (see *State (O'Connor) v. Larkin* [1968] I.R. 255, 258). Although such witnesses are, of course, confined to giving evidence, which is relevant and admissible, a determination as their ability to do so generally does not fall to be made in advance but rather as specific questions are asked. However, there can be circumstances, as the decision in *Herron v. Haughton*, Supreme Court, May 19, 2000, illustrates where it is open to a judge to query the purpose for which a witness is being called and to refuse to permit a party to call a witness where he or she is satisfied that the witness does not have any relevant evidence to give.

The appellant had been prosecuted for driving a car without having a current tax disc displayed and failing to wear a seatbelt and mounted a defence directed to showing that she was the victim of a campaign of harassment by the gardaí and that this was the reason why she had been prosecuted for these offences. She wished to call the prosecuting solicitor and when queried by the respondent District Judge as to the reason for this course of action, she explained that she believed that he was a party to a conspiracy to pervert the course of justice. The respondent thereupon refused to allow her to call the prosecutor as a witness because he took the view that this allegation was irrelevant to the particular proceedings. A submission that the respondent had erred in law in so ruling was rejected by Geoghegan J. in the Supreme Court who stated that:

> "There is no doubt that in general a defendant in a criminal case is entitled to call any witness he or she thinks fit. However normally a defendant will either bring his or her witnesses to court with their consent or serve a *subpoena* on them. It is unusual in the extreme for a defendant to call the prosecuting solicitor as his/her witness. In such circumstances it is perfectly in order in my view for the trial judge to be alert to the possibility that the witness is being called for frivolous or irrelevant reasons or in an abuse of the process of the court. In such circumstances the judge not only is entitled to, but I think that under his obligation to conduct a fair trial is obliged to probe to some limited extent at least the purpose for which the witness is being called."

He, thus, concluded that the respondent had been "absolutely right" to question the appellant as to why she wished to call the prosecuting solicitor and, in the light of her answers he was "perfectly right" to refuse to allow her to call him as a witness.

UNRELIABLE EVIDENCE

Road Traffic Offences   Section 105(1) of the Road Traffic Act 1961 provides that where the commission of an offence involves the proof of speed, the uncorroborated evidence of one witness stating his opinion as to the speed at which a vehicle was travelling shall not be accepted as proof of that speed. This provision is thought necessary because opinion evidence of speed, though admissible, is acknowledged to be unreliable. In addition, the usual means for identifying error, namely cross-examination, is not very effective in relation to such evidence. The subsection is, *per* Bingham LJ in *Crossland v. DPP* [1988] 3 All E.R. 712, 715, merely "intended to prevent the conviction of a defendant on evidence given by a single witness of his unsupported visual impression of a defendant's speed". Therefore, subsection (2) goes on to provide that speed may, *prima facie,* be established by tendering evidence of indications from which that speed can be inferred which were given by a watch or other apparatus (including photographic apparatus) and it is not necessary to prove that the apparatus was accurate or in good working order.

The application of section 105 arose for consideration in *People (DPP) v. Connaughton,* Court of Criminal Appeal, April 5, 2001. The applicant had been convicted of dangerous driving causing serious bodily harm. On appeal, objection was taken, on the basis of section 105, to the admission by the trial judge of the evidence of a number of witnesses who gave evidence to the effect that the applicant had been driving at speed. The Court, however, took the view that that section was not relevant in the circumstance of the case because the evidence of the witnesses was confined to a general impression of speed and no witness had actually given evidence of an enumerated speed of the applicant.

Sexual Offences   Two cases in 2001 confirm the dramatic change in the law in relation to sexual complainants and the requirement to give a corroboration warning which has been effected by the decision of the Court of Criminal Appeal in *People (DPP) v. JEM*, Court of Criminal Appeal, February 1, 2000 (*Annual Review of Irish Law 2000*, p.216) where the principles laid down by the English Court of Appeal in *R v. Makanjuola* [1995] 3 All E.R. 730 were endorsed.

In *People DPP v. C* [2001] 3 I.R. 345, one of the grounds of appeal advanced by the applicant against his conviction on a charge of rape was that the trial judge had erred in failing to exercise his discretion to give the jury a warning on the issue of corroboration. The Court of Criminal Appeal, however, emphasised that it was "no longer a rule of law or practice that a jury must be warned of the dangers of convicting of the uncorroborated evidence of a complainant in a trial concerning a sexual offence by reason of the nature of the offence". Turning to the exercise by the trial judge of his discretion on the facts of the case, Murray J. pointed out that the case was not one where the only evidence against the applicant was that of the complainant. On the contrary, there was a substantial body of evidence capable of constituting corroboration including the applicant's own testimony. He went on to say that:

> "Corroborative evidence does not mean that evidence of the complainant must be corroborated in every material respect. The fact that there is a conflict of evidence between witnesses or between what one witness has said on one occasion or on another occasion does not mean that the trial judge is required to direct the jury on the dangers of convicting on uncorroborated evidence. This is a matter for his discretion."

He was, thus, satisfied that it had not been demonstrated to the court that there was any ground on which the trial judge could be said to have exercised his discretion in this case improperly.

It was also submitted that the trial judge had erred in failing to hear arguments from counsel for the defence on the issue of corroboration. The court was satisfied that, in principle, a trial judge should allow counsel to argue in full any question arising concerning the kind of direction, if any, which he or she should give to a jury and that it was desirable that this occur in the absence of a jury before final speeches. However, the court was satisfied that, in the particular circumstances of the case, the trial judge had not erred in this regard.

The question of giving a warning also arose in passing in *People (DPP) v. Nolan*, Central Criminal Court, Herbert J., November 27, 2001. An unsuccessful submission of no case to answer had been made on the basis that the evidence was so weak and unreliable by reason of inconsistencies in the account given by the complainant that a jury properly directed could not convict on it. The learned judge was then requested by counsel for the defendant to give a corroboration warning but he refused to do so stating that:

> "I have thought about this a lot. [I] intend to give a very mild direction that the jury, conscious of these inconsistencies, should only convict after assessing the complainant's evidence with great care. I think that is sufficient to meet any problems that arise here because I think that the medical evidence is capable of corroboration of the fact that there was no consent, but nonetheless, I think that justice demands that some sort of warning be given....Then, having drawn...the jury's attention to the inconsistencies, I'll tell them that that they must assess her evidence with great care."

Identification evidence In *People (DPP) v. Cahill*, Court of Criminal Appeal, July 31, 2001, the two applicants had been convicted of the armed robbery of a jeweller's shop in Galway. The prosecution case against the first applicant was based exclusively on the evidence of two eye witnesses who identified him as the driver of the car used by the two robbers when they were escaping from the scene and the evidence of another witness who identified him as one of two men whom he had seen in a jeep, linked by other evidence to the robbery, in Clarinbridge on the morning of the robbery. The second applicant was also identified by that witness as the other man in the jeep but, in addition, there were several other pieces of evidence linking him to the commission of the offence.

The first eyewitness, Ms Kearns, had seen the two perpetrators of the robbery running from the scene on foot and get into a car. The second witness, Ms Burns, saw the driver of the getaway car as it sped past her. The two witnesses were brought to a gardaí station for the holding of identification parade but the applicants refused to participate in the parade and, instead, an informal identification procedure took place whereby the persons on parade were marched past the witnesses. Ms Kearns thought she recognised the person who had been driving the car but she wasn't sure and she failed to pick anyone out. For her part, Ms Burns picked out a person other than the first applicant as the driver of the car. Both witnesses were subsequently taken to the District Court in Galway where they identified the applicant as the driver of the getaway car. The other witness, Mr Bannon, also failed to pick anyone out at the garda station but purported to identify the first named applicant as one of the persons whom he had seen in the jeep in Clarinbridge.

It was submitted that the trial judge had given an inadequate warning as to the dangers of the visual identification in the case and, in particular, that although he had recited the relevant passage from the decision in *People (AG) v. Casey (No.2)* [1963] I.R. 33, he had not directed the attention of the jury to factors in the identification evidence which were peculiar to the instant case. However, the Court rejected the criticisms made of the directions given by the trial judge. The trial judge had summarised in detail the evidence of each of the three witnesses and had recited in full the relevant passage from *Casey*. In those circumstances, the Court was satisfied that the directions were careful and comprehensive and that the jury could not have been in any doubt as to the care with which they were required to approach the issue of visual identification.

It was further submitted that the frailties in the identification evidence were such as to render the verdict unsafe and unsatisfactory and that the trial judge had erred in not acceding to an application for a direction. The court referred to the authorities, which, it said, established that there was no rule of law, or practice that required an identification parade to be held and that each case had to be considered on its own facts. Where an alternative method of identification was adopted, its acceptability depended on the circumstances of the case. The court was satisfied that, in the case of the first named applicant, once he had refused to participate in a formal identification parade, it was appropriate to arrange for an information identification procedure. However, each of the witnesses had failed to identify the first named applicant on that occasion and the court was of the view that the subsequent purported identifications at Galway District Court were compromised by the informal procedure and were of such negligible value that a jury verdict which depended solely on such evidence could not be regarded as safe or satisfactory. Keane C.J. stated that:

> "Each of these witnesses was aware, when they went to the garda station, that a person whom the gardaí suspected of being concerned in the robbery would be taking part in the informal parade. Each of them, accordingly, saw the person concerned in the informal parade and their subsequent identification of him in the courthouse was irremediably flawed by the fact that they had previously seen him in the garda station and knew him to be a suspect."

He went on to highlight the inconsistencies in the evidence given by the witnesses *inter se* and between the descriptions given by them to gardaí and their evidence in court. The identification evidence was the only evidence connecting the first named applicant to the crime and, having regard to the dangers inherent in cases of visual identification, the court was satisfied that, in the circumstances, the case against him should have been withdrawn from the jury at the conclusion of the prosecution case. The situation in respect of the second named applicant was, however, different in that there was other evidence linking him to the commission of the offence, which the jury were entitled to consider.

The reliability of an identification made by a witness in court is crucially dependent on the quality of the pre-trial identification procedures, which should act as a means of screening out unreliable identification evidence. Thus, if improper or suggestive pre-trial identification procedures are used, the probative value of such evidence is undermined significantly. This was the case in *Cahill* where the Chief Justice rightly focused on the fact that the purported pre-trial identification of the accused by the witnesses had been compromised by the fact that they had previously seen him in the garda station. The problems created by the identification procedures used by the gardaí were not dissimilar to those created by the use of photographs. It has been observed by Mason J. in *Alexander v. R* (1981) 145 C.L.R. 395 that there is a tendency for a witness who is shown photographs "to substitute a photographic image once seen for a hazy recollection of the person initially observed". Thereafter, as Glanville Williams, *The Proof of Guilt* (3rd ed., London: Stevens, 1963), p.122, has pointed out, "his recollection of the culprit and recollection of the photograph are likely to be so merged that he can no longer separate them, even though in fact his identification was mistaken". Similarly, once the witnesses had seen the first named applicant in the garda station in circumstances where they knew him to a suspect, it was highly likely that they would identify him subsequently in the District Court as one of the perpetrators of the robbery.

As for the withdrawal of the case from the jury, it is clear from the case law including *People (DPP) v. O'Reilly* [1990] 2 I.R. 4 (*Annual Review of Irish Law 1990*, p.207) and *People (DPP) v. Duff* [1995] 3 I.R. 296 that one of the most important considerations in the exercise by a trial judge of his or her discretion to withdraw identification evidence from the jury is the conduct and adequacy of the pre-trial procedures. In particular, the holding of an identification parade can prove crucial in giving an *imprimatur* of reliability to evidence of identification where the opportunity for observation was not particularly good. Conversely, as in *Duff* and *Cahill*, the failure to hold a formal parade, or at least to conduct satisfactory identification procedures, can render weak identification evidence sufficiently unreliable to warrant its withdrawal from the jury.

Recognition evidence The courts have accepted that the general requirement to hold an identification parade is redundant in the case of recognition evidence i.e. where a witness purports to recognise a person previously known to him or her as opposing to identifying an unknown person (*People (DPP) v. O'Reilly* [1990] 2 I.R. 415 (*Annual Review of Irish Law 1990*, p.207)). The logical corollary, which emerges from the decision in *People (DPP) v. McDonagh,* Court of Criminal Appeal, April 6, 2001, is that, such evidence will not be rendered inadmissible by the shortcomings of an identification parade if one is actually held. The applicant in that case was a member of the travelling community who had been convicted of murder submitted. He submitted that an identification parade had been held in an unfair manner because he was the only traveller participating in the parade. The court was, however, satisfied that this ground of appeal had not been made out because the witness in question knew the applicant and the holding of an identification parade was, therefore, superfluous.

Cautionary instructions In *People (AG) v. Casey (No.2)* [1963] I.R. 33, 37, Kingsmill Moore J., delivering the judgment of the Supreme Court, stated that:

> "It is the function of a judge in his charge to give to the jury such direction and warnings as may in his opinion be necessary to avoid the danger of an innocent man being convicted, and the nature of such directions and warnings must depend on the facts of the particular case. But, apart from the directions and warnings suggested by the facts of an individual case, judicial experience has shown that certain general directions and warnings are necessary in every case and that particular types of warnings are necessary in particular types of case."

One such category of case, which was suggested in *People (DPP) v. McKenna,* Court of Criminal Appeal, October 19, 2001, is where the evidence of a sexual complainant is based on "recovered memory". The applicant in that case sought leave to appeal against his conviction in relation to 29 accounts of sexual assault arguing, *inter alia*, that the case involved "recovered memory" on the part of the complainant which, it was argued, should have been the subject of a warning by the trial judge. Delivering the judgment of the court, Geoghegan J. stated that if the case before the court had indeed been a recovered memory case then there might have been a good argument in favour of such a warning. However, the court was satisfied that this was not a case involving recovered memory and declined to express any view on the matter.

Withdrawal of case from the jury   The principles to be applied where an application is made to withdrawn the case from the jury at the conclusion of the prosecution case are well settled in England but, despite the importance of this application in practice, had received relatively little consideration in this jurisdiction. It is, therefore, notable that this issue was considered in two cases in 2001, *People (DPP) v. Nolan*, Central Criminal Court, November 27, 2001 and *People (DPP) v. M*, Court of Criminal Appeal, February 15, 2001.

The starting point for a consideration of this issue is the decision in *R v. Galbraith* [1981] 2 All E.R. 1060, where the English Court of Appeal considered the two schools of thought which existed at the time as to the proper approach to be adopted by a judge where a submission of no case to answer was made at the conclusion of the prosecution case. The first was that the judge should stop the case if, in his or her view, it would be unsafe or unsatisfactory for the jury to convict as where the judge thought that the main witnesses for the prosecution were not telling the truth. The second was that the judge should only do so if there was no evidence on which a jury properly directed could convict.

The Court of Appeal emphasised that a balance had to be struck between "on the one hand a usurpation by the judge of the jury's functions and on the other the danger of an unjust conviction". It, therefore, preferred the second of the two schools of thought, endorsing the views of Widgery C.J. in *R v. Barker* (1977) 65 Cr. App. R.287, 288, that:

> "It cannot be too clearly stated that the judge's obligation to stop the case is an obligation which is concerned primarily with those cases where the necessary minimum evidence to establish the facts of the crime has not been called. It is not the judge's job to weigh the evidence, decide who is telling the truth, and to stop the case merely because he thinks the witness is lying. To do that is to usurp the function of the jury."

In an oft-cited passage, Lord Lane C.J. laid down the principles, which should be applied by a trial judge in dealing with an application for a direction or a submission of no case to answer:

"(1) If there is no evidence that the crime alleged has been committed by the defendant, there is no difficulty. The judge will of course stop the case. (2) The difficulty arises where there is some evidence but it is of a tenuous character, for example because of inherent weakness or vagueness or because it is inconsistent with other evidence. (a) Where the judge comes to the conclusion that the Crown's evidence, taken at its highest, is such that a jury properly directed could not properly convict on it, it is his duty, on a submission being made, to stop the case. (b) Where however, the Crown's evidence is such that its strength or weakness depends on the view to be taken of a witness's reliability, or other matters which are generally speaking within the province of the jury and where on one possible view of the facts there is evidence on which a jury could properly come to the conclusion that the defendant is guilty, then the judge should allow the matter to be tried by the jury....There will of course, as always in this branch of the law, be borderline cases. They can safely be left to the discretion of the judge."

A gloss was subsequently placed on the *Galbraith* principles in *R v. Shippey* [1988] Crim. L.R. 767. The defendants were charged with rape and the prosecution case against them was based effectively on the uncorroborated evidence of the complainant. At the conclusion of the prosecution case, a submission of no case to answer was made. While the defence conceded that there was undoubtedly some evidence that showed that the alleged offences had been committed, it was argued that the evidence was so inherently weak and inconsistent that no jury properly directed could properly convict. For its part, the prosecution conceded that there were weaknesses and inconsistencies in the evidence. However, it was argued that, consistent with *Galbraith*, it was a matter for the jury to assess its strength or weaknesses. Taking the evidence at its highest, it was submitted that it could not be said that a jury properly directed could not properly convict.

Turner J. rejected the proposition that the effect of *Galbraith* was that, if there are parts of the evidence, which go to support the charge then no matter what the state of the rest of the evidence, that is enough to leave the matter to the jury. He stated that taking the prosecution case at its highest "did not mean picking out the plums and leaving the duff behind" and it was necessary to assess the evidence as a whole. He emphasised that it was not a sufficient basis for the withdrawal of the case from the jury that there were issues as to the credibility of individual witnesses or evidential inconsistencies between their evidence. On the other hand, if the evidence was self-contradictory or contained such inherent weaknesses that it lacked a foundation in reason and common sense, it might be regarded as so tenuous and weak as to justify withdrawal from the jury. Having examined the evidence before him, he was satisfied that parts of the complainant's evidence were "incredible" and were wholly inconsistent with the allegation of rape. He was, therefore, satisfied that the submission of no case to answer should be allowed and he withdrew the case from the jury.

The principles in *Galbraith* were approved as representing the law in this jurisdiction by Flood J. in *People (DPP) v. Barnwell*, Central Criminal Court, January 24, 1997, who linked them to the cardinal rule that the prosecution bears the onus of proof in a criminal trial. Applying them to the case before him, the learned judge was satisfied that there were serious inconsistencies and a clear conflict of evidence within the evidence adduced by the prosecution, which rendered it "tenuous in the extreme". In the circumstances, he had no doubt but that the case should be withdrawn from the jury. The application of the *Galbraith* principles in the context of inconsistencies in the evidence adduced by the prosecution has now been further considered in *Nolan* and in *M*.

In *Nolan*, the accused was charged with rape and, at the conclusion of the prosecution case, an application to withdraw the case from the jury was made on the basis that the evidence was so weak and unreliable by reason of inconsistencies in the account given by the complainant that a jury properly directed could not convict on it. Herbert J. engaged in a comprehensive review of the relevant authorities and, in particular of cases, which had applied the Galbraith principles to cases involving inconsistencies in the evidence, adduced by the prosecution case including *R v. Cameron*, *The Times*, May 3, 2001. In that case, the Court of Appeal refused to interfere with the decision of the trial judge not to withdraw the case from the jury on the basis that:

> "[T]he submission of no case to answer was essentially one for the judge who had had the advantage of seeing and assessing the complainant and the manner in which she gave her evidence. It was classically a case where the strength or weakness of the prosecution evidence depended on the view to be taken of the witnesses' reliability….the appellant….of course, denied the rape and the essential matter of doubt upon which the reliability of the complainant's evidence fell to be assessed was her assertion that rape had taken place. She had offered explanations as to why she had later indicated to others that it had not taken place, and the judge was fully entitled to take the view that the assessment of her evidence and credibility as a whole should properly be left for the jury to decide."

Herbert J. emphasised that, in order for a case to be withdrawn from the jury in accordance with principle 2(a) laid down by Lord Lane CJ, there must be something, as clearly was the case in *Barnwell*, going beyond questions of credibility; there must be no basis on which the jury could properly find the accused guilty. He had no doubt that the case before him was one, which should be left to the jury who would have to be properly directed in respect of it.

In *M,* the applicant sought leave to appeal his conviction on a charge of sexual assault on the ground that the trial judge had erred in refusing to withdraw the case from the jury because of the inconsistent versions of the incident given by the complainant both during and prior to the trial. Having examined the transcript of the evidence, the Court was satisfied that although different descriptive terms had been used by the complainant in her evidence and there were inconsistencies, the complainant remained consistent in the basic story that she told. Further, the inconsistencies in the case went to issues of credibility and reliability and these, as issues of fact, were for the jury to determine. Applying the principles laid down in *Galbraith* as interpreted in *Shippey,* the court was satisfied that the trial judge had not erred in refusing to withdraw the counts of sexual assault from the jury:

> "If there is no evidence that an element of the crime alleged had been committed, the situation would be clear. The judge would have to stop the trial. However, that is not the situation here. The judge comes to the conclusion that the prosecution evidence taken at its highest is such that a jury properly directed could not properly convict, it is his duty to stop the trial. However, that is not the case here. Here there is lengthy evidence from the complainants in which there are some inconsistencies. These inconsistencies are matters which to the issues of reliability and credibility and thus, in the circumstances, are solely matters for the jury. The learned trial judge therefore was correct in letting the trial proceed. These are matters quintessentially for the jury to decide. However, if the inconsistencies were such as to render it unfair to proceed with the trial then the judge in the exercise of his or her discretion should stop the trial. However, this is not the situation here."

It seems clear from the decisions in *Nolan* and *M,* when taken together with *Barnwell* that a submission of no case to answer will not be successful merely because the defence can identify inconsistencies, even serious inconsistencies, in the prosecution case provided that there is evidence that supports the charges. However, if it is possible to point to inherent conflicts in the prosecution case of a kind, which render the evidence, adduced tenuous or which cast serious doubt on whether the defendant committed the alleged offences, then the trial judge is under a duty to withdraw the case from the jury.

HEARSAY

Judicial review proceedings   In *McQuaid v. McBride*, High Court, Kearns J., February 21, 2001, the applicant instituted judicial review proceedings seeking to quash his conviction by the respondent District Judge for two offences under the Road Traffic Act 1961. In a number of decisions, the courts had questioned the propriety of joining District Judges as parties to judicial review proceedings where their conduct was impugned and the view had been taken that it would be inappropriate for the judge to participate in the proceedings by swearing an affidavit (see *O'Connor v. Carroll* [1999] 2 I.R. 160 (*Annual Review of Irish Law 1998*, p.91)). For this reason, Kearns J. acceded to the application of the notice party that he should receive a note of the evidence taken by the respondent. While the learned judge accepted that this was hearsay evidence, he agreed with the submission made by counsel for the DPP that "there need be no exclusionary rule for such evidence in judicial review where it is relevant and where there are public policy considerations which preclude the respondent from swearing an affidavit". In his view, it would be "quite wrong that the only person who could not be heard was the judge himself". He, thus, had recourse to the note of evidence which was exhibited in an affidavit sworn by the District Court clerk in deciding the matters before him though he did signal that he was conscious "of the fact that it is not, for reasons of public interest, in affidavit form as that would leave the respondent open to cross-examination in relation to the judicial process".

CONFESSIONS

Custody Regulations   The effect of a breach of the Criminal Justice Act 1984 (Treatment of Persons in Custody in Garda Síochána Stations) Regulations 1987 (the "Regulations") is governed by section 7(3) of the Criminal Justice Act 1984 which stipulates that a failure to observe them shall not "of itself" affect the admissibility in evidence of any statement made by an accused. That subsection was considered by O'Hanlon J. in *DPP v. Spratt* [1995] 1 I.R. 585, [1995] 2 I.L.R.M. 117 (*Annual Review of Irish Law 1995*, p.244) who interpreted its effect as follows:

> "The phrase 'of itself' is obviously an important one in the construction of the statutory provisions, and I interpret the sub-section as meaning that non-observance of the Regulations is not to bring about automatically the exclusion from evidence of all that was done and said while the accused person was in custody. It appears to be left to the court of trial to adjudicate in every case as to the impact the non-compliance with the regulations should have on the case for the prosecution."

Subsequent cases have emphasised that in addition to adjudicating as to whether there has been a breach of the Regulations, the trial judge must go on to consider whether there is a causative link between the breach of the regulations and whatever prejudice is alleged to have been suffered by an accused as a result thereof (*DPP v. Devlin*, High Court, Budd J., September 2, 1998 (1998 Review,

389); *DPP (Lenihan) v. McGuire* [1996] 3 I.R. 586 (*Annual Review of Irish Law 1996,* p. 262).

These principles were applied in the context of a challenge to the admissibility of a confession in *People (DPP) v. Murphy,* Court of Criminal Appeal, July 12, 2001. The applicant argued that a confession made by him to gardaí whilst in custody should have been excluded because of a failure by the gardaí to keep a record of the entirety of the interview as required by Article 12(11) of the Regulations. It was common case that, prior to making the confession at issue, the applicant had engaged in what was termed "a general chat" none of which had been recorded. It is not alleged that anything of significance had occurred during this period and there had not been any evidence before the trial judge which would have warranted a conclusion that the absence of the record had prejudiced the position of the applicant.

The Court referred to section 7(3) and the authorities in relation to its interpretation including *Spratt* and *McGuire* and endorsed the necessity for an accused to establish a causal connection between the failure to comply with the relevant regulation and whatever prejudice was alleged to have been suffered. In the instant case, there was a lacuna in the record but there was no evidence of any event occurring during that time to prejudice the applicant and the court was, accordingly, satisfied that this lacuna was insufficient to render inadmissible the inculpatory statement of the applicant.

Video recording of interviews　In *People (DPP) v. Murphy,* Court of Criminal Appeal, 12 July 2001, Denham J. observed in passing that the gap in the record of the interview with the applicant at issue highlighted the benefits of video recording interviews. She pointed out that: "The benefits from such recording accrue to the arrested person, the gardaí and the community in that the process becomes more transparent." It is, therefore, disappointing to note the lack of progress in the installation of the necessary equipment. According to an article in *The Irish Times* (April 8, 2002), as of that date, only 97 garda stations of a total of 700 have had the equipment installed. In addition, the target for the number of stations to have the equipment installed has been reduced to 150 which is a matter of serious concern given that, under the Criminal Justice Act, 1984 (Electronic Recording of Interviews) Regulations 1997, the obligation to video record interviews only applies to those stations where the equipment is installed.

Fundamental fairness　In *People (DPP) v. C* [2001] 3 I.R. 345, one of the grounds on which the applicant sought leave to appeal was that certain statements made by him in custody should have been excluded as having been obtained in breach of the standards of fundamental fairness. Reliance was placed on the well-known passage from the judgment of Griffin J. in *People (DPP) v. Shaw* [1982] I.R. 1, 60-61 where he stated that:

"The primary requirement is to show that the statement was voluntary, in the sense in which that adjective has been judicially construed in the decided cases. Thus, if the tendered statement was coerced or otherwise induced or extracted without the true and free will of its maker, it will not be held to have been voluntarily made. The circumstances, which will make a statement inadmissible for lack of voluntariness, are so varied that it would be impossible to enumerate or categorize them fully. It is sufficient to say that the decided cases show that a statement will be excluded as being involuntary if it was wrung from its maker by physical or psychological pressures, by threats or promises made by persons in authority, by the use of drugs, hypnosis, intoxicating drink, by prolonged interrogation or excessive questioning, or by any one of a diversity of methods which have in common the result or the risk that what is tendered as a voluntary statement is not the natural emanation of a rational intellect and a free will....Secondly, even if a statement is held to have been voluntarily obtained in the sense indicated, it may nevertheless be inadmissible for another reason....although a statement may be technically voluntary, it should nevertheless be excluded if, by reason of the manner or of the circumstances in which it was obtained, it falls below the required standard of fairness....Whether the objection to the statement be on constitutional or other grounds, the crucial test is whether it was obtained in compliance with basic or fundamental fairness..."

Applying those principles to the facts of the instant case, it was argued on behalf of the applicant that the trial judge should have exercised his discretion to exclude the statements of the applicant because he had only slept for approximately one hour in the previous thirty and had consumed a large quantity of alcohol in the period prior to questioning.

The Court of Criminal Appeal accepted that, under the decision in *Shaw*, the trial judge had a discretion to exclude the applicant's statements but, as stated in that case, that discretion fell to be exercised in accordance with the facts of the particular case. In the instant case, the trial judge had accepted the evidence by the investigating gardaí and a doctor that the applicant was in a perfectly coherent condition at all stages and was unaffected by tiredness or alcohol consumption and the Court was satisfied that there was ample evidence before him to support his findings.

In an interesting aside, the Court rejected the submission advanced by the applicant that there was an equivalence between the situation where a detainee had suffered from lack of sleep for reasons which had nothing to do with the investigating gardaí and that where the gardaí had deliberately deprived a detainee of his sleep. Murray J. stated:

"The two situations are not the same. If investigating gardaí had resorted to such tactics statements so obtained would be excluded on the grounds of public policy and breach of fair procedures by the State by reason of the use of such methods independent of any question concerning the voluntariness of a statement."

By way of contrast, it might be noted that one of the factors taken into account by the Court of Criminal Appeal in *People (DPP) v. Connell* [1995] 1 I.R. 244 (*Annual Review of Irish Law 1995*, p.246) was the applicant's lack of sleep while in custody even though the lack of sleep was not attributable to any acts or omissions on the part of the gardaí. The merits of this approach were questionable and it may that a different conclusion might be reached now.

PRIVILEGE

Identity of a client and legal professional privilege   The proceedings in *Miley v. Flood* [2001] 2 I.R. 50, [2001] 1 I.L.R.M. 489, arose out of the investigations of the Tribunal of Inquiry into Certain Planning Matters and Payments (better known as the Flood Tribunal) into allegations that monies had been paid to politicians for the purpose of securing the rezoning of lands at Carrickmines, County Dublin, owned by an English domiciled company called Jackson Way Properties Ltd. The Tribunal wished to discover the identities of the persons who were the beneficial owners of the company and, to that end, the applicant, a partner in the firm of solicitors which represented the company, was summonsed to appear before the Tribunal and asked to disclose the names of the persons from whom he had received instructions on behalf of the company. He refused to do so on the basis that this information was confidential and protected by legal professional privilege and that his client had given him specific instructions not to reveal it. However, the respondent ruled that legal professional privilege did not cover the identity of persons providing instructions to the applicant and the applicant sought judicial review of this determination. Given that the issue could have implications for the solicitor's profession, the Law Society was joined as a notice party and argued strongly that privilege applied.

In deference to the elaborate and comprehensive submissions made to him, Kelly J. engaged in a comprehensive review of the authorities on the issue. These were generally against the proposition advanced by the applicant and the Law Society but the learned judge said that he ultimately derived little assistance from these authorities. Instead, he decided the issue by reference to the principles laid down by the Supreme Court in the seminal decision of *Smurfit Paribas Bank Ltd v. AAB Export Finance Ltd* [1990] 1 I.R. 469, [1990] I.L.R.M. 588 (*Annual Review of Irish Law 1990*, p.435). In that case, the plaintiff sought disclosure of correspondence and instructions passing between the defendant and the solicitors then acting for it in relation to a charge taken by the defendant over the assets of a third party. The trial judge found that the documents in question did not request or contain any legal advice and were not, therefore, privileged and this conclusion was upheld on appeal by the Supreme Court where a distinction was drawn between 'legal advice' and 'legal assistance'. Finlay C.J. set forth the basic principle to be applied in dealing with claims of privilege as follows:

> "The existence of a privilege or exemption from disclosure for communications made between a person and his lawyer clearly constitutes a potential restriction and diminution of the full disclosure both prior to and during the course of legal proceedings which in the interests of the common good is desirable for the purpose of ascertaining the truth and rendering justice. Such privilege should, therefore, in my view only be granted in instances which have been identified as securing an objective which in the public interest in the proper conduct of the administration of justice can be said to outweigh the disadvantage arising from the restriction of disclosure of all the facts."

Having regard to the rationale for legal professional privilege, he was satisfied that legal advice satisfied this test but legal assistance did not because it was not "closely and proximately linked to the conduct of litigation and the function of administering justice in the courts".

Kelly J. viewed the decision in *Smurfit* as authority for the proposition that where communications between a client and his or her lawyer are at issue, privilege can only be claimed for a communication if it seeks or contains legal advice and that the communication of any other information is not privileged. Further, if a claim of privilege is challenged, the onus is placed upon the person invoking privilege to justify the claim. Applying these principles, he was satisfied that the applicant was not entitled to maintain a claim of privilege over the identity of persons who provided him with his instructions on behalf of the company. Neither did the applicant's claim that the information had been given to him in confidence affect the situation. Kelly J. pointed out that the confidentiality of information does not, of itself, create a privilege from disclosure. An exemption from disclosure will only apply where the conditions for privilege are met.

A number of the authorities examined by the learned judge declined to lay down an absolute rule that the identity of a client could never be privileged acknowledging that there might be circumstances where such a claim might be appropriate (*Ontario (Securities Commission) v. Greymac Credit Corporation* (1983) 146 D.L.R. (3d) 73, 84), as for example, where naming the client would incriminate him or her or where the identity of the client is so bound up with the nature of the advice sought that to reveal the client's identity would reveal that advice (*Federal Commissioner of Taxation v. Coombes* [1999] F.C.A. 842; (1999) 164 A.L.R. 131). However, it was not necessary for Kelly

J. to decide whether such exceptions existed in this jurisdiction because they did not arise on the facts before him.

Taking a definitional approach, it is clear that a solicitor claiming privilege in respect of the identity of his or her client faces significant difficulties in satisfying a court that the essential prerequisites for a claim of legal advice privilege are satisfied. It must, first of all, be established that the communication was made to or by a lawyer during the currency of a professional legal relationship (*Greenough v. Gaskell* (1833) 1 My. & K. 98, 101). Obviously, in order to satisfy this condition, it must be proved that a lawyer-client relationship exists and this would appear to require revelation of the identity of the client (*Bursill v. Tanner* (1885) 16 Q.B.D. 1, 5; *Federal Commissioner of Taxation v. Coombes* [1999] F.C.A. 842; (1999) 164 A.L.R. 131). Second, it is a fundamental prerequisite for privilege that the communication was intended to pass in confidence (*Webster v. James Chapman & Co* [1989] 3 All E.R. 939, 944) and the identity of a client will rarely be disclosed to a solicitor on that basis (*Re Cathcart, ex parte Campbell* (1870) 5 Ch. App. 703, 705). Furthermore, even if a court is willing to accept the assertion of a solicitor that he or she acts on behalf of an unnamed client and that the identity of the client has been imparted on a confidential basis, there still exist formidable difficulties in establishing that the identity of the client is a 'communication' within the rubric of privilege.

There is a long line of authority that restricts privilege to information which passes between a lawyer and client, rather than facts which a lawyer may learn in the course of his professional relationship with a client. A distinction is, thus, drawn between facts communicated to a lawyer by the client (whether orally or otherwise) and those which are patent to the senses (see *Sandford v. Remington* (1793) 2 Ves. Jun. 189; *Greenough v. Gaskell* (1833) 1 My. & K. 98, 104). As Baron Martin stated in *Brown v. Foster* (1857) 1 H. & N. 736, "what passes between counsel and client ought not to be communicated, and is not admissible in evidence, but with respect to matters which the counsel sees with his own eyes, he cannot refuse to answer." The identity of a client is a fact, which will often be patent to the solicitor, and not a fact actually communicated to him or her.

Further, even if the client is unknown to the solicitor and thus, his or her name is a fact which only becomes known to the solicitor by virtue of his or her professional relationship with the client, there is the added and, in most cases, insurmountable difficulty, that this is not a fact which is communicated to the solicitor for the purpose of obtaining legal advice. As Kelly J. makes clear in his judgment, not all communications that pass between a lawyer and client are privileged, only those made of the purpose of giving or receiving legal advice. Thus, no protection will be given to a mere 'collateral fact' such as the address of the client imparted by the client to the solicitor which is not relevant to the discharge by the lawyer of his or her professional functions (*Re Cathcart, ex parte Campbell* (1870) 5 Ch. App. 703, 705). Although, the identity of a client may well constitute vital information for the purpose of establishing and maintaining a professional relationship between a solicitor and client, it is only in exceptional circumstances that it will be required by the solicitor in order to give legal advice.

Turning to the broader policy considerations on which the decision of Kelly J. in *Miley* was ultimately based, there is a strong argument to be made that the identity of a client is information, which should not, ordinarily, be protected from disclosure. In order to justify the extension of privilege to the identity of the client, it would have to be shown that, having regard to the particular context in which he or she consulted a solicitor, knowledge that his or her identity could be disclosed would have dissuaded the client from instructing a solicitor or had a 'chilling effect' on the relationship. It is only in rare circumstances that this could be shown and these did not arise on the facts in *Miley*. The company instructed the applicant solicitor in relation to proceedings in which it was involved and it must be regarded as most unlikely that if the promoters of the company had been aware of the possibility of future disclosure of their identity that they would have declined to instruct solicitors. It is not surprising that this vague and unquantifiable danger should give way to the very evident public interest in having that information disclosed to a court or, in this case, the Tribunal.

Although the decision in *Miley v. Flood* dealt with a very net point, the judgment of Kelly J. has broader ramifications for the development of legal professional privilege in this jurisdiction and underscores its fundamental status in Irish law. The learned judge referred with approval to decisions in other jurisdictions which have taken the view that the privilege is more than a rule of evidence and have ascribed to it a substantive content which is capable of application in pre-trial and non-curial contexts and reiterated the view previously taken by him in *Duncan v. Governor of Portlaoise Prison* [1997] 1 I.R. 558, 575, [1997] 2 I.L.R.M. 296, 311 (*Annual Review of Irish Law 1997*, p.423) that: "Legal professional privilege is more than a mere rule of evidence. It is a fundamental condition on which the administration of justice as a whole rests." These comments echo those of Hamilton C.J. in *Quinlivan v. Governor of Portlaoise Prison*, Supreme Court, March 5, 1997 (*Annual Review of Irish Law 1997*, p.425), that the privilege has "always been regarded by the courts as absolutely essential and of paramount importance in the administration of justice" and Finlay C.J. in *Bula Ltd v. Crowley (No. 2)* [1994] 2 I.R. 54, 59 who referred to "the important confidence in relation to communications between lawyers and their clients which is a fundamental part of our system of justice and is considered in all the authorities to be a major contributor to the proper administration of justice." These *dicta* raise the possibility that, at some future date, the privilege may receive some measure of protection on the constitutional plane.

Records of proceedings and legal professional privilege   In *MFM v. PW*,

High Court, Finnegan J., June 22, 2001, the issue arose as to whether privilege could be claimed in respect of notes taken by a solicitor of the evidence in previous proceedings. The case had been part-heard before Moriarty J., but because of his tribunal commitments he had been unable to complete the hearing of the matter and, in the circumstances, the plaintiff wished to have the hearing recommenced before another judge. The defendant subsequently obtained an order for discovery requiring the plaintiff to make discovery of any note taken by the solicitor or counsel of the evidence heard before Mr Justice Moriarty. However, legal professional privilege was claimed over these notes prepared by the solicitor for the plaintiff on the basis that they had been prepared in contemplation of legal proceedings. In an affidavit filed on behalf of the plaintiff it was averred that the notes were prepared for the purpose of drawing the attention of certain points in the evidence to counsel and to the client. It was further averred that the notes were prepared specifically with the function of the solicitor in mind and assisted in its execution.

In the absence of any decided authority on the point in Ireland, Finnegan J. embarked on a comprehensive review of the English authorities on the point. The main authority in favour of granting the privilege claimed was *Nordon v. Defries* (1882) 8 Q.B.D. 508. In that case, the plaintiff had taken a shorthand note of the evidence in an action entitled *Nordon v. Nordon* with a view to its use in that action but also for the purposes of the instant case. Mathew J. stated that:

> "It is probable in this case that the notes of the evidence were taken as well with a view to ulterior proceedings in the case of *Nordon v. Nordon* as for the purpose of this action. If so the notes would seem to have been clearly privileged in that suit, and it is difficult to see why the privilege in one suit should destroy the privilege in another arising out of the same subject matter. It seems unreasonable that the privilege in each should become a privilege in neither."

A similar approach was taken by Channelle A. in *Lambert v. Home* (1914) 3 K.B. 86 who accepted that the shorthand notes at issue should be protected as forming part of the brief:

> "That which was said in the witness in the box is, I agree, relevant and it was public property in the sense that it might have been heard and might have been recorded by anyone; but words are evanescent, other people did not record them, and I did, and I did so solely for my use and protection in the present litigation which I then anticipated. I brought it into existence as a document of which inspection is asked, and I brought it into existence through my solicitor for the express purpose of instructing my solicitor and Counsel both as to advising me whether I should defend the present claim and to enable them to conduct my

defence for me if I did defend. It is part of my brief and I claim privilege for it. The record is not public property although the words which it records may have been."

However, the majority in that case took a different approach stressing the public nature of such a note. Cozens Hardy MR stated:

"It is admitted that the transcript relates to the matters in question in this action, but it is contended that the document is privileged – that is in substance a part of the defendant's brief, as a statement of what some, or possibly all, of the witnesses who were present at the collision have sworn, and that it is not fair to require the defendant to produce that which has been brought into existence under the instructions and at the cost of the defendant in anticipation of the present litigation. Now the proceedings in the County Court were public. Anyone present could listen and take a note of what the witnesses said. The transcript does not involve any such "professional knowledge, research and skill"....There is no original composition in the documents. It is a mere transcript of that which was *publici juris*. A defendant who has obtained at his own cost a copy of a document, not in his possession, which is not itself privileged, cannot decline to produce the copy, although he obtained it in anticipation of future litigation. So here a mere reproduction in a physical form of material which was *publici juris*, cannot, I think, be privileged."

A similar approach was advocated in Buckley L.J. who criticised the decision in *Nordon*:

"The shorthand notes had been taken in an action of *Nordon v. Nordon*. Discovery of them was asked for the purpose of using them in an action of *Nordon v. Defries*. Mathew J. says that in that action of *Nordon v. Nordon*, shorthand notes would seem to have been clearly privileged. In my judgment they would not have been privileged at all. If there had been subsequent proceedings in *Nordon v. Nordon*, as upon an inquiry as to damages or a reference before the Master or any subsequent step, the notes taken at the trial of *Nordon v. Nordon* would not have been privileged."

The learned judge also referred to the decision in *Robson v. Worswick* (1888) 33 C.D. 370 where Knorr J. had stated:

"It has been put in argument that supposing the shorthand notes had been taken by the solicitor's clerk – or the solicitor himself – they would have been privileged. I do not admit that would be so. A mere verbatim report of the evidence, whether by the solicitor's clerk, the solicitor or counsel, would not in my opinion be privileged."

On the basis of this review of the authorities, Finnegan J. regarded it as well settled that transcripts or solicitor's notes of proceedings and evidence are not privileged in a subsequent action. With regard to the question as to whether they were privileged in the action in which they were taken, he preferred the approach of the majority in *Lambert v. Home* as being more consistent with principle. He also took the view that insofar as a solicitor's notes are of evidence and proceedings they are a record of what was *publici juris* and so are not entitled to privilege in the action in which they were taken.

His analysis of the case law also indicated that insofar as there was a note which was a mixture, being in part a note of proceedings and/or evidence and in part notes made by a solicitor for purpose of litigation, the practice of the courts had been to allow production with the latter parts covered up (see *Ainsworth v. Wilding* (1900) 2 C.D. 315). Thus, he proposed to examine the note of evidence taken to determine the extent to which it contained other material designed to assist the plaintiff in the prosecution of the action which should be covered up as privileged prior to inspection.

The application for discovery in the instant case had arisen in unusual circumstances where the case had been part-heard. In the ordinary course of events, Finnegan J. did not regard it as likely that in the course of an action which ran without interruption the court would likely exercise its discretion and order discovery such as this during the course of the action. However, he did acknowledge that it might be appropriate to do so in special circumstances.

Legal professional privilege In *Buckley v. Bough*, High Court, Morris P., July 2, 2001, the plaintiff brought proceedings against the defendant claiming damages for medical negligence. An order for discovery was made and the defendant claimed legal professional privilege over a number of documents. That claim of privilege was challenged insofar as it related to documents concerning a hearing held by the Fitness for Practice Committee pursuant to the Medical Practitioners Act 1978.

Applying the law in relation to legal professional privilege laid down in the Supreme Court in *Smurfit Paribas Bank Limited v. AB Export Finance Limited* [1990] 1 I.R. 469; [1990] I.L.R.M. 588 (*Annual Review of Irish Law 1990*, p.435), and restated by Kelly J. in *Miley v. Flood* [2001] 2 I.R. 50, [2001] 1 I.L.R.M. 489 (above), the learned judge was satisfied that the claim of privilege failed. The bulk of the documentation consisted of correspondence passing between the defendant's solicitors and the Medical Council or its representatives and he stated that it was not possible that in this correspondence the defendant's solicitors were communicating legal advice to the defendant so as to attract privilege.

Of the remaining documents, two were a transcript of the hearing held by

the Fitness to Practice Committee and it was submitted on behalf of the
defendant that, on the authority of *Barry v. Medical Council* [1998] 3 I.R. 368
(*Annual Review of Irish Law 1998*, p.450), proceedings before the Fitness to
Practice Committee or the Medical Council were confidential and, thus,
transcripts of the evidence of these hearings were privileged. However, Morris
P. took the view that there was nothing in that decision to support the submission
made that the hearing before the Committee was privileged. Such support as
could be identified therein was based entirely upon patient-medical practitioner
privilege. This ground of privilege has not been claimed by the defendant but,
in any event, the plaintiff was the patient involved and she had expressly waived
any privilege of this nature. The learned judge was, therefore, satisfied that
there was no basis on which the defendant could claim privilege for these
documents.

Establishing a claim to legal professional privilege   In *Irish Haemophilia
Society Ltd v. Lindsay*, High Court, Kelly J., May 16, 2001; *Irish Times*, June
11, 2001, the applicant brought judicial review proceedings seeking to challenge
a ruling made by the respondent, the sole member of the Tribunal of Inquiry
into circumstances of infection of people with haemophilia with HIV and
hepatitis C, that a claim of legal professional privilege by the Irish Blood
Transfusion Service had been properly made. Three grounds were advanced
by the applicant in support of the application: (i) that the respondent had erred
in holding that the documents had been described in sufficient detail in the
affidavit of discovery, (ii) that the respondent had reversed the onus of proof
in respect of the challenge to the claim of privilege, and (iii) that the respondent
had erred in refused to carry out an inspection of the documents or to allow
cross-examination of the deponent.

Dealing with the first ground, Kelly J. was satisfied, having examined the
affidavit, that it complied with the directions of the Supreme Court in *Bula Ltd
v. Tara Mines Ltd* [1991] 1 I.R. 217 (*Annual Review of Irish Law 1990*, p.432)
and *Bula Ltd v. Crowley* [1991] 1 I.R. 220; [1990] I.L.R.M. 756 (*Annual Review
of Irish Law 1990*, p.432) that, where a claim of privilege is made, the proper
format is to list each document individually with a description of the general
nature of the document. He, thus, rejected the submission advanced by the
applicant that it was necessary to go further and describe the documents in
respect of which privilege was claimed in greater detail. In his opinion, to do
so "would run the risk of diluting or perhaps even destroying the privilege that
is being asserted". Although he did not expand further on his reasoning, it
seems clear that the learned judge was animated by the concern that to require
any greater level of specificity than a general description of a document would
be to reveal or, at least, give some indication of its contents which would
undermine significantly the protection conferred thereby.

The contention that the respondent had erred in holding that the onus was
on the applicant to adduce evidence, which would question the validity of the

privilege claimed, was dismissed by the learned judge in summary fashion. In his opinion, it was clear from the decision in *Smurfit Paribas Bank Ltd v. AAB Export Finance Ltd* [1990] 1 I.R. 469; [1990] I.L.R.M. 588 (*Annual Review of Irish Law 1990*, p.435), that the onus is on a party asserting legal professional privilege to prove that such claim is justified but, as in the instant case, when this is done, the onus then devolves upon the person seeking to challenge the claim of privilege to adduce some evidence to show that the claim is improperly made.

The disposition of the third ground advanced that the respondent should have inspected the documents at issue or permitting the deponent of the affidavit of discovery to be cross-examined did not unduly trouble the learned judge either. He referred to and endorsed the principles laid down by him in *Duncan v. Governor of Portlaoise Prison* [1997] 1 I.R. 558; [1997] 2 I.L.R.M. 296 (*Annual Review of Irish Law 1997*, p.423) as to the extremely rare circumstances in which cross-examination would be appropriate and the requirement, before a court would inspect documents, for cogent evidence to be adduced to suggest that the claim to privilege was being wrongfully asserted. No such evidence had been adduced in this case and he was satisfied that no arguable case had been made out that there were circumstances which would possibly justify either cross-examination or inspection.

In the course of his judgment, Kelly J. repeated the description previously given by him of legal professional privilege in *Miley v. Flood* [2001] 2 I.R. 50; [2001] 1 I.L.R.M. 489 (discussed above at 287–290) as a "fundamental condition on which the administration of justice as a whole rests" and it is clear that this proposition underpins his decision in *Irish Haemophilia Society*. Thus, while the courts must be alert to ensure that privilege is not improperly claimed, it is important that the substantive protected afforded by the privilege is not undermined by the procedural requirements governing its exercise. As he cautioned in his judgment, "[c]are must be taken to ensure that privilege is not abused on the one hand and on the other that the requirements for its assertion are not such as to in effect dilute or destroy it."

Waiver of public interest privilege   Because of its nature, public interest privilege does not fit easily within the conceptual framework of a privilege, which requires that a privilege exist for the benefit of an identified person, or persons who can choose to assert it or waive it as they see fit. Public interest privilege exists to further the public interest and, therefore, in so far as a holder of the privilege can be identified, it is the public as a whole. For this reason, the view has been taken that it can be invoked by any party to litigation or, if no objection is otherwise taken, the issue can and should be raised by the court of its own motion in an appropriate case (*AG v. Simpson* [1959] I.R. 105, 133).

A controversial question is whether the privilege may be waived. In England, the view has been taken that because it involves an adjudication of where the balance of public interest lies, the doctrine of waiver has no application (*Rogers v. Secretary of State for the Home Department* [1973] AC 388, 407, [1972] All E.R. 1057, 1066; *Air Canada v. Secretary of State for Trade* [1983] 2 A.C. 394, 436; [1983] 1 All E.R. 910, 917) and this is one of the principal reasons why the term "public interest immunity" is favoured in that jurisdiction. However, it appears from two decisions of the Supreme Court in 2001, *McDonald v. RTE* [2001] 1 I.R. 355, [2001] 2 I.L.R.M. 1 and *Hannigan v. DPP* [2001] 1 I.R. 378, [2002] 1 I.L.R.M. 4 that the Irish courts have taken a different approach.

In *McDonald*, the plaintiff had brought libel proceedings against the defendant broadcaster arising out of a radio broadcast which, it was alleged, had accused him of membership of the Provisional IRA and involvement in the murder of a Co. Louth farmer in 1991. The defence delivered by the defendant denied that the broadcast referred to the plaintiff, denied any libellous content and included a plea of public interest qualified privilege. The matter was listed for hearing but no judge was available and the matter was adjourned to the following day. The defendant had served *subpoenas* on a number of garda witnesses and, at the request of the defendant's legal advisors, they consulted with the defendant and its legal advisors. The following day, the defendant indicated that it wished to amend its defence to plead justification and, leave having been granted, an amended defence and detailed further particulars were delivered claiming that the plaintiff and associates had aided and abetted in the murder of the farmer.

The trial of the matter was adjourned and the plaintiff subsequently sought discovery from the defendant of all documents grounding the plea of justification. The plaintiff also sought discovery from notice parties, the Commissioner of the Garda Síochána and the garda superintendent of the area in which the murder was committed, of documents relating to his arrest along with other men in 1989 on land owned by the farmer near to where an arms dump had been found. Certain documents were disclosed but privilege was claimed over two files on the ground of public interest privilege.

The plaintiff contended that any claim of public interest privilege in the files had been waived because it was clear from the circumstances surrounding the delivery by the defendant of its amended defence and particulars that, at its consultations with the gardaí, the defendant had had sight, and possibly temporary possession, of these files. It was submitted that, by their action either in giving the relevant files to the defendant's legal advisers or in transmitting the contents of the files to the notice parties, the notice parties had waived any public interest privilege they might otherwise have asserted in the documents. In response, counsel for the notice parties submitted that what he termed public interest immunity was there to protect the public as a whole and that it was not open to members of the gardaí, or indeed the State itself, to waive the immunity in any way.

Having considered the affidavits filed in the matter, McGuinness J., with whom the other members of the Court concurred, concluded that the trial judge had been correct in holding that the participation by the gardaí in a consultation with the defendant, even if some reference to the files was made by them, did not amount, on the facts, to waiver by the notice parties of any public interest privilege which might attach to the documents in question. Although the learned judge does not expressly hold that it is possible to waive a claim of public interest privilege, her judgment seems to proceed on the basis that this is possible. The issue was not adverted to by Murphy J. but Fennelly J. in his concurring judgment reserved his position, emphasising that "if the facts were otherwise, it would not necessarily follow that a privilege of this character could be effectively waived by the action of individual officers of the Garda Síochána."

With regard to the substantive issue as to whether the files were clothed with public interest privilege, McGuinness J. referred to and approved as the most relevant, the principles laid down by Keane J. in *Breathnach v. Ireland (No.3)* [1993] 2 I.R. 458 (*Annual Review of Irish Law 1991*, p.341). Having examined the documents, she applied those principles and identified a number of documents, which should be produced.

The doubt remaining in the wake of the decision in *McDonald* as to whether it is possible to waive a claim of public interest privilege appears, however, to have been resolved by the decision of a differently constituted Supreme Court less than a week later in *Hannigan*. The applicant in that case sought inspection of a letter between the DPP and the gardaí containing directions as to the prosecution of the applicant in District Court proceedings impugned in judicial review proceedings brought by the applicant. The respondent claimed public interest privilege over the document but the applicant argued that privilege did not apply or, alternatively, had been waived by the disclosure of a considerable portion of the letter in an affidavit filed on behalf of the respondent.

Delivering the judgment of the Supreme Court, Hardiman J. took the view that the disclosure of the letter in an affidavit supported the proposition that disclosure of the terms of the letter could occur without deleterious effect from the DPP's point of view. Apart from this consideration, he held that the status of a document from the point of view of privilege from disclosure changes once it has been referred to in a pleading or affidavit. He approved of a passage in Matthew and Malek, *Discovery* (London: Sweet & Maxwell, 1992), para. 9.15, where it is stated that:

> "The general rule is that where privileged material is deployed in court in an interlocutory application, privilege in that and any associated materials is waived..."

He also referred with approval to a passage from the decision in *Nenea Karteria Maritime Company Ltd v. Atlantic and Great Lakes Steamships Corporation (No.2)* [1982] Com LR 139 where the basis of this rule had been explained as follows:

"[T]he opposite party...must have the opportunity of satisfying themselves that what the party has chosen to release from privilege represents the whole of the material relevant to the issue in question."

In the opinion of the learned judge, the letter at issue had indeed been deployed in the instant proceedings because it had been referred to and its contents summarised for litigious purposes by the party entitled to claim privilege in it. This deployment was inconsistent with an assertion of harmful effects following from its disclosure and privilege could not be claimed in respect of it.

It is not entirely clear whether the conclusion of Hardiman J. that the letter at issue was not privileged from disclosure is predicated on a finding that privilege did not apply because the deployment of the letter in an affidavit fatally undermined the argument that the requisite public interest in non-disclosure was present or, whether, it constituted an act of waiver of the privilege which would otherwise have existed. There are, as indicated above, difficulties with accepting the contention that an individual servant of the State can waive a privilege, which belongs to the public. However, that is very far from saying that public interest privilege can never be waived because, in practical terms, this proposition is unsustainable. The solution to this conundrum is, it is submitted, signposted by the judgment of Hardiman J. Thus, whenever a claim of public interest privilege is made, the court should be astute to ensure that the requisite ingredients for its assertion including confidentiality and a balance of public interest in favour of withholding the information are present. Where, as in *Hannigan*, the contents of a document in respect of which a claim of public interest privilege is made, have been disclosed, it will be very difficult to convince a court that those ingredients are present and thus, the claim of privilege will have been effectively 'waived'.

Determination of claim of public interest privilege In *Murphy v. Dublin Corporation* [1972] I.R. 215, 235, it was held that once a particular document is established to be relevant, the burden of satisfying the court that it should be privileged from production lies upon the party making the claim of privilege. In any case where a claim of privilege is made, the court has the power to examine the documents (*Ambiorix Ltd v. Minister for the Environment (No.1)* [1992] 1 I.R. 277, 283 (*Annual Review of Irish Law 1991*, p.338)) and will generally do so before upholding the claim. Indeed, in *Corbett v. DPP* [1999] 2 I.R. 179 (*Annual Review of Irish Law 1999*, p.274), O'Sullivan J. took the view that once a *prima facie* claim of privilege has been established, then the courts should proceed to examine the documents to ascertain whether the claim is properly founded.

However, in *McDonald v. RTE* [2001] 1 I.R. 355; [2001] 2 I.L.R.M. 1, Murphy J. sounded a cautionary note in relation to the examination of documents, stating that although this procedure will generally be the best method for adjudicating on a claim of privilege, there are circumstances where it will not be. In particular, there were cases where the examination of documents by a judge without any information as to the significance of particular documents or any explanation as to how they might benefit one party or embarrass the other could lead to an injustice. These comments were not, however, applicable in the instant case because, having examined the documents at issue, he was satisfied that examination was the appropriate procedure to employ to enable the court to exercise its function in determining whether privilege should apply.

Without prejudice privilege   In *Ryan v. Connolly* [2001] 2 I.L.R.M. 174, the plaintiff had sustained personal injuries in a collision with a car owned by the first named defendant and driven on the occasion in question by the second named defendant. He subsequently issued proceedings but was met with the defence that the proceedings were statute barred. In response, it was pleaded that the conduct and representations of the defendants from the time of the notification of the accident to the institution of proceedings had induced the plaintiff to refrain from issuing proceedings with the limitation period and that the defendants were, therefore, estopped from relying on the Statute of Limitations. This issue was directed to be tried as a preliminary issue.

In order to establish the plea of estoppel, the plaintiff sought to rely on the contents of correspondence between the parties which had been conducted on a 'without prejudice' basis and the first issue which, therefore, fell for determination was whether this correspondence could be opened to the Court.

Delivering the judgment of the Court, Keane C.J. began by approving the following statement of law in relation to without prejudice privilege contained in *Halsbury's Laws of England* (4th ed., Vol. 17, para. 212):

> "Letters written and oral communications made during a dispute between the parties, which are written or made for the purpose of settling the dispute and which are expressed or otherwise proved to have been made 'without prejudice', cannot generally be admitted in evidence."

That passage identifies the two basic conditions which must be satisfied for a claim of without prejudice privilege to be made, viz. the communication must be made (i) in a *bona fide* attempt to settle a dispute between the parties; and (ii) with the intention that, if negotiations failed, it could not be disclosed without the consent of the parties.

The learned Chief Justice went on to identify the policy basis for the privilege in terms which echoed those articulated by Oliver LJ in the leading English authority, *Cutts v. Head* [1984] Ch. 290; [1984] 1 All E.R. 597:

> "It is clear that this rule has evolved because it is in the public interest that parties should be encouraged, so far as possible, to settle their disputes without resort to litigation. If parties were in a position that

> anything they said or wrote in the course of negotiations, even where expressly stated to be 'without prejudice' could subsequently be used against them, they would undoubtedly be seriously inhibited in pursuing such negotiations."

The privilege, thus, promotes the settlement of disputes by enabling parties to discuss their dispute and the relative strengths and weakness of their cases with complete candour secure in the knowledge that anything said in the course of the negotiations cannot be used to their prejudice in the course of the proceedings. In the absence of such a privilege any concession made in the course of settlement negotiations or even the fact that an offer of compromise was made, would be admissible as an admission and *per* Romilly MR in *Jones v. Foxall* (1852) 15 Beav. 388, 396, "[i]f this were permitted, the effect would be that no attempt to compromise a dispute could ever be made".

Although not specifically mentioned by the Chief Justice, it should be noted that this public policy justification is reinforced by a convention or implied agreement that when parties embark on settlement negotiations on a without prejudice basis they do so on the understanding that the contents of those discussions will not be used to the prejudice of either party (*Cutts v. Head* [1984] Ch. 290, 313; [1984] 1 All E.R. 597, 611).

The courts have endeavoured to control the notable propensity of parties, and particularly their solicitors, to mis-characterise their communications as being without prejudice, by insisting that a party seeking to assert privilege must show that the communication in question was made in a genuine attempt to further negotiations to settle a dispute in respect of which legal proceedings had commenced or were contemplated. Thus, it has been held that the words 'without prejudice' "possess no magic properties" (*per* Costello J. in *O'Flanagan v. Ray-Ger Ltd,* High Court, April 28, 1983) and a court will not, therefore, hesitate to go behind that label and examine a communication in order to ascertain whether a communication actually owes its genesis to an attempt to compromise a dispute (*South Shropshire District Council v. Amos* [1987] 1 All E.R. 340, 344; *Dixons Stores Group Ltd v. Thames Television plc* [1993] 1 All E.R. 349, 351). This approach was approved by Keane C.J. in *Ryan v. Connolly* who took the view that it was clear from the authorities that:

> "[T]he presence of the heading 'without prejudice' does not automatically render the document privileged. In any case where the privilege is claimed but challenged, the court is entitled to look at the document in order to determine whether it is of such a nature as to attract privilege."

The learned Chief Justice does not appear to have entertained any doubts as to whether the correspondence at issue was subject to privilege because he went on to address the circumstances in which it would be permissible for a court to look at communications which were made on a without prejudice basis:

> "The rule, however, although firmly based on considerations of public policy, should not be applied in so inflexible a manner as to produce injustice. Thus, where a party invites the court to look at 'without prejudice' correspondence, not for the purpose of holding his opponent to admissions made in the course of negotiations, but simply in order to demonstrate why a particular course had been taken, the public policy considerations may not be relevant. It would be unthinkable that the attachment of the 'without prejudice' label to a letter which expressly and unequivocally stated that no point under the Statute of Limitations would be taken if the initiation of proceedings was deferred pending negotiations, would oblige a court to decided, if the issue arose, that no action of the defendant had induced the plaintiff to refrain from issuing proceedings."

He held, therefore, that the court was entitled to look at the without prejudice correspondence for the purpose of determining whether the circumstances were such that the defendants should not be allowed to maintain their plea under the Statute of Limitations.

The passage from the judgment of Keane C.J. set out above is of considerable interest insofar as it appears to endorse a narrow view of the ambit of the privilege, confining its application to admissions as to liability made in the course of settlements negotiations. The narrow view can be justified by reference to the genesis of the privilege, which evolved to protect parties from being prejudiced by any admission made in the course of settlement negotiations (see *Waldridge v. Kennison* (1794) 1 Esp. 143). It follows that the application of the privilege is confined to circumstances where it is sought to admit a without prejudice communication as an admission of liability at the trial of the action. This viewpoint has, perhaps, been best articulated by Hoffmann LJ in *Muller v. Linsley* (1994) 139 S.J. L.B. 43 who stated that:

> "If one analyses the relationship between the without prejudice rule and the other rules of evidence, it seems to me that the privilege operates as an exception to the general rule on admissions (which can itself be regarded as an exception to the rule against hearsay) that the statement or conduct of a party is always admissible against him to prove any fact which is thereby expressly or impliedly asserted or admitted. The public policy aspect of the rule is not in my judgment concerned with the admissibility of statements which are relevant otherwise than as admissions, i.e. independently of the truth of the facts alleged to have been admitted."

Thus, according to this theory, the privilege does not prevent the admission of without prejudice communications where the relevance of the communication lies in the fact that it was made rather than in the truth of any fact asserted therein as, for example, where it is admitted to explain delay (*Marron v. Louth County Council* (1938) 72 I.L.T.R 101, 103; *Family Housing Association (Manchester) Ltd v. Michael Hyde and Partners* [1993] 1 W.L.R. 354, 363) or, as in *Ryan v. Connolly*, to establish a plea of estoppel.

However, other cases have taken a broader view based on the public policy and convention rationales outlined above and have applied the privilege so as to protect a party from being prejudiced in any way by anything said in the course of settlement negotiations (see *Walker v. Wilsher* (1889) 23 Q.B.D. 335, 337). This view has recently been endorsed by the English Court of Appeal in *Unilever plc v. Proctor & Gamble* [2000] F.S.R. 344; [2001] 1 All E.R. 783. The claimant instituted proceedings seeking a declaration of non-infringement of the defendant's patent and sought to admit evidence of a claim of right and threat to bring enforcement proceedings made by the defendant during a without prejudice meeting between the parties. The defendant applied to strike out the proceedings as an abuse of process on the basis that the statement in question was privileged. Walker L.J., who delivered the leading judgment in the Court of Appeal, stated that the privilege "has a wide and compelling effect" and took the view that: "One party's advocate should not be able to subject the other party to speculative cross-examination on matters disclosed or discussed in without prejudice negotiations simply because those matters do not amount to admissions."

It is submitted that, ultimately, the question is one of policy and the parameters of the privilege should be dictated by the balance of public interest. In general, it is submitted that the balance of public interest will favour giving an expansive interpretation to the privilege. The privilege achieves its objective of promoting settlements by guaranteeing non-disclosure of the contents of the negotiations. This guarantee fosters the candour which is critical to the settlement process and which is undermined by disclosure for any purpose. It is only where parties can be sure that they can speak their minds and give their views in confidence that nothing said can be used to their prejudice that the necessary candour will be forthcoming. Thus, the privilege should be applied to exclude evidence of without prejudice negotiations except where it can be clearly shown that greater damage to the interests of justice would be effected by non-admission than by disclosure. The decision in *Ryan v. Connolly* can be explained on this basis. It is clear that the Court took the view that it would be unfair and would be contrary to the interests of justice if it could be abused so as to conceal representations which would ground a plea of estoppel.

Privilege against self-incrimination In *People (DPP) v. Finnerty* [1999] 4 I.R. 364; [2000] 1 I.L.R.M. 191 (*Annual Review of Irish Law 1999*, p.259), Keane J. regarded it as beyond dispute that:

"[T]he exercise by an accused person of his right not to give evidence in his own defence cannot lead to any inferences adverse to him being drawn by the court and that, in the case of the trial by jury, the jury must be expressly so advised by the trial judge."

However, a breach of this basic principle was identified by in *People (DPP) v. Coddington*, Court of Criminal Appeal, May 31, 2001. The applicant had been convicted of possession of a controlled drug, cannabis, for the purpose of supply. One of the main planks of the prosecution case against him was evidence of the finding of a large sum of cash hidden in two locations at his residence and, in relation to the inferences to be drawn from this evidence, the trial judge instructed the jury as follows:

"The defence say to you that as far as the cash that was found in the house there are inferences to be drawn from that which I have already described to you. The defence say to you that you don't know who lives in that house apart from Mr Coddington, though the fact that this was his residence was not disputed, that there is no evidence of who else may have access to the house or whose money it was. They say that there may be a totally innocent explanation as to why the cash was in the house. You are invited then to speculate as to what the perfectly innocent explanation may be. You have had no evidence from the accused in so far as that is concerned. There is no contest about where he lives, there is no contest that it was his money, and yet you are invited to speculate as to what the explanation there might be for the money being there."

This passage was criticised by the Court of Criminal Appeal on two grounds. The first was that the direction was inconsistent with the duty of a trial judge to instruct the jury that the onus to establish its case, including inferences, beyond reasonable doubt, remains at all times with the prosecution. The second was that it suggested to the jury that there was some onus on the accused to provide evidence of an innocent explanation for the presence of the money, and further, that an adverse inference should be drawn from the failure of the accused to give evidence in respect of a possible innocent explanation for the finding of the money. However, this was clearly impermissible having regard to the principles laid down in *Finnerty*:

"While the trial judge may remind the jury of the fact that the accused had, as was his right, not given evidence in the trial, they had to be expressly instructed not to draw any inference from the exercise of that right. In this case, the learned trial judge not only recalled that the accused had not given evidence but did so in the context of the failure of the defence to provide evidence of an innocent explanation for the

presence of the money and without any direction that no inference was
to be drawn from his failure to give this evidence."

In the circumstances, the court had little difficulty in reaching the conclusion
that it would be unsafe to allow the verdict to stand.

DOCUMENTARY EVIDENCE

Business records   In *Company Sergeant Berigan*, Courts Martial Appeal
Court, November 1, 2001, one of the grounds of appeal advanced by the
appellant was that documents had been admitted into evidence at the Court
Martial without proper formal proof. It particular, complaint was made that
the documents had been admitted without proof that they were originals
emerging from proper custody, identified by those responsible for their creation,
and that they had maintained carefully before being produced at the Court
Martial. In response, the prosecution sought to rely on section 5 of the Criminal
Evidence Act 1992, which provides that information contained in a document
is admissible in criminal proceedings as evidence of any fact therein of which
direct oral evidence would have been admissible if the information was
compiled in the ordinary course of business and was supplied by a person
(whether or not he so compiled it and is identifiable) who had, or may reasonably
be supposed to have had, personal knowledge of the matters dealt with.

The court, however, rejected the submission that section 5 addressed the
difficulty identified by the appellant. The evidence produced on behalf of the
prosecution went no further than identifying the documents and, although it
was arguable that the information contained therein had been compiled in the
ordinary course of business, evidence had not been led that the documents
were, in fact, compiled in the ordinary course of business or that the information
was supplied by a person who had or might reasonably be supposed to have
had personal knowledge of the matters contained in the documents.

Certificate evidence   In *DPP v. Syron* [2001] 2 I.R. 105, the respondent had
been arrested for drunk driving and taken to a garda station where he was
tested using an intoxilyser. At the trial of the respondent in the District Court
for an offence pursuant to section 49 of the Road Traffic Act 1961, a certificate
was presented to the court that showed that the first breath specimen given by
the respondent gave a reading of 93 micrograms of alcohol per 100 millilitres
of breath, the second breath specimen gave a reading of 89 micrograms of
alcohol per 100 millilitres of breath. The certificate then went on to state that
the specimen to be taken into account for the purposes of section 49 was
specimen number 2 and that the concentration of alcohol in the breath for the
purposes of that section was 73 micrograms of alcohol per 100 millilitres of
breath.

On an appeal by way of case stated it was submitted by the respondent that in the absence of clear regulations governing the calculation of the concentration of alcohol in an accused's breath which set out a scientific formulation or manner in which a sample of breath was calculated for the purposes of grounding a prosecution for drink driving, that the case against the respondent should be dismissed. The respondent pointed out that at the end of the prosecution case in the District Court the respondent was confronted with a certificate which contained three different readings and that the basis on which the figure of 73 micrograms of alcohol per 100 millilitres of breath was correct or admissible was not identifiable in any law passed by the Oireachtas or any Statutory Instrument enacted by the Minister. It was argued that this was a breach of the respondent's constitutional right to know fully the case being made against him and to fully and adequately defend himself. Reliance was based on the decision of the Supreme Court in *State (Healy) v. Donaghue* [1976] I.R. 325 and on the decision in *O'Callaghan v. Clifford* [1993] 3 I.R. 603 (*Annual Review of Irish Law 1993*, p.227) where Denham J. stated:

> "Where the State seeks to prosecute offences by way of a certificate which encompasses the entire prosecution case of which a factor or factors (for example, the mode of service of the notice stated to have been served on the applicant herein) are not set out on the certificate then the District Court has a special duty to ensure that due process of law is applied and that the applicant has an informed opportunity if he so wishes to raise any such matter at the hearing of the case."

However, O'Higgins J. took the view that the facts of the case did not show that the accused had been deprived of any of the rights identified by Gannon J. in *State (Healy) v. Donaghue* [1976] I.R. 325:

> "In this case there has been no denial that the right of the accused to challenge the evidence, and in particular the certificate in whatever the appropriate manner he sees fit. That might include, in appropriate cases, cross-examination of the Gardaí as to the accuracy and provenance of the device used, the investigation as to whether the device has been properly calibrated by the appropriate person and such other matters as might be relevant to the assessment of the accuracy of the evidence generated by the device. In this case there was no such cross-examination. Moreover there is nothing that would preclude the calling of witnesses on subpoena, if necessary to impugn the *prima facie* evidence. Moreover, I do not consider either the charge on the certificate to be in any way un-precise – although no doubt it could contain more information."

While O'Higgins J. accepted that there were no regulations under the Road

Traffic Act which set out in scientific formulation the manner in which a sample of breath was to be calculated for the purpose of making out an offence, the absence of such regulations did not in his view preclude the certificate from being the *prima facie* evidence it purported to be.

RES JUDICATA

Planning decisions In *Ashbourne Holdings Limited v. An Bord Pleanála* [2002] 1 I.L.R.M. 321, the applicant had been granted planning permission for the development of a golf club house and ancillary facilities subject to conditions providing for limited public access to the land. Subsequently, by reason of various changes in the location and layout of the development, it became necessary to make an application for retention permission. Permission was granted on appeal by An Bord Pleanála and again was subject to conditions requiring public access to various parts of the land although on different terms. The applicant issued judicial review proceedings seeking to quash the conditions. However, the Respondent contended that the decision to impose the conditions was *res judicata* because the applicant had not challenged by way of judicial review any of the conditions attached to the previous permission.

Kearns J. took the view that no question of *res judicata* arose on the facts of the case. He was satisfied that there had been a change in circumstances between the grant of the first permission in 1993 and the grant of the retention permission in 1997. The golf club development had taken place other than in conformity with the original planning permission and at least one golf hole had been moved to a new location. In addition, a new Cork County development plan had been introduced in 1996. He also placed some emphasis on the fact that, at no time had the board raised this point for the purpose of shutting out the appeal but, on the contrary, the board had proceeded to determine the matter.

Although it was well established that the decisions of planning authorities and the Board to grant or refuse permission or grant it subject to conditions are decisions, which are potentially subject to the doctrine of *res judicata* (*State (Kenny and Hussey) v. An Bord Pleanála*, Supreme Court, December 20, 1984), the decision in *Ashbourne* illustrates that they will rarely do so in practice. This is because an estoppel will only arise where the issues are identical. Thus, unless the applications submitted are identical or virtually identical the planning issues involved in adjudicating the application will be different (see *Delgany Area Residents Association Ltd v. Wicklow County Council*, High Court, May 28, 1998 (*Annual Review of Irish Law 1998*, p.420)). Furthermore, even if exactly the same application is submitted, the matter will not be *res judicata* if the planning considerations relevant to the area have changed as in *Ashbourne* where a new development plan had been adopted.

MISCELLANEOUS

Discretion to exclude relevant evidence In *R v. Sang* [1980] A.C. 402; [1979] 2 All E.R. 1222 the House of Lords endorsed the long established principle that, as part of the judge's function in a criminal trial is to ensure that the accused receives a fair trial, the judge always has a discretion to exclude evidence if, in his opinion, its prejudicial effect outweighs its probative value.

The existence of that discretion appears to have been first received an imprimatur at appellate level in this jurisdiction in *People (AG) v. O'Neill* [1964] Ir. Jur. Rep. 1 where Kenny J. confirmed that: "In a criminal trial the judge has a discretion to exclude relevant evidence when he is of opinion that its probative value is small but its prejudice-creating effect is considerable." The principle has now been reaffirmed in *People (DPP) v. Meleady,* Court of Criminal Appeal, March 20, 2001, where Geoghegan J. stated that:

> "It is well established that although there is no authority to permit a criminal court to admit, as a matter of discretion evidence which is inadmissible under an exclusionary rule of law, the converse is not the case. A judge, is part of inherent power, has an overriding duty in every case to ensure that the accused receives a fair trial and always has discretion to exclude otherwise admissible prosecution evidence if, in his opinion, its prejudicial effect, in the minds of the jury outweighs its true probative value."

The actual exercise of this discretion arose for consideration in *People (DPP) v. Coddington*, Court of Criminal Appeal, May 31, 2001. The applicant had been convicted of possession of a controlled drug, cannabis, for the purpose of supply and one of the grounds on which he sought leave to appeal his conviction was that the trial judge had erred in admitted evidence of the finding of a large sum of cash hidden in two locations at his residence.

At the trial, counsel for the applicant had objected to the admissibility of this evidence on the ground that its probative value was outweighed by its prejudicial nature. However, counsel for the prosecution stated that the evidence would be called to establish that when the notes were subjected to forensic examination, they were found to contain traces of cannabis resin. The trial judge accepted that this was a sufficient basis for the admission of the evidence and ruled that it was admissible. Subsequently, the trial judge ruled inadmissible the evidence of the forensic scientist called on behalf of the prosecution on the ground that the traces of cannabis resin were so minute as to be of no probative value in the circumstances of the case.

At the application for leave, counsel for the applicant renewed his argument that the prejudicial effect of this evidence outweighed its probative value pointing out that it was common knowledge that drug dealers have large amounts of cash. However, the court's view was that this was actually a reason why the finding of a substantial sum of cash in a case such as this might have sufficient probative value to be admissible. The court pointed out that the admissibility of evidence was a matter, which fell to be decided within the discretion of the trial judge in the circumstances of each case. In this particular case, it was satisfied that the trial judge had exercised his discretion correctly and that the evidence was not so prejudicial as to outweigh its probative value. Ultimately, it was a matter for the jury to decide what, if any, inference should be drawn from the finding of the cash having regard to the totality of the evidence.

The conclusion of the court on the facts is unremarkable but it does illustrate the circularity that is often involved in the application of the balancing test of probative value and prejudicial effect, whether in the context of the general discretion enjoyed by the trial judge or more specifically in relation to misconduct evidence. This is because the basis of the probative value of evidence i.e. the unlikelihood of coincidence that a person who was accused of being a drug dealer should happen to have large amounts of cash concealed at his home, is also the source of its prejudicial effect. Therefore, in many cases, although the courts do not acknowledge the fact, the application of this balancing test involves an assessment by the trial judge as to whether the evidence in question shows that the accused is guilty. If it does, then it is proper to admit it, notwithstanding any prejudicial effect it might have.

Circumstantial evidence   In *People (DPP) v. Cahill*, Court of Criminal Appeal, July 31, 2001, one of the grounds of appeal advanced by the applicants was that the trial judge had failed to properly explain the law as to circumstantial evidence to the jury. The trial judge had instructed them that:

> "For you to accept [circumstantial evidence] in establishing the prosecution's case, you must be satisfied that it is consistent with the guilt of the accused and inconsistent with any other rational hypothesis, that is to say, the explanation for this is consistent with the guilt of the accused and it doesn't have an innocent explanation. While that is the yardstick you must apply in assessing whether or not the circumstantial evidence is to be accepted by you as going any way in establishing the guilty of the accused, it must also be said – it has also been said that circumstantial evidence is, very often, the best of evidence. It is evidence of surrounding circumstances which by undesigned coincidence is capable of proving a proposition with the accuracy of mathematics."

The court, however, was of the view that the last proposition set out in this passage, the genesis of which was traced to an *ex tempore* judgment of the English Court of Appeal in *R v. Taylor* (1928) 21 Cr. App. Rep. 20, overstated the status and effect of circumstantial evidence. In the opinion of the court, the effect of circumstantial evidence had been more acceptably stated by Pollock

CB in *R v. Exall* (1866) 4 F. & F. 922, 929 as follows:

> "There may be a combination of circumstances, no one of which would raise a reasonable conviction or more than a mere suspicion; but...taken together may create a conclusion of guilt with as much certainty as human affairs can require or admit of."

The court was concerned that the direction of the trial judge could have given the jury an erroneous impression as to the weight of circumstantial, as distinct from direct, evidence and it was, accordingly, satisfied that this ground of appeal had been made out.

Libel In *Hill v. Cork Examiner Publications Limited*, Supreme Court, November 14, 2001, the plaintiff had succeeded in an action for libel against the defendant arising out of an article that conveyed the impression that the plaintiff, who had been imprisoned on another offence, was a sex offender. One of the grounds of appeal was that the trial judge had erred by imposing an "excessive limitation" on the evidence that the defendant had been permitted to adduce in relation to the offence in respect of which the plaintiff had been serving a sentence at the time of publication of the article. When counsel for the defendant had indicated his intention to the trial judge to put to the plaintiff the publicity which the offence of which he had been incarcerated had attracted, the trial judge ruled that this evidence was admissible but warned counsel for the defendant that he was "treading on delicate ground" and running the risk of having the jury discharged. Murphy J., delivering the judgement of the Supreme Court, stated that the observations of the judge were unobjectionable:

> "Those observations made, as they were, at the commencement of the case and not directed to any specific application to tender any particular evidence or to rule on any question put in cross-examination, are very helpful and entirely unobjectionable. Furthermore, the warning that a particular line of cross-examination might lead to the jury being discharged was not, in the context, a threat by the judge by a fair reminder by him to counsel of the delicate balance which the law requires to be preserved between giving evidence of general reputation and excluding the matters of specific misconduct (other than criminal convictions)."

The learned judge went on to confirm the rule laid down in *Scott v. Sampson* (1882) 8 Q.B.D. 491 that evidence adduced in mitigation of damages for defamation must be confined to the reputation of the plaintiff and may not consist of evidence of specific misconduct. He identified as the primary basis for this restriction that the admission of such evidence "would lead to innumerable subsidiary trials of collateral issues concerning the reputation of the plaintiff". It was clear that evidence of specific previous convictions was an exception to the general rule and was justified on the basis of the certainty with which a conviction could be proved.

Res gestae   The inclusionary doctrine of *res gestae* was long been the subject of academic and judicial criticism due to its unsatisfactory foundation in principle, uncertain ambit and its elasticity in the hands of judges seeking to admit what would otherwise be inadmissible evidence. In *Holmes v. Newman* [1931] 2 Ch. 112, Lord Tomlin described *res gestae* as "a phrase adopted to provide a respectable legal cloak for a variety of cases to which no formula of precision can be applied" while, speaking extra-judicially, Lord Blackburn went so far as to advise that: "If you wish to tender inadmissible evidence, say it is part of the res gestae" (quoted in Cross, *Evidence* (5th ed., London: Butterworths, 1979), p.43, n.13). These criticisms were endorsed by Hardiman J. in *People (DPP) v. O'Callaghan*, Court of Criminal Appeal, 18 December 2000 (*Annual Review of Irish Law 2000*, p.232) and it is, therefore, of interest that the doctrine of *res gestae* was invoked as the basis of admissibility of disputed evidence in *DPP v. Byrne*, Supreme Court, December 6, 2001.

The defendant had been found asleep in the driver's seat of a car with his keys in the ignition by a member of the Gardaí. The defendant was awakened by the Garda and arrested on suspicion of being drunk while being in charge of a car. The sample subsequently tendered by the defendant showed that he had a quantity of alcohol in his body in excess of the legal limit and he was prosecuted pursuant to section 50(3) of the Road Traffic Act 1961 (as amended) for the offence of being in charge of a motor vehicle with intent to drive when he had in his body a quantity of alcohol in excess of the legal limit. The defendant was convicted in a District Court and, on appeal to the Circuit Court, it was submitted that, as he was asleep, he could not be said to have been "in charge of a vehicle" or to have had an intention to drive the vehicle. One of the questions posed by the Circuit Judge on a case dated to the Supreme Court was whether he could consider the intentions of the defendant before he fell asleep to determine whether he had an intention to drive.

The decision of the Supreme Court was delivered by Murray J. who took the view that it was clearly open to the Circuit Court judge to draw such inferences as he thought proper as to the defendant's intention before he fell asleep. With regard to the relevance of those intentions and their admissibility, he stated that they were admissible under the doctrine of *res gestae*:

> "The circumstances pertaining to the presence of the defendant in the car prior to falling asleep and his intentions at that time are directly connected in material to the defence to which he is charged and in particular the issue as to whether he had, an irrelevant time, an intent to drive. It is a matter for the Circuit judge to determine what those circumstances and intentions were. These matters, which occurred

before the defendant fell asleep are in my view part of the *res gestae*. They are an intrinsic part of the circumstances being investigated in connection with the offence charged. Evidence which forms part of the *res gestae* includes acts or incidents which themselves constitute or accompany and explain the facts of the matter in issue. Items of evidence are said to be part of the *res gestae* owing to the nature and strength of their connection with the matters in issue and as such are admissible."

Although there is undoubted support for the proposition that an item of evidence may be admitted as part of the *res gestae* where it forms part of the same transaction as some fact or matter at issue (see, for example, *R v. Moore* (1914) 10 Cr. App. Rep. 54), invocation of the doctrine of *res gestae* is generally unnecessary because such evidence can be admitted simply as circumstantial evidence. It is thus difficult to disagree with the criticism levelled by Hardiman J. in *O'Callaghan* that: "The term is merely an expression of the general proposition that there is no universal formula for all kinds of relevancy. This proposition is not elucidated by the use of this Latin term which, unlike others, has no virtue of precision or historical connotation."

Omnia praesumuntur contra spoliatorem Under the maxim of *omnia praesumunter contra spoliatorem* (literally translated as "everything is presumed against a wrongdoer"), a court will draw inferences adverse to a wrongdoer from his destruction of or failure to produce relevant evidence or documents. The classic example of the application of this principle can be seen in *Armory v. Delamirie* (1722) 1 Stra. 504 where the defendant, a goldsmith, was held to have converted a jewel from a ring brought to his shop by the plaintiff. Pratt C.J. directed the jury in relation to the issue of damages that, "unless the defendant did produce the jewel, and show it not to be of the finest water, they should presume the strongest against him, and make the value of the best jewels the measure of their damages". The principle was stated in similar terms by Staughton J. in *Indian Oil Corporation Ltd v. Greenstone Shipping SA* [1988] 1 Q.B. 345; [1987] 3 W.L.R. 869: "If the wrongdoer prevents the innocent party proving how much of his property has been taken, then the wrongdoer is liable to the greatest extent possible in the circumstances."

The application of this presumption to the assessment of damages for proved wrongful acts is, thus, well established and in *Seager v. Copydex Ltd* [1969] 2 All E.R. 718; [1969] R.P.C. 250, where damages were claimed for misuse of confidential information, Winn L.J. stated that:

"[S]ince the basis on which damages are to be recovered in this case is a tortious basis, where there is insoluble doubt between two possible versions or assessments, when the tribunal of fact is pursing the factual issues, it should be borne in mind that there is a general principle that *omnia praesumuntur contra spoliatorem.*"

More controversial is the application of the presumption to the destruction or non-availability of evidence in deciding whether wrongdoing has occurred in the first place. In a number of cases, the view has been taken that the presumption should not be applied unless and until a party is proved to have been a wrongdoer (see *Dobson v. North Tyneside Health Authority* [1996] 4 All E.R. 474 and *General Tire & Rubber Co v. Firestone Tyre & Rubber Co Ltd (No.2)* [1974] F.S.R. 122; [1975] R.P.C. 203). However, there are a number of authorities indicating that strong adverse inferences can be drawn from the spoliation of documents.

In *Gray v. Haig & Son* (1855) 20 Beav. 219, the plaintiff had acted as agent for the defendant. After the termination of the agency, a dispute arose as to the amount of commission due to the plaintiff and an account was ordered. It was then discovered that the plaintiff had destroyed his books, which were essential to the taking of the account, after the dispute had arisen. In the absence of a satisfactory explanation for the destruction of the books, the Master of the Rolls felt compelled to apply the principle laid down in *Armory v. Delamirie* to "presume, as against the person who destroyed the evidence, every thing most unfavourable to him, which is consistent with the rest of the facts, which are either admitted or proved." He, thus, proceed on the assumption that the books, if available, would have supported the defendant's case. Another example is furnished by the decision in *The Ophelia* [1916] 2 A.C. 206 where Sir Arthur Channell referred with approval to the general principle that:

> "If any one by a deliberate act destroys a document which, according to what its contents may have been, would have told strongly either for him or against him, the strongest possible presumption arises that if it had been produced it would have told against him, and even if the documents is destroyed by his own act, but under circumstances in which the intention to destroy evidence may fairly be considered rebutted, still he has to suffer. He is in the position that he is without the corroboration which might have been expected in his case."

The application of the presumption of *omnia praesumunter contra spoliatorem* to proof of wrongdoing was accepted by the Court of Appeal in *Malhotra v. Dhawan*, Court of Appeal, February 26, 1997, but Morritt L.J. indicated some limitations as follows:

> "First, if it is found that the destruction of the evidence was carried out deliberately so as to hinder the proof of the plaintiff's claim, then such finding will obviously reflect on the credibility of the destroyer. In such circumstances it would enable the court to disregard the evidence of the destroyer in the application of the principle....Second, if the court

has difficulty in deciding which party's evidence to accept, then it would be legitimate to resolve that doubt by the application of the presumption. But, thirdly, if the judge forms a clear view, having borne in mind all the difficulties which may arise form the unavailability of material documents, as to which side is telling the truth, I do not accept that the application of the presumption can require the judge to accept evidence he does not believe or to reject evidence he finds to be truthful."

Although this decision was not considered, a similar approach is evident in the decision of the Supreme Court in *O'Mahony v. Bon Secours Hospital*, Supreme Court, July 13, 2001. The plaintiff had instituted proceedings against the defendants claiming damages for medical negligence arising out of his birth at the defendant hospital. Part of the trace recording the heart rate of the plaintiff in the period prior to his birth was not available and the plaintiff, thus, sought to rely on the maxim of *omnia praesumuntur contra spoliatorem* as shifting the burden of proof on to the defendant.

Dealing with this submission, Keane C.J. began by quoting a passage from *Halsbury's Laws of England* (4th Edition, Vol. 17, para. 120), under the heading "Unexplained circumstances and suppression of evidence" as follows:

"As between an innocent and guilty party, unexplained circumstances are presumed unfavourably to the wrongdoer. Thus a person, who having converted property, refuses to produce it so that its exact value may be known, is liable for the greatest value such an article could have; an unfavourable inference would be drawn in the case of one who destroys or suppresses, or fails to produce, evidence, or who declines to give evidence in support of his case, even though he is in court."

The Chief Justice also referred to *Williamson v. Rover Cycle Company* [1901] 2 I.R. 615 where the maxim was considered but not applied. The plaintiff in that case was injured when the steering post of a bicycle manufactured by the defendant broke. After the accident, the plaintiff had the damaged bicycle examined by three persons who each concluded that the break had not been caused by defective materials or workmanship. The plaintiff then sent the bicycle to the defendants 'for inspection'. They replaced the broken parts and threw them away and it was argued that the presumption of *omnia praesumuntur contra spoliatorem* operated to shift the burden of proof onto the defendant. However, the Court of Appeal held that the principle had no application because there was no evidence of any intention to suppress damaging evidence and the plaintiff had not been prejudiced by the actions of the defendants. Holmes L.J. stressed the limitations of the doctrine:

"There is no doubt that the plaintiff has been prevented by the action of the defendants from producing at the trial the broken parts of the machine; and that in certain circumstances the plaintiff would have been entitled to rely strongly on this fact is undoubted....But I know of neither authority nor principle for the proposition that in a case like the present the destruction of withholding by one party of something which, if produced, might or might not afford evidence on a particular issue, will in itself supply evidence which would otherwise be entirely wanting."

The Court in *O'Mahony* also held that the presumption was inapplicable to the facts before it. Keane C.J. pointed out, firstly, that there was nothing to indicate that the part of the trace in question had in fact been destroyed the defendant. Secondly, the trace was not critical to the issues, which had to be resolved in the case. The learned Chief Justice observed that:

"The maxim is intended to ensure that no party to litigation, be they plaintiff or defendant, is subjected to a disadvantage in the presentation of his or her case because his or her opponent had acted wrongly by destroying or suppressing evidence. Its application will, accordingly ... depend entirely on the circumstances of the particular case in which it is invoked. Not surprisingly, there is no authority for the proposition that it could be invoked so as to produce a clear injustice, i.e. an obligation in a court of trial to disregard the weight of the evidence which it has heard, because some of the documents, although of no significance in the outcome of the case, has been, for no sinister reason mislaid or destroyed or because some documents never existed in the first place."

Family Law

CHILDREN

Access In *In re R.B. and R.B. Minors; R.B. v. A.G. (otherwise known as A.B.),* High Court, February 28, 2001, Lavan J. had to determine the question of access of a 13-year-old boy, who was (and, under an order of Lavan J, continued to be) in the custody of his father. The mother's relationship with her son and the father was unhappy: Lavan J. observed that there appeared 'to be a conflict on the part of the [mother] with every matter concerning this child'. He regretfully came to the conclusion that she was:

> "not concerned for the welfare of [the boy]. She is blind to his needs, and has been for some two years. She sees only her own needs. She is a law onto herself. She has no idea of the affront she has caused her child."

Lavan J. decided that the boy needed 'a breathing space'. While remaining in his father's custody, the boy should go for counselling to an agreed psychologist with his mother. It would be for the psychologist to determine whether to interview both together or separately. The mother's participation in the counselling would be under the psychologist's direction. The matter might be re-listed on July 20, 2001 (five months later), supported by a report from the psychologist together with his recommendations, at which stage Lavan J. hoped to be in a position to make the orders in relation to access.

On appeal, the Supreme Court, December 19, 2001, did not disturb the custody and access decisions made by Lavan J. Keane C.J. (Denham and Murphy JJ. concurring) noted that the only matter on which the Supreme Court had been asked to rule was whether it had been appropriate for the child to have been seen by the trial judge in his chambers. The Chief Justice stated:

> "While I can understand the approach adopted by the trial judge to this matter in proceedings of this nature, the fact remains that, as a matter of principle, the only evidence which a trial judge, in family law proceedings as in other proceedings, can receive is evidence on oath or affirmation given in the presence of both the parties or their legal representatives.
>
> It has long been recognised that trial judges have a discretion as to whether they will interview children who are the subject of custody or

access disputes in their chambers, since to invite them to give evidence in court in the presence of the parties or their legal representatives would involve them in an unacceptable manner in the marital disputes of their parents. Depending on the age of the children concerned, such interviews may be of assistance to the trial judge in ascertaining where their own wishes lie and that would undoubtedly have been the case with [the child] in these proceedings. It is, however, sufficient to say that, while the objection to the trial judge having seen [the child] in his chambers was well founded, as there is no serious issue as to the legal custody of [the child] and the question of access, if it cannot be agreed, must be determined now in the High Court, no order is required in respect of the proceedings under the Guardianship of Infants Act."

In *T. v. T.*, High Court, November 28, 2001, where the father of a 12-year-old boy, in divorce proceedings, sought access on terms that would take account of the father's circumstances, in a new relationship with a new child, Lavan J, having interviewed the boy, adjourned the application so that a report from a person professionally qualified in childcare could be obtained. He considered that the case was one 'patently' calling for this step to be taken.

PARENTAL AUTONOMY

Introduction In the *Annual Review of Irish Law 2000*, pp.78-82, we discussed McCracken J.'s judgment in *North Western Health Board v. H.W. and C.W.,* High Court, October 27, 2000. It will be recalled that the case raised a simple issue on its facts but one involving a profound constitutional question: whether the refusal by parents to consent to the administration of the PKU test on their infant child is such a failure on their part to vindicate the infant's personal rights as to warrant the intervention of a State agency. McCracken J. held that it was not. On appeal, the Supreme Court, on November 8, 2001, affirmed by a four (Denham, Murphy, Murray and Hardiman JJ.) to one (Keane C.J.) majority: [2001] 3 I.R. 622. For analysis of the decision, see Arthur, "Medical Treatment: The Welfare of the Child v. The Wishes of the Parents" [2002] Ir. J. of Family L 20, Arthur, '*North Western Health Board v. H.W. and C.W.* – Reformulating Irish Family Law' (2002) 20 Ir. L. Times (n.s.) 39.

It may be useful to describe the PKU test briefly. It is a screening test designed to identify the presence of four metabolic conditions and one endocrine condition in infants. It involves a blood test, the blood being usually extracted from the heel of the infant.

Among the conditions which the test can identify is phenylketonuria. This may cause severe mental handicap, but which may be treated primarily by diet throughout the person's lifetime. It has an incidence of 1 in 4,500 in Ireland. Another condition is homocystinuria. This may cause intercranial bleeding or strokes. It also can result in severe mental handicap. It can be treated by diet control for life and the incidence in Ireland is 1 in 49,000. A third condition is hypothyroidism, which also results in mental handicap. It can be treated and controlled by medication and its incidence in Ireland is 1 in 3,500. All these conditions are treatable, but once the damage has been caused by the condition it is usually irreversible.

The parents' objection was originally based on religious grounds (and was so described in McCracken J.'s judgment) but ultimately rested on their view that it was wrong to subject their child to the invasive process of puncturing a blood vessel. They were willing to have his hair or urine tested: this would be a less efficacious way of testing for these conditions.

McCracken J. had 'no doubt that medical opinion would emphatically state that it is in [the infant]'s interest to have the PKU test done…' He considered, however, that Articles 41 and 42 of the Constitution made it inappropriate for a court to override the parents' refusal:

> "The framers of the Constitution used the words 'exceptional' in Article 42.5, and one must assume that they did so after very careful consideration. Indeed, the use of that word is totally consistent with the provisions of Article 41.1. There are of course cases in which the State may interfere with parental rights, and many of these are detailed in the Child Care Act, 1991. They are exceptional cases. In my view the decision in the present case by the defendants, who are acknowledged to be caring and conscientious parents, could not be said to constitute an exceptional case, even though the general medical opinion would be quite clear that such decision was wrong. If the State were entitled to intervene in every case where a professional opinion differed from that of parents, or where the State considered the parents were wrong in their decision, we would be rapidly stepping towards the Brave New World in which the State always knows best. In my view that situation would be totally at variance with both the spirit and word of the Constitution."

The Supreme Court judgments provided a comprehensive analysis of the constitutional issues. It may be useful first to refer to the core passages in each of the judgments before going on to analyse some of the crucial themes in greater detail.

Denham J. observed that 'any intervention by the courts in the delicate filigree of relationships within the family has profound effects. The State (which includes the legislat[ure], the executive and the courts) should not intervene so as to weaken or threaten these bonds unless there are exceptional circumstances.'

Murray J. observed that:

"[i]f the State had a duty or was entitled to override any decision of parents because it concluded, established or it was generally considered that the decision was not objectively the best decision in the interest of the child, it would involve the State, and ultimately the courts, in a sort of micro-management of the family. Parents with unorthodox or unpopular views or lifestyles with a consequential influence on their children might for that reason *alone* find themselves subject to intervention by the State or by one of the agencies of the State."

Murphy J. stated:

"In relation to the education of their children the relationship between the State and the family is clearly and expressly dealt with in Article 42. The corresponding rights and duties of the State in relation to matters of general medical welfare are unenumerated and ill defined but the subsidiarity of the State to the parents is clearly established. Clearly it would be incorrect to suggest that the State could or should intervene merely because by doing so it could advance significantly the material interests of a child. If such a crude test were permitted then children of less well off parents might be given readily in fosterage to others who, it could be demonstrated, had the capacity to advance the material, and even moral, welfare of the child.

The Thomistic philosophy – the influence of which the Constitution has been so frequently recognised in the judgments and writings of Mr. Justice Walsh – confers an autonomy on parents, which is clearly reflected in these express terms of the Constitution, which relegate the State to a subordinate and subsidiary role. The failure of the parental duty that would justify and compel intervention by the State must be exceptional indeed. It is possible to envisage misbehaviour or other activity on the part of parents, which involves such a degree of neglect as to constitute abandonment of the child and all rights in respect of it. At the other extreme lies the particular decision, made in good faith, which could have disastrous results. In the present case the parents did not present a refusal to the proposed PKU test. Indeed they positively agreed to the test provided it could be carried out on hair or urine samples. The objection of the parents centres exclusively upon the invasion or puncture – as they see it – of the blood cells of the child. No reasoning based on any scientific view or religious doctrine or practice was cited in support of this firmly stated objection. Nevertheless I do not accept that a particular ill advised decision made by parents (whose care and devotion generally to their child was not disputed) could be properly categorised as such a default by the parents of their moral and constitutional duty so as to bring into operation the supportive role of the State.

If the State had an obligation in the present case to substitute its judgment for that of the parents, numerous applications would be made to the Courts to overrule decisions made by caring but misguided parents. Such a jurisprudence and particular decisions made under it would tend to damage the long term interests of the child by eroding the interest and dedication of the parents in the performance of their duties. In my view the subsidiary and supplemental powers of the State in relation to the welfare of children aris[e] only where either the general conduct or circumstances of the parents is such as to constitute a virtual abdication of their responsibilities or alternatively the disastrous consequences of a particular parental decision are so immediate and inevitable as to demand intervention and perhaps call into question either the basic competence or devotion of the parents."

Hardiman J.'s judgment is the most detailed of those of the majority. Its central thesis is captured in the following passage:

"Article 42.5 is in the nature of a default provision. Under its terms, the State may in exceptional circumstances, upon a failure of parental duty of physical or moral reasons, become a default parent. The sub-Article does not constitute the State as an entity with general parental powers, or as a court of appeal from particular exercises of parental authority. Nor does it, in my view allow a court to derive uniform rules for the exercise of that authority in default.

It does not seem to be possible to hold that the respondent parents have failed in their duty towards their children. ... I do not view a conscientious disagreement with the public health authorities as constituting either a failure in duty or an exceptional case justifying State intervention."

Keane C.J.'s dissenting judgment is the longest of the five. He did:

"not accept the submission ... that, because of the particular provisions of the Constitution of the family, the court, in a case such as this, is obliged to allow the wishes of the parents, however irrational they may be, to prevail over the best interests of [their child], which must be the paramount concern of the court under the Constitution and the law. Far from giving effect to the values enshrined in Article 42, such an approach would gravely endanger his right, so far as human endeavours can secure it, to a healthy and happy life and would be a violation of those individual rights to which he is entitled as a member of the family and which the courts are obliged to uphold."

In a passage indicating the sharpness of his dissent from the majority's approach, the Chief Justice observed:

> "What is beyond doubt is that, if this test is not administered and in the
> course of the next few years, he suffers death or serious brain damage
> as a result, the responsibility will not be that of the defendants alone. In
> this case, the defendants have refused to protect and vindicate, so far as
> practicable, the constitutional right of [their child] to be guarded against
> unnecessary and avoidable dangers to his health and welfare. The courts,
> in my view, can and should."

Let us now try to unravel the issues that are at the core of this case. They
involve big questions, whose answers depend on taking particular stances on
the role of the family in society, the protection of individual family members'
rights, the function of the State and its agencies and the proper remit of the
courts. While naturally all of the five judgments address aspects of these issues,
the most fundamental debate was between Keane C.J. and Hardiman J. This is
particularly interesting since these two judges appear to be largely agreed, at a
philosophical level, on the courts' role relative to the other organs of State, as
is evidenced by their judgments in *Sinnott v. The Minister for Education* [2001]
2 I.R. 545 and *T.D. v. Minister for Education*, October 31, 2001.

The respective roles of the family and the State The issue at the centre of the
case might appear to the one of determining the respective roles of the family
and the State. Thus, for Denham, Murphy and Murray JJ., the case could be
satisfactorily resolved by holding that the parental default in this case was not
sufficiently egregious to constitute a failure warranting State intervention in
accordance with Article 42.5. Keane C.J. and Hardiman J. fought a different
contest. This concerns the relationship between the rights of the family and
the rights of the individual members of the family, especially the children. Of
course where the State acts as champion of the rights of the child the two
issues can seem identical, but they are not since it seems clear that the State is
not the only legitimate champion of these rights.

This brings us back to the jurisprudence of the 1980s. Three decisions are
of particular relevance: Ellis J.'s judgment in *PW v. AW*, High Court, 21 April
21, 1980 and the Supreme Court judgments in *In re J.H. (an infant)* [1985]
I.R. 375 and *In re Article 26 of the Constitution and the Adoption (No 2) Bill
1987* [1989] I.R. 656. In *P.W. v. A.W.*, Ellis J. expressed the opinion that:

> "the inalienable and inprescriptible rights of the family under Article
> 41 of the Constitution attach to each member of the family including
> the children. Therefore in my view the only way the 'inalienable and
> inprescriptible' and 'natural and imprescriptible' rights of the child can
> be protected is by the courts treating the welfare of the child as the
> paramount consideration in all disputes as to its custody , including

disputes between a parent and a stranger. I take the view also that the child has the personal right to have its welfare regarded as the paramount consideration in any such dispute as to its custody under Article 40.3 and that this right of the infant can additionally arise from 'the Christian and democratic nature of the State.'"

There is a clear emphasis in Ellis J.'s analysis on the centrality of the child's rights. The role of the family and its zone of autonomy is less emphasised.

A starkly different emphasis is apparent in *In re J.H. (an Infant),* where Finlay C.J. defined the rights of a child belonging to a family based on marriage as including, in addition to the rights of every child, the right:

> "(a) to belong to a unit group possessing inalienable and inpre-
> scriptible rights antecedent and superior to all positive law (Article
> 41, section 1);
> (b) to protection by the State of the family to which it belongs (Article
> 41, s.2);
> (c) to be educated by the family and to be provided by its parents
> with religious, moral, intellectual, physical and social education
> (Article 42, s.1)."

Finlay C.J. went on to say that he accepted the contention that in the case before the Court:

> "s. 3 of the Act of 1964 must be construed as involving a constitutional
> presumption that the welfare of the child, which is defined in section 2
> of the Act in terms identical to those contained in Article 42.1, is to be
> found within the family, unless the court is satisfied on the evidence
> that there are compelling reasons why this cannot be achieved, or unless
> the court is satisfied that the evidence establishes an exceptional case
> where the parents have failed to provide education for the child and to
> continue to fail to provide education for the child for moral or physical
> reasons."

This analysis removed the doubts that had been growing as to be constitutional validity of section 3 of the 1964 Act which had given paramountcy to the welfare of the child, but the price paid for this assurance was to modify the focus of that goal by a strong 'presumption', which translates in practice as a value preference in favour of continuing the custodial nexus between the parents and the child save in limited circumstances.

The Supreme Court decision in *In re Article 26 of the Constitution and the Adoption (No 2) Bill 1987* is important in this context for three reasons. First, it made it clear that the rights of a child who is a member of a constitutionally defined family 'are not confined to those identified in Articles 41 and 42 but are also rights referred to in Articles 40,43 and 44.' Secondly, it held that the State's role in endeavouring to supply the place of parents under Article 42.5 was not restricted to cases of the failure of parental duty to educate but extended also to those involving the failure of the parental duty 'to cater for the other personal rights of the child.' Thirdly, it elaborated on the concept of parental failure in duty.

Undoubtedly it is very difficult to reconcile the approach of Ellis J. in *P.W. v. A.W* with that favoured by the Supreme Court in *In re J.H. (an infant).* Hardiman J. considered that in cases such as the instant one, not governed by statute:

> "even more obviously than in custody cases where there is a statutory framework, a presumption exists that the welfare of the child is to be found in the family exercising its authority as such. If this presumption applies in the construction of a statute which makes no express reference to the authority of the family, it must, *a fortiori*, apply where the contest is between the parents of the child and a stranger, in this case a statutory body, outside any statutory framework."

One may perhaps question why the presumption in favour of the parents should necessarily be stronger in cases where their alleged failure does not raise an issue of custody. There are empirically supported reasons favouring continuity of a custodial relationship between parents and child which have no parallel in respect of a once-off decision in relation to their child by parents who are, and are likely to continue to be, custodians of the child.

Keane C.J.'s approach Keane C.J.'s analysis of *P.W. v. A.W.* and *In re J.H. (an Infant)* is radically different from that of Hardiman J. He stressed the fact that the latter decision had been concerned with a dispute as to the custody of a child between its parents and putative adoptive parents. He observed:

> "Those issues do not arise in this case: irrespective of its outcome, [the infant] will remain in the custody of his parents and his right to remain a member of the family whose authority is protected by the Constitution will be unaffected. The statement of the law by Ellis J. [in *P.W. v. A.W.*] that the rights of the family under Article 41 attach to each member of the family, including the children, and that the only way that those rights can be protected in the case of children is by the courts treating the welfare of the child as the paramount consideration do[es] not have to be read in cases other than custody cases subject to the qualification laid down by the court in *In re J.H. (an infant)*."

The Chief Justice did not further elaborate on the clash of philosophies between *P.W. v. A.W.* and *In re J.H. (an infant).* While making it plain that the qualification expressed *In re J.H. (an infant)* should be limited to the custodial issue, he did not present a detailed analysis of the relationship between Article 42.5. the welfare principle and the rights of the child in *non*-custodial contexts. What he had to say was limited to giving express endorsement to the jurisdiction of the court to protect and vindicate the personal rights of the child under Article 40.3 and Article 41, with the possible implication, and no more, that the court and, it seems the State, should have the power to intervene to provide that protection and vindication even where there has not been a parental failure falling within the terms of Article 42.5.

In this context it is useful to read closely what the Chief Justice had to say about the family under the Constitution. His words were elegant and humane, but were noteworthy for what they failed to include:

> "Article 41.1 acknowledges the primary role of the family in society. In philosophical terms, it existed as a unit in human society before other social units and, in particular, before the unit of the State itself. The philosophical origins of the modern system of democracy are to be found in the beliefs of Locke and Rousseau that civil government is the result of a contract between the people and their rulers: the family existed before that unit and enjoys rights which, in the hierarchy of rights posited by the Constitution, are superior to those which are the result of the positive laws created by the State itself. As the trial judge noted, this is an express recognition by the framers of the Constitution of the natural law theory of human rights, but the belief that the family occupies that philosophic status in contrast to the role of the State is by no means confined to those thinkers who subscribe to that particular philosophy.
>
> What is beyond argument is that the emphatic language used by the Constitution in Article 41 reflects the Christian belief that the greatest of human virtues is love, which, in its necessarily imperfect human form, reflects the divine love of the creator for all his creation. Of the various forms which human love can take, the love of parents for their children is the purest and most protective, at least in that period of their development when they are so dependent on, and in need of, that love and protection. I believe that Article 41, although couched in the language of '*rights*', should not be seen as denying the truth to be derived from the experience of life itself, that parents do not pause to think of their '*rights*' as against the State, still less as against their children, but rather of the responsibilities which they joyfully assume for their children's happiness and welfare, however difficult the discharge of those responsibilities may be in the sorrow and difficulties almost inseparable from the development of every human being . The rights acknowledged in Article 41 are both the rights of the family as an institution, and the rights of its individual members, which also are guaranteed in Article 42, under the heading 'Education', and which

derive protection from other articles of the Constitution, most notably Article 40.3.

Again, the Article speaks, not of the authority of parents, but of the authority of the family. While the family, because it derives from the natural order and is not the creation of civil society, does not, either under the Constitution or positive law, take the form of a juristic entity, it is endowed with an authority, which the Constitution recognises as being superior even to the authority of the State itself. While there may inevitably be tensions between laws enacted by the State for the common good of society as a whole and the unique status of the family within that society, the Constitution firmly outlaws any attempt by the State in its laws or its executive actions to usurp the exclusive and privileged role of the family in the social order."

This passage is important in acknowledging that the framers of the Constitution expressly recognised the natural law theory of human rights. It does, moreover, accept that the family is endowed with an authority 'which the Constitution recognises as being superior even to the authority of the State itself' and that the Constitution 'firmly outlaws any attempt by the State in its laws or its executive actions to usurp the exclusive and privileged role of the family in the social order.' What it does not do is investigate in any detail the notion of the family as a centre of autonomous decision-making, separate from the State, or consider the criteria whereby the courts may override or modify the decisions emerging from that source. At some point, a naked welfare test, determined by the courts, collides with the notion that deference be given to family decision-making. Unless one is to give an unqualified right of way to the welfare test, one has to have some principled basis for articulating the nature and scope of these qualifications.

The majority's approach It is interesting to contrast the Chief Justice's approach on this matter to that of the majority. Hardiman J. considered that the presumption expressed by Finlay C.J. in *In re J.H. (an infant)* was:

"not, of course, a presumption that parents are always correct in their decisions according to some objective criterion. It is a presumption that where the constitutional family exists and is discharging its functions as such, and the parents have not for physical or moral reasons failed in their duty towards their children, their decisions should not be overridden by the State and in particular by the courts in the absence of a jurisdiction conferred by the statute. Where there is at least a statutory jurisdiction, the presumption will colour its exercise, and may preclude it.

The presumption is not of course conclusive and might be open to displacement by countervailing constitutional considerations as perhaps in the case of an immediate threat to life."

This passage might suggest that for Hardiman J. Article 42.5 does not represent the limits of authorised intervention by the State or by the courts: the presumption may be displaced by 'countervailing constitutional considerations' of which, 'perhaps ... the case of an immediate threat to life' – presumably the child's life – is one. Thus, the child's constitutional rights can, in some instances at least, have sufficient weight to displace the presumption. One can conceive of cases where the child's life might be imperilled by an unimpeachable, though mistaken, parental decision which could not be characterised as involving any failure of parental duty. Yet, later in his judgment, Hardiman J. appeared content to let Article 42.5 represent the only basis justifying judicial overruling of parental decison-making.

We have already quoted from the central part of Murphy J.'s analysis of the issue. It rested strongly on the view that the autonomy conferred by the Constitution on parents 'relegate[s] the State to a subordinate and subsidiary role' and that '[t]he failure of the parental duty which would justify and compel intervention by the State must be exceptional indeed.'

Denham J.'s judgment made it clear that '[t]he rights of parents in exercising their responsibility are not absolute; the child has personal constitutional rights. The child has rights both as part of the unit of the family and as an individual.' Denham J. acknowledged that:

> "[i]nitially cases were more protective of parental authority and the family in all but very exceptional cases. However, in recent times the child's rights have been acknowledged more fully. It is settled law that the courts have a constitutional jurisdiction to intervene to protect the constitutional rights of a child ... whether legislation exists or not."

The task, in Denham J.'s view, is to ensure that the constitutional principles found in Articles 40.1, 41 and 42.5 'should be construed harmoniously.' (The reference to Article 40.1 would appear to be to Article 40.3, in view of earlier observations in the judgment.) She went on to state:

> "Thus, the child has personal rights: Article 40.1 of the Constitution of Ireland. The State has a duty to respect, and, as far as practicable, by its laws to defend and vindicate these rights. The State has a duty to vindicate the life of the person of the child. Thus, the Guardianship of Infants Act, 1964 and the Child Care Act, 1991 advanced the concept of the welfare of the child as the first and paramount consideration.
>
> However, the legislation and the rights of the child have to be construed in accordance with Article 41, which places the family at the centre of the child's life and as the core unit of society. The language of Article 41 ... is clear and strong. The family is the fundamental unit group of society and the State (which includes the courts) guarantees to protect the family in its constitution and authority.

Article 42.5 envisages, in exceptional cases, where the parents fail
in their duty to the child, that the State as guardian of the common
good shall be appropriate means endeavour to supply the place of the
parents, but this is subject to the rights of the child. It is clear that under
Article 42.5 the State is the default parent and not the super parent.

The Constitution clearly envisages the common good requiring the
State to take the place of parents where they for physical or moral reasons
fail in their duty towards their children. When taking this approach due
regard must be given to the right of the child to its family. However, the
child at all times retains his or her personal rights also."

This passage would suggest that, when construing the rights of the child, the
court must do so 'in accordance with Article 41,' thus qualifying the scope
that they would otherwise have. On this approach, the court should not first
seek to identify the personal rights of the child and then see how they can be
harmonised with the requirements of Article 41 but should instead immerse
itself with the values underlying Article 41 before engaging in the task of
identifying those rights.

In order to assess with accuracy Denham J.'s precise understanding of the
relationship between the child's rights, as a member of a family and as a citizen,
and the limitation on State intervention contained in Article 42.5, we must
give an extended quotation from her judgment:

"The Constitution clearly places the family as the fundamental unit of
the State. The family is the decision maker for family matters – both
for the unit and for the individuals in the family. Responsibility rests
fundamentally with the family. The people have chosen to live in a
society where parents make decisions concerning the welfare of their
children and the State intervenes only in exceptional circumstances.
Responsibility for children rests with their parents except in exceptional
circumstances. In assessing whether State intervention is necessary the
fundamental principle is that the welfare of the child is paramount.
However, part of the analysis of the welfare of the child is the wider
picture of the place of the child in the family; his or her right to be part
of that unit. In such a unit the dynamics of relationships are sensitive
and important and should be upheld when possible as it is usually to a
child's benefits to be part of the family unit.

In seeking the balance to be achieved between the child's rights
within and to his family, and the family (as an institution) rights, and
the parents' right to exercise their responsibility for the child, and the
child's personal constitutional rights, the threshold will depend on the
circumstances of the case. Thus, if the child's life is in immediate danger
(e.g. needing an operation) then there is a heavy weight to be put on the
child's personal rights superseding family and parental considerations

...

In assessing the balance to be achieved in this case it is relevant to consider the threshold which it would set for this and other medical tests and for matters such as inoculations. If the responsibility for making this decision is transferred from the parents to the State then it would herald in a new era where there would be considerably more State intervention and decision making for children than has occurred to date. Every day, all over the State, parents make decisions relating to the welfare, including physical, of their children. Having received information and advice they make a decision. It may not be the decision advised by the doctor (or teacher, or social worker, or psychologist, or priest or other expert) but it is the decision made, usually responsibly, by parents and is abided by as being in the child's best interest. Having been given the information and advice, responsibility remains with parents to make a decision for their child. The parents are responsible and liability rests with them as to the child's welfare.

In exceptional circumstances – such as where a child needs acute medical or surgical care – the expert may be part of an application for a court order to protect the welfare of the child by seeking a judicial decision different from that of the parents. This arises only in exceptional circumstances. Even if acute medical care is advised by some medical experts and the parents consider that the responsible decision may be to refuse such care it may be within the range of responsible decisions. This may occur where a child is suffering a terminal illness and parents may decide responsibly that he or she has suffered enough medical intervention and should receive only palliative care ...

There is a constitutional presumption that the welfare of a child is to be found within the family unless there are compelling reasons why that cannot be achieved or unless there are exceptional circumstances where parents have failed to provide education for the child: *In re J.H. (an infant)* [1985] I.R. 375. It is not suggested that the child be removed from the defendants in this case; the child will remain with the family no matter what the decision. However, any intervention by the courts in the delicate filigree of relationships within the family has profound effects."

Certainly this passage suggests a philosophy of considerable restraint on the part of the courts in exercising the power to intervene in the process of decision-making in the family. It would be wrong to interpret Denham J. as holding that intervention is restricted to the circumstances prevailing in cases where Article 42.5 applies: she specifically stated that:

"[t]he State – the Health Board – may intervene in the family, may interfere with the rights of family as a unit, and the rights of the child

and the parents pursuant to Article 41 of the Constitution, if it is justified
pursuant to Article 42.5 when parents have failed for physical or moral
reasons in their duty to their children or when other constitutional rights
of the child are breached or are in danger of being breached.

    The test to determine when there should be in intervention by the
courts is established in light of the Constitution, especially Article 40.3,
41 and Article 42.5."

In contrast to the Chief Justice, Murray J. lay considerable stress on the family
as an autonomous centre of decision-making separate from the State:

> "One of the inherent objects of the Constitution is the protection of
> liberties. Article 41.2, in providing that 'the State, therefore guarantees
> to protect the Family in its Constitution and authority ...' provides a
> guarantee for the liberty of the family to function as an autonomous
> moral institution within society and, in the context of this case, protects
> its authority from being compromised in a manner which would
> arbitrarily undermine the liberty so granted."

Murray J. thought it:

> "well established in our case law that the authority and autonomy
> explicitly recognized the Constitution as residing in the family as an
> institution in our family means that the parents of children have primary
> responsibility for the upbringing and welfare generally of their children.
> When exercising their authority in that regard they take precedence
> over the State and its institutions."

The established case-law, in Murray J.'s view, led to the conclusion that:

> "the family as a moral institution enjoys certain liberties under the
> Constitution which protect it from undue interference by the State
> whereas the State may intervene in exceptional circumstances in the
> interest of the common good or where the parents have failed for
> physical or moral reasons in their duty towards their children."

To give the State a general power of intervention:

> "would risk introducing a method of social control in which the State
> or its agencies would be substituted for the family. That would be a[n]
> infringement of liberties guaranteed to the family. Decisions which are
> sometimes taken by parents concerning their children may be a source
> of discomfort or even distress to the rational and objective bystander,
> but it seems to me that there must be something exceptional arising

from a failure of duty, as stated by this Court in *In re Article 26 and the Adoption (No 2) Bill 1987*, before the State can intervene in the interest of the individual child.

It would be impossible and undesirable to seek to define in one neat rule or formula all the circumstances in which the State might intervene in the interests of the child against the express wishes of the parent. It seems, however, to me that there must be some immediate and fundamental threat to the capacity of the child to continue to function as a human person, physically, morally or socially, deriving from an exceptional dereliction of duty on the part of parents to justify such an intervention."

In the instant case, '[u]nwise and disturbing' as the decision' might be, Murray J. was nonetheless satisfied that it was one that the parents had the liberty to take and that there had not been 'such an abdication of responsibility, moral or otherwise as would justify the State's view being substituted for that of the parents.'

Murray J.'s analysis cleaves closely to Article 42.5 as the criterion for intervention by the courts or the State. The emphasis on parental failure and their abdication of responsibility as representing the basis for the substitution of another judgment is notable.

If one had to summarise the effect of the four majority judgments, one could say that their approach, while involving some conceptual differences between the judges, is that the family under the Constitution is a zone of autonomous decision-making, which is subject to limited overruling by the State or its agents. These agencies undoubtedly may intervene in cases of parental failure under Article 42.5 but that concept should be given a narrow interpretation. There would also appear to be a power of intervention in a narrow band of cases based on urgent necessity. The majority take the view that the price of recognising such autonomy is that the State should not intervene in other cases, even where the parents' decision is mistaken and has negative implications for their child. Keane C.J.'s dissenting judgment places less emphasis on the autonomy of family decision-making and allows a consequentially greater remit for State intervention to protect the welfare of the child.

For an insightful analysis of the general subject, written nearly a decade ago, see Duncan, 'The Constitutional Protection of Parental Rights: A Discussion of the Advantages and Disadvantages of According Fundamental Status to Parental Rights and Duties', Chapter 29 of Eekelaar & Šarcevic eds., *Parenthood in Modern Society* (Martinus Nijhoff, Dortrecht, 1993).

The instant decision raises a range of important further issues, which require consideration.

The implications for families not based on marriage First let us consider what the implications of this decision may be for families not based on marriage. It is well-established law that Articles 41 and 42 refer to the family based on marriage. They do not apply to a cohabiting couple with children, however long that cohabitation may have existed. What is the position, therefore, where such a couple refuse to consent to the PKU test for their infant child?

It would appear that the Court's answer would have to proceed on the basis that the parents could not invoke Articles 41 or 42 in their aid. Does this mean that their values as to the upbringing of their child must be gives no weight whatsoever? That would seem to be a curious and insensitive approach for the Court to take but in order for it not to do so it would have to ascend a veritable mountain of jurisprudential analysis. This is because its thinking so far on the constitutional dimensions of the family not based on marriage has been undeveloped and paternalistic, at times harsh, at other times sentimental.

It is worth recollecting that much of this thinking was done at a time when birth outside marriage involved a strong social stigma and where lone parenthood involved a serious struggle for the mother with virtually no social supports. The father was regarded as a seducer, presumed to have little interest in his child. The mother was seen as being implicated in the breach of social norms. If she was vulnerable and unsupported, that was considered to be her fate, which should not greatly disturb society.

The starting point is, of course, *The State (Nicolaou) v. An Bord Uchtála* [1966] I.R. 567, in which the Supreme Court made it plain that the 'family' receiving constitutional protection under Article 41 was that based on marriage and that the unmarried father had no distinctive constitutionally protected rights. It seemed that the Supreme Court in *K v. W* [1990] I.L.R.M. 121 might have opened the door to the possibility that an unmarried father committed to his child and the mother had 'rights of interest or concern' grounded in the Constitution. This door was, however, firmly closed in *W. O'R v. E.H.* [1996] 2 I.R. 248 (analysed in *Annual Review of Irish Law 1996*, pp.367-75). Whatever else they might be, these rights of interest or concern were held not to be rights of the unmarried father rooted in the Constitution. Hamilton C.J. and the other Supreme Court judges speculated as to whether they should more convincingly be regarded as relevant to the children's welfare rather than to the juridical status of their father.

The constitutional position of the unmarried mother is different but still not based on Article 41. In *G. v. An Bord Uchtála* [1980] I.R. 32, O'Higgins C.J. observed that the unmarried mother:

> "is not the mother of a family, in the sense in which the term is used in the Constitution. Article 41 of the Constitution, which recognizes the family as the natural, primary and fundamental unit group of society and as a moral institution possessing inalienable and imprescriptible rights antecedent and superior to all positive law, refers exclusively to the family founded and based on the institution of marriage. It is this

family which, under Article 41, s.1, subs. 2, the State guarantees to protect in its constitution and authority as the necessary basis of social order and as indispensable to the welfare of the nation and the State.

But the plaintiff is a mother and, as such, she has rights, which derive from the fact of motherhood and from nature itself. These rights are among her personal rights as a human being and they are rights, which, under Article 40, section 3, subs. 1, the State is bound to respect, defend and vindicate. As a mother, she has the right to protect and care for, and to have the custody of, her infant child.... This right is clearly based on the natural relationship that exists between a mother and child. In my view, it arises from the infant's total dependency and helplessness and from the mother's natural determination to protect and sustain her child. How far and to what extent it survives as the child grows up is not a matter of concern in the present case. Suffice to say that this plaintiff, as a mother, had a natural right to the custody of her child who was an infant, and that this natural right of hers is recognized and protected by Article 40, section 3, subs. 1 of the Constitution. Section 6. subs. 4 and section 10, subs. 2(a) of the Guardianship of Infants Act 1964 constitutes a compliance by the State with its obligation in relation to the mother of an illegitimate child to defend and vindicate in its laws this right to custody. These statutory provisions made the mother guardian of her illegitimate child and give the mother statutory rights to sue for custody.

However, these rights of the mother in relation to her child are neither inalienable nor imprescriptible as are the rights of the family under Article 41. They can be alienated or transferred in whole or in part and either subject to conditions or absolutely, or they can be lost by the mother if her conduct towards the child amounts to an abandonment of her rights and duties."

In an important passage, O'Higgins J. went on to say that:

"[t]he child also has natural rights. Normally these will be safe under the care and protection of its mother. Having been born, the child has the right to be fed and to live, to be reared and educated, to have the opportunity of working and of realizing his or her full personality and dignity as a human being. These rights of the child (and others which I have not enumerated) must equally be protected and vindicated by the State. In exceptional cases the State, under the provisions of Article 42, section 5, of the Constitution is given the duty, as guardian of the common good, to provide for a child born into a family where the parents fail in their duty towards that child for physical or moral reasons. In the same way, in special circumstances the State may have an equal obligation in relation to a child born outside the family to protect that child, even against its mother, if her natural rights are used in such a way as to endanger the health or life of the child or to deprive him of his rights. In my view this obligation stems from the provision of Article 40, section 3 of the Constitution."

Even today, there is a considerable uncertainty on this question. In *E.F. and F.F. v. An Bord Uchtála*, Supreme Court, July 17, 1997, Keane J., delivering the Court's judgment, had to acknowledge that '... divergent views have been expressed in this court as to whether the right of the natural mother to the custody of her child, save where its welfare demands otherwise, is a constitutional right or derives from some other source ...'

How would the courts treat the issue of a refusal by unmarried parents to the administration of the PKU test on their child? The distinctive provisions of Articles 41 and 42, which guided the Supreme Court in *North Western Health Board v. H.W. And C.W.* can have no guiding effect in this context. Undoubtedly the child's constitutionally protected personal rights would have to be vindicated; but have the parents, as two individuals and by virtue of their role as members of a family, albeit one not based on marriage, any constitutionally-based entitlement to have their judgment afforded some weight against that of the State agency?

One may predict that the courts would find some verbal formula giving an element of deference to their judgment but let us confront the philosophical issue squarely. The reason why Article 41 pushed the State into secondary role was the belief that the common good was advanced by giving a zone of autonomy to families based on irrevocable commitment. That belief included the view that the children's welfare would generally be best advanced by their continuing contact with their parents, whose day-to-day decision-making would not be overruled save in egregious cases. It was not the fact of the parents' cohabitation alone that gave distinctive value and authority to the decisions they made regarding their children; it was the character of their commitment to each other.

Of course the formalities of marriage are neither necessary to generate a lifelong irrevocable commitment nor sufficient to assure that such a commitment, once given, will be adhered to. Nor does marriage give any assurance that the spouses will be better parents than if they had not married. Yet society, when formulating Articles 41 and 42, did so on the basis that irrevocable commitment was something to be encouraged and supported because it was likely to advance the common good. The Supreme Court decision in the instant case appears to be consistent with that premise. The judges said almost nothing about the position of unmarried parents; the little that Denham J. had to say on the subject would not give much support for the argument that the same degree of deference should be given under the Constitution to the decision-making of unmarried parents as is given to that of married parents.

Let us try to address the issue in practical contexts. One child whose parents are not married to one another at the time of birth may be fortunate enough to be reared by two loving, committed parents whose relationship is that of marriage in all but name. Another may be reared by the mother with no contact from the father. A third may be reared by the father with the mother's contact having ended shortly after birth. A fourth may be reared by the mother with limited connections with the absent father. Is the welfare of each of these children best served by affording to their parents (or, perhaps, one of them) the same degree of deference as to that afforded by Article 41 and 42 to married parents?

Of course, the statutory dimension should not be ignored. Married parents are automatically guardians of their children. The mother of a child born outside marriage similarly is automatically the child's guardian. The father of that child will be guardian only if the court so orders on the basis of the child's welfare. Our courts have yet to analyse the precise relationship between the statutory rights of guardianship, the constitutional protection afforded to married parents by Articles 41 and 42, the constitutional protection afforded to mothers of children born outside marriage and the absence of constitutional protection afforded to unmarried fathers. It may be that the courts will hold that the scope of that statutory protection is in all cases as broad as that afforded under Articles 41 and 42 but such an interpretation would be difficult to harmonise with the philosophical basis of those Articles.

Judges are no doubt conscious of the general political climate in which they make their decisions. A judgment that the PKU test maybe administered against the wishes of some or all unmarried parents but not married parents is politically unacceptable. Whether the courts would seek to provoke public debate by making such a distinction or cover it over by an expanded interpretation of the rights of unmarried parents is not clear. And how should the courts approach a difference of opinion as to their child's welfare by unmarried parents in this context?

Decision-making by divorced or separated parents When one turns to consider the implications for Article 41 and 42 of the constitutional changes that occurred in 1995 in relation to divorce, the position becomes still more complicated. Speaking broadly, one may describe the replacement of Article 41.3.2° as involving the insertion of a norm that is not merely lacking in harmony with the rest of that Article and Article 42 but is actually at variance with the norms underlying these original provisions. It may be plausible to describe the family based on lifelong marriage as 'the natural primary and fundamental unit group of society, and as a moral institution possessing inalienable and imprescriptible rights, antecedent and superior to all positive law.' It is less plausible to use such language to describe a model of a family which excludes irrevocable commitment as a component element but which insists on there being a marriage (defined in terms of revocable commitment) before constitutional recognition is afforded to it. Certainly no other constitution in the world asserts that such a model of a family is 'antecedent and superior to all positive law.' Nor do the international human rights instruments make such a claim.

Yet in *North Western Health Board v. H.W. and C.W.* the deference accorded to the decision-making autonomy of parents was attributed to the norms underlying Articles 41 and 42. Let us envisage a situation that can exist under the present constitutional dispensation, where spouses with a child divorce and each spouse enters into a second marriage. Article 41 will protect the family based on the second marriage; whether it continues to identify and protect the former spouses and child as members of a separate family based on marriage, albeit a dissolved one, is less clear. If Article 41 no longer protects the former spouses and their child, does that not damage the rationale for deference to the former spouses' joint decision-making in relation to the rearing of their child? If it continues to do so, does this mean that the State must defer to decisions made by the former spouses in relation to their child to an extent greater than it has to do in relation to decisions taken out for the same child by one of the former spouses and his or her new spouse? And what is the position under Article 42? It is perhaps easier to argue that the constitutional protection it affords to parents continues after a divorce but, if Article 41 ceases to extend its protection after a divorce, it is hard to see how the 'family' to which reference is made in Article 42.1 should not also suffer the same fate.

More generally there is a problem in cases where spouses separate and the child remains in the custody of one of them – overwhelmingly, in practice, the wife. Presumably Articles 41 and 42 protect the joint decision-making by the parents relating to their child's welfare, but what is the position where one parent wishes to approve of the PKU test and the other does not? Of course the matter can be resolved, *as between the spouses themselves* by an application under the Guardianship of Infants Act 1964 but what is the constitutional position? Is there a greater deference due to the unilateral, contested, decision by one parent in these circumstances and does the answer depend on which parent happens to have custody? The courts might take the view that deference should be limited only to cases of joint parental decision-making and that the welfare test should not be mediated by considerations that affected the Supreme Court in the instant case. How this solution could be applied to unmarried custodial parental decision-making is not easy to assess.

The welfare test dissected Let us now consider the merits of the Supreme Court's analysis of the welfare issue. 'Welfare' is defined in section 2 of the Guardianship of Infants Act 1964 as embracing 'religious and moral, intellectual, physical and social welfare'. This language is derived from Article 42.1 of the Constitution where it divides 'education' into these five categories. The Supreme Court made no attempt to provide a segmented test for State intervention into parental decision-making affecting the welfare of a child yet that was surely an option worth investigating further. Of course parents can make faulty decisions in respect of any of the five categories but it seems clear that certain kinds of decision, if made badly, are likely to be less immediately damaging to the child than others. Faulty decisions can be made by parents in relation to the intellectual or social welfare of their child, which might be considered less eligible for being overruled than those about the child's physical welfare. On this approach, parents who leave their children play outside on November evenings without enough clothing to protect them from the elements would have their decisions overruled more quickly than parents who let their children watch too much rubbish for too long on television. Certainly, concern for protecting 'the delicate filigree of relationships' should not stay the hand of the court where the child is placed at physical risk. So far as physical risk is concerned, the majority articulated a criterion for intervention at a surprisingly late and urgent point of danger to the child.

A number of the judges referred to the fact that the case did not involve a consideration of the religious views of the parents. Denham J. noted that 'this is not a case where there is a faith factor or a balancing of a religious element.' Hardiman J. noted that the religious issue might 'be central in another case'. He considered it 'more than arguable' that the health board's stance, which would in effect make the PKU test compulsory, involved as a logical corollary the proposition that section 4(2) of the Health Act 1953 was unconstitutional. Section 4 provides as follows:

> "(1) Nothing in this Act or any instrument thereunder shall be construed as imposing an obligation on any person to avail himself of any service provided under this Act or to submit himself or any person for whom he is responsible to health examinations or treatment.
>
> (2) Any person who avails himself of any service provided under this Act shall not be under any obligation to submit himself or any person for whom he is responsible to a health examination or treatment which is contrary to the teaching of his religion."

On the other hand, Keane C.J. found it 'not easy to understand' the purpose of section 4(2) since it appeared to deal with a situation already covered by section 4(1). In any event, it was in his view not relevant to the instant case concerning a function of the health board – promoting the welfare of children – which did not fall within the remit of the section.

We have yet to have a detailed analysis of the concept of the religious welfare of a child in Irish law. So far, the courts have sought to take a neutral stance, studiously avoiding any preference of one religion over another and tending, in custody cases, to invoke religion when it assists a conclusion justifiable on independent welfare grounds. (This profession of neutrality is not limited to Ireland: see Ahdar, "Religion as a Factor in Custody and Access Disputes" (1996) 10 Int. J. of L. Policy & the Family 177.)

When the courts confront cases involving a potential conflict between a child's physical welfare and the religious norms or beliefs of the parents how should they approach their resolution? The reality is that the concerns of Jehovah's Witnesses about blood transfusions are overridden by courts, here and in other countries, without compunction. The danger for the child is so stark and immediate that the courts do not hesitate to make the requested order. It is interesting to note that, in the United States of America, lobbying by adherents to the Christian Science Church has resulted in religious exemption statutes not dissimilar to section 4 of the Health Act 1953: see Wadlington, "Medical Decision Making for and by Children: Tensions Between Parent, State and Child" [1994] U. Illinois L. Rev. 311, at 331, Stanfield, "Current Public Law and Policy Issues; Faith Healing and Religious Treatment Exemptions to Child-Endangerment Laws; Should Parents Be Allowed to Refuse Necessary Medical Treatment for their Children Based on their Religious Beliefs?" 22 Hamline J. of Public L. & Policy 45 (2000), Dwyer, "The Children We Abandon: Religious Exemptions to Child Welfare and Education Laws as Denials of Equal Protection to Children of Religious Objectors" 74 N. Carolina L. Rev. 1321 (1996).

Let us move away from cases where a child's life is in immediate danger to consider a less urgent instance where the parents' decision regarding the child is considered by the court to be potentially damaging to the child's welfare and would just fall outside the protection afforded by Articles 41 and 42 to the autonomy of parental decision-making if no religious dimension were involved. The parents, however, invoke a religious basis for their decision. Does this extra factor require the court to reassess the question of deference to parental autonomy, with the possibility that a decision, which the court would otherwise decide to overrule from the standpoint of the child's welfare, may perhaps now be upheld? The judges in the instant case who referred to the fact that the parents were not invoking a religious justification for their refusal to authorise the PKU test must surely have been implying that the Court's decision *could* have been otherwise had that factor been taken into account. If a child's physical welfare can be affected by decisions based on religious factors the question will arise as to the extent to which the courts in the future will permit these factors to have such effect. For detailed consideration of the subject, see Hamilton, *Family, Law and Religion* (Sweet & Maxwell, London, 1995), Chapter 4. See also Kilkelly, *The Child and the European Convention on Human Rights* (Ashgate, Aldershot, 1999), pp.244–6, analysing *Hoffmann v. Austria*, (1993) 17 E.H.R.R. 293.

Can legislation curtail parental decision-making? Let us now turn to consider an aspect of the judgment, which raises important issues of a juridical character as to the relationship between the doctrine of the separation of powers and the protection of constitutional rights. A number of the judges hinted that legislation requiring parental content for the PKU test might well be constitutional. They were agreed that the question of the constitutional validity of such legislation had not been resolved by the Court's determination in the instant case. On the face of it, this poses a constitutional conundrum: how can a proposed intervention by a State agency that was identified in the instant case as an unconstitutional invasion on the family be transformed into compliance with the Constitution by reason of having received the benediction of the Oireachtas?

A number of reasons, some less plausible than others, can be posited for this magical transformation. One formal and unconvincing rationale is that legislation is presumed to be constitutional and that therefore the Court, when embarking on its analysis of the issue of constitutionality, is starting from a different position, which is closer to accepting the validity of the proposed intervention than is the case at common law. This presumption of constitutionality may be a useful strategy for the courts to adopt when approaching a constitutional issue *de novo* in the context of a specific statutory provision: the courts should give respect to the legislative organ of State by presuming that it does not seek to violate the provisions of the Constitution. Yet, in a case where the courts have specifically addressed the issue as to the constitutionality of an intervention of a particular type by the State and have held that the intervention is not compatible with the requirements of the Constitution, it is very hard to see how the presumption of constitutional validity relating to legislation should represent more than the most fragile of barriers. It is possible that a court might take the view that the legislation was based on access to facts not available to the courts in the earlier litigation. Undoubtedly this could be so in certain contexts where sophisticated scientific data might be decisive. In the instant case, however, there was no dispute as to the scientific facts: what was in issue was a question of values as to the extent to which parental decision-making, even involving bad decisions, should be respected under Articles 41 and 42.

Wardship, jurisdiction and the Constitution Finally let us consider the relationship between the exercise of the courts' wardship jurisdiction and the protection of constitutional rights. A number of the judges in the majority mentioned that the instant case did not involve the courts' wardship powers. The implication was that, had it done so, the outcome might have been different. The report of the legal argument before the Supreme Court makes it clear that the judges were fully aware of the Supreme Court of Canada's decision in *Re Eve* (1987) 31 D.L.R. (4th) 1 and the High Court of Australia's decision in *Secretary, Department of Health and Community Services v. J.O.B.* (1992) 106 A.L.R. 385.

In wardship proceedings, the best interests of the ward are paramount. The court takes account of the constitutional rights of the ward and the other parties, such as family members, but the goal of promoting the ward's best interests appears to be sufficiently strong to have the effect of putting those constitutional rights in second place. This seems to be the effect of the Supreme Court's holding in *In re a Ward of Court* [1996] 2 I.L.R.M. 401.

The Irish courts have yet to address the question as to how the exercise of wardship jurisdiction can have such a stark effect on constitutional rights. Why should the fact that the court is called on to exercise this paternalistic role result in the restriction of, or interference with, these rights? Where in the Constitution is the authorisation for this phenomenon? Courts have the constitutional responsibility to deliver justice in harmony with the constitutional rights of its citizens, not to circumscribe those rights in the search for the 'best interests' of a particular citizen whose fate comes under scrutiny through the adventitious circumstance of wardship proceedings having been commenced.

The historical provenance of wardship scarcely gives one confidence that it is in harmony with contemporary constitutional norms. Wardship was an aspect of feudal property relationships. It was only in recent years that the practice of settling a small sum of money on the minor as a prelude to commence proceedings was quietly set aside: see Shatter, *Family Law* (4th ed., Butterworths, Dublin, 1997), para 13.140.

Of course, the courts in the exercise of their *parens patriae* jurisdiction, seek to protect the welfare of children which is an entirely worthy goal. The origins and rationale of this jurisdiction have been debated (cf. Seymour, *'Parens Patriae* and Wardship Powers: Their Nature and Origin' (1994) 1 Oxford J. of Legal Studies 159; Abrahamowicz, 'Note, English Child Custody Law, 1660–1839: The Origins of Judicial Intervention in Parental Custody' (1999) 99 Columbia L. Rev. 1344). A strong argument can be made that this ancient jurisdiction has been overtaken by a new constitutional order in which the welfare of children is fully recognised and protected, not in isolation and subject to the contingent intervention of the courts in wardship proceedings, but rather as part of a comprehensive tapestry of rights in which welfare is calibrated in conjunction with other values, inculding the autonomy of children and their parents. The retention of the ancient jurisdiction, with its contingent impact, is arguably incompatible with this new constitutional order.

If the health board in the instant case had elected to take wardship proceedings and the court, applying the 'best interests' test with a reduced emphasis on Articles 41 and 42, had authorised the carrying out of the *PKU* test, how could such an outcome be justified? Can constitutional rights be sidelined by the choice of proceedings in which the same issue is to be addressed?

CHILDREN ACT 2001

The Children Act 2001 is an important and substantial measure, containing 271 sections, reforming the Children Act 1908 and other legislation relating to juvenile justice as well as amending the Child Care Act 1991. We examine its examine its main features in the Criminal law Chapter, above, 180. Particularly noteworthy substantive provisions include the raising of the age of criminal responsibility to 12 years (section 52 (17)) and the raising of the *doli incapax* presumption to 14 (section 52(2)).

For criticism of the weakening of the presumption, in that the legislation does not require that the child should have been aware that his or her conduct was seriously wrong, see "Power, 'The Children Bill 1999" [2001] Ir. J. of Fam. L. 23, at 23. More generally, see Douglas, 'The Child's Right to Make Mistakes: Criminal Responsibility and the Immature Minor,' Chapter 15 of Douglas & Sebba eds., *Children's Rights and Traditional Values* (Dartmouth, Aldershot, 1998).

A greater emphasis on parental roles and the responsibilities is evident throughout the legislation. Where a child has been found guilty of an offence, the court is empowered to make an order for the supervision of the parents – a 'parental supervision order' – if satisfied that a wilful failure on their part to take care of or control the child contributed to his or her criminal behaviour: section 111(1). This may in some cases involve the parents' undergoing treatment for alcohol or substance abuse or participating in courses to improve their parental skills: section 111(6). Section 111 empowers the court to order the parent (or parents) to pay compensation instead of the child where the wilful parental failure to take care of or control the child contributed to the child's criminal behaviour. Regard must be had to the parental means before making the order and determining its amount. Section 113(5). Conor Power (*op cit*, at 23) criticises these provisions as 'reflect[ing] a popularised and knee-jerk response rather than a considered attempt to tackle juvenile crime.'

CHILDCARE: JURISDICTIONAL ASPECTS

In *The Western Health board v. K.M.* [2001] 1 I.R. 729, on a Consultative Case Stated, the Supreme Court was called on to determine aspects of the international remit of section 47 of the Child Care Act 1991, which provides as follows:

> "Where a child is in the care of the health board, the District Court may, of its own motion or on the application of any person, give such directions and make such orders on any question affecting the welfare of the child as it thinks proper and may vary or discharge any such directions or orders."

The factual background concerned a five-year-old child whose mother was unable to take care of him on account of her psychiatric condition. A married couple living in England expressed an interest in fostering the boy on a long-term basis. The wife was a cousin of the boy's mother. The two questions in the Consultative Case Stated were:

> "1. Whether the District Court could lawfully direct the placement of a child with relatives or foster parents outside the State pursuant to section 47, and
> 2. if so, whether the period for which the child was so placed could be limited."

Finnegan J. answered both questions in the affirmative. For analysis of his decision, see Power, [2001] 3 Ir. J. of Fam. L 27. The Supreme Court affirmed. McGuinness J. (Denham, Murphy, Murray and Hardiman JJ. concurring), adopted a liberal construction of section 47 in view of the 'remedial social' purpose of the 1991 Act. Her analysis merits quotation *in extenso*:

> "In this jurisdiction both children and parents enjoy constitutional rights. The Oireachtas has rightly drawn attention to these rights in several sections of the 1992 Act. It is ultimately for the court and not for the health board to protect and enforce these constitutional rights in respect of children who are in care. This can conveniently be done through the powers given in s.47 of the Act. In my view these powers include a power to direct or permit the placement of a child outside the State where the evidence before the court indicates that such a placement is truly in the best interest of the child.
>
> Such an order, however, should be made rarely and with considerable caution. The child in question is ... in the care of and under the supervision of the health board, and the health board will continue to have responsibility for his welfare. The original care order was made by the District Court; the supervisory role of the court should to the greatest degree possible be maintained.
>
> Before any order placing a child outside the State is made, therefore, the judge of the District Court to whom such an application has been made should carefully weigh all relevant factors. These would include, *inter alia*, the following:
> 1. The constitutional rights both of the child and of his or her parents
> 2. The parameters of the law regarding children in the jurisdiction in which it is proposed the child should live. For example, does the principle that the welfare of the child is paramount apply? Are the normal principles of the comity of courts accepted? Is it likely that the orders of the Irish court will be recognised and enforced?
> 3. Is the country concerned a signatory to the Hague and/or Luxembourg Conventions on Child Abduction?
> 4. Is there already in place a system of co-operation between the child care authorities in the proposed jurisdiction and the health boards in their role as child care authorities in this jurisdiction or can such a system be readily established?

5.   If the child is placed abroad will access to the child by the natural parent or parents be a practical possibility in terms both of distance and of expense?

6.   Is there a reasonable possibility of using either undertakings or mirror orders (the use of which has been accepted by this court in Hague Convention cases) to make the position of the child and of the relevant health board more secure?

This list is by no means exhaustive. All factors relevant to the welfare of the child and to the constitutional rights of all parties must form a crucial part of the consideration of the District Court when deciding whether or not to make the order proposed. Relevant evidence should be provided to the District Court on the lines suggested above to enable the Court to make an informed decision as to which course is most conducive to the welfare of the child."

McGuinness J. acknowledged that, in the final event, the District Court was bound by section 24 of the Act of 1991. If, after careful scrutiny, the evidence before the court showed that a placement outside the jurisdiction was in the best interests of the welfare of the child concerned, the District Court had under section 47 to permit or direct such a placement. It was clear that the District Court must also have the power to limit the period for which the child was so placed if, in the opinion of the court, such a limitation was in the best interests of the child.

A question arose as to whether the power exercisable by the District Court under section 47 of the 1992 Act might be negatived in the case of a child under the age of seven by the terms of section 40 of the Adoption Act 1952, which, as originally passed by the Oireachtas, read as follows:

"1.   No person shall remove out of the State a child under seven years of age who is an Irish citizen or cause or permits such removal.

2.   Sub-section (1) shall not apply to the removal of an illegitimate child under one year of age by or with the approval of the mother or, if the mother is dead, of a relative for the purpose of residing with the mother or a relative outside the State.

3.   Sub-section (1) shall not apply to the removal of a child (not being an illegitimate child under the age one year of age) by or with the approval of a parent, guardian or relative of the child.

4.   A person who contravenes this section shall be guilty of an offence and shall be liable on summary conviction to imprisonment for a term not exceeding twelve months or to a fine not exceeding £100 or to both."

In *The State (M. & D.) v. The Minister for Foreign Affairs and Others* [1979] I.R. 73, Finlay P. held that the provisions of sub-section (2) and the words in parenthesis in sub-section (3) of section 40 of the Act of 1952 were an infringement of the personal right of the citizen to travel outside the State and, accordingly, should be declared invalid having regard to the provision of the Constitution. That case concerned a child of an unmarried couple where it was proposed with the consent of both parents that the child should travel to Nigeria and reside there. However section 40 (1) and the substantive part of sub-section (3) remained in force.

McGuinness J. stated:

> "Having regard to the definition of 'guardian' in the Adoption Act 1952 s.2, I am satisfied that a health board in respect of which a care order has been made is a guardian for the purposes of s.40 (3) of that Act and with the Health Bard's approval a child (other than an illegitimate child under one year of age) may be removed out of the State. In relation to a child in care to whom s.40 (2) applies, while the health board has the like control as if it were his parent under the Child Care Act 1991 s.18(3)(a) this has not the effect of displacing the mother for the purposes of approval: the approval of the mother and not the health board is required in respect of such a child"

The question, which needed to be answered, was whether a health board was a proper person to give approval under section 40(3). McGuinness J. held that it was. Again, in view of the importance of the issue, her analysis merits extended quotation:

> "At the time of the enactment of the Adoption Act 1952, which was the first legislation permitting legal adoption in this State, a particular problem had arisen by which perspective adopters from other jurisdictions, the majority from the United States, were taking Irish infants abroad for the purpose of adoption. In the main these were infants born to unmarried mothers who in the circumstances of the time felt themselves unable to care for their own children. There was little or no enquiry or assessment as to the suitability of the families or environments to which these infants were being brought and no evidence as to whether their removal from the State was in the best interests of their welfare. It was to cure that particular mischief that the Oireachtas enacted s.40. It is, of course, many years since any such situation existed in this country, although parallel situations have arisen in other jurisdictions.
>
> It is clear that s.40 is not addressed to the situation which applies in the instant case where the proposal is that the child be placed with relatives who have been fully assessed by the competent child care authority in the United Kingdom, and where the entire situation is being fully investigated by the District Court. The powers of the health board in regard to a child who is the subject of a care order are set out in

s.18(3) of the Act of 1991 ... The health board is stated to have 'the like control over the child as if it were his parent', may decide the type of care to be provided for the child and may give consent to the issue of a passport.

'Guardian' in relation to a child is defined in s.3 of the Adoption Act 1952 as meaning 'a person appointed, according to law, to be guardian of his person by deed or will or by order of a court of competent jurisdiction'. Under the provisions of the subsequent 1991 Act the District Court is the court of competent jurisdiction to make a care order, which transfers the majority of the powers of a parent or guardian to the relevant health board. Under s.47 the District Court has the requisite power to 'give such directions and make such order on any question affecting the welfare of the child as it thinks proper'. In my view, in a situation where a child is in care pursuant to a care order, this power in the District Court would be sufficient to enable the District Court itself to consent to the placement of the child outside the jurisdiction within the terms of s.40 of the Adoption Act 1952."

FAMILY HOME

In *Ulster Bank Ireland Ltd v. Fitzgerald*, High Court, November 9, 2001, O'Donovan J. rejected the argument by a wife that the plaintiff bank had been aware of the undue influence allegedly exercised on her by her husband in executing guarantees relating to a business in which she had her husband had a financial stake. O'Donovan J. was prepared to accept that the husband might have exercised inordinate pressure on his wife to execute the guarantees but there was 'no evidence whatsoever' to suggest that the bank's employees had any inkling as to why she might not have been a free agent. O'Donovan J. accepted the evidence of the bank manager that he had told the wife that she could obtain legal advice with regard to the guarantees.

O'Donovan J. distinguished *Barclay's Bank Plc v. O'Brien* [1994] 1 A.C. 1809 and *Bank of Ireland v. Smyth* [1995] 2 I.R. 459 on the basis that:

> "both of those cases were concerned with a direct threat to a family home; the *Barclay's Bank v. O'Brien* case arising from a bank's attempt to force a surety executed by a wife with regard to a transaction in which she had no financial stake and the *Bank of Ireland v. Smyth,* arising from a bank's attempt to recover possession of a family home in respect of which the wife was alleged to have executed a consent pursuant to the Family Home Protection Act 1976. In this case, however, as I have already indicated, I am satisfied that no threat to [the] family home resulted from the guarantees ... executed by her and, in any event, she had a financial stake in both of those guarantees. In those

circumstances, I reject the contention that the said guarantees are not enforceable against her."

This decision is to be welcomed. There is something distasteful about invoking undue influence to save family homes from the consequences of financial misfortune affecting the business of the husband or of the spouses. In the twenty-first century, it is not appropriate to use nineteenth century perceptions of inter-spousal relationships to mitigate the full force of commercial realities of the family home. The Family Home Protection Act 1976 adopted a sensible strategy in requiring the prior consent of the non-owning spouse to any alienation of an interest in the family home.

This approach is surely preferable to placing an elaborate and unconvincing obligation on commercial third parties to monitor the dynamics of the relationship between husband and wife or to engage in elaborate warnings and explanations premised on a perception of women as financially naïve and emotionally vulnerable beings, which should have no place in the law today. In the Contract Law Chapter, above, Eoin O'Dell analyses the decision in considerable detail, referring also to developments in Britain.

MAINTENANCE AND PROPERTY ENTITLEMENTS

The philosophy of financial provision Who gets what, and why, has always been a problem for the law when dealing with matrimonial property. The answer must depend on the philosophy underlying society's approach to a number of questions: the extent to which society should seek to encourage, or reward, permanent commitment; the propriety, or injustice, of ascribing differing parental roles based on gender; the scope of autonomy for spouses as an authoritative source of decision-making; and the wider question of the value to be ascribed to the autonomy of the individual, whether acting alone or in relationships of his or her choice. For a comprehensive analysis of the issues, see Buckley, "Matrimonial Property and Irish Law: A Case for Community?" (2002) 53 N.Ir.L.Q. 39

In Ireland, we have seen the courts in the past two decades striking down legislation dealing with the family home because it was considered to interfere retrospectively with mutual spousal decision-making (*Re Matrimonial Home Bill 1993* [1994] 1 I.R. 305; see further Woods, "The Matrimonial Home Bill 1993 – Should the Government Try Again?" [2001] 4 Ir. J. of Fam. L. 8), upholding a joint parental veto over the administration of a medical test on an infant child, even where this veto was not considered to be a sensible one (*North-Western Health Board v. H.W. and C.W.*, Supreme Court, November 8, 2001, discussed in this Chapter, above, 316), finding a term in a separation agreement whereby the spouses agreed to obtain a divorce to be contrary to public policy (*Dalton v. Dalton* [1982] 2 I.L.R.M. 418 – a decision which would seem no longer to represent the law in view of the constitutional change of 1995), holding that the State's recognition in Article 41.2.1° of the Constitution that 'by her life within the home, woman gives to the State a support without which the common good cannot be achieved' does not translate into a guarantee of any share in the beneficial ownership of the family home which the courts can identify (*BL v. ML* [1992] 2 I.R. 77, analysed in the *Annual Review of Irish Law 1991*, pp.216-22) and rejecting the concept of 'palimony', again on public policy grounds, even after the introduction of divorce (*Ennis v. Butterly* [1997] 1 I.L.R.M. 28, analysed by Eoin O'Dell in *Annual Review of Irish Law 1996*, 182-95).

One also finds that rhetoric was not always matched by reality. Thus, for example, in the 1950s, when the emphasis on permanence in marriage and the importance of women's role in the home was strong, wives living with their husbands had no entitlement to be awarded maintenance by a court, no share in their husbands' property and only limited entitlements by way of succession. The Succession Act 1965 remedied the latter problem with a radical reform, going well beyond that adopted in the statutory regimes of most other common law jurisdictions. The Family Law (Maintenance of Spouses and Children) Act 1976 provided a straightforward jurisdiction for awarding maintenance (to either spouse) without requiring the unmaintained spouse to separate as a precondition of entitlement to apply. See Binchy, "Family Law Reform in Ireland: Some Comparative Aspects" (1976) 25 Int. & Comp. L.Q. 901, at pp. 906-7.

The broader social and economic picture must not be ignored. In its day, the nineteenth century legislation providing for a separate property regime was seen as a reform of what had gone before, which was a matrimonial property regime in which the husband was the dominant force. Moreover, it is only in the past fifty years or so, with the phenomenon of inflation, that house ownership has become a means of acquiring substantial wealth over time. Furthermore, the increase of marital instability has brought the question of property interests into focus; when spouses remained together, that question did not often present itself to the courts for resolution.

Internationally, two dominant cultural shifts have been in progress in recent decades: the move towards gender equality, with an associated increase in the proportion of married women in the workplace, and the move away from permanent commitment in intimate relationships towards models involving cohabitation or divorce. Both of these shifts have major implications for legal policy on matrimonial property. The old model, however one may regard its merits in the light of contemporary norms, was at least simple. Marriage was a lifelong commitment. The wife prejudiced her own economic interests by rearing the children in the home, thus creating a position of economic dependency on her husband. He was therefore obliged to support her and the children. This policy was admittedly somewhat fuzzy in regard to the wife's entitlement to property rather than maintenance. She was considered undoubtedly entitled to an expectation of having a family home provided for her and the children but it was not the courts' policy to recognise any proprietary interest in her part in the home, still less in other property owned by her husband. Nor was her occupation in the family home secure. Up to the enactment of the Family Home Protection Act 1976, a husband could sell the family home over his wife's head, without her knowledge, and could mortgage it or otherwise imperil the stability of its occupation without consulting her.

Matters today are far less simple. The effect of the introduction of a divorce regime in 1995 has been to withdraw societal support for permanent commitment in marriage. A spouse who marries without such a commitment or who chooses to act inconsistently with it has a constitutional entitlement to a divorce, subject only to the requirement of living apart from the rejected spouse and satisfying a court that the proper provision exists or will be made for the spouses and children. The Constitution does not require that the spouse applying for the divorce need necessarily make that provision; nor does it confer any express obligation on the court to encourage, or even support, the norm of permanent commitment when addressing the question of financial provision.

Against a background of constitutional silence (if one ignores the cacophony of philosophies now underlying the patchwork sequence of words that make up Article 41), the legislation prescribes a multitude of circumstances to which the court is to 'have regard' when ordering financial provision, while giving no indication as to their relative weights or the normative framework in which the court is to come to its decision. What we have is a flood of detail with no guidance as to the spring that represents its philosophical source. Section 20 of the Family Law (Divorce) Act 1996 provides (in part) as follows:

> "(1) In deciding whether to make an order under sections 12, 13, 14, 15(1)(a), 16, 17, 18 or 22 and in determining the provisions of such an order, the Court shall ensure that such provision as the Court considers proper having regard to the circumstances exists or will be made for the spouses and any dependant member of the family concerned.
> (2) Without prejudice to the generality of subsection (1), in deciding whether to make such an order as aforesaid and in determining the provisions of such an order, the Court shall, in particular, have regard to the following matters:
>   (a) the income, earning capacity, property and other financial resources which each of the spouses concerned has or is likely to have in the foreseeable future,
>   (b) the financial needs, obligations and responsibilities which each of the spouses has or is likely to have in the foreseeable future {whether in a case of the remarriage of the spouse or otherwise),

(c) the standard of living enjoyed by the family concerned before the proceedings were instituted or before the spouses commenced to live apart .from one another, as the case may be,

(d) the age of each of the spouses, the duration of their marriage and the length of time during which the spouses lived with one another,

(e) any physical or mental disability of either of the spouses,

(f) the contributions which each of the spouses has made or is likely in the foreseeable future to make to the welfare of the family, including any contribution made by each of them to the income, earning capacity, property and financial resources of the other spouse and any contribution made by either of them in looking after the home or caring for the family,

(g) the effect on the earning capacity of each of the spouses of the marital responsibilities assumed by each during the period when they lived with one another and; in particular, the degree to which the future earning capacity of a spouse is impaired by reason of that spouse having relinquished or foregone the opportunity of remunerative activity in order to look after the home or care for the family,

(h) the conduct of each of the spouses, if that conduct is such that in the opinion of the Court it would in all the circumstances of the case be unjust to disregard it,

(i) the accommodation needs of either of the spouses,

(j) the value to each of the spouses of any benefit (for example, a benefit under a pension scheme) which by reason of the decree of divorce concerned, that spouse will forfeit the opportunity or possibility of acquiring,

(k) the rights of any person other than the spouses but including a person to whom either spouse is remarried,

(3) in deciding whether to make an order under a provision referred to in sub-section (1) and in determining the provisions of such an order, the Court shall have regard to the terms of any separation agreement which has been entered into by the spouses and is still in force ...

(5) The Court shall not make an order under a provision referred to in sub-section (1) unless it would be in the interests of justice to do so."

The terms of section 20(2) are largely similar to those in section 20 of the Judicial Separation and Family Law Reform Act 1989 and section 16 of the Family Law Act 1995.

The role of conduct as a factor in determining financial provision has faded greatly over the past quarter of a century. Most people would probably welcome the desire to orient the spouses away from recrimination and name-calling in litigation and to encourage them to take a civilised and harmonious approach. Yet the question of fault cannot be airbrushed from the picture completely. Is it just that a spouse who engaged in violence or sexual abuse during the marriage should have a claim to the other spouse's property on divorce? If it is still normatively relevant to use the term 'desertion', why should a spouse who deserted the other spouse and abandoned the children share in the deserted spouse's wealth on divorce?

To speak of desertion forces us to confront the values question. Where marriage involves permanent commitment as an ingredient of its essence, then of course desertion violates that commitment. Once permanence is removed from the legal understanding of marriage and a constitutional entitlement to divorce is built on living apart for a sustained period of time, is not the law obliged to reassess the normative premises of the new model of marriage?

What we find internationally are several competing theories, some echoing the former model of marriage as a permanent commitment, others adopting the rhetoric of no-fault divorce while being slow to confront its substance. The theory of marriage as an equal partnership has inspired some courts when addressing financial provision, encouraging them to adopt a presumption of equal distribution of assets. This can work well in the case of long marriages where the wife played a traditional role but seems a curious starting point to deal with short marriages where the wife has worked outside the home. There is a difference between respect for the principle of equality and the adoption of the principle of equal shares. Why should those who have had short marriages be obliged to share their property equally with their former spouses? Can such an intention be inferred by the court in the face of the fact that the spouses retained their separate property? When marriage does not involve a lifelong commitment, why should the phenomenon of going through a ceremony of marriage have such a radical effect on an individual's property entitlements?

When one revisits the equal partnership approach in its application to long marriages involving wives who worked in the home, one can understand it better if one recognises the element of recognition that it tacitly gives to the contribution that these wives made to the marriage over the years. That contribution has been traditionally undervalued, notably in Irish law, where no recognition has been given in proceedings under section 12 of the Married Women's Status Act 1957 to 'indirect' contributions of this character to the acquisition of property by the husband.

A completely opposite approach is that of the 'clean break'. On this view, spouses, having departed from the marriage, should be encouraged to wind up their property relationships with each other, leave them behind them and plan separate futures. This is entirely consistent with the philosophy of no-fault divorce. The difficulty with it is that it can result in serious financial hardship for wives who are not in good employment, especially where the assets will not yield a secure capital base for the future. In *J.D. v. D.D.* [1997] 3 I.R. 64, analysed by Power, "Maintenance: No Clean Break with the Past" [1998] 1 Ir. J. of Fam L 15, and in *Annual Review of Irish Law 1997*, pp.453–4, McGuinness J. noted that 'the "clean-break" policy has been criticised as causing future hardship to dependent wives.' It should be noted that McGuinness J. was critical about the manner in which the Family Law Act 1995 and the Family Law (Divorce) Act 1996 prevented the spouses from reaching closure in their financial arrangements.

Let us for a moment address what may seem like a collateral issue but which is nonetheless of considerable relevance. This is the conflict between the norms of spousal autonomy and paternalism. The conflict is most appropriate in relation to the legal effects of separation agreements. Such agreements embody general contractual norms: that the contracting parties as individuals know what is best for them financially and can come to their own agreement as to their future financial relationships, without the State looking over their shoulders, save to insure that the agreement is not vitiated by duress or undue influence. The norm of paternalism treats separation agreements with suspicion, being concerned about the relative inequalities of bargaining power that can occur between husbands and wives. These inequalities were of course far greater when most wives worked within the home but few would argue even today that all spouses contract on the basis of economic equality.

The traditional approach has been to protect wives against signing away their right to apply for maintenance (*cf.* section 27 of the Family Law (Maintenance of Spouses and Children) Act 1976) and to give courts the power to make orders for financial provision which can override the intended effects of separation agreements. This paternalistic protection of wives is bought at the price of weakening the attraction of separation agreements since the spouses cannot be given the assurance by their legal advisers that the courts will not at some time in the future make orders that are inconsistent with their terms. For an incisive analysis of the broader policy issues, see Crowley, "Pre-Nuptial Agreements – Have They Any Place in Irish Family Law?" [2002] 1 Ir. J. of Fam L 3.

All of these issues come together in the case of a marriage involving spouses with very considerable assets. If the husband is worth (let us assume) 10 million euro and the wife has the security of a home worth 1 million euro, what should be the basis on which a court in divorce proceedings should make an order for financial provision?

In England courts used to take the view that a principle of 'reasonable requirements' should apply. This meant, of course, that a wife in the scenario mentioned above would not be likely to be awarded half of the 10 million euro since such a sum would be well beyond her reasonable requirements. In *White v. White* [2001] 1 A.C. 596, the House of Lords, dealing with what was described as a 'big money' case where the spouses had built up very substantial assets in a farming partnership, rejected the approach based on 'reasonable requirements'. Lord Nicholls emphasised the need for fairness, which in turn required the court to be conscious of the principle of equality. He observed that:

> "there is one principle of universal application which can be stated with confidence. In seeking to achieve a fair outcome, there is no place for discrimination between the husband and wife in their respective roles."

While the yardstick of equality of division would help the parties and the court to focus on the need to ensure the absence of discrimination and would sometimes lead to 'a more or less equal division of the available assets', more often it would not. Lord Nicholls rejected the 'reasonable requirements' approach in robust terms:

> "Where the assets exceed the financial needs of both parties, why should the surplus belong solely to the husband? On the facts of a particular case there may be a good reason why the wife should be confined to her needs and the husband left with a much larger balance. But the mere absence of financial need cannot, by itself, be a sufficient reason. If it were, discrimination would be creeping in by the back door. In these cases, it should be remembered, the claimant is usually the wife. Hence the importance of the check against the yardstick of equal division."

White provoked an avalanche of commentary, including Eekelaar, "Back to Basics and Forward into the Unknown" [2001] Fam. L. 30; Hodson & Duckworth, "*White* – Bringing Section 25 Back to the People" [2001] Fam. L. 24; Brasse "*White v. White* – A Return to Orthodoxy?" [2001] Fam. L. 191; George, "Fair is Fair – After *White*" [2002] Fam. L. 307; Barton & Hibbs, "Ancillary Financial Relief and Fat Cat(tle) Divorce" (2002) 65 Modern. L. Rev. 79; Horgan, "Practical Problems Arising in Ancillary Relief Proceedings" [2001] 3 Ir. J. of Fam. L. 3, at 7-8 and Power, "Equality in Ancillary Relief" [2001] 1 Ir. J. of Fam. L. 24.

In the subsequent decision of *Cowan v. Cowan* [2001] 2 F.L.R. 192 the English Court of Appeal interpreted *White* somewhat less radically than had some of the commentators. *White* had made fairness rather than equality the court's objective. Thorpe LJ observed:

> "The decision in *White v. White* clearly does not introduce a rule of equality. The yardstick of equality is a cross check against discrimination. Fairness is the rule and in its pursuit the reasons for departure from equality will inevitably prove to be too legion and too varied to permit of listing or classification. They will range from the

substantial to the faint but that range can be reflected in the percentage of departure. However it would seem to me undesirable for judges to be drawn into too much specificity, ascribing precise percentage points to the various and often counterbalancing reasons which the facts of individual cases render relevant."

Furthermore the decision in *White* had been directed to 'the abnormal case', involving 'big money'. Even within the relatively narrow sphere of the big money case the infinite variety of facts and circumstances thrown up in individual instances made it dangerous to generalise or to attempt to distil principles." Thorpe L.J. summarised what he perceived to be the consequence of *White*:

"(i) Approved is the frequent theme of decisions in this court that the trial judge must apply such criteria as are to be found in section 25.

(ii) Approved also is the almost inevitable judicial conclusion that the unexpressed objective of the exercise is to arrive at a fair solution.

(iii) Disapproved is any discriminatory appraisal of the traditional role of the woman as homemaker and of the man as breadwinner and arbiter of the destination of family assets amongst the next generation. A calculation of what would be the result of equal division is a necessary cross-check against such discrimination.

(iv) Disapproved is any evaluation of outcome solely or even largely by reference to reasonable requirements.

(v) Insofar as the yardstick of reasonable requirements was a judicially created tool to enable negotiators and judges respectively to predict and calculate conclusions it introduced an element of predictability and accordingly curtailed the width of the judicial discretion conferred by parliament. Thus the prohibition on the future use of the tool extends the judicial discretion at the very moment when government policy has seemingly moved in the reverse direction, in harmony with international trends, academic and specialist commentaries and such research as is available. Therein lies the heightened case for legislation. If that case was clear when judges applied the yardstick of reasonable requirements …, subjective judicial perception of fairness after a careful appraisal of the section 25 criteria."

In spite of *Cowan's* rationalisation of *White*, there is research evidence indicating that the *White* principles have filtered down to have some effect on cases where the money at issue could not be considered 'big': see Fisher, "The Unexpected Impact of *White* – Taking 'Equality' Too Far?" [2002] Fam. L. 108, at 108-9.

In Ireland, in *M.K.v J.P. (otherwise S.K.)* [2001] 3 I.R. 371, analysed by Power, [2001] 4 Ir. J. of Fam. L. 22, and Buckley, *op. cit.,* at p.68, the subject fell for consideration. The spouses had married in 1963. They had six children. They separated in 1980 and entered a separation agreement in 1982, under which the husband undertook to make maintenance payments for his wife and children, the wife residing with them in the family home. The spouses renounced their respective succession rights. The wife obtained some part-time employment but was 'in the main ... fully involved in her role as a mother to her children' (*per* McGuinness J., with whose judgement Murphy and Murray JJ. concurred).

The husband began a second relationship with another woman. After obtaining a Haitian divorce from his wife and remarrying in the United States of America, he and the other woman lived together as husband and wife, holding the vast majority of their financial assets jointly. The other woman made substantial contributions to the acquisition of these assets. During their period together they accumulated considerable wealth. The husband was paid a high salary by his employers.

The parties divorced in Ireland in 2000 and the husband then married the woman with whom he had been living. So far as the ancillary orders were concerned, Lavan J. ordered the husband to pay his former wife £1,500,000, as well as maintenance equal to half his salary (including bonuses). He also required him to transfer his interest in the family home to her. The lump sum represented about half of the assets held by the husband and the woman who later became his second wife. Lavan J. subsequently ordered that 80% of the husband's Irish pension be paid to former wife when it fell due.

In his judgment, Lavan J. laid considerable stress on the manner in which the husband had obtained the Haitian divorce and remarried in the United States, described him as having "driven a coach and four through Irish legislation". He acknowledged however, that there had been adultery "on both sides." Lavan J. approached the law on financial provision when granting divorce in the following terms:

> "Accepting the submissions made by [counsel for the wife] in relation to the Law Lords' view of how to deal with these circumstances in their judgment in *White v. White*, I am happy that in current phraseology the Court may use the term 'equality'. In my view, however, the Court should continue to adopt the fundamental rules that had been in existence for nearly two hundred years in determining whether a wife is entitled to be maintained according to the style of her husband."

McGuinness J, on appeal, observed that this appeared 'to be the key passage, and indeed the only passage, in which the learned judge indicated the basis in law on which he exercised his discretion.'

The main grounds of appeal were that Lavan J. had failed to have due regard, pursuant to section 20(3) of the 1996 Act, to the deed of separation executed by the parties in 1982, that he had failed to have proper regard to the period of parties' separation of more than twenty years and that he had failed to consider and balance properly the matters set out at section 20(2)(a)–(l) of the Act of 1996.

So far as the separation agreement was concerned, both spouses had received full legal advice at the time they entered into the deed. Section 20(3) was mandatory in form, providing that, in deciding whether to make an order under a provision referred to in sub-section (1) and in determining the provisions of such an order, the Court "shall have regard to the terms of any separation agreement which has been entered into by the spouses and is still in force". Counsel for the husband submitted that, in exercising his discretion, Lavan J. had relied solely on his own, erroneous, interpretation of *White v. White* [2000] 3 W.L.R. [2001] 1 All E.R. 1, and on "fundamental rules" that had been in existence for nearly two hundred years. These so-called rules of two hundred years standing were unknown to the law. Central to the application of the constitutional and statutory principles in the consideration and determination of the issue of proper provision for a spouse on divorce was the reliance on judicial discretion. Section 20 of the 1996 Act set out the statutory guidelines to be followed by the Court in the exercise of its discretion in making ancillary orders. In the instant case Lavan J. had failed even to consider these statutory guidelines.

Counsel for the wife argued that, although Lavan J. had not made explicit reference to sub-section (3) and other provisions of section 20 in his judgment, it was clear from the whole course of the proceedings that he had in fact had regard to the matters set out in the statute. The law, including the statutory provisions, had been opened to him. Both counsel had made full legal submissions to him at the close of the evidence. In a judgment given *ex tempore* it was not to be expected that the judge would set out in explicit detail all the factors which he had considered in reaching his decision. Counsel for the wife also submitted that, in making reference to the principle of equality as set out by the House of Lords in *White v. White*, Lavan J. had been using the correct principle, which was also found in Ireland in *J.D. v. D.D.* [1997] 3 I.R. 64.

McGuinness J. referred to Lavan J.'s express reliance on ' the fundamental rules that had been in existence for nearly two hundred years in determining whether a wife is entitled to be maintained according to the style of her husband.' She commented:

> "Given the orders which he made one must presume he understood these fundamental rules to prescribe an equal division of both income and assets between divorcing or separating spouses. While I would of course accept that the wife of a rich man (or the husband of a rich woman) could always expect a substantially greater award both in income and in capital than the parties to the average marriage, I very

much doubt that a policy of equal division of assets between husband
and wife has prevailed under common law rules since the beginning of
the 19th century, or even the 20th century, either in this jurisdiction or
in England. In both jurisdictions the division of matrimonial assets on
separation or divorce has, since the mid 20th century at least, been
governed by statute. Explicit mandatory guidelines for the Court have
been set out in these statutes."

McGuinness J. went on to observe that, while Lord Nicholls of Birkenhead in
White had certainly stressed the importance of equality as a check or yardstick,
he was not suggesting that the individual circumstances of each case, or the
statutory guidelines, should be ignored. The husband and wife in *White*, were
'not a couple with a traditional roles' but were business partners in a large
farming enterprise. Throughout his speech Lord Nicholls had stressed that the
overall objective of the Court should be fairness.

In *White* the members of the House of Lords had been reacting to the
'reasonable requirements' yardstick, which had prevailed in 'big money' cases
in the English courts for many year. It had been discriminatory in its nature, in
particular against wives who fulfilled the traditional role of wife and mother
throughout a long marriage. *White* might therefore be seen as a 'useful
corrective in English matrimonial law', as the Court of Appeal in *Cowan* had
acknowledged.

McGuinness J. went on to set out the position in Irish law:

> "The concept of a single capital payment to the wife to meet her
> 'reasonable requirements' for the remainder of her life has never in
> fact formed a part of Irish family law. There are two main reasons for
> this. Firstly, such a capital payment is inevitably a part of a 'clean break'
> settlement in divorce proceedings. In this jurisdiction the legislature
> has, in the Family Law (Divorce) Act 1996, laid down a system of law
> where a 'clean break' solution is neither permissible nor possible.
> Secondly, the approach of the Irish courts, in accordance with both
> Article 41.2 of the Constitution and the statutory guidelines, has been
> to give full credit to the wife's contribution through the work in the
> home and as a mother to her children. (See, for example, *J.D. v. D.D.*,
> [1997] 2 I.R. 64). In this jurisdiction the overriding requirement of a
> fair outcome is governed by section 20(5) of the 1996 Act:
>
> > 'The Courts shall not make an order under a provision referred to
> > in sub-section (1) unless it would be in the interests of justice to do
> > so.'
>
> The provisions of the 1996 Act leave a considerable area of discretion
> to the Court in making proper financial provision for spouses in divorce
> cases. This discretion, however, is not to be exercised at large. The

statute lays down mandatory guidelines. The Court must have regard to all the factors set out in section 20, measuring their relevance and weight according to the facts of the individual case. In giving the decision of the Court, a judge should give reasons for the way in which his or her discretion has been exercised in the light of the statutory guidelines. In his judgment in the instant case the learned trial judge has notably failed to do this."

The instant case was not an ordinary or average one. In deciding what was proper provision for the wife, the Court was required to take into account the separation deed entered into by the parties, the fact that they had lived apart for twenty years, the wife's financial needs, the role which she had played in caring for the children, and the fact that the entire of the husband's wealth had been accumulated subsequent of the parties. 'These questions and others, and their relation both to the statutory guidelines and to the facts of the case should be set out in the judgment of the Court', McGuinness J. observed.

The Supreme Court's task of deciding whether the trial judge had correctly exercised his discretion under the statute had been rendered impossible, since no indication had been given in his judgment as to what regard he had to the various factors set out in section 20 of the 1996 Act. In particular, despite the mandatory requirement of section 20(3), no reference had been made to the effect of the 1982 separation agreement. Accordingly, the Supreme Court returned the matter to the High Court so that the question of proper provision for the parties to the divorce might be considered in the light of the mandatory provisions of the statute.

The Supreme Court holding that the case should be returned to the High Court is unproblematic in view of the lack of specificity in the High Court judgment. No doubt many a High Court judge who has been found not to have given sufficient explanation in his or her judgment for the basis of the conclusion arrived at will feel that he or she is being required to go through a formulaic recitation, especially in the context of the factors specified in section 20(2). Nevertheless a bald reference to the equality principle, even in an *ex tempore* judgment, might be considered not to provide sufficient explanatory clarification of the basis of the holding. Certainly a judge who proceeded on the basis of such a principle in the absence of considering all of the factors listed in section 20(2) would not be discharging the function prescribed by that provision.

Yet there have to be some guiding principles underlying the calibration of the respective weights to be given to each of the ten factors specified in subs. (2), bearing in mind that these are to be given regard without prejudice to the generality of subs (1), which requires the court to 'ensure that such provision as the Court considers proper having regard to the circumstances exists or will be made for the souses and any dependent member of the family.' For example, factor (k) requires the court to have regard to 'the rights of any person other

than the spouses but including a person to whom either spouse is remarried.'
It is entirely silent as to the provenance, nature or scope of these rights.
Assuming that they extend beyond legal rights (bearing in mind that cohabitees
do not have legally enforceable maintenance rights or obligations relative to
each other), the rights in question must be derived from the moral order. A
judge is inevitably required to address normative questions and must resolve
them according to some set of principles. The judicial function under section
20 cannot be reduced to one of fact. Of course each factual set of circumstances
is unique to the family concerned but general principles have to be applied to
these facts.

So the question remains. To what extent should a model of equal partnership
guide the court in exercising its function under section 20? Has it no role
simply because Irish law contains no 'clean break' principle? If it is to have
some role, are there paradoxical dangers to divorced wives in applying it to
'small money' cases? The Supreme Court decision in the instant case has not
resolved these questions.

It is frankly hard to see how Irish law can be considered to have given full
practical effect to the constitutional recognition of the work of women in the
home. The Supreme Court decisions in the *Matrimonial Homes Bill 1993* case
and *B.L. v. M.L.* give no encouragement to that view and McGuinness J.'s
decision in *J.D. v. D.D.* scarcely advanced the position, since it was dealing
with the court's powers in relation to proceedings for a change of status –
judicial separation. In that case, McGuinness J. asked the question:

> "In [the] division of the family assets should the 'stay at home' wife be
> treated differently from the wife who works outside the home?"

If 'big money' is generated by the business acumen of both spouses, a question
had to arise as to whether the equality norm, whatever weight it may have,
should yield the same outcome in terms of determining that divorced wife's
share, as it would in a case where the wife had worked within the home. And
what of the situation where the acquisition of the assets is largely attributable
to the business acumen of a woman with whom the husband is having an
affair? How extensive are her rights for the purposes of factor (k)?

The failure by the trial judge in the instant case to have addressed the
separation agreement was unfortunate. Very often in 'big money' cases, the
husband's assets will have multiplied geometrically after the spouses have
separated. This means that the wife's share on divorce will depend equally on
the degree of emphasis placed by the court on the terms of the separation
agreement. Of course section 20(3) is peremptory but that means no more
than that the court is obliged to have regard to these terms. The subsection is
silent on the intensity of regard that the court is to have. Here yet again is an
instance of why section 20 is not reducible to a normless infinity of factual
circumstances. A crucial value judgment must be made by the court: to what

extent should spouses be held to bargains they have freely made?

In *T. v. T.*, High Court, November 28, 2001, decided three weeks after the Supreme Court decision in *M.K. v. J.P. (otherwise S.K.)*, Lavan J. revisited the question of financial provision on divorce. The spouses had married in 1980. They had three dependent children. Their relationship broke down in 1989, the husband leaving the home in 1994. At the time of the divorce proceedings he was in a relationship of two years standing. He and his new partner had a child.

The husband's assets were around £20 million, the wife's around £1 million. The wife had largely 'devoted herself to her home and family', The professional work in which she was engaged placed a considerable strain on her. She was anxious that a lump sum provision be made in order to secure her own and her children's future.

Lavan J. gave a detailed analysis of counsels' arguments and referred to a number of Irish and English cases, including *White* and *Cowan*. He went on to state that he had had regard to the provisions of section 20 of the 1996 Act in respect of the proper provision to be made for the spouse and children and that he had paid particular regard to all of the matters contained in section 20(2). He added:

> "In my view I have no difficulty with section 20(2) ((a) through to (h)). This is a family where the husband has assets in excess of £20,000,000 and the wife has assets of some £1.5 million. In the later years of their married life they enjoyed an exceptional standard of living. Section 20(2)(i) causes me some difficulty which I will deal with later in this judgment. Section 20(2)(j), (k) and (l) I have also taken account of."

Lavan J. referred to *J.D. v. D.D.* He observed that he did:

> "not see the making of a lump sum payment as introducing the 'clean break' concept into Irish law. In my view it is making provision for the financial security of the [wife]. The [husband] has, before order of this Court, established a second family relationship and now has a daughter of same. What the future holds is therefore uncertain from all parties' points of view."

Lavan J. went on to say:

> "In relation to the English authorities relied upon I have found them extremely helpful and interesting. Where it is possible I ought to follow a decision of the High Court. In this case I do follow the above judgment. The decisions of the English courts are of strong persuasive value warranting great respect and evaluation. It goes without saying that they represented most interesting assessments by leading English jurists and I find them of assistance in this case."

He referred also to McCracken J.'s decision in *McA v. McA* [2000] 1 I.R. 457 and Budd J.'s decision in *P. O'D. v. J. O'D.* High Court. March 31, 2000.

Lavan J. went on to express 'wholehearte[d] concur[rence]' with a passage from the speech of Lord Nicholls in *White*, 'notwithstanding the difference in law between the two jurisdictions.' Quoting further passages from the speech, Lavan J. observed:

> "Whilst clearly distinguishing [*White*] as a 'clean break' case, I nonetheless find the principles therein enunciated as helpful in the interpretation of sections 22(1) and (2) of the Family Law (Divorce) Act 1996.
>
> Likewise I make a similar assessment of the Court of Appeal's decision in *Cowan v. Cowan* dated the 14th May, 2001 applying the *White v. White* decision. The extensive opinions expressed therein highlight the need for a thorough assessment of the criteria set out in the English statute by each trial judge.
>
> On one particular point I have no hesitation in following the Court's decision in the above case, namely, that the assessment of assets must be at the date of trial or appeal. I am much taken with the view expressed by Mance LJ ... and accept the point and apply it in this case."

Lavan J. went on to give a very detailed review of the evidence. He expressed his conclusions as follows:

> "Turning to the provisions for the [wife], the infant and the second son, which I consider proper having regard to the [husband]'s claim for a decree of divorce, and bearing in mind the views I have expressed on the statutory provisions and the Irish and English case law relied upon both parties, it seems to me that the [wife] has made an overall greater contribution to the marriage than the [husband]. None the less, I am mindful of the need for care and discretion when dividing a fortune as substantial as that with which I am now dealing....
>
> I am impressed with the case, the evidence, and the submissions made by and on behalf of the [wife] and do accept them ...
>
> One outstanding matter that has given me much difficulty is the specific provision of section 20(2)(i) of the Family Law (Divorce) Act, 1996. It seems to me on the evidence that I am obliged, in exercise of the discretion, which undoubtedly arises, to take it into account. In doing so this creates a further difficulty, namely how to quantify it and in this regard I note that the particular provision does not offer any formula for its proper assessment. I note that McGuinness J. in her judgment [in *J.D. v. D.D.*] and McCracken J. in his judgment [*McA. v. McA.*] did not deal with this aspect.
>
> In these circumstances I propose, from a monetary point of view to

deal with it by way of what I consider to be a proper adjustment of pension provisions in favour of the [wife].

Finally, and of significance, I note that the [husband] is in a new relationship and has a baby daughter born during the hearing of this case. It seems to me to be a compelling factor to be taken into account in determining the amount of a 'lump sum' which the Court ought to consider appropriate for the [wife] and the youngest child of the marriage. Especially from the [wife]'s point of view in that same permits both parties to begin anew.

Having regard to the foregoing and conscious that I ought to take a conservative view of such 'lump sum' for the reasons stated, I propose to award the [wife] the sum of £5 million without the payment of continuing maintenance, in the special circumstances of this case ....

In respect of the pension provisions as set out in the Delaney Bacon Woodrow Report dated the 10th July, 2001, I would have been disposed to divide this to the [husband] as to 49% and the [wife] as to 51%. However, having regard to the view I have expressed as to the taking into account of section 20(2)(i) of the aforesaid Act of 1996 I will in deference to my findings thereunder allow a finding of 45% to the [husband] and 55% to the [wife]."

While Lavan J. made no reference to the Supreme Court's judgment in *M.K. v. J.P. (otherwise S.K.)*, his judgment in *T. v. T.*, contains the clearest of recitals that he had specifically addressed all of the factors mentioned in section 20(2). It seems plain that on an appeal against the judgment on the ground that succeeded in the earlier decision would fail in the instant case.

In *M. v. M.*, Circuit Court, June 18, 2001, analysed by Power, [2002] Ir. J, Fam. L. 29, Judge Buckley made some important observations on the concept of matrimonial property regimes in Irish law. The husband in this case, which involved proceedings for judicial separation, had inherited a farm with £1,400,000. He argued that he should be entitled to retain the entirety of the proceeds of its sale on the basis that this sum did not form part of the 'matrimonial property'. Judge Buckley responded:

"The difficulty I have with this argument is twofold. Firstly there is no concept of matrimonial property in Irish law as there is in other legal systems and secondly there is nothing in the Judicial Separation and Family Law Act 1989 or the Family Law Act 1995 (or indeed in the Family Law (Divorce) Act 1996) which puts any limit on the extent of the assets of the spouses to which the court can have recourse when making periodical or lump sum orders, property adjustment orders, financial compensation orders or pension adjustment orders.

The range of 'matrimonial property regimes' which exist in civil and common law jurisdictions is dealt with in Chapter 4 of Paul A.

O'Connor's book *Key Issues in Irish Family Law*. Mr O'Connor's account shows that there is a wide range of different types of matrimonial property regimes, ranging from one where all the assets of the spouses, whether owned before the marriage or acquired by either or both [of the] spouses during the course of the marriage goes into a single pool, at one extreme, to one where only the property which the spouses agree should be regarded as matrimonial property is to be so categorised by the other. The history of the development of the protection of the interests of married women in our legislation has been a policy of increasing the entitlement to separate property as Mr. Alan Shatter points out at pages 832 ff. in the fourth edition of his book on Family Law. As Mr. Shatter points out, successive Reports of Committees on the Status of Women, the most recent that of 1993, have recommended that the desirability of legislation providing for a community of property regime be investigated. The first step the 1993 Commission suggested was the provision of automatic joint ownership of the family home. This recommendation was followed by the introduction of the ill-fated Matrimonial Homes Bill of 1993 which provided for the application of automatic ownership as joint tenants to every dwelling occupied as a married couple. The judgment of the Supreme Court that the Bill was unconstitutional has no doubt discouraged Governments from tackling the more general issue of matrimonial property. Mr. Shatter expresses considerable doubt, at page 836, as to the likelihood of a legislative initiative by government to provide for a regime of community property."

Judge Buckley went on to mention that, at a recent Judicial Studies Institute seminar for Circuit Court Judges on Family Law matters 'an experienced Judge' had put forward the idea that initially a judge should consider working on the principle that whatever assets one spouse brought into a marriage should be given to that spouse on judicial separation or divorce. Such an approach might be considered appropriate where the asset brought in consisted of a farm or a family business, though a question might well arise as to whether such an asset should really be given to the spouse with the intention that it should be available for passing on to the children of the marriage. While recognising that such an approach, particularly in the case of a farm or family business, might well be appropriate, Judge Buckley observed that it was 'clear that under the legislation all the assets of the parties are available for distribution by the Court'.

Judge Buckley went on to make some observations on the House of Lords decision in *White v. White*:

"While there are a number of reasons why *White v. White* is not directly comparable with this case: it was a divorce case, it was being decided on the 'clean break' principle and the parties had been partners in carrying on a farming business, none of which apply in this case, nonetheless there are passages in the judgments, particularly that of Lord Cooke, where he reviewed the development of the law in his native New Zealand and Australia which are of interest in showing how the law has developed in those jurisdictions. In New Zealand legislation had been introduced to impose guidelines on the trial judges and in Australia the High Court had introduced such guidelines. Each of these jurisdictions, as indeed had England and Wales, commenced with judges required to take a number of factors, not dissimilar from those contained in Section 16 of the Family Law Act 1995 into account, but given wide discretion in applying those factors.

However desirable it may be to have guidelines, and it is not clear that those suggested in *White v. White* are self-explanatory, none have been laid down in this jurisdiction and I must therefore exercise my own discretion. I have given custody of the two children to the [husband]. It was agreed by the parties that the family home should be sold. The [husband] will therefore have to spend a substantial sum on the purchase of suitable accommodation for himself and the children. His income is modest. As a long time, but temporary, employee of the State he has no present entitlement to any pension arising out of that employment. During the currency of the marriage the income from the lands was used as part of the income of the family, and it seems to me that the [husband] will require to invest the proceeds of the sale partly to provide an income to supplement his own earnings, but also to provide for a more substantial pension for himself. As against that the [wife] will also have to fund the purchase of an alternative residence which should be of sufficient size to enable the children to stay with her on access visits.

I do not believe that the [husband] should be entitled to retain the entire proceeds of sale, but I do not think that an equal division of this substantial sum should be equitable. The net sale price will probably be in the region of £1,400,000 and I would propose to award the [wife] approximately 25% of that sum. I say approximately because I propose to allow the [wife] to receive the entire sale price of the family home of which she is a 50% owner, and which has been valued at £500,000, the [husband] to discharge all encumbrances on the family home. This should give her an additional £250,000 and I will direct payment by the [husband] of a sum of £100,000 to make up the approximate 25% share."

M. v. M. was, of course, decided before the Supreme Court judgment in *M.K. v. J.P. (otherwise S.K.)* and Lavan J.'s judgment in *T. v. T.* It is interesting to compare Judge Buckley's solution with that adopted by Lavan J. in the latter decision.

Interim maintenance *V.C. v. D.C.*, High Court, November 16, 2001 is a clear example of the caution displayed by courts when hearing applications for interim maintenance. The spouses had married in 1981 and separated on or before 1996. They entered into an agreement in 1997 whereby the husband was to pay the wife £24,600 gross maintenance per annum to the wife with £4,000 net for each of the three children, as well as the children's education expenses. The wife and children got the family home, in which they resided. At the time of the proceedings, the husband was paying £30,245 to the wife taking into account changes in the consumer price index. The wife sought an interim order for the payment of £111,673.68 for a proposed re-roofing of the home, which was in an advanced state of disrepair, as well as the sum of £59,000 representing the amount of two loans she had been obliged to obtain, from her brother and another man. She also sought increases in the amounts of maintenance for her and the children. The husband produced an estimate for less than £20,000 from roof restoration specialists of repair work and stated that he had been advised that if this work was carried out and the roof maintained in a normal fashion, it would 'give no trouble' for decades to come.

Morris P. ordered that the work be carried out on the basis of the husband's estimate. He stressed the interim character of his jurisdiction. It would not be appropriate, in his view, to make the order for re-roofing work costing more than £100,000 on the hearing of an interim application. If the lesser work turned out not to be satisfactory problems would have manifested themselves by the time the case came on for full hearing and could be addressed at that stage.

So far as the debts incurred by the wife were concerned, Morris P. declined to make an order for their payment. Neither creditor was pressing for payment. At the full hearing the degree to which it had been necessary for the wife to incur the debts in order to maintain herself and the children could be examined, in the context of the claim by the husband that the debts were attributable to the wife's 'lavish lifestyle'.

So far as the claim for an increase in maintenance was concerned, Morris P. noted that the husband had claimed to have a pre-tax income of £111,189 and expenditure of £131,927, of which £73,817 was payable under the terms of the 1997 settlement. If these figures were correct, Morris P considered that there would be 'no justification for increasing the interim payments even if I were satisfied that [the wife] was hard pressed to live on the present maintenance payments. There simply .... would not be sufficient income available.' The only justification would be if the husband was failing to disclose his full wealth.

The husband's affidavit of means showed assets of between £2.5 million and £3 million with liabilities of £1.3 million. (The wife's house was valued at £2.5 million). The wife brought a discovery motion for the purpose of enquiring further into the assets. Morris P. observed:

"If I were trying this case on suspicion I would strongly suspect that [the wife] is correct. This is not the basis upon which I must determine this application. I must be satisfied that on the balance of probabilities [the wife] is correct and that [the husband] has not disclosed his income."

The wife in her affidavit had identified a number of factors 'which would suggest that there are greater assets available to [the husband] than he is disclosing.' These were denied by the husband. Morris P. was:

"not satisfied that it has been established to my satisfaction that [the husband]'s assets are greater than were originally stated. I do acknowledge that a lifestyle which includes the holidays and recreational activities emerging from this case indicate that there is no shortage of money and it may well be that at the hearing of this matter this will be established to the satisfaction of the court. At this stage in the proceedings it has not been established to my satisfaction that consistent with a capacity to pay there is a need for an increase in the interim payments to be made to [the wife]."

The message of this judgment appears to be plain: applications for interim maintenance are not appropriate proceedings, in Morris P.'s view, for the court to take a strong position, either on substantive or evidential issues. For a broad analysis of the decisions dealing with the duty to make full disclosure, see Horgan, "Ancillary Relief Applications in Separation and Divorce" [2001] 2 Ir. J. of Fam. L. 2.

Role of judicial review proceedings In *R.McC. v. Judge Yvonne Murphy*, Supreme Court, March 23, 2001, the applicant sought leave to apply by way of judicial review for an order of *certiorari* quashing an order of the respondent Circuit Court Judge referring his application for a review of periodic maintenance proceedings payable by him under an order of the Circuit Court in 1998 granting a divorce decree in respect of the applicant's marriage. The spouses had married in 1982. When the divorce decree was granted, an order by consent was made providing *inter alia* for the making of periodic payments by the applicant for the benefit of the three children of the marriage.

In November 1999, the applicant applied for an order varying the order in relation to periodic payments. Counsel for his wife submitted that the court had no jurisdiction to review the consent order. The respondent Judge, giving judgment in January 2000, said that under section 22(2) of the 1996 Act, she could vary the order as to periodical payments only if she considered it proper to do so having regard to any change in the circumstances of the case and to any new evidence. The only change she discerned in the applicant's circumstances since the consent order was that he had himself acquired a larger mortgage for his own requirements. She said that she was satisfied that in these circumstances it would not be proper to alter the maintenance arrangements. She accordingly refused the application.

When seeking leave to apply by way of judicial review, the applicant argued, *inter alia*, that he had been prevented from procuring particulars of his former wife's property and income arrangements by virtue of the respondent's ruling, that the respondent had been in error in stating that there were no grounds for review of the periodic maintenance in his mortgage repayments and that the decision flew in the face of fundamental reason and commonsense.

O'Neill J. in the High Court was of the view that the respondent had heard the applicant's case and that she was entitled to come to the conclusion on the merits of the applicant's case, having read the affidavit and heard submissions, and that, in the result, there had been no denial to him of natural justice. He was also of the opinion that, if there had been any error on her part, it was an error within her jurisdiction and could only be corrected on appeal. The Supreme Court affirmed. Keane C.J. (Murphy and Murray JJ. concurring) was:

> "satisfied that the learned High Court judge was entirely correct in so holding and that none of the additional grounds urged in this court entitled the applicant to the relief he was seeking. The respondent arrived at the conclusion, having read the affidavit of the applicant and heard the submissions, that it would not be proper to review the periodical payments in the light of the allegedly changed circumstances and evidence adduced by the applicant. That was plainly a finding which it was within her jurisdiction to make and which, if mistaken, could be corrected only by way of appeal. Had the applicant pursued an appeal to the High Court, the view might have been taken that the applicant had demonstrated a sufficient change in circumstances and had adduced sufficient evidence to warrant the making of an order pursuant to section 22(2) of the 1996 Act. The applicant having failed to take that course cannot succeed in having the respondent's order set aside where it was plainly made within her jurisdiction."

It seems plain that the strategy of seeking judicial review to attack Circuit Court judgments in family litigation is not likely to be a useful one, save in the most egregious cases. Two factors encourage the judicial resistance to this approach. First, an appeal to the High Court involves a complete rehearing. Secondly judicial review proceedings may raise problems as to the privacy of the proceedings. This aspect was dealt with as a preliminary matter in the instant proceedings: see below, 366. The Supreme Court did not attempt to resolve the matter definitively so some shadows must remain.

MEDIATION

The Family Support Agency Act 2001 establishes the Family Support Agency, whose functions include providing family mediation through the Family Mediation Service, which came into existence in 1985. That service now has centres in Dublin, Cork, Limerick, Galway, Athlone, Castlebar, Dundalk, Tralee and Wexford. Among the other functions of the Agency is that of supporting, promoting and developing the Family and Community Services Resource Centre Programme and administered by the Department of Social, Community and Family Affairs. There is a Government commitment for establishing 100 centres, of which 80 have come into operation or have been approved: 168 Seanad Debates, col. 1385 (December 11, 2001).

The subject of mediation is given a comprehensive analysis in Sinéad Conneely's *Family Mediation in Ireland*, published in March 2002 (Ashgate, Aldershot). It combines theoretical insights with a strong empirical dimension, examining the position in both parts of the island.

NULLITY OF MARRIAGE

In the 2002 Review, we shall give an analysis of the important Supreme Court decision in *P.F. v. G. O'M. (otherwise G.F.) (Nullity: consent)* [2001] 3 I.R. 1. The case is comprehensively considered by Fergus Ryan, 'Family Law – Reversal of Fortune – Nullity Law in the Age of Divorce' (2000) 22 D.U.L.J. 224.

In *McG. v. F. (otherwise McG.)* [2001] 1 I.R. 599, affirming High Court, 28 January 2000, short shrift was given to the petitioner's contention that a psychiatrist appointed by the Master in respect of a petition for nullity based on the incapacity of both parties to enter and sustain a normal marital relationship as a result of their mental and emotional condition should be entitled to interview, not only the parties themselves, but also five other people – the petitioner's brother and four of the petitioner's friends. Denham J. (Murray and Geoghegan JJ. concurring) had no hesitation in distinguishing nullity proceedings from wardship proceedings, where hearsay evidence is admissible on the basis that the proceedings, designed to protect the best interests of the ward, are inquisitional in character. She stated:

> "Nullity proceedings give rise to an action to determine an issue or issues. There are parties to the action. It is adversarial proceeding. It is not similar to matters of wardship, which are heard by the President of the High Court when conducting the jurisdiction previously exercised by the Lord Chancellor. Consequently, case law relating to wardship of children is of no relevance or assistance."

Counsel for the petitioner had indicated that the five people interviewed by the medical inspector could subsequently be called at the trial and, if they were not, then the judge could determine the appropriate weight to be given to the medical inspector's report. Denham J. commented:

> "Such a vista raises many problems. First, the medical inspector would in fact be conducting a preliminary hearing of persons other than the parties. Secondly, the fact that such persons would then be called to give evidence in court would mean that there would be many additional matters to address in court, for example, what such persons had said to the medical inspector, how it stands up on cross-examination, what was omitted, etc. All of this is quite apart from any consideration of rules of evidence, including the hearsay rule. Further, the weight to be given to such a report, if the additional interviewees of the medical inspector were not called to give evidence in court, or gave evidence contrary to the information they had given to the medical inspector, would be seriously undermined ....
>
> While the medical inspector has indicated that it is common practice in achieving a medical diagnosis, this is a report for the Court prior to a court hearing. To enable the medical inspector interview persons other than the parties would be to endorse a preliminary hearing by the doctor. Further, it would cause serious difficulties in the running of the nullity action in Court and it would take the action from the Court and place it partially in the hands of the doctor. The medical evidence of the medical inspector is an important aspect of the hearing. However, the determination is a judicial function and the evidence should be tendered in accordance with the law and fair procedures.
>
> Whilst the medical inspect was of the view that it was standard psychiatric practice to seek information from third parties and that such was warranted in this case the proceedings are judicial [, at] issue is the status of the parties. The inspector has been asked to examine the parties only. This is in keeping with the necessity for the nullity suit to be conducted in a court of law and not a doctor's clinic."

Denham J. made it clear that this holding was not intended to inhibit a court, if deemed appropriate, from giving additional authority to the medical inspector on consent of both parties.

The decision is to be welcomed. There was a regrettable tendency in some decisions over the previous decade to surrender to psychiatrists the function of determining the 'ultimate issue' on the basis of large doses of hearsay evidence.

PRIVACY OF PROCEEDINGS

In *R.McC. v. Judge Yvonne Murphy*, Supreme Court, March 23, 2001, the question arose as to whether an application seeking leave to issue proceedings for judicial review arising out of family litigation should fall within the scope of the *in camera* rule. The applicant sought leave to apply by way of judicial review for *certiorari* quashing the order of the respondent Circuit Court Judge, refusing his application for a review of periodic maintenance payments payable by him under an earlier order of the Circuit Court grant a divorce decree. The applicant was unsuccessful in the High Court. On appeal to the Supreme Court, the applicant made a preliminary application to the Court that the hearing of the appeal should be in public. While he accepted that, under section 38(5) of the Family Law (Divorce) Act 1996, proceedings under that Act were to be heard otherwise than in public, he invoked article 34.1 of the Constitution in support of his argument that the judicial review proceedings should be in public.

The Supreme Court rejected this argument, deciding that the appeal from the High Court would be heard otherwise than in public in order to ascertain *in limine* whether there was a sustainable ground for granting leave to issue judicial review proceedings. As Keane C.J. (Murphy and Murray JJ. concurring) explained:

"The application for leave to issue judicial review proceedings had been refused in the High Court on the ground *inter alia* that, if the respondent had erred in the order which she made, it was an error within the jurisdiction. If the learned High Court judge was correct in so holding, it would follow that, if the applicant were aggrieved by the determination of the Circuit Court, his appropriate remedy was by way of appeal to the High Court. The intention of the Oireachtas that proceedings under the 1996 Act were to be heard *in camera* would be frustrated if an unsustainable application for judicial review in respect of the Circuit Court order, grounded as here on affidavits setting out in detail evidence heard by the Circuit Court, had to be heard in public."

The Supreme Court was satisfied that the Circuit Court Judge had acted within her jurisdiction and that leave to issue proceedings for judicial review should not be granted. It accordingly dismissed the appeal. Keane C.J. went on to observe that:

"[i]t follows that, in these circumstances, it is unnecessary for this court to review its preliminary finding that this matter should be heard otherwise than in public, for the reasons I have given at an earlier part of this judgment. Unless and until the relevant legislation is found to be invalid having regard to the provisions of the Constitution, the High Court and this court must give effect to the requirement in the legislation – in this case section 38(5) of the 1996 Act – that proceedings of this nature be heard otherwise than in public."

For general consideration of the subject, see Horgan, Shannon and Gallagher, 'Reform of the *In Camera* Rule' (2002) 7 Bar Rev. 278.

SUCCESSION

The judicial response to applications by children of deceased testators under section 117 of the Succession Act 1965 gives us interesting glimpses into changing social mores, about the moral duty of parents to their children, certainly, but also about other social concerns. For a perceptive analysis, see Breen, "Children These Days – Section 117 of the Succession Act 1965 and the Moral Obligations of Parenthood" in Breen, Casey & Kerr eds., *Liber Memorialis Professor James C. Brady* (Round Hall Sweet & Maxwell, Dublin, 2001), p.72. The late Professor Brady had addressed this them in *Succession Law in Ireland* (2nd ed., Butterworths, Dublin, 1995), paras 7.48–7.79. See also Keating, *Probate Law and Practice* (Round Hall Sweet & Maxwell, Dublin, 1999), paras. 6–96—6–102 and Keating, *Probate Causes and Related Matters* (Round Hall Sweet & Maxwell, Dublin, 2000), Chaps.9-10.

It will be recalled that the broad principles favoured by Kenny J. in *G.M. deceased; T.M. v. T.A.M.* (1972) 106 I.L.T.R. 82, at 37 were narrowed somewhat by the Supreme Court in *The Estate of I.A.C. Deceased; C and F v. WC and TC* [1989] I.L.R.M. 815, where Finlay C.J. observed that it was:

> "not apparently sufficient ... to establish that the provision for a child was not as great as it might have been, or that compared with generous bequests to other children or beneficiaries in the will, it appears ungenerous. The Court should not, I consider, make an order under the Section merely because it would on the facts proved have formed different testamentary dispositions. A positive failure in moral duty must be established."

See further *Annual Review of Irish Law 1989*, pp.307-10.

In *In re M.S.H. Deceased; M. McC. and B.N. v. D.H.M. and E.H.*, High Court, October 31, 2001, McCracken J. quoted this passage when refusing applications under section 117 taken by two daughters aged 47 and 49 respectively who argued that their late father had failed in his moral duty to them as they grew up in the 1960s by denying them the opportunity for further education. One daughter had been required to start work as a shop assistant rather than train to be teacher, as she wanted. The other daughter had left school without having sat the Leaving Certificate examination and had gone to study to be 'a sick children's nurse', qualifying in 1972. Both daughters had married.

The first was living with her husband and children. She had acquired secretarial qualifications at her own expense and had worked for eighteen years with 'a major business'. The combined income of herself and her husband was £68,000. The other daughter's husband had received brain injuries in an accident. He was on a disability pension. Their combined income was £50,000. The applicants had eight other siblings, one of whom had Downs Syndrome and was well looked after in their father's will. McCracken J. analysed the issue as follows:

"The applicants' greatest complaint is that the testator did not make proper provision for them during their lifetime, which is of course one of the matters to be taken into account. Certainly both the applicants here had a very Spartan upbringing and were expected to go and work the moment they left school. However, only one of the testator's ten children was given a third level education, and the others all appear to have been treated in a similar way to the applicants. It is indeed a credit to the family that so many of them did manage to give themselves further education on their own initiative. However, what I have to determine is not whether the testator failed in some way in his moral obligation to the applicants thirty years before his death, but whether, at the time of his death, he owed any moral obligation to the applicants, and if so whether he failed in that obligation. This is the extent of the court's powers under the Act ....

Both applicants here are married with families, and at the relevant time had a reasonable family income, although I appreciate that part of the income was contributed by the applicants themselves. However, they are both capable of earning a reasonable amount of money. I do not think that the first applicant could in any way be said to have any special need either at the time of making the will or indeed now. The second applicant can point to the fact that her husband is disabled and unable to work, but he does have a permanent government pension. I do not consider that she has any immediate need such as would give rise to a moral obligation by the testator. As long as her husband is alive he will have a reasonably substantial pension, and of course she is in the same position as everybody else, in that if her husband dies there will be a loss of income. However, in my view this does not constitute a special need."

The case raises an interesting question as to how a court should address changing social norms when considering the issue of parental moral duty. If in the 1960s it was considered right and proper for young women not to be given the same opportunities for higher education as their brothers, should a court today hold that a generation of parents whose bequests reflected that norm was in breach of its moral duty? Should there be a duty on parents from that era who are fortunate enough to live into the twenty first century to compensate their adult daughters in their wills for the parents' complicity in what is now seen as a societal discrimination and injustice to young women three and four decades ago? McCracken J. appears to believe that the answers to this question should be in the negative.

If that is so, are there some other matters involving changing norms where the court might apply contemporary norms with retrospective effect? It seems that there may be. If a parent forty years ago treated a child harshly because of conduct or orientation that offended the norms of the time – premarital pregnancy or homosexual orientation, for example – a court would be likely to take that into account in a section 117 application. The rationale for this distinction is difficult to articulate coherently. It may be that, when it comes to determining moral duty as between a parent and child, the courts will tolerate the norms of an earlier social and economic culture but will not take the same attitude to more distinctively intimate aspects of morality. Harshness, insensitivity and judgmentalism are seen as significant departures from parental duty today even if, in the past, they may have been regarded as acceptable qualities for parents to show towards their children. It may well be that the contemporary high regard for individual privacy and autonomy makes the courts somewhat impatient with parental attitudes in the past, which failed to respect these norms.

For a recent consideration of practical aspects of section 117 applications, see Hourican, "Section 117 Claims: Practice and Procedure and Matters to Bear in Mind" (2001) 6 Conveyancing & Property L.J. 62.

Gaming and Lotteries

HORSE AND GREYHOUND RACING

Horse Racing Ireland   The Horse and Greyhound Racing Act 2001 established a new entity, Horse Racing Ireland (HRI), to take over the functions previously performed by the Irish Horseracing Authority (IHA) under the Irish Horseracing Industry Act 1994 (*Annual Review of Irish Law 1994*, pp.15-16). HRI, like the IHA, is concerned primarily with the overall administration of horseracing and horseracing in Ireland, including the authorisation and regulation of racecourses, the operation of totalisator (Tote) betting, and the provision of certain prize money and other financial supports for racecourses under the aegis of the Department of Agriculture. Section 8 of the 2001 Act sets out the main functions of HRI. These include the overall administration of racing including the authorisation of racecourses, the setting of fixtures, control of on-course bookmakers and, *inter alia*, the development and promotion of the industry as prescribed in the 1994 Act. Certain functions previously carried out by the Racing Regulatory Body (comprising the Turf Club and the National Hunt Steeplechase Committee) through a Registry Office were transferred to HRI by the 2001 Act. These include functions in relation to horse racing passports, race entries, declarations, stakeholding of race entry funds and prize-money. In addition, new functions have been conferred on HRI, namely: to negotiate media rights to the racing pictures and information as well as providing support towards the improvement of the health status of the Irish horse and the specialised education and training requirements of the sector.

Other changes made over the 1994 Act include the extension of the remit of HRI to greyhound racing. This latter required making amendments to the Greyhound Industry Act 1958. In addition, the 2001 Act provided for: the abolition of the 0.3% betting turnover charge and the flat rate charges on off-course bookmakers shops introduced in 1999; the removal of the restrictions in the legislation governing totalisators and betting generally which prohibited the operation of the IHA and Bord na gCon tote betting services from off-course bookmakers shops and the introduction of provisions to authorise the co-mingling of their tote pools with foreign tote pools; and the removal of the general prohibition in the Betting Act 1931 on people in Ireland placing bets abroad (the latter in effect recognising the reality of internet betting facilities).

Human Rights

ROSEMARY BYRNE, Trinity College, Dublin*

2001 is marked as much by a gradual infusion of international human rights law into the domestic Irish legal system as by a staggering lack of governmental progress in creating the core mechanisms to bring national norms into harmony with international standards. In the first instance, constitutional referenda were held to enable Ireland to ratify the Rome Statute for the establishment of the International Criminal Court and abolish the death penalty; while the future of the Special Criminal Court was called into question by a decision issued against Ireland by the United Nations Human Rights Committee, and by the publication of the interim Report by the Committee for the Review of the Offences Against the State Acts 1935-1998. The UN Committee on Economic, Social and Cultural Rights presented the government with a list of issues it wished to be addressed in connection with the State's implementation of the International Covenant on Economic, Social and Cultural Rights. The European Court of Human Rights delivered a judgment finding that the Irish doctrine of state immunity did not violate fair trial rights under the European Convention on Human Rights; and decisions from the Supreme and High Courts continue to define the parameters of refugee protection in the State. In the second instance, contrary to governmental promises, the European Convention on Human Rights and Fundamental Freedoms remains unincorporated, and with over a year since the enactment of the Human Rights Commission Act, the body was only established towards the end of the 2001, and has yet to play any visible role in national human rights debates.

This overview of human rights deals specifically with the legislative and judicial developments affecting the rights and liberties that are anchored in international instruments. Because, properly defined, human rights law deals with the convergence of national and international norms, an overview of developments in this area of law requires a focus on domestic, regional and international fora. In many instances, the developments overlap with other areas of constitutional and administrative law, and these are examined in more detail elsewhere in this volume.

*I would like to express my appreciation to Kirsten Roberts for her invaluable research assistance in preparing this contribution.

23RD AMENDMENT TO THE CONSTITUTION

Ratification of the Rome Treaty to establish the International Criminal Court   On June 7, 2001 a referendum was held on the 23rd Amendment to the Constitution (Constitution of Ireland 1937 (Bunreacht na hÉireann)) to pave the way for the State's ratification of the Rome Statute of the International Criminal Court. (UN Doc. A/CONF. 183/9) (1998). The result of the referendum showed 64% of all voters favouring ratification of the Rome Statute.

The International Criminal Court (ICC) is the first permanent international tribunal that will investigate and try individuals for the violations of genocide, crimes against humanity and war crimes. The creation of the ICC reflects the success of the international human rights movement in establishing individual criminal responsibility for the most serious crimes, which are considered to violate international norms and principles. The historic judgements delivered by the Nuremberg and Tokyo trials in the aftermath of the Second World War laid the foundation stones for the establishment of an international criminal justice system. It was nearly five decades, however, before the United Nations Security Council was able to generate the solidarity and will required to create the *ad hoc* criminal tribunals that dealt with crimes arising from the conflicts in the Former Yugoslavia and Rwanda. Although these temporary courts established in 1993 and 1994, respectively, ushered in an epoch of international criminal justice, their creation by Security Council Resolutions, rather than by international treaty, and their tightly framed jurisdictional powers required significant steps forward by the community of nations if an independent and universal system for international criminal justice was to be created. The establishment of a permanent international criminal court removes the final strings in the protective veil of national sovereignty that has for so long shielded perpetrators of widespread and gross atrocities around the world from prosecution.

Although Ireland failed to ratify the Rome Statute in 2001, on April 1, 2002 it submitted its ratification in New York, realizing the Government's intent to be among the first 60 countries to ratify the Treaty. The ratification of the Rome Statute and its implementation requires national authorities in signatory states to undertake constitutional reform and legislative enactments in order for the State to ensure compliance with its international obligations. The referendum enabled the relevant government agencies to begin the ratification process.

While the work of the ICC builds upon the important precedents established by the *ad hoc* International Criminal Tribunals for the Former Yugoslavia and Rwanda, the ICC will have jurisdiction over crimes committed in the territories of all ratifying states and over crimes committed by nationals of ratifying states. Non-ratifying states may choose to accept the court's jurisdiction in some cases. The obligation to co-operate with the Court's investigations and prosecution rests with all State Parties. The Court, however, acts on the principle of complementarity, whereby it will only prosecute crimes in instances where individual states fail to exercise their obligation. Like the *ad hoc* Tribunals, the ICC has no enforcement powers and no police force; hence its work depends upon co-operation with national authorities.

The delayed ratification of the Rome Statute among signatory states is the result of the complex constitutional issues in many jurisdictions that must be resolved for the treaty to be given effect in national law. The Rome Statute transfers certain sovereign powers in the administration of criminal justice to an international tribunal, and its implementation into Irish law required a Constitutional amendment. The Irish Constitution, like many of its continental European counterparts, provides an immunity to the Head of State with respect of acts done in the exercise and performance of the powers and functions of his or her office, an immunity which conflicts with the terms of the Rome Statute. Lesser immunities are conferred on Members of Parliament by the Constitution, yet are sufficiently limited as to comply with the terms of the treaty. The constitutional immunity conferred upon the President, however, is in conflict with Article 27 of the Rome Statue, which states:

> "This Statute shall apply equally to all persons without any distinction based on official capacity. In particular, official capacity as a Head of State or a Government, a member of a Government or parliament, an elected representative or a government official shall in no case exempt a person from criminal responsibility under this Statute, nor shall it, in and of itself, constitute a ground for reduction of sentence. Immunities ... which may attach to the official capacity of a person, whether under national or international law, shall not bar the Court from exercising its jurisdiction over such a person." (Rome Statute, Art. 27(1)(2))

Under the Rome Statute, an official position does not preclude the jurisdiction of the Court, nor does it constitute a ground for the reduction of sentence.

The Irish government, as a State Party to the treaty, can refer a situation to the court for investigation, an option that may also be exercised by the Security Council. Additionally, the prosecutor of the ICC may on his or her own initiative start an investigation based on information received from non-governmental and individual sources. The Prosecutor of the ICC is elected by the State Parties that have ratified the Rome Statute.

In its analysis of the progress taken in implementing the Rome Statute submitted to the Council of Europe in 2001, the Department of Foreign Affairs indicated that it remains uncertain as to whether Ireland would grant immunity to the Head of State or Government accused of a crime under the Rome Statute, "where that person's State is not a party to the Rome Statute" and that further research into customary international law relating to Head of State immunity was required, highlighting the fact that this is an undeveloped area of law in the jurisdiction. To date, there is no case law or relevant legislation relating to

Head of State immunity in criminal cases. ("The Implications for Council of Europe Member States of the Ratification of the Rome Statute of the International Criminal Court," Strasbourg, 9 August 2001, Consult/ICC (2001) 16).

In addition to the area of immunities, legal issues also arise with respect to obligations to surrender Irish nationals to the custody of the ICC. With legislation enacted enabling co-operation with the International Criminal Tribunal for the Former Yugoslavia, a legislative model for parallel co-operation with the ICC is in place.

It is envisioned by the Department of Foreign Affairs that the expanded provisions of the crimes encompassed in Article 7 (crimes against humanity) and Article 8 (war crimes) cover a wide range of areas that are not currently included in Irish law and hence will require the creation of new offences in Irish Law. ("The Implications for Council of Europe Member States of the Ratification of the Rome Statute of the International Criminal Court," Strasbourg, 9 August 2001, Consult/ICC (2001) 16).

Pursuant to the terms of the treaty, following the 60th ratification of the Rome Statute it will enter into force on July 1, 2002 ("first day of the month after the 60th day following the date of the deposit of the 60th instrument of ratification, acceptance, approval or accession with the Secretary General of the United Nations, Article 126 Rome Statute) and the Court, which will be located in The Hague, is expected to be fully functional by mid-2003. Ratification prior to June 2000 enables complying states to be eligible to nominate a judge to the Court. The ICC will have 18 judges elected by ratifying State Parties, and it is anticipated that elections will take place during the second meeting of the Assembly of State Parties in early 2003. Although Ireland to date has no permanent judges at ICTR and ICTY, there is one serving Irish *ad litem* judge, Maureen Clarke, S.C. at the International Criminal Tribunal for the Former Yugoslavia.

21st Amendment to the Constitution: Abolition of the death penalty
Pursuant to a constitutional referendum, the death penalty was finally abolished under Irish law with the 21st Amendment of the Irish Constitution, which states: "The Oireachtas shall not enact any law providing for the imposition of the death penalty." Although the death penalty was removed from the statute books in July 1990 (Criminal Justice (Amendment) Act 1990) and the State had not executed the sentence of death since 1954, the provision for the death penalty, albeit unused, remained in the Constitution. The Constitutional Review Group recommended that the Constitution should prohibit the re-introduction of the death penalty, along with amendments to Article 28.3.3, which permits the declaration of a State of Emergency together with legislation in pursuance of a State of Emergency "which might authorise the imposition of a death penalty as it did in the past" (Constitution Review Group, Report of the Constitution Review Group (Dublin: Government Publications) 1996, pp.286).

The referendum, which passed with 62% of the voters in favour, brings Irish domestic law into closer harmony with its international treaty obligations. In 1983 Ireland signed and ratified Protocol No. 6 of the European Convention on Human Rights and Fundamental Freedoms concerning the abolition of the death penalty (done at Strasbourg, on April 28, 1983). In 1993 Ireland acceded to the Second Optional Protocol to the International Covenant on Civil and Political Rights, Aiming at the Abolition of the Death Penalty (adopted and proclaimed by General Assembly resolution 44/128 of December 15, 1989). Article 1 of the Second Optional Protocol creates the obligation upon State Parties not to execute any individual within their jurisdiction and to "take all necessary measures to abolish the death penalty within its jurisdiction."

INTERNATIONAL COVENANT FOR CIVIL AND POLITICAL RIGHTS

Offences Against the State Acts The decision of the Human Rights Committee in the case of *Kavanagh v. Ireland* (Communication No. 819/1998: Ireland 26/04/2001. CCPR/C/71/D/819/1) constitutes the fourth finding by an international tribunal that the State's implementation of the Offences Against the State Act (1939) is in violation of international human rights treaty obligations. In the "views" expressed by the Human Rights Committee, it considered that in the circumstances of Mr. Kavanagh's trial before the Special Criminal Court his right to equality under law, protected by Article 26 of the International Covenant on Civil and Political Rights (ICCPR), had been violated. This follows three judgements last year by the European Court of Human Rights, adding further pressure for amendments to, or arguably the repeal of, the 1939 Act.

While this was the first case brought to the Human Rights Committee concerning the operation of the Special Criminal Courts, it is not the first time that the body has condemned the legislation. In response to the Irish First and Second Reports Submitted Under Article 40 of the International Covenant on Civil and Political Rights, the Human Rights Committee recommended that the Act be amended. Earlier criticism of the emergency legislation had been made by the Human Rights Committee in its "Concluding Observations" on the compliance of the Irish government with its obligations under the ICCPR (Consideration of Reports submitted by States Parties Under Article 40 of the Covenant, Concluding Observations of the Human Rights Committee, Ireland (CCPR/C0/69/IRL; http://www.irlgov.ie/iveagh/policy/hr/hrcobs.htm). The non-binding observations commented on the 1939 Act under its section identifying "Principal subjects of concerns and recommendations". In paragraph 13 the Committee recommends that the jurisdiction of the Special Criminal Court should be ended, echoing its views expressed in 1993 in response to Ireland's First Report under the ICCPR. At that time, the Human Rights

Committee stated that there was no justification for the continued operation of the Special Criminal Court. (Concluding Observations of the Human Rights Committee: Ireland, 03/08/93. CCPR/C/79Add.21 (Concluding Observations/ Comments)) para. 11).

The shortcomings of the Offences Against the State Act (1939) were further highlighted last year with three judgements of the European Court of Human Rights. In *Heaney and McGuinness v. Ireland* (European Court of Human Rights, Application no. 34720/97, judgment delivered 21 December 2000), and *Quinn v. Ireland* (European Court of Human Rights, Application no. 36887/ 97, judgment delivered 21 December 2000), the European Court of Human Rights unanimously held that the applicants' conviction and imprisonment under section 52 of the 1939 Act was in violation of the right to a fair trial and presumption of innocence guaranteed under Article 6 of the European Convention on Human Rights and Fundamental Freedoms.

Although the limitations of international human rights bodies are commonly critiqued, the collective voice of the Human Rights Committee and the European Court of Human Rights is highlighting the capacity for the human rights treaty regime to complement domestic human rights mechanisms. The Government has been awaiting the recommendations of the Committee to Examine the Offences Against the States Acts, which was established in 1999 under the chairmanship of Mr. Justice Anthony Hederman, retired Judge of the Supreme Court and former Attorney General. The interim report of the Committee released this year foreshadowed the extensive legal analysis of the legislation and options for reform, which the Committee released in its Final Report in 2002. The Final Report is written against the backdrop of international human rights standards, as well as the changing demands of international security in the aftermath of the terrorist attack on the World Trade Centre on September 11, 2001. It will be discussed in next year's *Annual Review of Irish Law*. The role of international bodies in this process of legislative reform and debate is noteworthy.

In the case of *Kavanagh v. Ireland*, the discretion afforded to the DPP in bringing cases before the Special Criminal Court was found to be a violation of the ICCPR. The powers of the DPP set forth in the Offences Against the State Act (1939) allows the DPP to determine which cases he or she "thinks proper" should be tried before the Special Criminal Court. The Human Rights Committee considered this to constitute "unfettered discretion" of the DPP, permitting him or her to find that additional offences should be tried in the Special Criminal Court, other than those explicitly prescribed by law, simply upon a determination that a trial by the ordinary courts would be "inadequate" (*Kavanagh v. Ireland*, para. 10.2.). It then goes on to find that the State Party had failed to demonstrate that the decision to try the author before the Special Criminal Court was based on reasonable and objective grounds.

It is notable that the majority of the Human Rights Committee did not find that Mr. Kavanagh had suffered a violation of Article 14 of the ICCPR, which guarantees fairness of trial and equality of arms. Mr. Kavanagh claimed that the abridged safeguards, which operate under the Special Criminal Court system, deprived him of his right to have his trial by jury, as well as the possibility of preliminary examinations of witnesses. The complainant highlighted the denial of the right to cross-examination, as the assessment of credibility of several key witnesses would be critical to the outcome of his case. The Committee rejected this argument, stating that "trial before courts other than the ordinary courts is not necessarily, *per se*, a violation of the entitlement to a fair hearing and the facts of the present case do not show that there has been such a violation) (*Supra,* para. 10.1) However, five of the sixteen Members of the Committee signed jointly a separate individual opinion, which considered the principle of equality, enshrined in the first para. of Article 14 to also have been violated. They argue that the principle of equality in the judicial system "goes beyond and is additional to" the specified fair trial principles included in Article 14 which govern the fairness of trials, proof of guilt, procedural and evidential safeguards, rights of appeal and review, and double jeopardy. They conclude: "The principle of equality is violated where all persons accused of committing the very same offence are not tried by the normal courts having jurisdiction in the matter, but are tried by a special court at the discretion of the Executive. This remains so whether the exercise of discretion by the Executive is or is not reviewable by the courts." (Individual Opinion of the Committee Members Louis Henkin, Rajsoomer Lallah, Cecilia Medina Quiroga, Ahmed Tawfik Khalil and Patrick Vella, *Kavanagh v. Ireland*, supra, para. 1-2.)

In spite of the split between the majority of the Committee and the 5 individual members as to whether the different treatment of individuals having committed like offences within the justice system violates the overarching principle of equality in Article 14 of the ICCPR, the Committee is unanimous that there is a violation of the right of equal treatment under Article 26. This is on the grounds of the excess discretion afforded to the DPP, which does not require the provision of specific or objective reasons for his or her determination that an individual be tried in the Special Criminal Court.

While the Human Rights Committee, as the monitoring body of the ICCPR, is not a judicial body and its views are not formally binding upon State Parties, compliance with its decisions is understood be in accordance with a State's obligations under the ICCPR. The Human Rights Committee is composed of 18 human rights experts nominated by States but serving in their personal capacity (Art. 28(3) ICCPR). It is the interpreting body for obligations under the ICCPR, which are legally binding upon State Parties. (S. Joseph *et al, The International Covenant on Civil and Political Rights* (Oxford: OUP, 2000), pp.13-15, *see also* L. Heffernan, "A Comparative View of Individual Petition Procedures under the European Convention on Human Rights and the International Covenant on Civil and Political Rights" (1997) 19 *Human Rights Quarterly* 78). The Committee states that the Irish government has the duty to provide the author of the complaint with an effective remedy, and also to "ensure that similar violations do not occur in the future: it should ensure that persons are not tried before the Special Criminal Court *unless reasonable and objective criteria for the decision are provided"* [emphasis added].

The *Kavanagh* opinion strengthens the body of international jurisprudence calling for reforms in the emergency legislation in order to bring Irish law into normative harmony with the increasingly more defined universal standards for civil and political rights. The marginal status of international human rights treaties in Irish law, however, is highlighted by outcome of Mr. Kavanagh's application for leave to apply for relief by way of judicial review subsequent to the favourable outcome of his case before the Human Rights Committee *In the Matter of Article 40.4 of the Constitution and in the Matter of Habeas Corpus Act, 1782 and In the Matter of the International Covenant of Civil and Political Rights; Joseph Kavanagh v. The Governor of Mountjoy Prison, The Special Criminal Court, The Director of Public Prosecutions, The Minister for Justice Equality and Law Reform, Ireland and the Attorney General,* High Court, June 29, 2001. Arising out of the decision of the Human Rights Committee and by way of judicial review, the applicant sought an Order of Certiorari quashing his earlier conviction as well as a declaration that section 47(2) of the Offences Against the State Act 1939 is incompatible with the ICCPR and "is accordingly to repugnant to the Constitution in particular, Articles 29.2 and 3 thereof."

Mr. Kavanagh's application for leave to apply for judicial review is constructed around a range of legal arguments aiming to give legal authority to an international human rights convention that is not incorporated into domestic law. This is the familiar strategy of litigants urging courts to follow precedential decisions of the European Court of Human Rights, which like the ICCPR still remains to be incorporated into Irish law. Under the Irish Constitution, international and domestic law constitute two discrete legal regimes. While in many civil law countries which have adopted a monist system, international human rights treaties are automatically incorporated into domestic law, in Ireland whether a treaty shall form part of Irish law is a decision resting solely with the Oireachtas. The obstacles for Mr. Kavanagh in this application for judicial review were considerable, as the Human Rights Committee, unlike the European Court of Human Rights, is not even a judicial body. In his refusal of the application, Finnegan J. rejects Mr. Kavanagh's submission that the ICCPR is justiciable at suit of the plaintiff. Mr. Kavanagh argues that while not incorporated into domestic law by statute, the ICCPR is part of customary international law, and hence part of common law. Citing *Re O'Laighleis* [1960] I.R. 93 at 124, Finnegan J. holds that Article 29 applies only to the relations between states and confers no rights upon individuals. He also rejects the characterization by the Applicant of the Human Rights Committee as a "competent judicial tribunal" and states that its "expression of views" have "the moral authority of the Committee but nothing more than that" as it is not a Court under the Constitution and without a constitutional amendment cannot affect the administration of justice in the Courts established under the Constitution."

The judgment also provides extensive consideration of the doctrine of "legitimate expectation." The applicant argued that the ratification of the ICCPR and its Optional Protocol by the State "created a legitimate expectation that its executive and judicial branches would adhere to the Covenant's requirements" and where the Committee communicates its views of a violation of an ICCPR right, the "State would promptly take steps to enforce the right which has been violated and grant the victim redress." Finnegan J., relying upon the legal reasoning of the judgments of Mason C.J. and Dean J. in the Australian High Court of Appeal, *Minister of State for Immigration and Ethnic Affairs v. Teoh* (1994-1995) 183 C.L.R. 272, states that "the judicial development of the common law must not be seen as a back door means of importing an unincorporated convention..."

As Kavanagh's unsuccessful application for judicial review confirms, entrenched in the constitutionally structured dualist system the Irish courts are not legally positioned to ensure normative harmony between international and domestic human rights. Absent a whole scale incorporation of all international human rights treaties to which the State is party, this burden falls instead upon the shoulders of Irish policy makers and legislators. Should legal normative harmony be an objective pursued by the State, as might be inferred from the commitments it has undertaken in the *Good Friday Agreement*, along with its international human rights profile, there is a call for a systematic and comprehensive analysis of the potential mechanisms available to the government for implementing human rights obligations. The strategy employed by the Norwegian government in 1989 when it agreed in principle to make binding international human rights treaties part of Norwegian law offers an instructive model for a more coherent approach to the State's human rights obligations. An appointed Committee provided an extensive report addressing, *inter alia*, the methods of implementing treaties in Norwegian law, a survey of the position of human rights conventions in other Nordic and Western European jurisdictions, and the criteria for determining which human rights treaties should be incorporated into domestic law. A detailed assessment was provided of the effects that the embodiment of human rights conventions could be expected to have in domestic law, with considerations ranging from the symbolic implications of constitutional provisions, to the practical ramifications of the proposed measures on the work of civil servants, law makers and the courts. The report contained legislative proposals with commentary, along with more long term suggestions for the promotion of human rights, providing recommendations to address the need for more accessible source material, and enhanced knowledge of human rights through mandatory course offerings of university curricula. (*Lovgivning om menneskerettigheter, Norges Offentlige Utredninger*, 1993:18, pp.193-199).

The *Report of the Constitution Review Group* provided a cursory consideration of select international human rights treaties in relationship to fundamental rights enshrined in the Constitution. Although the incorporation process for the European Convention on Human Rights is well underway, it is unfortunate that it was not preceded by the rigorous preparatory analysis that the Norwegian government undertook when confronting a similar task. The nascent Human Rights Commission is well positioned to carry out such valuable work.

INTERNATIONAL COVENANT ON ECONOMIC, SOCIAL AND CULTURAL RIGHTS

The Committee on Economic, Social and Cultural Rights officially disseminated a "List of issues to be taken up in connection with the consideration of the second periodic report of Ireland concerning the rights referred to in Articles 1-15 of the International Covenant for Economic, Social, and Cultural Rights (IESCR) (E/1990/6/Add.29). (List of Issues: Ireland. 18/05/2001. E/C.12/Q/IRE/2.) The list of concerns expressed by the Committee provides an interesting insight into the role of the Committee and the focus of its agenda with respect to assessing Ireland's compliance with the international human rights treaty. In 1999 the Committee on Economic, Social and Cultural Rights issued its 'Concluding Observations' on Ireland's first national report submitted under the International Covenant for Economic, Social and Cultural Rights (reprinted in International Covenant for Economic, Social and Cultural Rights, Second National Report by Ireland, Department of Foreign Affairs (2000) at Appendix IV).

The lists of queries for the Irish government that is set forth by the Committee provides an interesting example of the "constructive dialogue" that the body attempts to establish with States in order to enhance the enforcement of the rights protected under the treaty. Under the IESCR, there is a striking absence of enforcement provisions, and without an Optional Protocol, like that of its sister Convention, the ICCPR, there is no right of petition for individuals alleging breaches of IESCR rights. Because of the complicated nature of promoting and protecting economic, social and cultural rights as compared to civil and political rights, it is the quality and impact of this dialogue that will mark the success that this marginalised human rights body has on State Parties to the IESCR.

There are several types of questions set forth that are a follow-up to the *Committee's Concluding Observations* in 1999. These are divided into three sections, the first requesting general information, the second pertaining to issues related to the general provisions of the IESCR in Articles 1 through 5, and the third pertaining to specific substantive rights that are recognized in the Covenant in Articles 6-15. The structured engagement with the Irish authorities manifested in this document demonstrates a multi-stranded approach to rights protection. It requires, on the one hand, that the government report on its success in ratifying the International Convention on the Elimination of All Forms of Racial Discrimination, the enactment of the Employment Equality Bill and Equal Status Bill, and to state its position on repealing reservations to the IESCR, which deal with non-discrimination and compulsory education. Other queries, however, mandate a more in-depth and critical reporting by governmental sources. Central among the general queries, as well as among those pertaining to specific rights, the State is not only asked about the implementation of certain programmes, such as Partnership 2000, Government Strategy on Travellers and the National Poverty Strategy, but is also asked to assess their effectiveness. Some queries further ask authorities to provide views on areas where a specified policy could be strengthened. This focus highlights the "programmatic" nature of economic, social and cultural rights that are promoted and protected through non-legislative policies as well as through the enforcement of justiciable rights.

Other queries require that the state provide extensive data, which would reveal the varying levels to which economic, social and cultural rights are realized in the State. For instance, statistical information is required on the number of "negotiation licences" granted and denied that are required for trade unions and employers' associations to be able to enter into negotiations on pay and conditions of employment; on asylum seekers disaggregated by sex and age; on domestic violence; on the incidence of child labour; on annual percentage increases in rents and house prices (with a further query as to whether data are available on housing-related costs as a percentage of income); and on suicide and literacy rates for children and adults for the general population, and for Travellers, disaggregated by sex.

More controversial questions are included in the overall request for information–providing a possible insight into the views of Members of the Committee. A pointed question is included which asks about how the new "Relationships and Sexuality Education" is being taught in schools and whether the "initiative met with significant resistance from parents, teachers or the Catholic Church?" Further information is requested on mortality rates arising from illegal abortions and on whether there is case law with respect to prosecutions.

Internationally, although a rights based approach has been adopted by a number of aid organizations, the are very few non-governmental human rights organizations that exclusively address economic, social and cultural rights. This is in stark contrast to the large number of international and grassroots organizations whose mandate covers civil and political rights. In Ireland, while there are several prominent organizations that deal with economic and social justice issues, with the notable exception of the Commission for Justice and Peace none have availed of the State reporting process under the IESCR as an additional forum for increasing pressure on the government to improve the realization of IESCR rights in line with the increased resources enjoyed by the State in this period of economic prosperity. One of the first questions presented to the government by the Committee asks about the mandate of the Human Rights Commission and the priority that it attaches to economic, social and cultural rights in its programme of work. It remains to be seen if the Human Rights Commission will contribute its expertise in this area of rights protection.

The government's response to the 37 questions put forth by the Committee was received on 8 March 2002 and provides a comprehensive overview of state progress in tackling some of the most controversial areas of economic and social policy. It will be examined in *Annual Review of Irish Law 2002*.

EUROPEAN COURT OF HUMAN RIGHTS

There was a downward trend in 2001 in the number of provisional files opened against Ireland at the European Court of Human Rights, with 51 files, as compared to 61 in 2000. However, the overall number of applications registered reflected only a minor downturn, with 16 in 2001, as opposed to 18 registered last year. (Council of Europe, European Court of Human Rights, Survey of Activities, 2001, VII. Statistical Tables by State) Compared to other State Parties to the European Convention on Human Rights, the Irish record at the Court is a strong one. It remains to be determined whether the absence of a sizeable volume of complaints is reflective of advanced constitutional protections in Ireland, or rather the lack of will or knowledge by practitioners to utilize the mechanisms available under the ECHR. If one compares the small number of applications that are ultimately deemed admissible (this year there was only one) with the number of claims admitted against Scandinavian countries, then Ireland's record appears less remarkable. The temptation to contrast the Irish record in Strasbourg to that of the United Kingdom leads to misleading conclusions. While Ireland has had 6 admissible cases from 1999-2001, the United Kingdom has had 98. When one considers the dramatic differential in populations, in conjunction with the absence of a constitution in the United Kingdom, these figures seem less useful as a barometer of the comparative standards of rights protection in the two jurisdictions. Looking instead to the records of the Nordic countries, a different scenario emerges. The final number of applications admitted against Finland, Sweden and Denmark for the past three years totals 15, 8, and 13 respectively. These are all higher than those declared admissible for Ireland. Norway had six applications against it declared admissible, and statistically is the most similar to Ireland. Like Ireland, it was also among the last of the Council of Europe states to incorporate the European Convention on Human Rights into domestic law.

The most telling statistics from the European Court of Human Rights relate to the annual number of provisional files opened against State Parties. This figure pertains to the number of complainants that have taken preliminary steps to file an application with the Court in Strasbourg. Although only a fraction of these provisional files are typically registered, it reflects to some degree the extent of the awareness and accessibility of Strasbourg to lawyers and victims in national systems. For instance, although Denmark has a population not that much greater than Ireland's, three to four times as many provisional files are opened against Denmark than against Ireland. Yet, in spite of the increase in approaches to the Court with specific grievances, the Court admitted only three more applications against the Danish government. More strikingly, although 13 applications against Sweden were determined admissible, in individual years during this time period between seven and 10 times as many provisional files were opened at the Court against Sweden than against Ireland. *(Supra)* One can infer from these data that the legal communities in the Scandinavian countries are more inclined to approach Strasbourg than their Irish counterpart.

With the forthcoming incorporation of the European Convention on Human Rights into Irish law and an increased familiarity with Strasbourg case law and procedures, there may be an increase in the number of cases against Ireland in the court. One of the disappointments of 2001 was the delayed introduction of the European Convention on Human Rights Bill, 2000. It is anticipated that the Bill will be enacted in 2002. The relevance of this regional human rights protection regime is likely to become far more central for practitioners and policy makers after incorporation.

The doctrine of state immunity under Irish law sustained scrutiny by the Grand Chamber of the European Court of Human Rights when its application by the courts in the case of *McElhinney v. Ireland* (2002) 34 E.H.R.R. 114 was found by a majority of 12 votes to five not to violate the right to a fair trial protected under Article 6 of the European Convention on Human Rights. The applicant claimed that a member of the United Kingdom armed forces on Republic of Ireland territory assaulted him. The Supreme Court held that there was no doubt that the soldier accused of the assault was "acting in the sphere of governmental or sovereign activity, rendering the acts complained of *jure imperii.*" After reviewing international conventions and state practice, along with Irish case law, Hamilton C.J., with O'Flaherty J. and Blayney J. in agreement, dismissed McElhinney's appeal, stating "I am not satisfied that it is a principle of public international law that the immunity granted to sovereign states should be restricted by making them liable in respect to tortious acts, committed on their behalf by their servant or agent, causing personal injuries to the person affected by such act or omission, when such act or omission is committed *jure imperii* ..." (*McElhinney v. Ireland,* December 15, 1995). He submitted in his petition to the European Court of Human Rights that by invoking and applying the doctrine of sovereign immunity, the United Kingdom and the Irish courts denied him the right of judicial determination of his compensation claim arising out of the allegations of assault. In his application on admissibility, McElhinney complained of a violation of Articles 5 (right to liberty and security), 6 (right to a fair trial) and 13 (right to an effective remedy). He also complained of discrimination, invoking Article 14, because the British courts would not have applied the same doctrine in an action for assault committed by an Irish soldier in the United Kingdom. The Grand Chamber decided that the complaints under Articles 5 and Articles 13 were manifestly ill-founded, yet his complaint under Articles 6 and 14 raised serious questions of fact and law that are of such complexity that their determination should depend on an examination on the merits. Although the Article 14 claim of discrimination was found to be admissible, the applicant before the Grand Chamber did not pursue it.

In considering the application on its merits, the Court states that the right of access to court under Article 6 of the European Convention on Human Rights is not absolute and subject to limitations. It then establishes that in its opinion the granting of sovereign immunity to a State in civil proceedings pursues the legitimate aim of complying with international law to promote comity and good relations between States and that the generally recognised rule of public international law on State immunity cannot in principle be regarded as a disproportionate restriction on the right of access to court as embodied in Article 6(1) of the ECHR. Although the judgment accepts that there is a trend in international law towards limiting State immunity in respect of personal injury caused by an act or omission within the forum State, it asserts that this practice is by no means universal, and adds the qualification that this trend tends, in distinction to the facts of the *McEhlinney* case, to apply to "insurable" personal injury, rather than to incidents that relate to the core area of State sovereignty, which would apply in this case to the acts of a soldier on foreign territory. In delivering its judgment the Court also notes that it would appear that while the doctrine of sovereign immunity barred access to courts in Ireland, there was no evidence before the Grand Chamber that there would be any procedural or other bar to bringing an action in Northern Ireland.

This year one application, *Bosphorous Hava Yollari Turizm ve Ticaret AS against Ireland* was determined to be admissible by the fourth section of the European Court of Human Rights (European Court of Human Rights (fourth section), Decision as to the Admissibility of Application no. 45036/98, delivered September 13, 2001). The forthcoming decision on the merits will consider whether the impounding of the complainant's leased aircraft in Ireland constitutes a violation of the right to property enshrined in Article 1 of Protocol No. 1. The applicant in the case is a Turkish airline charter company, which leased an aircraft in 1992 from JAT, the national airline of the former Yugoslavia. This case arises from the adoption by the United Nations Security Council of a Resolution imposing sanctions on the Former Yugoslavia (UNSC Resolution 757 (1992)), which was subsequently implemented by a European Community Council Regulation (EC Regulation 1432/92).

The outcome of this case warrants close consideration. Firstly, as the Court concludes, it raises complex and serious issues under Article 1 of Protocol

One. Secondly, beyond the narrow ambit of the interpretation of Protocol One, for Irish and international lawyers it addresses the tensions that arise in current legal practice when international, regional and national legal standards are expected to converge, but instead may collide. This case deals with the balance between the fate of a Turkish air charter company, which claims its airline business was destroyed as a result of the actions of the Irish government, and the measures undertaken by the international community to stop the devastating conflict in the Former Yugoslavia and its widespread atrocities. The legal actors in this dispute highlight the interaction between international legal and political bodies – the United Nations Security Council, the UN Sanctions Committee, and the UN legal office – and regional ones – the European Community, European Court of Justice and the European Court of Human Rights – and how these international and regional norms are translated on the domestic level, by the governments of Ireland and Turkey, in the first instance, and then by the High and Supreme Courts of the State. As the Irish High Court acted pursuant to an opinion sought of the European Court of Justice, the forthcoming judgment will provide the opportunity to witness how both regional tribunals balance competing rights.

1951 CONVENTION RELATING TO THE STATUS OF REFUGEES

The competing agendas of the protection of refugees and the control of immigration continue to remain in the arena of legal and political controversy. 2001 sees the field of refugee protection in the State in a curious position. The Courts are being called upon with increasing frequency to define the standards and norms that shall apply to refugee law in the jurisdiction. Within the next three years, one will be looking also to European Court of Justice for rulings on the standards governing substantive and procedural refugee law. The directives and regulations that are now being proposed by the European Commission will soon be adopted to construct the Common Asylum System for the European Union.(*See* Communication from the Commission to the Council and the European Parliament, Scoreboard to review Progress on the Creation of an Area of "Freedom, Security and Justice" in the European Union, COM (2000) 167 final; Amended Proposal for a Council Directive on minimum standards on procedures in Member States for granting and withdrawing refugee status, COM (2002) 326; Proposal for a Council Regulation establishing the criteria and mechanisms for determining the Member State responsible for examining an asylum application lodged in one of the Member States by a third country national, COM (2001) 447 final; Proposal for a Council Directive on minimum standards for the qualification and status of third country nationals and stateless persons as refugees, or as persons who otherwise need international protection, COM (2001) 510 final; Amended proposal for a Council Directive on the right to family reunification; COM (2000) 624 final; Proposal for a Council Directive laying down minimum standards on the reception of applicants for asylum in Member States, COM (2001) 181 final.)

While many of the cases seeking judicial review in 2001 deal with matters of statutory interpretation and administrative law, there are two cases that raise interesting issues from the perspective of international refugee law. The first addresses the area of humanitarian leave to remain, and the second, manifestly unfounded claims.

The absence of legislative criteria for the granting of humanitarian leave to remain for those asylum seekers denied refugee status creates a lacuna in domestic refugee law that mirrors the situation throughout many jurisdictions in Europe. Humanitarian leave to remain is a form of subsidiary protection. As asylum regimes tightened throughout the continent, this complementary status was given with increased frequency while refugee recognition rates plummeted. The decline in refugee recognition rates in developed countries is attributed by authorities to the abundance of weak applications. The use by authorities of humanitarian leave as an alternative to refugee status may also reflect the changing protection needs of modern migrants forced to flee from their countries of origin. In the context of contemporary conflicts, individuals fleeing persecution may not fulfil the narrow criteria of the 1951 Convention Relating to the Status of Refugees, which was drafted in the context of the population displacements, which followed the Second World War. Hence, in circumstances where governments do not consider it possible to return an individual to their country of origin for reasons of safety, or broader humanitarian considerations, legislative provisions providing for complementary forms of protection represent an important safety net. There is another less altruistic explanation, whereby the granting of humanitarian status over full refugee status in many states generally entails a lessened commitment to the recipient by the host state. For example, these lessened commitments may relate to the length of time that an individual has leave to remain in the state without a reassessment of their situation, and rights to family reunification and employment. While some Member States have explicitly defined legislative criteria for designating humanitarian leave to remain, others leave its granting to the discretion of governmental authorities.

In Ireland, there is no procedure within the refugee determination system for individuals to automatically have their applications considered for humanitarian leave. Although this would be cost-efficient for authorities, the current framework requires that consideration by the Minister of humanitarian considerations be examined separately at the stage of deportation. Under section 3(6) of the Illegal Immigrants (Trafficking Act 2000), "humanitarian considerations" is one of eleven criteria that the Minister shall have regard to in determining whether to make a Deportation Order in relation to a person. With the current ruling by the Supreme Court in *P v. Minister for Justice Equality and Law Reform.* [2001] I.E.S.C. 53 (July 30, 2001), it is unlikely, absent legislative amendment, that the decisions of the Minister granting humanitarian leave will offer concrete guidance on the criteria applied in reaching his or her determinations. Hardiman J. found the current practice of providing denied asylum seekers with standardized communications without detailed reasons supporting the decision to be adequate. This case illuminates the ambiguity surrounding criteria for subsidiary forms of protection and the protection gap it creates in the Refugee Act 1996 [amended].

The full implementation of the Refugee Act 1996 [amended] in November 2000 meant that a number of cases that came before the Courts seeking judicial review in 2001 concern the interim refugee determination procedures set up by the *Hope Hanlon* letter. These procedures are set out in a communication of December 1997, amended in March 1998, sent by the Minister to the Representative of the United Nations High Commissioner for Refugees at the time. Criteria and procedures for manifestly unfounded claims contained in the *Hope Hanlon* letter are now in section 12 of the Refugee Act 1996 [amended]. The significant distinction between claims designated as "manifestly unfounded" and other asylum applications is that with the former, claimants do not have the right to an oral hearing upon appeal. Although considering the procedures set out under the *Hope Hanlon* letter, the decision by Finnegan J. upholds the current practice by finding that there is no entitlement to an oral hearing on appeal for "manifestly unfounded" claims. *In the Matter of the Illegal Immigrants (Trafficking) Act 2000 between Valerie Zgnat'ev and The Minister for Justice Equality and Law Reform, James Nicholson Seating as the Appeals Authority Ireland and the Attorney General*, High Court, July 17, 2001. In his careful deliberation, Finnegan J. reaches his conclusion after consideration of the status of "manifestly unfounded" procedures in international and regional law, with particular reference to the position of the United Nations High Commissioner for Refugees (UNHCR). The judgment mistakenly identifies the origin of "manifestly unfounded" procedures with the UNHCR Executive Committee Conclusions on International Protection no. 30/1983. Manifestly unfounded procedures were being used by the Swedish authorities in the 1950s and made a reappearance in domestic asylum systems when Europe began to experience a climb in applications in the 1980s. Drawing from the standards on manifestly unfounded procedures set forth in the UNHCR Executive Committee Conclusion cited above, the judgment upholds the denial of an oral hearing on appeal on the grounds that they "only apply to applications which are so obviously without a foundation as not to merit full examination at every level of the procedure and which are clearly fraudulent or not related to the criteria for the granting of refugee status under the Convention." This formula clearly accepts the abridgement of safeguards in circumstances that are circumscribed by tightly defined criteria. This judgment is flawed in that it fails to consider whether the criteria for manifestly unfounded claims, set forth in the *Hope Hanlon* letter, satisfy the requirement that such claims are "obviously without foundation" or "clearly fraudulent." There are two criteria included in the *Hope Hanlon* letter that are clearly overbroad and do not meet the narrow standards set by the UNHCR Executive Committee. Among the grounds upon which it may be determined that an application is manifestly unfounded, is an applicant's provision "of clearly insufficient details to substantiate an application." Another ground is where an "applicant is a national of or has a right of residence in a state party to the Geneva Convention in respect of which the applicant has failed to adduce evidence of persecution." (*Hope Hanlon Letter*, December 10, 1997, as amended March 28, 1998, para. 14 (a)(j)) The mere absence of sufficient detail in an interview, which commonly has trans-cultural and linguistic obstacles to communication, and the failure to generally adduce evidence of persecution, may indeed constitute grounds for rightly denying an asylum claim in the first instance. However, in the context of the dynamics of asylum determinations, these grounds are hardly reflective of claims that are obviously without foundation or clearly fraudulent.

HUMAN RIGHTS COMMISSION

The birth of the Human Rights Commission has been marked by an inexcusably prolonged labour. Almost 12 months after the controversial process of selecting the Commissioners to serve, and the decision to expand the number of Commissioners from eight to 14 in response to an outcry from the NGO community, the government did manage to pass amending legislation (Human Rights Commission (Amendment) Act 2001). Initially, the amendment for expansion of the Human Rights Commission was attached to the European Convention on Human Rights Bill 2001. This approach had two detrimental effects. The first was that it delayed the creation of the Commission, which required only simple amending legislation. The second effect of attaching the creation of the Commission to the passage of the ECHR incorporation bill was that it would have prevented the Commission from contributing to the discussion on incorporation-arguably one of the most important current human rights developments. In 2002, the Commission did present a brief commentary on the European Convention on Human Rights Bill. With the large number of Commissioners and the vast expertise they bring with them, the document is disappointingly thin in its analysis. As the institution was only set up in November 2001, the body played no role in human rights debates for the year. It is hoped that it will soon take large strides towards catching up with its Northern Irish counterpart in the breadth and depth of its engagement with human rights issues in the State.

CONCLUSION

The disappointments of 2001 in the area of human rights arise from delay. The Review Committee of the Offences Against the State Acts 1939-1998 did not offer its final report for public debate and reform. It was published in 2002, three years after the Committee's creation and after four decisions were delivered by the Human Rights Committee and the European Court of Human Rights finding provisions of the legislation to be in violation of treaty obligations. Four years after the signing of the Good Friday Agreement, Ireland remains the final state within the Council of Europe yet to incorporate the European Convention on Human Rights. In spite of the slow progress in the introduction and passage of the legislation, there has been no authoritative body offering a comprehensive and

focussed analysis of the implementation of human rights instruments into Irish law. The near doubling of the number of Human Rights Commissioners, and the energy expended in the battle concerning their nominations, has seemingly not inspired any visible productivity on the part of this much heralded institution. It remains to be seen if the Human Rights Commission will fulfil its mandate and serve as the central conduit for the convergence of domestic and international human rights law in Ireland.

Information Law and the Ombudsman

ESTELLE FELDMAN, Trinity College, Dublin

CONSUMER INFORMATION

(S.I. No. 15 of 2001) Life Assurance (Provision of Information) Regulations 2001 require suppliers of life assurance to provide information to clients resident in Ireland before they sign a proposal or an application form in respect of life assurance and also throughout the term of the policy. The information is to include details of the policy, its appropriateness to the needs of the client, early encashment consequences, projected benefits and charges, intermediary/sales remuneration, review of premium, cancellation rights, together with other general and additional information, some of which is already subject to disclosure pursuant to the Third Life Assurance Framework Directive (92/96/EEC) as implemented by S.I. No. 360 of 1994.

S.I. No. 339 of 2001 European Communities (Consumer Information on Fuel Economy and Co, Emissions of New Passenger Cars) Regulations 2001 give effect to Council Directive 1999/94/EEC relating to the availability of consumer information on fuel economy and CO_2 emissions in respect of the marketing of new passenger cars. The regulations specify the requirements for consumer information to be displayed on new car labels and posters at points of sale. A consumer information guide is required to be produced by an authorised body (the Society of the Motor Industry of Ireland) and to be made available centrally and at all points of sale. Promotional literature and material must also include relevant consumer information and may not contain information which may confuse customers.

INFORMATION COMMISSIONER

All statutory references in this section are to the Freedom of Information Act 1997 unless otherwise stated. The Act has been previously considered in *Annual Review of Irish Law1997*, p.2 *et seq*; *Annual Review of Irish Law1999*, p.1 *et seq*; p.350 *et seq*; *Annual Review of Irish Law2000*, p. 273 *et seq*. In addition to hard copy all documents referred to may be found at the Information Commissioner's website http://www.irlgov.ie/oic unless otherwise stated.

Investigation into compliance by public bodies   An investigation by the Information Commissioner into the practices and procedures adopted by public bodies generally for the purpose of compliance with the provisions of the Act was conducted in accordance with section 36. The report is included in full in *Annual Report of the Information Commissioner 2001,* Chapter 6. In compliance with section 36(2) the first investigation had to be carried out not later than three years after the commencement of the Act. The report is based on an examination of twelve public bodies spread across the civil service, local authorities and health boards, concentrating for the most part on those bodies, which have received the largest number of requests for access to records (section 7) since the commencement of the Act.

The importance of these findings should not be underestimated. Certainly legal practitioners for whom the Act is assuming increasing importance might find cause for concern in comments such as: "The Act is complex and often requires the balancing of competing interests. It contains twelve detailed exemption and exclusion sections which, unfortunately, ... can be seen simply as twelve opportunities to refuse access." Moreover, those practitioners representing public bodies, of which there are now some 350 covered by the Act, would be advised to pay particular attention to the Commissioner's findings in relation to failure to give reasons, see below, 393 and *Courts Service* case, 403 *et seq.*, and the preparation of accurate schedules in respect of requested records, see below, 393 *et seq.*, and *EH v Information Commissioner*, 399 *et seq.*,

It can be noted that of the four High Court Appeals decided in 2001, see 396 *et seq.*, only one, which was a delayed judgment of 2000, does not relate to fundamental legal procedures. The Courts Service was one of the appellants in an appeal relating *inter alia* to a request for access to the book of evidence. Other procedural issues considered include discovery, *in camera* proceedings and records of the Director of Public Prosecutions. All of these fall to be considered under exemptions to the right of access conferred by the Act.

Openness and transparency   The Commissioner concluded that generally the Act has brought about major gains in terms of greater openness and transparency notwithstanding a high rate of refusal of requests. He found the level of refusals a little surprising in the context of a regime which is designed to give access to information to the greatest extent possible, subject to the requirement of the public interest and the right of privacy. The Commissioner also found an unnecessary use of exemption clauses having examined specifically section 19 (meetings of the Government), section 20 (deliberations of public bodies) and section 26 (information obtained in confidence):

> "It is possible to make a prima facie case for exemption under these or other provisions in relation to many records but whether it is worth doing so, in some cases, is an entirely different matter. In my view the cause of greater openness is not served by trying to rely on an exemption to refuse information simply because the exemption is there or because,

while the record sought is innocuous, it is feared that release will, from the public body's point of view, create an unfortunate precedent", *Annual Report of the Information Commissioner 2001*, Chapter 6.

The Commissioner discovered widespread failure, when refusing information, to give reasons that meet the requirements of the Act (section 8(2)(d)). The Act is intended to provide access to information held by public bodies to the greatest extent possible consistent with the public interest and the right to privacy (Long Title). Release should be the norm; refusal the exception. In this context, it is, according to the Commissioner, hardly too much to expect a public body which is refusing access to go to the trouble of properly documenting that refusal.

Effectiveness of internal review In practice, based on figures supplied by all public bodies for 2000, about 7% of initial decisions proceed to internal review (section 14). However, that internal review is not fully effective in many public bodies. Some of the internal review decisions examined in the course of the investigation bore all the hall marks of rubber stamping - there was no evidence of independent consideration of the issues and little or no attempt to improve the explanations given to the requester. Even in public bodies where there was no evidence of rubber stamping, a significant number of the internal review decisions examined in the course of the investigation, almost 40%, did not meet the full requirements of the Act in terms of quality of response. Without wishing to overstate the problems in this area, the Commissioner expressed concern that on a second attempt and even with the input of a more senior official, some public bodies are failing to accord requesters their full statutory rights by either releasing the information requested or by providing clear and comprehensive explanations for not doing so.

Failure to give reasons and prepare schedules of records The Act obliges a public body which is refusing a request (*e.g.* section 8) whether wholly or partly, to give the requester a statement of the reasons for the refusal and, other than in cases where those provisions of the Act which permit a refusal to confirm or deny the existence of a record are being invoked (*e.g.* section 19(5)), to specify: any provision of the Act pursuant to which the request is refused; the findings on any material issues relevant to the decision; and particulars of any matter relating to the public interest taken into consideration for the purposes of the decision.

Where information is refused, statements of reasons, which fail to meet the requirements of the Act, are reasonably common. The sample would suggest that such failures occur in about 50% of cases. Without a proper statement of reasons a requester cannot make an informed decision as to whether to seek a further review. There is clear evidence that unnecessary reviews by the Commissioner are being generated as a result of the failure to give proper statements of reasons.

The Commissioner notes that the Central Policy Unit of the Department of Finance, which is responsible for training personnel in freedom of information procedures, has advised public bodies that a statement of reasons should show a connection, supported by a chain of reasoning, between the decision and the decision maker's findings on material issues. It has also strongly recommended that, other than in cases involving no more than a few records, decision makers should prepare a schedule listing the records sequentially by number and containing the following information: the date of the record; the title of the document or the name of its author or addressee; a brief but sufficient description of the record or its contents to show a prima facie claim for exemption; the exemption claimed; and where the claim relates to parts of a record, a clear indication of the parts involved.

In the case of the Department of Justice, Equality and Law Reform, where adequate explanations had not been given in a number of the cases examined, two particular problems were noted. The first was a tendency to rely on an exemption but to give no indication as to why it was appropriate in the particular case. The second was failure to provide a schedule of the records at issue. The failure to provide a schedule meant that in some cases the requester had no indication of how many records were being refused and often was given little real information about the nature of the records held by the Department.

Records management   The Act does not impose specific requirements on public bodies in relation to records management, although provision has been made in section 15(5) for the making of regulations by the Minister for Finance in relation to this matter. Despite the absence of specific requirements it is clear that proper records management is vital to the success of the Act. Unfortunately, on the basis of the current sample, the Commissioner found that record keeping in public bodies is not of a particularly high standard.

Failure to meet time limits   With a few exceptions, the Commissioner found procedures adopted for the processing of requests under the Act have been satisfactory. This conclusion is based on the findings that most public bodies process most requests within the statutory deadline (not later than four weeks: section 8). Failures that went beyond the occasional breach were noted in the case of three public bodies - the Department of Education and Science, the Department of Health and Children and, to a lesser extent, the Department of Justice, Equality and Law Reform. In the case of the Department of Health and Children, failure to take the initial decision within the deadline appears to happen often enough to give the Commissioner cause for serious concern.

The most serious problem is in the Department of Education and Science. It is of interest to note that the Department has records of over 41,000 former residents of 59 industrial and reformatory schools of which about 13,000 are specific personal files: of the 230,000 documents held by the Department in relation to these institutions, 100,000 documents relate to these individual personal files. As a consequence of the search and retrieval issues arising from about 1400 requests under the Act and a number of High Court actions which involve the release of these records, the Department moved in August 1999 to scan all the records on to a computer database. However, in relation to other requests, unconnected with industrial schools, deadlines were not met by significant margins in about half the cases examined.

Exemptions (i) The Commissioner expressed the concern following examination of exemptions claimed under section 19 (meetings of the Government) that this exemption, which is clearly intended to be applied with discretion, is regarded, in practice, as mandatory. Further, the refusal of access to records whose contents are already largely in the public domain is not an encouragement to the creation of a more open public service. The exercise of the exemption appears to place the emphasis on finding the correct "technical" basis for refusal rather than making information available "to the greatest extent possible consistent with the public interest and the right to privacy". The Commissioner noted that such a minimalist approach can easily spill over into the use of other exemptions resulting in an overly cautious approach to the release of other information.

The Commissioner found that, in practice, it appears that decision makers rarely, if ever, consider exercising their discretion to release. This has resulted in situations in which decision makers appeared to feel obliged to refuse access to Government memoranda even though their contents had already been released in their entirety by way of press release.

(ii) In considering section 20 (deliberations of public bodies), the Commissioner found that some decision makers displayed a basic misunderstanding of the nature of the public interest test which section 20 requires, confusing it with the public interest balancing test contained in sections such as 21 (functions and negotiations of public bodies), 26 (information obtained in confidence) and 27 (commercially sensitive information). Further, a number of reviews conducted by the Information Commissioner have been settled on the basis that, by the time the review came to be dealt with, the information had been released because the deliberative process had concluded. This gives rise to suspicion among some users of the Act that refusals under section 20 are tactical, designed to defer access until it suits the public body decision makers that material relating to the deliberative process should not be released until that process has concluded.

(iii) The Commissioner noted that section 26 (information obtained in confidence) is a complex exemption and it would appear that many decision makers experience difficulty in applying it correctly. In some cases the exemption is invoked in circumstances where it is inappropriate to do so. In some cases what the public body seeks to protect is the identity of the person who has provided information to it in confidence, as opposed to the contents of the information. In such cases, access may more appropriately be refused under section 23(1)(b) or section 46(1)(f) which provide that access may be refused if it could reasonably be expected to reveal or lead to the revelation of the identity of a person who has given information in confidence to a public body in relation to the enforcement or administration of the civil law or in relation to the enforcement of the criminal law.

A second set of circumstances in which it may not be appropriate to invoke section 26 is where the information at issue is intended to influence policy making or legislation. In such circumstances, it is most unlikely that a legal duty of confidence is owed to the provider of the information. However, public bodies may feel that refusing to treat such information in confidence will reduce the flow of information to them:

> "In my view this is a consequence which must be suffered in the interests of democracy. The alternative is to permit policy to be formulated and legislation to be enacted on the basis of secret representations - something which is wholly at odds with the concepts of openness and transparency which the FOI Act was intended to foster", *Annual Report of the Information Commissioner 2001*, Chapter 6.

Recommendations   The compliance report that was published in July 2001 includes a number of practical recommendations The *Annual Report of the Information Commissioner 2001* published in June 2002 notes the extent to which progress has been made based on these recommendations.

HIGH COURT APPEALS

Section 42 governs the right to take an appeal from a decision of the Information Commissioner on a point of law to the High Court. Such decisions issue consequent on a section 34 review, (see *Annual Review of Irish Law1999*, p. 351 *et seq*). Judgments were delivered in four such appeals in 2001. All are reported on the Information Commissioner's website at www.irlgov.ie/oic.

School League Tables **case**   *Minister for Education and Science v. the Information Commissioner*, High Court, July 31, 2001, the *School League Tables* case, (see *Annual Review of Irish Law1999*, p. 354 *et seq.*; *Annual Review of Irish Law 2000,* p. 274), was an appeal against the Commissioner's decision directing the Minister to give *The Sunday Times*, *The Sunday Tribune* and *The Kerryman*, access to certain records held by the Minister concerning the results of the Leaving Certificate Examinations held in 1998. The substantive matter was already moot by the time of the High Court hearing in July 2000.

During the period from initial request commencing in July 1998 coincidentally a new education Bill was passing through the Oireachtas. The newspapers had declared their intention of publishing league tables of secondary schools, a matter that caused considerable controversy and resulted in a number of interests such as teachers and parents unions presenting submissions to the Commissioner for the purposes of his review, see Information Commissioner's composite Decision No. 98104, 98130, 99024. The Minister took the opportunity presented to tack on section 53, (*Annual Review of Irish Law 1999*, p. 354 *et seq*), which provided that the Minister had discretion in relation to examinations, to refuse access to any information which would enable the compilation of information (that is not otherwise available to the general public) in relation to the comparative performance of schools in respect of academic achievement of students notwithstanding any other enactment. Section 53 of the Education Act 1998 came into effect on February 5, 1999, and the Commissioner's decision issued on October 7, 1999. This raised the question of whether section 32 was to apply to the new legislation. By virtue of this section a request shall be refused if disclosure of the record concerned is prohibited by any other enactment.

RETROACTIVITY v RETROSPECTION

Thus, the issue for determination was whether the Information Commissioner was required to apply section 53 in his determination so as to preclude granting the information as requested. Relying on the statement of Barron J. in *O'H v. O'H* [1990] 2 I.R. 558, (see *Annual Review of Irish Law 1990*, p. 309 *et seq*.), where he drew a distinction between applying the new law to past events and taking past events into account, Ó Caoimh J. found that the Commissioner was so required and upheld the appeal. Ó Caoimh J. concluded that in the instant case the application of section 53 was retroactive rather than retrospective being satisfied that if the request for information was one made to the head of the Department on October 7, 1999 that he would have been entitled to refuse access to the information sought in the instant case:

> "Clearly if section 34 of the Act were to be construed narrowly as involving merely a review of an earlier decision and not involving a rehearing then the provisions of Section 53 could not apply to the determination of the Information Commissioner without it having a retrospective effect. In particular I conclude that the provision of Section 53 must apply in conjunction with Section 32 of the Freedom of Information Act of 1997 which permits a head to refuse to grant a request under Section 7 in circumstances where 'the disclosure of the record concerned is prohibited by any enactment or the non disclosure of the record is authorised by any such enactment'."

RIGHT TO APPLY FOR INFORMATION

The respondent and the appellants had argued that the Freedom of Information Act conferred a vested statutory right for the benefit of every person with the existence of an independent Commissioner vindicating that right where he makes a decision in favour of disclosure. Possibly the aspect of the judgment which raises most concern is Ó Caoimh J.'s finding that: "such a right as does exist involves an application for the information in question and a positive determination to entitlement of the right." With respect, this reasoning reduces the right of access to a right to apply for access, albeit the application should be positively considered. If such reasoning were applied say to a person's right to enter a public building, it would mean that the right to walk through the entrance had been reduced to the right to knock on the door. Clearly, just as with the exemptions to access in the Act, there are occasions when entry to the building may be prohibited, but the role of doorkeeper is to bar entry only when these situations arise not to act constantly as guardian of the entryway benevolently deciding whether or not there is a right to knock. Such a decision renders the philosophy behind the Freedom of Information Act meaningless. By contrast see below *Deely v. Information Commissioner*, 405 *et seq.*,

DISREGARD OF REASONS FOR REQUEST

Given the controversy that had surrounded the *School League Tables* case, Ó Caoimh J. sensibly commented that the Court is not concerned with whether there should or should not be access to information to permit league tables to be published in regard to performance of schools. Unfortunately, he failed to take his reasoning a step further and invoke section 8(4) which requires that the reasons of a requester be disregarded, another fundamental support of the freedom of information philosophy. By contrast see below *EH and EPH v Information Commissioner*, 399.

The judgment did not issue until July 2001 and, even had the judgment found in favour of the Information Commissioner, the issue of the information at this stage would have been valueless to the requesters. Primarily, therefore, this case represents a lost opportunity to highlight the importance of the rights conveyed by the Freedom of Information Act. Furthermore, within that context the behaviour of the Minister for Education and Science in slipping through section 53 went unremarked apart from what might, but failed to be, a damning judicial comment: "I am satisfied that, even if Section 53 were to be construed as being retrospective in its effect, the intention of the provision was such that it should apply to the situation pertaining in the instant case." In effect this judgment has applied a statutory provision that specifies what the requester's purpose would be to an Act that prohibits any consideration of such purpose.

TIMELY REVIEW

Due to a lack of resources in the early years of the Act's operation the Commissioner has been unable to conduct reviews within the time limit prescribed, (*Annual Review of Irish Law 2000*, p.274). In this context, in relation to this judgment, in the *Annual Report of the Information Commissioner 2001* Chapter 3 the Commissioner noted: "it is, perhaps, unfortunate that the requesters lost the right of access because of unavoidable administrative delays."

EH and EPH v. The Information Commissioner The cases of *EH and EPH v. the Information Commissioner*, High Court, May 6, 2001, and December 21, 2001 (*Annual Review of Irish Law 2000* , p. 274), are a composite judgment by O'Neill J. The appellant was seeking access to all records held by the Minister for Health and Children and the Eastern Health Board relating to himself, his former partner and his daughter. This was in relation to allegations of sexual abuse, which he strenuously denied. The Commissioner had upheld the refusal to grant access on the basis that:

(a) Disclosure of certain records was prohibited under sections 22(1)(a), legal professional privilege, and 22(1)(b), contempt of court,

and

(b) Under the provisions of sections 6(4) and (5) access was denied to other records on the grounds that these did not relate to personal information about the Appellant and access to these was not necessary or expedient in order to understand a record created after the commencement of the Act. (See *Annual Review of Irish Law 1997*, p. 3; see *Salve Marine Ltd. v. Information Commissioner, Annual Review of Irish Law 2000*, p. 273 *et seq.*)

The first judgment of May 2001 dealt with section 22(1)(b) and the later judgment on sections 6(4) and (5) was delivered in December following further submissions and an examination by the court of the records in question. The refusal on grounds of legal professional privilege was not appealed. The judgment on section 6(5) in particular, records which relate to personal information, may well have significant consequential effects in increasing access to information.

DISCOVERY UNDERTAKINGS

In order to understand the case it is important to appreciate that whereas the appellant was already in possession of a significant portion of the records sought, apparently in the region of 200 records, these had been discovered to the appellant in Court proceedings in which he had sued the Board and the Minister for negligence. For the purposes of obtaining such discovery the appellant had given the court an express undertaking "to preserve the total confidentiality of all documents hereinafter discovered and to obtain a similar undertaking from each and every person to whom the documents or any of them are submitted in the course and preparation for the hearing of this action." In addition to this undertaking, another potential restriction on the use of documents emanating from the Board arose from the judgment and order of Barr J. *in camera, Eastern Health Board v. Fitness to Practice Committee of the Medical Council* [1998] 3 I.R. 399, (see *Annual Review of Irish Law1998*, pp. 448-9). The express undertaking and Barr J.'s order had been given to protect the interests of the children referred to in the Fitness to Practice Inquiry. The appellant found himself in the paradoxical situation of wishing to have unrestricted access to the documents in issue so that he could demonstrate his innocence of the offences with which he had been charged and so as to enable him to pursue his case before the Fitness to Practice Inquiry. The appellant was supported in his appeal by his daughter and former partner.

In the first judgment O'Neill J. upheld the Commissioner's findings in refusing to release records under section 22. At the outset he noted that during the proceedings some attention was given to the reasons of the appellant for seeking disclosure under the Act. He held that as section 8(4) makes absolutely clear any reasons are entirely immaterial and must be disregarded in dealing with a request for access. O'Neill J. found section 22(1)(b) to be mandatory in its effect allowing for no discretion once either the head or the Commissioner is satisfied that the disclosure of a record would constitute a contempt of court. He held further that the concept of disclosure is there in the widest sense and interpreted that as meaning "any disclosure" be it disclosure by the public body itself or disclosure by the person seeking the record or either of them. Since neither a head of public body nor the Commissioner has any jurisdiction under the Act to impose any conditions on the type or extent of disclosure or the use of the documents after disclosure it must be assumed that permitting disclosure of a record will be to the world at large.

In the circumstances in which the Act operates, there is an untrammelled right to information based on a philosophy of disclosure wholly different to that which is at the root of the discovery process in Court proceedings:

> "If it were the case that one could under the provisions of the Act obtain documents disclosure of which was prohibited by the ruling of a Court or by a undertaking given to a Court, I have no doubt that this would amount to a gross and constitutionally impermissible interference in the administration of justice. In my view section 22(1)(b) is there to ensure that this does not happen, and it must operate accordingly. ... I have come to the conclusion that where a head of a public body or the

Commissioner is aware that there is in existence an undertaking to a Court be it expressed or implied, that disclosure must be refused on the basis of section 22(1)(b)."

O'Neill J. continued with general comments on the likely future relationship between discovery and the right of disclosure under the Act which are of interest to quote *in extenso*:

"I think it will undoubtedly be the case that as the public grow accustomed to the opportunities of disclosure contained in the Act, as time goes by and where litigation may be contemplated or indeed where it has even occurred they may opt to seek disclosure of documents via the Act rather than via the traditional method of discovery. Thus it is to be anticipated that a difference of practice may emerge where a defendant or plaintiff is a public body. That is not of course to say the existing policy of requiring an implied undertaking in relation to discovered documents should change. The vast majority of defendants or indeed plaintiffs will not be public bodies and will be entitled to privacy in respect of their confidential documents save to the extent that they are required to be discovered under order of the Court. Therefore it is easy to foresee that there will be a rational and harmonious co-existence between the two regimes of disclosure."

EVIDENTIAL BASIS FOR APPEAL ON POINT OF LAW

With regard to the balance of the records, O'Neill J. accepted the appellant's submission that in relation to those documents to which access was refused by virtue of sections 6(4) and (5) a practical problem existed in the context of a High Court appeal under section 42(1). Such an appeal can only be taken on a point of law but the grounds for refusal of access under these subsections are essentially questions of fact, *i.e.* was the record created before the commencement of the Act, if so does it refer to the requester or is its disclosure necessary or expedient for interpreting a record created after the commencement of the Act. Without knowing the identity of the document or its content, neither the appellant nor the court can know whether or not the refusal based on these subsections is an error of law. To constitute an error of law there would have to be either no evidence at all to support the conclusion to refuse access, or alternatively the decision must be one which on the basis of the facts, flies in the face of reason and common sense, the test set out in the case of *The State (Keegan) v. The Stardust Tribunal* [1986] I.R. 642. On that basis, O'Neill J. concluded that the only solution was for the court to examine the relevant documents in order to be satisfied that there did not exist grounds of appeal on a point of law.

RECORDS WHICH RELATE TO PERSONAL INFORMATION DEFINED

In the second judgment delivered in December 2001, O'Neill J. varied the Commissioner's findings in relation to the section 6 refusal and directed disclosure of some of the documents requested. In so doing, O'Neill J. interpreted section 6(5)(b) which permits disclosure of records created before the commencement of the Act which relate to personal information about the person seeking access to them. He noted as a starting point that it seemed absolutely clear from the use of the phrase "relates to" that a document need not itself contain "personal information" about the requester, "personal information" in this context, as defined in section 2 of the Act. He adopted as the appropriate test to be applied to determine whether or not a record "relates to" as that postulated by Mr O'Donnell, counsel for the respondent, namely "whether there is a sufficiently substantial link between the requester's personal information (as defined in the Act) and the record in question". O'Neill J. specifically discounted the following as determinative factors:

> "The circumstances in which the record was created, the purposes behind the creation of the record and in particular whether it was created with the affairs of the particular individual in question in mind notwithstanding the fact that the record may not specifically mention or refer to that individual and what was in the mind of the author at the time of creation of the record and in particular whether or not the requester was in the mind of the author."

In the words of O'Neill J:

> "A requester has a right of access to "records". The record will generally speak for itself. Where a doubt or ambiguity exists, as to the connection of the record to the requester, a consideration of factors may inter alia, assist in determining whether there is a sufficiently substantial link between the requester's personal information (as defined in the Act) and the record in question. ... If the record contains an express reference to the requester, be it however insubstantial or trivial then clearly it "relates to personal information", about the requester. Here one would have in mind records such as letters which contained no personal information but are about or refer to the requester, such as holding type letters or pro forma or replies. Where the record does not name or has no express reference to the requester a substantial link will be established, if the record relates to something in which the requester

has a substantial personal interest, as distinct from something in which he has an interest as a member of the general community or of large scale class of the same."

SCHEDULE OF RECORDS

O'Neill J. referred in some detail to the Commissioner's schedule of records noting the very accurate description of their contents. Whilst none of the documents in themselves contained personal information about the appellant, they did make express reference to him by name and as such came within the ambit of the test set out above. "Documents of this sort, whilst not as [the Commissioner] said, containing in themselves personal information may assist in achieving a complete picture from the point of view of an Appellant." As has been noted, O'Neill J. varied the Commissioner's decision upholding his refusal in some instances and ordering disclosure of one affidavit and 8 of the requested documents.

Courts Service case   *Minister for Justice, Equality and Law Reform and the Courts Service v. Information Commissioner* [2002] 2 I.L.R.M. 1, (*Courts Service* case) a judgment delivered by Finnegan J. (as he then was) on March 14, 2001 is one of the two reported appeal cases. At one level, that of the courts, this is a relatively straightforward judgment that discharged the decision of the Information Commissioner to disclose the complete transcript and associated materials relating to Circuit Criminal Court proceedings. A disclosure order was substituted to disclose two documents deemed not to fall within the records under section 46(1)(a) and (b) to which the Act does not apply.

COURT PROCEEDINGS IN PUBLIC

Under section 46(1) the Act does not apply *inter alia* to (a) a record held by the courts relating to a court or to proceedings in a court nor to (b) a record held or created by the Attorney General or the Director of Public Prosecutions or the Office of the Attorney General or the Director of Public Prosecutions. An exception arises, section 46(1)(a)(I), and the Act will apply where the record relates to proceedings in a court; and relates to proceedings held in public; and was not created by the court and whose disclosure to the general public is not prohibited by the court. The Act applies to records concerning the general administration of the courts, 46(1)(a)(II) and the general administration of either of those Offices, 46(1)(b), see also *Deely v. Information Commissioner*, 405.

The complexity in the case as seen from the standpoint of a requester of records arises from a need to understand the important legal technicalities that underlie "proceedings in public" and both the express and implied Rules of the Superior Courts. According to Finnegan J. the phrase "held in public" refers to the word "proceedings" and not to the word "court". He was satisfied that in the present context the word "proceedings" is not used in the sense of an action but rather that it means any step in an action. For this step to come within the exception it must be a step taken in public.

RULES OF THE SUPERIOR COURTS

Finnegan J. held that the Information Commissioner was incorrect insofar as he found that section 46(1)(a)(I) is concerned with a specific prohibition imposed by the court which has dealt with or is dealing with the matter to which the record relates:

> "I am satisfied that the provision equally applies to the situation here where there is a general prohibition express or implied in the Rules of the Superior Courts with specified exceptions and a discretion in the court where appropriate to relieve from that prohibition. ... While not relevant here I would hold that as the courts are entitled to regulate the conduct of court business a practice not having its origin in the Rules of the Superior Courts would likewise amount to a prohibition e.g. the practice of confining access to Central Office files to parties and their representatives."

He held further that the Court Officers Act 1926 section 65 created a general prohibition on the disposal of documents held by the Court but from which the Judge can dispense. Without such a dispensation the prohibition in place within the meaning of section 46 (1) (a) (I) applied.

ACCESS TO RECORDS CREATED BY THE DIRECTOR OF PUBLIC PROSECUTIONS

Finnegan J. was satisfied that the compilation of the documents mentioned in the Criminal Procedure Act, 1967 section 6 as amended by the Criminal Evidence Act, 1992 section 12 even if the same were to consist solely of the photocopying of documents prepared elsewhere and putting same into a book is the creation of a record having regard to the definition of record contained in the Freedom of Information Act. Thus, section 46(1)(b) applies to the book of evidence and documents contained therein, a record created by the Director of Public Prosecutions or the Office of the Director of Public Prosecutions. Significantly, he found that if such documents were also held by a public body other than the Director of Public Prosecutions or his Office subject to other provisions of the Act these may be accessible on application to that body.

FAILURE TO JUSTIFY REFUSAL OF REQUEST

Finnegan J. noted that the Commissioner quite properly granted access to certain records where it had not been shown to the Commissioner's satisfaction that the refusal to grant a request was justified, section 34(12)(b). Finnegan J. concluded that the information available to him was the same as that available to the Commissioner. However, he pointed out that upon full information in relation to the nature of these documents being available they may well be documents falling within the exemptions in section 46(1)(a) or (b). This seems to reaffirm how critical it is for public bodies not only to give proper reasons for refusal of requests for access but also to create comprehensive schedules of records requested.

Deely v. The Information Commissioner In *Deely v. The Information Commissioner*, High Court, May 11, 2001, McKechnie J. also examined the Act's relationship with records of the Director of Public Prosecutions. The appellant had been charged with an offence under section 52 (1) of the Road Traffic Act, 1961 as amended. Being aggrieved at being so prosecuted and being further aggrieved at being the only driver to face any criminal charge, the appellant sought to invoke the provisions of the Freedom of Information Act in order to obtain the reasons for his prosecution. Section 18 provides for a right, in the case of a person affected by an act of a public body, to be given reasons for that act. However this right is qualified by section 18(2)(a) to the extent that reasons need not be given where to do so would involve the giving of information contained in an exempt record. Since the appellant made no case that the records requested concerned the general administration of the Director of Public Prosecution's office McKechnie J. was satisfied that the records were exempt records by virtue of section 46, see *Courts Service* case above, 403. McKechnie J. found that the appellant failed to present any case which would justify any variation or annulment of the decision reached by the Information Commissioner.

This is an expansive judgment in which McKechnie J. considered statutory interpretation of the Act in general terms and specifically examined the correct interpretation and interplay between certain sections of the Act. He examined sections 2 (definition of exempt record); 6 (right of access to information); 7 (request for records); 8 (decisions on requests); 14 (internal review); 18 (information regarding acts of public bodies affecting the requester); 34 (review by the Commissioner); 37 (powers of the Commissioner) and 46 (restrictions of Act). In addition he considered statutory publications under sections 15 and 16 and Freedom of Information Act, 1997 (Section 18) Regulations 1998: S.I.

No. 519 of 1998 which regulates a decision to refuse to grant an application under section 18.

STATUTORY INTERPRETATION

McKechnie J. stated that the purpose of the Act's enactment was to create accountability and transparency to an extent not heretofore contemplated let alone available to the general public: "Many would say that it creates an openness which inspires a belief and trust which can only further public confidence in the Constitutional organs of the State. It is on any view, a piece of legislation independent in existence, forceful in its aim and liberal in outlook and philosophy." With regard to interpretation he cautioned as to how this might be done in a complete way:

> "Being a creature of the Oireachtas, of a type without direct or parallel precedent, it is not possible to cite Acts, *pari passu*, upon which the Courts have expressed a view as to the correct method of statutory interpretation. ... I am not therefore certain that given the vision of the 1997 Act, it is altogether a complete statement to suggest, that, the provisions thereof in their entirety can adequately be interpreted, for the purpose of implementation, simply by a straightforward application of *Howard* [*v. Commissioners of Public Works* 1994 1 I.R. 101]."

INFORMATION COMMISSIONER'S DISCRETION

With regard to a section 34 review or section 36 investigation conducted by the Commissioner, McKechnie J. held that under section 37(6) of the Act, the Commissioner has an extensive discretion as to the procedures which he may adopt or follow, (*Annual Review of Irish Law 1999*, p.353):

> "Certainly, when dealing with a refusal the Commissioner can only be encouraged to pursue a solution to the joint satisfaction of the public body and the requester, and in so doing he must be free, in accordance with the underlying intention of the Act, to perform the preparatory work to his decision in whatever way he wishes, informally if that be his choice. It need hardly be said, however, that in so doing he must not compromise the due and proper performance of his function."

ONUS OF PROOF

As was noted in the *Courts Service* case above, 403, it must be shown to the Commissioner's satisfaction that the refusal to grant a request was justified, section 34(12)(b). When a person exercises his right to request information under section 18 that presumption does not appear to apply. However, McKechnie J. felt that this may not mean that the public body concerned can passively await the discharge by an applicant of some sort of onus and then only react. It would be much more desirable and more in keeping with the spirit of the legislation for a fuller engagement between the Commissioner and the public body as happened in the instant case. Nevertheless, generally the appellant correctly and necessarily assumed the onus and obligation of proving that the impugned decision of the Commissioner was erroneous on a point of law.

RIGHT OF ACCESS

Of great significance, especially given the decision in the *School League Tables* case above, 396, McKechnie J. held as follows:

> "The essence of the Act is that when a person comes within Section 6(1) *he may exercise that right, not out of grace and favour of the public body in question, but rather pursuant to the force of law*. It is a legal right, which he is exercising, indeed under Section 8(4) of the Act the reasons why he wishes to exercise that right are entirely immaterial. So what is crucial is that a requester must show that his request for access is made pursuant to a right of access, this right being one founded on, and contained within, the provisions of the 1997 Act itself." (emphasis added)

McKechnie J. held further that all sections from section 7 onwards are dependant upon the existence of the right of access created by section 6 and are designed to facilitate the implementation of that right. However, unless the right itself exists in the first instance, any further reference to or consideration of the other sections would appear to be irrelevant. Echoing Finnegan J. in *Deely* above, but in more specific terms, he held that section 46(1)(b) operates both independently of and conjunctively with section 2(1). This comprehensive judgment is to be welcomed as a thoughtful and reasoned interpretation of many critical aspects of the Act.

ABSENCE OF APPEAL TO SUPREME COURT

As was noted in *Annual Review of Irish Law 2000,* p. 274 *et seq.,* there is no appeal under the Act to the Supreme Court. It is worthwhile in considering the issues involved to repeat some of the points made: "In the first instance, the absence of the higher appeal mechanism may contribute negatively to the speed of the delivery of the High Court appeal judgments. It is also the situation that there is a developing use of the Act as a part of legal proceedings in preference, or in addition, to discovery. More significantly, however, it precludes the possibility of developing a coherent body of law in relation to the Freedom of Information Act." The experience of the four High Court appeal cases as analysed above appears to bear out these concerns.

To date six different High Court judges have delivered six appeal judgments of which two are now reported: *Minister for Agriculture and Food v. Information Commissioner* [2001] 1 I.L.R.M. 40, (*Annual Review of Irish Law1997,* p.350 *et seq.*), and *Minister for Justice, Equality and Law Reform and the Courts Service v. Information Commissioner* [2002] 2 I.L.R.M. 1, (*Courts Service* case) analysed above, 403. One of the judgments was delivered *ex tempore, Salve Marine Ltd. v. Information Commissioner,* High Court, July 19, 2000, *The Irish Times,* July 20, 2000, (*Annual Review of Irish Law2000,* p. 273 *et seq.*). It is clear from the analyses that while there is clear agreement on some elements of the Act's application, there is conflict between the earlier and later judgments on matters of crucial interpretation.

A problem confronted by the litigants in the *School League Tables* case related to the decision in the earlier judgment in Minister for Agriculture in which it was held that the Commissioner did not engage in *de novo* review. As was submitted in the analysis in the 1999 Review, this latter case was, in this respect, wrongly decided. The former judgment and the judgments in *EH,* the *Courts Service* and *Deely* cases support that opinion. Unfortunately, in *School League Tables* this issue influenced counsels' argument and may have overshadowed the substantive issue. Nevertheless, allowing that *School League Tables* was correctly decided with regard to the substantive issue, it is still a lost opportunity to have highlighted the manner in which conflicting and extraordinarily damaging legislation was slipped through the Oireachtas. The fact that any legislation can be passed in this manner without comment from the courts imposes an enormous if not impossible burden on the Information Commissioner to be a watchdog on all legislation going through the Houses of Oireachtas to assess its potential implications. One would hope that notwithstanding the series of judgments presaged in *Sinnott,* (see above in Constitutional Law chapter, 68), the Supreme Court, if it were involved, would not be as averse to bringing to the fore the need to protect the legislative vision of the Freedom of Information Act.

CERTIFICATES OF EXEMPTION

A Government Minister may exempt a record from the application of the Freedom of Information Act, (*Annual Review of Irish Law 2000*, p. 275 *et seq.*). In 2001 one such certificate was issued by the Minister for Justice, Equality and Law Reform. A copy of the report issued by the Minister in respect of this certificate is included in Appendix II of *Annual Report of the Information Commissioner 2001*.

OMBUDSMAN

In addition to hard copy all documents referred to may be found at the Ombudsman's website http://www.irlgov.ie/ombudsman/ unless otherwise stated.

Information Commissioner and Ombudsman compared   Both the Information Commissioner and the Ombudsman deal with matters of administrative accountability. The current office-holder, Mr. Kevin Murphy, is also the Information Commissioner. This combination continues to be advantageous for both functions, (*Annual Review of Irish Law 2000*, p. 276 *et seq.*). It should, however, be noted that there are significant differences in the statutory role and responsibility of each Office not least of which is the confusion for the general public that of the increasing number of bodies that now come within the Information Commissioner's ambit, many remain outside the purview of the Ombudsman. Moreover, the Information Commissioner's decisions have binding effect, subject solely to an appeal to the High Court on a point of law, see above, 401. This is in contrast to the Ombudsman who is governed by the Ombudsman Act 1980, and whose recommendations need not be accepted. The Ombudsman is currently reviewing the effectiveness of his Office's procedures for dealing with enforcement issues, see *Annual Report of the Ombudsman 2001*.

Local authority planning complaints   In 2000 the Ombudsman noted very considerable delays on the part of local authorities in furnishing reports to his Office on planning complaints, (*Annual Review of Irish Law 2000*, p. 277). He reports in the 2001 Annual Report that his comments were based on a national perspective built up over recent years from complaints from all parts of the country about failure, on a consistent basis, to take action against developers who did not adhere to the terms of planning permissions given to them or who engaged in other unauthorised environmental/planning activities. "Indeed, the public and my Office have been very frustrated that such actions have not been pursued with sufficient vigour, including court action, where appropriate." In the weeks following publication of his *2000 Annual Report* there was a significant increase in the number of telephone calls to the Ombudsman's Office and a 39% rise in complaints to his Office during 2001 about planning matters.

The Ombudsman comments that the new Planning and Development Act, 2000, (*Annual Review of Irish Law2000,* p.32 *et seq.*), and Regulations made under the Act (Planning and Development Regulations 2001) together consolidate all planning and development legislation. He anticipates that these will help to ensure that circumvention of regulations will be less likely to occur in the future and that the application process is even more open and transparent. Nevertheless, he is putting all local authorities on notice that he will be highly critical of any local authority that, in his view, fails to use the provisions of the Act effectively to ensure compliance or to initiate court proceedings in cases of non-compliance. See *Annual Report of the Ombudsman 2001,* p.8 *et seq.*

Section 6(7) investigations   In June 1999 the Ombudsman published the first of a number of investigative reports presented to the Dáil and Seanad under the Ombudsman's investigative functions in accordance with section 6(7) of the 1980 Act. These investigations arose from individual complaints, generally of individuals who lack the ability to act on an organised basis to lobby successfully for redress, (see below, 411 and *Annual Review of Irish Law2000,* p.277 *et seq.*). Similar themes of denial of individual statutory rights and disproportionate penalties, as well as wider issues such as abuse of secondary legislation and delegated powers run through these reports.

REPRESENTING COMPLAINANTS

***Lost Pension Arrears Report,* June 1999**   The Ombudsman's approach to representing complainants as described in this report has general application. He does not always agree with the complainant's perception of having been wronged and the statistics published in each year's Annual Report show that in roughly 50% of all cases the complaint is either not upheld or discontinued. He notes that one of the connotations of the term "Ombudsman", which is borrowed from the Swedish context, is that of being a "representative" of a particular group. Further consideration of the chapter entitled *Sense of Grievance* is of value to understanding his general attitude in relation to those aggrieved by the actions of public bodies.

UNFAIR OPERATION OF THE LAW

The fact that the Ombudsman cannot uphold a complaint does not necessarily mean that he does not share the complainant's sense that an injustice has been done:

> "It may well be the case that the action complained of is fully in line with the law but that the law itself, in certain contexts, gives rise to an injustice or an unfairness. In such situations, an Ombudsman is generally unable to uphold the complaint but can draw attention to the unfair operation of the law."

INABILITY OF AGGRIEVED CLASS TO PURSUE LEGAL CHALLENGE

It is appropriate for an Ombudsman to give expression to the sense of grievance which is being articulated by complainants. This is particularly the case where the grievance in question is a recurring one and where those affected are, whether because of age or social status or for other reasons, unable to organise themselves at the political or lobby group level. The Ombudsman was struck not only by the very strong and enduring sense of grievance which characterises almost all complainants, but by the remarkably similar ways it has been expressed over the years.

> "It also comes across that many of these complainants recognise their inability to organise a common platform with other similarly affected people; that, in effect, they are on their own. By definition, the people affected here are either elderly or widowed and this must at least diminish the chances of being able to lobby successfully on an organised basis. This sense of being on their own appears to compound the underlying grievance.
>
> It is noteworthy in the present context that *no High Court action has ever been taken by an aggrieved pensioner who has been refused arrears of contributory pension. Perhaps this inaction is not so much a reflection of weak legal arguments as a reflection of the inability of those concerned to muster the resources to mount a legal challenge."* *Lost Pensions Arrears*, p. 14 emphasis added.

This comment is especially significant given the Ombudsman's opinion that the regulations that formed the basis of the actions of the Department of Social, Community and Family Affairs, the Department concerned, in relation to late pension claims "*would have been struck down had they been challenged in the High Court.* [emphasis added] But because these regulations were never challenged, we shall never know now what attitude the Court would have taken. It is not for an Ombudsman to *decide* that a particular regulation is invalid; but he is entitled to take a view on the matter and to be guided by that view in dealing with individual complaints." *Lost Pensions Arrears*, p. 26.

SECRET DISCRETION UNCOVERED

As noted in *Annual Review of Irish Law 2000* (p.277), all the complainants the subject of this particular investigation were pensioners who, with one exception, were inadvertently late in claiming their pension entitlements. The Department of Social, Community and Family Affairs was inactive in efforts to resolve the difficulties during the period 1985 to 1996. Rules were applied rigidly and without equity. Throughout this period the Ombudsman's Office reluctantly took the view that, whereas the pensioners in question were being treated unfairly, the Ombudsman had to recognise that the Department's actions were in accordance with the regulations. However, in 1996:

> "the Ombudsman's Office discovered, by chance, that the Department had a long-standing arrangement with the Department of Finance under which lost arrears of contributory pension could be paid on an extra-statutory basis. In effect, this was a recognition that the regime laid down by regulation could give rise to unfair outcomes in certain situations." *Lost Pensions Arrears*, p. 9.

It would be unfair to suggest that the Department ever actively abused these powers. Indeed, it was only because it chose to use them in a particular case that the arrangements came to the Ombudsman's attention. Nevertheless, it is instructive to quote the Ombudsman's conclusions:

> "A disquieting feature reported on in the 1997 Investigation Report [an earlier section 4(2) report into three complaints] was the fact that the Department's extra-statutory discretion to pay pension arrears, as agreed with the Department of Finance, was effectively kept secret. The arrangement dated back to 1961 in the case of the old age pension and even earlier in the case of widow's pension. Certainly, the arrangements were agreed at a time when a culture of secrecy prevailed; but they continued to exist, unpublicised, long after the Department had adopted a customer-focused approach to its claimants. It would seem that these arrangements amounted to a supplementary set of rules that could be invoked, or not invoked, at the discretion of the Department. Because pensioners, and the public generally, were unaware of the existence or details of these rules, it was not possible to seek to rely upon them. In effect, the Department retained to itself the powers to decide that these rules should be invoked." *Lost Pensions Arrears*, p. 32.

As a consequence of the 1997 investigation the primary law was amended by section 32 of the Social Welfare Act 1997.

PROPORTIONALITY AND PENALTIES

In his final *Annual Report* (for 1993) the first Ombudsman, Michael Mills, applied the test of proportionality to the penalty system then in place. He noted that the principle of proportionality is a feature of European Union Law and one that may evolve as a feature of Irish public law. He concluded that the Department's practice clearly failed to meet this test and that: "there was no reasonable proportion between the penalty being imposed on the pensioner (substantial arrears lost) and whatever detriment might result for the Department where a pension claim is made out of time." *Lost Pensions Arrears*, p. 19.

REDRESS

The Ombudsman notes that redress might only be possible following amendment of a regulation. Also, the Ombudsman's jurisdiction does not extend to judicial or legislative actions. With these restrictions in mind, the Ombudsman raised the question as to whether it would be within his powers in recommending, following investigation, that a regulation be amended. It can be noted that the theme of the Ombudsman's 2001 Annual Report is redress, and each copy of the report includes a pamphlet which is a Guide to the provision of redress when public bodies make mistakes in their dealings with the citizen, see *Annual Report of the Ombudsman 2001* and p. 13 *et seq.*

As a result of the instant investigation, redress was obtained for some 200 pensioners with, in one case, a widow receiving IR£36,000 of arrears and in another case, a solution that paid all outstanding arrears for a period of 19 years during which the pension had been refused. The Ombudsman noted that in fairness to the Department, where a case is well made it is prepared to look afresh at the matter and, in many instances, give the pensioner the benefit of the doubt.

JURISDICTION TO CHALLENGE *ULTRA VIRES* ACTS AND OTHER MALADMINISTRATION

In the context of the pension regulations which governed the "late claims" issue up to 1997, it appeared to the Ombudsman that these regulations may have been made *ultra vires* the delegated authority given to the Minister by the Oireachtas. This is one of the specific categories of maladministration against which, under section 4(2)(b) of the Ombudsman Act 1980, actions must be tested. Alternatively, if the Ombudsman concluded that the decisions required by the regulation were unfair or unreasonable then those decisions might be found to be "contrary to fair or sound administration" which is the residual category covered by this section.

SECONDARY LEGISLATION

A real concern for the Ombudsman, and adverted to on a number of occasions, is that where primary law is to be made operational by way of secondary law, there should not be any unauthorised restriction on the putting into effect of primary law. In the report he repeats an earlier comment:

> "I have found that restrictions or qualifications, not specifically provided for in the primary legislation, are often incorporated into statutory regulations, which as we all know receive very little scrutiny…I detect an attitude which sees delegated legislation as a means of fine tuning in areas which might prove controversial if included in the primary legislation."

The Ombudsman noted that the overall difficulty is compounded by the absence of any effective monitoring or control of secondary legislation within the Oireachtas. He suggested that a mechanism is needed which acknowledges the utility of secondary legislation in terms of the flexibility it provides for voluminous and often complex regulations while enabling the Oireachtas to supervise effectively the exercise of the powers which it has delegated. *Lost Pensions Arrears*, p. 29 *et seq.*

INEQUITY IN OBTAINING REDRESS

The Ombudsman's conclusions in relation to the *Lost Pensions Arrears* investigation continue to have relevance in relation to how complainants are treated by the public service:

> "Perhaps the first conclusion is that the penalty system was excessively harsh and inequitable and this harshness and inequity was allowed continue for far too long. The reforms introduced in 1997 might have been introduced at any point after the issue was first raised in 1985. The reforms were introduced in response to the Ombudsman's 1997 Report; but there was nothing in that report of which the Department had not been aware for many years. The inherent inequity of the system should have been enough to prompt change. But it seems that change would have to wait until the Department was forced to act in the face of sustained criticism from the Ombudsman. Of course the Department did not have a free hand in all of this. It needed the approval of the Department of Finance to the relaxation of the penalty as any change in arrangements would have spending implications. In the context of the annual budgetary negotiations between the two Departments, it would seem that there were always other developments whose funding should

take priority. The fact that the affected pensioners have never been organised as a lobby group must have adversely affected their case.

A related question, for the Ombudsman's Office itself, is whether it could have been more proactive in pursuing the issue at an earlier stage. The Office was initially reluctant to investigate a policy and practice, which was firmly rooted in secondary legislation. The Office did have a view that it could do no more than express criticism of the policy and its unfair consequences. It was some time before the issue of investigating individual 'late claims' complaints, and confronting the regulation on which the penalty was based, emerged as a real option." *Lost Pensions Arrears*, p. 36.

HOUSING FUNCTION OF LOCAL AUTHORITIES

***Local Authority Housing Loans Report*, July 2000** The housing function of local authorities is, to a large extent, determined by statute. The principal pieces of legislation are the Housing Acts of 1966 and 1988. The housing activity of local authorities may be divided into direct provision of housing for persons who are unable to provide their own accommodation, and assistance to persons purchasing or improving their own dwellings. Houses are sold by local authorities in accordance with the provisions of section 90 of the Housing Act 1966, as substituted by section 26 of the Housing (Miscellaneous Provisions) Act 1992. Housing Authorities are responsible for the promotion and administration of the Tenant Purchase Scheme in their areas. All tenants who apply to purchase their houses are given assistance by housing authorities to enable them to decide on the purchase option suitable to their circumstances. See *Local Authority Housing Loans*, p. 3.

In summary, the investigation revealed 6,411 accounts, involving refunds of approximately IR£547,000, ranging from IR£1 to approximately IR£3,500 in individual cases. One local authority made refunds totalling IR£122,823; one local authority had a credit balance remaining on an account for almost 19 years and one borrower made 46 consecutive monthly instalments on a fully paid-up loan. Seven local authorities reported no overpayments. See *Local Authority Housing Loans*, p. 2.

FAILURE TO INFORM

The Ombudsman noted that in some local authorities it was a requirement of audit to issue a refund to a borrower only on the receipt of a written application from the borrower.

"However, no evidence was presented to me to suggest that the local authorities concerned actually notified the borrowers that they were due a refund. In these circumstances, for such a policy to be justified, it is important that the borrower be informed of the existence of such a credit and also be notified of the audit requirement." *Local Authority Housing Loans*, p. 13.

Nursing Home Subventions Report, January 2001   This Report deals with the payment by health boards of subsidies or subventions to patients in private nursing homes as provided for in the Health (Nursing Homes) Act 1990 (the 1990 Act). The majority of these patients are elderly people and, by definition, unable to care for themselves or be cared for at home by their families. The Report is a case study in public administration, which examines the operation of the subvention scheme by the health boards; it deals also with the role of the Department of Health and Children (the Department) in making regulations (as provided for in the 1990 Act) and in overseeing the introduction and operation of the scheme nationally. In addition, the report considers the nature of the relationship between the Department and the Oireachtas on the one hand, and that between the Department and the health boards, on the other.

The report identified a failure to allow a pocket money provision in the calculation of the elderly person's means and the erroneous calculation of family circumstances in the calculation of those means. As a result of the investigation, fundamental changes, which mirrored the Ombudsman's concerns, were made to the regulations and appropriate arrears were paid in affected cases, *Annual Report of the Ombudsman 2001*, p. 37 *et seq.*

UNWARRANTED DELAYS IN OBTAINING REDRESS

As noted with earlier investigations, yet again the Ombudsman encountered several difficulties in his efforts to deal with the complaints received:

> "These difficulties were reflected in delays, on the part both of the health boards and of the Department, in dealing with issues raised by the Ombudsman and in the consistent re-iteration of explanations and arguments which were, in his view, without merit. Only in January 1999 were the two most significant of the subvention problems eventually resolved. As the Ombudsman now knows from documentation seen in the course of preparing this present report, it took the Department more than five years to acknowledge and address defects *of which it was aware prior to September 1993.*" *Nursing Home Subventions*, p. 6, emphasis included.

NEGATIVE LEGAL ADVICE

The Ombudsman reported that:

> "[B]oth the 'pocket money' issue and the family assessment issue were the subject of detailed and repeated legal advice in the period 1995 - 1998. Some of these advices were requested by individual health boards and some by the Department. Whereas the health boards were always quick to inform the Department (and generally the other boards) of such advice, the Department appears not to have circulated the advice it was receiving."

The Ombudsman is quite critical of the attitude of the Department. It is noted in his report that the Department, having been given sight of the draft report, rejected his conclusions with regard to their attitude to legal advice. Nevertheless, the Ombudsman strongly maintained his view that positions taken appeared to have been contrary to the legal advice received, *Nursing Home Subventions*, p. 57 *et seq.*, quotation at p.57.

Passengers with Disabilities Report, August 2001 This Report investigated the refusal by the Revenue Commissioners to grant tax relief on vehicles adapted for the transport of passengers with disabilities. The Report gave details of how three carers, responsible for the transport of close family members suffering from a qualifying disability, were refused the tax reliefs available under the Disabled Drivers and Disabled Passengers (Tax Concessions) Regulations, 1994.

POSITIVE RESPONSE OF REVENUE COMMISSIONERS

It is clear from both the Ombudsman's and the Information Commissioner's Annual Reports that the Revenue Commissioners rank highly among those public bodies concerned to ensure fairness and administrative best practice in their dealings with citizens. Thus, it is no surprise that there was a positive outcome not only to the particular complaints but also to a recommendation from the Ombudsman for a review of other similar refusals. The review carried out by the Revenue involved an initial examination of 10,500 files of which 103 files were selected for further investigation. Of the cases reviewed Revenue said that while it was not possible to give an exact statement of the amounts involved, based on the current average claim size for disabled passengers, the total repayment involved in respect of those applicants who had so far responded to its approaches under the review was of the order of €590,000 (£464,663). When the review process is finally completed Revenue estimate that the final amount repaid, including fuel repayment and repayment of road tax will be of the order of €850,000 (£669,429). See *Annual Report of the Ombudsman*, p.38 *et seq.*

Protecting the weakest   In each of the investigations mentioned it should be noted that it is the weakest in society who have been inadvertently and, in the view of the Ombudsman in the case of the Nursing Home Subventions, deliberately, deprived of statutory entitlements involving relatively significant sums of money necessary for their daily living.

FREEDOM OF INFORMATION ACT 1997

Over 50 additional bodies came within the scope of the Act during 2001 by way of four statutory instruments. These included a number of bodies within the enterprise sector, such as FÁS, IDA Ireland, Forfás and Enterprise Ireland. Specified functions of the Labour Relations Commission and the National Standards Authority of Ireland are also included. From October 2001 the scope of the Act was extended to a further 43 bodies including the constituent universities of the National University of Ireland, Trinity College, Dublin City University, University of Limerick, the Institutes of Technology, other educational institutions, Comhairle and the Regional Authorities and Assemblies. By the end of 2001 the total number of bodies covered by the Act is almost 350 and it is anticipated that a further 35 bodies will be added during 2002.

S.I. No. 126 of 2001 (Prescribed Bodies) Regulations 2001   These prescribe the Industrial Development Agency (Ireland), Enterprise Ireland, the National Authority for Occupational Safety and Health, Forfás, An Foras Áiseanna Saothair, FÁS International Consulting Limited, Shannon Free Airport Development Company Limited and Údaras na Gaeltachta as a public body for the purposes of the FOI Act, by their inclusion in subparagraph (5) of paragraph 1 of the First Schedule to the Act.

S.I. No. 127 of 2001 (Prescribed Bodies) (No. 2) Regulations 2001   These prescribe The National Standards Authority of Ireland as a public body for the purposes of that FOI Act by its inclusion in subparagraph (5) of paragraph 1 of the First Schedule to the Act. In accordance with section 3 subparagraph 5 of that Act, these Regulations provide that the FOI Act shall apply to The National Standards Authority of Ireland only as respects specified functions of the body.

S.I. No. 128 of 2001 (Prescribed Bodies) (No. 3) Regulations 2001   These prescribe the Labour Relations Commission as a public body for the purposes of the FOI Act by its inclusion in subparagraph (5) of paragraph 1 of the First Schedule to the Act. In accordance with section 3 subparagraph 5 of that Act, these Regulations provide that the FOI Act shall apply to the Labour Relations Commission only as respects specified functions of the body.

S.I. No. 475 of 2001 (Prescribed Bodies) (No. 4) Regulations 2001   These prescribe each of the bodies listed in the schedule (these are the 43 educational institutions, Comhairle and the Regional Authorities and Assemblies referred to above.) as a public body for the purposes of the FOI Act by their inclusion in subparagraph (5) of paragraph 1 of the First Schedule to the Act.

S.I. No. 368 of 2001 (Classes Of Health Professionals) Regulations 2001 These prescribe classes of health worker and social worker for the purposes of section 28(7) of the FOI Act. Their effect is to widen the meaning of "health professional" in section 28 of the FOI Act to include persons holding either the National Qualification in Social Work (N.Q.S.W.) issued by the National Social Work Qualifications Board, the Certificate of Qualification in Social Work (C.Q.S.W.) issued by the Validation Body on Social Work Qualifications and Training, a letter of accreditation from the National Social Work Qualifications Board or a qualification in clinical psychology recognised by the Minister for Health and Children where the person concerned has been practising as a clinical psychologist for a minimum of three out of the last five years following the award of the qualification concerned.

SOCIAL WELFARE ACT 2000

S.I. No. 242 of 2001 Social (Consolidated Payments Provisions) (Amendment) (No. 3) (Sharing Of Information) Regulations 2001   These prescribe the information which a specified body may be required to share with the Department of Education and Science in relation to the use of the Personal Public Service Number as a unique student identifier at all levels of the education system. In addition, information which may be shared in relation to a person between the Department of Social, Community and Family Affairs and any other specified body for the purposes of seeking or giving that person's Personal Public Service Number, is specified. The Regulations also specify the information which may be shared between the Department of Social, Community and Family Affairs and Local Authorities in relation to tenancies supported through the Supplementary Welfare Allowance system in order to assist those authorities in carrying out their statutory responsibilities in relation to private rented accommodation.

Law Reform

THE LAW REFORM COMMISSION'S SECOND PROGRAMME

The Law Reform Commission was established by the Law Reform Commission Act 1975. It was part of a wave of such agencies, which engulfed the common law jurisdictions in the period from the mid-sixties onwards.

Law reform in Ireland began slowly after Independence. It was not really until the arrival of Mr. Charles Haughey in the Department of Justice that the pace quickened: see Haughey, "Law Reform in Ireland" (1964) 13 I.C.L.Q. 1300. The Department established a special division for law reform. Guided by Roger Hayes, the Department developed close links with international scholars of world repute. Our Civil Liability Act 1961 is largely modelled on Glanville Williams's draft Bill contained in his *Joint Torts and Contributory Negligence*, published in 1951, and the strong German flavour to the compulsory share provisions of the Succession Act 1965 is attributable to the influence of Dr Ernst Cohn, author of the *Manual of German Law*. Matters slowed down in the late 1960s and it took the initiative of Declan Costello as Attorney General to establish the Law Reform Commission: see O'Connor, "The Law Reform Commission and the Codification of Irish Law" (1975) 9 Ir. Jur. (ns) 14.

The 1975 legislation gives the Commission wide-ranging powers, on its own initiative or that of the Attorney General, to formulate proposals for law reform.

The Commission established its First Programme of Work, which was adopted by the Government in 1977. It led to the publication of over sixty documents – Working Papers, Consultation Papers and Reports – culminating to a large degree in legislation, mainly in the areas of family law, torts, criminal law, evidence, private international law, limitation of actions, land law and conveyancing law.

There have been some notable instances where legislative reform has not yet followed the publication of Commission's proposals, perhaps most controversially that of defamation, where it is surely only a matter of time before a new law is passed. In some other cases, the Commission produced proposals, which, far from being perceived as unduly radical, were regarded as too conservative. The most controversial of these was the Commission's recommendation, in its *First Report on Family Law* (LRC1 –1981), that adultery should generate an action for damages for the benefit of the family. The immediate legislative response was to abolish the old actions for criminal conversation, enticement and harbouring of spouses, in the Family Law Act 1981: see McMahon & Binchy, *Law of Torts* (3rd ed, Butterworths, Dublin 2000), para. 33.01. The Commission's proposals on nullity of marriage, contained in its *Report on Nullity of Marriage* (LRC9 – 1984) have been allowed to languish, overtaken by an ideological shift to divorce.

The Commission's *Second Programme of Law Reform* was approved by the Government on 19 December 2000: *Second Programme for Examination of Certain Branches of the Law with a View to their Reform 2000 – 2007* (PN 9459 2000). It identifies thirty-one topics, grouped under twelve general branches of the law. It considers that these topics 'reflect the rapid pace of social and political change in Ireland and internationally': p. 3. It enlarges on this context as follows: (pp 2-3):

> "In Ireland there is an increasing emphasis on the importance of government accountability; and on the need to improve the interface between the citizen and the law. There is also greater sensitivity towards the plight of vulnerable groups such as children, the disabled (including those with legal incapacities) and the elderly. On the scientific and technological front, new dilemmas for law and society are emerging; and the information revolution is already affecting the way we live our lives and conduct our business."
>
> On the international plane, the issue of law reform is necessarily affected by the trend towards economic globalisation and greater European integration. The problems that arise if there are differences between national legal systems have become more acute; often, they require the conflict of laws aspect of a law reform problem to be considered as well as its substantive features.
>
> Hence, too, as a separate matter, it is ever more important that the Commission should pay close attention to the law and practice of our fellow EU Member States, while keeping in constant touch with developments in other common law jurisdictions. And, of course, the Commission must always bear in mind the common standards in the field of human rights set out by the European Convention on Human Rights."

It is interesting to reflect on the strong emphasis, overt and implicit, on the protection of human rights in this analysis. With the establishment of the Human Rights Commission in 2000 (analysed *Annual Review of Irish Law 2000*, p.272 ff) and its expansion in 2001 (above, 389), as well as the introduction of a Bill incorporating the European Convention on Human Rights (albeit on the mild interpretative model favoured in Britain), the prospect of enhanced protection of human rights in Ireland is surely a real one.

Among the thirty-one topics identified in the Second Programme, the following may be mentioned as being likely to have particular impact, though of course one must await the actual content of the recommendations to make a more accurate assessment: tribunals of inquiry; class actions and representative actions taken in the public interest; the law of privacy; homicide; restorative justice; corporate criminal liability; aspects of the law of compensation for personal injury; succession law; the law of trusts, including the law of charities; the law relating to the elderly; the law affecting persons with physical, mental or learning disabilities; adoption and the rights and duties of cohabitees.

Ireland has yet to experience a large debate on the values that should underlie law reform and the criteria for assessing the 'success' of law reform agencies. A rare exception is the contribution by Mr. (now Chief) Justice Keane shortly after his appointment as President of the Commission in 1987: 81 Incorp. L. Soc. Gazette of Ireland 131 (1987). Obvious questions that need to be addressed include the following. Should the Law Reform Commission limit its remit to 'black letter' law? Should it, on the contrary, adopt a left-leaning, liberal agenda? Ought it to be capable of proposing radical constitutional amendments? Should it have a 'position' on the integration of Irish law within a European model? Should it aim to produce proposals that have the greatest prospect of implementation or should it not hesitate to be radical in the fairly sure belief that its proposals will not be translated into legislation? Should it ignore lobbies or seek to negotiate with them?

All of these questions have been widely discussed in Britain, which established Law Commissions in England and Scotland a decade before we did. The position here is far from identical but it is nonetheless interesting to read the varying opinions of those with experience as Law Commissioners, including Peter North, 'Law Reform: Processes and Problems" (1985) 101 L.Q. Rev. 339 and Stephen Cretney, "The Politics of Law Reform – A View from the Inside" (1985) 48 Modern L. Rev. 493.

THE LAW REFORM COMMISSION'S REPORTS AND CONSULTATION PAPERS

Elsewhere in this Review we examine a number of Reports and Consultation Papers published by the Law Reform Commission. In the Chapter on Limitation of Actions (below, 423), we analyse the Commission's *Report on the Statutes of Limitations: Claims in Contract and Tort in Respect of Latent Damage* (other than Personal Injury) (LRC 64 – 2001). In the Torts Chapter (below, 554), we consider its *Report on Aggravated, Exemplary and Restitutionary Damages* (LRC 60-2000). In the Criminal Law Chapter (below, 180), we discuss the Commission's *Consultation Paper on Homicide: The Mental Element in Murder* (LRC CP 17-2001).

Limitation of Actions

ACCRUAL OF CAUSE OF ACTION

In *O'Donnell v. Kilsaran Concrete Ltd* [2002] 1 I.L.R.M. 551, Herbert J. confronted important issues as to when the limitation clock begins to run against the plaintiff in relation to latent defects in property. The second defendant built a dwelling house for the plaintiff in 1987. An architect's certificate of practical completion was issued in March 1988. Some defects were identified in a 'snags list'; the second defendant attended in them in 1989. In 1991 cracks appeared in the outside wall of the house in the area of the garage wing. These were attributed to settlement and the problem was removed by replastering the affected area.

In 1998, an architect whom the plaintiff consulted with the intention of having a window in the lounge area replaced advised the plaintiff that there was cracking in the plaster of the lower section of the outside wall of the main structure of house adjoining the garage block and the garage itself. The problem was attributed to the presence of more than 0.5% of iron pyrites in the concrete blocks with which the wall was constructed. This mineral undergoes a chemical reaction if the wall becomes water saturated in the presence of oxygen and the reaction results in splitting and rust staining of the blocks. The deterioration is accelerated by increased temperature.

The plaintiff issued a plenary summons in June 1999. A preliminary issue of law arose as to whether the summons had been issued within the periods prescribed by the Statute of Limitations.

So far as the plaintiff's claim for breach of contract was concerned, Herbert J. was satisfied that 'any cause of action ... accrued prior to March 1988 when the architect issued his certificate of practical completion' and was consequently time-barred.

The Statute did not defeat the plaintiff's claim in negligence, however. On the evidence, Herbert concluded that the cracking due to the excess of iron pyrites in the block work of the dwelling house had not developed until 'well within the limitation period of six years' prior to the issue of the plenary summons.

An interesting question – not previously answered in an Irish decision – was whether Irish law should favour the approach adopted by the House of Lords in *Pirelli v. Oscar Faber and Partners* [1983] 2 A.C. 1, where Lord Fraser of Tullybelton, delivering the unanimous verdict of their Lordships, observed:

"There is an element of confusion between damage to the plaintiff's body and latent defect in the foundations of a building. Unless the defect is very gross it may never lead to any damage at all to the building. It would be analogous to a predisposition or natural weakness in the human body, which may never develop into disease or injury. The plaintiff's cause of action will not accrue until damage occurs, which will commonly consist of cracks coming into existence as a result of the defect even though the cracks or the defect may be undiscovered or undiscoverable. There may perhaps be cases where the defect is so gross that the building is doomed from the start and where the owner's cause of action will accrue as soon as it is built, but it seems unlikely that such a defect would not be discovered within the limitation period. Such cases, if they exist, would be exceptional."

Counsel for the defendants argued that, if these principles applied, the action for negligence was time-barred as the defective block work rendered the dwelling house a building doomed from the start, so that the cause of action began to run in 1988 and expired six years later. The civil engineer called to give evidence by the plaintiff agreed in cross-examination that the blocks had been unsuitable from the start and should not have been used. Their unsuitability related only to the danger of the eventuality that in fact occurred. The blocks were otherwise capable of functioning but carried a risk, which any competent building would find unacceptable and which could not be eliminated by the use of plastering or pebble dashing. Herbert J, referring to the civil engineer's evidence, noted that:

"[t]his risk was that a sufficiently rapid chemical reaction could occur within the blocks if they became water saturated in the presence of oxygen – a not unusual occurrence in the climatic conditions of the West of Ireland – and this would result in cracking and rust staining of the blocks."

Herbert J. considered that this evidence did not support a characterisation of the plaintiff's house as a building doomed from the start. On the contrary, the presence of the iron pyrites was a latent defect in the structure which, though predisposing the building to damage, might never have led to any actual damage to the building at all. Lord Keith's remarks in *Ketteman v. Hansel Properties Ltd* [1987] A.C. 189 were authority for the proposition that a building should not be so characterised merely because it had a latent defect which must inevitably result in some damage at some later stage.

Herbert J. did not accept the invitation of counsel for the defendants to become embroiled in the issue whether a claim for negligently caused pure economic loss was sustainable, since the sole issue of the trial of the preliminary point of law was one of limitations. It is interesting that he did not refer to the decision of the Supreme Court, less than four months previously, in *Glencar Exploration plc v. Mayo County Council* [2002] 1 I.L.R.M. 481 which cast a long shadow over such claims. Herbert J. was surely right to avoid the siren call in this direction. To have responded to it would have taken him towards such formidable issues as the present status of the principles favoured in *Junior Books v. Veitchi* [1983] 1 A.C. 520 and distinctions between cases where economic loss is incurred in remedying non-dangerous defects and those where the loss is sustained in order to preserve the physical safety of persons coming into contact with the product or building.

Nor did Geoghegan J.'s decision in *Irish Equine Foundation Ltd v. Robinson* [1999] 2 I.L.R.M. 289 assist the defendants since the damage in the instant case came into existence only 'not long prior to October 1998 or in the terminology used by Geoghegan J. was not manifest until then'. It was not necessary for the court to express an opinion, therefore, 'on the vexed question of "discoverability"'. One may perhaps question whether *Irish Equine Foundation* can be distinguished so easily. In that case, Geoghegan J. considered that, if the roof had been defectively designed for the reasons suggested by the plaintiff, this would have been manifest at any time to any expert who examined it. If the negligence alleged in the instant case was the decision to use the blocks in the circumstances in which they were used, it can be argued that this negligence (if such it was) was 'manifest' in 1988. One would thus have the position that the second defendant was negligent, with that negligence being of a character to start the clock for a claim by the plaintiff for negligently caused pure economic loss assuming that such a claim is sustainable in Irish law in these circumstances. After *Glencar*, such an assumption cannot easily be made.

A question arises as to whether the time-barring of a right of action for negligently caused pure economic loss has any effect on a right of action for negligently caused property damage, which would not otherwise be time-barred, where the negligence in question consists of a single act or omission by the defendant. In other words, is the plaintiff's later claim for negligently caused property damage capable of being treated as a separate claim with its own distinct date of accrual?

The answer surely has to be in the affirmative. Otherwise legitimate claims for negligently caused property damage will be defeated by the time-barring of essentially hypothetical claims for negligently caused pure economic loss which were of no concern to the plaintiff and which, on the basis of a test of 'manifestation' of defective design adopted in *Irish Equine Foundation*, would actually involve the defeat of claims in many instances where the plaintiff would not be expected to have become aware of the existence of the factual (or, as the case might be, legal) basis for making a claim.

More importantly, there seems no principled reason why one should not sever claims for negligently caused pure economic loss from those for negligently caused property damage even where there is a common act of negligence grounding both claims. The decision of *Brunsden v. Humphrey* (1884) 14 Q.B.D. 141 recognises that separate causes of action – even for the same category of tort – may be appropriate to vindicate separately protected rights. In *Hayes v. Callanan*, High Court, 25 March 1999, noted *in Annual Review of Irish Law 2000*, pp.475-6, Smith J. applied the principles recognised in *Brunsden v. Humphrey*. A similar approach was adopted by O'Donovan J. in *Kerwick v. Minister for* Defence, High Court, March 19, 1999, noted in *Annual Review of Irish Law 1999*, pp.401-2. The problem lies in determining what constitutes a separate interest in this regard. In the context of injury to human beings, we have seen the courts grappling with the question whether a distinction can be drawn between physical and mental injury (see McMahon & Binchy, *Law of Torts* (3rd ed, Butterworths, Dublin, 2000), Chap. 17). In *Brunsden v. Humphrey*, Coleridge C.J., dissenting, considered that the logical consequence of the majority's approach was that a person should be regarded as having distinct interests in a leg and an arm but one of that majority, Lord Esher MR, disagreed with this interpretation of its holding, in *Macdougall v. Knight*, (1890) 25 Q.B.D. 1.

Fleming, *The Law of Torts* (9th ed, Law Book Company, Sydney, 1998), p.150, when analysing the development of the doctrine of the duty of care in negligence, observes that:

> "[i]t might have been more elegant to speak, as Civilians do, of a plaintiff's protected rights rather than of a defendant's duty, especially when the focus is on the kind of injury the plaintiff has suffered, for example whether liability extends to purely economic loss or mere mental distress rather than physical injury. The choice of nomenclature was due to historical accident and has no substantive implications."

Perhaps the philosophy of compartmentalising the duty of care, favoured in *Glencar*, will encourage more interest-based analysis in the law of negligence. From the standpoint of prospective plaintiffs, it would be a double blow to have their claims segmented for the purpose of identifying a cause of action but merged for the purposes of limitation of actions.

LATENT DAMAGE

In February 2001, the Law Reform Commission published its *Report on the Statutes of Limitations: Claims in Contract and Tort in Respect of Latent Damage (other than Personal Injury)* (LRC 64 – 2001). The Report follows a request from the Attorney General under section 4(2)(c) of the Law Reform Commission Act 1975.

The Commission favours the introduction of a discoverability test for claims in respect of latent damage. It is anxious that this test be sufficiently subjective to take account of the particular circumstances in which the plaintiff finds himself or herself, but that it should not be so lax as to excuse naivety or unreasonable failure to be observant:

> "Thus, even where the plaintiff is not an engineer, has no interest in DIY and the like, he would still not be excused for taking no action in response to the rapid spread of a large damp green mouldy patch in his wall. The reasonable person would have taken some action. He would have known something was wrong because he would have used his standard intelligence to draw from his store of standard past experience. (Para. 2.36)."

The Commission considers that taking into account the individual circumstances of the plaintiff will mean that, in cases where the plaintiff has 'superior knowledge, intelligence [or] experience', these factors will be relevant, 'so that the engineer will be expected to infer the appropriate facts from the cracks on the walls of a house sooner than the ordinary householder lacking in such professional experience': para 2.38. The Commission is surely correct in its view of how the test should be applied to a person with professional qualifications or experience. Whether superior intelligence should be a factor may be debated: it is not taken into account in determining the negligence or contributory negligence of adults, though it is relevant in relation to that of children: see McMahon & Binchy, *op cit.*, paras. 40.05ff. It would seem a little rough on geniuses that their claims should expire sooner than for the generality of humanity.

The Commission proposes (paras 2.39, 2.40) that the discoverability test should apply in relation to tort, contract, breach of statute 'or independent of any such provision', including claims for infringement of constitutional rights. Exceptions proposed by the Commission are actions for libel, slander and injurious falsehood. In this context it is worth noting that the Commission is of the view (para.2.42) that ' .... it would be too audacious to attempt to define damage. There as so many variations of damage that to define it would only serve unnecessarily to restrict the scope of loss or damage.'

The Commission proposes that the discoverability formula should be so drafted as to prevent the discoverability of trivial damage from triggering the limitation period. To start the limitation clock on the basis of such a level of damage 'would inevitably cause hardship to numerous plaintiffs. This would be so particularly in construction cases where the full significance of a minor hairline crack might not be evident for four or five years': para 2.43. Perhaps it would be useful for the legislation to make it clear that, in cases where an awareness of trivial damage should apprise the plaintiff of the likelihood that the damage will worsen, this should be enough to trigger the limitations clock.

As to the drafting model for translation of its proposals for a discoverability test, the Commission recommends that Alberta's Limitation Act 1996 should be followed. This requires that the plaintiff ought to be aware 'that the loss, assuming liability on the part of the defendant, warrants bringing proceedings.' The Commission is conscious that the departure from the model provided by the Statute of Limitations (Amendment) Act 1991 could conceivably encourage courts to infer that differences in drafting were intended to introduce substantive changes. Nevertheless it favours the Alberta legislation because its relative simplicity is in harmony within the Commission's 'plain language' philosophy. To allay any possible concerns, it proposes that the new legislation should include a provision referring courts to its Report when interpreting the Act.

The Commission goes on to recommend (para. 3.05) that the plaintiff should be entitled to take action within six years from the accrual of the cause of action or three years from the date when the cause of action is or ought to be discoverable by the plaintiff, whichever expires later. The Commission proposes, however, that there should be a long-stop date, after which a plaintiff would not be permitted to sue, regardless of whether the damage was discoverable by then. It summarises in para. 4.12, the factors that led to this conclusion:

> "We are of the opinion that, in non-personal injury cases, the need for certainty in the law and also the economic considerations which affect not only the defendant but society in general are of greater weight when pitched against the purely economic claims with which we are dealing. In such cases, we are essentially weighing up two economic interests: that of the plaintiff in being able to bring a potential action; and that of the defendant in having to maintain insurance cover indefinitely (which can be significant, especially in construction cases) or bear the risk if he does not, as well as the costs inherent in storing the relevant documents. In addition, underlying the consideration of these opposing interests is the overriding concern of ensuring certainty and confidence in the law."

The Commission recommends (para 4.16) that the longstop period should be ten years. While some Commissioners were in favour of a period of twelve years as it is more generous to the plaintiff and consistent with limitation period for contracts under seal, the perceived advantage of ten years is that it is consistent with the growing trend in the construction industry to take out insurance cover for ten years, the Liability for Defective Products Act 1991, section 7(2)(a) (see *Annual Review of Irish Law 1991*, pp.430-2) and the Home Bond guarantee scheme. The proposed starting-point for the ten-year period is the date of accrual rather than 'the date when the harmful act or omission took place' – if one can so describe an omission.

The Commission recommends (para 5.13) that the limitation period should generally start to run from the time the first item of loss resulting from the wrongful act becomes discoverable, even in respect of any other damage which becomes discoverable after that date. Exceptional cases would be those where a single act causes *distinct* damage on two separate occasions or where a continuing tort, actionable only on proof of damage, is involved.

The Commission turns to consider the important question whether the accrual of a right of action to an owner of property against the designer or builder of a building should have the effect of preventing a subsequent purchaser from having a right of action against the defendant in respect of that damage. The English Court of Appeal so held in *Sparham – Souter v. Town & Country Developments (Essex) Ltd* [1976] Q.B. 858 and its approach received Lord Wilberforce's blessing in *Anns v. Merton London Borough Council* [1978] A.C. 728, at 758. The position was reversed there by the Latent Damage Act 1986, section 3. There is no Irish authority in which the issue has been separately addressed. The Commission, writing five months before the Supreme Court handed down its judgment in *Glencar Exploration plc v. Mayo County Council* [2002] 1 I.L.R.M. 481, considered that there was apparently 'no substantive rule in Irish law which prevents a claim in tort for damage to property, where the plaintiff had no interest in the property at the time of the damage being inflicted.;: para 5.20. In any event, the Commission recommends that legislation should be enacted to this effect.

If the subsequent purchaser is not to be deprived of a right of action by reason of the fact that the first purchaser had a right of action, how should the discoverability principle operate in respect of the subsequent purchaser's claim? One approach, favoured by the Alberta Law Reform Institute and the Ontario Law Reform Commission, treats the limitation period as having started to run when the damage was discoverable by the first owner. Another approach, favoured by the English and New Zealand Law Commissions, is that the slate is wiped clean and that a new discoverability test applies to the subsequent purchaser. In para 5.34 of its Report, the Commission acknowledges that the arguments for either of these approaches are 'evenly balanced'. It prefers the former. We suggest that the equities tilt rather towards the latter. The subsequent purchaser's right of action is a distinct, rather than inherited, one. It should have its own discoverability test, especially where the Commission has taken the view that discoverability should be determined by having regard to the plaintiff's particular circumstances. If the first purchaser was an engineer, the clock may well have started to tick against him or her in circumstances where it would not for a lay purchaser. That is entirely just in respect of his or her claim but it is far from just that the subsequent purchaser, a layperson with no such professional expertise, should have his or her right of action affected by the personal circumstances of another claimant in respect of a separate claim. It is of course true that the building and defect represent common denominators in the two claims but tort law generally regards wrongs as being done to individuals rather than groups of claimants. A robust argument that a builder would be open to endless litigation if the law did not, as it were, pass the baton of a right of action from one purchaser to a later purchaser is surely weakened by the equally robust strategy, favoured by the Commission, of a ten-year long-stop.

The Commission considers that the balance of equities lies in favour of making the legislation non-retrospective in its effect: 'many professionals and other potential defendants will have made insurance provision for action against them involving latent damage based on the present limitations legislation' (Para. 5.56). Similar concerns did not win the day in relation to the 1991 Act, where claims for personal injuries and death were involved.

The Commission recommends (para 6.18) that, in construction liability claims, a cause of action in contract should accrue for all of the participants in the construction process at the date of the completion or purported completion. So far as such claims are concerned, the starting point of the long stop in both tort and contract should also be this date: para. 6.41.

Turning to legal incapacity (a term it prefers to 'disability') the Commission recommends (para. 7.04) the removal from the Statute of Limitation 1957 of section 48(1)(c) which suspends the operation of the Act in cases where a person is a convict subject to the operation of the Forfeiture Act 1870. The 1870 Act was repealed by the Criminal Law Act 1997.

The Commission recommends (para. 7.13) that unsoundness of mind be replaced with a definition, based on the Canadian Uniform Limitation of Actions Act 1931, which refers to a person who is 'incapable of the management of his or her affairs because of disease or impairment of physical or mental condition'. It proposes (para. 7.15) that, if, on the date when a right of action became discoverable, the person to whom it became discoverable was under a legal incapacity, the action may be brought at any time before the expiration of three years after the legal incapacity has ceased. A *supervening* legal incapacity should suspend the accrual and the proposed discoverability periods: para. 7.20. A thirty-year long stop for claims in respect of physical damage would apply to cases where the limitation period is postponed because the plaintiff is under a legal incapacity attributable to his or her mental or physical condition: para. 7.24. Where the accrual or the discoverability limitation period is postponed on account of minority the Commission proposes a long-stop of ten years commencing when the plaintiff reaches the age of majority: para 7.26.

The Commission recommends that legislation be enacted providing for the guardianship of adults under a legal capacity, which would include the power to commence, compromise or settle litigation that does not relate to the adult's estate: para 7.30.

The Commission enters a zone of controversy in making proposals that evince a certain dissatisfaction with the Supreme Court decision in *O'Brien v. Keogh* [1972] I.R. 144, which struck down the distinction, for limitation purposes, between children in the custody of a parent or guardian and children who are not. The Commission notes (para. 7.33) that '[a] question-mark was raised over the correctness of this decision by O'Higgins C.J. in the subsequent case of *Moynihan v. Greensmyth* [1977] I.R. 55.' The Commission states in paras. 7.31–7.32:

> "The fact that an action may be brought on behalf of the plaintiff by a
> guardian is not currently taken into account by section 49 [of the 1957
> Act]. In cases where this is possible it appears unnecessary to subject a
> defendant to a long and indefinite period of liability in situations where
> there is a guardian who could take the action within the limitation period.
> The Commission is of the view that this is unduly unfair to the defendant.
>
> Thus the Commission recommends that the limitation period should
> not be postponed unless the person under a legal incapacity can show
> that at the time of the incapacity he was not in the custody of a parent
> or guardian. At present and until the appropriate legislation concerning
> incapacitated adults is enacted, this recommendation can only be applied
> to minors."

The Commission considers that 'the difficulty highlighted in *O'Brien v. Keogh*',
concerning cases where a child has a right of action against a parent who has
custody of the child, can be avoided by providing that the limitation period
will be postponed where the claimant is actually taking an action against the
parent or guardian.

One may wonder whether these recommendations represent the best way
of responding to the difficulties that result from *O'Brien v. Keogh*. The
assumptions underlying the impugned distinction were crude and unsatisfactory
but they surely were more plausible in a society, nearly half a century ago,
where the incidence of marital breakdown and birth outside marriage was far
lower than today. It would seem premature to reintroduce the concept of a
child's being in the custody of his or her parent or guardian as a criterion for
reducing the scope of the child's legal right of action, without first having
considered how it would work, or be intended to work, in practice in cases
where married parents have separated, divorced or remarried or, in the case of
unmarried parents, where the father has close associations with the child but
has not been appointed guardian under the provisions of the Status of Children
Act 1987.

A further difficulty should be noted. The Supreme Court in *O'Brien v.
Keogh* did not limit its condemnation of the provision to cases where the child
is suing a parent. It also had concerns about cases were the parents died shortly
after the accrual of the right of action, leaving an orphan behind them who, by
reason of the drafting of the provision, was treated as a child in the custody of
the parents, since the relevant time was that of accrual; thus, if the parents and
the child were in a traffic accident in which all were injured and the parents
died as week later, the child was treated as one in the custody of his or her
parents.

On the relationship between fraud and discoverability, the Commission
recommends (para. 7.50) that a supervening fraudulent concealment should

suspend only the remainder of the limitation period, until the fraudulent concealment becomes discoverable. A long stop should not apply in the context of fraud: para 7.52. The Commission proposes (para. 7.54) that a long stop of thirty years should be applied to the postponement under section 72 on account of mistake.

CONSTITUTIONAL ASPECTS

In *White v. Dublin Corporation*, High Court, May 25, 2001, which Garrett Simons analyses in the Chapter on Planning Law, below, 451, applicants for judicial review also sought a declaration that section 82 (3B)(a) of the Local Government (Planning and Development) Act 1963, inserted by section 19 of the Local Government (Planning and Development) Act 1992, was invalid having regard to Articles 40.3 and 43 of the Constitution. The provision contained a two-month limitation period for taking proceedings to question the validity of a decision of a planning authority on an application for permission under Part IV of the 1963 Act. This provision was an absolute bar, with no provision for extension of the period of limitation. One of the grounds of invalidity asserted by the applicants was that an aggrieved party could be denied the right to take proceedings even where he or she could not have known within the two-month period of his or her entitlement to take proceedings.

The case arose from a situation where, the applicants claimed, a neighbour's application for planning permission, which they had not contested because it did not involve serious detriment to their own privacy, had subsequently been modified to their disadvantage, without their knowledge, with the approval of the Corporation.

Having emphasised the need for transparency in the decision-making process, Ó Caoimh J. noted that the uncontroverted evidence adduced by the applicants made it clear that substantial grounds existed for contesting the planning permission in question. Furthermore it was clear that the time limit provided in section 82 had elapsed before the applicants became aware of the terms of the decision:

> "In the absence of further notification or advertising in the terms of the 'modifications' sought under Article 35, the applicants would have had to have been inspired to know of the terms of the decision in question before the two month period had elapsed. However, having regard to the terms of Section 82 itself, even if the applicants had become aware of the decision in question one day after the expiry of the two month period in question the same factual position would essentially present itself to the applicants as presented itself in fact to them in the summer of the year 2000. It is apparent from the state of the planning file that it was not clear to the applicants what the status of the planning permission

was in the absence of any indication of an extension of time having been given in favour of the local authority at a time prior to that decision being made where on inspection the planning file did not reveal the existence of any such extension of time."

Counsel for the Attorney General argued that the applicants' lacked *locus standi* because they had failed to move within a period of two months from the date of becoming aware of the decision. Ó Caoimh J. acknowledged the 'superficia[l] attracti[on]' of this argument but he noted that the applicants were still out of time to bring any challenge to the planning decision in question. In these circumstances no mechanism existed for a late application to be made outside of the two month time limit. This in effect called into question the provisions of the section which had been found by Costello J. in *Brady v. Donegal County Council* [1989] I.L.R.M. 282 to be unreasonable and therefore unconstitutional.

If the section had contained a provision requiring the application to be made within two months of when the applicants knew or ought to have known of the decision in question, the applicants might well have found themselves to be in a position where they were out of time. This was not the position, however. The section 'made no provision whatsoever to deal with the situation in which they found themselves'. It was on this basis that they sought to challenge the validity of the provision in question having regard to the Constitution. Accordingly Ó Caoimh J. held that the applicants had the necessary *locus standi* to bring a challenge to the provisions of section 82. Ó Caoimh J. considered it 'clear', in the context of any such challenge, that the courts would have to consider whether the time limit contained in section 82 'was such as to undermine or compromise the substantive right guaranteed by the Constitution of access to the court.'

The whole question of short limitation periods with no provision for extension to deal with hard cases is a troubling one from the standpoint of constitutional law. Of course there is a real social need to expedite the planning process but this should not be at the price of justice to individuals. Costello J.'s analysis of the dilemma, in *Brady v. Donegal County Council*, offers a potential argument in favour of some modification of the existing law. Hogan & Morgan, *Administrative Law in Ireland* (3rd ed, Round Hall Sweet & Maxwell, Dublin, 1998), p.456 observe that Costello J.'s reasoning 'casts considerable doubt on the validity of this subsection (and, indeed, by implication, other unqualified time bars of this kind).' See also Brady & Kerr, *The Limitation of Actions* (2nd ed, Butterworths, Dublin, 1994), p212.

An open-ended entitlement to extend the limitation period where justice so requires could create its own difficulty, however. Experience with the judicial power to *dismiss* proceedings on this broad ground shows how elastic are the principles that apply and how difficult it is to predict outcomes in specific cases. Yet if the legislature were to attempt to prescribe the cases where an extension should be permitted, going beyond a 'discoverability' test, it would be very hard to predict the variety of contingent circumstances in which justice would require an extension. A limited list of such cases would create new, and possibly unconstitutional, anomalies in the law.

ISSUE OF WRIT

In *Bula Ltd v. Crowley*, High Court, February 20, 2001, Barr J. was required to make rulings prior to the trial of issues relating to the limitation of actions. This complex litigation, involving several actions with different parties, has been before the courts for well over a decade.

Barr J. had no difficulty in accepting the proposition that issuing a writ to prevent the running of the Statute of Limitations could not be classified as an abuse of process. He referred to *Baulk v. Irish National Insurance Co.*, [1969] I.R. 66, where Walsh J. had expressed the view that it was:

> "erroneous to compare the position of proceedings which have been commenced by the issue of a plenary summons that has not been served within the necessary 12 months with the position where no proceedings have been issued at all. Section 11 subs. 2(b) of the Statute of Limitations, 1957 requires that the action in this case be brought before the expiration of 3 years from the date on which the cause of action accrued, but it does not require that the proceedings should be served within that time. If the proceedings, for one reason or another, cannot be served or are not served within that time, then a plaintiff may find himself in a position where he cannot pursue his action and the alternative course of issuing fresh proceedings may be useless to him if more than three years from the date of the cause of action have already elapsed."

Barr J. considered it to be of interest that Order 8, rule 1 of the *Rules of the Superior Courts 1986*, which deals with the renewal of summonses, provides that:

> "... a summons so renewed shall remain in force and be available to prevent the operation of any statute whereby a time for the commencement of the action may be limited and for all other purposes from the date of issuing of the original summons."

This clearly implied that the efficacy of a plenary summons was not dependent on service and that issuing it would stop time running under the Statute of Limitations.

TRESPASS TO THE PERSON

In *Devlin v. Roche* [2002] 2 I.L.R.M. 192 (Supreme Court, affirming High Court, Morris P.), the question of the limitation period for claims for assault and battery fell for consideration. The plaintiff claimed damages for assault and battery, negligence, breach of duty and breach of statutory duty in relation to the alleged attack on him by a member of An Garda Síochána. The proceedings were launched more than three, and less than six, years after the incident. The plaintiff conceded that his claims for negligence and breach of statutory duty were statute-barred but he argued that the claim for assault was still viable.

Section 3(2)(a) of the Statute of Limitations (Amendment) Act 1991 provides that '[a]n action founded on tort shall not be brought after the expiration of six years from the date on which the cause of action accrued.' This is subject to section 3(1), which provides:

> "An action, other than one to which Section 6 of this Act applies, claiming damages in respect of personal injuries to a person caused by negligence, nuisance or breach of duty (whether the duty exists by virtue of a contract or of a provision made by or under a statute or independently of any contract or any such provision) shall not be brought after the expiration of three years from the date on which the cause of action accrued to the knowledge (if later) of the person injured."

The question before the court, therefore, was whether an action based on intentional assault was one 'claiming damages in respect of personal injuries to a person caused by negligence, nuisance or breach of duty (whether the duty exists by virtue of a contract or of a provision made by or under a statute or independently of any contract or any such provision).' If it was, the plaintiff's action was barred. If not, then the six-year limitation period applied.

In the absence of any relevant Irish authorities, Morris P. referred to two English decisions. In the first, *Letang Cooper* [1959] 1 Q.B. 23, the plaintiff, when sunbathing on the grass, had been run over by the defendant's car. The defendant had failed to see her in his path. More than three years elapsed before the plaintiff commenced her proceedings. She based her claim both on negligence and 'the commission by the defendant of a trespass to her person.' The Court of Appeal found that in the circumstances of the case there was only one cause of action, which lay in negligence, and that it was accordingly statute barred. Lord Denning stated:

> "Where the injury is not inflicted intentionally but negligently I would say that the only cause of action is negligence and not trespass."

In *Stubbings v. Webb* [1993] A.C. 498, the plaintiff sued for damages for personal injuries arising out of alleged sexual assaults and other physical abuse on the part of the first and third named defendants. These actions were alleged to have taken place three decades previously. It was necessary for the court to determine whether the plaintiff's cause of action was one claiming damages for assault, in which case the claim was statute barred as having long exceeded the six-year limitation period, or was one for damages for negligence, nuisance or breach of duty, in which case a discretion was vested in the court under English law to extend the limitation period.

In the House of Lords Lord Griffiths, speaking on behalf of all their Lordships, said as follows:

> "I accept that *Letang v. Cooper* was correctly decided in so far as it held that negligent driving is a cause of action falling within section 2(1) of the Act of 1954 but I cannot agree that the words 'breach of duty' have the effect of including within the scope of the section all actions in which damages for personal injuries are claimed, which is the other ground upon which the Court of Appeal decided *Letang v. Cooper*. If that had been the intention of the draftsman it would have been easy enough to say so in the section. On the contrary the draftsman has used words of limitation; he has limited the section to actions for negligence, nuisance and breach of duty and the reason he did so was to give effect to the recommendation of the Tucker Committee that the three year limitation period should not apply to a number of causes of action in which damages for personal injuries might be claimed, namely damages for trespass to the person, false imprisonment, malicious prosecution or defamation. There can be no doubt that rape and indecent assault fall well within the category of trespass to the person."

Lord Griffiths went on to observe:

> "Even without reference to Hansard I should not myself have construed breach of duty as including a deliberate assault. The phrase lying in the juxtaposition with negligence and nuisance carries with it the implication of a breach of duty of care not to cause personal injury rather than an obligation not to infringe any legal right of another person."

Morris P was satisfied that the wording of section 3(1) of the 1991 Act could not be interpreted as embracing an action for damages based upon a deliberate assault:

> "In my view assault is a separate cause of action to an action based on negligence, or as it was originally described 'on case'. The distinction lies in the fact that in the one case there is a deliberate intention to cause the injury. In the other such an intention need not exist. In my

view an action based on assault is neither based on nuisance nor on a breach of duty but on the assertion of a deliberate intention to cause the injury. In these circumstances the limitations imposed by Section 3(1) of the 1991 Act have no application.

I am left in no doubt whatever that the views of Lord Griffiths in *Stubbings v. Webb* are correct and I respectfully adopt them."

Accordingly Morris P. held that the plaintiff's claim for damages for assault was not barred by virtue of the provisions of section 3(1) of the Statute of Limitations (Amendment) Act 1991.

The Supreme Court affirmed Morris P. Geoghegan J. (McGuinness and Hardiman JJ. concurring) acknowledged the strength of the competing interpretations of the expression 'breach of duty' but agreed with the approach adopted by Lord Griffiths in *Stubbings v. Webb*, subject to 'a small proviso'. Geoghegan J. would have preferred if Lord Griffiths had used the words 'particular breach of duty' rather than 'breach of duty of care'. Geoghegan J. explained:

"A breach of duty of care is really the same thing as negligence. But the law of tort traditionally recognised particular breaches of duty, which were governed by their own principles rather than by *Donoghue v. Stevenson*. The *Rylands v. Fletcher* duty, the duty to an invitee at common law and the absolute duty in respect of dangerous goods or articles are all examples of breaches of duty which would not always be accurately described as breaches of duty of care but which nevertheless clearly come within the statutory provisions.

But I cannot accept that a breach of some general duty not to commit a civil wrong of any sort could come within the expression 'breach of duty' in the statutory provision which clearly has to be interpreted in the context of the words next to it, i.e. negligence and nuisance. A breach of contract is, of course, also included but that is perfectly logical as that does not arise from a general duty but rather from a particular duty undertaken by a promise to another party. A breach of statutory duty is clearly analogous to a breach of a common law duty of care."

This passage is of considerable interest for a number of reasons. First, Geoghegan J. was right to emphasise that a doctrinal concept of duty, based on the language of the duty of care, is too narrow and anachronistic to capture faithfully the breadth of duties that can arise, or have arisen prior to statutory modification, under the common law of negligence. (As to the latter, the old duty to invitees, prescribed in *Indermaur v. Dames* (1867) L.R .2 C.P. 311, has been expunged by the Occupiers' Liability Act 1995.) What Geoghegan J. appears to envisage is that cases of strict liability, without the requirement of proof of any fault, should also come within the scope of the concept 'breach of duty'. The instances he cites – *Rylands v. Fletcher* liability and 'the absolute duty in respect of dangerous goods or articles' - appear to give this view some support.

Rylands v. Fletcher was traditionally interpreted as a decision articulating a rule of strict, though not absolute, liability. It has more recently been reinterpreted and restated by the High Court of Australia, in *Burnie Port Authority v. General Jones Pty Ltd*, (1994) 179 C.L.R. 520, in terms of negligence, albeit with a broad application of the concept of a 'non-delegable duty', which is in truth vicarious liability under another name. See further McMahon & Binchy, *op. cit.,* paras. 25.45 – 25.55. It is not entirely clear whether Geoghegan J.'s reference to 'the absolute duty in respect of dangerous goods or articles' refers to the strict liability regime prescribed by the Liability for Defective Products Act 1991 or the common law principle of vicarious liability in respect of extra-hazardous activities: see McMahon & Binchy, *op.cit.*, paras. 43.50 ff. Perhaps the latter is more probable since Geoghegan J. appears to be addressing his remarks to old common law rules rather than recent statutory innovations.

At all events we should note the difference between imposing vicarious liability on a person for the wrongful conduct of another and imposing strict liability on a person for his or her own conduct. In neither case is the person guilty of fault but in the former there will generally have been fault on the part of the other person in respect of whose conduct vicarious liability is imposed.

Does it really make sense to say that a person held strictly liable, without proof of any fault on his or her part, has been in 'breach of duty'? What duty existed in the first place? None surely. Indeed, it makes much more sense to say that we have a duty not to injure another intentionally than that we have a duty not to injure another without any fault on our part. Yet the effect of the instant decision is to interpret 'breach of duty' precisely in the reverse way. If this conclusion is a matter for criticism, the target of the criticism should not be the Supreme Court but rather the Tucker Committee which produced an incoherent recommendation for reform in England (*Report of the Committee on the Limitation of* Actions Cmd. 7740, 1949), leading to legislation there which (as, sadly, so often was the case) was transcribed unreflectively into Irish law.

One should not ignore another traditional pocket of strict liability: that relating to animals. Cattle trespass and *scienter* liability do not require proof of fault in the sense of negligence but are, perhaps, good examples of where the liability could reasonably be described as being premised on a 'breach of duty'. Neighbouring landowners can plausibly be considered to be in a relationship of ongoing duty towards each other: were not the metaphors of neighbourhood and proximity central to Lord Atkin's analysis in *Donoghue v. Stevenson*? Similarly, if one chooses to own an exotic and dangerous species of animal or to continue to possess a domestic animal when aware of its particular mischievous propensity, it seems consistent with ordinary language to say that one has a duty towards others in relation to the animal. The fact that liability is not premised on proof of negligence in respect of the particular circumstances in which the animal caused the injury is not decisive. By having, or retaining, the animal under one's control in circumstances where the animal was a danger to others one had a duty towards those others, of protection if not technically 'of care'. The strict liability regime applying to injuries caused by dogs, prescribed by section 21 of the Control of Dogs Act 1986, clearly comes within section 3(1), on Geoghegan J.'s analysis of the nature of a breach of statutory duty.

It is interesting to note that there is an ongoing debate as to whether personal injuries are recoverable under the rule in *Rylands v. Fletcher* and as to how to characterise a claim for personal injuries in the law of nuisance. The answer will depend on whether the courts are willing to categorise these two torts as essentially interferences with rights of property rather than harbingers of the action for negligence. So far as the tort of nuisance is concerned, the House of Lords in *Hunter v. Canary Wharf Ltd* [1997] A.C. 655 held that only those with an interest in the land might sue. Compensation might be awarded for physical injury, but on the basis that it interfered with an amenity, reducing the value of the proprietary right. One has to agree with Tony Weir's observation (*Tort Law* (Oxford University Press, Oxford, 2002), 147) that is 'odd to say that noises and smells affect the land itself, which has neither ears nor nose.' Whether Irish law has fully embraced this limitation is not entirely clear: see *Molumby v. Kearns*, High Court, January 19, 1999, McMahon & Binchy, *op cit.*, paras 24.59-24.71, Dunleavy, (2000) 6 Ir. Planning & Envir. L.J. 8. If the rationale for awarding damages for personal injury in nuisance actions were truly based on the interference with a proprietary interest, this would make the inclusion of nuisance claims within section 3(1) hard to justify.

One should also consider briefly the position in relation to claims for damages for infringement of constitutional rights. These may sometimes consist, in part or in whole, of claims in respect of personal injury, such as where the right to health or bodily integrity has been violated. On the basis of Geoghegan J.'s analysis, it seems that such claims are capable of falling within section 3(1). It may seem odd to describe an infringement of a constitutional right as a 'breach of duty' but is it any more curious than giving the same description to torts of strict liability? Indeed a Hohfeldian analysis of rights and duties would appear to support this conclusion.

Perhaps matters are not quite so simple. Our courts have yet to develop a sophisticated jurisprudence on the requisite components of liability for infringements of constitutional rights, either in general or in specific cases. It is therefore not clear whether liability should be premised on intention or negligence on the part of the infringer or, indeed, whether strict liability for an infringement may be imposed. However broad the answer may be, it seems clear that intentional infringement will at all events generate liability. In cases where the infringement of a particular constitutional right can involve liability when committed intentionally or negligently, it is possible that the courts would adopt the analogy with trespass to the person and apply section 3(1) to the latter, but not the former, mode of infringement.

Geoghegan J. went on to address, but not attempt to resolve, some wider issues relating to the tort of trespass. The whole question of the relationship between trespass, intention and negligence is complicated by the fact that the genus of the tort of trespass is ancient whereas the conceptual basis of negligence was not stated clearly until less than a century ago, in *Donoghue v. Stevenson* [1932] AC 562: see further the Torts Chapter below. Moreover, the ingredients of trespass have changed radically over the centuries. Originally, trespass to the person was a tort of strict liability based on the directness of the contact. Gradually, a defendant was permitted to escape liability on the ground of lack of voluntariness, intention or negligence on his or her part but the onus rested firmly on the defendant to establish such lack. The effect in England of Diplock J.'s decision in *Fowler v. Lanning* [1959] 1 Q.B. 426 has been to place the onus of proof on plaintiffs alleging an intentional trespass. In *Letang v. Cooper*, Lord Denning MR acknowledged that forcing a claim for negligent trespass into the category of a cause of action for negligence involved 'go[ing] one step further' than what had been decided in *Fowler v. Lanning*. The position in England has not yet been finally resolved: *Street on Torts* (10th ed., by Brazier and Murphy, Butterworths, London, 1999), 25–6, observes that 'even today we cannot conclusively assert that trespass has no relevance when negligent conduct is relied on'.

Although courts in the United States of America have long gone down the path favoured in these two English cases, courts in some other common law jurisdictions have been more circumspect. In the recent decision of the Supreme Court of Canada in *Scalera v. Non-Marine Underwriters, Lloyds of London* [2000] 1 S.C.R. 551, the majority of the Court regarded the tort of trespass as having continuing vitality in protecting personal autonomy from direct infringement. Echoing some of the arguments made by Sullivan in "Trespass to the Person in Canada: A Defence of the Traditional Approach" (1987) 19 Ottawa L. Rev. 533, and by Linden J. in *Bell Canada v. Cope (Sarnia) Ltd*, 11 C.C.L.T. 170 (Ontario High Court, 1980), McLachlin J. observed:

> "When a person interferes with the body of another, a *prima facie* case of violation of the plaintiff's autonomy is made out. The law may then fairly call upon the person thus implicated to explain, if he can. If he can show that he acted with consent, the *prima facie* violation is negated and the plaintiff's claim will fail. But it is not up to the plaintiff to prove that, in addition to directly interfering with her body, the defendant was also at fault."

McLachlin J. was anxious to stress that she was not opposed to the possibility of 'future growth in this area of the law', which would require proof of something more than 'the minimum' of non-trivial contacts. It is worth noting that much of the discussion on this issue in many cases throughout the common law world (including *Stubbings v. Webb)* is connected with the question of limitation periods in litigation involving claims for sexual abuse. That matter has been dealt with in Ireland by the Statute of Limitations (Amendment) Act 2000, which we analysed in *Annual Review of Irish Law 2000* , pp.315-8. Another context in which the boundaries between trespass and negligence have been debated is that of informed consent to treatment. A negligence characterisation won the day in *Walsh v. Family Planning Services* [1992] 1 I.R. 486 (see *Annual Review of Irish Law 1992*, pp.560-1). Undoubtedly cases will arise where the non-disclosure will fall on the wrong side of section 3(1), on the basis that it was motivated by self interest rather than paternalism. For a comprehensive analysis of this area of the law see John Healy, *Medical Negligence: Common Law Perspectives* (Sweet & Maxwell, London, 1999), chap. 6.

Uncertainties remain in this area. The onus of proof is of course a crucial question. Moreover, it is not at all clear what 'negligence' means in the context of negligent trespass: specifically whether it carries with it any requirement of a breach of duty of care over and above carelessness and, if so, whether the duty must have been owed to the plaintiff. Similarly the scope of 'intention' has yet to be determined. On one view it should not be necessary for the plaintiff to show that the defendant's intention was directed towards the plaintiff. In this regard, *Winfield and Jolowicz on Tort* (15th ed, by Rogers, Sweet & Maxwell, London, 1998), p.84, fn. 87, refer to the Northern Ireland Court of Appeal in *Livingston v. Ministry of Defence* [1984] N.I. 356 which applied the doctrine of 'transferred intent' to the tort of battery. This was Winfield's own preferred interpretation of English law ((1935) 83 U. of Pennsylvania L. Rev. 416 fn 15) and has deep American roots: Prosser, "Transferred Intent" (1967) 45 Texas. L. Rev. 650. There is, however, a formidable argument in principle against making the ineffectively directed malevolence of the defendant towards one person the basis of liability in trespass to another, not an intended or foreseeable victim of that hostility. For further consideration of this theme, see McMahon and Binchy, *op. cit.*, paras 22.07–09.

In *Devlin*, Geoghegan J. made it clear that his judgment was based on the claim being one of intentional trespass. He expressed no opinion on what the situation would be if it were one for unintentional trespass; while the view that such an action should be treated as one for negligence was attractive because it forestalled an anomaly, it seemed clear that the law relating to unintentional trespass was not settled in Ireland. Not only would there be the question as to whether negligence was an essential ingredient but also the question as to the onus of proof in relation to such negligence.

If an important distinction is to be made between intentional and unintentional trespass, the courts will in the future have to distinguish between intention as to the direct contact with the plaintiff and intention as to its injurious consequences on the other: see Oughton, Lowry & Merkin, *Limitation of Actions* (LLP, London, 1998), pp.279–80. If a plaintiff pleads battery and the defendant acknowledges an intent of direct contact but denies an intent of injury, is there not a case for holding that the claim falls within section 3(1), regardless of the substantive law relating to negligent trespass, on the basis that the injury was unintended?

TRUST

In *Jobling – Purser v. Jackman*, High Court, November 27, 2001, Kinlen J. following the principles set out in Esher M.R's judgment in *Joar v. Ashwell* [1893] 2 A.C. 390, at 393, applied section 44 of the Statute of Limitations 1957 to the complex facts of the case, holding that the defendant was an express trustee.

DISMISSAL FOR WANT OF PROSECUTION

In *Brennan v. Fitzpatrick,* Supreme Court, November 23, 2001, affirming High Court, March 20, 2000, medical negligence proceedings initiated in 1989 in relation to events occurring in 1986 were dismissed for want of prosecution. The statement of claim had been delivered in 1990. A reply to a motion for particulars raised by the defendants was made in 1992. The defendant's defence was filed in March 1996. This was struck out in December 1998.

A solicitor had represented the plaintiff until February 1998. After a gap of seventeen months, another solicitor represented him. By the time of the hearing of the appeal to the motion for dismissal for want of prosecution, the plaintiff was again a lay litigant.

Applying the principles set out by the Supreme Court in *Primor plc v. Stokes Kennedy Crowley* [1996] 2 I.R. 459, Denham J. (Murray and McGuinness JJ. concurring) had no doubt that the delay in the instant case had been inordinate. It was also inexcusable. The main excuse given before the High Court had been that a medical report was being awaited from a consultant in Britain. Denham J. pointed out, however, that obviously a medical opinion had been obtained when the proceedings had been launched. Moreover the plaintiff's first solicitor had served notice of trial in May, 1996 and the medical report in question had not been sought until February, 1999 (and had still not been obtained at the time of the swearing of an affidavit on March 2, 2000).

The plaintiff had also complained about the documents furnished on discovery. The defendants had submitted that they had made a full discovery. Denham J. considered that a problem on discovery could have dealt with by either of the solicitors for the plaintiff.

The plaintiff also had submitted that he had not known of the actual orders that were being sought or of the affidavits filed on behalf of himself and on behalf of the defendants. This did not avail him, however, as, at the relevant time, he had legal representation.

The inordinate delay had given rise to a substantial risk that it would not be possible to have a fair trial and the delay was 'likely to have caused serious prejudice to the defendants'. On balance, the justice of the situation was in favour of dismissing the proceedings, as Johnson J. had ordered in the High Court.

The problem of how the principles relating to dismissal for want of prosecution (or other delay) should operate in the context of litigation claiming damages for child abuse arose in *Kelly v. O'Leary* [2001] 2 I.R. 526. It will be recalled that the Statute of Limitations (Amendment) Act 2000 enables victims of sexual abuse to take proceedings many years later where they can show that the abuse caused psychological injury of such significance as to substantially impair his ability to initiate the litigation. See the *Annual Review of Irish Law 2000*, pp. 314–8. In *Kelly v. O'Leary*, the plaintiff was alleging physical rather than sexual abuse, when she was a child in an orphanage run by the defendants, an order of nuns. Her statement of claim alleged systematic beatings and dreadful humiliations. A difficulty with the claim was the great delay that had occurred since the time of the alleged events, during the period from 1937 to 1947. Most of the key witnesses were long deceased and the nun against whom some of the most serious allegations were made was 82 years old.

Kelly J. acknowledged that a question arose as to whether the test set by *Ó Domhnall v. Merrick* [1984] I.R. 152 and *Toal v. Duignan (No. 1)* [1991] I.L.R.M. 135 was more indulgent to defendants than that prescribed by *Primor.* He did not seek to resolve this question, however, preferring to apply the putatively more stringent *Primor* test with its threefold criteria.

There was no doubt that the delay had been inordinate; it was also inexcusable, in Kelly P.'s view, since little or no evidence had been put forward as to the presence of exercising circumstances:

> "The plaintiff has been free of the dominion, if dominion there was, of the Sisters of Mercy for well over 50 years. During that time she married and had a large family. No medical or psychological evidence has been given in her support by way of affidavit although ample time was afforded to enable such an affidavit or affidavits to be sworn."

The balance of justice lay in favour of dismissing the action. The 82-year-old nun's memory was likely to fade and become distorted during the period before the litigation would come to trial. She had care for over a thousand children over the years that she was at the orphanage and it was, in Kelly J.'s view, 'therefore hardly surprising that there is evidence to the effect that she cannot remember specific incidents'. Virtually all the witnesses who might be available to the defendant had died. While the case was not dependant on documents, they did nonetheless play an important role in it. The plaintiff's medical records relating to the three nervous breakdowns she had suffered as an adult no longer existed. These would have been relevant to the issue of the causation of her medical complaints. Without them the defendant was unable properly to investigate the cause of the plaintiff's mental distress, The defendant had not contributed to the delay. Kelly J. observed:

> "There is here a real and serious risk of an unfair trial. As a matter of probability the trial may amount to an assertion countered by a bare denial. Indeed even the ability of this defendant to make a denial is doubtful in respect of a number of allegations. Such an exercise would be far removed from the form of forensic inquiry which is envisaged in the notion of a fair trial in accordance with the law of this State.
>
> Constitutional principles of fairness of procedure require that the action not proceed. To allow the action to go on would put justice to the hazard."

As we have already noted, *Kelly v. O'Leary* did not involve any claim relating to sexual abuse. Let us nonetheless try to assess the implications of the decision for claimants in litigation involving sexual abuse who fulfil the disability requirements of the Statute of Limitations (Amendment) Act 2000. Is what has been given to them by that legislation to be taken away by the common law rules developed by *Ó Domhnall v. Merrick, Toal v. Duignan (No. 1)* and *Primor plc v. Stokes Kennedy Crowley*? We suggest that *Kelly v. O'Leary* does not present an insuperable hurdle in the generality of cases. The plaintiff's case foundered largely on account of her failure to convince Kelly J. that the delay was excusable. In cases complying with the liability requirements of the 2000 Act, the constituent elements of that disability are likely, either in most cases or in all *a priori,* to be considered to render the delay excusable.

Of course, if the more generous criterion afforded to defendants by *Ó Domhnall v. Merrick* and, more particularly, *Toal v. Duignan (No. 1)* were to be applied, rather than the *Primor* test, the issue of the inexcusability of the plaintiff's delay would not be isolated, considered and resolved as a precondition of addressing the broader discretionary factors such as the availability of witnesses or documentary evidence in support of the defendant. It is possible that a court would regard section 3 of the 2000 Act as prescribing a distinctive new statutory criterion, not reducible either to the *Primor* stream of jurisprudence or that of *Ó Domhnall v. Merrick* and *Toal v. Duignan (No. 1)*. We suggest that a close reading of that provision does not permit of an entirely new test, since it refers to an assumed pre-existing 'power of a court to dismiss an action on the ground of there being such delay between the accrual of the cause of action and the bringing of the action as, in its interests of justice, would warrant its dismissal'. If the issue of statutory interpretation is narrowed to the question of which of the two judicial streams is captured by this language, it has to be acknowledged that the latter seems closer to it. Nonetheless, the policy thrust to the 2000 Act would so obviously be thwarted by an unduly lenient criterion for dismissal that the pressure will be on the court to apply the *Primor* test.

ESTOPPEL

In the chapter on Evidence, above, 269, Declan McGrath analyses the Supreme Court decision in *Ryan v. Connolly* [2001] 2 I.L.R.M. 174, [2001] 1 I.R. 627. Eoin Ó'Dell in the Contract Law Chapter, above, 125, also subjects the decision to critical consideration.

More generally, see Anthony Barr, 'Estoppel and the Right to Plead a Defence under the Statute of Limitations' (2001) 6 Bar Rev. 445.

ADVERSE POSSESSION

In *Mulhern v. Brady,* High Court, February 14, 2001, a claim of adverse possession of agricultural land failed. Carroll J. found that there had been no open assertion of title as evidence of intent to extinguish the title of the registered owner. She adopted the observations of O'Hanlon J., in *Doyle v. O'Neill*, High Court, January 13, 1995 that "the adverse user must be of a definite and positive character and such as could leave no doubt in the mind of a land owner alert to his rights that occupation adverse to his title was taking place". This was particularly the case when the piece of land in question was "for the time being worthless or valueless for the purposes of the original owner".

Local Government

LOCAL GOVERNMENT ACT 2001

Introduction   The Local Government Act 2001 represents the culmination of a major process of legislative and constitutional reform, begun in the late 1980s, intended to produce a complete restatement of local government law in Ireland. With the enactment of the 2001 Act, this process can be said to have reached a conclusion, at least in terms of major reform. It also marks the final eclipse of the Local Government (Ireland) Act 1898, which until the 2001 Act remained the major landmark law in this area. The 2001 Act also replaced the Municipal Corporations (Ireland) Acts 1840 and 1843, the Commissioners Clauses Act 1847, the Towns Improvement (Ireland) Act 1854 and various post-1922 Local Government Acts. It is not possible in the present context to do full justice to an Act comprising more than 240 sections and over 200 pages; what follows is a broad overview of its main provisions. It is also necessary to mention that, given the scope of the 2001 Act, it will be phased in by means of various Commencement Orders over a period of years.

General overview   The 2001 Act follows from the Twentieth Amendment of the Constitution Act 1999, which inserted a new provision into the Constitution, Article 28A, and gave specific recognition to local government as well as fixing a five-year interval between local elections. Prior to the 1999 amendment, local authority elections were frequently postponed, which in turn reflected poorly on the importance of local government. Under the 2001 Act, local authorities will generally be titled county councils, city councils and town councils in line with everyday language, though the title 'borough' was also reinstated during the passage of the Act in response to suggestions during the debate in the Oireachtas. The 2001 Act contains a general statement of local authority functions; a comprehensive code on local authority membership; provides for the office of Cathaoirleach for all local authorities (to which the title mayor may be assigned and which will, from 2004, be an elected full-time office for a five year term) and for the holding of local elections and filling of casual vacancies; and provides flexible arrangements for local authority co-operation and joint service provision.

Other provisions include a corporate plan for county/city councils; a framework for the introduction of new financial management and accounting systems; local government audit; and flexible powers for the making of byelaws. A comprehensive new general ethics framework will apply for both staff and councillors; and modern provisions concerning local authority staffing and related matters are also incorporated. Provision is made for introduction by regulations of a salary for councillors. The 2001 Act includes provision for an independent commission to deal with local authority boundary changes and local electoral reviews. Provision is made for establishment of new town councils, change of place names and public local inquiries.

The 2001 Act emphasises that the elected council determines policy, and sets out an updated range of mechanisms to oversee, monitor and direct implementation of policy by the executive. The manager operates within this policy framework and under a duty to carry into effect decisions of the elected council. A new framework is provided for local authority meetings with right of media and public access. The partnership model is introduced for county and city councils via strategic policy committees (SPCs) with representation from relevant sectoral/community interests. The SPC chairs and the Cathaoirleach form a corporate policy group which must be consulted in preparation of the corporate plan and annual budget for submission to the council, in effect a form of local cabinet.

The 'dual mandate' One of the most-publicised proposals in the legislation when initially proposed was to end, from 2004, the 'dual mandate', by which local authority councillors may also be members of the Oireachtas. This proposal was not included in the 2001 Act as enacted, primarily due to successful lobbying by a number of non-party independent Tads who were also local authority councillors and whose support the government required. It remains to be seen whether this issue will be revisited at some future date. Until then, the dual mandate is still permissible.

Local authority divisions Part 2 of the 2001 Act contains key provisions establishing local authorities within a modern legislative format. The State is divided into local government areas of counties and cities. Within the counties, and forming part of them, are the town local authorities. Each of these areas – county, city or town – has a local authority known, as appropriate, as a county council, city council or town council; or borough council in some cases. In accordance with the 2001 Act, some major local authorities have engaged in significant name changes. By way of example, Dublin Corporation has become Dublin City Council.

Local authority membership and elections Parts 3 and 4 of the 2001 Act deal with local authority membership and local elections. Any person 18 years or over and a citizen of Ireland or ordinarily resident in the State qualifies to become a councillor. Eligibility is subject to certain disqualifications, set out in sections 13 and 14 of the 2001 Act. Local elections are fixed at five yearly intervals to be held in the month of May or June, with the next local elections in 2004. A mechanism is included to allow for alteration in the number of members of a local authority. As regards co-options, the 2001 Act provides that in future, co-optees to a local authority must be nominated by the party for which the departing member concerned was elected.

Cathaoirleach (mayor)   Part 5 of the 2001 Act deals with the position of the Cathaoirleach, which, under existing law, is the generic title. Existing mayors and lord mayors continue and it will be open to any local authority to adopt the title mayor or Cathaoirleach. From 2004, the Cathaoirleach of counties and cities will be elected by direct vote for the life of the council, this is, likely to be five years. The Cathaoirleach will be a full-time position.

Meetings and committees   As regards meetings of local authorities, Part 6 of the 2001 Act establishes a statutory right of public access, and restricts the right to meet in committee to special cases and subject to special procedures. Schedule 10 sets out a comprehensive, consolidated, code for local authority meetings. It provides for annual, ordinary and special meetings. Prior to meetings it requires notification of members and public notice and availability of agenda; and with special arrangements for budget (estimates) meeting and annual meeting and for convening of special meeting. At meetings it provides for quorum, chairing of meeting, business of meeting; deciding of questions; right of public and media access; minutes; appointments to other bodies; etc. And for standing orders to be made by the local authority, to regulate such other matters as it may consider appropriate, as well as certain matters to be incorporated in such orders. It also allows for the issue of guidelines by the Minister to promote the objective of appropriate gender balance in the making of appointments by local authorities to committees or other bodies.

The framework for local authority committees and joint committees is set out in Part 7 of the 2001 Act. The relevant provisions specify that county and city councils establish strategic policy committees (SPCs), chaired by an elected member but comprising both councillors and sectoral/community interests. SPCs are to advise the council on policy matters and are established in accordance with guidelines issued by the Minister. It was pointed out during the Oireachtas debate that SPCs have been in operation on an administrative basis for some time. Guidelines in place prior to the coming into force of the 2001 Act provide for the drawing up of an SPC scheme by a local authority and include guidance on: representation of sectoral interests and selection procedures, the term of office of SPC members and chairs, and procedures to be followed in appointing chairs and other positions. In effect, the SPCs form the core of a type of local authority cabinet.

Local authority functions   Part 9 of the 2001 Act contains a general statement of local authority functions, including a general obligation to provide a forum for the democratic representation of the local community and to provide civic leadership. Specific functions, which are carried out under relevant legislation, are listed in Schedule 12 of the Act. These include functions directly conferred on local authorities, such as planning, housing, sanitary (waste) services, fire, water pollution and roads. Also included are matters for which Ministers other than the Minister for Local Government are responsible but which involve local authorities, such as higher education grants and the control of horses. The Act also provides a range of broad powers to promote the community interest, including provision of local amenities such as public parks and library services. Part 9 also includes updated arrangements for: making bye-laws to regulate matters of local concern; land acquisition and disposal; establishment of a community fund to support local projects; discretion to introduce a community initiative scheme whereby an annual contribution can be introduced for a specific community initiative, but only following extensive local consultation; and the conferral of civic honours and other matters concerning the ceremonial role. Part 10 of the 2001 Act allows for necessary inter-authority co-operation in the performance of functions. It provides the flexibility for service arrangements, such as fire services, to be made on foot of local agreements between town and county authorities or between adjoining counties and cities.

Local Government Commission   Part 11 of the 2001 Act provides for the establishment of an independent Local Government Commission, which is responsible for the review of local electoral areas under Part 4; the alteration of local authority boundaries under Part 8; and the establishment of new town councils.

Financial management and budget   Part 12 of the 2001 Act allows for the modernisation of financial management, accounts and audit to provide transparent, user-friendly and comparable data for all authorities. Thus, it is provided that, each year a local authority shall prepare a draft budget (formerly known as local authority estimates). The manager must consult the corporate policy group (CPG) for this purpose. Provision is also made for a Local Government Audit Service and the Director of Audit; and that local government auditors shall be independent in the performance of their professional functions. In an era where corporate governance is becoming increasingly significant, no doubt Part 12 of the 2001 Act will take on increasing importance in the years ahead.

Community development   In the context of the general obligation on local authorities to ensure democratic participation, Part 13 of the 2001 Act provides a statutory basis for the establishment, composition and functions of the County/ City Development Boards (CDB), which had already been set up in some areas prior to the 2001 Act. It also provides for the preparation by such Boards of a strategy for the economic, social and cultural development of its area; and that other bodies shall have regard to such strategy.

Local government service and management   Part 14 sets out the respective roles of the elected council, manager and staff. It provides that the policy role of the elected council is expressed by it in the exercise of its reserved functions. These include the functions listed in Schedule 14, such as the striking of a rate. Further specific functions may be designated as reserved functions by the Minister. Part 14 also sets out the duty of the manager in relation to the elected council: to carry into effect the decisions of the council and to advise and assist the council. It also provides for the establishment by each county and city council of a corporate policy group (CPG), comprising the Cathaoirleach and chairpersons of the SPCs to advise and assist the elected council in the formulation, development and monitoring of policy for the local authority. The CPG must be consulted by the manager in the preparation of the authority's draft budget and may involve additional persons to assist it. It must also be consulted in the preparation of the corporate plan. The corporate plan, or statement of strategy, will normally have effect for the life of the council. It will set out the principal activities of the local authority, its objectives and priorities, proposals to work towards improved customer service and human resource activities. The plan must be drawn up in consultation with the CPG, in accordance with any Ministerial guidelines, and must be adopted by the elected council. An annual progress report must be submitted by the manager.

Ethical framework   Part 15 provides a comprehensive new ethics framework for members and officials. It involves: disclosure of interest in any matter which arises, an annual statement of interests and a public register of interests which is overseen by the Public Offices Commission. Codes of conduct for staff and members are also envisaged.

Non-performance of functions; removal from office   Part 21 of the 2001 Act restates previous law as regards the non-performance of certain functions, including dissolution of a Council, in effect removing the elected officials from office. The circumstances in which the Minister may order a dissolution include situations where: the Minister is satisfied, after the holding of a public local inquiry, that a local authority is not effectually performing its functions, a local authority fails to comply with a decree of court, a local authority fails to adopt a budget (formerly an estimate) sufficient for its expenses. In recent years, such orders have been made under pre-2001 legislation where councils have failed to adopt draft estimates, which have included certain charges for services, notably refuse charges.

HOUSING

Gaeltacht   The Housing (Gaeltacht) Amendment Act 2001 amended the Housing (Gaeltacht) Acts 1929 to 1979 to update the arrangements for housing grants and assistance in Gaeltacht areas.

Planning Law

GARRETT SIMONS, B.L., Lecturer in Administrative and Planning Law, King's Inns

PLANNING AND DEVELOPMENT ACT 2000

PLANNING AND DEVELOPMENT REGULATIONS 2001

Introduction   The Planning and Development Act 2000 still represents the single most significant source of change in relation to planning law. Although passed in the year 2000, the Act has been commenced on a staggered basis only: for this reason, and given the scale of the task otherwise involved, it is intended to confine this commentary to those parts of the Act which had been commenced in the year 2001. In this regard, those provisions of principal interest are in relation to the acquisition of lands (including the acquisition of protected structures), and the licensing of events and funfairs. (See S.I. No. 449 of 2000; S.I. No. 153 of 2001; and S.I. No. 335 of 2001.) These are discussed in further detail below. Before turning to that task, however, it is proposed to make a few brief remarks in relation to the Planning and Development Regulations 2001.

Planning and Development Regulations 2001   The Planning and Development Regulations 2001 (S.I. No. 600 of 2001) represent a consolidation of the regulations in relation to the planning legislation. In particular, the 2001 Regulations will replace the previous principal regulations, the Local Government (Planning & Development) Regulations 1994 – 1999. As these earlier regulations were not revoked until March 11, 2002, and the Planning and Development Regulations 2001 themselves only came into force on January 21, 2002, and March 11, 2002, discussion of these regulations is, strictly speaking, outside the purview of the present annual review (S.I. No. 599 of 2001). For this reason, it is intended only to provide a very brief sketch in relation to these regulations.

One theme, which emerges clearly from the Planning and Development Regulations 2001, is that of (increased) public participation. This is particularly evident in those provisions in relation to the making of an application for planning permission, and any subsequent appeal. The site notice, and newspaper notice are to be more user-friendly. For example, where the application is for permission consequent on the grant of outline permission, it will be necessary to state the register reference number of the relevant outline permission. The notices must also state that the planning application may be inspected or purchased at the offices of the planning authority, and that a submission or observation in relation to the application may be made to the authority in writing on payment of the prescribed fee within the period of five weeks beginning on the date of receipt by the authority of the application. Where the applicant for planning permission is a company, certain information including the names of the directors, and the address and registration number of the company, must also be submitted with the application.

A planning authority is also required to approve a list of newspapers, including national newspapers, it considers have a sufficiently large circulation in its functional area. This exercise might well avoid the difficulties which had arisen on the facts of *Brady v. Donegal County Council* [1989] I.L.R.M. 282.

A site notice is required to be inscribed or printed in indelible ink and affixed on rigid durable material and secured against damage from bad weather and other causes. Where there is more than one entrance to the lands from public roads, a site notice must be erected or fixed on or near all such entrances. The planning authority may also require additional site notices.

Where a subsequent application for planning permission is made within six months from the date of the making of a previous application in respect of substantially the same lands, then the site notice must be on a yellow background.

The importance of the public notices is elevated in that the (former) discretion of the planning authority in circumstances where there is some defect in either a newspaper notice, or a site notice, is removed under the regulations. Under the Local Government (Planning & Development) Regulations 1994, a planning authority had discretion to allow a defect to be remedied by the giving of further notice of the application for planning permission. Under Article 26 of the 2001 Regulations failure to comply with the requirements in relation to notice renders the application invalid; nor can the planning authority rescue the application by a request for further information (Article 33). The one exception to this is where the planning authority is satisfied that the applicant complied with the requirements in relation to his site notice but that any site notice erected by the applicant has been maliciously defaced or destroyed by any person other than the applicant.

Much criticism has been made of the fact that it is now necessary to pay a fee (€20) when making a submission or observation. As against this, the level of service provided to a person making a submission or observation in relation to an application is greatly enhanced. For example, such a person is entitled to an acknowledgement of the submission or observation; to notification in circumstances where an application is returned as invalid (Article 29); to notification of the decision on the application (Article 31); and to notification of the fact of an appeal (Article 69). Moreover, where further information or revised plans are submitted which contain '*significant additional data*' then an observer is entitled to notification of the fact of the submission (Article 35). (Similarly a person making a submission or observation on an appeal is entitled to notice of the decision of An Bord Pleanála (Article 74)).

The minimum period for the determination of an application is extended to a period of five weeks (Article 30). It should also be noted that any submissions or observations received after this time cannot be considered (Article 29).

The notification of the decision on the application will have to be a more meaningful document. In particular, the planning authority must specify, *inter alia*, the main reasons and considerations on which the decision is based, and, where conditions are imposed on the grant of planning permission, the main reasons for the imposition of any such condition. In the case of a decision to grant or refuse planning permission where the decision by the planning authority is different, in relation to the granting or refusal of permission, from the recommendation in the report or reports on the application, the main reasons for not accepting the recommendation in the report or reports must be specified.

Similar provisions apply with respect to the decision of An Bord Pleanála on an appeal (Article 74). In addition, where An Bord Pleanála grants planning permission in circumstances where the planning authority had refused planning permission on the basis of an (alleged) material contravention of the development plan, the planning authority must state the main reasons and considerations for materially contravening the development plan.

The provisions in relation to further information, and revised plans, are also tightened up (Articles 33 and 34). In the event that a request for further information is not complied with, the application shall be declared to be withdrawn after the period of six months from the date of the requirement for further information or evidence has elapsed. The further information or revised plans are to be available for inspection or purchase. Again, a person making a submission or observation is entitled to notification. Further, a fresh newspaper notice may also be required.

ACQUISITION OF LAND

Introduction   Significant amendments are introduced under Part XIV of the Planning and Development Act, 2000 in relation to the acquisition of land. These amendments can be considered under two headings as follows. First, a number of amendments are introduced to the substantive law in relation to the acquisition of land. Secondly, the compulsory purchase procedure has been considerably modified.

Acquisition of land   The general powers of a local authority to develop or to secure or facilitate the development of land are replicated, under Part XIV of the Planning and Development Act 2000, in broadly similar terms to that which had applied under the previous legislation (section 77 of the Local Government (Planning & Development) Act 1963.) In addition, it is expressly provided under section 212(4) that a planning authority may use powers in relation to the compulsory acquisition of land, in particular, to facilitate the assembly of sites for the purposes of the orderly development of land.

The nature and extent of a local authority's power to acquire land is also regulated. Of particular interest is the fact that a distinction is drawn between acquisition effected by agreement, and that effected compulsorily. It appears from a reading of section 213(3) that whereas lands may be acquired by agreement where the local authority has not determined the manner in which or the purpose for which it will use the land, the compulsory purchase power is only available if the local authority is of the opinion that the land will be required for a particular purpose (although not necessarily immediately required).

A local authority is afforded a greater level of flexibility in relation to lands in its ownership. Local authority land may be sold, leased or exchanged, by a local authority, subject to such conditions as it may consider necessary, where the local authority no longer requires the land for any of its functions, or in order to secure: (a) the best use of that or other land, and any structures or works which have been, or are to be, constructed, erected, made or carried out on, in or under that or other land, or (b) the construction, erection, making or any carrying out of any structures or works appearing to it to be needed for the proper planning and sustainable development of its functional area. (Section 211) (Ministerial consent is not needed in all cases: see Article 206, Planning and Development Regulations 2001.)

These provisions are open to the criticism that they appear to de-couple the acquisition of land from the underlying public purpose. More specifically, given the constitutional protection afforded to property rights, it would seem that the power of a local authority to acquire lands by way of compulsory purchase must be limited to circumstances where there is a countervailing public interest. If there is no such countervailing public interest, or if, for whatever reason, it becomes spent after the acquisition has occurred, then it would seem that the original land owner should be entitled to retain, or offered the opportunity of recovering, his lands. (cf. *Crosbie v. Custom House Dock Development Authority* [1996] 2 I.R. 531.) One danger of the wording of the new provision is that the fact that lands acquired even by way of compulsory purchase may be put to another use, or sold leased or exchanged, might be relied upon by a local authority as lessening the burden otherwise upon it to demonstrate a particular purpose in respect of which compulsory purchase is necessary, before the confirming authority. (The argument being that if the land can be put to other use subsequently, the importance of demonstrating a particular purpose is less significant.)

Compulsory purchase procedure   Turning now to the compulsory purchase procedure, this has been modified so as to transfer the confirming function from the Minister for the Environment and Local Government, to An Bord Pleanála. This applies to a wide range of compulsory purchase powers under legislation such as, for example, the Housing Acts, the Roads Acts, and the Dublin Docklands Development Authority Act 1997.

The provisions of Part XIV of the Planning and Development Act 2000 in this regard are open to the very serious criticism that they fail to state expressly what considerations it is that An Bord Pleanála should take into account in deciding whether or not to confirm a compulsory purchase order. The fact that the confirming function has been transferred to An Bord Pleanála would seem to suggest that the adjudication must involve a consideration of proper planning and sustainable development. This inference is borne out by the fact that in performing its functions in this connection, An Bord Pleanála is required to have regard to the policies and objectives for the time being of, *inter alia*, planning authorities and any other body which is a public authority whose functions have, or may have, a bearing on proper planning and sustainable development. (See section 218(4) and section 143.) All of this would seem to suggest that the decision in *Crosbie v. Custom House Dock Development Authority* [1996] 2 I.R. 531 is of little or no relevance to the new procedures. It seems that the function of An Bord Pleanála is much wider than the function previously exercised by the Minister for the Environment and Local Government. (The decision in *Crosbie v. Custom House Dock Authority* is also distinguishable on the basis that, on the peculiar facts of that case, the need for redevelopment and regeneration had been determined, in principle, by the legislation itself.)

Protected structures   A different form of acquisition procedure applies in relation to protected structures. Under section 71 of the Planning and Development Act 2000 the test for acquisition (whether by agreement or compulsorily) is that it appears to the planning authority that it is necessary to do so for the protection of the structure. Any person, on whom a notice of the proposed compulsory acquisition has been served, may submit to the planning authority concerned an objection. If the objection is not withdrawn, the planning authority must apply to An Bord Pleanála for consent. Again, the legislation is silent as to what matters An Bord Pleanála should take into account in making its adjudication in this regard. In particular, it is not clear on what basis An Bord Pleanála should assess the necessity of acquiring structures. It is also to be noted that unlike the position obtaining in relation to a conventional compulsory purchase order, an objector does not have a right to an oral hearing.

The power of acquisition extends to any land which forms part of the attendant ground of the protected structure, and, is, in the planning authority's opinion, necessary to secure the protection of the structure, whether or not the land lies within the curtilage of the structure or is specified as a feature in the record of protected structures.

DEVELOPMENT PLAN

Material contravention Under section 39 of the Local Government
(Planning & Development) Act, 1963, a local authority is prohibited from
carrying out development, in its functional area, which would represent a
material contravention of the development plan. (See now section 178, Planning
and Development Act 2000). A novel aspect of this provision was considered
by McKecknie J. in his decision in *Byrne v. Fingal County Council,* High
Court August 2, 2001. The applicant sought to prohibit the development of a
travellers' halting site by the local authority. One of the grounds put forward
in support of the application was that the proposed development involved a
material contravention of the development plan. McKecknie J. ruled that as
the use of land as a halting site was expressly included as one of the acceptable
uses under the relevant zoning, there was no question of a material contravention
of the land use provisions of the development plan. McKecknie J. then went
on to consider whether or not a breach of an express obligation under the
development plan to follow a consultation procedure with the local community
in relation to the provision of a halting site could *per se* represent a material
contravention of the development plan. McKecknie J. held that lack of
consultation could not amount to a material contravention. In so holding, it
appears that McKecknie J. considered that a material contravention would
have to involve a (physical) breach of a planning objective or planning policy.
    McKecknie J. held that notwithstanding the fact that a failure to consult
did not represent a material contravention, the obligation to consult could
nevertheless be enforceable. McKecknie J. held that it could be said to be a
condition precedent to the finality of any proposal in relation to a halting site,
and, accordingly, held that the intended works could not proceed in the absence
of the commitment being satisfied.

Emergency situation The decision in *Byrne v. Fingal County Council,* High
Court August 2, 2001 is also of interest in that the relationship between the
prohibition on material contravention and the procedures under the (then)
Section 2 of the City and County Management (Amendment) Act 1955 (as
amended), was considered too. In brief, the provisions of section 2 allowed
for a procedure whereby the manager was required to inform the elected
members of an intention to carry out works. It was then open for the elected
members to direct by resolution that such works not proceed, subject to certain
exceptions. (See now sections 138, 139, and 140 of the Local Government
Act 2001.) One of the exceptions to this procedure was where the works were
necessary to address an emergency situation. In this regard, emergency situation
had an artificial definition and an emergency situation was deemed to exist
where, in the opinion of the manager, the works concerned were urgent and
necessary in order to provide a reasonable standard of accommodation for any
person.

McKecknie J. held that the prohibition under section 39 of the Local Government (Planning & Development) Act 1963 (see now section 178, Planning and Development Act 2000) was not affected by the deemed emergency provisions. McKecknie J. held that these latter provisions regulated the internal affairs of the local authority and defined the relationship between the manager and the elected members. The provisions did not by-pass the prohibition in relation to a local authority carrying out development in material contravention of the development plan.

The findings of McKecknie J. in this respect would seem to be borne out by consideration of the transitional provisions under section 27 of the Housing (Traveller Accommodation) Act 1998. Specifically, the 1998 Act had introduced an express requirement that a local authority include, in its development plan, objectives in relation to the provision of accommodation for travellers. The transitional provisions stipulated that any thing done, or act carried out, by a housing authority for the purpose of implementing an accommodation programme shall be deemed not to contravene a development plan in the period between the coming into operation of this (new) obligation and compliance with same. The absence of any other provision under the housing legislation disapplying the prohibition on local authority development in material contravention of the development plan would suggest that the prohibition remains intact in all other cases. (cf. *Ward v. Donegal County Council,* High Court, November 30, 2000.)

The findings of McKecknie J. are also supported by reference to the provisions of the Waste Management (Amendment) Act 2001. The fact that specific provision was made under that legislation to by-pass the material contravention prohibition might be taken as indicative of the fact that but for such express provision, same would continue to apply.

The decision in *Byrne v. Fingal County Council* highlights the following anomaly in the planning legislation: whereas a local authority is in one sense in a privileged position in that it is, generally, exempted from the requirement to obtain planning permission, it is actually in a worse position insofar as material contravention of the development plan is concerned. It is open, in principle at least, to grant planning permission to a private sector developer in respect of a material contravention of the development plan. In the case of local authority exempted development, conversely, generally speaking there is no such 'out'.

Waste Management (Amendment) Act 2001   The relationship between the waste management plan, and the statutory development plan, is regulated under the Waste Management (Amendment) Act 2001. Reference is made, in particular, to the provisions of section 22(10C) of the Waste Management Act, 1996 (as inserted by section 4 of the Waste Management (Amendment) Act 2001). The manager has a discretion to proceed with development which would materially contravene the development plan in circumstances where the development is consistent with the provisions of, and is necessary for the implementation of, the waste management plan. There is a requirement that the manager shall publish notice of the intention of the local authority to carry out the proposed development, and to allow for the making of submissions or observations. In respect of applications for planning permission, section 34(6) of the Planning and Development Act, 2000 does not apply in similar circumstances.

Reference is also made to the provisions of Section 22 (10) of the Waste Management Act 1996 (as inserted by section 4 of the Waste Management (Amendment) Act, 2001). A local authority shall not, by resolution, under sections 3 or 4 of the City and County Management (Amendment) Act 1955 give a direction that works not be proceeded with, or require any act, matter or thing to be done or effected, where the effect of such direction or requirement would be contrary to, or inconsistent with, any provision of a waste management plan or would limit or restrict the proper implementation of such provision. (See now sections 138, 139, and 140 of the Local Government Act 2001.)

Content and procedure   Insofar as the concept of a development objective is concerned, it is to be noted that the very restrictive approach taken by Blayney J. in the High Court in *Glencar Exploration plc. v. Mayo County Council* [1993] 2 I.R. 237 was queried by Keane C.J. in the Supreme Court decision on the applicants' claim for damages. (*Glencar Exploration plc v. Mayo County Council* [2002] 1 I.L.R.M. 481). Blayney J. in the High Court had suggested that in order to represent a valid development objective, an objective would have to be positive in character and have as its aim the carrying out of works on, in or under land. Keane C.J. expressly reserved for another occasion the question as to whether the decision of the High Court on the substantive issue was correct in point of law. In particular, Keane C.J. drew attention to the fact that various other matters which a planning authority had discretion under statute to include in its development plan did not require the carrying out of works of any sort.

The decision in *Glencar Exploration plc v. Mayo County Council* [2002] 1 I.L.R.M. 481 is also of interest in that the duty of the planning authority in or about the making of the development plan was considered. The function of a planning authority was characterised in the following terms. Same constituted the exercise of a power vested in the planning authority by law for the benefit of the public in general. It was not the fulfilment by the planning authority of a duty imposed by statute for the specific protection of particular categories of persons, the breach of which may lead to an action for damages. Accordingly, the *ultra vires* exercise of the power could not of itself provide the basis for an action in damages.

TRAVELLERS' HALTING SITES

Under section 21 of the Housing (Traveller Accommodation) Act 1998, a local authority is required to appoint a committee to be known as the local traveller accommodation consultative committee. Under section 21 (3) a local consultative committee may, *inter alia*, advise in relation to the preparation and implementation of any accommodation programme for the functional area of the local authority. This provision was considered in the decision in *Jeffers v. Louth County Council,* High Court, April 5, 2001. Murphy J. held that consultation with the local consultative committee is required so as to allow the committee to advise, not only in relation to the preparation of, but also in relation to the *implementation* of, any accommodation programme. On the facts of the case, Murphy J. ruled that the local authority should be restrained from carrying out any further development of a travellers' halting site unless and until the procedures prescribed under the Housing (Traveller Accommodation) Act, 1998 had been complied with. The decision in *Byrne v. Fingal County Council* High Court August 2, 2001 has already been discussed above, under the heading 'Development plan'.

APPLICATION FOR PLANNING PERMISSION

Request for further information The ambit of a planning authority's discretion to request further information was considered in some detail in the decision in *Murphy v. Navan Urban District Council*, High Court, July 31, 2001. The planning authority had sought, by way of a request for further information, and by way of a clarification, the following. First, the applicant was requested to submit revised public notices arising from an (alleged) deficiency in the existing public notices in relation to the description of the nature and extent of the proposed development. Secondly, documentary evidence was sought in relation to the ownership of the entire application site.

The applicant for planning permission contended that neither of these matters constituted a proper request for further information, and accordingly, argued that the request for clarification was invalid and thus did not stop time running for the purposes of a default planning permission. The applicant accordingly argued that he was entitled to a default planning permission. In particular, the applicant argued that the only procedure whereby a further public notice could be required was that provided for under Article 17 of the (then) Local Government (Planning & Development) Regulations 1994. In connection with the request for information in relation to the title to the lands, it was submitted that the question of ownership had been clarified in the context of a previous application for planning permission, and that in circumstances where the instant application was simply for retention of alterations to development authorised by that planning permission, it was not a *bona fide* request for clarification of further information supplied. It was also suggested that the planning authority was seeking to require the applicant to make material statements to his detriment in a matter with which the planning authority itself was materially concerned and in a manner which could only be of benefit to the planning authority. (There was a dispute as between the applicant and the planning authority as to the ownership of a ten-foot strip of land along the boundary between his property and that of the local authority.)

Ó Caoimh J. rejected these submissions, and held that the planning authority was entitled to make a request for such further information as to the estate or interest in or right over the land, which it considered necessary to enable it to deal with the application for planning permission.

In relation to the argument as to the public notices, Ó Caoimh J. accepted that the notices were inadequate. As for the argument that any requirement to publish new site notices should have been made under Article 17, at the time at which the planning authority first considered the application for planning permission, Ó Caoimh J. ruled that he would not be disposed to grant the applicant a declaration in relation to a default planning permission in circumstances where this alleged failure to invoke Article 17 had not been pleaded in the statement of grounds.

ENFORCEMENT

Enforcement notice   The procedures which a local authority must undertake in relation to the issue and service of an enforcement notice were considered by Herbert J. in his decision in *Dublin Corporation v. O'Callaghan,* High Court, February 13, 2001. Although this decision is in relation to the requirements of the previous legislation, it is submitted that at least some of the comments therein may be relevant to the new enforcement mechanism. (The procedure in relation to the issue and service of an enforcement notice is streamlined under the Planning and Development Act 2000. The provisions in this regard came into force on March 11, 2002 and will be considered in further detail in next year's Annual Review.)

Herbert J. held that the (then) legislation envisaged two separate and distinct steps being taken by a planning authority in relation to an enforcement notice: first, the making of a decision that it is expedient to serve an enforcement notice; secondly, the preparation and service of that notice. The wording of the (then) provisions of section 31 of the Local Government (Planning and Development) Act 1963, indicated that in determining whether or not it was expedient to serve an enforcement notice, the planning authority was not at large, but restricted to considering the proper planning and development of the area including the preservation and improvement of the amenities of the area; the provisions of the development plan; any Special Amenity Area Orders relating to the area; any relevant ministerial directives; the terms of any planning permission (if any); and the probable effect which the decision might have on any place which is not within or is outside the area of the planning authority. Herbert J. held that it must clearly have been intended that the making of a decision by a planning authority that it was expedient to serve an enforcement notice must be attended by some formality, by some recording of the fact that a decision to serve a notice had been taken, and of the basis upon which it had been determined that it was expedient so to do. In the absence of such a record, the High Court would find it difficult, if not entirely impossible, to review a decision of a planning authority to serve an enforcement notice. Herbert J. further held that this formal record must have come into existence prior to the enforcement notice being signed or served on the relevant owner and occupier: the enforcement notice cannot itself constitute this record which must both *ante* date, and be entirely separate from it.

This judgment represents a robust defence of the rights of a person affected by an enforcement notice. By requiring the planning authority to lay bare its decision-making process, it allows such a person to consider whether or not there might be grounds for challenging the legality of the enforcement notice by way of an application for judicial review. (It is one of the curious features of the planning legislation that the decision to issue and serve an enforcement notice is not subject to any form of administrative appeal.)

It is not entirely clear as to the extent to which these principles might be applied to the new enforcement notice procedure under Part VIII of the Planning and Development Act 2000. The legislation is largely silent as to the matters which a planning authority must take into account in deciding whether or not to serve an enforcement notice. Section 153 (3) baldly states that a planning authority, in deciding whether to issue an enforcement notice, shall consider any representations made to it or submissions or observations made to it, and *'any other material considerations'*. As a matter of first principle, one might have thought that the same considerations which apply in relation to a decision on an application for planning permission should operate: in a sense, the decision as to whether or not to serve an enforcement notice is the obverse of the decision to grant or refuse planning permission, in that given the draconian effects of an enforcement notice, it would seem inappropriate to issue an enforcement notice in circumstances where the development was not objectionable in planning terms, and planning permission would inevitably have been granted had an application in that regard been made. The matter may not, however, be as clear-cut under the new legislation in that it is elsewhere provided that no enforcement action shall be stayed or withdrawn by reason of the fact that an application for retention planning permission has been made, or even granted. (Section 162 (3)) This might be taken as suggesting that the two issues are separate and that the primary purpose of an enforcement notice is now regulatory, in the sense of penalising failure to apply for planning permission in a timely fashion.

Liability of directors   The decision in *Sligo County Council v. Cartron Bay Construction Limited,* High Court, May 25, 2001 is of interest in relation to the appropriate respondents to an application for a planning injunction. There had been a failure by a company to comply with the terms of an order made by the High Court under the (then) section 27 of the Local Government (Planning and Development) Act 1976 (as amended). Ó Caoimh J. held that insofar as the affairs of the respondent company were inextricably linked to the actions of the two director respondents, if the company had been in wilful default it had been through the medium of the actions of the directors. Insofar as a company can have a will, it must be by those in control of the company. In this connection, Ó Caoimh J. held that whereas the failure of a corporate entity will not necessarily give rise to a conclusion of wilful default on its part or on the part of its directors, on the facts, the directors were guilty of a substantial wilful failure to account to the company in respect of rent.

The decision is also of interest in that Ó Caoimh J. held that matters relating to the manner in which the directors had carried on the affairs of the company and, in particular, in relation to allegations that they had siphoned off monies, could be dealt with in the context of an application for a planning injunction. Ó Caoimh J. held that while it was clear that a plenary hearing in a case such as this would be preferable to one on affidavit, none of the parties had sought such a hearing. Furthermore, Ó Caoimh J. was satisfied that all of the respondents knew the nature of the case against them, and that the director respondents were afforded every opportunity of meeting the case against them. In this regard, Ó Caoimh J. appears to have distinguished the decision in *Dublin County Council v. O'Riordan* [1985] I.R. 159.

Contempt of court   The decision in *Curley v. Galway Corporation,* High Court, March 30, 2001 provides a dramatic example of the teeth of the planning injunction. The facts were unusual in that the respondent was itself a local authority: the development was being carried on outside its functional area, and, accordingly, subject to the requirement to obtain planning permission in the ordinary way. Various orders had previously been made under section 27 of the Local Government (Planning and Development) Act 1976 (as amended). An application to attach and commit the manager, and for the sequestration of the local authority's assets, had been brought arising out of breaches of those orders. Kelly J. held that the object of the contempt proceedings was coercive. In the light of undertakings received on oath, and subject to conditions, Kelly J. ruled that it was not necessary or appropriate to make orders of committal or sequestration at that juncture. Kelly J. instead adjourned the application for sequestration on terms and directed the appointment of an independent engineer, at the expense of the respondent local authority, to report to the High Court as to the level of compliance with its obligations under the terms of the existing court order. Kelly J. also imposed a fine of IR£50,000 and directed that the respondent local authority pay costs on a solicitor and own client basis.

Onus of proof The debate as to whether or not the onus of establishing an exempted development lies with the respondent in enforcement proceedings continues. In the decision in *Fingal County Council v. Crean,* High Court, October 19, 2001, Ó Caoimh J. held that he was satisfied that the onus rests upon the respondents to satisfy the court that the exemption contended for is one to which they are entitled. This decision is consistent with earlier authorities such as *Dillon v. Irish Cement Ltd.,* Supreme Court, November 26, 1986. As against this, other decisions such as *Westport Urban District Council v. Golden* [2002] 1 I.L.R.M. 439 suggest that the onus resides with the applicant, as moving party. This latter approach has much to recommend it. As a matter of first principle, it would seem that as the requirement to obtain planning permission represents as interference with constitutionally protected property rights, the availability of exempted development merely represents the restoration of the *status quo* and does not entail any benefit or privilege. Accordingly, there would appear to be no special reason which would justify shifting the onus to the respondent and away from the applicant as moving party.

JUDICIAL REVIEW: PROCEDURE

Substantial grounds The requirement that an applicant for judicial review establish '*substantial grounds*' for challenging the validity of a decision has been considered in a number of cases. Of particular interest, is the growing case law in relation to the similarly worded provisions of the Illegal Immigrants Act 2000. In *P. v. Minister for Justice, Equality and Law Reform* [2002] 1 I.L.R.M. 16, Smyth J., in the High Court, appeared to favour a much higher standard than has, to date, been applied under the planning legislation. Specifically, relying on the decision of the Court of Appeal in *Mass Energy Limited v. Birmingham City Council* [1994] Env. L. R. 298, Smyth J. appeared to suggest that an applicant might have to show that his case was not merely arguable but was strong; that is to say, was likely to succeed. It was not necessary for the Supreme Court to address this aspect of the decision in that it decided the case on narrower grounds. See generally "Judicial Review under the Planning Legislation – the case for the abolition of the leave stage" (2001) 8 I.P.E.L.J. 55.

Time limits The application of time limits in relation to judicial review proceedings had been considered in two decisions in 2001. In *Henry v. Cavan County Council* [2001] 2 I.L.R.M. 161, Ó Caoimh J. had to consider the relevant date from which time runs in circumstances where the decision of a planning authority is challenged. Section 82(3B) of the Local Government (Planning & Development) Act 1963 (as inserted by section 19(3) of the Local Government (Planning and Development) Act 1992), provides that an application for leave to apply for judicial review shall be made within the period of two months commencing on the date on which the decision is given. The applicant sought to challenge a decision of a planning authority to grant planning permission. The application for judicial review had not been made within two months of the date of the making of the decision to grant planning permission. The applicant argued that the date when the grant is made is the date from which the planning permission will apply and that it is this latter date which is the critical date. This argument was rejected by the High Court. It was held that a distinction must be drawn between a *decision* of a planning authority to grant planning permission, and the *grant* itself. On the facts, as the application for leave to apply for judicial review had not been made within the period of two months from that (earlier) date, the proceedings were inadmissible.

With respect, it is submitted that this approach is correct. It is trite law that judicial review is concerned with the decision-making process. In this regard, it would seem that the making of the grant of planning permission is a mechanical function only. Once the decision has been made to grant planning permission, then the planning authority or An Bord Pleanála, as the case may be, exercise no further discretion in the matter but must proceed to make a formal grant, once the relevant time periods have passed.

The decision does serve to highlight an anomaly in the legislation. It is this. In the ordinary course of events, the planning authority shall make a grant of planning permission only where no appeal has been brought to An Bord Pleanála against the decision within the appropriate period. If there is an appeal, then generally it is An Bord Pleanála who will make the final decision, and, where relevant, make a grant of planning permission. If, however, an appeal is made, but subsequently withdrawn or dismissed, then the decision of the planning authority, in effect, revives and the planning authority is required to make a grant. This could leave an objector stranded in the following circumstances. An objector dissatisfied with the decision of a planning authority might nevertheless forgo an opportunity to seek to challenge the validity of the planning authority's decision by way of judicial review, on the basis that an appeal has been brought, by another party, to An Bord Pleanála. If this appeal is subsequently withdrawn however, there is a risk that the decision of the planning authority will revive. The objector might then find himself in a situation where the time specified for bringing judicial review proceedings has expired, and thus by reliance on the appeal may have forfeited his opportunity to challenge the decision of the planning authority.

The second decision then is that of *O'Connell v. Environmental Protection Agency* [2002] 1 I.L.R.M. 1. Although this case concerned a challenge to a decision of the Environmental Protection Agency, and not a challenge under the planning legislation, it is of interest for the following reason. A challenge to a decision on an application for an integrated pollution control licence is subject to a two-month statutory time limit, although the application itself may be made by way of conventional judicial review. The notice party developer in *O'Connell v. Environmental Protection Agency* sought to argue that, notwithstanding the fact that the application for leave to apply for judicial review had been made within the statutory two month period, nevertheless the applicant had not moved promptly as required under Order 84 rule 21. Herbert J. held that the Environmental Protection Agency Act 1992, while imposing a non-expandable upper time limit within which an application for leave to apply for judicial review must be brought, does not in any way suspend or lessen the requirement under Order 84, rule 21 that every application for judicial review must be made promptly. On the facts, however, Herbert J. ruled that the applicant had fully excused any seeming delay on her part.

It is questionable as to whether this decision would be followed in the context of the special judicial review procedure under the planning legislation. If, as the decision in *K.S.K. Enterprises Ltd. v. An Bord Pleanála* [1994] 2 I.R. 128 seems to suggest, the interpretation of the requirements of the statutory time limit is to be guided by considerations of legal certainty, then it would seem unnecessary to undermine the certainty of the statutory time limit by reference to a concept as vague as promptness. Moreover, it is arguable that the finding in *Lancefort Ltd. v. An Bord Pleanála,* High Court, May 13, 1997 that the time period expires at midnight, and that the ordinary rules as to reckoning the date of service under Order 122 do not apply, indicates that the statutory time limit is the only restriction on time.

Time limit: constitutionality The fact that the two month time limit under the (then) provisions of section 82 (3A) & (3B) of the Local Government (Planning and Development) Act 1963 (as amended) admitted of no exception had raised a question mark over its constitutionality. The matter is now largely of academic interest only in that under Section 50 (4)(a)(iii) of the Planning and Development Act, 2000, the High Court is empowered to extend the prescribed eight-week period.

Nevertheless, the matter may still be relevant in respect of proceedings under the previous legislation. In *White v. Dublin Corporation,* High Court, May 25, 2001, the High Court held that the applicants had sufficient *locus standi* to challenge the constitutional validity of the two-month time limit.

The facts of the case were unusual. The notice party developer was a neighbour of the applicants for judicial review, and having been refused planning permission, appealed that decision and submitted a second application for planning permission in respect of a slightly modified development. The planning authority then invited the submission of revised plans under Article 35 of the Local Government (Planning and Development) Regulations, 1994. The planning authority did not, however, require that the application for planning permission be re-advertised. The applicants did not learn of the grant of planning permission until a date when the two-month time limit had already expired. The applicants contended that there were substantial grounds for challenging the validity of the planning permission, and that insofar as their application was barred by reference to the two-month time limit, the absence of any saver or exception rendered that time limit unconstitutional.

It was argued against the applicants that they did not have sufficient *locus standi* to bring the constitutional challenge in circumstances where they had failed to institute judicial review proceedings within two months of the date of their learning of the decision to grant planning permission. Ó Caoimh J. held that the applicants did have *locus standi*. This was presumably on the basis that as the High Court would not have power to rewrite the statutory provisions or to substitute a differently worded time limit, a finding in favour of the applicants would involve a finding of unconstitutionality *simpliciter*, and would result in the two month time limit being struck down. Provided that the applicants could demonstrate their ability to argue a live issue of prejudice within the meaning of *Cahill v. Sutton* [1980] I.R. 269 it would seem that they had *locus standi*. The fact that a saver *might* have been worded in such a way so as to pass muster constitutionally yet nevertheless have excluded the applicants on account of their delay in issuing proceedings once they learnt of the decision to grant planning permission, would seem irrelevant: the applicants still were in a position to put forward a concrete set of facts against which the validity of the actual statutory provisions could be tested.

(The point might still have been made against the applicants that the requirement to move promptly governs all judicial review proceedings (*O'Connell v. Environmental Protection Agency* [2002] 1 I.L.R.M. 1), and, accordingly, the principle of judicial restraint would seem to suggest that, just as it is appropriate to first determine whether or not the applicant has substantial grounds, this issue of delay should also have been determined before the High Court embarked on a consideration of the constitutional challenge (*Blessington & District Council Ltd. v. Wicklow County Council* [1997] 1 I.R. 273)).

Undertaking as to damages　　Order 84, rule 20(6) of the Rules of the Superior Courts, 1986 provides that if the High Court grants leave to apply for judicial review, it may impose such terms as to costs as it thinks fit, and may require an undertaking as to damages. These principles had recently been applied in the context of judicial review proceedings under the planning legislation in *Seery v. An Bord Pleanála (No. 2)* [2001] 1 I.L.R.M. 151. The decision in *O'Connell v. Environmental Protection Agency* [2002] 1 I.L.R.M. 1 provides a further example of the application of this rule to environmental litigation. Notwithstanding the fact that the judicial review proceedings raised various issues as to the procedures of the Environmental Protection Agency, and the implementation of Council Directive 85/337/EEC on environmental impact assessment, Herbert J. concluded that the real substance of the application was the preservation and protection of private property rights which were normally protected by private law remedies and that the apparent public law aspects of this challenge were, in fact, subsidiary though important issues. Accordingly, the applicant was required to give an undertaking as to damages.

Herbert J. declined, however, to require that the undertaking as to damages be fortified.

Types of decision protected The special judicial review procedure under the planning legislation applies only in respect of certain decisions of a planning authority or of An Bord Pleanála. For example, the decision of a planning authority to make or to vary a development plan is subject to conventional judicial review. Similarly, where, by way of planning condition, matters are left over for agreement as between a planning authority and the developer, the determination in this regard is also subject to conventional judicial review: *O'Connor v. Dublin Corporation* [2000] 3 I.R. 420; [2001] 1 I.L.R.M. 58 (*Annual Review of Irish Law 2000*, 336). It is well established that failure to use the special judicial review procedure where required will lead to proceedings being struck out: see, for example, *Goonery v. Environmental Protection Agency,* High Court, July 15, 1999. The question as to the propriety of invoking the special judicial review procedure in circumstances where it would have been sufficient to go by way of conventional judicial review remained open, however. This question was considered tangentially in the decision in *Neville v. An Bord Pleanála,* High Court, July 31, 2001. (See also decision of October 12, 2001.) Ó Caoimh J. held that it was not open to an applicant to seek to challenge, in the context of an application under the special judicial review procedure, a regular decision of a planning authority. More specifically, the applicant in those proceedings had sought to challenge the decision of An Bord Pleanála on an application for planning permission on the basis, *inter alia*, that the underlying provisions of the development plan were themselves invalid. Ó Caoimh J. held that it was not open to do so. With respect, it is arguable as to whether or not this ruling is correct. It would seem that the greater should include the lesser, and in circumstances where the basis of a challenge includes some matters which are not subject to the special statutory judicial review procedure, an applicant should be entitled to roll-up the relief sought in one set of proceedings. Indeed, it is difficult to see what possible prejudice could be suffered by a respondent in circumstances where an applicant has (voluntarily) undertaken the more onerous requirements of the statutory judicial review procedure.

Locus standi The decision in *Halpin v. Wicklow County Council,* High Court, March 15, 2001 provides a recent example of an applicant being refused leave to argue certain grounds of challenge on the basis that he did not have a sufficient interest in the matter. More specifically, the applicant was held not to have *locus standi* to challenge a decision to amend a development plan on the ground that a public notice was defective in circumstances where the notice had been sufficient, in fact, to draw his attention to proposed varied amendments to the development plan; where he actually responded to it and made such representations as he wished; and where he was not acting on behalf of anyone other than himself. The applicant was thus not permitted to raise a point against the public notice where he had not been prevented from making submissions.

Strictly speaking, a distinction should be observed in this context between the concepts of *locus standi* and *jus tertii*: the judgment appears to have elided the two concepts. In the particular circumstances of the instant case, the fact that the applicant was seemingly affected by the proposed development plan might have been thought sufficient to allow him standing to challenge a decision (*locus standi*); this would not necessarily mean that he is unrestricted in the arguments which he can make on the application (*jus tertii*). The practical significance of this elision may not be great, however: even if it did not go to the issue of *locus standi*, the fact that an applicant was not personally prejudiced by an alleged defect would in any event be relevant to the exercise of the High Court's discretion to withhold relief: *Cunningham v. An Bord Pleanála,* High Court, Lavan J., May 3, 1990. (Had the proceedings been taken under section 82(3A) & (3B) of the Local Government (Planning and Development) Act 1963, it would also go to the statutory requirement of 'substantial grounds'; *Blessington & District Community Council Ltd. v. Wicklow County Council* [1997] 1 I.R. 273).

JUDICIAL REVIEW: APPEALS TO SUPREME COURT

General   There is only a limited right of appeal to the Supreme Court in the case of the judicial review procedure applicable to certain types of planning decisions. Specifically, it is necessary to obtain the leave of the High Court in order to bring an appeal to the Supreme Court. See generally "Leave to appeal to the Supreme Court" (2002) 9 I.P.E.L.J. 3. These provisions were considered in detail in at least three reserved judgments in 2001. A number of principles emerged from these judgments which may be of universal application.

The Supreme Court in *Irish Hardware Ltd. v. South Dublin County Council* [2001] 2 I.L.R.M. 291 held that the provisions represented a regulation of the Supreme Court's appellate jurisdiction within the meaning of Article 34.4.3 of the constitution, and thus reaffirmed its previous decision in *Irish Asphalt Ltd. v. An Bord Pleanála* [1996] 2 I.R. 179. It was further held that the subsection, having excepted those cases from the appellate jurisdiction, went on to create an exception to this exception to allow an appeal if the case involved a point of law of exceptional public importance and it was desirable in the public interest that an appeal should be taken to the Supreme Court. In this connection, the decision of the High Court to grant or refuse leave to appeal is unimpeachable, and may not itself be the subject of an appeal to the Supreme Court. This second decision *viz.* to grant or refuse leave to appeal, was held not to represent a separate 'decision' of the High Court within the meaning of Article 34.4.3 of the constitution, so as to attract the general right of appeal.

A number of practical procedural issues were commented upon in the second judgment: *Kenny v. An Bord Pleanála* [2001] 1 I.R. 704; [2002] 1 I.L.R.M. 68, as follows. McKechnie J. noted that there is no statutory obligation to the effect that the certificate of the High Court on an application for leave to appeal must contain the point of law involved, though it was desirable that it should do so. McKechnie J. went on to state that an appeal is not confined to the point of law in question, and that indeed precedent showed that not infrequently such a point is abandoned during the currency of an appeal; rather the appeal is against the decision in its entirety with the appellant becoming *dominus litis* in the sense that he controls the scope of the appeal.

McKechnie J. also drew attention to the following paradox inherent in the statutory provision in respect of appeals. The requirement for leave to appeal applies not only in respect of the decision of the High Court on the substantive application for judicial review but also governs the application for leave to apply for judicial review. The High Court may only grant leave to apply for judicial review in circumstances where an applicant has demonstrated 'substantial grounds' for challenging the decision of the planning authority or An Bord Pleanála. Thus, the refusal of leave to apply carries with it the inference that such grounds as were raised were insubstantial. Before leave to appeal could be granted in such a case, it would be necessary for the High Court to certify that its decision involved a point of law of exceptional public importance and that it was in the public interest that an appeal be brought. McKechnie J. queried as to how it could logically be said that, within the same decision, one could have, on the one hand, a failure to establish substantial grounds and yet, on the other, on the same material, have a point of law of exceptional public importance? McKechnie J. went on to comment that if such a point existed, surely the ground thereof must have met the required threshold and therefore leave to apply for judicial review should have been granted.

It is respectfully submitted that the foregoing comments on the paradox are well made. It is submitted that the fact that leave to appeal is required even in respect of the decision on the application for leave to apply for judicial review is unfair. The effect of such requirement is that an applicant can be shut out from invoking the jurisdiction of the courts on the basis of a summary hearing before a single High Court judge. In the absence of the safeguard of an untrammelled right of appeal to the Supreme Court, this is open to serious criticism. Experience in relation to conventional judicial review indicates that leave to apply for judicial review is occasionally refused in error. In a number of cases where the applicant had initially been refused leave to apply by the High Court, only to be granted same by the Supreme Court, the applicant has gone on to succeed on the substantive hearing for judicial review. (See, for example, *O'Reilly v. Cassidy (No. 2)* [1995] 1 I.L.R.M. 311.) It is regrettable that the opportunity was not taken in relation to the reforms introduced under Section 50 of the Planning and Development Act 2000 to relax the requirements in this regard. At the very least, it is submitted that there should be a procedure whereby an applicant can renew his application for leave to appeal before the Supreme Court.

The third decision, *Ashbourne Holdings Limited v. An Bord Pleanála (No. 3)*, High Court, June 19, 2001, confirms that the point of law must arise out of the decision of the High Court itself, and not merely from discussion or consideration of a point during the hearing, be it of major or minor import, which did not go to the actual determination or decision itself. In other words, there is no place for a moot on some interesting point which may have arisen in the case.

Finally, the decision in *Neville v. An Bord Pleanála,* High Court, October 12, 2001 is authority, if authority were needed, for the proposition that an application for leave to appeal should be heard *inter partes.*

JUDICIAL REVIEW: SUBSTANTIVE

Reasonableness The decision in *Ashbourne Holdings Ltd. v. An Bord Pleanála* [2002] 1 I.L.R.M. 321 represents one of very few examples of a planning decision being quashed by reference to the concept of administrative unreasonableness.

The facts may be summarised as follows. The applicant company had previously applied for planning permission for the development of a golf clubhouse and ancillary facilities. It was accepted by all parties that there was no public right of way over the lands. As part of that earlier application, however, the applicant company had submitted various proposals for limited public access to the lands. Conditions to like effect had been attached to the planning permission. Subsequently, as a result of changes in the location and layout of the development, the applicant company made an application for retention planning permission. Planning permission was granted on appeal by An Bord Pleanála. Again, conditions were attached requiring public access to various parts of the lands (albeit in different terms), and, it was further provided that any charge for public access was to be agreed with the planning authority. The applicant company issued and served judicial review proceedings seeking to quash the relevant conditions of this second planning permission, and further sought an order of mandamus directing the grant of planning permission with the said conditions removed. It was urged on behalf of the applicant company that the impugned conditions were invalid on a number of grounds, including, *inter alia*, the following: the conditions did not fairly and reasonably relate to the permitted development; the conditions were directed at securing objects other than regulating the development and use of land and were irrelevant to planning; the conditions were unduly restrictive of constitutional rights; the conditions were void for uncertainty; and An Bord Pleanála had failed to have any or any adequate regard to the conclusions reached by its inspector.

Kearns J. agreed with a submission made on behalf of the respondents to the effect that the fact that the conditions were imposed largely as a result of representations and undertakings offered by the applicant was strong evidence to suggest that the conditions were reasonable. Kearns J. went on, nevertheless, to hold that certain of the conditions were invalid as unreasonable. Part of the conditions had the capacity to frustrate and/or render inoperable the use of the headland as a golf course. It could hardly be said that a peripheral condition, which had such damaging implications for the development as a whole, could be fairly or reasonably related to the development. Further, the reasons stated for the imposition of the conditions were not supported.

Kearns J. also held that there was no evidence to support the board's rejection of certain of the inspector's recommendations. This aspect of the decision is remarkable in that it involved the High Court finding that there was no material before An Bord Pleanála which would support the board rejecting the inspector's recommendation. In so doing, Kearns J. distinguished *O'Keeffe v. An Bord Pleanála* [1993] 1 I.R. 39; [1992] I.L.R.M. 237.

Perhaps the part of the judgment of most general application is as follows. Kearns J. held that by purporting to impose conditions in respect of public access, An Bord Pleanála sought to avoid the usual consequences of creating a public right of way and had effectively shifted responsibility on to the applicant. More specifically, Kearns J. held that the conditions imposed, whether intentionally or otherwise, worked to circumvent the existing statutory provisions in connection with the creation of a public right of way, whilst at the same time depriving the applicant both of compensation and of the right to derive a profit from its ownership: a vague right of public access may legitimately be considered as far more onerous on a property owner than a public right of way, which at least is confined to a dedicated or specified route.

DEVELOPMENT: EXEMPTED DEVELOPMENT

Planning permission   It is well established that in exercising its jurisdiction on an application for a planning injunction under section 27 of the Local Government (Planning and Development) Act 1976 (as amended) (see now section 160 of the Planning and Development Act 2000), a court enjoys a discretion to refuse relief in the case of trivial or technical breaches. It appears now from two decisions in 2001 that the nature of the breach of a planning permission may also be relevant to the question as to whether there has, in fact, been any unauthorised development at all, in that it seems that planning permissions are to be interpreted flexibly so as to allow for a tolerance in respect of what had been described as 'immaterial deviations'.

Reference is made to the decision in *O'Connell v. Dungarvan Energy Limited*, High Court, February 27, 2001. Finnegan J. appeared to approve of the following passage from the decision in *Lever (Finance) Limited v. Westminster Corporation* [1972] All E.R. 496.

"In my opinion a planning permission covers work which is specified in the detailed plans and any immaterial variation therein. I do not use the words *de minimis* because that would be misleading. It is obvious that, as the developer proceeds with the work there will necessarily be variations from time to time. Things may arise which were not foreseen. It should not be necessary for the developers to go back to the planning authority for every immaterial variation. The permission covers any variation which is not material."

Reference is also made to the decision in *Cork County Council v. Cliftonhall Limited,* High Court ,April 6, 2001. In that decision Finnegan J. again had regard to the materiality of the deviation:

"I must now look at the overall effect of deviations from the approved plans and in particular the altered footprint and the increased ridge height and determine whether the combined effect of the same is that there is a material non-compliance with the planning permission notwithstanding that each of the deviations on their own does not amount to a material non-compliance. With some diffidence I hold that there is not a material non-compliance."

Land reclamation   The spreading of spoil, clay and earth so as to lay a rough path or road does not constitute land reclamation within Part III, Class 9 of the Second Schedule of the Local Government (Planning and Development) Regulations 1994. Same could not be regarded as either field drainage, nor as the reclamation of land. Reclamation clearly meant that land, which was not otherwise available for significant agricultural use of any sort, was being put in a condition where it would be available for agriculture use by the carrying out of whatever works were necessary: *Dolan v. Cooke,* Supreme Court April 6, 2001.

Section 5 reference   The reference procedure has been radically altered under the Planning and Development Act 2000. In particular, the two-tier structure is changed so that a reference should generally be made to the planning authority at first instance, with an appeal to An Bord Pleanála. Under section 5 of the Local Government (Planning and Development) Act 1963, the reference was made to An Bord Pleanála, with an appeal to the High Court.

The reference procedure under the previous legislation was considered in the decision in *Fairyhouse Club Ltd. v. An Bord Pleanála,* High Court, July 18, 2001. Finnegan J. granted the applicants leave to argue, by way of an application for judicial review, that section 5 did not permit of a reference by a person other than the developer or owner of the lands in question. The applicants had argued that a reference could not be made by a third party, such as a local resident.

Finnegan J. refused leave to argue that An Bord Pleanála had no jurisdiction to decide on a reference where the event alleged to constitute the development had already taken place. Finnegan J. also held that An Bord Pleanála's statement of reasons was adequate.

Section 4(1)(g)   The decision in *Fingal County Council v. Crean,* High Court, October 19, 2001 appears to be authority for the proposition that the exemption under section 4(1)(g) of the Local Government (Planning and Development) Act 1963 (see now section 4(1)(h) of the Planning and Development Act 2000) is not available in respect of an unauthorised structure. If so, this may resolve the following apparent anomaly: unlike the position obtaining in respect of exempted development under the regulations, there was no express provision under section 4(1)(g) to the effect that the benefit of the exempted development was not available in the case of an unauthorised structure.

LICENSING OF EVENTS AND FUNFAIRS

Under Part XVI of the Planning and Development Act 2000, a special regulatory scheme is introduced in respect of events and funfairs. Events and funfairs, as defined, are not subject to the usual requirement to obtain planning permission but instead certain events are required to obtain a licence. An '*event*' is defined as a public performance which takes place wholly or mainly in the open air or in a structure with no roof or a partial, temporary or retractable roof, a tent or similar temporary structure and which is comprised of music, dancing, displays of public entertainment or any activity of a like kind. A licence is only required in respect of an event at which the audience comprises 5,000 or more people: Article 183 of the Planning and Development Regulations 2001. The same licence may permit a number of events at a venue within a specified period not exceeding one year. A licence is not required for the holding of an event by a local authority.

To an extent Part XVI serves to breach the gap in the previous legislation identified in the Supreme Court decision in *Butler v. Dublin Corporation* [1999] 1 I.R. 565; [1999] 1 I.L.R.M. 481. In that decision, the Supreme Court had indicated that a transient event such as a one-day pop concert might not constitute development within the meaning of the planning legislation. Under Part XVI it is now expressly provided that the holding of an event, as defined, and works directly or solely relating to the holding of such an event, shall not be construed as 'development' within the meaning of the Planning and Development Act 2000. A saver applies, however, in respect of existing planning permissions. Specifically, it would appear that where any planning permission has been granted for the holding of an event or events, a licence shall only be required for the holding of any *additional* event on the land concerned.

SECTION 38 AGREEMENTS

Under section 38 of the Local Government (Planning & Development) Act 1963, a planning authority was empowered to enter into an agreement with any person interested in land in its area for the purpose of restricting or regulating the development or use of the land, either permanently or during such period as may be specified by the agreement. These provisions, in effect, gave rise to a form of statutory restrictive covenant, which would run with the land. (See now section 47 of the Planning and Development Act 2000.) A serious drawback of such agreements from the viewpoint of the landowner was that there is no mechanism expressly provided whereby an application might be made to be released from the agreement where, for example, there was subsequently a change in the proper planning and development of the area.

The decision in *Langarth Properties Ltd. v. Bray Urban District Council,* High Court, June 25, 2001, may resolve these concerns in at least some situations. On the facts, the planning authority had refused planning permission on the basis of a section 38 agreement that prohibited further development of the lands. An Bord Pleanála subsequently granted planning permission, on appeal, and the planning authority then sought to enforce the restrictive covenant. Morris P. held that the planning authority when considering applications for future development of the land was limited to considering the proper planning and development of the area. It was not open to the planning authority to rely solely upon the fact that there was a section 38 agreement in existence. To prevent or inhibit the development of lands for any reason other than the proper planning and development of the area would be an unconstitutional interference with the rights of private ownership of land. It followed that the limitation and restrictions imposed by the section 38 agreement remained valid only for so long as the proper planning of the area required that the restriction be maintained. The fact that An Bord Pleanála had granted planning permission authorising development which would otherwise be in direct conflict with the section 38 agreement was a clear indication that the proper planning and development of the area no longer required observance of the covenant.

Practice and Procedure

HILARY DELANY, Trinity College, Dublin and RAYMOND BYRNE

ABUSE OF PROCESS

Established principles on the inherent jurisdiction of the court to strike out a claim on the grounds that it discloses no reasonable cause of action or that it is frivolous or vexatious have been applied on a number of occasions in 2001.

In *Jestdale Ltd v. Millennium Theatre Co. Ltd.*, High Court, July 31, 2001, the defendant applied to have proceedings brought against it struck out as an abuse of process on the basis that the plaintiff's claim must fail. An agreement made between the parties provided that the defendant would demise a property to the plaintiff on the completion of certain works. It also made express provision for rescission of the agreement if the works were not completed by a specified date. The works were not completed on time and the defendant served a notice of rescission. The plaintiff sought a declaration that the purported rescission notice was invalid and the defendant applied to have the proceedings struck out as an abuse of process. The defendant submitted that there was no conflict of fact, which disclosed a legal basis for dispute between the parties, and that there was no version of the facts as presented by the plaintiff which would entitle it to the relief which it claimed. The plaintiff relied on the *dicta* of Costello J. in *Barry v. Buckley* [1981] I.R. 306 that the court's inherent jurisdiction to strike out a claim should be exercised sparingly and only in clear cases and of McCarthy J. in *Sun Fat Chan v. Osseous Ltd* [1992] 1 I.R. 425 (*Annual Review of Irish Law 1991*, p.325) to the effect that generally the High Court should be slow to entertain an application of this kind. The plaintiff submitted that its inability to comply with its obligations under the agreement had been a direct result of the defendant's acts and/or omissions and that the disputes of fact could only be resolved at a full trial of the action. Lavan J. stated that the evidence before the court clearly demonstrated that the plaintiff had failed to honour its commitments under the agreement and that it now sought to frustrate the defendant's attempts to extricate itself from the situation. Although he was conscious of the principle that the inherent jurisdiction of the court to strike out proceedings should be exercised sparingly, Lavan J. concluded that the defendant had reached the required threshold in the proceedings and he was satisfied that the plaintiff's claim must fail.

In *Lawlor v. Seamus Ross Menolly Homes Ltd*, Supreme Court, November 22, 2001 the plaintiff brought proceedings against the defendants essentially alleging that they had failed to perform their obligations in relation to an alleged joint venture project for the development of land in West Dublin. The defendants appealed against the refusal of the High Court to accede to their motion to dismiss the plaintiff's claim as being an abuse of the process of the court. It was agreed between the parties that the court might exercise such jurisdiction only if it is demonstrated beyond argument that the plaintiff's claim must fail. Fennelly J. stated that the applicable principles were not in dispute and referred to the judgments of Costello J. in *Barry v. Buckley* [1981] I.R. 306 and of McCarthy J. in *Sun Fat Chan v. Osseous Ltd* [1992] 1 I.R. 425 (*Annual Review of Irish Law 1991*, p.325). He also referred to the *dicta* of Hardiman J. in *Supermac's (Ireland) Ltd v. Katesan (Naas) Ltd* [2000] 4 I.R. 273 (*Annual Review of Irish Law 2000*, p.362) and stated that these comments underline the strictness of the applicable test, namely that the plaintiff's claim must be bound to fail. As he stated, the question for the court is whether the plaintiff's claim is so deeply flawed that it cannot succeed. Fennelly J. stated that in his view the fatal defect in the plaintiff's claim was that there was clear evidence that an integral part of the agreement was that how the entire joint venture was to be financed was left open for discussion at a later date. While the parties might well have reached an agreement in principle to enter into a joint venture, they remained in negotiation so long as they had not agreed on finance. Fennelly J. held that there was no concluded contract and he allowed the appeal and dismissed the plaintiff's claim. Keane C.J. also stated that he would allow the appeal. While he accepted that the burden resting on the defendant in bringing such a motion is undoubtedly a heavy one, he held that even making every assumption in favour of the plaintiff, the contract relied on could not possibly constitute a concluded contract between the parties which would give rise to any action at law.

In *Kayfoam Woolfson v. Healthcare Materials Management Board,* High Court, June 29, 2001 the applicant commenced proceedings seeking a review of an award of a contract on the grounds that it was in breach of European Community principles on the award of public supply contracts and in breach of the applicant's legitimate expectation. The respondents brought an application seeking to have the claim struck out under the inherent jurisdiction of the court on the basis that the applicant's case could not succeed. Finnegan J. referred to the *dicta* of McCarthy J. in *Sun Fat Chan v. Osseous Ltd* [1992] 1 I.R. 425 (*Annual Review of Irish Law 1991*, p.325) and said that he was satisfied that the jurisdiction to strike out arises not only when facts are admitted, but also where the facts are clear and show that the claim is unsustainable. Having considered the circumstances of the case before him, he was not satisfied that the applicant's case, whether on agreed facts or on clear facts as established on the affidavits, must fail. Accordingly Finnegan J. refused to make an order striking out the applicant's claim.

Finally, in *Weldon v. Mooney,* High Court, January 25, 2001, the plaintiff's claim arose out of an accident, which is alleged to have occurred when the plaintiff apparently climbed into the luggage compartment of a bus. The defendants sought an order striking out the plaintiff's pleadings pursuant to Order 19, rule 28 of the Rules of the Superior Courts on the grounds that they showed no reasonable cause of action or alternatively sought an order that the claim should be struck out pursuant to the court's inherent jurisdiction. Counsel for the plaintiff relied on the *dicta* McCarthy J. in *Sun Fat Chan v. Osseous Ltd* [1992] 1 I.R. 425 (*Annual Review of Irish Law 1991*, p.325) to the effect that generally the High Court should be slow to entertain an application of this kind. Ó Caoimh J. concluded that if the defendants knowingly permitted persons to use the luggage compartment to be carried on the bus and the bus was driven in knowledge of that fact, he accepted that a cause of action might exist in favour of the plaintiff. In the light of this fact he was prepared to direct that the plaintiff's claim should proceed as against each of the defendants.

APPEALS

High Court appeal from Circuit Court: finality In *P. v. P.*, Supreme Court, July 31, 2001, the Supreme Court confirmed the finality of an appeal from the Circuit Court to the High Court under section 39 of the Courts of Justice Act 1936. The case involved family law proceedings and the applicant claimed that because he was effectively denied a hearing or a fair hearing in accordance with law, section 39 of the 1936 Act did not apply. The respondent submitted that section 39 prohibited any appeal from the High Court appeal, since section 39 provided that the High Court decision was 'final and conclusive and not appealable.' The Supreme Court agreed. The Court held that it was manifestly clear from the terms of section 39, as re-enacted by the Courts (Supplemental Provisions) Act 1961, that the Oireachtas intended the High Court to be the court of final instance in the hearing of appeals from the Circuit Court, and this provision was a recognition of the desire of public policy to determine the point in which proceedings *inter partes* had to be considered final. The Court accepted that there was an inherent jurisdiction at common law on which a final order could be impugned, but it noted that this was limited to correcting the final judgment to ensure that it accurately reflected the adjudication and intention of the court that made it and, in the exercise of a wider and more fundamental jurisdiction, to setting aside an order on the grounds that it had been obtained by fraud. The Court cited the decision of Murphy J. in *Din v. Banco Ambrosiano Spa* [1991] I.R. 569 (*Annual Review of Irish Law 1990*, p.451). Clearly, the Court accepted that a final order could be rescinded or varied where a party discharged the burden of establishing that there were exceptional circumstances showing that the interests of constitutional justice necessitated such a remedy. If such a remedy was available in respect of final orders of the Supreme Court (as the Court had accepted in *Bula Ltd v. Tara Mines Ltd*, Supreme Court, July 3, 2000 and in *Re Greendale Developments*

Ltd (No. 3) [2000] 2 I.R. 514), it had to be available for final and unappealable orders of the High Court. However, the applicant in the present case had not established such an exceptional case.

COSTS

Criminal appeal: 'follow the event'   In *The People v. Redmond (No. 2)*, Court of Criminal Appeal, March 29, 2001, the Court held that the practice that costs follow the event should apply in criminal proceedings no less than in civil cases. In this case, the Director of Public Prosecutions had sought to review the sentence imposed on the defendant pursuant to section 2 of the Criminal Justice Act 1993 as being unduly lenient. The Court of Criminal Appeal refused the application: *The People v. Redmond*, Court of Criminal Appeal, December 21, 2000 (*Annual Review of Irish Law 2000*, 143). The respondent, who was not legally aided, then applied for his costs of the review, contending that they should follow the event. The Director argued that the court had no jurisdiction to award costs under section 34 of the Courts of Justice Act 1924, as the power to review sentences was not introduced until 1993. The Court of Criminal Appeal disagreed and awarded the defendant his costs. The Court followed its approach in *The People v. Hughes*, Court of Criminal Appeal, March 27, 2000 in respect of applications for costs in cases of review of sentences under section 2 of the 1993 Act, noting that there were no circumstances to depart from the principles espoused in that case. It also noted that the jurisdiction of the Court to award costs had a separate basis in Order 99 of the Rules of the Superior Courts 1986. Moreover, justice would not be served if an applicant had to bear the costs of his own success before the courts.

Security for costs   The principles set out by Finlay P. in *Collins v. Doyle* [1982] I.L.R.M. 495 in relation to the factors which the court should consider where an individual, as opposed to a corporate plaintiff, seeks security for costs were applied by Barr J. in *Jahwar v. Owners and all Parties Interested in the MV Betta Livestock 17,* High Court, May 29, 2001. The plaintiff, who was a Syrian national and appeared to be domiciled in that country, brought a claim for disbursements and wages arising out of his function as master of a ship. Barr J. set out the following principles, which had been laid down in *Collins v. Doyle. Prima facie* a defendant establishing a *prima facie* defence to a claim made by a plaintiff residing outside the jurisdiction has a right to an order for security for costs. However, this right is not an absolute one and the court must exercise its discretion based on the facts. He also stated that poverty on the part of the plaintiff is not of itself automatically a reason for refusing the order and that the court may have regard to whether the plaintiff has made out a *prima facie* case that his inability to provide security flows from the defendant's wrong. Having regard to the fact that the plaintiff's earnings appeared to be modest, and that if he were ordered to provide security he would be prevented from pursuing a claim for a basic right, Barr J. concluded that it would be manifestly unjust to prevent the plaintiff from pursuing his claim and he held that the defendant was not entitled to security for costs.

The principles which apply where an application for security for costs is brought in relation to a corporate plaintiff were considered by Carroll J. in *Kerry Tree (Technology) Ltd v. Sun Alliance and London Insurance plc,* High Court, October 3, 2001. Carroll J. stated that the manner in which the discretion to require security for costs to be given in such cases and how the burden of proof is to be distributed have been laid down in a number of decisions including *Jack O'Toole Ltd v. MacEoin Kelly Associates Ltd* [1986] I.R. 277, *Bula Ltd v. Tara Mines Ltd (No.3)* [1987] I.R. 494, *Comhlucht Paipear Riomhaireachta Teo v. Udaras na Gaeltachta* [1991] 1 I.R. 320 and *Lismore Homes Ltd v. Bank of Ireland Finance Ltd* [1999] 1 I.R. 501. Carroll J. then stated that the following principles appeared to be relevant. Where it is established or conceded that the plaintiff company would be unable to meet the costs of a successful defendant, the onus of proof to establish special circumstances to justify refusal of an order lies on the plaintiff company. In addition, if the plaintiff company relies on the contention that its financial problems were brought about by the defendant's conduct it is not enough to make a mere bald statement to that effect and the plaintiff must establish at least a *prima facie* case of the existence of special circumstances. Further, while it must be established that the plaintiff has an arguable case, it is not necessary or proper to evaluate the prospects of success.

Given that the first two plaintiffs acknowledged that they were insolvent, the onus lay on them to establish that there were reasonable circumstances, which would require the court to exercise its discretion not to order security for costs. While the defendant claimed that there were no such special circumstances, the plaintiffs argued, *inter alia,* that they would not have become insolvent if the defendant had paid them within a reasonable time and that there had been a delay on the defendant's part in seeking security. Carroll J. concluded that on the facts before her, the plaintiffs had not discharged the onus of proving that they had a stateable case. She went on to say, that even if she were wrong in holding this, she considered that the claim that the first two plaintiffs would not have become insolvent if it had not been for the defendant's conduct did not outweigh the special circumstances favouring the defendant. These circumstances were that the defendant had already gone through arbitration on the contract and paid damages and costs, that the plaintiffs were alleging a claim unknown to law and that they were proceedings brought by two companies in receivership with no indication whether the receiver consented or not. In addition, Carroll J. held that the delay alleged by the plaintiffs was not such as to disentitle the defendant to the order sought. She therefore concluded that the plaintiffs had not discharged the onus of proving special circumstances, which would entitle them to resist an order for security being made, and she exercised her discretion to order security for costs by the first and second named plaintiffs.

The principles which apply where security is sought against corporate plaintiffs were also considered by Keane C.J. in an *ex tempore* judgment in *Irish Conservation and Cleaning Ltd v. International Cleaners Ltd.*, Supreme Court, July 19, 2001. He referred to the principles set out by Finlay C.J. in *Jack O'Toole Ltd v. MacEoin Kelly Associates Ltd* [1986] I.R. 277 in which the former Chief Justice had pointed out that a simple, bald assertion by an individual that he would not now be in a state of financial difficulty if it had not been for the actions of the defendants is not enough. However, in the case before him special circumstances arose which rendered an order for security inappropriate. It was not in dispute that the defendants were the plaintiff's only customer and the plaintiff asserted that because of the defendant's failure to pay its accounts it had got into serious financial difficulty and had been left in a position where it was unable to provide security for costs. The Chief Justice concluded that he was satisfied that the High Court judge had properly exercised his discretion in accordance with established principles in declining to make the order for security for costs.

The question of what will constitute 'sufficient security' within the meaning of section 390 of the Companies Act 1963 has recently been clarified by the Supreme Court in *Lismore Homes Ltd v. Bank of Ireland Finance Ltd* [2002] 1 I.L.R.M. 541. In the High Court McCracken J. had concluded that 'the section can only mean that the security required must approximate to the probable costs of the defendant should he succeed', a conclusion with which the Supreme Court effectively agreed. Murphy J. stated that he found himself disagreeing with the conclusions reached by the Court of Appeal in England on this point, although he added that he did so with hesitation. However, in upholding the conclusion reached by McCracken J. in relation to the measure of security which should be ordered, he stated that he was greatly comforted to find himself in full agreement with the views expressed by Kingsmill Moore J. in the earlier decision of the Supreme Court in *Thalle v. Soares* [1957] I.R. 182. Murphy J. expressed the view that the plain meaning of the words 'sufficient security' in section 390 of the Companies Act 1963 is clear. He stated as follows:

> "The word 'sufficient' in its plain meaning signifies adequate or enough and it is directly related in the section to the defendant's costs. The section does not provide – as it might have – a sufficient sum 'to meet the justice of the case' or some such phrase as would give a general discretion to the court. Harsh though it may be, I am convinced that sufficient security involves making a reasonable estimate or assessment of the actual costs which it is anticipated that the defendant will have to meet."

In the circumstances Murphy J. concluded that the amount fixed by the trial judge, as security was as realistic an assessment as could be made and he dismissed the plaintiff's appeal.

Taxation: comparators and breakdown of fees In *Gallagher v. Stanley*, High Court, March 23, 2001, Kearns J. made some important comments on the process of taxation. The case arose from taxation of the bill of costs presented by the plaintiff in a medical negligence action. The defendant had challenged the amounts awarded as excessive and Kearns J. remitted the case to the other Taxing Master for adjudication. He noted that the taxing master's figure was based solely on his own assessment of the value of the work done, rather than by reference to relevant comparators. This would have required him to set out in a reasoned and detailed way the basis for his assessment particularly when it marked such a departure from the comparators. In addition (reflecting views he had already expressed in *Superquinn Ltd v. Bray UDC*, High Court, May 5, 2000: *Annual Review of Irish Law 2000*, p.368), he held that, arising from the changes in section 27 of the Courts and Courts Officers Act 1995, there was a strong case for suggesting that, in addition to conducting an analysis and providing reasons for his conclusions, the Taxing Master had to also break up the solicitors fee into component elements; this would keep appeals to the High Court within manageable proportions.

Taxation: significance of case not fully taken into account In *Bloomer v. Law Society of Ireland (No.2)*, Supreme Court, July 30, 2001, the Supreme Court affirmed the views of Geoghegan J. in the High Court (*Annual Review of Irish Law 2000*, p.367). This was an appeal against the taxation of costs in a case in which the plaintiffs had successfully challenged the former exemption from the FE-1 'Entrance' examination of the defendant: see *Bloomer v. Law Society of Ireland* [1995] 3 I.R. 14 (HC); (1997) 6 IJEL 220 (SC) (*Annual Review of Irish Law 1996*, pp.567-8). In his judgment, Geoghegan J. held that the Taxing Master had acted correctly in many aspects of the taxation of the costs in this case, but that he had fallen into some error on a number of points, in particular by failing to take into account the significance of the case and its complexity. He thus increased the amount of the brief fee for the High Court action to be paid to senior and junior counsel, but otherwise confirmed the determinations of the Taxing Master. The plaintiffs appealed unsuccessfully to the Supreme Court. The Court held that Geoghegan J. had an abundance of evidence before him in regard to senior counsel's role in the proceedings and the Court agreed that increasing the brief fee to £21,000 seemed in every way reasonable. It also agreed that there was nothing in any of the evidence to suggest that a solicitor's instruction fee of £76,000 (substantially lower than claimed by the solicitors) was unfair or unreasonable.

COURT ORDER

Amendment: 'slip rule' In *Limerick City VEC v. Carr*, High Court, July 25, 2001, O'Higgins J. considered the extent to which a court could order the amendment of a final court order beyond the 'slip rule'. The case arose from a long dispute between the parties in which the plaintiff, who had suspended the defendant without pay, had been found to have acted *ultra vires* its statutory powers and had been ordered by the High Court to pay the salary arrears (this was affirmed by he Supreme Court): *Carr v. Minister for Education and Science* [2001] 2 I.L.R.M. 272 (SC) (*Annual Review of Irish Law 2000*, pp.287-8). The plaintiff then paid the defendant her salary on foot of the order of the High Court, as affirmed by the Supreme Court; but this sum, it appeared, also included the PAYE amounts, which the plaintiff had previously paid to the Revenue Commissioners on behalf of the defendant. In the present case, the plaintiff sought the return of those monies from the defendant or, alternatively, it claimed the amount as against the Revenue Commissioners. The plaintiff claimed, *inter alia*, that the High Court decree was awarded on the basis that the defendant would go to the Revenue Commissioners to be assessed for tax on the amount of the decree. As indicated, O'Higgins J. declined to amend the High Court order. He applied the decision of the Supreme Court in *Belville Holdings Ltd v. Revenue Commissioners* [1994] I.L.R.M. 29 (*Annual Review of Irish Law 1993*, p.446) that the Court's power above and beyond the provisions of the slip rule to amend an order of a court had to be exercised sparingly and only when the Court found that the order did not correctly state what the court actually decided or intended would it make an amendment. Apart from that the Court did not have the jurisdiction to interfere with an order of the court which correctly expressed the decision of the court and which was not appealed. He did not consider that this case did not come within the parameters of the slip rule in *Belville*. O'Higgins J. did not consider the, admittedly dissenting, views of Denham J. in *Attorney General (SPUC Ltd) v. Open Door Counselling Ltd (No. 2)* [1994] 1 I.L.R.M. 256 (*Annual Review of Irish Law 1993*, pp.160–5) that a wider discretion may exist to amend a final order under Article 34. See also the discussion in the House of Lords in *R v. Bow Street Magistrate, ex p Pinochet (No. 2)* [2000] 1 A.C. 119.

COURT FEES

Constitutionality of fees In *Murphy v. Minister for Justice, Equality and Law Reform* [2001] 2 I.L.R.M. 144 (SC), the Supreme Court held that reasonable charges for court services were not in breach of the right of access to the courts under Article 40.3 of the Constitution. In this case, the plaintiff challenged the power in the Courts of Justice Act 1936 by which fees were imposed on particular transactions involved in Court proceedings in the High

Court. The plaintiff submitted, *inter alia*, that the fees on notices of motion and affidavits were unconstitutional because they impeded him from proceedings with his case. The High Court and, on appeal, the Supreme Court, dismissed the claim. Delivering the unanimous decision of the Court, Murphy J. held that, provided the fees charged were proportionate and reasonable, they did not conflict with the Constitution. Indeed, Murphy J. appeared to envisage a future in which 'full cost' charges could be imposed on commercial entities in commercial disputes, though not necessarily on individuals. He commented that 'the concept of the entire cost of the judicial system being borne out of tax, including tax imposed on modest incomes, to exonerate substantial commercial organisations would seem absurd in principle and offensive in practice.' It is worth noting that the Courts Service for England and Wales has moved in the direction of charging a full commercial rate for civil cases, including the cost of judges, but it remains to be seen whether this model will be followed in Ireland. The Denham Working Group on a Courts Commission, in its *First Report: Management and Financing of the Courts* (1996) had leaned against full cost charges: see *Annual Review of Irish Law 1996*, p.480 and *Byrne and McCutcheon, The Irish Legal System*, 4th ed (Butterworths, Dublin 2001), para. 9.55–9.58.

DISCOVERY

General principles – meaning of 'possession, custody or power' The most widely accepted definition of when a document is in the 'power' of a person for the purposes of discovery is the one laid down by O'Flaherty J. in *Bula Ltd v. Tara Mines Ltd* [1994] 1 I.L.R.M. 111, 113 to the effect that 'a document is within the power of a party if he has an enforceable legal right to obtain from whoever actually holds the document inspection of it without the need to obtain the consent of anyone else.' The definition set out in *Bula* has been followed recently by the Supreme Court in *Johnson v. Church of Scientology* [2001] 2 I.L.R.M. 110 in which the defendant appealed against an order of the High Court that certain documents must be procured and discovered. Counsel for the defendants contended that a rule, which limits discovery to documents, which are or have been the property of a party, or are or have been in his physical custody or are under his absolute dominion where no other person has a legal right to interfere with disclosure, sets clear limits to the duty to disclose. He further submitted that a rule that requires a party to 'procure' documents which are not within these categories is potentially boundless and requires searches to be undertaken by people who are not under the control of the party for documents which the party has never seen and has no right to obtain. Denham J. stated that in relation to the discovery of documents the law evokes three concepts, possession, custody and power and that in order to be discoverable a document must be in possession, custody or power (in accordance with the enforceable legal right test) of a party. In allowing the defendants' appeal, she held that documents which are in the possession, custody or power of a party must be discovered and that a document is in the power of party when that party has an enforceable legal right to obtain the document. Denham J. concluded that the documents at issue in the case before her were not in the possession, custody or power of the defendants and that, as the defendants had no enforceable legal right to obtain them, the plaintiff was not entitled to the discovery sought.

Further and better discovery In *Hannon v. Commissioners of Public Works*, High Court, April 4, 2001, the plaintiff brought a motion for further and better discovery following the making of discovery by the defendant. McCracken J. stated that it was accepted by both sides that the principles set out by Brett L.J. in the decision of *Compagnie Financiere and Commerciale du Pacifique v. Peruvian Guano Co.* (1882) 11 Q.B.D. 55 still applied to such applications. McCracken J. then proceeded to summarize the principles which he felt should be taken into account in deciding whether to grant an application for further and better discovery. He stated that the court must decide as a matter of probability whether any document is relevant to the issues to be tried. He then went on to stress that relevance must be determined in relation to the pleadings in the specific case and not by submissions as to alleged facts put forward in affidavits unless such submissions relate back to the pleadings, or in the case of an application for further and better discovery, to previously discovered documents. It followed from these principles that a party might not seek discovery of a document in order to find out whether the document was relevant and that a general trawl through the other parties' documentation is not permitted under the rules. Finally McCracken J. stated that the court is entitled to take into account the extent to which discovery of documents might become oppressive, and should be astute to ensure 'that the procedure of discovery is not used as a tactic in the war between the parties'. Applying these principles to the facts before him, McCracken J. set out in a schedule to his judgment the list of documents, which should be discovered.

New Order 31, rule 12 As previously noted (see *Annual Review of Irish Law 2000*, p.370) the Rules of the Superior Courts (No. 2) (Discovery) 1999 (S.I. No. 233 of 1999) altered the discovery process in a number of material ways. First, it provided that the written application seeking voluntary discovery must specify the precise categories of documents in respect of which discovery is sought and the reasons why each category of documents is required, although a proviso sets out that where, by reason of the urgency of the matter, the consent of the parties, the nature of the case or any other circumstances which to the court seem appropriate, the court may make an order as appears proper, without the necessity for such prior application in writing. Secondly, the notice of motion is required to specify the precise categories of documents in respect of which discovery is sought. Thirdly, motions for discovery must now be grounded on an affidavit which shall verify that the discovery sought is necessary for disposing fairly of the matter or for saving costs and shall furnish the reasons why each category of documents is required to be discovered.

In *Swords v. Western Proteins Ltd* [2001] 1 I.R. 324 Morris P. stated that S.I. No. 233 of 1999 imposed a clearly defined obligation upon a party seeking discovery to pinpoint the documents or category of documents required and to provide reasons why they were being sought. As he stated 'blanket discovery became a thing of the past'. Keane CJ echoed these views in his judgment in *Burke v. Director of Public Prosecutions,* Supreme Court, June 21, 2001 where he commented that a practice had developed whereby orders for discovery were being obtained unnecessarily and delaying litigation. He stated that he had no doubt that Morris P. in *Swords* had been entirely correct in the view which he had expressed as to the object of the new rule and its importance. In *Burke*, the Supreme Court had to consider an appeal from an order of the High Court refusing to grant discovery against the respondent in relation to categories of documents identified in the grounding affidavit. Keane C.J. concluded that he was satisfied that the documents sought were clearly specified and that the applicant was not attempting to go on a 'general trawl or fishing expedition'. He therefore made an order that the High Court had been in error in declining to make an order of discovery in respect of two categories of documents and allowed the appeal to that extent.

It should also be pointed out that the decision in *Swords* was reached without Morris P. being required to consider the terms of the proviso to rule 12(4)(1) set out above, which allows the court to make an order for discovery without the necessity for prior application in writing in limited circumstances. This point is illustrated by the decision of McKechnie J. in *Brian Greene & Co. Ltd v. Instruelec Services Ltd* [2002] 1 I.L.R.M. 237 in which he made an order for discovery notwithstanding the Master's refusal to do so on the grounds that the letter seeking voluntary discovery was insufficiently precise. McKechnie J. held that the facts of the case before him came within the terms of the proviso in rule 12(4)(1), on the basis that the parties had consented to an order for discovery being made, and in such circumstances he held that there had been compliance with the rules and the court clearly had jurisdiction to make the order sought.

Non party discovery   In *Enright v. Finn,* Supreme Court, May 17, 2001, the applicant sought non-party discovery against the Law Society in an action seeking judicial review of the decision of the respondent district judge refusing to strike out proceedings involving allegations of fraudulent misconduct on the basis that sections 6 and 7 of the Criminal Procedure Act 1967 had not been complied with. The applicant sought discovery of two categories of documents, namely all those concerning the Law Society's investigation into his practice and those concerning the communication of information relating to an investigation by agents of the DPP into allegations made against the applicant to the Law Society. Murphy J. stated that it was clear that documents generated by the inquiry undertaken by the society had no relevance to any matter in dispute. However there was an issue as to whether the director or his agent communicated to the society in such a manner as might have instigated the inquiry, which took place. It was a part of the applicant's case that the DPP or his agents had acted wrongfully and unlawfully in furnishing information to the society and in causing the statutory investigative powers of the society to be invoked. To that extent the documents relating to this issue would be relevant and material in the sense those words were used in the *Peruvian Guano Co.* case (1882) 11 Q.B.D. 62 which he said continues to govern the law as to what is relevant or material for the purposes of an affidavit of discovery. In this limited way and subject to a number of conditions Murphy J. allowed the appeal.

Inspection Order 31, rule 18 of the Rules of the Superior Courts 1986 provides that the court may make an order for inspection in such place and in such manner as it may think fit and that the application should be grounded on an affidavit, unless the documents are ones referred to in the pleadings or affidavits of the party against whom the application is made or disclosed in his affidavit or list of documents, which must set out what documents are sought, that the applicant is entitled to inspect them, and that they are in the possession or power of the other party. In addition, rule 18(2) makes it clear that the court ought not to make an order if it is not necessary for disposing fairly of the cause or matter or for saving costs. In *Barry v. Director of Public Prosecutions,* High Court, April 2, 2001 the applicant sought an order for further inspection contending that the case had altered so substantially that this was now required. The respondent argued in favour of the privileges claimed and also placed reliance on the provisions of rule 18(2), claiming that the order sought was not necessary for disposing fairly of the action of for saving costs. O'Neill J. concluded that there was no basis in the fresh affidavits served for contending that the case had been materially altered and that it was therefore not necessary either for disposing fairly of the cause or matter of for saving costs that further inspection be ordered.

INTEREST ON AWARDS

Award of statutory compensation tribunal In *M.O'C. v. Minister for Health,* Supreme Court, July 31, 2001, the Supreme Court leaned in favour of the contention that the Hepatitis C Compensation Tribunal had been empowered by section 5(1) of the Hepatitis C Compensation Tribunal Act 1997 to order interest pursuant to section 22 of the Courts Act 1981 on an award under the 1997 Act. The appellant was refused her claim for the payment of interest pursuant to section 22 of the 1981 Act in the High Court. On appeal, the Supreme Court remitted the matter to the High Court. The Court considered that, even on a literal interpretation of section 5(1) of the 1997 Act, it vested in the Hepatitis C Compensation Tribunal the jurisdiction under section 22 of the 1981 Act. Moreover, applying a purposive interpretation to section 5(1) of the 1997 Act, it was clear that the fundamental purpose of the 1997 Act was to compensate the claimants. Further, it was intended that the Tribunal should make those awards and that an award of the Tribunal should be made on the same basis as an award of the High Court, calculated by reference to any relevant statutory provision including the Courts Act 1981.

Interest from date of judgment or date of taxation In *Clarke v. Garda Commissioner*, Supreme Court, July 31, 2001, the Supreme Court dealt again with the issue of whether interest on costs runs from the date of judgment or from the date on which costs are taxed. The plaintiff's claim had been settled on May 15, 1996, on condition, *inter alia*, that the defendants "pay to the plaintiffs their costs of the said action when taxed and ascertained." A certificate of taxation was issued on March 20, 1997, certifying £130,388.27 as the sum due for party and party costs. This was paid on May 8, 1997. No interest was paid. Interest at the prevailing rate of 8% from May 15, 1996 to May 8, 1997 was agreed to amount to £10,215.01. The plaintiffs claimed this sum as due from the date of the settlement. The defendants argued that interest was payable only to the extent that the plaintiffs were out of pocket. The plaintiffs had paid £64,000 to their solicitors on account of fees in February 1996. The Circuit Court stated a case to the Supreme Court, asking whether interest was payable on costs from the date of judgment or order awarding them, or only from the date of taxation. In answering the case stated, the Court held that interest on costs, just as much as interest on the amount of the judgment, is to be collected by operation of the machinery for execution of judgments, that is, sections 26 and 27 of the Debtors (Ireland) Act 1840, a procedure that does not envisage any inquiry as to matters that concern essentially the relationship between a party and his solicitor, counsel or others. The Supreme Court rejected the argument that the extent of the right to interest should depend on the extent to which a party has discharged costs, whether comprising the fees of his legal advisers, expert witnesses or others, matters of which the officer executing the order of the court is in the ordinary way necessarily unaware. It also noted that taxation is concerned only with the measure of the costs of the successful party as of the date of judgment and has no function to inquire into payments made after that date. Since costs which constitute a liability of the unsuccessful party from the moment of judgment, they are not payable until quantified but from that point the debt relates back to the date of the judgment, with interest running from that earlier date.

INTERROGATORIES

A fairly flexible interpretation of what will be considered 'necessary for disposing fairly of the action or for saving costs' within the meaning of meaning of Order 31, rule 2 in line with that suggested by Walsh J. in *J. & L.S. Goodbody Ltd v. Clyde Shipping Company Ltd,* Supreme Court, 9 May 1967 has been accepted by O'Sullivan J. in *Crofter Properties Ltd v. Genport Ltd.* High Court, November 30, 2001. The defendant brought an application authorising it to deliver interrogatories to the plaintiff in relation to the defendant's counter claim in the proceedings in which it was alleged that certain telephone calls had been made by the plaintiff or it servants or agents to the British police which were of a malicious, untrue and defamatory nature. The defendant believed that it had identified telephone numbers from which these calls had been made and sought to raise interrogatories to oblige the plaintiff to confirm under oath the owners of these telephone lines and their connection with the plaintiff. O'Sullivan J. quoted with approval the following *dicta* of Walsh J. in *J. & L.S. Goodbody Ltd v. Clyde Shipping Company Ltd*:

> "While Order 31 rule 2 of the Rules of the Superior Courts provides that leave to deliver interrogatories shall be given only when it is considered necessary either for disposing fairly of the action or for saving costs, it is well established that one of the purposes of interrogatories is to sustain the plaintiff's case as well as to destroy the defendant's (see the judgment of this Court in *Keating v. Healy*) and that interrogatories need not be confined to the facts directly in issue but may extend to any facts, the existence or non-existence of which is relevant to the existence or non-existence of facts directly in issue. Furthermore the interrogatories sought need not be shown to be conclusive on the questions in issue but it is sufficient if the interrogatories sought should have some bearing on the question and that the interrogatory might form a step in establishing the liability. It is not necessary for the person seeking leave to deliver the interrogatory to show that it is in respect of something he does not already know."

O'Sullivan J. stated that the matters which he had to consider were, first, whether the interrogatories were necessary either for disposing fairly of the matter or for saving costs, secondly, whether they were relevant in the sense explained above, thirdly, whether they should not be allowed because they were simply fishing, and fourthly, whether they prejudiced the plaintiff unfairly. He concluded that he had no doubt that considerable time and cost would be saved by the delivery of interrogatories provided they were permissible under the other headings set out above. In relation to the question of relevance, O'Sullivan J. stated that he was going to be asked to draw inferences from the replies to the interrogatories and he thought that they were clearly relevant for that purpose. In addition, he was not satisfied that they would unjustly prejudice the plaintiff, and he stated that in so far as they were proper interrogatories to be asked, they should be allowed. However, O'Sullivan J. stated that some of the interrogatories could be considered to be too wide or simply fishing and would have to be disallowed. He concluded that there were in his view a considerable number of interrogatories which exceeded the permissible scope for such questions and that the generalised nature of some of the queries went beyond achieving a saving of costs or doing justice between the parties. O'Sullivan J. therefore allowed some of the interrogatories and refused leave to deliver the remainder.

JUDICIAL ETHICS

Proposed Judicial Council   Against the background of the *'Sheedy Case'* in 1999 (see *Annual Review of Irish Law 1999*, pp.448-52), a Committee on Judicial Conduct and Ethics, chaired by Hamilton CJ until his retirement and thereafter by Keane C.J., was established in 2000. The *Report of the Committee on Judicial Conduct and Ethics* (Pn 9449) was published in January 2001. For a more extensive discussion, see Byrne and McCutcheon, *The Irish Legal System*, 4th ed (Butterworths, Dublin 2001), para 4.145 et seq. It recommended the establishment of Judicial Council, largely on the lines of the arrangements in place in New South Wales in Australia. The proposed Judicial Council would be empowered to deal with three areas: judicial conduct and ethics; judicial studies and publications; judicial remuneration and conditions of work generally. The Report concluded that the existing provisions for dealing with concerns about judicial misconduct, namely impeachment, were inadequate. The Report noted that other instances of judicial misconduct, falling short of the 'misbehaviour' currently regulated by Article 35 of the Constitution, merited some form of investigation. The proposed Judicial Council, of which all judges would be members, would be the mechanism for dealing with such matters. It would carry out its functions through a Board and three committees. The Board of the Council would consist of the Chief Justice, the Presidents of the High Court, the Circuit Court and the District Courts, four ordinary judges, one from each of these courts to be elected by their colleagues, and a co-opted judge. The three committees would be: a Judicial Conduct and Ethics Committee, a Judicial Studies and Publications Committee and a General Committee. They would have the same structure and representation as the Board.

Judicial Conduct and Ethics Committee   The Report recommended that a complaint against a judge made by a member of the public or of the legal profession would be considered by the Judicial Conduct and Ethics Committee. There might be cases where no action was required, either because the complaint disclosed no inappropriate behaviour, or where an appeal or judicial review was the more appropriate response. Where the complaint was of a serious nature, and could not be disposed of informally or through the appeal mechanism in the courts, it would be dealt with by a Panel of Inquiry. This would comprise three members, two of them judges nominated by the committee and a layperson drawn from a panel of three 'people of standing in the community' appointed by the Attorney General. Where misconduct was established by the Panel of Inquiry, this could recommend any of the following actions be taken: a private reprimand by the Conduct and Ethics Committee to the judge; a public reprimand by the Conduct and Ethics Committee to the judge; a recommendation by the Conduct and Ethics Committee to the Attorney General that the government consider the tabling of a resolution in both Houses of the Oireachtas calling for the removal of the judge from office for stated misbehaviour or incapacity.

Judicial Studies Committee   The Judicial Studies Committee would be responsible for judicial training and education and for the publication of a journal. It would supercede the existing Judicial Studies Institute, which was established in 1996 with a view to providing continuing education for all judges. The Judicial Studies Institute was established against the background of section 16 of the Courts and Court Officers Act 1995 (*Annual Review of Irish Law 1995*, p.398), which introduced for the first time a mandatory requirement that candidates for judicial appointment undertake to agree to take any course of training or education as may be required by the Chief Justice or the President of the court to which the person is appointed. The Judicial Studies Committee would also publish 'bench books', which would include specimen directions for criminal trials and guidelines on sentencing.

General Committee   The General Committee would be responsible for keeping under review questions of remuneration and the working conditions of judges. Any reports presented by the Committee to the Board would, where appropriate, be referred to the Attorney General, the Minister for Justice or the Courts Service.

Response to the Report   The Government indicated that it would bring forward the necessary constitutional amendment to Article 35 and enact the necessary legislation to place the Judicial Council on a statutory basis. The 22nd Amendment to the Constitution Bill was published in 2001 with a view to having the issue put to a referendum in June 2001. However, the proposal was withdrawn in May 2001 when the Opposition parties disagreed with the connected proposal in the 22nd Amendment Bill that the impeachment procedure would, in future, require a two thirds vote in the Oireachtas, rather than the current position where a simple majority suffices. At the time of writing, no further moves in the establishment of the proposed Judicial Council have been made.

Standards in Public Office Commission The Standards in Public Office Act 2001 (see the Administrative Law chapter, 1, above) provides for the furnishing of tax clearance certificates to the Standards in Public Office Commission by persons upon appointment to judicial office.

JUDICIAL REMUNERATION

The Courts (Supplemental Provisions) Act 1961 (Increase of Judicial Remuneration) Order 2001 (S.I. No. 44 of 2001) and the Courts (Supplemental Provisions) Act 1961 (Increase of Judicial Remuneration) (No.2) Order 2001 (S.I. No. 302 of 2001), made under section 46(9) of the Courts (Supplemental Provisions) Act 1961, twice increased the salaries of members of the judiciary, with effect from March 2001 and July 2001, respectively. The first increase reflected the increases under the programme for Prosperity and Fairness (PFP), while the second referred to the most recent report of the Review Body on Higher Remuneration in the Public Sector.

LEGAL AID

Attorney General scheme In *Murphy v. GM, PB and PC Ltd*, Supreme Court, April 3, 2001, the Supreme Court dealt with the application of an *ad hoc* scheme operated by the Attorney General in connection with applications by the Criminal Assets Bureau under the Proceeds of Crime Act 1996. In the present case, the High Court had made an order in 1999, pursuant to the Proceeds of Crime Act 1996, prohibiting the respondents from disposing or dealing with certain monies which the second respondent claimed represented the proceeds of unlawful activities by the first respondent. An application by the second and third respondents for the payment out of those monies and for a recommendation under the *ad hoc* legal aid scheme was refused by the High Court, from which the respondents appealed. In relation to the *ad hoc* legal aid scheme, the Court held that the grant of legal aid was a matter for the Court itself, which had to be satisfied that the means of the applicant were insufficient to enable him to obtain legal representation on his own behalf and that by reason of exceptional circumstances, it was essential, in the interests of justice that the applicant should have legal aid in the preparation of the conduct of his case. In the present case, the Court felt that inadequate steps had been taken to dispute the second respondent's assertion as to his present inability to discharge legal costs. The alteration of the normal onus of proof, in relation to substantive applications under the 1996 Act, did not appear to have been extended to applications for a recommendation in relation to the legal aid scheme. In the circumstances of the case, the Court concluded that it was in the interests of justice that the respondent be legally represented.

PRIVILEGE

Legal professional: identity of client In *Miley v. Flood* [2001] 1 I.L.R.M. 489 (HC), Kelly J. held that the concept of legal professional privilege doe not extend to an entitlement to claim privilege in respect of the identity of one's client. The case arose against the background of the Tribunal of Inquiry into Planning Matters, of which the respondent was sole member. The applicant was a solicitor for a company called Jackson Way Properties Ltd ('the company') and he had been ordered by the respondent to disclose to the tribunal of inquiry the names of persons from whom the applicant had received instructions on behalf of the company. On judicial review, the applicant submitted that this was a matter, which was protected by solicitor-client privilege. As indicated, Kelly J. dismissed the application. He referred to his own judgment in *Duncan v. Governor of Portlaoise Prison* [1997] 1 I.R. 558 to the effect that legal professional privilege was more than a mere rule of evidence. It was a fundamental condition on which the administration of justice as a whole rested. Nonetheless, the mere confidentiality of information did not confer in itself an entitlement to claim privilege. On the specific situation in this case, Kelly J. relied on the leading decision of the Supreme Court in *Smurfit Paribas Bank Ltd v. AAB Export Finance Ltd* [1990] 1 I.R. 469 to the effect that privilege would only be granted if it could be identified with some public interest in the administration of justice which would outweigh the disadvantage arising from restrictions on disclosure; the onus being on the person claiming the privilege. Having reviewed the Irish authorities, Kelly J. concluded that the applicant had not established that he was entitled as a matter of Irish law to maintain a claim of privilege over the identity of persons who provided him with instructions on behalf of the company. Any such claim would, he concluded, be inconsistent with the views of the Supreme Court in the *Smurfit Paribas* case. He also referred extensively to other common law jurisdictions in this area. He noted that in many of the foreign jurisdictions, the law of privilege was not the same as in this jurisdiction, and indeed in some mere confidentiality appeared to confer privilege: he noted that this simply was not the law in Ireland. Even in those jurisdictions, however, there was, nonetheless, a strong body of legal authority reaffirming the general principle that a solicitor was not entitled to maintain a claim to privilege in respect of the identity of his client.

RULES OF COURT

The following rules of court were made in 2001.

District Court: Criminal Justice The District Court (Criminal Justice) Rules 2001 (S.I. No. 194 of 2001), as amended by the District Court (Criminal Justice)

(No.2) Rules 2001 (S.I. No. 448 of 2001), provide for the amended procedures in the District Court for sending forward in indictable matters consequent on the abolition of the preliminary examination procedure by the Criminal Justice Act 1999, which came into effect in October 2001: see the Criminal Law chapter, 180, above.

Circuit Court: Sex offenders The Circuit Court Rules (No.1) (Sex Offenders Act 2001) 2001 (S.I. No.433 of 2001) prescribe the procedures for the Circuit Court in applications under sections 11, 16 and 19 of the Sex Offenders Act 2001: see the Criminal Law chapter, 180, above.

High Court: Chief prosecution solicitor The Rules of the Superior Courts (Chief Prosecution Solicitor) 2001 (S.I. No. 585 of 2001) provided for the use of the title chief prosecution solicitor, consequent on the transfer of the criminal prosecution functions of the Chief State Solicitor to the Director of Public Prosecutions, as recommended by the Nally Report on the Public Prosecutor System (1999).

Child abduction The Rules of the Superior Courts (Child Abduction and Enforcement of Custody Orders Act 1991) 2001 (SI No.94 of 2001) revised the procedures in relation to proceedings under the Child Abduction and Enforcement of Custody Orders Act 1991, with effect from March 20, 2001.

Euro changeover The Rules of the Superior Courts (Euro Changeover) 2001 (S.I. No. 585 of 2001) amended a number of provisions in the Rules of the Superior Courts 1986 to provide for convenient euro equivalents of various sums referred to in the Rules. They came into effect on January 1, 2002.

Investor compensation The Rules of the Superior Courts (Investor Compensation Act 1998) 2001 (S.I. No. 270 of 2001) sets out the procedures for an application under the Investor Compensation Act 1998. They came into effect on July 16, 2001.

Lodgment: Investment The Rules of the Superior Courts (Amendment to Order 77) 2001 (S.I. No. 268 of 2001) amended O.77, rr.43(1)-(2) of the Rules of the Superior Courts 1986, which deal with the investment of monies lodged in court and the appropriate titles of relevant Stock Exchanges. They came into effect on July 16, 2001.

Special summons procedure The Rules of the Superior Courts (Amendment to Order 3) 2001 (S.I. No. 269 of 2001) amended O.3, r.21 of the Rules of the Superior Courts 1986, the 'catch-all' provision allowing for the use special summonses. They came into effect on July 16, 2001.

THIRD PARTY PROCEDURE

Meaning of 'as soon as is reasonably possible' Section 27(1)(b) of the Civil Liability Act 1961 provides that a concurrent wrongdoer who is sued for damages or for contribution and who wishes to make a claim for contribution under the Act shall, if the person is not already a party to the action, serve a third party notice upon such person 'as soon as is reasonably possible' and, having served such notice, he shall not be entitled to claim contribution except under the third party procedure. It has been made clear that section 27 of the Act of 1961 is intended to ensure that, as far as possible, all questions relating to the liability of concurrent wrongdoers should be tried in a single proceeding and as Murphy J. has recently reiterated in *Molloy v. Dublin Corporation* [2002] 2 I.L.R.M. 22 its purpose is to prevent a multiplicity of actions. In his view such a procedure has attractions for all the parties and is desirable in the public interest. However, the legislation made it clear that where the defendant in the original proceedings failed to serve the third party notice 'as soon as is reasonably possible' the court had a statutory discretion to refuse to make an order for contribution in his favour. The meaning of the words 'as soon as is reasonably possible' have recently been examined in some detail by Murphy J, delivering the judgment of the Supreme Court in *Molloy*. Murphy J. stated as follows:

> "The terms in which the time limit was expressed do appear severe. The use of the word 'possible' rather than the words 'practicable' as is invoked elsewhere, suggests a brief and inflexible time limit. It might suggest that if it is physically possible to serve the appropriate notice within an identified period that any further delay would be impermissible. However, such a draconian approach would be inconsistent with the nature of the problems to be confronted by a defendant and of the decisions to be made by him or his advisors. The statute is not concerned with physical possibilities but legal and perhaps commercial judgments. Proceedings cannot and should not be instituted or contributions sought against any party without assembling and examining the relevant evidence and obtaining appropriate advice thereon. It is in that context that the word 'possible' must be understood. Furthermore the qualification of the word 'possible' by the word 'reasonable' gives a further measure of flexibility."

In the circumstances, the court concluded that it had been possible for the second named defendant on the information available to it to make a 'prudent and responsible decision' to apply to join the third party several months before it had done so and on that basis, the court agreed that the third party order should be set aside.

Prisons

DISCIPLINARY PROCEDURES

In *Gilligan v. Governor of Portlaoise Prison*, High Court, McKechnie J., April 12, 2001, a prisoner brought an application for judicial review regarding alleged breaches of natural and constitutional justice and fair procedures by the Governor of Portlaoise Prison. This application arose as a result of certain sanctions imposed in accordance with rule 69 of the Rules for the Government of Prisons 1947 in respect of breaches of discipline by the appellant in the course of his term of imprisonment.

McKechnie J., held, in refusing leave to apply for judicial review, that the exercise by the respondent of his functions under rules 68 and 69 of the 1947 Rules was an exercise of a power and function of a limited nature in a matter other than a criminal matter and was therefore valid by virtue of Article 37 of the Constitution (*State (Murray) v. McRanh* [1979] I.R. 133 was applied). It was for the respondent to decide the most suitable and satisfactory way, from his point of view, to run his prison and the areas within it in an organised and coherent manner. McKechnie J., was of the opinion that in the circumstances of this case no right existed to an opportunity for the appellant to consult his legal advisor (*Campbell v. U.K.* (A/80) (1984) E.H.R.R. 165 distinguished).

EARLY RELEASE (BELFAST AGREEMENT)

Qualifying persons In *Doherty v. The Minister for Justice*, High Court, McKechnie J., November 24, 2000, the applicant was convicted of firearm offences by the Special Criminal Court in 1995, and sentenced to eight years imprisonment. He sought early release either under the "Multi-Party Agreement" or under the Criminal Justice (Release of Prisoners) Act 1998. In January 2000, he sought and was granted leave to apply for judicial review by Geoghegan J. for an order of mandamus compelling the Minister to respond to his request for early release. The respondent wrote to the applicant in April 2000 refusing his application for early release on the grounds that he was not a qualifying person. The applicant was granted leave to judicially review this refusal.

McKechnie J., held, in refusing the relief sought, that the requirement that the applicant be a member of a subversive organisation in order to apply for early release is an unlawful requirement and accordingly *ultra vires* the powers of the respondent. Any consideration of such a stance could only mean that a prisoner must join an illegal organisation or must maintain his membership thereof. That would be to insist on the commission of a criminal offence. No court in a State with democratic institutions could ever stand over such a proposition. The third ground of refusal, namely that the relevant offences are not similar offences to schedule offences in Northern Ireland, could not be sustained. The location of the offence is irrelevant, unless it can be shown that location itself is a core element of the offence.

The respondent was acting *intra vires* in his insistence upon a connection between similar offences and the Northern Ireland troubles. He is entitled to do so when exercising his powers to specify persons to be "qualifying prisoners" under section 3(2) of the 1998 Act. The primary and predominant purpose of the legislation must have been to deal with the troubles in Northern Ireland.

In *O'Hare v. Minister for Justice, Equality and Law Reform*, High Court, Ó Caoimh J., August 10, 2001, the applicant, a member of the Irish National Liberation Army, applied for release from prison in May 2000 under the Criminal Justice (Release of Prisoners) Act 1998, which implemented the Belfast Agreement. In November 2000 the Minister for Justice specified the applicant to be a qualifying person for the purposes of the Agreement. In accordance with the Act, the case was then referred to the Release of Prisoners Commission, which requested the Minister to provide an up-to-date security report and psychiatric and psychological assessments on the applicant. The Minister forwarded the psychological assessment to the Commission in February 2001 but, according to an affidavit sworn on his behalf, he was considering legal advice with respect to the transmission of the security report and the psychiatric assessment. The applicant was given leave to apply by way of judicial review for, *inter alia*, an order of mandamus directing the respondent to release the applicant from prison under the terms of the Belfast Agreement.

O'Caoimh J., held, in refusing the relief sought, that the language in which the Belfast Agreement was couched was not to be construed in the same manner in which one would construe an Act of the Oireachtas, as its terms were essentially political in nature. The respondents were required to consider the applicant's position under the terms of the review process and there was no automatic entitlement to a qualifying prisoner to be released from custody at the conclusion of the two-year period referred to in the Agreement, which only envisaged such release where "the circumstances allowed it." Once the Minister has invoked the provisions of section 3 of the 1998 Act and has requested the advice of the Commission, he must have regard to the advice concerned given by the Commission and must await the receipt of this advice before determining the applicant's request;

The Minister was not entitled to bypass the provisions of the Act and he was not entitled to influence the Commission in the performance of its functions in so far as the Act provides that it shall be independent in the performance of those functions under the Act. Once the Minister received advice from the

Commission, he was required to have regard to it in considering whether to exercise any power of release in relation to the applicant. No suggestion had been made in the course of the proceedings that in seeking psychiatric, psychological and security reports the Commission acted in any way improperly, and it was clear that such matters might be of assistance in determining whether a particular prisoner should be released under the terms of the Agreement, having particular regard to the necessity to protect the community in the context of any proposed release. The applicant had not demonstrated that the Minister had failed to have regard to the relevant provisions of the Belfast Agreement in his approach to the applicant's request for an early release.

PRISON DESIGNATION

Wheatfield Prison The Prisons Act 1972 (Section 3) Order 2001 (S.I. No. 461 of 2001) made under the Prisons Act 1972 (No. 7), section 3; specified Wheatfield Place of Detention, Cloverhill Road, Clondalkin, Dublin, as a prison to be known as Wheatfield Prison and became operative on October 10, 2001.

TEMPORARY RELEASE

The sole circumstance in which the courts will intervene in relation to a decision to grant temporary release will be where the powers to grant temporary release are being exercised in a manner, which is in breach of the constitutional obligation of the executive not to exercise them in a capricious, arbitrary or unjust way. It is not permissible for the court to intervene merely on the ground that it would have reached a different conclusion on the appropriateness of temporary release.

In *Kinahan v. The Minister for Justice Equality and Law Reform*, Supreme Court, February 21, 2001, the applicant was serving a four-year sentence for receiving stolen cheques. The applicant made an application for temporary release in March 2000, which was refused by letter dated May 26, 2000. The applicant sought an order by way of judicial review quashing this refusal on the basis that the notification of the decision to refuse temporary release did not contain adequate reason for such refusal; that the reasons actually given suggested that the decision had been come to in an irrational or unreasonable fashion; that the criteria set out in the letter dated May 26, 2000 were themselves inadequate and inconsistent with modern penal policy; and that the criteria were being applied in a discriminatory fashion. The High Court refused the application. The applicant appealed to the Supreme Court.

The Supreme Court held, in refusing the relief sought, that the sole circumstance in which the courts will intervene in relation to a decision to grant temporary release will be where the powers to grant temporary release are being exercised in a manner which is in breach of the constitutional obligation of the executive not to exercise them in a capricious, arbitrary or unjust way. It is not permissible for the court to intervene merely on the ground that it would have reached a different conclusion on the appropriateness of temporary release. (*Murray v. Ireland and the Attorney General* [1991] I.L.R.M. 465 applied.)

The letter of May 26, 2000 properly set out the six criteria used to assess applications for temporary release. This letter stated a rational policy, which the Minister was entitled to lay down, and evidences a decision rationally based on those criteria. The criteria were not in any way deficient. Although the recommendations of the Committee of the Council of Europe, to which Ireland is a party, are clearly not binding, they have in fact been complied with in relation to the applicant. There is nothing in the recommendations referred to which, either in its own terms, or as a matter of law, creates a presumption that the applicant or any prisoner is entitled to a temporary release. The applicant had established no discriminatory application of the relevant criteria. In any event, the essence of the temporary release provision is that it is based on a consideration of the individual circumstances of the prisoner.

In *Lynch v. The Minister for Justice, Equality and Law Reform*, High Court, Herbert J., March 26, 2001, prisoner, brought an application by way of Judicial Review seeking to compel the Minister to grant his application for temporary release. Herbert J. held, refusing the relief sought, that a prisoner had no constitutional or inherent right to early release from prison or to temporary release. (See *Ryan v. Governor of Limerick Prison* [1988] I.R. 198.). After conviction the powers of commution and of temporary release were vested in the executive and were administrative matters in which the Court had no function and in respect of which the relevant authorities had a wide discretion. (See *Boyle & Rice v. The United Kingdom* [1988] 10 E.H.R.R. 425. See also *McHugh v. The Minister for Justice* [1997] I.R. 245).

Transfer of detainees from Saint Patrick's Institution   The Prisons Act, 1970 (Section 7) Order, 2001 (S.I. No. 297) made under section 7(1) of the Prisons Act 1970; continues for a further 24 months the operation of section 7 of the Prisons Act 1970, which provides for the transfer to prison of persons serving sentences in Saint Patrick's Institution for the purpose of relieving overcrowding in that Institution It became operative on June 28, 2001.

VOTING

Prisoner's right to vote   In *Breathnach v. Ireland*, Supreme Court, July 11, 2001, a prisoner sought, *inter alia*, declaratory relief to the effect that the State's failure to enable him to exercise his franchise unfairly discriminated against him and was in breach of the Constitution. The applicant was granted declaratory relief in the High Court. The respondent appealed. The Supreme Court held, allowing the appeal and setting aside the High Court order, that the State was not under a constitutional duty to provide the appropriate machinery in order to enable prisoners to exercise their right to vote. Article 40 of the Constitution did not forbid discrimination; on the contrary, to legislate was on occasions necessarily to discriminate.

The State had to have regard to differences of capacity, physical and moral, and that such differences existed between persons detained because they had broken the law and other citizens was beyond argument. As a consequence of lawful custody, many of the applicant's constitutional rights were suspended and he had no absolute right to vote under the Constitution. The lack of facilities to enable the applicant to vote was not an arbitrary or unreasonable situation, and the absence of such provisions did not amount to a breach by the State of the applicant's right to equality.

Restitution

EOIN O'DELL, Trinity College, Dublin

The concept of unjust enrichment is at the heart of the decision of Barr J. in *Kelly v. Cahill* [2001] 2 I.L.R.M. 205 (HC) (noted Hourican, (2001) 6 (2) C.P.L.J. 49; O'Dell, (2001) 23 D.U.L.J. (*n.s.*) 71; Peart, (2001) 95 (4) *Law Society Gazette* 18). Here, Barr J. held that a nephew who was the beneficiary of property under his uncle's will would be unjustly enriched by the receipt of that property and therefore held it on a remedial constructive trust for the testator's widow to whom the testator had intended to direct the property. Two interrelated issues arise. First, was the nephew in fact unjustly enriched at the expense of his aunt, the testator's widow? If so, then the second issue is whether the remedial constructive trust was an appropriate remedy.

In *Kelly v. Cahill*, by will dated October 23, 1969, the deceased had left his property jointly to his wife and brother for life, with remainder in trust for his nephew. However, having changed his mind, in January 1994 he instructed his solicitor that he wanted to leave all of his property to his wife instead of to his nephew. The solicitor advised that the most tax-efficient means to achieve this end would be to leave the will unaltered and instead to put the property into the names of himself and his wife, as joint tenants. A deed of transfer to achieve this end was drawn up by the solicitor and executed by the deceased and his wife. All parties believed that the deed covered all of the deceased's property. However, due to the solicitor's inadvertence – without the knowledge of the testator and his wife, and contrary to the testator's express intentions – the deed excluded much of the testator's property. Hence, when the testator died, these excluded lands passed under the will ultimately for the benefit of the nephew.

Barr J. found that the evidence established a clear, positive intention on the part of the testator that his wife should inherit all of his property on his death, that he took all appropriate steps to bring that about, and that he could not reasonably have known of his solicitor's error. As a consequence, he held that

> "'Justice and good conscience' require[d] that the [nephew] should not be allowed to inherit the testator's property or any part of it on the death of his widow and that his interest in remainder under the will should be deemed to be a constructive trust in favour of the widow. In my opinion a 'New Model' constructive trust of that nature the purpose of which is to prevent unjust enrichment is an equitable concept which

deserves recognition in Irish law."

On the issue of whether the nephew was in fact unjustly enriched at the expense of his aunt, the testator's widow, four questions arise: whether there has been (i) an enrichment of the defendant, (ii) at the expense of the plaintiff, (iii) in circumstances in which the enrichment can be regarded as 'unjust' and (iv) whether there are any reasons why restitution should nevertheless be denied to the plaintiff (see the *Bricklayers' Hall* case: *Dublin Corporation v. Building and Allied Trades Union* [1996] 1 I.R. 468, 483-484; [1996] 2 I.L.R.M. 547, 557-558 *per* Keane J.; see *Annual Review of Irish Law 1996*, p.502; (1993) 15 D.U.L.J. (*ns*) 27; (1997) 113 L.Q.R. 245; (1998) 20 D.U.L.J. (*ns*) 101). These enquiries will organise the analysis here of whether the nephew was unjustly enriched at the expense of his aunt.

ENRICHMENT

As Keane J. observed in the *Bricklayer's Hall* case, there is often little difficulty in determining whether a defendant has received a benefit, whether in money or in money's worth. Hence, in that case Keane J. held that it is clear that, at Irish law, a defendant can "be obliged to effect restitution of money *or other property* to another where it would be unjust for him to retain the *property*" ([1996] 1 I.R. 468, 483; [1996] 2 I.L.R.M. 547, 557; emphasis added). So it is that, on the facts of *Kelly v. Cahill*, the property received by the nephew undoubtedly constitutes an enrichment.

AT THE PLAINTIFF'S EXPENSE

Direct and interceptive subtraction The nephew having received an enrichment, a more difficult question arises: at whose expense did he receive it? This is functionally a causation enquiry, linking the defendant who has received an enrichment with the appropriate plaintiff at whose expense he been enriched (see, *e.g.*, *Commissioner v. Royal Insurance* (1994) 182 C.L.R. 51 (HCA); *Kleinwort Benson v. Birmingham City Co* [1996] 3 All E.R. 733, 742 *per* Evans L.J., 749 *per* Morritt L.J.). There is little difficulty in a case of a straightforward direct transfer from a plaintiff to a defendant – it is clear that the defendant's receipt is at the plaintiff's expense. Birks describes this as an enrichment of the defendant by direct subtraction from the plaintiff (see, e.g., Birks, *An Introduction to the Law of Restitution* (rev ed., OUP, Oxford, 1989), p.23). More difficult is the case where a transferor intends to benefit the plaintiff but the benefit instead arrives with the defendant. On the one hand, one school of thought argues that here the defendant is just as much enriched at the expense of the plaintiff as if there had been a direct subtraction from the plaintiff (see, *e.g.*, Birks, pp.133–134; see also Birks and Mitchell 'Unjust Enrichment' in Birks (ed.), *English Private Law* (OUP, Oxford, 2000) vol., II, 525; 530, para 15.13; 538, para. 15.35). Birks characterizes this as an "interceptive subtraction", both where the defendant has intercepted the enrichment and where it has been (mis)directed to the defendant; and he has been followed in this by La Forest .J in the Supreme Court of Canada in *LAC Minerals v. International Corona Resources* (1989) 61 D.L.R. (4th) 14 (SCC) 45. On the other, a second school of thought argues that there must be a direct connection between a plaintiff and a defendant in a restitution action, which there would not be where the enrichment was conferred not by the plaintiff but by a third party (see, *e.g.*, Burrows, *The Law of Restitution* (Butterworths, London, 1993), pp.46-54; Virgo, *Principles of the Law of Restitution* (OUP, Oxford, 1999), p.106); in such cases, the defendant's enrichment would not at be the expense of the plaintiff but – if at all – of the third party (Smith, (1991) 11 O.J.L.S. 481).

Though controversial, Irish law seems to have adopted the concept of interceptive subtraction (see, *e.g.*, *McMechan v. Warburton* [1896] 1 I.R. 435 (Chatterton VC and CA); *In re PMPA Insurance Co Ltd* [1986] I.L.R.M. 524 (HC; Lynch J.); *HKN Invest OY v. Incotrade PVT Ltd* [1993] 3 I.R. 152 (HC) 162 *per* Costello J.; *Shanahan v. Redmond,* High Court, June 21, 1994, Carroll J.; noted O'Dell, [1997] L.M.C.L.Q. 197); *Behan v. Bank of Ireland* (High Court, Morris J., unreported, 15 August 1997 [affd. on other grounds: [1998] 2 I.L.R.M. 507 (SC)] all discussed in *Annual Review of Irish Law 1997* pp.611–616). An ingenious example of such interceptive subtraction in the context of secret commissions has recently been suggested by Rotherham, [1997] C.f.i. L.R. 42, 46–47 discussing cases where a payor is prepared to pay a given price for a good or service, part of which ends up with the principal as the formal price, and part of which is diverted by the agent as his secret commission. Though the purchaser is not legally obliged to pay the combined sum, he plainly intends to pay it to secure the good or service in question, so that the part diverted by the agent would otherwise certainly have ended up with the principal. On Rotherham's view, such cases come within the concept of interceptive subtraction.

Any doubts about the status of interceptive subtraction as a matter of Irish law must now be convincingly stilled by *Kelly v. Cahill*. There, the enrichment of the nephew was held to be at the expense not of the testator but of his aunt. The nephew's receipt would have been directly from the testator but only interceptively from his aunt to whom the testator had intended to direct the property. Given that Barr J. held that the nephew was indeed unjustly enriched at the expense of his aunt, this must constitute a strong endorsement of the concept of interceptive subtraction. Of course, the court must be able to hold with sufficient certainty that the third party (here the testator) had intended to benefit the plaintiff (here his wife, the nephew's aunt) so as to hold that the enrichment of the defendant (here the nephew) is at the plaintiff's expense (see, *e.g.*, Birks, pp.133, 136). Smith objects that it is difficult to say the least to make such a determination of fact; however, as is demonstrated by Barr J's finding in *Kelly v. Cahill* that the testator had positively intended to benefit his wife and had taken all appropriate steps to bring that about, it is a finding that can be made in an appropriate case. As a consequence, Irish law seems to have decisively adopted the concept of interceptive subtraction.

UNJUST

The principle against unjust enrichment has often been criticised on the grounds that the concept of an "unjust" enrichment was too discretionary, too open-textured, for precise judicial deployment (see, *e.g.*, *Baylis v. Bishop of London* [1913] 1 Ch. 127 (CA) 140 *per* Hamilton L.J.; *Sinclair v. Brougham* [1914] A.C. 398 (HL) 453–454 *per* Lord Sumner; *Holt v. Markham* [1923] 1 K.B. 504 (CA) 513 *per* Scrutton L.J.; *Attorney General v. Ryan's Car Hire* [1965] I.R. 642 (SC) 664 *per* Kingsmill-Moore J.). The law in this area could indeed have gone the road of discretion – there are occasional traces of it in Irish cases (a recent example is provided by *Goodman v. Minister for Finance* [1999] 3 I.R. 356 (HC; Laffoy J) see *Annual Review of Irish Law 1999,* pp.458-465, 473-477) – but it has in fact taken an entirely different path. As Keane J. commented in the *Bricklayers' Hall* case "the law, as it has developed, has avoided the dangers of 'palm tree justice' by identifying whether the case belongs in a specific category which justifies so describing the enrichment: possible instances are money paid under duress or as a result of a mistake of fact or law or accompanied by a total failure of consideration ([1996] 1 I.R. 468, 484; [1996] 2 I.L.R.M. 547, 558). In other words, the law has not committed itself to a prescriptive notion of "unjust"; instead, to characterize an enrichment as unjust is simply to conclude that there exists on the facts a recognised cause of action, such as mistake, or duress, or failure of consideration.

Mistake   If "a person pays money to another under a mistake of fact which *causes* him to make the payment, he is *prima facie* entitled to recover it as money paid under a mistake of fact" (*Barclays Bank v. Simms* [1980] Q.B. 677, 695 *per* Goff J.; see also *National Bank v. O'Connor & Bowmaker* (1969) 103 I.L.T.R. 73 (HC; Budd J.); *David Securities v. Commonwealth Bank of Australia* (1992) 175 C.L.R. 353 (HCA); *Kleinwort Benson v. Lincoln City Council* [1999] 1 A.C. 153 (HL)). The plaintiff having established the mistake, the defendant's enrichment is thereby properly characterised as unjust.

Hence, where a social welfare authority has mistakenly overpaid benefits, it could in principle recover the overpayment on the ground of mistake (see, *e.g.*, *Holt v. Markham* [1923] 1 K.B. 504; *Avon CC v. Howlett* [1983] 1 All E.R. 1073; [1983] 1 W.L.R. 605 (CA); noted Burrows (1984) 100 L.Q.R. 31) though in such cases, as a restitutionary cause of action, it would be subject to restitutionary defences, such as the recently developed defence of change of position, or the longer established and more general defence of estoppel, which was in fact successful in both *Holt v. Markham* and *Avon CC v. Howlett* (on that issue, see now Key, [1995] C.L.J. 525; *Phil Collins v. Davis* [2000] 3 All E.R. 808 (Ch. D; Parker J.); *Scottish Equitable v. Derby* [2001] 3 All E.R. 818 (CA); *Nat West v. Somer* [2002] 1 All E.R. 198 (CA)).

This common law action, arising on general principles, would – unless excluded by the social welfare code – co-exist with any specific right of recovery conferred by the social welfare code. For example, benefits have long been recoverable on the grounds of fraud or wilful concealment (see section 46(1) of the Social Welfare Act 1952) though on no other ground (see section 46(5)(b) of the 1952 Act). This ground has been substantially re-enacted in section 300(1) of the Social Welfare (Consolidation) Act, 1981, section 31(1) of the Social Welfare Act 1993, and section 248(1)(a) of the Social Welfare (Consolidation) Act, 1993 and supplemented with a further ground of recovery where there are new facts or new evidence (see section 35 of the Social Welfare Act 1991 (inserting section 300(5)(aa) of the Social Welfare (Consolidation) Act 1981)) though again there is the statutory injunction that there be recovery on no other ground (see section 300(5)(b) of the 1991 Act). However, according to section 40 of the Social Welfare Act 1992, the expanded ground in section 35 of the Social Welfare Act 1991 can apply to periods prior to the commencement of the 1991 Act.

In *Minister for Social, Community and Family Affairs v. Scanlon*, the respondent had ceased employment in 1985, and from that date had been in receipt of disability benefit until 1994, when it was discontinued on the basis of new evidence that the respondent not at any stage been disabled from work. The Minister's claim for the return of the benefit failed before Laffoy J. (High Court, May 11, 1999), and the Minister appealed (Supreme Court, January 16, 2001). Fennelly J. (Keane C.J., Denham, Murray and McGuinness JJ. concurring) allowed the appeal and held that no constitutional right was infringed by the retrospective application of the recovery provisions. The benefit received, he said:

> "is an entitlement created by statute. It is subject, from the outset, to the condition that a Deciding Officer award. That decision, in turn was at all times subject to the infirmity that a Deciding Officer might revise that decision … leading to an obligation to repay all benefit received … The bar on recovery [in s300(5)(b) of the 1991 Act] contains at most a statutory concession that money already paid should not be recoverable at the suit of the Minister even though it has been established through the applicable statutory machinery that it had been wrongly paid in the first place. I cannot identify any constitutional right to retain the benefit of a concession of that sort."

No Irish case similar to *Avon CC v. Howlett* seems to have tested whether the statutory concession in section 46(5)(b) of the 1952 Act or section 300(5)(b) of the 1991 Act, precluding recovery except on the statutorily stated grounds of fraud, wilful concealment, or new evidence, excluded the common law action based on mistake. The language is clearly wide enough to do so; but the robust attitude of Fennelly J. in *Scalon* might indicate the contrary.

One reason for the absence of such an action based on mistake might be the old rule that a mistake of law was not actionable; after all, the mistaken overpayment of benefit could be said to be a mistake as to a statutory entitlement. This argument was successful in *Holt v. Markham*, but it was given decidedly shorter shrift when it failed in *Avon CC v. Howlett*; and the mistake of law bar itself has since been abrogated throughout the common law world (*Air Canada v. British Columbia* (1989) 59 D.L.R. (4th) 161 (SCC); *David Securities v. Commonwealth Bank of Australia* (1992) 175 C.L.R. 353 (HCA); *Kleinwort Benson v. Lincoln City Council* [1999] 1 A.C. 153 (HL)). Although it seemed that this development had been replicated at Irish law (see *Annual Review of Irish Law 1996*, pp.509-510; *Annual Review of Irish Law 1997*, pp.616-624; *Annual Review of Irish Law 1999*, pp.471-473) the curious reasoning of the majority in the Supreme Court in *Duff v. Minister for Agriculture (No 2)* [1997] 2 I.R. 22 threatened to breathe new life into a properly interred corpse (see Gannon "The Rise and Fall of the Mistake of Law Rule" (2000) 3 T.C.L.R. 73).

In *Duff*, the Minister erroneously implemented a European Regulation and excluded the plaintiff farmers from milk quotas. What is certain is that the Supreme Court held that the plaintiffs were entitled to damages, and remitted the matter to the High Court (where Laffoy J. impressively completed the Herculean assessment of such damages (High Court, March 25, 1999; June 3, 1999, August 11, 1999, August 24, 1999; discussed in *Annual Review of Irish Law 1999*, pp.471-473)). Still uncertain, however, is the basis of this liability. The Minister's erroneous implementation of the Regulation was characterized by Barrington and O'Flaherty JJ. in the Supreme Court as a "mistake of law". However, it was argued in *Annual Review of Irish Law 1997*, pp.619-623 that the appropriate basis of liability was the fact that the farmers had a legitimate expectation as a matter of national law which the Minister's error had frustrated, though this in turn ran into difficulties with the judgment of Henchy J. in *Pine Valley v. Minister for Environment* [1987] I.R. 23 (SC) requiring that to sound in damages an *ultra vires* action must independently constitute a wrong (such as negligence or malice). These concerns have been vindicated by comments of Fennelly J. in *Glencar Exploration v. Mayo Co C,* Supreme Court, July 19, 2001. The applicants had been successful in having the respondent's ban on their mining set aside as *ultra vires* (see *Glencar Exploration v. Mayo Co Co* [1993] 2 I.R. 237 (HC; Blayney J.)) but their subsequent claim for damages had been dismissed in the High Court (Kelly J., August 20, 1998). On appeal, in judgments delivered by Keane C.J. (Denham, Murray and McGuinness JJ.

concurring) and Fennelly J., their appeal was dismissed (see the Administrative Law chapter, above; and the Contract Law chapter, above). Fennelly J. commented that:

> "the considered statements of the law made in *Pine Valley* remain the law, despite apparent inconsistency with some dicta in the majority judgments in *Duff v. Minister for Agriculture (No. 2)* [1997] I.R. 22, which appear to treat liability for damages as automatically flowing from a mistake of law said to have been made by a Minister. ... I do not believe that it can have been intended [in *Duff*] to depart from such an important principle as that laid down in *Pine Valley*". (11; see also 21–26).

If this is correct, and it surely is, then it is still open then to decide the extent to which a breach of a legitimate expectation can give rise to a claim for damages. Furthermore, this shot across the bows of *Duff* must also call into question its unfortunate "mistake of law" reasoning (which is at best regrettable, at worst indefensible).

Failure of consideration   Where "a plaintiff has paid money in pursuance of his obligations under a contract and the consideration for which he entered into the contract totally fails, he may bring an action for the return of the money so paid (as money had and received to his use) ..." (*United Dominions Trust v. Shannon Caravans* [1976] I.R. 225, 231 *per* Griffin J.; *cp Fibrosa Spolka Ackyjna v. Fairbarin Lawson Combe Barbour* [1943] A.C. 32, 65 *per* Lord Wright; and now generally *Roxborough v. Rothmans* (2002) 76 A.L.J.R. 203 (HCA)). For example, where a deposit has been paid to secure a contractual counter-performance which does not materialise, the deposit is recoverable as having been paid for a consideration which has failed (see, *e.g.*, *Foran v. Wight* (1989-1990) 168 C.L.R. 385 (HCA)), unless the contract has provided or the parties intended that the deposit be non-returnable (though even here equity might relieve against such forfeiture and nevertheless order the return of the deposit; see, *e.g.*, *Coyle v. Central Trust* [1978] I.L.R.M. 211 (HC; McWilliam J.); see generally *Stockloser v. Johnson* [1954] 1 Q.B. 476 (CA); *Stern v. McArthur* (1988) 165 C.L.R. 489 (HCA); *Workers Trust v. Dojap* [1993] A.C. 537 (PC); Harpum, [1984] C.L.J. 134; Robertson, (1989) 23 U.B.C.L.R. 301; Pawlowski, [1994] .J.B.L. 372; Chin, (1995) 25 U.W.A.L.R. 110; see now also *cp On Demand Information v. Michael Gerson (Finance)*[2000] 4 All E.R. 734 (CA)). Hence, in *In re Edenfell Holdings,* High Court, July 30, 1997, Laffoy J. restrained a receiver's sale of property and ordered the return of a deposit paid by the putative purchaser (see *Annual Review of Irish Law 1997*, PP.658-659). However, on appeal (Supreme Court, April 23, 1998) Keane J. (O'Flaherty and Barron JJ. concurring) reversed and directed the receiver to complete the sale.

The issue arose again in *Forbes v. Tobin,* High Court, McCracken J., March 8, 2001. The plaintiff agreed to purchase from the defendant premises comprising a filling station, shop and workshop, and paid a deposit. The contract of sale provided that the plaintiff was to pay any exigible value added tax but the plaintiff disputed that any such tax was payable. The defendant also required that the plaintiff take over its agreements with its oil suppliers, but the plaintiff refused. The defendant then purported to serve two completion notices and sought to forfeit the deposit. The plaintiff sought specific performance of the contract, McCracken J. found that value added tax was indeed payable on the sale, and held that as a consequence the plaintiff was not ready willing and able to close and was therefore not entitled to an order for specific performance. However, he went on to hold that the defendant was not entitled to require the plaintiff to take over the oil supply contracts, and that, as a consequence, the defendant was also not ready willing and able to close at the time that the completion notices was, so that the contract for sale was not properly rescinded and the deposit was not properly forfeit. He therefore made an order requiring the return of the deposit plus interest (on the role of interest in the reversal of unjust enrichment, see *Annual Review of Irish Law 1999*, pp.473–477; to the discussion there of *Cooke v. Walsh* [1989] I.L.R.M. 322 (SC) see now *Clarke v. Commissioner of An Garda Síochána,* Supreme Court, July 31, 2001, Fennelly J. (Keane C.J., Murray, Hardiman and Geoghegan JJ. concurring) at pp.6-11; Edelman, (1999) 27 A.B.L.J. 211; Edelman, (2000) 28 A.B.L.J. 115; Ridge, (2000) 28 A.B.L.J. 275).

Ignorance   In the *Bricklayer's Hall* case, Keane J. gave as possible examples of unjust factors "mistake of fact or law or accompanied by a total failure of consideration" ([1996] 1 I.R. 468, 484; [1996] 2 I.L.R.M. 547, 558; *cp Moses v. Macferlan* (1760) 2 Burr. 1005, 1012; 97 E.R. 676, 681 *per* Lord Mansfield; *Fibrosa Spolka Akcyjna v. Fairbairn Lawson Combe Barbour* [1943] A.C. 32 (HL) 63 *per* Lord Wright; *Pavey & Matthews v. Paul* (1986) 162 C.L.R. 221 (HCA) 256 *per* Deane J.; *David Securities v. Commonwealth Bank of Australia* (1992) 175 C.L.R. 353 (HCA) 379; *Kleinwort Benson v. Lincoln City Council* [1999] 2 A.C. 349 (HL) 408-409 *per* Lord Hope). Linking these three causes of action, there is the single thread that the plaintiff had no real intention to enrich the defendant, so that the enrichment was unintended, non-consensual or involuntary. By parity of reasoning, therefore, if some other factor were to mean that a defendant's enrichment was equally unintended or unconsented to by a plaintiff, then the defendant would be unjustly enriched at the plaintiff's expense. Hence, where a plaintiff does not intend to enrich because he is unaware of (ignorant of) the defendant's enrichment, that enrichment should likewise be characterised as unjust. For example, the victim of a theft is unaware of (ignorant of) the thief's enrichment at the plaintiff-victim's expense, but can obviously have restitution from the thief. Similarly, in *Kelly v. Cahill*, the testator's widow, the plaintiff aunt, was entirely unaware of the facts, which gave rise to the defendant's enrichment. If an enrichment is unjust because it has been received without the claimant's consent, then, since the intended beneficiary, the plaintiff aunt, plainly did not consent to the nephew's enrichment, it can be said that this enrichment is unjust. This unjust factor, "which calls for restitution when wealth is transferred to a defendant wholly without the knowledge" (Birks, p.140) of the claimant, Birks has christened 'ignorance' (*ibid.*). Though it has proved a controversial unjust factor, it is entirely defensible both on principle and as a matter of authority (see *Annual Review of Irish Law 1996*, pp.519-520; *Annual Review of Irish Law 1997*, pp.625-646). It is the most appropriate unjust factor upon which an intended beneficiary can rely against an unintended recipient (see O'Dell, (2002) 65 (3) M.L.R. 360, 371-372). Since Barr J. held that the plaintiff along with her husband could not reasonably have known of the solicitor's error, which had the effect of enriching the nephew, this must constitute a strong endorsement of ignorance as an unjust factor as a matter of Irish law.

DEFENCES

Fiscal chaos In claims for restitution against public authorities, many courts have been sufficiently attracted by defendants' arguments that plaintiffs' claims would lead to fiscal chaos to countenance not only generous applications of defences such as change of position (*Murphy v. AG* [1982] I.R. 241 (SC) 320 per Henchy J.; see *Annual Review of Irish Law 1996*, pp.522-523; *Annual Review of Irish Law 1997*, pp.659-665; (1998) 20 D.U.L.J. (*ns*) 101, 141-152), or passing on (*Air Canada v. British Columbia* (1989) 59 D.L.R. (4th) 161 (SCC) 193-194 *per* La Forest J.) but also to directly to preclude claims in its own right as a matter of policy (*ibid.*). However, such policy arguments have not found favour in the European Court of Justice (Case 199/82 *State Finance Administration v. San Giorgio SpA* [1983] E.C.R. 501), the High Court of Australia (*Commissioner v. Royal Insurance* (1994) 182 CLR 51 (HCA)), or the English courts (*Woolwich v. IRC (No 2)* [1993] A.C. 70 (HL); *Kleinwort Benson v. Birmingham City Council* [1996] 4 All ER 733 (CA); *Kleinwort Benson v. Lincoln City Council* [1999] 1 A.C. 153 (HL)). In the Irish courts, the policy bolstered the application of a defence already available on the facts in *Murphy*, but it has not been accepted as a free-standing reason to refuse an otherwise valid claim. Hence, in *Tate v. The Minister for Social Welfare* [1995] 1 I.L.R.M. 507 (HC) Carroll J. held that "for the State to try and avoid its responsibilities on the basis of cost would not be acceptable in the Courts of this State" ([1995] 1 I.L.R.M. 507, 516). Again, in this year's *Dekra Erin Teo v. Minister for the Environment,* High Court, November 2, 2001) O'Neill J. (at p.43) again rejected the fiscal chaos policy as an answer to private law claims.

Nevertheless, strong public policy considerations can provide sufficient reasons to deny restitutionary claims. For example, in *Banque Financière de la Cité v. Parc (Battersea)* [1999] 1 A.C. 221 (HL) 234, Lord Hoffmann commented that there could be "reasons of policy for denying a remedy". An example more secure than that of La Forest J. in *Air Canada* is provided by Keane J. in the *Bricklayers' Hall* case, who denied the Corporation's claim for policy reasons which both underlay the defence of *res judicata* and operated more generally in their own right as grounds of public policy arising out of the planning code (see (1998) 20 D.U.L.J. (*n.s.*) 101, 165-167). In *Kelly v. Cahill*, it might have been argued that the plaintiff's remedy ran foul of the strong public policy in favour of the finality of testamentary instruments upon which the Succession Act, 1965 is based (Langbein, 88 *Harv L Rev* 489, 491-503 (1975); Davey, [1980] *Conv.* 64, 67–70; Lang, (1985) 5 Melb. U.L.R. 82, 85-89; Critchley, [1999] C.L.J. 49, 51–53). However, though strong, the policy is not always determinative; and claims succeed despite it in the context of trusts arising out of mutual wills or joint deposit accounts. Hence, in *Seagrave v. Kirwan* (1828) 1 Beatt. 157, 163–165 Hart L.C. brushed aside such policy objections that the will was being undercut where a constructive trust for the benefit of the next of kin was imposed on the lawyer who had drafted the will and had then as executor succeeded to the undisposed residue of the estate. On balance, it seems that the policy ought not to preclude claims similar to that which was successful in *Kelly v. Cahill*.

Res judicata In the *Bricklayers' Hall* case, the plaintiffs' claim for restitution was successfully met with a plea of *res judicata*. In what was in many ways a re-run of that case, a similar claim was similarly successfully met in *Limerick VEC v. Carr and The Revenue Commissioners,* High Court, O'Higgins J., July 25, 2001. The first defendant had succeeded in an action against the plaintiff, and, on foot of an order of Barron J. in the High Court, the plaintiff paid the first defendant a sum of £112,816.14 to represent gross unpaid salary, and paid tax and PRSI on that amount to the second defendant. In the present proceedings, the plaintiff maintained that the decree of Barron J. was made on the basis that Ms Carr would go to the Revenue Commissioners to be assessed for tax on the amount of the decree, that she had not done so, and that, as a consequence, it was entitled to recover at least the amount of the tax and PRSI either from the first defendant or from the second.

The plaintiffs first attempted to vary the earlier order of Barron J. to provide expressly that Ms Carr should go to the Revenue Commissioners to be assessed for tax. However, O'Higgins refused to exercise the power in Order 28, rule 11 (RSC) to correct clerical mistakes or errors arising from accidental slips or omissions on the ground that Barron J. had in fact made no such order and had not been asked to do so. (*Concorde Engineering v. Bus Atha Cliath* [1996] 1 I.L.R.M. 533 (HC), 535–536 *per* McCracken J. considered at 5–6). Similarly, although he accepted that there exists at common law a power to amend an order where the court itself finds that it does not correctly state what the court had actually decided and intended, he held that it is a power to be exercised sparingly and refused to exercise it here because whilst it was probable that Barron J. would have made an order directing Ms Carr to seek an assessment from the Revenue Commissioners it was by no means certain that it was his actual intention that she do so (*Belville Holdings v. Revenue Commissioners* [1994] 1 I.L.R.M. 29 (SC) considered).

Assuming that the plaintiffs could nevertheless make out a cause of action, the first defendant relied on the *Bricklayer's Hall* case for the argument that the matter was *res judicata* as a consequence of Barron J.'s earlier decision. It is a fundamental principle that final decisions cannot be reopened except on appeal, and if there has been no appeal, as here, the matter cannot afterwards be relitigated between the parties or their privies (see, e.g., *White v. Spendlove* [1942] I.R. 224 (SC); *Tassan Din v. Banco Ambrosiano SpA* [1991] 1 I.R. 569 (HC); *Belton v. Carlow Co. Co.* [1997] 1 I.R. 172 (SC) 182; *McCauley v. McDermot* [1997] 2 I.L.R.M. 486 (SC); *Blackall v. Blackall,* Supreme Court, June 18, 1998)). They are prevented from relitigating either a cause of action (cause of action estoppel; *Chamberlaim v. Deputy Commissioner of Taxation* (1988) 164 C.L.R. 502 (HCA))) or, more broadly, an issue which has been adjudicated upon in the earlier proceedings (issue estoppel; see, e.g., *D. v. C.* [1984] I.L.R.M. 173 (HC; Costello J.)). Indeed, issue estoppel has been extended to preclude subsequent litigation of issues which ought to have been adjudicated upon in the earlier proceedings (estoppel by omission; see, e.g., *Yat Tung Investment Co. v. Dao Heng Bank* [1975] A.C. 581 (PC); *Arnold v. National Westminster Bank* [1991] 2 A.C. 93 (HL)); while contiguous with these *res judicata* estoppels is the more general discretionary power to strike out actions as an abuse of process. Both of these extensions are less absolute than cause of action estoppel, and have be traced back to the decision of Wigram VC in *Henderson v. Henderson* (1843) 3 Hare 100; 67 E.R. 313 (see, e.g., *Hoystead v. Commissioner of Taxation* (1921) 29 C.L.R. 537 (HCA) *rvsd.* [1926] A.C. 155 (PC); *Yat Tung*). However, Handley (2002) 118 L.Q.R. 397 argues that *Henderson* itself is an example of cause of action estoppel, which is now accepted to be an absolute bar to subsequent litigation, and that the extension of such absolutist principles to include estoppel by omission by Kilbrandon in *Yat Tung* was an error properly corrected by Lords Bingham and Millett in *Johnson v. Gore-Wood* [2001] 2 W.L.R. 72 (HL) and by Lord Bingham in *Gairy v. AG of Grenada* [2001] 3 W.L.R. 779 (PC) by bringing cases of estoppel by omission within the realm of abuse of process. There is force in this argument; as Handley argues, "strike-out applications based solely on cause of action or issue estoppels can usually be determined summarily on minimal evidence. On the other hand the abuse of process issue which ... calls for 'a broad merits-based approach' requires a discretionary judgment and this will tend to generate extensive evidence and lengthy argument" ((2002) 118 L.Q.R. 397, 407). However, there are strong affinities between issue estoppel and estoppel by omission, and such omission is not the only reason why there might be an abuse of process. Consequently, there is a strong reason to retain a category of *res judicata* estoppel by omission, separate on the one hand from cause of action estoppel and issue estoppel by being less absolute, and separate on the other hand from abuse of process by being more precisely defined in its application to preclude subsequent litigation.

On whatever species of estoppel or abuse of process it could have been based, the defendants' plea of *res judicata* in *Limerick VEC v. Carr and The Revenue Commissioners* was plainly very strong. However, the plaintiffs argued that Ms Carr was herself in turn estoped from relying on the doctrine of *res judicata* because of the representations made by an accountant called on her behalf in the original proceedings before Barron J. In such a case of counter estoppel (see, e.g., *Cassidy v. O'Rourke,* High Court, May 18, 1983, Carroll J.; *Republic of India v. India Steamship Co* [1993] A.C. 410; *Showlag v. Mansour* [1995] 1 A.C. 431 (PC); *Littondale v. Wicklow Co. Co.* [1996] 2 I.L.R.M. 519) the party against whom the plea of *res judicata* is made does not seek to deny that he or she would be estoped, but insists that the other party is estoped from saying so (McDermott, *Res Judicata and Double Jeopardy* (Butterworths, Dublin, 1999), p.163)). However, O'Higgins J. held that neither the accountant nor the first defendant had given an undertaking that she would go to the Revenue Commissioners to be assessed in respect of the award, so that she was not precluded from relying on the doctrine of *res judicata,* and the plaintiff's claim against her therefore failed.

However, had the first defendant's plea of *res judicata* been unsuccessful, either because no species of estoppel or abuse of process could be made out or because the cross-estoppel prevent it from being raised, the question would then have arisen, in what did the first defendant's unjust enrichment consist? To put it another way, given that she had received the money from the plaintiffs, she had plainly been enriched at their expense, but what factor would have rendered it unjust? It is hard to find any. All of the examples given by Keane J. in the *Bricklayers' Hall* case – mistake, duress, failure of consideration – would seem inapplicable because the money was paid pursuant to a valid court order; similar unjust factors based on the impairment of the plaintiff's consent would seem equally inappropriate for the same reason. Neither could it be said that the defendant's receipt pursuant to the court order was unconscientious. Nor is there a strong policy elsewhere in the law pulling in favour of the return of the monies (on these three families of unjust factors, vitiated consent, unconscientious receipt, and policy, see *Annual Review of Irish Law 1996,* 506–521; O'Dell (1998) 20 D.U.L.J. (*n.s.*) 101, 108–111 with references). Indeed, as O'Higgins J. held, *res judicata* provides an insuperable contrary policy, and the plaintiff's claim against the first defendant failed.

As for the plaintiff's claim against the second defendant, the Revenue Commissioners, it proceeded on the basis that the Revenue should have made an assessment against Mrs Carr, but on an interpretation of the relevant statutory provisions, O'Higgins J. rejected that claim. Parallel with this statutory claim, there may have been a common law claim upon which the plaintiffs could have relied, consisting in the argument that the plaintiffs, having been compelled to pay tax and PRSI to the Revenue in respect of the first defendant, had discharged a debt owed to the Revenue by the first defendant, and having so compulsorily discharged the first defendant's debt, it was entitled to have restitution from the first defendant in the amount of the debt so discharged, by analogy with *East Cork Foods v. O'Dwyer Steel* [1978] I.R. 103 (SC) (see *Annual Review of Irish Law 1996*, 511–515, *Annual Review of Irish Law 1999*, 461–471). However, had there been substance in the plaintiff's statutory claim against the second defendants, or had this common law argument been raised, they would almost certainly have been met with a successful abuse of process argument. Since the Revenue were not parties to the original proceedings between the plaintiff and the first defendant, neither cause of action nor issue estoppel, nor even estoppel by omission, could have been relied upon by them against the plaintiff. Nevertheless, the Revenue should have been able to argue that the claim against them was in substance nothing more than an end run around the original judgment of Barron J, and thus constituted an abuse of process. (This provides one example of where the doctrine of abuse of process is wider than estoppel by omission; they should be kept separate for that reason). In the end, then, it is difficult to disagree with O'Higgins J.'s observation that it would have been open to the plaintiffs "to appeal the order of Barron J. if they were dissatisfied with it. They consciously decided not to adopt that course. They cannot successfully circumvent that decision in these proceedings" against either of the defendants.

PROPRIETARY CLAIMS

Unjust enrichment of the defendant, of itself and without more, is simply a legal, personal claim, giving rise simply to a personal obligation to make restitution in the amount of the enrichment. It does not give rise to a proprietary liability. For this, there must be something more than merely an unjust enrichment of the plaintiff at the expense of the plaintiff, or there must be something else which would give rise to a separate but parallel proprietary claim (see (1998) 20 D.U.L.J. (*n.s.*) 101, 160-180; (2001) 23 D.U.L.J. (*n.s.*) 71, 74–82, 87–90). The trust, often characterised as a constructive trust or even a remedial constructive trust, is regularly pressed into service to justify proprietary restitution, on the basis that it provides that something more or something else to give rise to a proprietary liability. Unfortunately, in *Kelly v. Cahill*, Barr J. did not conduct an enquiry as to whether there was something in addition or alternative to unjust enrichment to justify the imposition of a remedial constructive trust; for him, unjust enrichment was a sufficient trigger. This is unfortunate if not pernicious. Unjust enrichment and the remedial constructive trust must be carefully separated. Both are potent chemicals; separately used, they serve important functions; mixed together, however, they can be explosive. Liability in unjust enrichment is a strict and personal liability, which arises at common law on the basis of recognised, causes of action. On the other hand, the remedial constructive trust is a discretionary equitable proprietary liability (and though unfocussed and largely insensitive to issues of policy, priority and timing, at least for so long as it is imposed whenever justice and good conscience require it, it seems nevertheless to be alive and kicking in Ireland (see (1998) 20 D.U.L.J. (*ns*) 101, 168-180; (2001) 23 D.U.L.J. (*ns*) 71, 74-82)). It is important to keep the distinction between personal and proprietary liability separate, because the former will for all practical purposes be lost in an insolvency, whereas the latter will generate a claim outside an insolvency. There was no question of an insolvency on the facts of *Kelly v. Cahill*, but the untrammelled application of a remedial constructive trust on the basis simply of unjust enrichment could have significant and unwelcome ramifications in another case where the defendant was insolvent. Consequently, these important concepts should not be conflated, but instead kept separate.

Given that unjust enrichment simply generates a personal claim, for there to be a proprietary one there would need to be on the facts something else which generated a separate parallel proprietary claim or something more which in conjunction with unjust enrichment would elevate the personal action into a proprietary one. On this basis, the result in *Kelly v. Cahill* may be explained as an example of a *Re Rose* trust (*Re Rose; Rose v. Inland Revenue Commissioners* [1952] 1 Ch. 499 (CA); *Vandervell v. IRC* [1967] 2 A.C. 291 (HL); *Corin v. Patton* (1990) 169 CLR 54 (HCA); *T. Choithram International SA v. Pagarnai* [2001] 1 W.L.R. 1 (PC)) or on the basis of rectification of the deed (*Walker v. Armstrong* (1856) 8 DeGM&G 531; 44 E.R. 495; *Lister v. Hodgson* (1867) LR 4 Eq. 30; *McMechan v. Warburton* [1896] 1 I.R. 435 (Chatterton VC); *aff'd* [1896] 1 I.R. 441 (Ir. CA)). The problem was with a misdrafted deed; better then that the solution should also have focused on the deed, by rectifying it, rather than imposing an imprecise remedial constructive trust.

Safety and Health

ADVENTURE ACTIVITIES STANDARDS AUTHORITY

The Adventure Activities Standards Authority Act 2001 provides for the establishment of the eponymous Adventure Activities Standards Authority (Údarás um Chaighdeáin do Ghníomhaíochtaí Eachtraíochta). Its purpose is to regulate adventure activities, whether land-based or water-based. Prior to the 2001 Act, no specific statutory authority had a standard-setting function in this area and, in light of the number of serious accidents and fatalities in such activities it was considered necessary to have a regulatory body in this area. At the time of writing a Commencement Order for the 2001 Act had not been made.

CHEMICAL SAFETY

Chemical weapons   The Chemical Weapons (Licensing of Scheduled Toxic Chemicals and Precursors) Regulations 2001 (S.I. No. 54 of 2001), made under the Chemical Weapons Act 1997 (*Annual Review of Irish Law 1997*, 666) established a detailed licensing system relating to the production, use, acquisition or possession of a toxic chemical or precursor listed in the First Schedule to the Chemical Weapons Act 1997. They came into effect on February 23, 2001.

CONSTRUCTION REGULATIONS 2001

Introduction   The Safety, Health and Welfare at Work (Construction) Regulations 2001 (S.I. No.481 of 2001), made under the Safety, Health and Welfare at Work Act 1989 (*Annual Review of Irish Law 1989*, 379-93), implemented the 1992 EC Directive on Temporary or Mobile Construction Sites and also some new provisions on construction site safety based on 'partnership' reports drawn up in 1999 and 2000. They also revoked and replaced the Safety, Health and Welfare at Work (Construction) Regulations 1995 (*Annual Review of Irish Law 1995*, 445-8)). The 2001 Regulations largely came into effect on 1 January 2002, subject to some important transitional provisions, which delay full implementation of some new provisions, mainly concerning training, until June 1, 2003. The Construction Regulations 2001 are rather more wide-ranging than their title might indicate. The Regulations apply, of course, to building projects, but they also include many civil engineering projects as well as maintenance activities connected with existing buildings, such as maintenance of equipment as well as cleaning and other decorating.

Principal changes in the 2001 Regulations   The principal changes in the 2001 Regulations over the 1995 Regulations they replaced were; the introduction of mandatory basic awareness training, known as Safe Pass training, for all construction workers; Construction Skills Certification Scheme (CSCS) training for specified workers, such as scaffolders and drivers of certain vehicles, including tower cranes; a new concept of Site Safety Representative, which is mandatory where more than 20 are at work on a site; the Project Supervisor for the Construction Stage (PSCS) required to co-ordinate arrangements to ensure that workers have Safe Pass and CSCS registration and to co-ordinate welfare facilities on construction sites; the extension of requirement on contractors to appoint safety officers.

Design and operational elements   The 2001 Regulations involve two major elements: requirements concerning the preparatory design and management of safety and health for construction work (Regulations 3 to 8); and detailed operational Regulations for construction work (Regulations 9 to 129). In this Review, we concentrate on the design and management elements of the 2001 Regulations.

Design stage and construction stage   Regulation 2 of the 2001 Regulations specifies that the 'design stage' means the period of time during which the design of a project is prepared, but *not* the design of temporary works by a contractor to facilitate the construction: this would form part of the construction stage. Regulation 2 also specifies that 'design' means the preparation of drawings, particulars, specifications, calculations, bills of quantities in so far as they contain specifications or other expressions of purpose, according to which a project, or any part or component of a project, is to be executed. Regulation 2 specifies that the construction stage means the time starting when preparation of the construction site begins, including the design of temporary works to facilitate the construction work and ending when construction work on the project is completed.

Duties concerning design and management of construction work   Part 2 of the 2001 Regulations (Regulations 3 to 8) contains the essential provisions concerning preparatory design and management:

Regulation 3 describes the duties of the Client.

Regulation 4 describes the duties of the Project Supervisor for the Design Stage (PSDS) (referred to in the British CDM Regulations as the Planning Supervisor).

Regulation 5 describes the duties of Designers.

Regulations 6 and 8 describe the duties of the Project Supervisor for the Construction Stage (PSCS) (referred to in the CDM Regulations as the Principal Contractor).

Regulation 7 describes the functions and powers of the Site Safety Representative (new in the 2001 Regulations).

Safety and health plan   The 2001 Regulations require that a Safety and Health Plan be prepared by the PSCS for *some but not all* construction projects. In developing the Safety and Health Plan, the PSCS must take account of the requirements of section 12 of the 1989 Act, which deals with the Safety Statement. Regulation 6 also states that the Plan must take account of other work activities taking place on the site and include specific measures concerning any of the ten work activities listed in the Second Schedule to the Regulations. Regulation 4(2) specifies that a Safety and Health Plan is required in two situations: where work will last longer than 30 working days or the volume of work will exceed 500 person-days (that is, where notification of the construction work to the HSA is required under Regulation 8); *or* where the construction work involves particular risks, including those specified in the Second Schedule to the Regulations.

Safety file   Regulation 6 of the 2001 Regulations specifies that a Safety File must be prepared where more than one contractor is engaged in a construction project. The Safety File must contain 'relevant health and safety information to be taken into account during any subsequent construction work following completion of the project.' By contrast with the Safety and Health Plan, the Safety File is intended to provide information for use during any *subsequent* construction work following *completion* of the project. It is an Operations and Maintenance File, so that it would include, for example, drawings as well as information on the completed project, including electrical work, pipe-work, the position of overhead lines and similar matters.

Duties of the client   Regulation 2 of the 2001 Regulations defines a 'client' as any person engaged in trade, business *or other undertaking* who commissions or procures the carrying out of a construction project for the purposes of such trade, business or undertaking. Regulation 3 of the 2001 Regulations specifies that the client has the following mandatory duties: appoint a project supervisor for the design stage of every project; appoint a project supervisor for the construction stage of every project; keep available any safety file prepared under Regulation 6 for inspection by any person who may need information in the file in order to comply with any duties imposed under 'the relevant statutory provisions'.

Duties of the project supervisor for the design stage (PSDS) We have already seen that the 2001 Regulations require the client to appoint project supervisors for the design and construction stages. Regulation 2 specifies that any project supervisor must be a 'competent person'. This indicates that such a person must have qualifications, training and experience appropriate to the functions they carry out under the Regulations. Regulation 4 of the 2001 Regulations specifies that, during the design of a project and when estimating the period of time required for completion of the project, and where appropriate for stages of the project, the project supervisor for the design stage (PSDS) must take account of the General Principles of Prevention contained in the Safety, Health and Welfare at Work (General Application) Regulations 1993 (*Annual Review of Irish Law 1993*, 491): these are a hierarchy of risk control measures. Regulation 4 also specifies that the PSDS must take account of any Safety and Health Plan or Safety File Also for this purpose, the PSDS must co-ordinate the activities of other persons engaged in design work related to the project. Regulation 4 specifies that, where a Safety and Health Plan is required by Regulation 6, the PSDS must prepare *on a preliminary basis* such a Plan to provide information for the project supervisor for the construction stage. Regulation 4 of the 2001 Regulations also requires the PSDS to provide the project supervisor for the construction stage (PSCS) with any available information that needs to be included in the Safety File required under Regulation 6.

Duties of designer Regulation 5 of the 2001 Regulations specifies the duties of any person who is engaged in work related to the design of a project *other than the project supervisor*. A designer is a person involved in the preparation of drawings or other material for the project.

Duties of project supervisor for the construction stage (PSCS) The most wide-ranging design and management duties under the 2001 Regulations are imposed on the project supervisor for the construction stage (PSCS). These fall under the following headings: notification of projects to the Health and Safety Authority; the Safety and Health Plan; the Safety File; co-ordination of day-to-day activities; co-ordination of arrangements for site safety representative (new in the 2001 Regulations); co-ordination of arrangements for welfare facilities (also new in the 2001 Regulations); co-ordination of records of Safe Pass and CSCS certificates (also new in the 2001 Regulations).

The PSCS is required by Regulation 8 to give advance written notice to the Health and Safety Authority in relation to work scheduled to last more than 30 working days or on which the volume of work is scheduled to exceed 500 person days. The PSCS must ensure that the particulars to be contained in the notice are clearly displayed on the site and, if necessary, periodically updated. The First Schedule to the 2001 Regulations specifies that the notice must include certain particulars. Regulation 6 of the 2001 Regulations specifies that the PSCS shall, before construction work commences, develop the Safety and Health Plan for the site, using the Plan that had been prepared on a preliminary basis by the PSDS; make adjustments to the Safety and Health Plan, where required, to take account of the progress of the work and any changes that occur during work; and prepare and, where required, adjust the Safety File; and on completion of the project, deliver the Safety File to the client. The PSCS must also: organise co-operation between contractors (including successive contractors on the same project) and co-ordination of their activities on a project with a view to protecting persons at work and preventing accidents and ill-health; facilitate the appointment of a site safety representative, co-ordinate arrangements which facilitate the provision and the maintenance, in an appropriate condition, of site welfare provisions; co-ordinate measures to ensure that relevant persons have received Safe Pass training; co-ordinate measures to ensure that relevant persons have CSCS certification; and to keep records relating to Safe Pass and CSCS.

Duties of contractors in construction work   Although the changes introduced by the 2001 Regulations alter to some extent the scope of the duties of contractors, they remain responsible for ensuring the day-to-day safety, health and welfare of their employees and/or those whom they merely supply as labour to a construction project. This is, of course, entirely consistent with the general principles contained in the Safety, Health and Welfare at Work Act 1989. Regulation 9 of the 2001 Regulations, which largely replicated Regulation 8 of the 1995 Regulations, specifies that contractors must comply with: the detailed provisions concerning operational safety, health and welfare contained in Regulations 15 to 129 of the 2001 Regulations (covering 16 major headings, such as scaffolding, use of equipment, trench work); and the appropriate requirements of the Fourth and Fifth Schedules as regards any place of work under the contractor's control (containing almost 30 additional headings, such as fire-fighting and evacuation procedures). The effect of this is that, as already noted, day-to-day responsibility for compliance with the detailed operational Regulations contained in the 2001 Regulations rests firmly on the contractor. The only detailed change is that responsibility for welfare facilities has been transferred to the sole responsibility of the PSCS; otherwise the contractor remains responsible. In addition to the duties under the 2001 Regulations, the contractor must comply with the duties imposed in some of the more significant Regulations made under the 1989 Act, such as those in the General Application Regulations 1993 (including manual handling training and electrical safety).

MANUFACTURING STANDARDS

Machinery The European Communities (Machinery) Regulations 2001 (S.I. No. 518 of 2001) implemented the 1998 EU Technical Standards ('CE' Marking) Machinery Directive (98/37/EC), which updated the original 1989 Technical Standards Machinery Directive (89/392/EEC). The 2001 Regulations replaced the European Communities (Machinery) Regulations 1994 and 1995 (*Annual Review of Irish Law 1994*, 403 and *Annual Review of Irish Law 1995*, 443) (and which had in turn replaced the European Communities (Machinery) Regulations 1992 (*Annual Review of Irish Law 1992*, 539)). In general terms, the 2001 Regulations prohibit placing on the market and putting into service any machinery (as defined in the Regulations) unless, when properly installed and maintained and used for its intended purpose, it does not endanger the health or safety of persons and, where appropriate, domestic animals or property. Machinery as defined must comply with the safety and health requirements in the Annexes to the 1998 Directive, as amended, which in essence provide specific headings dealing with the safety design and operation of machinery. While the Annexes to the Directives are self-executing in legal terms, many of the headings have been fleshed out in considerable detail in the detailed technical standards or European Norms, which have been developed by the European Standards Organisations, such as CEN and Cenelec, which enjoy the recognition of the EC though not a formal part of the EC institutions.

Medical devices The European Communities (In Vitro Diagnostic Medical Devices) Regulations 2001 (S.I. No. 304 of 2001) implemented Directive 98/79/EC on *in vitro* diagnostic medical devices. The European Communities (Medical Devices) (Amendment) Regulations 2001 (S.I. No. 444 of 2001) amended the European Communities (Medical Devices) Regulations 1994 (*Annual Review of Irish Law 1994*, 403) to assign the function of the competent authority in the State to the Irish Medicines Board.

Petroleum coke The National Standards Authority of Ireland Act 1996 (Section 32) Regulations 2001 (S.I. No. 484 of 2001) enable local authorities to summarily prosecute an offence in respect of the sale, manufacture and assembly for domestic use of petroleum coke and other solid fuels in contravention of the conditions and composition set out in the Industrial Research and Standards (Section 44) (Petroleum Coke and other Solid Fuels) Order 1991.

OCCUPATIONAL SAFETY

Carcinogens The Safety, Health and Welfare at Work (Carcinogens) Regulations 2001 (S.I. No. 78 of 2001), made under the Safety, Health and

Welfare at Work Act 1989 (*Annual Review of Irish law 1989*, 379-93), implemented Directive 90/394/EEC on the protection of workers from the risks related to exposure to carcinogens at work, as amended in 1997 by Directive 97/42/EC. The 2001 Regulations replaced the Carcinogens Regulations 1993 (*Annual Review of Irish Law 1993*, 504), which had implemented the 1990 Directive. The 2001 Regulations impose obligations on employers in respect of chemicals designated as cancer causing under the EC Directives which regulate the manufacture, classification, packaging and labelling of chemicals. These Classification, Packaging and Labelling (CPL) Directives have been implemented in Ireland by the European Communities (Classification, Packaging and Labelling of Dangerous Preparations) Regulations 1995 (*Annual Review of Irish law 1995*, 438) and the European Communities (Classification, Packaging, Labelling and Notification of Dangerous Substances) Regulations 2000 (*Annual Review of Irish Law 2000*, 391). Among the chemicals designated as cancer-causing in these CPL Directives (carrying the 'risk phrase' R45) are: acrylonitrile (used in the manufacture of synthetic yarn), benzene (used as a solvent) and vinyl chloride monomer (VCM, used in the manufacture of plastics and as a refrigerant). In addition, the First Schedule to the 2001 Regulations contains a listing of certain substances and activities to which they apply. These include: rubber manufacturing and processing which give rise to dust and fumes; work involving exposure to aromatic polycycil hydrocarbons from coal soot, coal tar or coal pitch; work giving rise to dusts from electro-refining of cupro-nickel materials; work involving exposure to hardwoods. Under the 2001 Regulations, employers must carry out an assessment of the risks associated with the use of any of these carcinogens or mutagens in the workplace, and take steps to control such risks by eliminating or minimising exposure. A significant change in the 2001 Regulations over the 1993 Regulations is that employers must not only be aware of carcinogens which have been formally designated at EU level as cancer-causing under the CPL Directives, but also any carcinogen where the manufacturer has information that the substance in question is a category 1 or category 2 carcinogen. In order to comply with this requirement, employers will need to consult the information contained in the Material Safety Data Sheet (MSDS) supplied by the manufacturer/supplier. Under the 2001 Regulations, employers must also ensure that employees who are at possible risk of exposure to carcinogens are consulted and provided with information and training on the nature of the hazards and risks of carcinogens. Employees must also be provided with the facility to undergo health surveillance if desired. The Regulations require employers to maintain records on the results of assessments, measurements of exposure and health surveillance. Such records must kept for 40 years and be available to the Health and Safety Authority.

Chemical agents The Safety, Health and Welfare at Work (Chemical Agents)

Regulations 2001 (S.I. No. 563 of 2001), also made under the Safety, Health and Welfare at Work Act 1989 (*Annual Review of Irish Law 1989*, 379-93), implemented the 1998 EC Directive on Chemical Agents and revoked and replaced the Safety, Health and Welfare at Work (Chemical Agents) Regulations 1994 (*Annual Review of Irish law 1994*, 405). The 2001 Regulations also revoked the European Communities (Protection of Workers) (Exposure to Lead) Regulations 1988 (*Annual Review of Irish Law 1988*, 376), whose provisions have been incorporated into the 2001 Regulations. In the main, the 2001 Regulations replicate the principal terms of the 1994 Regulations and impose a general duty on employers to make an assessment of risk in connection with any chemical substance present at work and likely to be hazardous to health. Unlike the Carcinogens Regulations 2001, discussed above which apply to a limited range of chemical substances, the Chemical Agents Regulations 2001 thus apply to all chemical substances and preparations, in whatever form they appear. The Chemical Agents Regulations thus apply not merely to substances that appear in liquid form in a container, such as certain acids, but also any chemical agent that has a solid form, such as asbestos. It is estimated that there are over 100,000 chemical substances and preparations known to exist within the European Community that come within the definition of 'chemical agent' in the 2001 Regulations. The 2001 Regulations also state that where measurement of exposure to chemicals is necessary after the required risk assessment, the employer must use appropriate sampling and measuring procedures as well as procedures for evaluation of results. The employer must also ensure that an occupational exposure limit (OEL) set out in a relevant Approved Code of Practice (ACoP) from the Health and Safety Authority is not exceeded. The Health and Safety Authority has published an ACoP for the Chemical Agents Regulations 2001, which supersedes the previous ACoPs for the 1994 Regulations. The 2001 Regulations also impose obligations concerning health surveillance, specifically in connection with exposure to lead and lead compounds (such as in crystal glass manufacturing), to record and retain results of chemical exposure monitoring and health surveillance and to provide appropriate information and training for employees.

Confined spaces   The Safety, Health and Welfare at Work (Confined Spaces) Regulations 2001 (S.I. No. 218 of 2001), made under the Safety, Health and Welfare at Work Act 1989 (*Annual Review of Irish Law 1989*, 379-93), impose general duties on employers concerning entry into confined and other similar spaces, such as closed tanks, vessels, ships' bulkheads and sewers. Unlike most other recent Regulations made under the 1989 Act, the Confined Spaces Regulations do not involve implementation of an EC Directive; instead they are, in general, modelled on the British Confined Spaces Regulations 1997, made under the Health and Safety at Work Act 1974. The 2001 Regulations impose general duties on employers in respect of confined space entry. These include: that no person should enter a confined space for any work purpose unless it is not reasonably practicable to achieve that purpose without entry; that, if confined space entry is required, no person shall enter or carry out work in a confined space unless an identification and evaluation of the risks to safety and health arising from this work has been carried out; that, if entry is required, a safe system of work must be planned, organised, performed and maintained so as to render that work safe and without risks to health; that any person involved in carrying out the system of work required by the Regulations must be provided with adequate information, instruction and training appropriate to the particular characteristics of the work activity involved; and that suitable and sufficient arrangements must be in place for the rescue of a person in the event of an emergency. More specific details on the general duties imposed by the Regulations are to be found in an Approved Code of Practice (ACoP) on Confined Space Entry, published by the Health and Safety Authority in 2001.

Construction The Safety, Health and Welfare at Work (Construction) Regulations 2001 (S.I. No.481 of 2001) are considered separately, above, 514.

Dangerous goods transport The Regulations made in 2001 on the transport of dangerous goods by road and rail are discussed below, 523.

Work equipment The Safety, Health and Welfare at Work (General Application) (Amendment) Regulations 2001 (S.I. No.188 of 2001) implemented Directive 95/63/EC, which had amended the 1989 Directive on Work Equipment (implemented by Part IV of the Safety, Health and Welfare at Work (General Application) Regulations 1993: *Annual Review of Irish Law 1993*, 494-6). The 2001 Regulations: require employers to take account of general design and ergonomic factors when placing work equipment in a specific work location; add a number of requirements on the inspection of work equipment; require employers to take account of the working posture and position of employees while using work equipment, in particular, ergonomic requirements; impose new obligations concerning the technical standards for work equipment generally, such as on the installation and location of work equipment and its erection and dismantling; and impose detailed obligations with respect to mobile equipment, whether self-propelled or not, such as cranes, fork-lift trucks. The extensive new provisions on lifting equipment supersede provisions that previously only applied to factories and other industrial premises.

Working time: hours The Organisation of Working Time (Records) (Prescribed Form and Exemptions) Regulations 2001 (S.I. No. 473 of 2001) were made under the Organisation of Working Time Act 1997 (*Annual Review of Irish Law 1997*, 502-8). They require employers to keep records of employees' working hours and annual leave. They also provide for certain exemptions in relation to keeping records of rest breaks and rest periods.

Protection of young persons   The Protection of Young Persons (Employment) Act 1996 (Employment in Licensed Premises) Regulations 2001 (S.I. No. 350 of 2001), made under the Protection of Young Persons (Employment) Act 1996 (*Annual Review of Irish Law 1996*, 543-5) make provisions for young persons aged 16 or 17 employed to carry out general duties in licensed premises. The Protection of Young Persons (Employment) Act 1996 (Bar Apprentices) Regulations 2001 (S.I. No. 351 of 2001), also made under the 1996 Act, restrict the working hours of apprentices aged 16 or 17 employed in a full-time capacity in licensed premises.

TRANSPORT

Carriage of dangerous goods by road The Carriage of Dangerous Goods by Road Regulations 2001 (S.I. No. 492 of 2001), (the CDGR Regulations), made under the Carriage of Dangerous Goods by Road Act 1998, set down extremely detailed requirements for those engaged in the transport of dangerous goods, including petroleum products, as defined in the UN's ADR Agreement on Carriage of Dangerous Goods. The 1998 Act implemented the general terms of the ADR Agreement, while the 2001 Regulations implement the ADR Agreement in detail. The 1998 Act had not been brought into force until the 2001 Regulations were finalised and the 1998 and 2001 Regulations both came into force on April 1, 2002: see Carriage Of Dangerous Goods By Road Act 1998 (Commencement) Order 2001 (S.I. No. 495 of 2001). The Carriage of Dangerous Goods by Road (Appointment of Competent Authorities) Order 2001 (S.I. No. 493 of 2001) made the HSA the main enforcement body for the CDGR Regulations. To indicate the scope and complexity of the 2001 Regulations, they replace a number of previous Regulations in this area, including: the Dangerous Substances (Conveyance of Petroleum by Road) Regulations 1979 and 1996; the Dangerous Substances (Conveyance of Scheduled Substances by Road) (Trade or Business) Regulations 1980 to 1997; and the European Communities (Training for Drivers of Vehicles Carrying Dangerous Goods) Regulations 1997. The Carriage of Dangerous Goods By Road (Fees) Regulations 2001 (S.I. No. 494 of 2001) entitle competent or designated authorities to charge for the provision of services required under the Carriage of Dangerous Goods by Road Regulations 2001.

Dangerous goods safety adviser   The European Communities (Safety Advisers for the Transport of Dangerous Goods by Road and Rail) Regulations 2001 (S.I. No. 6 of 2001) implemented the 1996 Directive on dangerous goods safety advisers (DGSA), which requires that employers must appoint a DGSA where involved in the transport of dangerous goods by road or rail. Such a DGSA must hold the relevant vocational qualification recognised by the Health and Safety Authority (for carriage by road) or the Department of Public

Enterprise (for carriage by rail).

Transport of dangerous goods by rail The European Communities (Transport of Dangerous Goods By Rail) Regulations 2001 (S.I. No. 500 of 2001) implemented Directive 99/48/EC on the transport of dangerous goods by rail within Ireland and between Ireland and other Member States of the European Union. They came into effect on November 8, 2001. The 2001 Regulations largely replace detailed arrangements in the byelaws of the State railway undertaking, Irish Rail.

Social Welfare Law

GERRY WHYTE, Law School, Trinity College, Dublin

LEGISLATION

As a result of the alignment of the financial year with the calendar year, two Budgets were introduced in 2001 and as a result two Social Welfare Acts were passed during that year.

Social Welfare Act 2001   In addition to providing for the annual changes in welfare and contribution rates, the Social Welfare Act 2001 also provides for a number of improvements in social welfare schemes and for the alignment of the income tax year with the calendar year. It also makes provision for the introduction of the Euro currency with effect from January 1, 2002.

Part 3 of the Act provides for a number of improvements in social welfare schemes, including an extension in the duration of payment of Maternity Benefit from 14 to 18 weeks and of Adoptive Benefit from 10 to 14 weeks – section 12. (S.I. No. 230 of 2001 brought this provision into effect). Various improvements are made in the means test for social assistance payments (section 13 and S.I. No. 407 of 2001) while by virtue of section 14, the annual Respite Care Grant is increased by £100 to £400 (and to £800 in the case of a carer looking after more than one person). Section 15 provides for a new allowance of £10 per week for pensioners living on certain islands off the coast of Ireland – see further S.I. Nos. 132 and 326 of 2001 – while section 16 removes the limitation on the amount of income support payable to married claimants in the case of a married person claiming Disability Allowance. Claimants of Disability Allowance, Invalidity Pension, Unemployability Supplement and Blind Pension may now qualify for an additional Living Alone Allowance – section 17 – while the payment after death arrangements are extended to allow the spouse/partner of a claimant of Carer's Benefit to continue to claim his/her benefit for a period of six weeks following the death of the claimant – section 18 and S.I. No. 103 of 2001. Section 19 provides for the introduction of a uniform rate of Constant Attendance Allowance, a supplement payable under the Occupational Injuries code, while, by virtue of section 20, the insurance contribution conditions for Maternity Benefit, Adoptive Benefit, Health and Safety Benefit, Disability Benefit and Unemployment Benefit are relaxed somewhat.

Part 4 effects a number of amendments to the social welfare code. Section

21 provides for a reduction in the assessment of maintenance payments for the purpose of One-Parent Family Payments and also empowers the Minister to provide for the continued entitlement to this payment of a claimant who has been in receipt of the payment for a period of 52 consecutive weeks and whose earnings now exceed the amount specified in section 158(3) of the Social Welfare (Consolidation) Act 1993 – see further, S.I. No. 103 of 2001. The section also provides that a person in receipt of a half-rate One-Parent Family Payment at the commencement of the section will continue to receive this payment for the duration of his or her entitlement. Section 22 (brought into effect on July 2, 2001 by S.I. No.300 of 2001) provides for the recovery from a financial institution of amounts of pension paid by way of electronic fund transfer to a claimant's account for any period after his/her death while section 23 provides for a change in the manner of calculating the rate of Pre-Retirement Allowance. Section 24 prohibits the payment of an increase in respect of a qualified adult who is participating in certain prescribed schemes while section 25 effects a technical amendment to the prosecution provisions of the welfare code, enabling an officer of the Revenue Commissioners (instead of the Collector-General) to sign a certificate stating that a debt is due and owing. This latter section was brought into effect on July 27, 2001 by S.I. No. 360 of 2001. Section 26 relaxes somewhat the conditions of eligibility for Carer's Benefit specifically in relation to determining whether a claimant was engaged in full-time remunerative employment and this was brought into effect on June 28, 2001 by S.I. No. 301 of 2001. Finally, section 27 provides for the payment of adult dependant allowances on a pro-rata basis where the claimant is in receipt of certain reduced rates of contributory pensions.

Part 5 introduces transitional arrangements to protect the entitlements of insured persons to social insurance payments and to calculate liability in respect of self-employment contributions, voluntary contributions or optional contributions in the light of the alignment of the tax and calendar years. This Part was brought into effect by S.I. No. 243 of 2001. See also S.I. No. 654 of 2001.

Part 6 provides for the adoption of convenient amounts in Euro in relation to welfare payments and PRSI thresholds and ceilings following the changeover to the Euro on January 1, 2002. See further S.I. Nos. 99 of 2001, 100 of 2001, 102 of 2001, 613 of 2001, 614 of 2001, 615 of 2001, 616 of 2001 and 618 of 2001.

Part 7 provides for the amendment of the Health Contributions Act 1979 in the light of the alignment of the income tax year with the calendar year and also the introduction of the Euro on January 1, 2002. Section 38 in this Part was brought into effect on May 29, 2001 by S.I. No. 244 of 2001.

Social Welfare (No.2) Act 2001   The Social Welfare (No.2) Act 2001 provides for the increases in the rates of social insurance and social assistance payments and the improvements in the Family Income Supplement scheme announced in the second Budget of 2001. In addition, it also provides for a reduction in the higher rate of employer social insurance, an increase in the earnings/income ceiling above which contributions are not payable by employed or optional contributors and a once-off payment from the Social Insurance Fund to the Central Fund of the Exchequer.

REGULATIONS*

Thirty-six regulations relating to income maintenance schemes were promulgated during 2001. They are as follows:

Social Welfare (Consolidated Contributions and Insurability) (Amendment) (Defence Forces) Regulations 2001 (S.I. No. 5 of 2001) – These Regulations provide for a reduction in the employer social insurance contribution Class H from 11.3% to 10.6%. Class H contributions are payable in respect of Non-Commissioned Army Officers and enlisted personnel of the Defence Forces. This reduction coincides with the introduction of the new National Training Fund Levy (0.7%) and thus there is no overall increase in the employer's PRSI contribution.

Social Welfare (Consolidated Contributions and Insurability) (Amendment) (No.1) (Credited Contributions) Regulations 2001 (S.I. No. 76 of 2001) – These Regulations provide that employment contributions will be credited to insured persons who avail of additional unpaid maternity leave, under the terms of the Maternity Protection Act 1994.

Social Welfare (Consolidated Payments Provisions) (Amendment) (Increase in Rates) Regulations 2001 (S.I. No. 99 of 2001) – These Regulations provide for increases in the reduced rates of Disability Benefit, Unemployment Benefit, Health and Safety Benefit, Old Age (Contributory) Pension, Retirement Pension, Widow's and Widower's (Contributory) Pension, Deserted Wife's Benefit, and also provides for increases in the rates of tapered increases in respect of Qualified Adults. They also provide for increases in the minimum and maximum weekly rate of Maternity Benefit and Adoptive Benefit and further provide for the conversion of the reduced rates of payment to Euro amounts to coincide with the introduction of the new Euro currency from January 2002.

Social Welfare (Rent Allowance) (Amendment) Regulations 2001 (S.I. No. 100 of 2001) – These Regulations provide for increases in the amount of means disregarded for people affected by the decontrol of rents and the minimum rent for the purposes of the Rent Allowance scheme. They also provide for the

*I am very grateful to the Planning Unit of the Department of Social, Community and Family Affairs for assistance in identifying all of the statutory instruments relating to the social welfare code promulgated by the Department during 2001.

conversion of the amounts disregarded to convenient euro amounts in line with the conversion to the new Euro currency from January, 2002.

Social Welfare (Consolidated Supplementary Welfare Allowance) (Amendment) Regulations 2001 (S.I. No. 101 of 2001) – These Regulations provide a disregard of £5 per week for pensioners in the assessment of means for the purposes of Rent or Mortgage Interest Supplement. They also increase the maximum amount of Rent Supplement payable to tenants in voluntary housing developments funded through the local authority Capital Assistance scheme from £21 to £31 for couples and £19 to £29 in all other cases.

Social Welfare (Occupational Injuries) (Amendment) Regulations 2001 (S.I. No.102 of 2001) – These Regulations provide for increases in the reduced rates of Disablement Gratuities, Disablement Pension, Injury Benefit and also provide for the conversion of the above rates to convenient euro amounts in line with the introduction of the new Euro currency from January 2002.

Social Welfare (Consolidated Payments Provisions) (Amendment) (No.1) (Miscellaneous Provisions} Regulations 2001 (S.I. No.103 of 2001) – These Regulations provide for various miscellaneous changes to the social welfare code. They provide for the disregard of foster care allowance received from a Health Board in calculating a spouse's income for the purposes of the Qualified Adult Allowance. They also provide for an amendment to the conditions regarding transitional payments in respect of One-Parent Family payments so that the maximum duration of payment of transitional payments under these Regulations may not exceed 12 months, whether in one period or an aggregate of periods, over the life of the claim. The Regulations further provide for an increase of £50 per week for single persons and £100 for couples in the weekly income disregards for the means test for Carer's Allowance and also provide for the extension of the payment after death provisions to include Carer's Benefit.

Social Welfare (Consolidated Payments Provisions) (Amendment) (No.2) (Miscellaneous Provisions) Regulations 2001 (S.I. No. 132 of 2001) – These Regulations provide for the extension of the sale of residence disregard, in the assessment of means, to Disability Allowance and recipients of Blind Pension aged under 66 years. They also specify a list of islands off the coast of Ireland in respect of which the new Island Allowance is payable to pensioners over 66 who are normally resident on those islands and amend the provisions regarding the payment day for Pre-Retirement Allowance to provide that the Allowance will be paid in the same manner as Unemployment Assistance and Farm Assist.

Social Welfare (Consolidated Contributions and Insurability) (Amendment) (No.3) (Refunds) Regulations 2001 (S.I. No. 133 of 2001) – Section 23 of the Social Welfare Act 2000 provides for the return of social insurance contributions in certain circumstances to a separated person making an enforceable maintenance payment. These Regulations outline the circumstances in which a return of contributions is made in such cases and the basis for calculating the amount of PRSI contribution to be returned.

Social Welfare (Consolidated Contributions and Insurability) (Amendment) (No.2) (Contribution Rates) Regulations 2001 (S.I. No.134 of 2001) – These Regulations provide for amendments, consequent on the Social Welfare Act 2001, to the regulations governing the payment and collection of insurance contributions.

Social Welfare Act 2001 (Section 12) (Commencement) Order, 2001 (S.I. No. 230 of 2001) – This Order brings section 12 of the Social Welfare Act 2001, into effect on March 8, 2001 for the purpose of extending the duration of entitlement to Maternity Benefit and Adoptive Benefit for persons in insurable self-employment and on February 8, 2001 for the extended duration to apply in the case of a father entitled to Maternity Benefit following the death of the mother, or to Adoptive Benefit following the death of the adoptive mother.

Social Welfare (Consolidated Contributions and Insurability) (Amendment) (No.4) (Modified Social Insurance) Regulations 2001 (S.I. No.231 of 2001) – These Regulations provide for the continuation of a modified rate of social insurance for persons who, on April 5, 1995 were employed by Eircom and who, immediately on ceasing to be employed by Eircom become employed by Eircell 2000 Plc under terms and conditions which provide that he or she continues to be employed in a permanent and pensionable capacity and for payment during illness on a basis considered adequate by the Minister.

Social Welfare (Consolidated Payments Provisions) (Amendment) (No.3) (Sharing of Information) Regulations 2001 (S.I. No.242 of 2001) – These Regulations prescribe the information which a specified body may be required to share with the Department of Education and Science in relation to the use of the Personal Public Service Number as a unique student identifier at all levels of the education system. They also specify information in relation to a person that may be shared between the Department of Social, Community and Family Affairs and any other specified body for the purposes of seeking or giving that person's Personal Public Service Number. The Regulations also specify the information, which may be shared between the Department of Social, Community and Family Affairs and local authorities in relation to tenancies supported through the Supplementary Welfare Allowance system in order to assist those authorities in carrying out their statutory responsibilities in relation to private rented accommodation.

Social Welfare Act 2001 (Part 5) (Commencement) Order, 2001 (S.I. No. 243 of 2001) – This Order brings Part 5 of the Social Welfare Act 2001, into effect from May 29, 2001.

Social Welfare Act 2001 (Section 38) (Commencement) Order, 2001 (S.I. No. 244 of 2001) – This Order brings section 38 of the Social Welfare Act 2001, into effect from May 29, 2001.

Social Welfare Act 2001 (Section 22) (Commencement) Order, 2001 (S.I. No. 300 of 2001) – This Order brings section 22 of the Social Welfare Act 2001, into effect from July 2, 2001.

Social Welfare Act 2001 (Section 26) (Commencement) Order, 2001 (S.I. No. 301 of 2001) – This Order brings section 26 of the Social Welfare Act 2001 into effect on June 28, 2001.

Social Welfare (Consolidated Payments Provisions) (Amendment) (No.4) (Island Allowance) Regulations 2001 (S.I. No.326 of 2001) – These Regulations provide for the addition of Island Roy in Co. Donegal to the list of prescribed islands for the purposes of the Island Allowance payable to pensioners over 66 who are normally resident on those islands.

Social Welfare (Miscellaneous Control Provisions) (Amendment) Regulations 2001 (S.I. No.327 of 2001) – These Regulations extend existing control provisions requiring employers in the construction industry to maintain on-site records.

Social Welfare Act 2001 (Section 25) (Commencement) Order, 2001 (S.I. No. 360 of 2001) – This Order brings section 25 of the Social Welfare Act 2001 into effect on July 27, 2001.

Social Welfare Act 1998 (Section 17) (Commencement) Order, 2001 – (S.I. No.361 of 2001) – This Order brings section 17 of the Social Welfare Act 1998 into effect on July 27, 2001.

Social Welfare Act 2001 (Sections 13 (1) (a) (iii), (2) (a) (iii), (3) (b) and (4) (b)) (Commencement) Order, 2001 (S.I. No. 407 of 2001) – This Order brings subsections (1) (a) (iii), (2) (a) (iii), (3) (b) and (4) (b) of section 13 of the Social Welfare Act 2001 into effect from the first week in September 2001.

Social Welfare (Consolidated Payments Provisions) (Amendment) (No.5) (Educational Opportunities) Regulations 2001 (S.I. No. 408 of 2001) – These Regulations provide for unemployed persons aged between 18 and 20 years to retain their entitlement to payment of Unemployment Benefit or Assistance while participating in an approved course of education, training or development where they have been (a) in receipt of Unemployment Assistance or Unemployment Benefit for not less than 156 days and (b) out of formal schooling for at least two years.

Social Welfare (Temporary Provisions) Regulations 2001 (S.I. No. 532 of 2001) – These Regulations provide for the payment of a Christmas Bonus to long-term social welfare recipients, equivalent to 100% of their normal weekly payments, subject to a minimum payment of £20.

Social Welfare (Consolidated Payments Provisions) (Amendment) (No.6) (Widowed Parent Grant) Regulations 2001 (S.I. No.548 of 2001) – This Regulation provides for an increase in the Widowed Parent Grant from £1,000 to euro 2,500 (£1,968.91), with effect from December 5, 2001, as announced in Budget 2002.

Social Welfare (Consolidated Contributions and Insurability) (Amendment) (No.6) (Euro) Regulations 2001 (S.I. No. 613 of 2001) – These Regulations convert certain PRSI rates contained in the Social Welfare (Consolidated Contributions and Insurability) Regulations 1996 to convenient Euro amounts in line with changes made to the PRSI rates in the 2001 Social Welfare Act.

Social Welfare (Consolidated Payments Provisions) (Amendment) (No.7) (Euro) Regulations 2001 (S.I. No.614 of 2001) – These Regulations provide for the conversion of certain rounding and means banding provisions contained in the Social Welfare (Consolidated Payments Provisions) Regulations 1994.

Social Welfare (Liable Relative) (Amendment) (Euro) Regulations 2001 (S.I. No. 615 of 2001) – The Liable Relative Regulations provide for the rounding of any amount of contribution due by a liable relative up or down to the nearest £1 where the amount is under or over 50 pence and for the payment of a minimum contribution of £2. These Regulations provide for the conversion of these amounts to convenient Euro amounts.

Social Welfare (Rent Allowance) (Amendment) (No.1) (Euro) Regulations 2001 (S.I. No.616 of 2001) – Regulations currently provide for the disregard of the qualified child weekly rate of £13.20 in the assessment of means in relation to the Rent Allowance scheme for people affected by the de-control of rents. These Regulations provide for the conversion of this amount to a convenient Euro amount of EUR 16.80.

Social Welfare (Occupational Injuries) (Amendment) (No.1) (Euro) Regulations 2001 (S.I. No. 617 of 2001) – These Regulations provide for the conversion of certain rounding provisions as well as an income limit of £24 provided for in the Rules of Behaviour and a £100 payment limit in relation to disablement benefit, contained in the Occupational Injuries Regulations.

Social Welfare Act 2001 (Section 37(6) (Commencement) Order 2001 (S.I. No. 618 of 2001) – This Order gives effect to the provisions of the Social Welfare Act 2001 dealing with the conversion of certain monetary amounts consequent on the introduction of the new Euro currency, and details the effective dates for the purposes of the relevant social welfare payments.

Social Welfare (Consolidated Payments Provisions) (Amendment) (No.8) (Increase in Rates) Regulations 2001 (S.I. No. 650 of 2001) – These Regulations provide for increases in the reduced rates of Disability Benefit, Unemployment Benefit, Health and Safety Benefit, Old Age (Contributory) Pension, Retirement Pension, Widow's and Widower's (Contributory) Pension, Deserted Wife's Benefit, Maternity Benefit and Adoptive Benefit and also provides for increases in the rates of tapered increases in respect of Qualified Adults.

Social Welfare (Rent Allowance) (Amendment) (No.2) Regulations 2001 (S.I. No. 651 of 2001) – These Regulations provide for increases in the amount of means disregarded for people affected by the decontrol of rents and the minimum rent for the purposes of the Rent Allowance scheme with effect from January 3, 2002.

Social Welfare (Occupational Injuries) (Amendment) (No.2) Regulations 2001 (S.I. No. 652 of 2001) – These Regulations provide for increases in the reduced rates of Disablement Gratuities (assessed at 19% or under from December 31, 2001), Disablement Pension payable in lieu of such gratuities from January 4, 2002, and Injury Benefit payable to persons under the age of sixteen.

Social Welfare (Consolidated Supplementary Welfare Allowance) (Amendment) (No. 1) (Income Disregards) Regulations 2001 (S.I. No. 653 of 2001) – These Regulations provide for an increase of euro 18.26 (from €31.74 (£25) to €50.00 (£39.38)) in the income disregard for part-time workers claiming Rent or Mortgage Interest Supplement under the Supplementary Welfare Allowance scheme as announced in Budget 2002. They also provide for an increase from £5 to euro 10 (£7.88) in the amount of pension income disregarded for the purposes of Rent and Mortgage Interest Supplement.

Social Welfare (Transitional Arrangements) (Alignment of Income Tax Year with Calendar Year) Regulations 2001 (S.I. No.654 of 2001) – With effect from January 1, 2002 the Income Tax year and the calendar year will be aligned and consequently, the period April 6, 2001 to December 31, 2001 will comprise a 'short' tax year. These Regulations contain the transitional arrangements necessary to preserve entitlement to social insurance based benefits, to ensure that people are not adversely affected by the 39 week Income Tax Year.

CASELAW

The Irish courts decided three cases dealing with the social welfare system during 2001, two of which are concerned with the control provisions of the social welfare code and the third with the status of share fishermen for social insurance purposes.

Control provisions *Minister for Social, Community and Family Affairs v. Scanlon* [2001] 1 IR 64; [2001] 2 I.L.R.M. 342 concerns the power of the welfare authorities to recover overpaid welfare. This power had been considered by the courts on a previous occasion in 1986, in *The State (Hoolahan) v. Minister for Social Welfare,* High Court, July 23, 1986. In that case, Barron J. held that section 300(5)(a) of the Social Welfare (Consolidation) Act 1981, pursuant to which the Department sought to recover deserted wife's benefit paid to a claimant who the Department subsequently believed was not entitled to such benefit, required the welfare authorities to establish that the original decision awarding payment was given by reason of a fraudulent mis-representation on the part of the claimant.[1]

---

1. Section 300(5) provided, in relevant part: "A revised decision given by a deciding officer or an appeals officer shall take effect as follows – (a) where any benefit ... will, by virtue of the revised decision, be disallowed or reduced ... and the revised decision is given owing to the original decision having been given ... by reason of any statement or representation ... which was to the knowledge of the person making it false or misleading in a material respect ... it shall take effect as from the date on which the original decision took effect ..."

Five years later, the Department began the process of amending the social welfare code so as to enhance its powers to recover overpaid welfare. First, section 35 of the Social Welfare Act 1991 amended section 300 of the 1981 Act by inserting a new paragraph – paragraph (aa) – in sub-section 5 which empowered a welfare official to backdate a revised decision based on new evidence or facts to such date as the official should determine, having regard to the new evidence or facts.[2] Then section 31(1) of the Social Welfare Act 1993 substituted new provisions for section 300, adding, *inter alia*, a provision [section 300B(c)] allowing a welfare official to backdate a revised decision, in any case not already covered by provisions corresponding to the former section 300(5)(a) and (aa), to any date considered appropriate by the official, having regard to the circumstances of the case and providing, in section 300D(4), for the repayment of overpaid welfare to the Social Insurance Fund, the Minister or a health board, as the case may be.[3]

The Social Welfare Acts 1981 to 1993 were then consolidated by the Social Welfare (Consolidation) Act 1993, section 249 of which deals with the effect of revised decisions and provides as follows:

A revised decision given by a deciding officer shall take effect as follows–

(a) where any benefit, assistance, child benefit or family income supplement will, by virtue of the revised decision be disallowed or reduced and the revised decision is given owing to the original decision having been given, or having continued in effect, by reason of any statement or representation (whether written or verbal) which was to the knowledge of the person making it false or misleading in a material respect or by reason of the wilful concealment of any material fact, it shall take effect as from the date on which the original decision took effect, but the original decision may, in the discretion of the deciding officer, continue to apply to any period covered by the original decision to which such false or misleading statement or representation or such wilful concealment of any material fact does not relate;

(b) where any benefit, assistance, child benefit or family income supplement will, by virtue of the revised decision, be disallowed or reduced and the revised decision is given in the light of new evidence or new facts (relating to periods prior to and subsequent to the commencement of this Act) which have been brought to the notice of the deciding officer since the original

---

2. Section 40 of the Social Welfare Act 1992 subsequently clarified that section 300(5)(aa) should apply to new facts or evidence relating to periods prior to and subsequent to the commencement of the paragraph.

3. Section 31(1) also empowered designated welfare officials to defer, suspend, reduce or cancel, in accordance with a prescribed code of practice, any amount of welfare due to be repaid by a welfare claimant to the welfare authorities.

decision was given, it shall take effect from such date as the deciding officer shall determine having regard to the new facts or new evidence;

(c) in any other case, it shall take effect as from the date considered appropriate by the deciding officer having regard to the circumstances of the case.[4]

Section 300D(4) of the 1981 Act as inserted by section 31(1) of the 1993 Act providing for a liability to repay overpaid welfare and various mechanisms for such repayment, was re-enacted by section 278 of the 1993 Consolidation Act.

Subsequently, section 31 of the Social Welfare Act 1997 provided that where a person is convicted of an offence under section 32 of the Larceny Act 1916, by virtue of having received any social welfare payment by way of personation, the amount involved could be recovered from any social welfare payment to which the person was or became entitled, while section 20 of the Social Welfare Act 1998 empowered the Department to recover overpaid welfare by obliging claimants to repay such monies on demand, without recourse to court proceedings.

These extended powers of the welfare authorities to recover overpaid welfare were considered by the Supreme Court in *Minister for Social, Community and Family Affairs v. Scanlon* [2001] 1 I.R. 64; [2001] 2 I.L.R.M. 342. The defendant had been in receipt of disability benefit from September 1985 until May 1994. In June 1994, the original decision to award disability benefit was revised and the benefit disallowed on the ground that the original decision was induced by fraud on the part of the claimant. Following an appeal, the appeals officer ruled that the benefit should be refunded, not on the basis that the claimant knowingly made a fraudulent claim, but rather because there was new evidence indicating that he had worked while claiming benefit. The Minister subsequently instituted legal proceedings against the defendant seeking to recover £43,088.25.

In the High Court, High Court, May 11, 1999 (see *Annual Review of Irish Law 1999*, pp.485-8), Laffoy J. held that, given the presumption against the retrospective application of legislation, benefit paid to the defendant prior to the commencement of the Social Welfare Act 1993 was not repayable pursuant

---

4. Sections 264 and 269 of the Social Welfare (Consolidation) Act 1993 make identical provision, *mutatis mutandis*, in respect of revised decisions of, respectively, appeals officers and health board officials dealing with claims for supplementary welfare allowance. The power of welfare officials to defer, suspend, reduce or cancel any welfare due to be repaid by a claimant was re-enacted by section 282 of the 1993 Act pursuant to which the Minister subsequently promulgated the Social Welfare (Code of Practice on Recovery of Overpayments) Regulations 1996 [S.I. No.227 of 1996].

to a revised decision based on new evidence.[5]

On appeal, however, the Supreme Court took a less restrictive interpretation of the legislation. Delivering the judgment of the Court, Fennelly J. accepted that, in relation to interpreting legislation with potential retrospective effect, one had to consider this in the light of both the Constitution and common law principles. In the instant case, he held that a retrospective reading of section 300(5)(aa) did not affect any constitutional right as the defendant's right to receive benefit and to retain benefit wrongly paid was statutory in origin and did not constitute a property right for the purposes of the Constitution.[6] Turning to the common law approach to the retrospective application of legislation, he held that this approach had two essential elements – first, it was designed to guard against injustice by preventing the unfair imposition of new burdens in respect of past actions; second, the presumption against retrospective effect was a rule of construction, not of law and so could be displaced by the clear words of the statute. In the instant case, Fennelly J. disagreed with the High Court judge in relation to the impact of section 40 of the Social Welfare Act 1992 which provided that section 300(5)(aa) was to apply to new facts or evidence relating to periods prior to and subsequent to the commencement of that paragraph. According to Fennelly J., this provision was clear and unambiguous in enabling decisions made pursuant to section 300(5)(aa) to have retrospective effect. It followed, further, from this that section 300D(4), which provided mechanisms for the recovery of overpayment in non-fraudulent cases, also had retrospective effect. Finally, he also disagreed with the trial judge's ruling that it was necessary for the Department to serve a fresh demand for payment following on the appeals officer's decision, taking the view that section 300H of the 1981 Act[7] implies that the Minister's claim for repayment

---

5. She also held that the welfare authorities were not able to recover benefit paid to the defendant between April 1993 and May 1994 as there was no evidence before the court of any demand for such repayment following on the decision of the appeals officer and consequently the liability of the defendant under section 278 of the 1993 Consolidation Act had not been made out.

6. He also rejected the contention that deciding and appeals officers were exercising judicial functions that, under the Constitution, should properly have been reserved to the judiciary.

7. Now section 283(b) of the Social Welfare (Consolidation) Act 1993. This provides in relevant part:
   "In any proceedings ... for the recovery of any sums due to the Minister or the Social Insurance Fund, a decision on any question relevant to the proceedings given in accordance with this Act shall, unless an appeal or reference in respect of the decision is pending or the prescribed time for appealing against the decision has not expired, be conclusive for the purpose of those proceedings and ... where any such appeal or reference is pending ... the court dealing with the case shall adjourn the proceedings until such time as a final decision on the question has been obtained."

can proceed on foot of the claim based on the original decision of the deciding officer, including the demand made on foot thereof.

In *McGinley v. Deciding Officer, Criminal Assets Bureau*, Supreme Court, May 30, 2001, the issue before the Supreme Court was whether the Circuit Court had jurisdiction to hear an appeal against a decision to withdraw disability allowance from the appellant, made by a deciding officer of the Department who was also a bureau officer of the Criminal Assets Bureau, where the decision had been made in the name of the Bureau. The appellant's challenge to the jurisdiction of the Court was based on the argument that the initial decision to withdraw the allowance was *ultra vires* the Bureau. By virtue of section 5(1)(c) of the Criminal Assets Bureau Act 1996, the functions of the Bureau include the taking of all necessary actions under the Social Welfare Acts for the investigation and determination of any claim in respect of benefit by any person engaged in criminal activity, while section 8(8) provides:

> "A member of the Garda Síochána, an officer of the Revenue Commissioners or an officer of the Minister for Social Welfare, who is a bureau officer, notwithstanding his or her appointment as such, shall continue to be vested with and may exercise or perform the powers or duties of a member of the Garda Síochána, an officer of the Revenue Commissioners or an officer of the Minister for Social Welfare, as the case may be, for purposes other than the purposes of this Act as well as for the purposes of this Act."

The respondents did not rely on section 5(1)(c), as they were not alleging that the appellant was engaged in criminal activity, but rather invoked section 8(8) in defence of its competence to act in the instant case. The Circuit Court judge held, however, that section 8(8) did not extend the powers of the Bureau but rather simply provided that appointment as a Bureau officer would not diminish the powers and duties that that individual had by virtue of his or her original appointment as, (in the instant case), a deciding officer of the Department. He went on to hold that section 5(1)(c), if relied upon, would render the Bureau's decision *intra vires* as it was most likely that the appellant had engaged in criminal activity in receiving the disability allowance when his means clearly disentitled him to receipt of this payment. He then stated a case to the Supreme Court essentially asking whether the actions of the Bureau officer in the instant case were *intra vires*.

Fennelly J., delivering the judgment of the Court, held that any infirmity flowing from the fact of the original decision having been expressed to have been made in the name of the Bureau was removed once the Circuit Court decided to hear the appeal *de novo*, i.e. as if the judge were the original deciding officer, pursuant to section 253A of the Social Welfare (Consolidation) Act 1993 (as inserted by section 34 of the Social Welfare (Amendment) Act 1997. Any challenge to the jurisdiction of the actual deciding officer to disqualify the appellant for receipt of this allowance should have been made by way of judicial review. Fennelly J. added that it was not possible to presume lack of jurisdiction of the deciding officer when making his decision from the concession made by counsel for the respondents at the hearing of the appeal that he would not rely on section 5 as the possibility could not be excluded that the argument would be made that section 5 had actually been relied on by the deciding officer when coming to his conclusion. He also opined that section 8(8) had no bearing on the jurisdiction of the Circuit Court as it simply preserved the normal functions of the Bureau officers and could not confer jurisdiction where none existed.

Insurability of share fishermen   The status of share fishermen for the purposes of social insurance was the focus of attention in the third case decided in 2001, *Griffin v. Minister for Social, Community and Family Affairs,* High Court, October 2, 2001. This issue had previously been addressed in two High Court cases, *Director of Public Prosecutions v. McLoughlin* [1986] I.R. 355; [1986] I.L.R.M. 493, and *Minister for Social Welfare v. Griffith,* [1992] 1 I.R. 103; [1992] I.L.R.M. 667, in which both Costello and Blayney JJ. respectively held that the relationship between share fishermen and the skipper of a boat was that of partnership, rather than employer-employee, with the result that the share fishermen were not subject to compulsory insurance. In the instant case, however, an appeals officer, whose decision was subsequently confirmed by the Chief Appeals Officer, held that share fishermen were employed under a contract of service and therefore were fully insurable as employees when their earnings were over a certain level per week. In coming to his conclusion, the appeals officer relied upon a UK authority, *Stephenson Jordan and Harrison Ltd. v. McDonald* [1952] I.T.R. 191, wherein Denning L.J. said that under a contract of service an employee's work was an integral part of the business whereas that was not the case under a contract for services. He also relied upon an American authority, *US v. Silk*, 331 US 704, which appeared to take the view that workers who are obliged to work as a matter of economic reality are to be regarded as employees. However, as Carroll J. in the High Court pointed out, the appeals officer did not attempt to apply either the *McLoughlin* or *Griffith* cases to the case before him and so it was hardly surprising that she set aside his decision. She also pointed out that the appeals officer had made mistakes of law in concluding (a) that there cannot be a partnership unless there is capital investment; (b) that an agreement to set off losses against the next fishing trip is not a commercial risk and (c) that there must be an equal coming together of partners in order to be self-employed. In addition, she also held that a number of findings of fact made by the appeals officer were not sustainable having regard to the evidence before him.

Sports Law

**NEVILLE COX, Law School, Trinity College Dublin and
CATHRYN COSTELLO, Law School, Trinity College Dublin**

INTRODUCTION

Given that this is the first year in which the *Annual Review of Irish Law* has contained a section on Sports Law, it is appropriate at this juncture to explain what is meant by the term. There is in fact some uncertainty as to whether it is valid at all to speak of *sports law* – that is a particular body of law specific to sport – or whether the appropriate term should be *sport and the law*, suggesting that whereas the law does interact with sport, this is not sufficient to ground a specific legal discipline. In short it remains a matter of debate as to whether the law in this area is issue driven or not.

Whereas there are arguments on both sides, it is submitted that the preferable view is the former – that we can legitimately speak of 'Sports Law' as a separate legal discipline, just as we speak of 'environmental law', rather than 'the environment and the law'. This is for a variety of reasons. First, sport is remarkably self-regulating for something with enormous social importance, and the courts give increasing prominence and acceptance to the decisions of sporting tribunals provided that such bodies operate within certain acceptable guidelines. Secondly, certain doctrines are starting to emerge on the playing field which are not found elsewhere, notably in respect of the individuated duty of care owed by participants in a sporting event (*McComiskey v. McDermott* [1974] I.R. 75) Thirdly, because of the nature of sport, this 'law' is international in operation and is not subject to the same geographical limitations as other forms of law, reflected in the ongoing importance of the Court of Arbitration for Sport in Lausanne, Switzerland. Perhaps most importantly though, the law increasingly treats sporting activity as different to other human activity for the purposes of legal regulation, most obviously in the fact that serious assaults may routinely be committed provided that the parties involved are engaged in a sporting contest, and despite the fact that absent the sporting context, such actions would attract criminal sanction.

The next question then is what areas within sport are of concern to the law? The answer is that as sport becomes more professionalised and moves from being a pastime into a business, the law's involvement therewith increases. First there is legal concern with the definition of sport. After all an activity benefits from being defined as a sport, and hence it is important that there be a clear legal definition of the concept. Secondly, the law limits the freedom of sports governing bodies to 'run sport,' especially where this involves admission to, disciplinary rules within (including disciplinary rules pertaining to the use of performance enhancing drugs) and indeed expulsion from such bodies. It is not certain whether such bodies may be susceptible to a challenge by way of judicial review, but it is certain that in their actions they must act in accordance with fair procedures and natural and constitutional justice.

Beyond this, the law is concerned with the business of sport. Particularly here we see the influence of European Union Law notably since the decision of the European Court of Justice in *Union Royale Belge des Societes de Football Association ASBL v. Bosman, Royal Club Liegois SA v. Bosman, Union des Associations Europiens de Football v. Bosman* Case C–415/93. This includes legal concern with players' contracts, with broadcasting of sporting events, with taxation and insurance aspects of sport, with sponsorship and marketing, with the intellectual property rights of sportspersons, with the competition law aspects of sport, and with the right to work and especially the right to travel beyond national boundaries to further one's work as a sportsperson.

Finally, there is a legal concern with the overall operation of sport on a Human Rights analysis. This includes a general concern that sport be governed and operated in accordance with principles of equality and also a specific concern with racism within sport.

As a final aspect of this short introduction to sports law, it is necessary to consider briefly the nature of the governmental structure of sport in Ireland. In this respect we can make a distinction between the governance of sport generally on the one hand, and the governance of the Olympic movement on the other. In respect of the latter, the Olympic Council of Ireland is affiliated to the most powerful body in sport the International Olympic Committee, which has jurisdiction over the running of the Summer and Winter Olympic games, but in reality has enormous power over sport generally. Outside of the Olympic movement, each sport will have its own national governing body, again affiliated to a European governing body and an overall International federation. Thus to take soccer as an example, the Football Association of Ireland is affiliated to UEFA (Europe's soccer governing body) and FIFA (the world governing body). Beyond self regulation, the Irish government is also involved in the governance of sport, most notably in the activities of the Irish Sports Council set up under the Irish Sports Council Act 1999. Finally the European Union and the Council of Europe have specific concern with sport.

CRIMINAL LAW

It is comparatively rare for criminal actions to arise out of on field sporting activity. Equally it is far from impossible and indeed there are several examples of this in practice (*R. v. Bradshaw*, (1878) 14 Cox C. 83, *R. v. Moore* (1891) 14 T.L.R. 229, *R. v. Billinghurst* [1978] 8 *Criminal LR*, 553, *Ferguson v. Normand*

[1995] S.C.C.R. 770, *People (DPP) v. McCarthy*, Circuit Court (Dublin), October 20-22, 1987). For present purposes, the most recent example of such activity occurred in late 2000. In 1999 a GAA player who had assaulted another in an off the ball incident causing him to suffer brain damage, was sentenced to nine months in prison. This sentence was suspended in October 2000 when the Circuit Court was informed that the victim had been compensated to tune of forty six thousand pounds from a combination of the GAA's disability and loss of earnings schemes, and a contribution of seventeen thousand pounds from the defendant, Mr. John Joe Greaney.

IRISH SPORTS COUNCIL

The Irish Sports Council was set up in 1999 under the terms of the *Irish Sports Council Act* of that year. Amongst the statutory objectives of the Sports Council is the creation and operation of anti-doping policy. In this respect, the Sports Council does not actually enforce drug testing in sport. Rather, with the consent of the sports federations it co-ordinates the drug testing programmes in various different sports. The target number of tests for 2001 was 660. In fact in excess of that number of tests was carried out, with 50% of such tests occurring outside of competition. Moreover, in August 2001, in an important development, the GAA signed up to the Sports Council programme. This is of particular significance in that GAA sports are amateur in nature, and hence the introduction of a drug-testing programme perhaps more tailored to the needs of professional sport was something of a shock. It is perhaps of little surprise that the operation of such mandatory drug testing within the GAA has been the source of much complaint by members of that body. The Council is also concerned with the distribution of financial aid within sport. Thus in 2001 it had a budget of just under €20 million, rising to €25.7 million in 2002.

EQUALITY LAW

The world of sport is highly segregated – men and women play and compete separately; seniors have separate tennis and golf tours; the fully-abled and the disabled have separate sporting events; national teams exclude foreigners. Much of this differentiation flows from the commitment to merit, which is inherent in competitive sport. The rationale is that as, for example, men are on average faster than women, competitive sport requires that the sexes be segregated in order to ensure a level playing field. The sporting metaphor has now been incorporated into the vocabulary of equal opportunity. However, the lesson of anti-discrimination law is that commonplace distinctions, which may appear commonsensical, often mask prejudicial treatment. Thus equality law should serve as a basis for the scrutiny for these measures. Other types of discrimination appear to be just as pernicious in the sporting context as any other. There is no 'level playing field' justification for discrimination on the basis of race, religion, sexual orientation or membership of the Traveller Community. Unfortunately, the Irish statutory regime does not reflect this position, and adopts a somewhat contradictory and piecemeal approach to non-discrimination and sport.

The purpose of this section is to highlight the recently enacted provisions of Irish equality law, which are of particular relevance to the sporting context. It does not purport to be an exhaustive survey, but rather serves to highlight the under-exploited potential of Irish equality law to challenge established practices. Until relatively recently Ireland's equality law was chiefly of EU origin and focused on employment discrimination on gender and nationality grounds. Since the late 1990s equality law has been extended to cover new grounds and new contexts. Prohibited grounds of discrimination now include gender, marital status, family status, sexual orientation, religion, age, disability, race and Membership of the Traveller Community. The Employment Equality Act 1998 ('EEA') prohibits each of these grounds of discrimination in the employment context. As much sporting activity involves employment relationships, the EEA is of relevance. In addition, the Equal Status Act 2000 ('ESA') prohibits discrimination in relation to following situations: the provision of goods and services, accommodation matters, educational establishments and clubs.

Gender Gender segregation and discrimination in sport is endemic. From the youngest age, when the physical abilities of boys and girls are comparable, sports activities are gender segregated. Even in the recreational context of the golf-course, separation of the sexes is pervasive. The provisions of the Employment Equality Act on gender equality, which are to be interpreted in line with the EC Gender Equal Treatment Directive (Directive 76/207/EEC on Equal Treatment for Men and Women as regards access to Employment, Vocational Training and Promotion, and Working Conditions, [1976] OJ L45/19.), prohibit direct and indirect discrimination and harassment.

The Irish authorities have inferred gender discrimination where interview questions suggest gender bias (*Rotunda Hospital & Mater Misericordiae Hospital v. Dr. Gleeson*, ODEI Determin. No. DEE003, 18/04/00). Thus contrasts sharply with the UK case of *Saunder v. Richmond Borough Council* [1977] I.R.L.R. 362, where a female golf champion was refused employment as a golf coach. Interview questions focused on her gender. Nonetheless the decision was held on the facts not to be discriminatory.

The Irish EEA does not provide any specific provisions legitimising gender differentiation in sport. However, section 25(2) provides that it is permissible to treat sex as an occupational qualification where on grounds of physiology or on grounds of authenticity for the purposes of entertainment, the nature of the post so requires. It is noteworthy in relation to gender that physiology is stated to exclude physical strength or stamina, unlike the analogous provision of section 37(3) in relation to other types of discrimination. This provision could provide much ammunition to challenge gender differentiation in sports employment.

One gender discrimination case arose in 2001, albeit under the provisions of the 1977 Employment Equality Act (now replaced by the 1998 EEA). In *Nelson v. Boxing Union of Ireland* (ODEI, DEC-E2001-018) a female licensed professional boxer in the UK was effectively refused permission to box in Ireland. The Equality Officer accepted that the decision was gender-based. In the absence of specific statutory exemption, this could not be justified. The respondent's health and safety arguments were characterised as invocation of 'gender-based stereotypes and assumptions.'

Nationality, locality and race   Sport is currently the vehicle for benign nationalistic sentiment. National teams are typically made up of nationals of the state concerned, defined as that State sees fit. European Community law prohibits nationality discrimination in the economic sphere, where Community nationals are at issue. However, it has been accepted that the composition of national teams is not subject to the provisions on non-discrimination on grounds of nationality. These nationality requirements may only be imposed in limited contexts. In *Dona* Case 13/76 [1976] E.C.R. 1333, the European Court confined it's ruling to certain matches, which for non-economic reasons relating to the particular nature and context of such matches, were "of sporting interest only." In *Bosman* (Case C–415/93 [1995] E.C.R. I-4921) the European Football Association attempted to argue that nationality discrimination should not be prohibited in relation to the composition of professional club teams. At issue was UEFA's 3+2 rule, whereby a maximum of 5 non-national players could play on any club team. The European Court rejected the argument that the composition of such teams required a national element. The impact of the Bosman case was dramatic and enduring – it resulted in a 1 800% increase in the number of non-British players in the English Premiership.

Nationality discrimination falls under the provision of the EEA dealing with race discrimination, race being defined as "race, colour, nationality or ethnic or national origins" (section 6(2)(h) EEA). In fact, this is broader than the EC provisions as EC law is principally concerned with discrimination against other Community nationals, the position or so-called third country nationals being in most instances outside its scope. The EEA thus treats nationality discrimination just as strictly as race discrimination. The EEA does not provide any specific exemptions for sporting activities. There is a general exemption where the criterion in question is an "occupational qualification for the post in question" (section 37(2) EEA). Thus any attempt to employ only nationals or even persons from a particular locality (which may be regarded as indirect nationality discrimination) requires justification on the basis of occupation qualification. It is difficult to see how this can be the case when what is really at issue is not an occupational requirement, but rather a requirement of the context of the activity. The EC provision does not override the Irish legislation, being facilitatory rather than mandatory.

Age, disability and race may all be regarded as occupational qualifications where "on grounds of physiology or on grounds of authenticity for the purpose of entertainment" the nature of the post would be materially different if filled by a person not having that relevant characteristic (section 37(3)(b) EEA). This somewhat convoluted provision may also be useful in the sporting context where merit criteria often indirectly exclude the aged and the disabled. The reference to race/nationality discrimination warrants more careful scrutiny however. It is difficult to see how nationality requirements can be regarded as occupational requirements – players of any nationality could play equally well. Rather the requirement is related to the employment context, rather than the employment role. Whether race could ever be a genuine physiological criterion is also to be doubted. While recruiting an Othello of African origin may be permissible under the section, recruiting a choosing a black basketball player on grounds of race would not.

In contrast to the EEA, the ESA has several significant exemptions from the general anti-discrimination regime for sporting activities. Differences in treatment on the basis of gender, age, disability, nationality or national origin in relation to the provision or organisation of a sporting event are permissible to the extent that the differences are reasonably necessary having regard to the nature of the facility or event and are relevant to the purpose of the facility or event (section 5(2)(f) ESA). Also potentially relevant is the section relating to privacy/embarrassment, which provides that where because of sex embarrassment of breach of privacy could reasonably be expected to happen on account of the presence of another gender. In the US the presence of female sports reporters in male dressing rooms has been litigated, to the detriment of the players' modesty, and to the benefit of gender equal opportunities.

Special provisions in relation to clubs   The EEA contains special provisions in relation to clubs, defined as bodies which have applied for or hold a certificate of registration under the Registration of Clubs Act 1904–1999 (section 8 ESA). This registration allows clubs to sell alcohol to members and certain visitors. Unlike the provisions in relation to goods and services, the Equal Status Act does not prohibit discrimination in all circumstances in relation to clubs. A balance was struck in the legislation between the importance of non-discrimination and the value of freedom of establishment.

In principle, a club will be considered to be acting in a discriminatory manner where it has a rule, policy or practice that discriminates against a member or applicant in relation to the affairs of the club. These include issues of admission, termination of membership and making reasonable accommodation for members with disabilities.

However, a club will not be regarded as discriminating where the principal purpose of the club is to cater only for the needs of persons of a particular group from within the nine grounds (Section 9(a) ESA). This provision allows freedom of association to effectively trump non-discrimination where the principal purpose of the association is to cater for the needs of the group. Whether this strikes the correct balance remains to be seen. Clearly the provision could not be availed of by, say, a tennis club which excludes women on the basis of 'tradition' or misogyny, as it would not be possible to demonstrate a link between the composition and purpose of the association. However, the section could have been more tightly worded, requiring a higher threshold in relation to the nexus between the activities and the purpose of the club.

Also permitted is the practice of confining benefits or privileges to particular categories of age or gender where it is not practicable for those outside the category to enjoy the benefit or privilege at the same time as members within the category (section 9(b) ESA). The clubs must make arrangements to offer the same or reasonably equivalent benefit or privilege to those members outside the category. This is the most troubling of the exemptions, as it appears to warrant such a low standard of justification – all that must be demonstrated is that it is not practicable to extend the benefits to all at the same time. This runs counter to the essence of anti-discrimination law, which requires equal treatment even where scare resources are at issue. If a club has categories of membership which are discriminatory, and only limited availability of its resources, the solution is to redraft those categories of membership, and reallocate in a rational manner to all. All that the subsection requires is a "reasonably equivalent benefit" to be made available to all. The section is an uneasy compromise which arguably aims to protect commonplace discrimination women by golf clubs in making available only inferior membership status to women. Whether it succeeds remains to be seen – the requirement of "reasonably equivalent benefit" when read in light of the object and purpose of the legislation, may allow for robust scrutiny of these measures.

While these provisions have yet to be litigated, it appears that a number of settlements with golf clubs were reached on foot of complaints brought by women golfers. (Equality Authority, *Annual Report 2001,* p.43).

It is also permissible to have different types of membership, access to which is not based on any discriminatory ground (Section 9(c) ESA.). Also allowed are measures to eliminate past discrimination by offering particular fee rates or membership arrangement to persons of a particular gender, by reserving places on the management board etc. (section 9(d) ESA). Finally, there is a sports-related permissive clause which allows clubs to provide reasonably necessary different treatment to member of a particular gender, age, disability, nationality or national origin as regards sporting facilities or events (section 9(e) ESA).

A special enforcement mechanism is available in the case of discriminating clubs. The Equality Authority may apply to the District Court in order to suspend the club's certificate, with the effect that it cannot sell alcohol for the duration of the suspension. There is an appeal to the Circuit Court, and clubs may re-apply to the District Court for a declaration that it is not longer discriminating.

Also of relevance is the EC Directive on Race & Ethnicity Directive (Council Directive 2000/43/EC implementing the principle of equal treatment between persons irrespective of racial or ethnic origin [2000] O.J. L180/22). This will provide an EC framework for issues of race and ethnicity (but not nationality) discrimination. The Directive requires implementation by July 19, 2003.

SPORTS GOVERNING BODIES AND FAIR PROCEDURES

The case *Kinane v. Turf Club* (High Court, McCracken J., July 27, 2001, *ex tempore*) concerned the jockey Michael Kinane who had been suspended for two days for careless riding of the Aidan O'Brien trained horse 'Sophisticat' at Leopardstown. If implemented this ban would have meant Kinane would have been unable to compete in the King George VI and Queen Elizabeth Diamond Stakes at Ascot. As such he appealed the decision of the Leopardstown Stewards before the Appeals and Referrals Committee of the Turf Club. It was agreed between all parties that, in the event of the committee upholding the decision of the stewards, it would hear representations from counsel for Mr. Kinane in respect of the penalty to be imposed.

In the event, after evidence, including video evidence was given in respect of the race, the committee adjourned to deliberate in the matter. Having done so, it called both parties in and announced both that the Stewards' decision *and* the two day ban imposed would stand. Counsel for Mr. Kinane, Ercus Stewart SC was not given the opportunity to make representations in respect of the penalty to be imposed as had been agreed. He objected to this, and after taking legal advice the committee allowed him to make submissions on the penalty imposed. Mr. Stewart argued that it would be impossible at this point for the committee to come to a different conclusion and hence sought an adjournment without a decision to allow a newly constituted committee to hear the appeal. The three man committee again deliberated in private and returned to inform the plaintiff that it had made its decision and was sticking to it.

The plaintiff then sought an interim injunction in the High Court restraining the implementation of this decision, and a declaration that the decision of the appeal committee was null and void and in breach of principles of natural and constitutional justice. In this respect it should be noted that in both Ireland and England, the courts have long been adamant that whether sports bodies are operating on a private or a public basis, they must act in accordance with fair procedures (*Moloney v. Bolger*, High Court, September 6, 2000, *Quirke v. BLE* [1988] I.R. 83, *Jones v. Welsh Rugby Union*, noted in Rose and Albertini,

'*Jones v. WRU*: New Law for the New Era', 5 (1) S.L.J. (1997) 20, *Dundalk Football Club v. Eircom League and Kilkenny City FC*, High Court, May 2, 2000, *Russell v. Duke of Norfolk* [1949] 1 All E.R. 109, *Modahl v. BAF*, (Court of Appeal, July 28, 1997.)). Especially this requirement has been imposed when disciplinary proceedings (with possible suspension) are on the line (*Modahl v. BAF*, (Court of Appeal, July 28, 1997) – although a notable exception continues to exist in respect of anti-doping policy, where the strict liability nature of most doping rules, are at least potentially unfair, yet are typically upheld both by civil courts (*Gasser v. Stinson*, High Court, June 15, 1988), *Wilander & Tobin v. ITF* [1997] 2 Lloyd's Rep. 293) and international arbitration panels (*NWBA v. International Paralympic Committee*, (CAS 95/122), *C v. FINA*, (CAS 95/141), *V. v. FINA*, (CAS 95/150), *USA Shooting and Q v. International Shooting Union*, (CAS 94/129).

Essentially the requirement of fair procedures in this context involves a requirement that rules are fair, that sports bodies stick rigidly to such rules (*Dundalk Football Club v. Eircom League and Kilkenny City FC*, High Court, May 2, 2000), that parties are given a right to be heard and potentially to cross examine witnesses and to be fully aware of all charges against them (*Quirke v. BLE* [1988] I.R. 83, *Jones v. Welsh Rugby Union*, noted in Rose and Albertini, '*Jones v. WRU*: New Law for the New Era', 5 (1) S.L.J. (1997) 20), the right to an appeal (*Clancy v. IRFU* [1995] 1 I.L.R.M. 193, *Newport Association v. Football Association of Wales (No. 2)*, High Court, April 12, 1995) and that the decision which is ultimately reached is not 'irrational' in the legal sense (*Bolger v. Osborne*, [2000] I.L.R.M. 250).

In the instant case the court *per* McCracken J. granted the interim injunction sought by Mr. Kinane, until August 15, 2001 (which period covered the date of the Ascot race meeting on July 27 and 28). The court concluded that the applicant had made out a stateable case that the committee decision was in breach of natural and constitutional justice. Having done so, there was little or no doubt that the balance of convenience in the matter would favour the applicant who frankly stood to lose a good deal more if the ban were imposed than did the Turf club if the injunction was granted. The ban was therefore temporarily lifted, and Mr. Kinane competed in and won the King George VI and Queen Elizabeth Diamond Stakes. The turf club subsequently agreed to a permanent injunction being granted against the decision, a declaration that the decision of the committee was null and void and to pay damages to the plaintiff and the costs of the proceedings. Finally, on August 27, a newly convened appeals and referrals committee upheld the finding of the stewards and a two day ban was finally imposed on Mick Kinane, which ban did not cover the date of any major race meeting. The decision is an interesting one, not least because from an outsider's point of view, it may well appear that the situation was manipulated by his legal team to allow a champion jockey to compete in a major event. Whether or not this is true, however, it is submitted that the High Court made entirely the right decision. A great deal was on the line for the applicant in this case; therefore the standards of propriety expected of the governing body were rightly very high. Here, both by failing to allow the applicant to address the panel on the sole point of real significance in the case and especially by failing to follow agreed procedures, the panel simply did not vindicate the interests of the applicant and the decision was therefore inconsistent with requirements of fair procedures. Clearly Mr. Kinane's legal team saw its chance and took it, but in the circumstances it was entirely entitled to do so.

One final point should be addressed. In this case, and with the urgency of the matter obvious, the applicant applied by way of the private mechanism of plenary summons. It remains a matter of some uncertainty, however whether a judicial review might lie in a case of this nature. Certainly, given the statutory nature of the horseracing industry, it seems likely that a judicial review action could lie against the Turf Club (*Bolger v. Osborne* [2000] I.L.R.M. 250), even though it may be convincingly argued that given that the dispute is a private rather than a public one, the case should still be brought by means of plenary summons. But what of the decisions of sports governing bodies generally? Can these be seen to be of such a public law dimension that their actions may be judicially reviewed, thereby ensuring that a remedy would exist for someone affected by a decision (e.g. a supporter) who has no contractual link with the body concerned, and also ensuring that the benefits of case management and the ready availability of a stay on proceedings are available to the applicant?

The English courts have, even since the seminal decision in *R. v. Panel on Mergers and Takeovers, ex p Datafin* [1987] Q.B. 699; [1987] 1 W.L.R. 699 insisted that sports governing bodies are private in nature and hence not legitimate respondents in a judicial review action (*R v. Disciplinary Committee of the Jockey Club, ex parte Massingberd Munday* [1993] 2 All E.R. 207, *R. v. Jockey Club, ex parte RAM Racecourses* [1993] 2 All E.R. 225, *R. v. Disciplinary Committee of the Jockey Club, ex parte Aga Khan* [1993] 1 W.L.R. 909). In Ireland the position is less clear cut. In *Murphy v. Turf Club* [1989] I.R. 172, the High Court per Barr J. appeared to rule out this possibility. In *Quirke v. BLE* [1988] I.R. 83, on the other hand, the same judge allowed an athlete successfully to judicially review a decision of the athletics governing body. In general, it is accepted that the decision in *Geoghegan v. Institute of Chartered Accountants* [1995] 3 I.R. 86, broadened the scope of the judicial review jurisdiction in Ireland, by allowing the courts to focus on the nature (and especially the monopolistic nature) of the power wielded by proposed respondents rather than the source of such power. Moreover in *Bolger v. Osborne* (a decision again involving the Turf Club and hence concerning a power which was statutory in nature) Macken J. appeared to accept the theoretical possibility that national governing bodies might be subject to judicial review. The position remains uncertain. Nevertheless, it is submitted that given that the power exercised by most governing bodies is fundamentally monopolistic in nature, and moreover that, sport being a business the power is also one which can impact sharply on the livelihood of 'workers', there is a very strong case for deeming such power to be public in nature and hence subject to a judicial review.

MISCELLANEOUS AND INTERNATIONAL MATTERS

In the international arena many developments have occurred in 2001 that will impact on the way in which sports law will operate in Ireland. The World Anti-Doping Agency, created in November 1999 continues to grow in stature and is leading to much needed harmonization in the approach within sport to its anti-doping policies. Nonetheless there is the disturbing and emerging realization that many positive tests (especially the inexplicable number of positive tests recorded in respect of top athletes for the banned steroid 'nandrolone') may be the result of athletes using legal dietary supplements. Indeed the International Olympic Committee has long warned athletes of the dangers that such supplements will lead to positive tests. Thus far the Court of Arbitration for Sport and the former arbitration panel of the IAAF have not accepted the claim made by certain athletes that their positive showing for nandrolone was the result of innocent ingestion of permitted supplements, and hence that disciplinary measures taken against them by Sports Federations should be lifted. (*In the matter of Douglas Walker* [2001] I.S.L.R. 264, and *In the Matter of Linford Christie* [2001] I.S.L.R. 270, *NWBA v. International Paralympic Committee*, (CAS 95/122), *C. v. FINA*, (CAS 95/141), *V. v. FINA* (CAS 95/150), *USA Shooting and Q. v. International Shooting Union* (CAS 94/129)). Equally it remains to be seen whether such rules could genuinely stand up to scrutiny under the Irish constitutional guarantee of fair procedures – especially where an athlete's livelihood is at stake.

Finally, it should be noted that the EU, which has always been active in sport and particularly in co-ordinating anti-doping policy, decided at the Nice Council meeting (December 2000) to adopt a declaration recognizing 'the specific characteristics of sport and its social functions in Europe which should be taken into consideration when implementing community policies'. Even without such declaration, the EU has revolutionized professional sport in Europe through the decision of the European Court of Justice in *Union Royale Belge des Societes de Football Association ASBL v. Bosman, Royal Club Liegois SA v. Bosman, Union des Associations Europiens de Football v. Bosman* Case C–415/93. In this case, *inter alia* existing rules which restricted the free movement of sports persons (in transfer situations) and limited, in particular the capacity of clubs to field teams composed in great part of (European) non-nationals, were deemed to be invalid under European Union Law.

In a 2001 reported decision, the European Court of Justice pulled back from this position somewhat in deciding that free movement of workers could be restricted, where this involved an essentially administrative rule with no economic motivation, but rather which was designed to protect some aspect of sport. The case in question is *Lehtonen and another v. Federation Royale Belge des Societes de Basket-ball ASBL (FRBSB) (Ligue Belge Belgische Liga ASBL, intervening)* (Case C–176/96). In this case, L., a basketball player of Finnish nationality, played in a team which took part in the Finnish championship during the 1995/1996 season. He then became engaged by a club affiliated to the Belgian basketball federation (FRBSB), to take part in the final stage of the 1995/1996 Belgian championship. To this end, he and the club signed a contract of employment on April 3, 1996. Under the FRBSB Rules, there were three different transfer periods for the 1995/96 season. Players could be transferred between Belgian clubs only before the start of the season, in the period from April 15 to May 15, 1995. Under the FIBA (World Basketball Governing Body) Rules, players from the European zone on the other hand, could be transferred until February 28,1996, and those from third countries until March 31, 1996. The FIBA Rules prohibited clubs from including in their teams, after the deadline fixed (February 28), players who had already played in another country in the same season (a rule not unlike that challenged in *Clancy v. IRFU*). On April 5, 1996 the FRBSB informed the team that L was not properly licensed and that sanctions could be imposed on the club if he was played. Despite that warning, on April 6, 1996, L was played in a game which his team won, and as a sanction, the FRBSB awarded the match to the other club. In the following match, the team, while it included L on the team sheet did not field him, yet it was again penalised by the award of the match to the other club. Subsequently, FIBA refused to register L on the ground that the transfer deadline of February 28, 1996 applicable to him had passed, and in order to avoid further punishment the team did not select or play L again that season. Subsequently, L and the team brought proceedings against the FRBSB in a Belgian court, in the course of which a preliminary reference was made to the EU for the purpose of determining whether the transfer rules in question constituted an unjustified obstacle to the freedom of movement for workers contrary to Article 48 of the EC Treaty (now Article 39 EC). The FRBSB submitted that the rules on transfer periods were justified on non-economic grounds concerning only sport as such.

In the event, the ECJ upheld the FRBSB argument, concluding that the Treaty provisions concerning freedom of movement for persons did not preclude rules or practices excluding foreign players from certain matches for reasons which were not of an economic nature, which related to the particular nature and context of such matches and were thus of sporting interest only, as in the case of matches between national teams from different countries. Equally, it concluded that restriction on the scope of the Treaty had to remain limited to its proper objective. As such, whereas the setting of deadlines for transfers of players by sports federations could meet the objective of ensuring the regularity of competitions, such measures could not go beyond what was necessary for achieving the aim pursued. In the instant case, the court was concerned with the fact that the deadline for transfers of European Zone players was earlier than that for non-European Zone players. On this basis the Belgian rule appeared arbitrary and indeed in violation of Article 39 of the treaty, unless it could be justified by objective reasons concerning only sport as such or relating to differences between the position of players from a federation in the European zone and that of players from a federation not in that zone. However, it was for the national court to ascertain the extent to which objective reasons justified such different treatment.

Finally in 2001 the Commission proposed an initiative (accepted in June 2002) to make 2004 the European Year of Education through Sport.

STATUTORY DEVELOPMENTS

In 2001 the Horse and Greyhound Racing Act was passed. Under the terms of sections 5 and 6 of this Act, a new body 'Horse Racing Ireland' (HRI) is created to replace the pre-existing Irish Horse Racing Authority created under the terms of the Irish Horseracing Industry Act, 1994. Under section 8 of the Act, the functions of HRI would include the following:

— Registry office functions (i.e. dealing with the naming of horses, racing passports and identification, horseracing entries and declarations, racing calendar publications, stake holding of race entry fund and prize money for horse races and registration of racehorse owners) in accordance with the rules of racing.

– Provision and maintenance of mobile track equipment, including for example photo finish equipment, and also the provision to the Racing regulatory body of any material generated by such equipment for their use.

— Representing Irish horseracing on an international basis.

— Negotiating all income from medial rights.

— Provision of financial and other necessary support to maintain and improve the health and welfare status of the thoroughbred horse and assist educational and other institutions and organisations in providing improved training and education facilities for the thoroughbred horse industry to satisfy the training and educational needs of that industry at all levels.

— Any other functions transferred to HRI from the racing regulatory body.

The Act also provides for the creation of a race goers' consultative forum for purposes of consultation relating to the operations of HRI in the context of developments or desired developments in the horseracing industry generally, and also for the creation of a media rights committee to negotiate on and in relation to all contracts or agreements with any person in relation to the broadcasting of photography for any commercial purpose of a race fixture.

Furthermore, under section 12, the Act creates a Horse and Greyhound Racing fund for the purpose of giving support to horse and greyhound racing. The fund shall have in 2001 monies paid into it by the Minister for Agriculture, Food and Rural Development equivalent to the revenue paid into the exchequer in the year 2000 from excise duty on off course betting, with a similar approach taken from 2002 onwards. From this fund annually, 80% of the money shall be paid to HRI and 20% to Bord na gCon for the furtherance of their functions.

Finally, and also in 2001 the Horse Racing Ireland (Membership) Act was enacted, amending the schedule to the Irish Horseracing Act of 1994 and dealing with the membership of the newly created HRI. The Act provides that the said body would consist of a chairman and 13 ordinary members to be appointed by the Minister, with of the thirteen members, five to be nominated by the Racing Regulatory Body, and one each from interests such as authorized racecourses, racehorse owners, racehorse trainers, racehorse breeders, authorized bookmakers, persons whom the minister considers to be representative of persons employed in the horseracing industry, persons directly employed in the industry and persons involved with the horseracing industry in Northern Ireland.

TORT LAW

In January 2001, a Turkish seaman who had lost his eye after being struck by a golf ball received two hundred and fifty thousand pounds as a result of the settlement of a High Court action. In July, 1998, the plaintiff, Mr. Erdal Sahin and two colleagues had gone for a walk and, as they passed an open area near a road, they sat down on a wooden bench, which was ten yards to the right of the 18th tee of Greenore Golf Club, Co. Louth. He was injured when a golfer, Mr. Gerry King hit his drive on the 18th hole. The judge divided liability on a 50-50 basis between the defendant golfer and the golf club.

A finding of liability in this case is broadly consistent with the approach to duty and standard of care taken by Irish (and more regularly by English) Courts when dealing with sports related matters. The general approach is to say that the duty owed by one participant to another is that he or she refrain from 'negligence in all the circumstances', with the circumstances of, for example a fast moving contact sport being such that liability would not be imposed for a dangerous tackle by a soccer player even though the same level of negligence would ground an action in tort had the incident occurred off the sports field (*McComiskey v. McDermott* [1974] I.R. 75, *Rootes v. Shelton* [1968] A.L.R. 33, *Condon v. Basi* [1985] 2 All E.R. 453, *Smoldon v. Whitworth*, Court of Appeal, December 17, 1996). Moreover, such analysis has been deemed to apply to non-contact sports such as golf (*Cleghorn v. Oldham*, (1927) 43 T.L.R. 465, *Brewer v. Delo* [1967] 1 Lloyd's Rep. 488, *Lewis v. Buckpool Golf Club*, [1993] S.L.T. 43, *Horton v. Jackson*, Court of Appeal, February 28, 1996, *Pearson v. Lightening, Court of Appeal, April* 1, *1998.*) In English law there is suggestion that the duty owed by a participant to a spectator is different to the inter participant duty, such that in the former the player must merely refrain from acting with 'reckless disregard' for the spectator's safety (*Wooldridge v. Sumner* [1963] 2 Q.B. 43, *Wilks v. Cheltenham Home Guard Motor Cycle and Light Car Club* [1971] 2 All E.R. 369). No such statement exists at Irish law (*Donaldson v. Irish Motor Racing Club & Thompson*, See McMahon & Binchy, *Casebook on the Irish Law of Torts* (Professional Books, Abingdon, 1983), p. 220). Equally, the Supreme Court has suggested that, because of the special circumstances of sport, an individuated duty of care (imposing on a sports person the specific duty of a 'reasonable sportsperson') might operate (*McComiskey v. McDermott* [1974] I.R. 75). In any event, this duty/standard of care analysis applies equally to the golfing situation as to a contact sport situation. In the specific context of the sport of golf, the English courts in deciding individual cases have also consistently held that the ability of the individual golfer is a relevant factor, such that the worse the golfer (and hence the greater the likelihood that his or her shot will deviate from its intended line of flight), the greater the duty of care owed by him or her to other persons in the area (*Pearson v. Lightening,* Court of Appeal, April 1, 1998).

Applying these considerations to the present case then, it may be argued that the defendant golfer should be liable if it is accepted that in playing the shot when he did, he was negligent in the circumstances. Similarly, the golf course could be seen as negligent for designing the course in such a fashion that a seat to which the public had access was located sufficiently close to the tee that an accident of this nature could occur.

We have a certain sympathy with the defendants in this case. It is arguable (and of course this being a settlement, it is impossible to know how the argument would have fared had the trial gone to term) that in sitting on a bench, ten yards from a golf tee, the plaintiff was guilty of some degree of contributory negligence – and certainly at English law, courts in looking at liability for injury caused on the golf course will bear in mind the potential for contributory negligence (*Feeney v. Lyall* (1991) S.L.T. 156) – a position consistent with the terms of the Civil Liability Act 1961. On the other hand of course, it is arguable that the club should not have located a seat in such a position and that the defendant should not have played until the seat was vacated (*Horton v. Jackson*, Court of Appeal, February 28, 1996). It is unclear, however from the facts what the precise circumstances of the case were and whether the golfer was aware of the plaintiff's position, whether he mis-hit his shot, whether he habitually 'shanked' his ball to the right of its intended line of flight, and especially whether he took any steps to alert the plaintiff as to his impending shot either before or after playing it.

Two final points on this case should be noted. First, as a result of the decision, the Golfing Union of Ireland issued a recommendation that all its members carry a personal injury insurance policy (in fact the defendant golfer in this case *did* carry such a policy). Secondly, the case is indicative of the fact that the golf course is a potential legal minefield, with golfers acting within both the rules and customs of their sport, yet finding that such actions cause serious injury and leave themselves open to legal action. Given that golf involves a lot of people concentrating on their own activities in a relatively small area, the risk of injury is ever present, and some clear judicial statement of what constitutes negligence by a golfer (which would constitute a blueprint of how to act in non-negligent fashion) would be welcome.

Torts

DUTY OF CARE

Restatement of conceptual components   The Supreme Court decision in *Glencar Exploration plc v. Mayo County Council* [2002] 1I.L.R.M. 481 represents the most important restatement of the principles of the duty of care in negligence since *Ward v. McMaster* [1998] I.R. 337. For the previous three decades, all the leading cases had represented new milestones in the expansion of the duty of care. *Glencar* is a giant step in the reverse direction.

The Atkinian formula of neighbourhood and proximity   Overshadowing these developments is the Lord Atkin's great speech in *Donoghue v. Stevenson* [1932] A.C. 562 in which for the first time the underlying principles were articulated at a deep conceptual level. Negligence litigation had formerly involved a bewildering accumulation of specific contexts in which a duty of care had been imposed. An attempt to provide conceptual order and generality was made by Brett MR in *Heaven v. Pender* (1883) 11 Q.B.D. 503, but this did not receive broad acceptance in the years that followed. It took Lord Atkin to articulate a general criterion for the duty of care capable of covering the variant of factual circumstance. His solution was far from perfect: its abstract and metaphorical language scarcely gives substantive guidance to a court in new situations and is based on circular logic. Nevertheless it was hugely important because it gave a conceptual unity to the tort and encouraged courts to reflect on crucial values concerning interpersonal relationships in society rather than applying the contingent instances of precedent in a mechanistic way. What Lord Atkin had to say is worth quoting *in extenso*:

> "It is remarkable how difficult it is to find in the English authorities statements of general application defining the relations between parties that give rise to the duty [of care]. The courts are concerned with the particular relations which come before them in actual litigation, and it is sufficient to say whether the duty exists in those circumstances. The result is that the courts have been engaged upon an elaborate classification of duties as they exist in respect of property, whether real or personal, with further divisions as to ownership, occupation or control, and distinctions based on the particular relations of the one side or the other, whether manufacturer, salesman or landlord, customer, tenant, stranger, and so on.

In this way it can be ascertained at any time whether the law recognizes a duty, but only where the case can be referred to some particular species which has been examined and classified. And yet the duty which is common to all the cases where liability is established must logically be based upon some element common to the cases where it is found to exist. To seek a complete logical definition of the general principle is probably to go beyond the function of the judge, for the more general the definition the more likely it is to omit essentials or to introduce non-essentials....

At present I content myself with pointing out that in English law there must be, and is, some general conception of relations giving rise to a duty of care, of which the particular cases found in the books are but instances. The liability for negligence, whether you style it such or treat it as in other systems as a species of 'culpa', is no doubt based upon a general public sentiment of moral wrongdoing for which the offender must pay. But acts or omissions which any moral code would censure cannot in a practical world be treated so as to give a right to every person injured by them to demand relief. In this way rules of law arise which limit the range of complainants and the extent of their remedy. The rule that you are to love your neighbour becomes in law, you must not injure your neighbour; and the lawyer's question, who is my neighbour? receives a restricted reply. You must take reasonable care to avoid acts or omissions which you can reasonably foresee would be likely to injure your neighbour. Who, then, in law is my neighbour? The answer seems to be – persons who are so closely and directly affected by my act that I ought reasonably to have them in contemplation as being so affected when I am directing my mind to the acts or omissions which are called in question."

Lord Atkin approved of the use of the word "proximity" in this context by AL Smith L.J. in *Le Lievre v. Gould* [1893] 1 Q.B. 491, provided that:

"proximity be not confined to mere physical proximity, but .... to extend to such close and direct relations that the act complained of directly affects a person whom the person alleged to be bound to take care would know would be directly affected by his careless act."

The Anns *'two-step' test*   In *Anns v. Merton London Borough Council* [1978] A.C. 728, Lord Wilberforce set down a 'two-step' test which he considered to represent the law as it had developed since *Donoghue v. Stevenson*. He observed (at pp.751-752) that:

"the position has now been reached that in order to establish that a duty of care arises in a particular situation, it is not necessary to bring the facts of that situation within those of previous situations in which a duty of care has been held to exist. Rather the question has to be approached in two stages. First one has to ask whether, as between the alleged wrongdoer and the person who has suffered damage there is a sufficient relationship of proximity or neighbourhood such that, in the reasonable contemplation of the former, carelessness on his part may be likely to cause damage to the latter – in which case a prima facie duty of care arises. Secondly, if the first question is answered affirmatively, it is necessary to consider whether there are any considerations which ought to negative, or reduce or limit the scope of the duty or the class of person to whom it is owed or the damages to which a breach of it may give rise...."

Lord Wilberforce's two-step formula can be interpreted as merely expressing Lord Atkin's 'neighbour' formula in more expansive language, without any implication of its embracing a *wider scope* of duty. On another view, Lord Wilberforce's formula hints at precisely this extension of scope of duty. The reference to a '*prima facie* duty of care' may suggest to some judges that the first step is one that should not give them cause to hesitate too long. Although the formula does not expressly state this, its overall effect may be to encourage the imposition of a duty of care in all situations, however novel, or, conversely, however strongly repudiated in earlier judicial precedents, unless there is some most unusual reason, based on public policy, not to do so or to do so only partially.

A still more radical (and heterodox) interpretation of Lord Wilberforce's test is that the first step actually *equates* the duty of care with reasonable foreseeability of injury. This would drain the expressions 'proximity' and 'neighbourhood' of all their traditional meaning, since the distinguishing feature of these concepts is that they demand something more than reasonable foreseeability.

The British retreat from Anns   Lord Wilberforce's formula initially received fairly widespread support. Relatively soon, however, the tide turned. In *Governors of the Peabody Donation Fund v. Sir Lindsay Parkinson & Company Ltd* [1985] A.C. 210 at 240, Lord Keith noted that there had been a tendency in recent cases to treat this formula as being of a definitive character. He added:

"This is a temptation which should be resisted ... [I]n determining whether or not a duty of care of particular scope was incumbent on a defendant it is material to take into consideration whether it *is just and reasonable* that it should be so." (Emphasis added).

The end for Lord Wilberforce's formula came with *Caparo Industries plc v. Dickman* [1990] 2 A.C. 605, and *Murphy v. Brentwood District Council* [1991]

1 A.C. 398. In these two decisions, the House of Lords made it clear that it would no longer proceed by broad strides, based on the concepts of proximity, neighbourhood and duty. Instead it would inch forward incrementally, sceptical of general principles and loose concepts, venturing cautiously by way of close analogy with what had gone before. Lord Bridge's observations in *Caparo* encapsulate this *volte-face*:

> "Whilst recognizing, of course, the importance of the undeveloping general principles common to the whole field of negligence, I think the law has now moved in the direction of attaching greater significance to the more traditional categorization of distinct and recognizable solutions as guides to the existence of the scope and limits of the varied duties of care which the law imposes. We must now, I think, recognize the wisdom of the words of Brennan J, in the High Court of Australia in *Sutherland Shire Council v. Heyman* (1985) 60 A.L.R. 1 at pp.43-44, where he said:
>
>> 'it is preferable in my view that the law should develop novel categories of negligence incrementally and by analogy with established categories, rather than by a massive extension of a *prima facie* duty of care restrained only by undefinable "considerations which ought to be negative, or to reduce or limit the scope of the duty of the class of person to whom it should be owed".'"

The incremental approach now in vogue in Britain is closely associated with a predilection to break the duty of care into three categories by reference to the consequences of negligent conduct. These are, first, cases of physical injury or damage, the infliction of which 'universally requires to be justified'; second, cases of pure economic loss, which should largely go uncompensated; and third, cases of psychiatric injury, in respect of which an elaborate (and unhelpful) distinction is now drawn between primary and secondary victims.

The Irish endorsement of the Atkinian test   In Ireland, Lord Atkin's 'neighbour' principle was applied without debate or, it has to be said, significant analysis for many years. The arrival of Mr. Justice Walsh to the Bench changed matters.

One finds that the language of proximity was the currency of several crucial decisions in which Walsh J. played a crucial role. These include *Curley v. Mannion* [1965] I.R. 543, *Purtill v. Athlone Urban District Council* [1968] I.R. 205 and *McNamara v. Electricity Supply Board* [1975] I.R. 1. It is not perhaps surprising that Walsh J. should have been attracted to the lexicon of proximity and neighbourhood. His deep analytic capacity (witness *Byrne v. Ireland* [1972] I.R. 241), his paternalistic concern for children (witness *Purtill* and *McNamara*) and employees (witness *Doherty v. Bowaters Irish Wallboard*

Mills Ltd [1968] I.R. 277) and a certain circumspection on his part about articulating the underlying policy factors in negligence litigation (witness *Moynihan v. Moynihan* [1975] I.R. 192 and *McComiskey v. McDermott* [1974] I.R. 75) combined to encourage him to articulate the duty of care in broad, abstract terms.

The impact of Ward v. McMaster   *Ward v. McMaster* must now be considered, since it represents such a significant milestone in the development of negligence law in Ireland. Much of its importance at High Court level lies in Costello J.'s rejection of the last vestiges of the immunity from negligence of vendors and builders and his enthusiastic endorsement of the principle of recovery of damages for non-dangerous defects. These matters did not arise directly on appeal to the Supreme Court. It will be recalled that Mr Ward bought a house from the first named defendant with the assistance of a loan granted by Louth County Council under regulations made by virtue of section 39 of the Housing Act 1966. The house turned out to be riddled with both dangerous and non-dangerous defects, which made it uninhabitable.

Mr Ward had no difficulty in bringing a successful claim against the builder-vendor, which was not appealed. He also sued the County Council in negligence. The essence of his claim was that the County Council, by requiring him to pay a fee with his loan application, had led him to believe that the fee was for a valuation of the house, which would be carried out carefully. In fact the fee was designed to discourage frivolous applications, though Mr Ward was not told this.

The Council employed the services, not of a surveyor but of an auctioneer, who was unable to discover the hidden defects in the bungalow. The auctioneer was acquitted of negligence in the High Court since he had done all that might be asked of one of his profession. The failure by the County Council to carry out the valuation with due care resulted, the plaintiff argued, in reasonably foreseeable loss to him.

Costello J. referred to Lord Wilberforce's 'two-step' test in and noted with approval the additional requirement, set down in *Peabody*, that the court should consider whether it is 'just and reasonable' to impose a duty of care. Applying these criteria, Costello J. imposed liability on the County Council on the basis that 'there was a sufficient relationship of proximity or neighbourhood between the plaintiff and the Council such that in the reasonable contemplation of the Council carelessness on their part in the carrying out of the valuation of the bungalow . . . might be likely to cause him damage'. The Council ought to have been aware, in view of Mr Ward's very limited means and his knowledge that they were going to value the premises, that he would not employ a professional valuer. Echoing Lord Wilberforce's two-step test for the duty of care in *Anns,* Costello J. held that there was nothing in the dealings between the parties which should restrict or limit the *prima facie* duty of care that arose. In particular no warning against reliance on the proposed valuation had been given. Going on to apply the *Peabody* additional requirement, Costello J. held that, since the Council must have been aware of Mr. Ward's reliance, "it would not be just to hold that no duty of care was imposed on the Council and it seems to me to be perfectly reasonable that it should be."

On appeal by the County Council, the Supreme Court unanimously affirmed Costello J.'s finding of liability. Two judgments were delivered: one by McCarthy J., Walsh J. concurring; the other by Henchy J. Finlay C.J. and Griffin J. concurred with both judgments.

McCarthy J. gave a wide-ranging review of cases in Ireland and other common law jurisdictions dealing with the duty of care in negligence. He did 'not seek to dilute the words' of Lord Wilberforce's 'two step' test in *Anns*. Whilst Costello J. had 'essentially rested his conclusion on the "fair and reasonable" test' McCarthy J. preferred 'to express the duty as arising from the proximity of the parties, the foreseeability of the damage, and the absence of any compelling exception based upon public policy.' McCarthy J. went on to observe:

> "I do not, in any fashion, seek to exclude the latter consideration, although I confess that such a consideration must be a very powerful one if it is to be used to deny an injured party his right to redress at the expense of the person or body that injured him."

McCarthy J. concluded that the County Council was under a duty of care to Mr Ward. He said:

> "The proximity of the parties is clear: they were intended mortgagors and mortgagee. This proximity had its origin in the *Housing Act 1966* and the consequent loan scheme. This Act imposed a statutory duty upon the County Council and it was in the carrying out of that statutory duty that the alleged negligence took place. It is a simple application of the principle in *Donoghue,* confirmed in *Anns* and implicit in *Siney,* that the relationship between [Mr Ward] and the County Council created a duty to take reasonable care arising from the public duty of the County Council under the statute. The statute did not create a private duty but such arose from the relationship between the parties."

McCarthy J. specifically rejected the 'incremental' approach which subsequently found full endorsement from the House of Lords. He said:

> "The elaborate analysis of Brennan J. in the High Court of Australia in *Sutherland Shire Council v. Heyman* led to the verbally attractive proposition of incremental growth in this branch of the law; such a proposition, however, suffers from a temporal defect – that rights should be determined by the accident of birth."

McCarthy J.'s approach seems to be premised on a view of the duty of care as being pointed inevitably in the direction of expansion. One may wonder whether any such a position should be favoured *a priori*. It is perfectly possible to conceive of occasions where, after further reflection and perhaps some difficult cases revealing previously unforeseen complexities, a court might wish to restrict the scope of the duty of care which it had articulated in a particular context. These concerns undoubtedly were partially responsible for the Supreme Court's *volte-face* in *Glencar Exploration Plc v. Mayo County Council.*

At all events, McCarthy J. in *Ward v. McMaster* stood four square behind the Wilberforce formula and evinced a considerable reluctance to weigh policy factors in the formula prescribing the duty of care. He expressed a preference:

> "to express the duty as arising from the proximity of the parties, the foreseeability of the damage, and the absence of any compelling exception based upon public policy. I do not, in any fashion, seek to exclude the latter consideration, although I confess that such a consideration must be a very powerful one if it is to be used to deny an injured party his right to redress at the expense of the person or body that injured him."

McCarthy J.'s approach in *Ward v. McMaster* may be contrasted with that which he adopted in *Sunderland v. Louth County Council* [1990] I.L.R.M. 658. In the latter case he sought to identify and effectuate the social policy underlying planning legislation. On one view this might seem to be no more than doing what any judge must do when addressing a claim for damages for breach of statutory duty, but the difficulty with this analysis is that the plaintiff's claim sounded in *common law negligence* and was so analysed by McCarthy J.

Henchy, J.'s judgment in favour of Mr Ward is of narrower scope than McCarthy J.'s. That much is tolerably clear. What is somewhat less clear is the precise basis of the imposition of liability. Henchy J. disdained the urge to embark on a broad analysis of the duty of care since he considered that the salient features of the case were 'sufficiently clear and distinctive to enable the point at issue to be decided on well-established principles'.

Henchy J. went on to state that the breach by the Council of its public duty under the Regulations made under section 39 of the Act 'would not in itself give a cause of action in negligence to the plaintiff'. It was necessary for the plaintiff to show that the relationship between him and the Council was one of proximity or neighbourhood which cast a duty on the Council to ensure that, regardless of anything left undone by him, he would not end up as the mortgagor of a house which was not a good security for the amount of the loan. A paternalistic or protective duty of that kind would not normally be imposed on a mortgagee in favour of a mortgagor, but the plaintiff was in a special position. To qualify for a Council loan, the plaintiff had to show first, that he was unable to obtain one from a commercial agency and, secondly that his circumstances were such that he would otherwise need to be re-housed by the Council. A borrower of that degree of indigency could not have been reasonably expected to incur the further expense of obtaining a structural survey of the house. The plaintiff, like the Council, had relied on the auctioneer's opinion. He considered that the Council would have the house approved by a surveyor and that it would be superfluous for him to engage a surveyor. That was an understandable attitude and one that ought to have been foreseen by the Council, particularly when one of the preconditions of the loan required the plaintiff to insure the home against fire for at least its full value. The council 'must be taken to have impliedly assured the plaintiff that the house would be a good security for the loan'.

Henchy J. considered that '[i]n the light of the special relations between the plaintiff and the Council, apart from their public duty in the matter', the Council owed a duty to the plaintiff to ensure by a proper valuation that the house would be a good security for the loan. 'In the light of the statutory rights and duties of the Council', it owed a duty to the plaintiff to observe due care in the valuation of the house; it had failed to carry out that duty. If the Council had wished to avoid the incidence of that duty, it could have so provided in one of the preconditions of the loan.

Henchy J.'s judgment is clearly narrower in its language than McCarthy J.'s. Its emphasis on the particular circumstances of the case contrasts with McCarthy J.'s broad statement of the duty of care.

Nevertheless, when one looks closely at the two judgments, the conceptual basis for imposing liability appears very similar. Both judges were content to articulate that basis in terms of the proximity of the relationship between the parties. While Henchy J. did not venture a comment, one way or the other, on McCarthy J.'s preference for a 'two-step' over a 'three-step' formula, Henchy J. did not seek to base his analysis on the 'three-step' model. The idea that his judgment gives any support for the retrenchment that began in *Peabody* seems mistaken. Far from seeking to articulate the duty of care in qualified and subtractive terms, he favoured the broad Atkinian language of proximity, not even broken into the two steps that Lord Wilberforce had proposed in *Anns*.

If one looks back over Henchy J.'s earlier judgments in which he analysed the duty of care, two elements are apparent. First, Henchy J. was willing to adopt the neighbour formula of *Donoghue v. Stevenson* and the language of proximity without seeking to gloss it in any way. In *Siney*, he considered that 'there was a proximity of relationship creating a general duty on the [defendant]'. Secondly, Henchy J. tended to lay greater emphasis in his analysis on the facts of the case so far as they impacted on the foreseeability of the plaintiff's being injured or the reasonableness of the defendant's precautions: both these elements generally feature in the assessment of the discharge of the standard rather than the duty of care: see McMahon & Binchy, *Law of Torts* (3rd ed., Butterworths, Dublin, 2000), Chapter 7. This tendency is apparent in

McNamara (in sharp contrast to Walsh J.'s approach) and in *Keane v. Electricity Supply Board* [1981] I.R. 44. In *McNamara*, he observed that the earlier law relating to trespassers ran 'counter to the principle that pervades the law of negligence since *Donoghue v. Stevenson*, which is that a man is liable in damages if he has failed to take all reasonable steps to avoid injuring those whom he ought to reasonably have foreseen as likely to be injured by his conduct.' Far from placing limits on the *Atkinian* test, this goes close to equiperating foreseeability with the duty of care.

In sum, Henchy J.'s judgment in *Ward v. McMaster* was supportive of a conceptual formulation of the duty of care based on proximity of relationship with no indication of any tendency to define the duty of care in qualified terms.

The Glencar *volte-face*   Let us now consider *Glencar Exploration plc v. Mayo County Council*. The facts, very briefly, concerned two companies engaged in prospecting for and mining ores and minerals, who had been granted prospecting licences by the Minister for Energy to explore for gold in an area south of Westport. After they had spent large sums, the respondent County Council adopted a mining ban in the County Mayo Development Plan. The applicants took judicial review proceedings, claiming, *inter alia* a declaration that the mining ban was *ultra vires* the legislation, an order for *certiorari* and the award of damages for negligence and breach of statutory duty. Blayney J. granted the declaration that the ban was *ultra vires*: [1993] 2 I.R. 237. The High Court, on 20 August 1998, dismissed the claim for negligence. Kelly J. held that, although the respondents were negligent in the sense that they had done something which no reasonable authority would have done, the applicants had no right to damages.

The Supreme Court affirmed Kelly J.'s judgment. We need not here enlarge upon the judgment of Keane C.J. on the question of *ultra vires* or legitimate expectation, other than to note that the Chief Justice's analysis of the first issue cast severe doubt on the conclusions reached by Blayney J. and his analysis of the legitimate expectation doctrine gave little indication of enthusiastic support for an expansive interpretation. For a comprehensive consideration of the latter issue, see Eoin O'Dell's Contract Law Chapter, above, 125. Eoin O'Dell also discusses the *ultra vires* issue in Glencar in the Restitution Chapter, below, 500.

The Chief Justice had no problem with Kelly J.'s conclusion that, in adopting the mining ban, the respondents had 'done something which no reasonable local authority would have done'. The uncontested evidence had been that the ban was adopted in the face of unequivocal advice from the respondent's officials that it was unnecessary in planning terms, would be contrary to the interests of the people of County Mayo and would operate in an arbitrary manner.

The novelty in the decision is the rejection, as *obiter*, of McCarthy J.'s statement of the duty of care in *Ward v. McMaster* and the enthusiastic embrace by the Supreme Court of the incrementalist approach adopted by the House of Lords in *Caparo*, following the High Court of Australia's lead in *Sutherland Shire Council v. Heyman*. The Supreme Court was concerned that the 'two step' test favoured in *Anns* and expanded upon by McCarthy J. in *Ward v. McMaster* might erode the distinction between liability for causing injury and liability for failing to prevent it and that it might extend unduly the scope of liability in negligence for pure economic loss. The Chief Justice considered it desirable to add the 'just and reasonable' test, favoured in *Peabody* and later decisions of the House of Lords (as well as by Costello J. in *Ward v. McMaster*) to the 'two step' test prescribed in *Anns*.

Keane C.J. stated:

> "For the purposes of this case, it is sufficient to say that the mere fact that the exercise of power by a public authority may confer a benefit on a person of which he would otherwise be deprived does not of itself give rise to a duty of care at common law. The facts of a particular case, however, when analysed, may point to the reasonable foreseeability of damage arising from non-existence of the power and a degree of proximity between the plaintiff and the defendant which would render it just and reasonable to postulate the existence of a duty of care. That approach is consistent with the reluctance of the law to impose liability for negligence arising out of an omission to act rather than out of the commission of positive acts which may injure persons or damage property. In the present case, the decision by the respondents that they would not grant planning permission for any mining development within the area covered by the ban was, on the assumption that it was *intra vires*, the exercise by them of a statutory power which would result in the withholding of a benefit from the applicants which would foreseeably result in their suffering financial loss. But, although such a loss was undoubtedly reasonably foreseeable, when one bears in mind that the powers in question were exercisable by the respondents for the benefit of the community as a whole and not for the benefit of a defined category of persons to which the applicant belonged (as in *Siney* and *Ward v. McMaster*), I am satisfied that there was no relationship of 'proximity' between the plaintiffs and the respondents which would render it just and reasonable to impose liability on the respondents.
>
> In considering whether such a relationship of 'proximity' existed and whether it would be just and reasonable to impose a duty of care on the respondents, I think one also has to bear in mind that this was not a case in which it could reasonably be said that the applicants, in incurring the expense of their prospecting activities, could be said to have been relying on the non-negligent exercise by the respondents of their statutory powers. Their position is in contrast to that of the plaintiffs in both *Siney* and *Ward v. McMaster* where, in each case, they belonged

to a category of persons for whose benefit a particular statutory framework had been created and who might reasonably be said to have relied on the local authority in each case taking reasonable care in the exercise of the statutory powers vested in them. The applicants in the present case could rely on no more than a general expectation that the respondents would act in accordance with the law which is not, in my view, sufficient to give rise to the existence of a duty of care."

Pointedly, the Chief Justice concluded his judgment as follows:

"In both [*Siney v. Dublin Corporation* [1980] I.R. 400 and *Ward v. McMaster*] the loss was held to be recoverable following the approach adopted by the House of Lords in *Anns*. While the same tribunal subsequently overruled its earlier conclusion to that effect in *Murphy v. Brentwood District Council*, we were not invited in the present case to overrule our earlier decisions in *Siney* and *Ward v. McMaster*. I would expressly reserve for another occasion the question as to whether economic loss is recoverable in actions for negligence other than actions for negligent misstatement and those falling within the categories identified in *Siney* and *Ward v. McMaster* and whether the decision of the House of Lords in *Junior Books Ltd v. Veitchi Company Ltd* [1983] 1 A.C. 520 should be followed in this jurisdiction."

Implications of the decision Let us now try to assess the implications of the Supreme Court's decision in *Glencar*. The actual holding was scarcely revolutionary, since it did no more than affirm Kelly J.'s judgment on a claim for pure economic loss that would at all stages have had an uncertain prospect of success. The importance of the decision lies in its reformation of the conceptual basis of the duty of care of negligence. This will have general and specific effects.

General effects The addition of the 'just and reasonable' requirement requires the plaintiff to surmount three hurdles rather than two and is designed to make it less likely, in novel situations, that the claim will succeed. While the Court placed this extra hurdle in a claim for pure economic loss, it did not limit its application to cases of that character: thus claims for personal injuries or damage to property will also be affected.

This does not mean, of course, that the test for plaintiffs has been rendered impossible. *Street on Torts,* (10th ed. by Brazier & Murphy, Butterworths, London, 1999), p.177, speaking of the equivalent British retrenchment, effected by *Caparo* and *Murphy*, states that:

"[a] plaintiff in an action for negligence will not fail because the duty – situation he relies on has never previously been recognised. The House of Lords have not closed the categories of negligence. A plaintiff seeking recognition of a novel duty situation *will* have to argue his case in the context of existing authority, to persuade the court that to extend liability into this new situation accords with previous analyses of policy and justice in analogous cases. Moreover a finding of no duty in analogous cases will tell against the plaintiff."

This source goes on to observe (*op. cit.*, 179) that:

"[j]udicial conservatism and the adoption by the House of Lords of Brennan J.'s dictum in *Sutherland Shire Council v. Heyman* may not close the categories of negligence. It does of course restrict their growth. First, by demanding that new duty – situations develop incrementally, it becomes harder to establish a new category of negligence significantly different from, and wide in scope than, its predecessors. Second, it may be that where a duty-situation is not entirely novel, but analogous to a category or case where earlier authorities refused to recognise a duty, the door is indeed closed to expansion of the classes of duty-situations."

The new approach adopted by the Supreme Court suffers from two conceptual weaknesses. The first is the redundancy of the third requirement, that the court be satisfied that it is 'just and reasonable' to impose a duty of care. If the court has addressed the first two components of the test, it will already have considered the justice and reasonableness of imposing a duty of care. These concepts are integral to an assessment of those components. Justice is at the core of the first, which is concerned with a normative assessment of the relationship between the parties; reasonableness (which is surely not a stranger to justice) clearly is central to the second requirement, especially if what Aristotle would call practical reasonableness is in consideration. In truth, having analysed the facts of the case in the light of these two requirements, the court has already done the work of assessing the justice and reasonableness of imposing liability.

Of course, the reason for requiring the court to go through the process of addressing the third factor is a frankly pragmatic one: to encourage future courts to hesitate before expanding (or even, maintaining the present dimensions of) the duty of care.

The second conceptual weakness of the new approach is the philosophy of incrementalism which it has imported from Australia, via London. The idea here is that courts should move incrementally 'by analogy with established categories' rather than by 'a massive extension of a *prima facie* duty of care restrained only be indefinable "considerations which ought to be negative, or to reduce or limit the scope of the duty or the class of persons to whom it is owed."' If the argument in favour of incrementalism is no stronger than that it is an antidote to the spectre of an untrammelled extension of the *prima facie* duty of care, one is entitled to examine the practical affects on a legal system of applying the broader approach in order to test whether these fears are well grounded. In England, the period where the broader approach prevailed lasted only six years, until *Peabody*. During that period, there was one decision of controversially broad scope: *Junior Books v. Veitchi* [1983] 1 A.C. 520. We shall be discussing that decision, and its present status in Irish law, below, 567. Suffice it here to observe that *Junior Books* has indeed received recognition in Irish jurisprudence: in the High Court judgment of Costello J., in *Ward v. McMaster*, where the 'just and reasonable' proviso was actually applied.

In Ireland, the broad approach prevailed for thirteen years. In that period, there is no obvious instance of undue expansion of the duty of care. The Supreme Court had little difficulty in rejecting the claims of plaintiffs in *Madden v. Irish Turf Club* [1997] 2 I.L.R.M. 148, *Smith v. Coras Iompair Éireann* [1991] 1 I.R. 314, *Coyle v. An Post* [1993] I.L.R.M. 508, *Sunderland v. Louth County Council* [1990] I.L.R.M. 658, *Sweeney v. Duggan* [1997] 2 I.L.R.M. 211 and *McCann v. Brinks Allied Ltd and Ulster Bank Ltd*, Supreme Court, November 41996 (analysed *Annual Review of Irish Law 1995*, 577–9) and *Convery v. Dublin County Council* [1996] 3 I.R. 153. There is no decision on pure economic loss that could be regarded as controversial. It is true that many Irish judges are reluctant to leave seriously injured plaintiffs go uncompensated (though Messrs Smith, Coyle, Sweeney and McCann all failed before the Supreme Court). Few would argue that this pro-plaintiff bias is driven by a cerebral reflection on the conceptual elements in the duty of care, however.

The problem with incrementalism is that, even if the court is to proceed by baby steps rather than in league boots, its decision to take those steps and its choice of direction have to be guided by some underlying philosophy of duty deriving from the myriad of personal, social and economic relationships which in sum, constitute society. If, for example, it is going to hold (as apparently the Supreme Court in *Glencar* would wish) that there is no duty on individuals to go to the assistance of others in physical danger, that is a decision which has to be based on a general normative philosophy. When confronted with a new case – a three-year-old child who drowns in a paddling pool in a city park because the adults sitting beside the pool did not want to get their feet wet, for example – of course the court will examine the precedents in detail in order to inform itself of their normative premises; but the idea that it should be discouraged from adopting a broad philosophical perspective seems mistaken. It is worth noting the observations of *Winfield & Jolowicz on Tort,* (15th ed, by WVH Rogers, Sweet & Maxwell, London, 1998), 111, speaking of the British retrenchment:

> "[w]here it is sought to extend the law into a new area the court must exercise a conscious choice in the matter and it would be surprising if the judge were to approach the matter without any general conception, however vague, of what ought to give rise to a duty of care. It can be

argued that *Anns*, properly understood, did offer such a general conception which was simpler and more coherent than what has taken its place."

Pure economic loss Let us now attempt to consider the implications of *Glencar* for claims of recovery for negligently caused pure economic loss. We have had few enough of these claims over the past couple of decades. In *McShane Wholesale Fruit and Vegetables Ltd v. Johnston Haulage Co Ltd* [1997] 1I.L.R.M. 86, Flood J. gave what might at first seem to be a broad interpretation of the scope of the duty of care in this context but, when one analyses his judgment more closely, it merely answers a simple question in simple terms. See further McMahon & Binchy, *op. cit.,* para 10–13.

There were a few cases that supported a broad approach: *Condon v. Coras Iompair Éireann*, High Court, 4 November 1984 and *Tulsk Co-operative Livestock Mart Ltd v. Ulster Bank Ltd*, High Court, May 13, 1983 are examples. But other cases took a restrictive line. *Sweeney v. Duggan* [1997] 2 I.L.R.M. 211 is an obvious instance. Nor has the *Hedley Byrne* principle been applied with great liberality, as is demonstrated by *Hazylake Fashions' Ltd v. Bank of Ireland* [1989] I.R. 601.

Two aspects of claims for pure economic loss need to be examined in some detail in view of Keane C.J.'s observations in *Glencar.* These are (1) liability based on *Junior Books* and (2) claims for economic loss sustained in preventing personal injury or damage. It may be best to examine first the British developments on these two matters and then to go on to consider the position in Ireland.

In the House of Lords decision in *Junior Books Ltd. v. Veitchi Co. Ltd* [1983] 1 A.C. 520, the majority held that the *Donoghue v. Stevenson* principle was capable of generating liability in appropriate cases, not only where a plaintiff suffers personal injury or injury to property but also where the plaintiff suffers economic loss resulting from a non-dangerous defect in property supplied to him or her.

Even in its formulation, the *Junior Books* principle was one intended to apply in only limited factual circumstances but, as soon as the decision had been handed down, the judges in the House of Lords quickly showed signs of unease that they might have opened a Pandora's box. This led to a full-scale retreat from *Junior Books* through various retrospective characterisations that are not easy to harmonise with what the majority of their Lordships actually said in that case.

Thus we find, in *Murphy v. Brentwood D.C.* [1991] 1 A.C. 398, Lord Keith's unapologetic statement that he regarded *Junior Books* as being 'an application of the *Hedley Byrne* principle', and Lord Bridge, in similar terms, observing that:

"there may, of course, be situations where, even in the absence of contract, there is a special relationship of proximity between builder and building owner which is sufficiently akin to contract to introduce the element of reliance so that the scope of the duty of care owed by the builder to the owner is wide enough to embrace purely economic loss. The decision in *Junior Books v. Veitchi Co. Ltd,* can, I believe, only be understood on this basis."

There are, indeed, some impressive policy reasons for arguing against the majority approach in *Junior Books*. First, it does involve a significant intrusion into the law of contract by the law of tort. People arguably should be let settle on the quality levels of a product or house by agreement rather than have the question of non-dangerous quality defectiveness policed by the law of tort. Secondly, and relatedly, it may be argued that the very concept of qualitative defectiveness is inevitably determined by the contractual context: you get what you pay for and the level of expectation is determined by the price paid. Thirdly, there are practical difficulties in having intermediate contractual relationships on the chain from producer to consumer, which often contain exemption clauses, rendered uncertain by the possibility of a negligence action in tort.

The British courts have grappled with the question whether, if the purchaser of a building discovers that it is in a dangerous state and decides to repair the building so as to prevent injury, he or she may be compensated by the one whose negligence caused this dangerous state to occur. In *Dutton v. Bognor Regis UDC* [1972] 1 Q.B. 373, at 396, Lord Denning M.R. said:

"Counsel for the council submitted that the liability of the council would, in any case, be limited to those who suffered bodily harm; and did not extend to those who only suffered economic loss. He suggested, therefore, that although the council might be liable if the ceiling fell down and injured a visitor, they would not be liable simply because the house was diminished in value I cannot accept this submission. The damage done here was not solely economic loss. It was physical damage to the house. If counsel's submission were right, it would mean that, if the inspector negligently passes the house as property built and it collapses and injures a person, the council are liable; but, if the owner discovers the defect in time to repair it – and he does repair it – the council are not liable. That is an impossible distinction. They are liable in either case. I would say the same about the manufacturer of an article. If he makes it negligently, with a latent defect (so that it breaks to pieces and injures someone), he is undoubtedly liable. Suppose that the defect is discovered in time to prevent the injury. Surely he is liable for the cost of repair."

This was an unfortunate way of dealing with the issue of principle. Lord Denning M.R. was, arguably, quite right from the standpoint of justice to hold that the defendant should compensate the plaintiff for the cost of repair but he was unwise, in doing so, to characterise the loss as 'physical damage'. Clearly it was not, and this error made it easy for the House of Lords in *Murphy*, when departing from Lord Denning on policy grounds, to stigmatise his position as involving legal error.

At all events Lord Denning M.R.'s policy preference on this issue found general support in *Anns* and specific endorsement in the Court of Appeal's decision of *Batty v. Metropolitan Property Realizations Ltd* [1978] Q.B. 554. See further Neyers, '*Donoghue v.* Stevenson and the Rescue Doctrine: A Public Justification of Recovery in Situations involving the Negligent Supply of Dangerous Structures', 49 U. of Toronto L.J. 475 (1999).

We have already seen that the House of Lords has for well over a decade been in substantial retreat from the position espoused in *Anns*. Its decisions in *Murphy* and *Caparo* have changed the law on recovery for pure economic loss, including in the areas covered by *Junior Books* and *Dutton*. In *Caparo* Lord Bridge observed that:

> "[o]ne of the most important distinctions always to be observed lies in the law's essentially different approach to the different kinds of damage which one party may have suffered in consequence of the acts or omissions of another. It is one thing to owe a duty of care to avoid causing injury to the person or property of others. It is quite another to avoid causing others to suffer purely economic loss."

The message here is clear: the move from the 'two-step' to the 'incremental' approach has very tangible negative implications for the delimitation of the scope of the duty of care in the context of pure economic loss. Their Lordships now favour a policy of generally refusing to countenance compensation for such loss, subject only to the exception of the *Hedley Byrne* principle, interpreted broadly.

These decisions are opposed to permitting recovery in an action for negligence (as opposed to contract) for *non-dangerous defects* in buildings and products. This was the effect of their Lordships' earlier decision in *D. & F. Estates Ltd. v. Church Commissioners for England* [1989] A.C. 177, and it received strong reiteration in *Murphy*.

Another major change brought about by these decisions is to deny compensation for expenses incurred in rendering a dangerous premises (or product) safe where the defendants' negligence caused this dangerous state. In *Murphy* the arguments marshalled in favour of this change were surprisingly weak. Take, for example, Lord Keith's analysis. He considered that to permit compensation in such circumstances:

> "would open on an exceedingly wide field of claims, involving the introduction of something in the nature of a transmissible warranty of

quality. The purchaser of an article who discovered that it suffered from a dangerous defect before that defect had caused any damage would be entitled to recover from the manufacturer the cost of rectifying the defect, and, presumably, if the article was not capable of economic repair, the amount of loss sustained through discarding it. Then it would be open to question whether there should not also be a right to recovery where the defect renders the article not dangerous but merely useless. The economic loss in either case would be the same. There would also be a problem where the defect causes the destruction of the article itself, without causing any personal injury or damage to other property. A similar problem could arise, if the *Anns* principle is to be treated as confined to real property, where a building collapses when unoccupied."

The idea that the court should not adhere to a just principle because it would be powerless to resist the extension of that principle to other related but ultimately different areas seems unattractive.

Lord Bridge argued somewhat differently, stressing that the product liability principles articulated in *Donoghue v. Stevenson* were premised on the latency of the defect that renders the product dangerous to persons or property. While this is a correct statement of what *Donoghue v. Stevenson* decided, it fails to reflect the gradual judicial extension beyond latency which was given statutory re-enforcement in Ireland by section 34(2)(f) of the Civil Liability Act 1961. Cf. McMahon & Binchy, *op cit*, paras. 11.27-11.29. (It is also significant that the Irish courts never accepted a latency test in occupiers' liability to invitees, in contrast to the House of Lords, whose willingness to do so partially explains the needs for the English Occupiers' Liability Act 1957.) Lord Bridge went on to argue as follows:

"If a dangerous defect in a chattel is discovered before it causes any personal injury or damage to property, because the danger is now known and the chattel cannot be safely used unless the defect is repaired, the defect becomes merely a defect in quality. The chattel is either capable of repair at economic cost or it is worthless and must be scrapped. In either case the loss sustained by the owner or hirer of the chattel is purely economic. It is recoverable against any party who owes the loser a relevant contractual duty. But it is not recoverable in tort in the absence of a special relationship of proximity imposing on the tortfeasor a duty of care to safeguard the plaintiff from economic loss. There is no such special relationship between the manufacturer of a chattel and a remote owner or hirer.

I believe that these principles are equally applicable to buildings. If a builder erects a structure containing a latent defect which renders it dangerous to persons or property, he will be liable in tort for injury to persons or damage to property resulting from that dangerous defect.

But, if the defect becomes apparent before any injury or damage has been caused, the loss sustained by the building owner is purely economic. If the defect can be repaired at economic cost, that is the measure of the loss. If the building cannot be repaired, it may have to be abandoned as unfit for occupation and therefore valueless. These economic losses are recoverable if they flow from breach of a relevant contractual duty, but, here again, in the absence of a special relationship of proximity they are not recoverable in tort. The only qualification I would make to this is that, if a building stands so close to the boundary of the building owner's land that after discovery of the dangerous defect it remains a potential source of injury to persons or property on neighbouring land or on the highway, the building owner ought, in principle, to be entitled to recover in tort from the negligent builder the cost of obviating the danger, whether by repair or by demolition, so far as that cost is necessarily incurred in order to protect himself from potential liability to third parties."

This analysis may be criticised for its attempt to resolve an important issue of principle by a process of formal characterisation. Nothing substantial is addressed or resolved by categorising a plaintiff's costs incurred in preventing injury as 'economic loss' relating to 'a defect of quality'. The question remains as to whether costs of this type, however formally categorised, should be compensated as a matter of justice or even good social policy. Lord Bridge's qualification relating to buildings near the boundary of the owner's land suggests that he is conscious of at least some instances where the injustice of a complete denial of compensation would be obvious; but clearly this specific qualification does not exhaust all such cases.

John Fleming's graphic critique ('Preventive Damages', Chapter 3 of N. Mullany ed., *Torts in the Nineties* (Law Book Company, Sydney, 1997), at pp.59–60) is worth recording:

"Instead of considering the problem of such 'preventive damages' in terms of policy, the *D & F Estates* Court retreated to sterile logic, based on a narrow view of a supposedly rigid dichotomy between economic and physical loss. While motivated to slay the dragon of tortious economic loss, their Lordships sacrificed its traditional protégé, the victim of physical risk."

How will the *Junior Books* principle fare in Ireland? Prior to *Glencar*, the answer might have seemed simple: it had been enthusiastically endorsed here in *Ward v. McMaster* where Costello J. said that he had "no difficulty" in following it. But there was at least some doubt as to whether the position was quite so clear. In *Ward v. McMaster* the plaintiffs had sustained damage from both dangerous and non-dangerous defects; it was easy to treat their claim for the latter as one more nail in the defendant builder's coffin. But if it had been the *only* nail, the issues of principle and policy might have seemed more stark. As we have noted, crossing the threshold into recovery of damages for non-dangerous defects has significant implications for the entire law of contract. This is not necessarily a reason to refuse to take that step but it is a good reason for hesitating before doing so and for analysing in detail what precisely that step will involve.

The Supreme Court decision in *Glencar* surely casts a huge shadow over the status of *Junior Books* in Ireland. The Chief Justice went out of his way to mention that he was reserving his position on that precise question

An aspect of contract law should not be ignored. The common law world is witnessing a clear move away from the strict rule of privity of contract: see O'Dell, 'Restitution, Rectification and Mitigation: Negligent Solicitors and Wills, Again', 65 *Modern L. Rev.* 360, at 375–376 (2002). It seems only a matter of time before the rule is even more substantially modified, after consideration by the Law Reform Commission. This development has two important effects in the context of builders' liability. First, it makes it easier for a court to endorse the *Junior Books* principle. A formidable barrier to such endorsement is that *Junior Books* subverts the purity of the privity rule. Once that purity has been compromised, this objection evaporates. Secondly, the modification of the privity rule carries with it important possibilities for drafting exemption clauses that will bind third parties. Whether a legislative modification of the privity rule, in itself, would be enough to encourage the present Supreme Court to take a more expansive approach may, however, be doubted. Moreover, it could be argued that such modification should be regarded as offering extended protection under the rubric of contract which obviates the need for a supplementary remedy in negligence.

With regard to the issue of preventive costs, it may be hoped that an Irish court will not take the same approach as the House of Lords by denying compensation to one who has discovered a danger in his or her product or premises and who has either repaired the dangerous defect, sold at a loss or simply discarded the product or abandoned the premises. The High Court decision in *Ward v. McMaster* seems quite inconsistent on its facts and holding with the House of Lords' approach. Apart from the question of precedent, the issues of principle and policy all point towards allowing recovery. To deny compensation encourages people to risk their own lives, limbs and property as well as those of others. This is anti-social and contrary to the norms of the law of negligence.

Nevertheless, there are strands of thinking in *Glencar* which make it conceivable that the Supreme Court could countenance going down the present British road. First, the Court happily followed British decisions on the general issue of the scope of the duty of care in negligence. The British courts reject claims of this character. That suggests that the Supreme Court may also follow their lead in this specific context. Secondly, the Supreme Court showed no interest in making distinctions between differing kinds of claims for economic loss, apart from the distinctive strand of liability based on the *Hedley Byrne* principle. Indeed the following passage from Keane C.J.'s judgment suggests a reluctance to countenance compensation, not only for non-dangerous qualitative defects, but also for economic loss sustained in preventing injury or damage:

> "The reason why damages for [economic] loss – as distinct from compensation for injury to persons or damage to property – are normally not recoverable in tort is best illustrated by an example. If A sells B an article which turns out to be defective, B can normally sue A for damages for breach of contract. However, if the article comes into the possession of C, with whom A has no contract, C cannot in general sue A for the defects in the chattel, unless he has suffered personal injury or damage to property within the *Donoghue v. Stevenson* principle. That would be so even where the defect was latent and did not come to light until the article came into C's possession. To hold otherwise would be to expose the original seller to actions from an infinite range of persons with whom he never had any relationship in contract or its equivalent.
>
> That does not mean that economic loss is always irrecoverable in actions in tort. As already noted, economic loss is recoverable in actions for negligent misstatement. In *Siney*, economic loss was held to be recoverable in a case where the damages represented the cost of remedying defects in a building let by the local authority under their statutory powers. Such damages were also held to be recoverable in *Ward v. McMaster*, the loss being represented by the cost of remedying defects for which the builder and the local authority were held to be responsible. In both cases, the loss was held to be recoverable following the approach adopted by the House of Lords in *Anns*. While the same tribunal subsequently overruled its earlier conclusion to that effect in *Murphy v. Brentwood District Council* [1991] 1 A.C. 398, we were not invited in the present case to overrule our earlier decisions in *Siney* and *Ward v. McMaster*. I would expressly reserve for another occasion the question as to whether economic loss is recoverable in actions for negligence other than actions for negligent misstatement and those falling within the categories identified in *Siney* and *Ward v. McMaster* and whether the decision of the House of Lords in *Junior Books Ltd v. Veitchi Co. Ltd* should be followed in this jurisdiction."

A third reason for apprehending that the Supreme Court might not allow recovery for economic loss sustained in preventing injury or damage is that the Court in *Glencar* seemed content to restrict the development of the duty of care so as to avoid the imposition of affirmative obligations of assistance to others. These obligations can relate to the protection of life and bodily integrity.

Perhaps the spirit of *Glencar* is more receptive to the rejection of claims for pure economic loss sustained in preventing physical injury than one might believe could be the case. A compromise that might commend itself to the Court is to make a distinction between the risk of damage to property and the risk of danger to persons and to restrict liability only to cases where economic loss is sustained in preventing the latter.

Witness immunity   The concept of witness immunity is well entrenched the law. in *Re Haughey* [1971] 217, Ó Dálaigh C.J. explained that this immunity:

> "does not exist for the benefit of witnesses, but that of the public and the advancement of the administration of justice and to prevent witnesses from being deterred, by fear of having actions brought against them, from coming forward and testifying the truth. The interest of the individual is subordinated by the law to the higher interest, *viz.*, that of public justice, for the administration of which it is necessary that witnesses should be free to give evidence without fear of consequences."

In *Looney v. The Bank of Ireland and Anor* [1996] 1 I.R. 157, O'Flaherty J. referred to:

> "the need to give witnesses (and also indeed, the judge) in court, a privilege in respect of oral testimony and also with regard to affidavits and documents produced in the course of a hearing. Such persons, either witnesses or those swearing affidavits, are given an immunity from suit. Otherwise, no judge could go out on the bench and feel that he or she could render a judgment or say anything without risk of suit. Similarly, witnesses would be inhibited in the way they could give evidence. The price that has to be paid is that civil actions cannot be brought against witnesses even in a very blatant case, which of course this case is not, but even in a case of perjury – which would be such a case – the law says that an action cannot lie."

O'Flaherty J. considered that a boundary must be set to this immunity:

> "If someone for a malicious purpose, or in order to abuse what he might have thought was a situation of immunity that he enjoyed in court, simply used that situation to make defamatory or malicious statements against others, in a manner that had nothing to do with the particular proceedings in which he was engaged, then it might well be that he would have no answer in an action for defamation or malicious falsehood, or whatever."

Barrington J., concurring, expressly agreed with the qualification that there might be some limit to the 'so called' absolute privilege of a witness in the case of flagrant abuse.

The witness immunity rule was also recognised in the context of civil proceedings, seeking damages for alleged perjury, in *Fagan v. Burgess* [1999] 3 I.R. 306, a decision of O'Higgins J.

In *E. O'K. v. D.K. (Witness: Immunity)* [2001] 3 I.R. 568 the issue arose in the context of negligence litigation against a psychiatrist who had carried out a psychiatric examination of the plaintiff in proceedings for nullity of marriage (in which she was respondent), by order of the Master of the High Court, and had delivered the report to the court and given evidence in the proceedings. A decree of nullity was made on the basis of the personality disorder of the plaintiff. The plaintiff later sued the psychiatrist, claiming that the psychiatrist had been negligent in failing to conduct a careful and thorough psychiatric examination, in failing to confirm with the plaintiff facts disclosed to her by others in the course of the assessment and in placing reliance in reaching her conclusion on inaccurate and incorrect information.

The psychiatrist sought to have the proceedings struck out on the basis that they did not disclose a cause of action against her. O'Sullivan J. made an order in her favour and the Supreme Court affirmed.

Witness immunity is traditionally part of a wider genus which has traditionally included the parties to litigation, judges, jurors and lawyers. So far as lawyers are concerned, we do not have clear authority in Ireland. Some Irish support can be found for the House of Lords decision of *Rondel v. Worsley* [1969] 1 A.C. 191 relating to the immunity of barristers from a duty of care in the discharge of their advocacy functions: see *W. v. Ireland (No. 2)* [1997] 2 I.R. 141, McMahon & Binchy, *op cit.*, para 14.164. The scope of the advocacy immunity was further clarified, and modified, in *Saif Ali v. Sydney Mitchell & Co. (a firm)* [1980] A.C. 198. The House of Lords revisited the issue in *Hall (Arthur JJ) & Co. v. Simons* [2000] 3 All E.R. 673. Their Lordships, by a majority, abolished advocates' immunity for both civil and criminal cases: see Williams, 'May There Be No Moaning of the Bar', (2000) 16 *Professional Negligence* 225, Todd, 'Tort' [2000] N.Z.L. Rev. 505, at 510–513.

In *E. O'K. v. D.K. (Witness: Immunity)* [2001] 3 I.R. 568 Murphy J. (Murray and Fennelly JJ. concurring) made it clear that the Supreme Court was not attempting to determine the issue of advocates' immunity in the instant case. Referring to *Hall*, he observed that:

> "[e]ven if that decision were to be followed in this jurisdiction it would not affect the outcome of these proceedings. The decision in *Hall v. Simons* was confined to the position of lawyers. It did not purport to strip witnesses of the immunity which had been conferred on them in the public interest. So far from it, the House of Lords appears to have reaffirmed the immunity of witnesses but rejected the argument that lawyers were entitled to entitled to immunity by analogy to that conferred on witnesses."

In this context Murphy J. quoted from Lord Hoffman's speech in *Hall* to the effect that:

> "[n]o one can be sued in defamation for anything said in court. This rule confers an absolute immunity which protects witnesses, lawyers and the judge, the administration of justice requires that the participants in court proceedings should be able to speak freely without being inhibited by fear of being sued, even unsuccessfully, for what they say. The immunity has also been extended to statements made out of court in the course of preparing evidence to be given in court. So it is said that a similar immunity against proceedings for negligence is necessary to enable advocates to conduct the litigation properly."

This seemed to Murphy J:

> "to be a classical restatement of the immunity which of necessity is conferred on witnesses who give evidence in the courts in the United Kingdom. Lord Hoffman declined to extend that principle to lawyers."

In the instant case, the psychiatrist's right to be protected from the proceedings by the plaintiff or anybody else in respect of the evidence given by her in the original matrimonial proceedings had been 'particularly strong'. She had not been retained by either party, nor had she advised either of them. The proceedings had not been instituted or defended as a result of what she had said or done. Her terms of reference had been dictated by the order of the Master of the High Court and her report had been made in a sealed envelope addressed to him. The evidence she gave had been based on her professional expertise and the investigations which she had undertaken. All of these matters had been open to examination, and were fully examined, in the course of the proceedings. The trial judge in the nullity petition had considered the expert evidence afforded to him in the light of the examination and cross-examination of the witness and submissions made to him by counsel. As O'Sullivan J. had pointed out in his judgment in the instant proceedings, it would be difficult, if not impossible, to conclude that any negligence on the part of the psychiatrist could be shown to be the cause of the decision ultimately made, even if it could be established that she had been guilty of negligence and that her negligence brought about the judgment and order of which plaintiff complained, Murphy J. was satisfied that O'Sullivan J. had been correct in concluding that Irish law:

> "confers upon a witness – whether expert or otherwise – immunity from proceeding in respect of a wrong committed in such circumstances. The immunity is subject to the qualification already noted that if a witness – or even a judge – so departed from duties which he or she

was purporting to perform as to abuse his position that he would forfeit the immunity which he was abusing. In the present case although it has been urged strenuously over many years that [the psychiatrist] erred, and [the plaintiff] alleges, acted negligently, it was not and could not be suggested, that she attempted to abuse the position of expert witness to which had been appointed by the High Court."

Accordingly, the Supreme Court dismissed the plaintiff's appeal.

EMPLOYERS' LIABILITY

Unsafe place of work In *Mackey v. Iarnród Éireann/Irish Rail*, High Court, May 31, 2001, Kinlen J. held the defendants liable in negligence for failing to provide a safe place of work for the plaintiff, an electrician who provided general maintenance for locomotive engines at Connolly Station in Dublin in a shed which was not properly equipped to deal with the exhaust fumes that came from running engines. Every time a locomotive came into the shed for fuelling or servicing, considerable amounts of fuel were discharged. There was no powered ventilation in the shed. The plaintiff developed asthma, attributable in part to his working environment.

Kinlen J. referred (with apparent approval) to a range of particulars of negligence sent in a letter by the plaintiff's solicitors to the defendants. (It is not clear, however, whether Kinlen J.'s judgment should be interpreted as involving an actual holding that these grounds had been established.) They included the following:

"Exposing the plaintiff and other operatives to excessive amounts of diesel exhaust fumes contrary to sections 13, 37 and 58 of the Factories Act 1955 (as amended by section 20 of the 1980 Safety in Industry Act) and Articles 5 and 17 of the 1993 General Application Regulations; failing to keep the premises sufficiently clean and free of dust and debris contrary to section 10 of the Factories Act 1955; permitting staff to wash locomotives with fluid containing known irritants without proper extraction or other facilities so as to ensure that other staff were not contaminated by the product contrary to the provisions of Article 2 of the Second Schedule of the 1993 General Applications Regulations; failing to warn electricians to wear suitable protective masks while examining over-heated batteries contrary to Articles 21 to 26 of the 1993 General Application Regulations; and failing to carry out a proper risk assessment of the dangers of the shed and failing to inform and consult with staff concerning them, contrary to provisions of Articles 10, 11 and 12 of the 1993 General Application Regulations ...."

Unsafe premises   In *Cassidy v. Wellman International Ltd,* Supreme Court,
October 31, 2000, the plaintiff employee working in a warehouse slipped on a
wet floor. O'Donovan J. found his employers liable, reducing the award by
25% to take account of the plaintiff's contributory negligence. The defendants'
appeal concentrated on two aspects of O'Donovan J.'s judgment. First, they
argued that he had left unresolved the factual issue of whether the accumulation
of water was attributable to a defective manhole cover which allowed water to
bubble through it. In an *ex tempore* judgment with which Hardiman and
Fennelly JJ. concurred, Keane C.J. interpreted O'Donovan J.'s finding
differently. His conclusion on the issue had not been:

> "in any vitiated by the fact that he did not decide the case on the basis
> that there was water bubbling from the manhole cover, because, as he
> correctly said on the evidence, it was clear that even if that were so that
> he could not have caused the accident, but he treated the crucial matter
> in the case as being, was there water on the floor at that point when the
> plaintiff fell to such a degree as to render the floor dangerous and he
> concluded that there was."

The defendants complained secondly about what they claimed was the too
perfunctory dismissal by O'Donovan J. of the expert technical evidence adduced
on their behalf. O'Donovan J. had observed:

> "If there was water on the floor at the material time, as I believe there
> was, it is my view, notwithstanding the results of the skid resistance
> test carried out by [the expert witness who was called by the defendants]
> that it was a danger to persons working in the warehouse. In this regard,
> I prefer the evidence of [the expert witness called by the plaintiff] for
> the simple reason that it has been my own experience that wetness
> under foot or virtually any hard surface threatens the stability of the
> pedestrian."

The Chief Justice commented:

> "There the trial judge is not, as I think [counsel for the defendants] was
> disposed to criticize him for, simply relying on his own experience and
> placing it ahead of expert engineering evidence. On the contrary he is
> saying that he prefers the evidence of another expert engineer, namely
> [the expert witness called by the defendants] who said that, given that
> the skid resistance tests were within acceptable limits, that would not
> conclude the matter because a floor can be skid resistant in that sense
> and still depending on the amount of water that accumulates on it can
> be slippery and therefore dangerous and he says that accords with his
> own experience and I think he is simply saying that it accords with

common sense, that that can be so. It is hardly possible in my view to fault the trial judge for preferring the evidence of one expert engineer to another where he finds the evidence of one engineer more closely according with the facts of human experience as he saw it."

Unreasonable system of investigating In *O'Rourke v. An Post and the Commissioner of An Gardaí Síochána*, Circuit Court, July 19, 2000, Judge McMahon imposed liability on an employer in negligence where the employer's investigative officer had an investigation into theft of money from boxes abstracted from public telephones which was carelessly carried out and which caused the Gardaí to arrest the plaintiff, who was entirely innocent of the theft. The investigative officer had concluded, wrongly, that shortfalls from particular boxes to which the plaintiff had access had not occurred when he was on vacation and that the thefts had not taken place over a particular period from certain boxes to which the plaintiff had no access. She had also failed to repeat a secret test of the plaintiff's honesty with marked coins when it showed that he had not taken any. She described the test as 'inconclusive' but Judge McMahon disagreed:

"What [the investigative officer] meant by 'inconclusive' was that it could not be said *with certainty* that the plaintiff was innocent. This, of course, is true. But this was because of the nature of the *test*. The test designed by [the investigative officer] could show that the plaintiff was a thief if there were shortfalls. If there were no shortfalls, however, one could only conclude that the plaintiff did not steal *on this occasion*. This limited conclusion was all the test could yield when no money was taken. For the defendant to say that it was 'inconclusive' suggests that the plaintiff did not pass the test, which is an improper suggestion. [The plaintiff] passed the test with flying colours. If the test had been repeated a couple more times (which would have been very easy to do within a short space of time) and if [the plaintiff] was shown not to have stolen on these further occasions, that would be further evidence of [his] innocence. Again, however, it would not conclusively prove that [the plaintiff] never took money, but it would strongly support such a conclusion. It would suggest that the investigators should 'look elsewhere' for the thieves.

The employer could be blamed, therefore, for drawing an unfair conclusion from the limited test it designed and for not repeating the test, which would have given the employer more reliable evidence of [the plaintiff's] innocence. As employers they had a duty, once the finger of suspicion pointed in their minds to [the plaintiff] and, once they commenced the investigation, to carry it out fully and carefully. Had they done so, they would have found no discrepancies in any test set for [the plaintiff], who is an honest man, and they would have had no reason to suspect an employee who had worked with them for sixteen years. they would have been in a position to give all of this information to the Gardaí, including the results of the additional tests. Had this been done, I have no doubt that the Gardaí would not have arrested [the plaintiff] first, or at all."

An Post argued that it had merely furnished information to the Gardaí and that the Gardaí had taken the decision to arrest. This, in Judge McMahon's view, was:

"unfairly to minimise the role as investigator. It must be remembered that the defendant had an Investigative Department; it had experience and expertise in such matters; it had assembled much information which it had studied; it designed the 'marked coins' test which it administered with the approval of the Gardaí; it had carried out such tests on many previous occasions and .... it had an experienced investigator who continued, even after the arrest, to make input in the interview process in the police station 'when clarification was required'. I pause here to say that if the Gardaí required clarification from [the investigative officer] at this stage, it indicates that the Gardaí were not fully *au fait* with the circumstances and the documentation involved and were obliged to rely on [her] knowledge of the circumstances. More significantly, An Post had in its possession voluminous documentation and records which it handed over to the Gardaí and which the Gardaí must have assumed were studied in detail by the defendant. The Gardaí only came into possession of this documentation on 27 January, 1998, shortly prior to the arrest of [the plaintiff] on the 28th, and they could not have studied them thoroughly in the short time available, and, accordingly, must have relied on the defendant as to what was in them. The defendant was much more involved in the final decision that it likes us to believe. Its investigation and its general conduct clearly impressed the Gardaí to some extent, and the Gardaí were clearly influenced by the first defendant's assurances in the matter. I have no doubt that they relied on the information presented to them by [the investigative officer] and I have no doubt that [she] must have realised this at the time."

Judge McMahon concluded that the investigation carried out by An Post had been 'incomplete and flawed'. It had proceeded on the false premise that certain boxes had not shown any shortfall while the plaintiff was on holiday. Once An Post commenced its investigation, it owed a duty to its employee to carry it out carefully and in a reasonably professional manner. In this it had failed and was in breach of its duty to the plaintiff in that regard. This was a causative factor in the Gardaí's decision to arrest the plaintiff and to deprive him of his liberty.

Judge McMahon went on to observe that, if there was defamation involved in the case, the first-named defendant would have available to it at least the defence of qualified privilege on the facts as found. There was no evidence of malice. Accordingly, the damages he awarded were not in respect of the damage to the plaintiff's reputation. Judge McMahon went so far as to state, by way of *obiter dictum*, that he 'would tend to the view that the first defendant would have a fuller defence to a defamation action in this case, in that I think its communication with the Gardaí, if accurate, were made on an occasion of absolute privilege.'

The Gardaí had done nothing wrong. They had 'reasonable suspicion' in arresting the plaintiff. They had been entitled to rely on the accuracy of the information given to them by experienced investigators of a public body. Full responsibility for the plaintiff's arrest had to rest with the first defendant. Judge McMahon awarded the plaintiff £25,000 general damages.

The decision is of particular interest because it deals with a common enough matter: the investigation of suspected wrongdoing of employees by their employer. Moreover, it does so under the rubric of negligence rather than defamation, malicious prosecution or false imprisonment. It appears to afford a remedy, in substance if not in form, for the non-malicious, negligent initiation of the arrest of an employee by an employer. This raises the broader question whether a non-malicious negligent initiation of an arrest could give rise to liability where the relationship between prosecutor and prosecuted was not one of employer-employee. The law of employers' liability does not have sharp edges: others in relationships close to that of employment can come within the same principles: see e.g., *White v. Burke*, Doyles Personal Injury Judgments: Hilary and Easter Terms 1995, p. 1 (High Court), *Allen v. Ó Súilleabháin*, High Court, July 28, 1995, *Shinkwin v. Quin-Con Ltd* [2001] 2 I.L.R.M. 154.

The relationship between negligence and defamation was explored by the House of Lords in *Spring v. Guardian Assurance plc* [1995] 2 A.C. 296 in the context of a reference given by a former employer regarding a former employee. The fact that qualified privilege affords a defence to defamation did not prevent the imposition of a duty of care. Similarly, the fact that the holding in the instant case imposed liability in circumstances where a claim for false arrest would have failed is not a reason for concern.

It is interesting to note that, in *Kelly v. Minister for Agriculture, Food and Forestry*, High Court, May 1, 2000, Butler J. made a ruling on a preliminary point of law that the facts as pleaded disclosed a good cause of action where the plaintiff, employed as a factory supervisor in a meat processing factory, was prosecuted and acquitted on a charge of conspiracy to defraud the first defendant, whose officers acted on his behalf in the administration of a scheme for deboning intervention beef. The plaintiff claimed that his signature had been placed upon the prescribed documentation by 'an officer, servant or agent' of the first defendant acting in concert with others. Applying McCarthy J.'s 'two step' test in *Ward v. McMaster* [1988] I.R. 337 (subsequently abandoned

by the Supreme Court in *Glencar Exploration plc v. Mayo County Council*
[2002] 1 I.L.R.M. 481), Butler J. stated:

> "It is argued, on behalf of the defendants that it would be contrary to
> public policy to impose a duty of care generally to act in such a way
> that no criminal prosecution could ever be initiated for the reasonable
> and probable cause against a person who claims damages in respect of
> it. I do not accept this argument. This case has nothing to do with
> wrongful or malicious prosecution"

Contributory negligence In *Mackey v. Iarnród Éireann/Irish Rail*, High
Court, May 31, 2001, Kinlen J. acquitted the plaintiff employee of any
contributory negligence in continuing to work in a locomotive shed where
large quantities of exhaust fumes were being discharged, after having had
pneumonia. The plaintiff developed asthma in part attributable to these fumes.
The working conditions were so unsatisfactory as to involve negligence on
the part of his employers: see 577, above. Kinlen J. noted that no particulars of
negligence had been supplied. He observed that the plaintiff:

> "knew he had a bad chest. He had had pneumonia but it had cleared...
> He had a wife and family to support [;] he had a good job. He was not
> provided with either gloves or masks nor made use of them. The court
> does not find any evidence of contributory negligence on the part of
> the plaintiff."

This brief analysis was sufficient to deal with the issue. It would seem harsh to
hold that an employee whose physical condition was weakened by a work
environment that implicated the employer in negligence should himself or
herself be found guilty of contributory negligence for continuing in the
employment. The position would be different if the employee's condition was
not attributable to the work environment and that working environment was a
safe and unsatisfactory one for other employees. Here difficult policy choices
are involved. If an employer is aware that an employee is no longer physically
capable of carrying out the work for which he or she was originally employed,
what is the employer to do?

One option would be to discharge the employee – an unpalatable solution
from the standpoint of the employee. In *Bolger v. Queally Pig Slaughtering
Ltd*, High Court, March 8, 1996, noted in *Annual Review of Irish Law 1996*,
586-7, where an employer ignored a complaint from an employee who had
developed a swelling around his left elbow was held negligent in letting the
condition worsen. Barron J. rejected the employer's argument that the only
person response could have been to discharge the employee. Barron J. was
satisfied that 'some arrangement would have been made to enable the plaintiff
to work but at the same time ... to work without injuring himself'. The issue

was left open, on the basis of the lack of a sufficient evidential grounding, in *Rafferty v. Parsons (CA) of Ireland Ltd* [1987] I.L.R.M. 98, analysed by Binchy '"Light Work": A Dilemma for Employers', (1988) 82 Incorp. L. Soc. of Ireland Gazette 47. In *Rafferty*, McCarthy J, dissenting, considered that the case should have been allowed to go to the jury with an ancillary issue as to voluntary assumption of risk.

PROFESSIONAL NEGLIGENCE

Solicitors   In *Ewing v. Kelly*, Supreme Court, October 31, 2001, the Supreme Court affirmed the rejection by the High Court of the contention that the action of the Law Society of Ireland in providing names of solicitors who would be prepared to act for the plaintiff instituted by him against solicitors 'was or could have amounted to negligence' (*per* Murphy J., McGuinness and Fennelly JJ. concurring).

Hospitals   In *O'Mahony v. Tyndale,* Supreme Court, July 13, 2001, the dismissal of a claim for negligence against a hospital on causal grounds was affirmed on appeal. We note the case below, 602.

OCCUPIERS' LIABILITY

The common law categories of invitees and licensees   The Supreme Court decision of *Thomas v. Leitrim County Council* [2001] 2 I.L.R.M. 385 was concerned with the common law rules as to the liability of occupiers to entrants onto property under this control. The common law has, of course, been overtaken by the Occupiers' Liability Act 1995; yet this judgment offers fascinating insights into the present philosophy of the Court regarding the fault principle in tort law.

The case involved a simple fact situation. The plaintiff was an English visitor to Sligo who had come with her husband and family to take part in a ballooning event. Weather conditions prevented this event from being held, so the party went sightseeing. They had read about Glencar Waterfall in County Leitrim in the Michelin Guide and decided to go there. The waterfall had formerly been in private ownership; a concrete footpath had been laid at that time. When the local authority became owner, it developed a car park with toilet facilities across the road from the area of the waterfall and renewed the footpath. It did not ascribe full-time maintenance staff to its upkeep.

The plaintiff and her party went up the footpath by the side of the waterfall to a viewing platform. Having proceeded to the top of the path they began to descend. Towards the bottom of a steep part of the pathway, they came upon a tree which had fallen across the path, completely blocking it. A row of trees made it impossible to pass the obstruction on the right had side. To the left was a very steep bank leading further downwards. This had been grassed but it had been used as a short cut to some extent and there were two distinct bare tracks on it, one on either side of a tree stump.

The various members of the party stepped off the path and on to the bank. The plaintiff's husband slipped shortly after leaving the path but was not injured. Just as he was getting up, the plaintiff stepped off the path higher up and almost immediately slipped and received a serious injury. She was sixty-two years old at the time of the accident.

McCracken J. held that the plaintiff was an invitee. He held that the defendant had breached its duty as invitor, but reduced the plaintiff's damages by two-thirds to take account of her negligence. The Supreme Court on appeal held that the plaintiff's status was that of licensee rather than invitee but that the defendant had breached its duty *qua licensee*. It affirmed McCracken J.'s reduction for contributory negligence.

As to the plaintiff's status, McCracken J. had ascribed the category of invitee to the plaintiff because he considered that her presence on the premises conferred a material benefit to the defendant. He observed that Glencar Waterfall was:

"clearly a tourist amenity and is designed to attract tourists into County Leitrim. The plaintiff and her party in fact went to the area because they read of it in a book dealing with tourist attractions.

The question remains whether attracting tourists is of sufficient material interest to bring entrants into the area under the heading of Invitees. On balance, I think it is. One of the main purposes, if not the principal purpose, of attracting tourists into an area is that they bring financial benefits to the area. While these benefits may initially put money in the pocket of local shopkeepers, nevertheless there is, at least indirectly a benefit to the local authority as well. Accordingly, in my view the plaintiff entered the area of Glencar Waterfall as an invitee."

The Supreme Court was not convinced by this analysis. Hardiman J. (Keane C.J. and McGuinness J. concurring) did:

"not accept that, when an amenity is developed, a local person visiting it would do so in the capacity of a licensee and a foreign visitor as an invitee. The evidence establishes only that the local authority has provided some amenities at a long-standing place of public resort to which anyone, tourist or local, can have free access. No doubt it is for the public benefit, and is certainly within the powers of the local authority, that such access is guaranteed by the public ownership of a conspicuous site but I do not accept that it has been shown on the evidence that the local authority has a material interest in the access of an individual to the site, anymore than the previous private owners would have had...."

Hardiman J. agreed with the submission of the defendant that the evidence was more consistent with the policy of bringing areas of natural beauty into the common ownership or enjoyment of everyone than one of obtaining tourist money. Hardiman J. considered that:

> "the act of developing an amenity by a local authority cannot be regarded as simply a means of 'putting money into the pockets of local shopkeepers'.... I do not accept that a person's status on a publicly owned amenity varies with whether he or she is a local or a foreign visitor. What is to be said, on that analysis, of the status of a person who comes from another part of Ireland?"

Hardiman J. went on to note that the law relating to occupiers' liability had been 'radically reformed' by the Occupiers' Liability Act, 1995. Had the law been in force at the time of the plaintiff's accident, her position 'would have been a less favourable one than under the old law, which applies to this case.'

The 'essence' of the common law had been a distinction between those whose presence on lands or premises was in pursuance of an interest common to them and the occupier, and all others. Since this concept of interest or benefit was at the heart of the distinction, it could not be ignored or unrealistically glossed without destroying the whole basis of the common law approach:

> "At an abstract level it is possible to gloss almost any permissive presence of a person on another's lands with an element of benefit. The private house guest was the classic licensee. But even the relationship of host and guest *might* be analysed in terms of benefit: social amenity, relief of loneliness, or hope of reciprocation. An occupier might not himself fully analyse his reasons for offering hospitality.
>
> But these putative benefits are simply too remote to amount to the material benefit which alone grounds the status of invitee. In cases governed by the common law, the distinction which lies at the heart of it must be given substance by realistic application. The provision of a public benefit to all comers is not less worthy of protection, by the attribution of a social or altruistic motive, than private hospitality. The provision of access to a naturally wild area should not require its being manicured to the degree required of commercial or industrial lands or premises."

Accordingly the plaintiff was characterised as a licensee rather than an invitee.

Hardiman J.'s analysis identifies the formidable difficulty attaching to a distinction between locals and foreigners (or visitors from elsewhere in Ireland).

No court would feel comfortable with denying the status of invitee to a local visitor to the waterfall. Yet it would be possible, having identified the development of tourism as a material benefit sufficient to confer invitee status on the generality of visitors, to extend that status to local visitors rather than deny it to all visitors. The courts throughout the common law world were happy to ascribe invitee status to all (save trespassers) who went into shops, on the basis of the potential material benefit brought to the shopkeeper, even where the particular entrant had no present intention of making a purchase or was penniless and likely to remain so.

Hardiman J.'s analysis is also noteworthy for its emphasis on the requirement of material benefit as a precondition of the imposition of an onerous duty on the occupier. His brief reference to the 1995 legislation betrays no indication of a desire to affirm, even retrospectively, the judicial trends, apparent since the Sixties, especially in the judgments of Walsh and McCarthy JJ., of expanding the scope of occupiers' duties towards entrants onto their property. Indeed, it seems unlikely that the Supreme Court today would be receptive to the argument that the 1995 Act should be interpreted restrictively so far as it rolls back the judicial extension of occupiers' duties over the previous three decades. It would be a brave plaintiff who would contend that the legislation is limited in its effects to 'occupancy' rather than 'activity' duties and that the proximity test articulated in *McNamara v. Electricity Supply Board* [1975] I.R. 1 governs the latter: cf McMahon & Binchy, *op cit*, paras. 12.67-12.73. We return to this theme in our discussion of Ó Caoimh J.'s judgment in *Weldon v. Mooney*, High Court, January 25, 2001, below, 591.

Hardiman J.'s insistence that social guests should be categorised as licensees is entirely consistent with the traditional doctrine. It may be contrasted with the approach adopted by McCracken J. in *Doyle v. Magill* [1999] 2 I.L.R.M. 66, analysed in *Annual Review of Irish Law 1999*, 506-8.

Turning to the plaintiff's status as a licensee, Hardiman J. adopted a test for liability which was remarkably generous from her point of view. He approached the issue 'on the basis of the statement most favourable to a licensee which can be found in the authorities'. This appeared to be that of Lord Sumner in *Mersey Docks and Harbourt Board v. Proctor* [1923] A.C. 253, at 274, where he said that licensor 'must act with reasonable diligence to prevent his premises from misleading or entrapping the licensee...'. Similarly, in *Aherne v. Roth* [1945] Ir. Jur. Rep. 45, the duty to licensees had been described as being a duty "to protect [them] against concealed dangers which [the licensor] actually knows to exist".

In applying this duty to the facts of the case, the fallen tree was not regarded as a concealed danger or trap, since it had actually been observed prior to the plaintiff's stepping off the path and was the reason for her doing so. The trap was found in the terrain rather than what was placed upon it. The plaintiff's decision to walk over unsurfaced terrain at the point where the accident took place, had been significantly influenced by the presence of tracks which had been permitted by the defendant to be made, and to remain, on the ground. Hardiman J. considered that they might have misled the plaintiff in altering her perception of the risk, though the course she embarked on was still obviously risky.

The Supreme Court affirmed the two-thirds reduction of the plaintiff's damages to take account of her contributory negligence.

Statutory duty to 'visitors' In *Heaves v. Westmeath County Council,* 20 Ir. L. Times (n.s.) 236, (Circuit Court, Mullingar, October 17, 2001), Judge McMahon gave important guidance on aspects of the Occupier's Liability Act 1995. The plaintiff was injured when he slipped on rustic steps when walking on the grounds of Belvedere House with his two children. Belvedere House had been opened to the public earlier that summer. It was in the occupation of the defendant. Although the house itself was closed to the public on the day of the accident – a Sunday – the gardens and surrounding grounds were open to visitors. Behind the House, a terrace overlooked the lawn. As one moved towards the water, formal steps led down to another lower terrace.

The accident occurred when the plaintiff's two children had strayed from his sight and the plaintiff was looking for them. As he was going down the steps, he slipped on an uneven indentation on the second step which was partly covered in lichen and moss.

The plaintiff sued the defendant as occupier, arguing that it had breached its 'common duty of care to him' as a visitor. The circumstances of the plaintiff's arrival onto the premises proved important. He had driven to the car park where he paid a one-pound entry fee for himself and 50 pence for each of his children. Two attendants in a wooden hut in the car park had taken the money.

Judge McMahon held that the plaintiff should be characterised as a visitor for the purposes of the Act. He stated:

> "In so far as the term 'visitor' includes an entrant who was present on premises by virtue of a contract, it would seem clear that the plaintiff in the present case should be classified as a visitor. After all, he paid an entry fee in respect of himself and his children. At common law he would have been classified as a contractual invitee. At common law he would be entitled to reasonable care. The history of the legislation in question indicates that there was no intention to downgrade the legal status of such an entrant. The Act was primarily introduced to reverse *McNamara v. ESB* [1975] I.R. 1 in respect of trespassers, and to create a new category for recreational users who were causing some concern to the agricultural community who feared that the common law might treat them too leniently by according to them the duty of reasonable care.
>
> 'Recreational users', on the other hand, was intended to cover people who entered premises with or without permission, *without a charge,* to

engage in a recreational activity conducted in the open air (including any sporting activity), or to engage in scientific research and nature study or to explore caves, visit sites and buildings of historical, architectural, traditional, artistic and archaeological or scientific importance (section 1 (1) of the 1995 Act).

From a careful reading of these definitions it is clear that, by entering under a contract the plaintiff is squarely in the category of 'visitor', and by paying a charge he is outside the category of 'recreational user'...."

Counsel for the defendant suggested that, since the money from the plaintiff had been paid in the car park, it constituted a charge in respect of parking the car only and, since it did not amount to an entry fee, it accordingly brought the plaintiff out of the visitor category and into the category of recreational user. Judge McMahon did not agree. He considered that there could be:

"little doubt, from the definition of recreational user, that a parking charge, if that is all it is, will not take the entrant out of that category. The weakness of this argument in the present case, however, was fully exposed when in answer to the question, whether the plaintiff and his children would have been charged if they arrived on foot, the defendant's counsel had to concede that they would have to pay in such an event also. In these circumstances, it is clear that the fees were not paid for the privilege of parking the car. They were clearly entry fees. And this made the plaintiff and his children 'visitors' under the Act.

That the plaintiff also wandered at his leisure enjoying the garden and the grounds is not in doubt. But engaging in a recreational activity does not necessarily and invariably make him a recreational user. The Act is clear in declaring that, if an entrant comes to the premises under contract and pays a charge he is a visitor, and only a visitor. In this legislative classification it is important to remember that there are *three*, and only *three* categories; these categories are exhaustive; there are no more categories. Furthermore, it is equally important to realise that an entrant cannot be in two categories at the same time. A careful study of the legislation compels one to this conclusion and, in this, it in no way departs from the common law.... To accept the defendant's argument, that because the plaintiff was enjoying the scenery he must therefore be a recreational user, would ignore these principles, would distort the statute and would lead to unwarranted and unreasonable conclusions. For these reasons I have little hesitation in rejecting it."

The question thus reduced itself to whether the defendant had discharged its duty under section 3(1):

"to take such care as is reasonable in all circumstances (having regard to the care which the visitor may reasonably be expected to take for his own safety and, if the visitor is on the premises in the company of another person, the extent of the supervision and control the latter person may reasonably be expected to exercise over the visitor's activities) to ensure that a visitor to the premises does not suffer injury or damage by reason of any danger existing thereon."

An engineer who gave evidence on behalf of the plaintiff pointed out that the step on which the plaintiff had slipped had a rough indentation. He considered that, when covered with moss, it might constitute a trap. He suggested that the steps might have been cordoned off, that a warning notice might have been placed at the head of the steps to alert visitors or that a handrail might have been constructed.

Emphasising that the duty imposed by section 3(1) was one of 'reasonable care and no more', Judge McMahon concluded that the precautions which the defendant had taken in all the circumstances were reasonable. It had appointed personnel to address the risk; the head gardener had a satisfactory cleaning system in place, and it had worked for several years without a problem. Moreover, in those matters where the gardener lacked competence he recognised his own limitations and engaged an outside expert to advise him. He had, moreover, duly implemented the advice he received.

The holding in this case should be welcomed by those in charge of open spaces whose concerns about their potential liability as occupiers led to the enactment of the 1995 legislation. Those fears, if not completely groundless, were exaggerated, since there is in this context a very real difference between reasonable care and strict liability.

In *Williams v. T.P. Wallace Construction Ltd* [2002] 2 I.L.R.M. 63, Morris P. held that the plaintiff was a trespasser when he fell from a ladder on a building site. Since the defendants had not acted with reckless disregard for his safety, Morris P dismissed the claim under the Occupiers' Liability Act 1995. (Morris P. also dismissed the plaintiff's claim under the Safety, Health and Welfare at Work Act 1989.

The facts were as follows. The first named defendant was a firm of building contractors. The second was a firm of roofing contractors. The third party distributed building materials, including a type of guttering which had been specified by an architect for use in the construction of a shopping centre. The first defendant was main contractor on site. The second named defendant was subcontractor on the job. The gutting was supplied to the Irish market through a builder's providers company.

When difficulties arose during the fitting of the guttering on the building site, the builder's providers company asked for the plaintiff who was the third party's general manager to come to Dublin to deal with the problem. The assistant manager of the builders' providers company took him to the site.

It was 'anticipated and expected' that the architect on site would be present when they arrived but he was not. The builder's tea break was on. The assistant manager of the builders' providers company told the site foreman that the party would go for a cup of coffee and return later when the tea break was over. What happened thereafter was 'not altogether clear'. The plaintiff said that, as they walked back towards the main road, they made contact with a workman and asked him whether it was possible to get on to the flat roof to gain access to the gutter and he said that it was. The assistant manager of the builders' providers company had another version: he said that the party was approached by a man who asked them whether they were there 'to see about the gutter' and, on being told that they were, he asked the group if they wanted to see the guttering and actually went with them up the stairs to the roof.

When they had gained access to the roof, the plaintiff saw a ladder, climbed up on to scaffolding, attempted to inspect the guttering, found that he could not because the scaffolding was incomplete and decided to descend the ladder but, when he returned to it, the ladder slipped away from the scaffolding because it was not tied or footed and the plaintiff fell.

Morris P. rejected the various accounts of how the party came to be on the roof, by virtue of their internal inconsistency and the unlikelihood that a workman, working during the tea break, would identify the group and take it upon himself to escort them on to the flat roof. He was not satisfied that the plaintiff was 'entitled to be regarded at law as a visitor ...' Presumably this was on the basis that the place where the party went was outside what in common law was termed the 'area of invitation': see further McMahon & Binchy, *op. cit.*, 2nd ed., (Butterworths, Dublin, 1990), pp.222-3. Since the plaintiff was thus a trespasser (though Morris P. did not expressly use that word), the question became one of whether the first defendant had injured the plaintiff intentionally or acted with reckless disregard for his person. Morris P. stated succinctly that he was satisfied that 'no case' had been made out to that effect. Morris P. also rejected the plaintiff's claim under section 8 of the Safety, Health and Welfare at Work Act 1989 on the basis that the 'place of work' in question had not been 'made available' to him.

In *Sheehy v. The Devil's Glen Tours Equestrian Centre Ltd*, High Court, December 10, 2001, Lavan J. held that the plaintiff, who was on the defendant's premises "to avail [herself] of the horse riding facilities provided on a commercial basis by the defendant", was a 'visitor', to whom the defendant had breached its duty under section 3 in exposing her to the risk of tripping on the saddle of a door, the metal strip of which was about two inches above ground level.

Who is a 'recreational user'?   The scope of the definition of 'recreational user' is a matter of uncertainty in its application to children who engage in what are undoubtedly recreational activities – playing football for example – in places where their entitlement to do so may be connected in some way with a broader relationship between them and the occupier. Pupils of a school who kick a ball around the yard before school opens would normally be considered visitors rather than recreational users but, if they do so at a time earlier or later than has been permitted by the school, their status is less clear. Cf. McMahon & Binchy, *op. cit.,* paras. 16.79-16.84, *Bauer v. Minidoka School District No 331* (1989) 116 Idaho 586, 778 P. 2d 336, *Alter v. City of Newton* (1993) 35 Mass. App. Ct. 142, 617 N.E. 2d 656. Similarly if they turn up there at the weekend or in the middle of the summer holidays, the point at which their ancillary relationship fades into the background and the prospect of their being characterised as recreational users (or trespassers) is not easy to identify.

Similar difficulties can arise in relation to public parks and other open areas. In *Byrne v. Dun Laoghaire/Rathdown County Council*, 20 Ir. L.T. (ns) 16 (Circuit Court, Smyth P.; November 13, 2001) the plaintiff, an adult, fell when training an Under-15 soccer team at the playing fields in Sallynoggin, County Dublin at the end of July. The defendant contended that he had not received its permission to use the playing fields at this time as it was off-season; Smyth P held that he was a 'recreational user' and he acquitted the defendant of liability in respect of the 'indentation' (rather than hole) in the ground where the plaintiff fell. One can understand the court's treating the use of areas specifically devoted to team games as falling under distinctive rules involving a separation between visitors and recreational uses as otherwise there would be no orderly management of the use of these areas for the benefit of all.

Non-stationary premises   In *Weldon v. Mooney*, High Court, January 25, 2001 the plaintiff was injured when he fell from the luggage compartment at the rear, of a bus owned by the second defendant and driven by the first defendant. He had climbed into the luggage compartment a short time previously. The accident occurred at 2:55 am. The plaintiff alleged that the door of the luggage compartment had no lock and that the second defendant or his servants or agents had been aware of the practice of young men such as himself using the luggage compartment as he had done to 'hitch' a lift home.

The defendants sought an order striking out the claim as showing no reasonable cause of action or being frivolous or vexatious. Ó Caoimh J. refused to make the order.

He considered that there was a possibility of a successful claim in negligence if the plaintiff could prove the allegation that the first named defendant had moved off from the bus stop when he knew or ought to have known that the plaintiff had boarded the luggage compartment of the bus and that therefore it was unsafe so to move.

A question arose as to whether the plaintiff should be characterised as a trespasser under the Occupiers' Liability Act 1995, to whom only a duty not to injure intentionally nor recklessly would arise. Ó Caoimh J. considered that the plaintiff's claim for negligence 'remain[ed]'. By this he appears to have meant that, in the light of the broader duty arising by virtue of the first defendant's alleged actual or constructive knowledge of his presence in the luggage compartment, the limitations on the duty of occupiers prescribed by section 4 of the Occupiers' Liability Act 1995 had to give way.

This raises an important issue as to the boundaries between the duty arising under common law, the duties arising under the 1995 Act and the limitations attaching to these latter duties. Section 2(1) of the Act provides that, subject to section 8, the duties, liabilities and rights provided for by the Act are to have effect in place of those, which previously attached by the common law 'to occupiers of premises as such in respect of dangers existing on their premises for entrants thereon.' Section 1(1) defines 'danger' in relation to any premises, as meaning 'a danger due to the state of the premises'. The same subsection defines 'premises' as including vehicles and other means of transport.

Under common law, when the duty owed to trespassers was a restricted one, the courts developed a distinction between 'occupancy' and 'activity' duties. The latter could involve a straightforward duty of care in negligence. So, for example, if a trespasser on a private driveway was injured by the householder who was driving home drunkenly from a day at the local public house, the duty would be defined in terms of 'activity', to which the negligence standard attached. The movement of the courts in this direction was not a smooth one. The activity duty was originally expressed in terms of an obligation not to act with 'reckless disregard' for the trespasser's presence; only gradually did it become one of negligence. Kingsmill Moore J.'s judgment in *Donovan v. Landy's Ltd* [1963] I.R. 441 and his attempt to interpret the ratio of *Breslin v. Brennan* [1937] I.R. 350 capture the complexity of this process.

It is interesting to note that the difficulty in making a coherent conceptual distinction between 'activity' and 'occupancy' duties led the High Court of Australia, in *Australian Safeway Stores Pty Ltd v. Zaluzna* (1987) 162 C.L.R. 479 to adopt a unified criterion, of negligence, in respect of occupiers' liability, whether relating to the state of the premises or activities taking place on them. The plaintiff, a customer in the defendant's store, had fallen on a slippy floor. Mason, Wilson, Deane and Dawson JJ. stated:

> "Is there anything to be gained by striving to perpetuate a distinction between the static condition of the land and dynamic situations affecting the land as a basis for deciding whether the special duty is more appropriate to the circumstances than the general duty? The present case illustrates the neat issue that such a question can raise: on the one hand, the appellant argues that because the condition of the floor was caused by wet weather it was unrelated to any activity of the appellant and therefore the special duty supplied the relevant test; on the other hand, it was the activity of conducting a commercial operation on the premises that provided the context for the accident and what could be more dynamic than the constant movement of rain-soaked shoppers

over the floor of a supermarket on a Saturday morning? If it was always the case that the formulations of an occupier's duty in specific terms contributed to the easy ascertainment of the law there would be a case for their retention ... but the pursuit of certainty in this way loses its attraction if its attainment depends on the resolution of difficult questions based on artificial distinctions."

Four features of the Irish legislation may be noted. First, section 2(1) sets up a new statutory regime of liability, in replacement of the common law, but only that attaching to 'occupiers of premises *as such....*' (emphasis added). If an occupier is sued in another capacity–as a driver, for example, who has an accident on the premises he or she occupies–it would seem that on this basis the Act does not apply. Secondly, the definition of 'danger', as we have seen, is restricted to a danger due to the state of the premises. This contrasts with section 1(1) of England's Occupiers' Liability Act 1984, which refers to 'any danger due to the state of the premises *or to things done or omitted to be done on them*' (emphasis added). A strong argument can be made that, for this reason also, 'activity' duties are unaffected by the 1995 Act and continue to be governed by the common law. Thirdly, 'premises' are defined as including 'vessels, vehicles, trains, aircraft and other means of transport'. There is no restriction to vehicles "not in operation" (as recommended by the Law Reform Commission in its *Report on Occupiers' Liability* para. 4.131 (LRC – 1993) and as provided for in equivalent legislation in Victoria and Western Australia.) This omission adds weight to the interpretation of the 1995 Act as excluding 'activity' duties. In a decision of the Full Court of the Federal Court of Australia in *Meth v. Moore* (1982) 44 .A.L.R. 409 Toohey J. observed that:

"[w]hile it may be logical, if somewhat unreal, to equate a stationary motor vehicle with a house or other structure, it is not logical to continue the equation once the vehicle is in motion. If the duty owed by the owner of a static vehicle to a passenger is comparable to that of the occupier of premises, there is no reason in law or logic why a different and broader duty should not arise in respect of a moving vehicle, the same duty as is owed to other users of the road."

It is interesting to read the Law Reform Commission's view (*op cit,* para. 4.129) that if the nature of the plaintiff's complaint 'is in regard to the condition of the particular structure, then it is appropriate to deal with the complaint under the principles of occupiers' liability. If it concerns the negligence of the operator – of a car or a train, for example, that is a claim that should be dealt with under ordinary negligence principles.' As we have mentioned, the decision of the Supreme Court in *Thomas v. Leitrim County Council* [2001] 2I.L.R.M. 385 makes it hard for plaintiffs to press the distinction between activity and occupancy duties and to contend that *McNamara v. Electricity Supply Board* still governs the former.

The fourth point worth noting about the 1995 Act is the curious way in which it defines the duty owed by the occupier to a recreational user or non-criminal trespasser. Section 4(1) states that, in respect of a danger existing on the premises, this duty is:

> "(a) not to injure the person or damage the property of the person intentionally, and
> (b) *not to act* with reckless disregard for the person or the property of the person." (Emphasis added)

If the duty is not to *act*, this casts some doubt on the interpretation that the Act excludes activity duties. More alarmingly, it opens the possibility that the legislation restricts the duty of occupiers in relation to recreational users and trespassers to such narrow confines that no duty is imposed to avoid being reckless with regard to dangers resulting from the state of the premises where the occupier is not engaging in any activity. That certainly seems to be what section 4(1) says but it is impossible to reconcile with the definition of 'danger' in section 1(1).

We are urgently in need of authorative clarification on this crucial question as to the application of the 1995 Act to 'activity' duties. The language of the statute is unacceptably ambiguous.

Premises let by public authority   In *O'Callaghan v. Dublin Corporation*, 18 I.L.T. (ns) 98 (Dublin Circuit Court, Judge Devally, February 8, 2000), a child plaintiff who slipped and fell when descending the steps from the third floor in the Balcurris flats, where she lived, failed in her action for negligence. There was evidence that the steps were wet and slippy at the time. The plaintiff's engineer gave evidence, on the basis of a test he had carried out, that the particular step was slippery when wet. He said that the edge of the step, which consisted of concrete inset with limestone, had been worn down over time so that it had become rounded and polished. Counsel for the defendant challenged the efficacy of the test. The report notes that 'there was some sparring before Judge Devally commented that he had heard sufficient evidence on the topic'. An engineer's report, contradicting the finding of slippiness, was submitted by the defendant to the court.

In holding against the plaintiff, Judge Devally is reported as having stated that the effect of the limestone would have been to make for a solid surface. He commented that there was no such thing as a perfect surface, but he had rarely seen such a well-aligned state-of-the-art landing as the one in the instant case.

PRODUCT LIABILITY

In *Annual Review of Irish Law 1999*, 497–502, we analysed *Cassells v. Marks and Spencer plc,* High Court, March 25, 1999, where Barr J. absolved the defendant of negligence in the sale of a dress, which injured the plaintiff when it caught fire when she was wearing it. The dress was highly flammable. It was sold with a label which contained a warning in red stating "Keep away from fire". A tag was attached with a warning stating "In the interest of safety it is advisable to keep your child away from fire". Barr J. held that the defendant had not been negligent in selling and marketing the dress without having it treated with a chemical fire retardant. He also held that the warning of the danger of fire was adequate.

The plaintiff appealed to the Supreme Court against the latter holding. Counsel for the plaintiff submitted that the warnings were 'mere platitudes' and did not tell purchasers anything that they did not already know. In view of Barr J.'s holding that the cotton material presented 'a major fire hazard', an ineffective general warning was equivalent to no warning.

Counsel for the plaintiff placed particular emphasis on *O'Byrne v. Gloucester* Supreme Court, November 3, 1988 (analysed in *Annual Review of Irish Law 1988*, 433–4) where, in similar circumstances, Finlay C.J. had suggested that the garment in question should have had attached to it 'a simple warning that it was dangerous if exposed to a naked flame and would burn rapidly'. This wording, said counsel, was much more effective than the somewhat bland warning provided by the defendant in the instant case.

Counsel for the defendant interpreted Finlay C.J.'s remarks differently. The ratio of the Chief Justice's judgment was simply that there should have been a warning label. The wording which he had suggested was *obiter*. It was unlikely that he saw himself as laying down the exact wording for future labels.

Counsel for the defendant pointed out that the evidence showed that two hundred thousand children's dresses had been sold in that season alone. The instant case was the only one known to the defendant where a child wearing one of the dresses had been injured by fire. This went to demonstrate that the defendant's fire warning was, in fact, both adequate and effective.

The Supreme Court affirmed Barr J. McGuinness J. (Murphy and Murray JJ. concurring) considered that the warning given by the defendant fully met the standards set out by Laffoy J. in *Duffy v. Rooney and Dunnes Stores (Dundalk) Ltd*, High Court, June 23, 1997, which had been approved by the Supreme Court on the appeal on April 23, 1998.

McGuinness J. agreed with Barr J.'s view that the warning required by the regulations as to children's nightwear was 'in its terms "Keep away from fire" a sufficiently clear warning to carers that a child wearing the garment to which the warning is attached should be kept away from unprotected fire.' She found it:

"somewhat difficult to follow the logic of the argument asserted on behalf of the plaintiff that a warning 'Keep away from fire' merely 'tells people what they already know' and is too bland. The warning clearly indicates that the garment is made of flammable material – otherwise there would be no need for the warning. Is it suggested that because the label does not warn that the material burns rapidly one might think that there was really no danger in allowing the garment to come in contact with a naked flame? Is it suggested that a child dressed in material which burns more slowly, but is nonetheless flammable, may safely be exposed to unprotected fire, or that in that case a 'Keep away from fire' warning may be ignored? Different materials have different properties when exposed to fire; it is well known that some emit fumes; others melt and may adhere to the flesh causing severe burns; others, like cotton, burn rapidly. When a purchaser is presented with a warning label 'Keep away from fire' the only logical reaction is to do precisely that, regardless of the nature of the particular garment or the material of which it is made. To her credit, the plaintiff's mother in this case accepted that she had seen the warning and knew of the danger of the unguarded fire."

McGuinness J.'s reasoning is completely logical and cannot be faulted on that account. Perhaps the plaintiff's argument can best be understood as addressing, not the logical substratum of the communication attached to the dress but rather its colourlessness. Sometimes people need to be jolted into attention in order to pay the care that the situation demands. Jolting customers in this way may be bad for business but necessary to achieve the goal of safety.

ROAD ACCIDENTS

In *McEneaney v. Monaghan County Council*, High Court, July 26, 2001, the first defendant, a road authority, was held negligent in failing to provide a French drain which would have collected water seeping from adjoining lands. This failure resulted in the creation of a localised hazard to the plaintiff, a motorist, who was not alerted to the possibility of ice on the road in the absence of any recent sign or warning and who was involved in an accident as a result.

MISREPRESENTATION

Negligent misrepresentation   In *Annual Review of Irish Law 2000*, 443–4, we noted that the Supreme Court, in *Wildgust* [2001] 1 I.L.R.M 24 had referred the proceedings back to the High Court to hear the plaintiff's amended claim based on a negligent misstatement. The matter again came before Morris P., who gave the judgment on August 17, 2001.

It will be recalled that the case concerned the non-payment of a premium of an insurance policy on the life of the wife of the plaintiff. Maintaining the policy was integral to the terms of a loan granted by Hill Samuel to the plaintiff. Because of the non-payment of the premium, the life policy lapsed and the insurer, Norwich Union, did not make any payment when the wife died. The plaintiff sued (*inter alios*) Norwich Union. His claim against the defendant, as has been mentioned, ultimately crystallised into one based on negligent misstatement.

An important issue of fact concerned the question whether a representative of Hill Samuel had been told by a representative of Norwich Union that a cheque for the premium had been received and that everything was 'correct and in order'. The Hill Samuel representative gave evidence that, if he had known that the premium remained unpaid, Hill Samuel would have paid it in order to keep the policy alive. Morris P. concluded on the evidence that this assurance had been given.

This finding did not, however, conclude the legal issue in favour of the plaintiffs. The evidence also established that, on account of a bank strike and a postal strike, the first-named plaintiff had not received notice form Norwich Union of the non-payment of the premium until some months had elapsed. At no stage up to the time when the policy lapsed was he aware of the conversation between the representatives of Norwich Union and Hill Samuel and thus he had never placed any reliance on it.

Morris P., applying the principles as to the duty of care set out by the Supreme Court a month previously in *Glencar Exploration plc v. Mayo County Council* [2002] 1 I.L.R.M. 481, dismissed the plaintiff's claim. He stated:

> "In my view the one major insurmountable difficulty for the plaintiff is that at no stage did he .... become aware of the fact that the misstatement had been made by the Norwich Union nor did he place any reliance upon it. He was not misled by the misstatement because he was not aware of it. He was not prejudiced by it. It was not until two months later that he became aware of the fact that the premium had not been paid. In my view the misstatement in no way influenced or contributed towards the conduct of the plaintiff. It did not influence him or cause him to act to his detriment. I do not believe that it would be reasonable that the law should impose a duty on the defendant for the benefit of the plaintiff in these circumstances. In my view to do so would, as Brennan J, said in *Caparo Industries Ltd plc v. Dickman* be a 'massive extension of a *prima facie* duty of care' which is not my understanding of the law in this jurisdiction."

This conclusion seems harsh on the facts of the case. First, let us dispose of a

small inaccuracy. Brennan J.'s remarks were made in the decision of the High
Court of Australia in *Sutherland Shire Council v. Heyman* (1985) 157 C.L.R.
424 rather than in the House of Lords judgment of *Caparo Industries Ltd v.
Dickman* [1990] 2 A.C. 605.

In principle, there should be no objection to imposing liability for negligent
misstatement where the misstatement is not made directly to the plaintiff
provided the plaintiff reasonably relies to his or her detriment on the carefulness
with which the statement is made to the third party in circumstances where the
making of a careful statement to that third party by the defendant is part of a
wider relationship of reliance between the plaintiff and defendant. If, for
example, the parties had agreed that the only mode of notification of default in
the payment of the premium was to be to Hill Samuel, who would then pay the
premium, a negligent failure to notify Hill Samuel would seem clearly to
constitute a negligent misstatement actionable at the suit of the plaintiff.

The fact that Norwich Union also had an obligation to notify the plaintiff
of default should not, of itself, be a reason for exempting Norwich Union from
liability, where the plaintiff was aware of the notification requirement to Hill
Samuel and where Norwich Union must have been aware in general of the
difficulties caused by the bank strike and the postal strike. Counsel for the
plaintiff argued that it was unrealistic to attempt to separate the coinciding
interests of Hill Samuel and the plaintiff since each had an identical and
corresponding interest in ensuring that the policy remained in place;
accordingly, a misrepresentation made to Hill Samuel had to prejudice the
plaintiff since, without this misrepresentation, the policy would have been
renewed by Hill Samuel. Morris P. appeared to proceed on the basis that the
plaintiff's failure to become aware of this misstatement until months later meant
that neither had he been misled by it nor had he relied upon it. Yet this
conclusion can be questioned. Of course he did not rely on the erroneous
communication directly, since he was unaware of it: what he relied on, to his
detriment, was that a system of communication to Hill Samuel would be
operated with care. He was fully aware that, if that system was not operated
with care, he would suffer. He did not have to be involved himself in that
system of communication to a third party in order to suffer damage.

Morris P.'s judgment contains no extended analysis of the implications for
the law relating to negligent misstatement of the radical revision of the
conceptual foundations for the duty of care brought about by *Glencar
Exploration plc v. Mayo County Council*. He appeared to accept as beyond
question the fact that, in proceedings for negligent misstatement, the new
principles relating to the duty of care applied. Referring to the McCarthy J.'s
test in *Ward v. McMaster*, which was repudiated in *Glencar*, Morris P. observed:

> "This is no longer the full test. I must add the further factor of asking
> myself 'Is it just and reasonable that the law should impose a duty of a
> given scope on a defendant for the benefit of the plaintiff?' I am satisfied

that this is the appropriate test in cases where negligent misstatement is alleged."

In *Williams v. Natural Life Health Foods Ltd* [1998] 2 All E.R. 577, Lord Steyn regarded *Henderson v. Merrett Syndicates Ltd* [1995] 2 A.C. 145 as settling the position:

"that the assumption of responsibility principle enunciated in *Hedley Byrne & Co Ltd v. Heller and Partners Ltd* [1964] A.C. 465 is not confined to statements but may apply to any assumption of responsibility for the provision of services. The extended *Hedley Byrne* principle is the rationalisation or technique adopted by English law to provide a remedy for the recovery of damages in respect of economic loss caused by the negligent performance of services. Secondly, it was established that once a case is identified as falling within the extended *Hedley Byrne* principle, there is no need to embark on any further inquiry whether it is 'fair, just and reasonable' to impose liability for economic loss. Thirdly, and applying *Hedley Byrne*, it was made clear that 'reliance upon [the assumption of responsibility] by the other party will be necessary to establish a cause of action (because the negligence will have no causative effect).' Fourthly, it was held that the existence of a contractual duty of care between the parties does not preclude the concurrence of a tort duty to the same respect."

If this approach were adopted in Ireland, liability could be imposed for negligence under the *Hedley Byrne* principle without the need to have recourse to the 'just and reasonable' test which Morris P. considered to be a necessary extra requirement.

If one nonetheless were to apply the 'just and reasonable' test to the facts of the instant case, the plaintiff should surely have succeeded. The parties were in a close relationship of mutual financial interdependence. Their respective interests in the payment of insurance premia pulled in the same direction.

RES IPSA LOQUITUR

In *Rothwell v. Motor Insurers Bureau of Ireland*, High Court, July 6, 2001, a case involving a claim under the MIBI Agreement of December 21, 1988, the plaintiff's vehicle had skidded on a patch of oil that was left on the road by an unknown driver of a truck or lorry 'on which the cap or cover of the fuel tank was missing, defective or not properly fitted'. There was, naturally, no evidence as to why the cap or cover was missing or defective.

The plaintiff argued that this was a case where the *res ipsa loquitur* doctrine applied. McCracken J. could not accept this submission:

> "because ... there may be circumstances in which a spillage of this nature occurs without any fault whatever on the part of the driver.
>
>   I think the problem can be best dealt with by considering the position in an ordinary case where the driver and owner of the vehicle are known, and are the defendants. In those circumstances, once the court was satisfied that the accident was probably caused by a fuel spillage from the defendant's vehicle, the onus would clearly shift on to the defendant to show that the spillage had occurred under circumstances which did not constitute negligence on his part. In an ordinary case there clearly would be no onus on the plaintiff to prove the negative, namely that there were no circumstances which would excuse the defendant from liability. These would be matters solely within the knowledge of the defendant and it would be for him to produce the necessary proofs. In the present case, in my view a similar situation arises. The plaintiff is in the position that he does not know what happened and could not know what happened. He has been able to satisfy the court that the probability is that this accident was caused by a fuel spillage, and there certainly are circumstances in which this could constitute negligent driving on the part of the driver of the vehicle from which the spillage occurred. Beyond that the plaintiff cannot go. Of course, unlike the ordinary case, there is also no way in which the defendant can know what happened, and therefore the defendant is unable to produce any explanation which might excuse liability, and therein lies the real difficulty of this case."

Nonetheless, McCracken J. thought that this problem had to be resolved in favour of the plaintiff:

> "The whole purpose of the MIBI Agreement and its predecessors is to compensate persons injured in road traffic accidents where no other compensation is available. In my view it would be quite wrong and quite contrary to the intention and purpose of the Agreement that a plaintiff should be put in a position that he will not receive compensation if he cannot prove that the driver could have no defence, where he would not have to have this burden of proof if the identity of the driver or vehicle was known. Accordingly, I find the issue of liability in favour of the plaintiff ..."

Perhaps the simplest approach would be to apply directly the *res ipsa loquitur* doctrine in these circumstances. The plaintiff was able to establish that the situation was one calling for an explanation by the driver under the principles set out by Erle C..J in *Scott v. London & St. Katherine's Docks Co* (1865) 3 H.

& C. 596 at 601, 159 E.R. 665 at 667. Accidents such as occurred to the plaintiff do not usually happen without negligence on the part of those in control of the 'thing' – the vehicle emitting the oil spillage – that caused the injury. The fact that the driver was unknown does not affect the liability of the MIBI, since it bears the responsibility for the negligence of unknown drivers. Its inability to produce evidence that might displace the onus imposed on it by the *res ipsa loquitur* doctrine is not a reason for exempting it from responsibility. Such an inability is a frequent consequence of the application of the doctrine, as, for example, where a plane disappears without trace. The company that owns the plane must compensate the families of the deceased passengers even though it may have no idea what was the true cause of the plane's disappearance. The position is no different in principle where vicarious liability is imposed in respect of the conduct of actors whose identity is not, and cannot in the circumstances be, known by the vicariously liable party.

It is interesting that McCracken J. proceeded on the basis of the rationale for *res ipsa loquitur* favoured by the Supreme Court in *Hanrahan v. Merck Sharp & Dohme Ireland Ltd* [1988] I.L.R.M. 629, which grounded the doctrine on the 'palpable unfair[ness]' of requiring the plaintiff to prove that which is 'peculiarly within the range of the defendant's capacity of proof'. This rationale is controversial and not easy to harmonise with the great body of cases on *res ipsa loquitur* which are based on commonsense principles of inferential evidence rather than on a normative ascription of the burden of proof. The *Hanrahan* rationale does not provide a solution for the kind of situation that arose in *Rothwell v. Motor Insurers Bureau of Ireland* since clearly the MIBI had no more access to knowing how the accident occurred than the plaintiff. The traditional approach, based on a commonsense process of inferential reasoning from circumstantial evidence, yields a simpler solution to this type of case.

In *Murray v. Millar*, Circuit Court, Roscommon, November 14, 2001, where a traffic accident occurred when the first and second defendant's cow jumped out in front of the plaintiff's car, Judge McMahon imposed liability on the basis of section 2 of the Animals Act 1985. He summarised the effect of the earlier case law as follows:

> "[T]he effect of this statutory provision is that reasonable care must now be taken to ensure that animals do not stray onto the highway and cause damage thereon. This normally translates into an obligation to ensure that the land is stock proofed and that the fencing is sufficient to prevent animals from breaking out. Moreover, in relation to proof, the case law indicates that the onus of proof, that the land was properly fenced, is now on the landowner or the owner of the animal who seeks to evade liability. In *O'Reilly v. Lavelle* [1990] 2 I.R. 372) and again in *O'Shea v. Anhold and Horse Holiday Farm Ltd*, (Supreme Court, 23 October 1996) the courts in this jurisdiction have clearly accepted that

the principle of *res ipsa loquitur* applies to these situations. Accordingly, in cases such as the present, to escape liability, the first and second defendants must provide the evidence to show that they took reasonable care in the management of the land to ensure that the fencing was secure. … [T]he first and second defendants …. tendered no significant evidence in this regard, and on this ground, I have little hesitation in holding them liable for the damage which their straying animal caused to the plaintiff."

CAUSATION

Negligence claim against hospitals In *Annual Review of Irish Law 2000*, 433, we noted Quirke J.'s decision in *O'Mahony v. Tyndale*, High Court, April 7, 2000, dismissing a claim for negligence by a child who suffered from a serious mental disability, taken against a hospital in respect of the treatment he was given at the time of his birth. Quirke J. held that the hospital system for recording the condition and treatment of neonates immediately after birth had been 'wholly inadequate' but that the plaintiff had not established on the balance of probabilities that his disability had been caused because he had developed hypoglycaemia by reason of inadequate nursing and monitoring with the '24-hour nursery' during the hours after his birth.

The Supreme Court affirmed on July 13, 2001. Keane C.J. (Murphy and Hardiman JJ. concurring), applying the principles set out in *Northern Bank Finance v. Charleton* [1979] I.R. 149 regarding the functions of an appellate court in relation to findings of fact by trial judges, held that Quirke J.'s findings should not be disturbed. The maxim *omnia praesumuntur contra spoliatorem* had no application. There was nothing to indicate that a trace which had been taken had been destroyed by the defendants. In any event, the missing trace would not have been critical to the issue whether an episode of bracycardia had led to hypoxia in view of the evidence that had been given by two witnesses. For detailed consideration of this aspect of the case, see Declan McGrath's Evidence Chapter, above, 269.

Novus actus interveniens In *Breslin v. Corcoran and Motor Insurers' Bureau of Ireland*, High Court, July 17, 2001, Butler J. had to make an important legal determination of a kind of situation that crops up with depressing regularity. The first defendant had left his car, unlocked with the keys in the ignition, outside a coffee shop in Talbot Street, Dublin, as he dropped into the shop to get a sandwich. When he was coming out, an unknown person jumped into the car and drove off at high speed, turning into a lane where the car struck and injured the plaintiff. Undoubtedly the first defendant had been guilty of carelessness and breach of statutory duty, but had the causal connection between his wrong and the plaintiff's injury been severed by a *novus actus interveniens*?

In the Circuit Court decision of *Dockery v. O'Brien* (1975) 109 I.L.T.R. 127, Judge McWilliam, on similar facts, had held that the causal connection had not been thus severed and that the damage suffered by the plaintiff was reasonably foreseeable. In the English Court of Appeal case of *Topp v. London Country Bus (South West) Ltd* [1993] 3 All E.R. 448, however, the defendant was held not to have breached a duty of care to the injured plaintiff.

Butler J., bound by neither decision, had no hesitation in finding that the chain of causation had been 'clearly broken'. The first defendant's negligence had been merely a *causa sine qua non*, rather than a *causa causans*. The only type of circumstances in which Butler J. could envisage a successful claim against the owner of a stolen vehicle would be where there was 'actual and clear evidence that the vehicle was left in an area where it should be known to the owner that people routinely stole cars for the purpose of driving them around in a reckless and dangerous fashion.'

This holding in this decision may well be in harmony with the philosophy of *Glencar Exploration plc v. Mayo County Council*, where the Supreme Court evinced a certain hostility to affirmative obligations in negligence. Of course there are different types of affirmative obligations. They embrace cases (such as mentioned by the Supreme Court) where the party falling under a moral duty to act had no prior responsibility for creating this situation of danger to another. What arose in the instant case, however, did involve such prior responsibility: the first defendants had created a situation where, human nature being what it is, danger to others was made more likely. While the case in favour of imposing liability can be grounded on solid philosophical foundations (cf. Moore, 'The Metaphysics of Casual Intervention' (2000) 88 Calif. L. Rev. 827), it has to be acknowledged that decisions in Canada are slow to find careless car owners liable (cf. Tong v. Bedwell, 112 A.C.W.S. (3d) 795 (Alberta Q.B. 2002).

The question whether liability should be imposed on car drivers who leave the keys in the ignition could be resolved by a totally abstract analysis: inevitably values as to the proper remit of negligence law will affect the answer. If emphasis is placed on the deterrent function of tort law and on communitarian norms, Butler J's judgement may appear too narrow: cf. Fleming, "Note: Injury Caused by Stolen Motor Vehicle" (1994) 110 L.Q.Rev. 187, Howarth, "My Brothers' Keeper? Liability for Acts of Third Parties" (1994) 14 Legal Studies 88. If, however, one is concerned, as the Supreme Court in *Glencar* clearly was, to prevent court authority from becoming so vast as to risk leaning 'to remain stable and to retain its moral focus intact' (Stapleton, "Duty of Care: Peripheral Parties and Alternative Opportunities for Deterrence" (1995) 111 L.Q.Rev. 301, at 316), then Butler J. may well seem to have drawn the line at the best point. Doubters may still regard this type of case as easily distinguishable from the general run of third party interventions in that the foreseeability of the intervention is precisely the reason that the defendant's conduct may be stigmatised as negligent in the first place: cf. *Stansbie v. Troman*

[1948] 2 KB 48.

In *Murray v. Millar*, Circuit Court, Roscommon, November 14, 2001, Judge McMahon gave a detailed analysis of the doctrine of *novus actus interveniens*.

The third defendant, when driving on the main road from Roscommon to Lanesboro one winter's evening, was suddenly confronted by a black pedigree cow which jumped out in front of his car from his left side of the road. He was unable to avoid a collision. After he had struck the cow, he pulled into his own side of the road, turned his lights to dims, put on his hazard lights and checked the state of the animal. From the absence of any movement, he concluded – mistakenly, as it transpired – that she was dead.

Aware of the hazard that the cow represented, the third defendant tried to stop passing cars. Several passed him without stopping and the one that did stop 'was not too helpful'. Having considered his options, he decided to go for help to a house no more than four hundred yards away. In his absence, the plaintiff, driving down the road, collided with the cow. The cow was owned by the first defendant and kept by her and her husband, the second defendant, in a field adjoining the road.

The issue of the first and second defendants' liability in relation to the cow's escape onto the road was not problematic. The common law immunity from liability for damages caused by animals straying onto the highway had been abolished by section 2 of the Animals Act 1985 and the circumstances called for the application of *res ipsa loquitur* principle: see above, 599.

Counsel for the first and second defendants argued that, even if they had been negligent initially, the force of their negligence was spent, because of the subsequent conduct of the third defendant in leaving unguarded the injured animal which was a hazard to other traffic. Judge McMahon's analysis of this defence, of *novus actus interveniens*, merits extensive quotation since it represents the first detailed discussion of its nature and limits. He stated:

> "The Latin phrase usually used by lawyers to describe the situation when the intervening act relieves the original actor, i.e., *novus actus interveniens,* is of course an insufficient abbreviation to indicate the legal consequences when the principle comes into play. Lawyers frequently say, in a shorthand and misleading way, that the defendant is not liable because of a *novus actus interveniens*, as if any intervening act will have this disruptive effect. Nothing could be further from the truth. It is only some intervening acts that possess this disruptive quality. In so far as the three Latin words *novus actus interveniens* are intended to describe the circumstances when it will provide the original wrongdoer with a full defence, it should more meaningfully translate as an *intervening act which is of such a kind that it attracts sole liability for the plaintiff's injury or is of such a kind that it becomes the sole legal cause of the plaintiff's injuries.*
>
> In these circumstances we should first ask what is the general nature

of the intervening act if it is to have this effect in these types of cases.

It can be said with some confidence that if the intervening act is predictable and inevitable, the original actor cannot shrug off responsibility since he practically programmed the intervention.... In this case it can be truly said that the third party's act is not voluntary or independent. Similarly, if the original actor intended the intervention he will be responsible. [citing *O'Rourke v. An Post*, Circuit Court, Dublin, July 19, 2000; discussed above, 579]. At the other end of the scale, however, it is equally clear that, if he could not reasonably foresee any intervening act, after his initial action, then he will not be responsible for the unpredictable intervention.... In between these two extremes, the courts have been less sure-footed in defining when the intervening act will in effect hijack the causal element and erase the significance of the original wrong. The courts will prefer to determine each case on its own facts. In examining the circumstances where the intervening act will have the effect of relieving the original perpetrator, two facts feature in the judge's approach: first whether, and to what extent the intervening act was foreseeable by the original actor, and second, how does one characterise the attitude of the subsequent intervener – was he careless, negligent, grossly negligent, reckless or, did he intend to do damage? .... If the intention of the intervener can be properly characterised as being criminal or subjectively reckless, then it is likely (though not inevitable) that it would have the effect of breaking the chain that leads back to the initial wrongdoer.... Where the conduct of the intervener does not invite such opprobrium, however, the courts are not inclined to exonerate the first act of all causative relevance..... A third factor should also be noted: the greater the delay there is between the original conduct and the intervening act, the more likely is the latter to be considered as the sole operative cause.... If, on the other hand, the intervening act is close in time to the original act the courts are more likely to say that the original conduct still possesses a causative relevance. The temporal proximity of the two acts to each other, therefore, is frequently relevant, although in truth it is only one of several factors which the courts will consider in coming to a conclusion."

The instant case was 'not particularly difficult to resolve' since it was clear that the original wrongdoers could reasonably foresee the kind of intervention that occurred; moreover, the intervener's act was not unreasonable in the circumstances.

Judge McMahon considered that, in the instant case, the liability of the first and second defendants was so clear that it could be rationalised in terms of their duty of care, remoteness or principles. He observed that "in a different and more difficult pattern one might have to embark on a deeper analysis of the degree of foreseeability required, the nature and quality of the intervening act, and even then it might not be possible to avoid resort to policy considerations in coming to a just decision but not here."

In analysing the matter Judge McMahon thought that it 'must be relevant to acknowledge that the predicament in which [the third defendant] found himself was caused by the very people who now want to place the liability on him.' The first and second defendants must have foreseen that if their cow escaped onto the road it was likely to cause an accident and that more than one vehicle might eventually become involved. Accordingly, Judge McMahon held that they were responsible to the plaintiff's loss.

Consecutive injuries   In *In re the Hepatitis Compensation Tribunal Act 1997; R.L. v. The Minister for Health and Children*, [2001] 1 I.R. 744, O'Neill J. grappled impressively with the complex conundrum of consecutive injuries. This is a subject which has not previously come before an Irish court. In England, it has occasioned much controversy, with two attempts by the House of Lords to resolve the difficulties having left the present law in a state of considerable confusion.

In *R.L* the applicant had been infected with the Hepatitis C virus. This made him so lacking in energy that his employment prospects in the catering industry were damaged. He was later involved in a traffic accident which resulted in the amputation of his right knee. A question arose as to the impact of this new element in the compensation of his damages for loss of earnings.

It may be useful first to refer to the English cases, since they reveal, if not resolve, the difficult issues of principle and policy.

In *Baker v. Willoughby* [1970] A.C. 467, the plaintiff's leg had been negligently injured by the defendants. Before his action against them had reached the doors of the court, the plaintiff suffered the further misfortune of being the victim of burglary, in which the burglars shot his injured leg, resulting in its amputation. A question naturally arose as to how the damages in relation to his leg should be calculated.

The defendant argued that his liability was limited to the time of the amputation. The Court of Appeal agreed but the House of Lords reversed. Their Lordships were concerned lest a lacuna in compensation should be created since the robbers, if sued, would have been liable only for having deprived the plaintiff of a leg that had already been damaged. They did not accept that the robbers should be responsible, in addition, for having deprived the plaintiff of the element of his claim against the defendant that consisted of the difference between a sound leg and a damaged one from the time of the robbery. They considered that the proper way of looking at the situation was that the plaintiff had suffered a loss of amenity in the original accident and that this loss was unaffected by the amputation of his leg resulting from the robbery. Lord Reid observed that a plaintiff:

"is not compensated for the physical injury: he is compensated for the loss which he suffers as a result of the injury. His loss is not in having a stiff leg; it is his inability to lead a full life, his inability to enjoy those amenities which depend on freedom of movement and his inability to earn as much as he used to earn or could have earned if there had been no accident. In this case the second injury did not diminish any of these. So why should it be regarded as having obliterated or superseded them?"

In the later decision of *Jobling v. Associated Dairies Ltd* [1982] A.C. 794, a somewhat different factual scenario led to a situation not dissimilar to that in *Baker v. Willoughby*. The defendant's negligence caused the plaintiff to suffer a back injury with a continuing disability. Some years later he developed a physical condition of myelopathy, unconnected with the accident, which would also have had the effect of rendering him totally disabled had he not been already. Their Lordships showed no enthusiasm for making this defendant compensate the plaintiff for his entire loss.

Beyond this, it is hard to find unanimity to viewpoint among the several speeches. O'Neill J. in *R.L.* observed that in *Jobling*:

"the speeches of their Lordships explore the various principles and indeed policies which have a bearing on whether or not a supervening event is to be disregarded or not. It can fairly be said that the outcome generally of their extensive consideration of the subject is defeat in the sense that they were unable individually or collectively to convincedly adopt a principle or a set principles to apply both in circumstance of the supervening event being tortious and non-tortious."

He referred to Lord Wilberforce's pragmatic approach which disdains any attempt at conceptual coherence:

"Without any satisfaction I draw from this the conclusion that no general logical universally fair rules can be stated which will cover in a manner consistent with justice cases of supervening events whether due to tortious, partially tortious, non culpable or wholly accidental events. A court can only deal with each case as best they can in a manner so as to provide just and sufficient but not excessive compensation taking all factors into account."

Crucial to their Lordship's analysis in *Jobling* was what came to be described as the 'vicissitudes principle', summarised by Lord Russell of Killowen as follows:

"[I]t is well established that in assessing compensation for damage caused to a plaintiff by a tortfeasor among other considerations is the consequent loss or reduction in earning capacity in the working life of the plaintiff. It is also well established that it is appropriate in arriving at an estimated figure under that head that some allowance or discount should be made for the ordinary vicissitudes of life. It is also well established that if by the time of trial facts emerge which make known a vicissitude of life as applicable to the plaintiff, that knowledge should replace that which would have been only an estimate: where there is knowledge estimation has no part..."

O'Neill J. considered it necessary to set out well settled principles generally governing the assessment of damages:

"The object of every award of damages is to put the party wronged as far as possible in the same position, no better or worse, as he would be in, if he had not suffered the wrong in respect of which he claims.

The defendant must compensate for the loss caused by his wrongful act and no more.

The defendant must take the plaintiff as he finds him.

The court must not speculate or estimate when it has knowledge of the facts and must have regard to relevant events which have occurred before the trial."

The problem with causation as a general governing principle, and in particular the necessary finding that the original tort and supervening event became concurrent causes of the damage, was that this would apply with equal force whether the supervening event was either a tortious act or a non-tortious event such as the occurrence of natural disease. The application of this principle to the facts in *Jobling* would have involved bring the court into conflict with the well settled principle that the occurrence of natural illness was one of the vicissitudes of life to which a court must have regard in the assessment of future damages. For that reason their Lordships in *Jobling* had rejected causation as a general principle governing the treatment of all supervening events. O'Neill J. agreed . Such an approach 'would clearly be in conflict with the judgments of the Supreme Court in *Reddy v. Bates* [1984] I.L.R.M. 197.' Thus any approach to this problem which had the effect of excluding the occurrence of natural illness from the assessment of future damage 'would be wrong and in principle unworkable.'

It had long been part of the common law that a court when assessing damages for loss of income into the future should have regard to the vicissitudes would could in the normal course of life befall people, resulting in a diminution in their earning capacity or the duration of their working life. This principle found expression in the judgments of the Supreme Court in *Reddy v. Bates* [1984] I.L.R.M. 197, where Griffin J. listed the matters to which regard must be had as 'unemployment, redundancy, illness, accident and the life'.

O'Neill J. analysed the issue as follows:

"Logically it would seem hard to argue against the inclusion of tortiously caused accidents. Events of that kind are undoubtedly part of the 'slings and arrows of outrageous fortune' and thus, why in principle should they be excluded? The argument against including tortious accidents seems to be one of a practicable nature rather than a principled one....

[I]f the respondents in this case are permitted to say that the road traffic accident was one of the vicissitudes of life the consequence of which was that regardless of the occurrence of hepatitis C, the plaintiff's participation in the catering industry would have ended, in any event, then the applicant in this case would find himself in the situation of being unable to claim any damages in respect of his loss of income from the time of the road traffic accident onwards. To many that would seem an unacceptable and indeed unjust result. Why, it may be asked, should the original wrongdoers ... be relieved of a liability which they undoubtedly had, because of the infliction on the unfortunate applicant of a second tort by another party? Should the clean and clinical lines of logic be permitted to run that far?

In my opinion, to permit principle to go that far is to allow it run into the realm of caprice. There is no good reason when the respondent in this case or in similar cases should have this relief from liability arising directly out of a second misfortune tortiously visited on the applicant. Instead it should be said that, as a matter of policy, tortious events should not be considered to be amongst the 'vicissitudes of life', which a court should have regard to in the assessment of future loss.

Where a claimant has suffered injuries from two or more successive and independent tortious acts, policy should lean against the application of any rule or principle which would have the effect of preventing a claimant from being fully compensated for the aggregate effects of all his injuries. Hence the necessity in my view to remove subsequent tortious acts from the list of life's vicissitudes."

Thus, if the supervening event was a tortious act, the critical consideration became one of causation of the specific items of damage. In the instant case, the plaintiff's loss of income as a result of exclusion from the catering industry after the road accident could be wholly attributable either to the accident or to the respondents' conduct. In O'Neill J.'s opinion, it was appropriate to invoke section 11(1) and (2) of the Civil Liability Act which provides as follows:

"For the purposes of this part, two or more persons are concurrent wrong-doers when both or all are wrong-doers and are responsible to a third person (in this part called the injured person or the plaintiff) for the same damage, whether or not judgment has been recovered against some or all of them.

With prejudice to the generality of subsection (1) of this section –

persons may become concurrent wrongdoers as a result of the vicarious liability of one for another, breach of a joint duty, conspiracy, concerted action to a common end or independent act causing the same damage; ...

The wrong on the part of one or both may be a tort, breach of contract or breach of trust, or any combination of them;

It is immaterial whether the acts constituting concurrent wrongs are contemporaneous or successive."

The respondent and the driver of the motor vehicle which struck the plaintiff were 'wrongdoers' within the meaning of the Act (assuming there was some degree of fault on the driver's part). The wrongs in both instances could be regarded as independent acts causing the same damage and both wrongs might be regarded as torts. The Act made it clear that it was immaterial that they occurred successively rather than contemporaneously.

Either the respondents or the driver could invoke the provisions of the Act in order to seek contribution from each other in respect of the plaintiff's loss of earnings, but each of them was liable to the applicant for the entire amount of this loss. It was open to a respondent to contend that a supervening event was not tortious at all; if that defence succeeded, the supervening event 'would have to be regarded as non-tortious accident or one of the vicissitudes of life with all the consequences which flow from that, including the removal of that event from the scope of section 11 of the Civil Liability Act, which proceeds on the basis that those responsible for both events are "wrong-doers".'

As a consequence of this the applicant was entitled in the instant proceedings to recover the full amount of his loss in respect of his exclusion from the catering industry after the road traffic accident from the respondents.

O'Neill J.'s interesting holding gives rise to a couple of observations. The first is that it offers a very satisfactory and fair solution to the problem of successive causes where both causes are tortious in character. The plaintiff has the practical protection of being able to recover damages of the solvent defendant where the other (as would have been the case in *Baker v. Willoughby*) is insolvent. A second point worth noting is that the principle of concurrent fault can apply only in respect of the *same injury*. This can result in difficulties of computation – not in theory but in practice. If the plaintiff receives an injury in 2002 caused by wrongdoer A and in 2005 is the victim of a tort which constitutes a concurrent cause of his or her injury thereafter, section 11 of the 1961 Act can apply only in respect of injury occurring from the time of the second tort. Thus, A will, as a wrongdoer in his or her own right, will have to compensate the plaintiff for the loss between 2002 and 2005.

Problems of scientific proof   If the success or failure of a plaintiff's claim depends on the resolution by the court of a scientific or medical theory disputed by scientists or doctors what is the court to do? Is it required to adjudicate on the merits of the theory? In *Best v. Wellcome Foundation Ltd* [1992] I.L.R.M. 609, Finlay C.J. thought not. He was:

> "satisfied that it is not possible either for a judge of trial or for an appellate court to take upon itself the role of a determining, scientific authority resolving disputes between distinguished scientists in any particular line of technical expertise. The function which a court can and must perform in the trial of a case, in order to achieve a just result, is to apply common sense and a careful understanding of the logic and likelihood of events to conflicting opinions and conflicting theories concerning a matter of this kind."

This approach is frankly unconvincing. In achieving 'a just result' the trial judge has to resolve all relevant factual issues in the case rather than sidestep them or deny that he or she is resolving them. Of course the court is not itself a scientific authority and its adjudication may be unlikely to have any influence within the scientific community but it is nonetheless required, to the best of its ability, to determine, one way or the other, an issue on which scientific opinion is divided.

This problem arose in *Curran v. Finn*, High Court, January 29, 2001 where O'Neill J. had the courage to confront, and resolve, a difficult contested issue relating to medical theory. In 1993, the plaintiff, who suffered from multiple sclerosis, was involved in a fall in the defendant's shop caused by the defendant's negligence. She claimed that the fall aggravated her condition, and that surgery to relieve cord compression caused by her prolapsed thoracic disc, carried out in 1994, had further aggravated that condition.

The main dispute was between expert witnesses on whether trauma to the central nervous system could aggravate multiple sclerosis; if so, whether it had done this in the instant case; and whether the surgery had aggravated her condition. The experts when giving evidence referred to the literature on the subject; O'Neill J.'s judgment discusses the evidence and the literature in some detail. O'Neill J. concluded his analysis of the first, and crucial, issue as follows:

> "Clearly the ultimate scientific resolution of this controversy is not something with which this court need concern itself. However, the great weight of the expert evidence I heard was in favour of the proposition that trauma to the central nervous system can cause an aggravation of MS through the mechanism of a breach of the BBB. It is of course very unsatisfactory that there are not clear answers as to what is the entire causative pathway leading up to a breach of the Blood Brain Barrier and beyond. However, the opinion in favour of the proposition that trauma to the CNS can aggravate MS is long standing amongst neurologists and was shared by all but one of the experts who gave evidence before me.

> I am therefore inclined to prefer the view that as a matter of
> probability this theory is more likely to be correct."

On the question whether surgery could exacerbate the condition of those with
multiple sclerosis, O'Neill J. again came to an unambiguous conclusion that,
as a general proposition, it was 'likely or probable that surgery on the central
nervous system in patients who already have MS carries with it the substantial
risk of making the MS worse'. As to whether the surgery had had this effect in
the instant case, the evidence was conflicting. O'Neill J. acknowledged that
the interpretation of MRI scans clearly required great expertise and that the
discipline of neuro-radiology in this regard was 'a remote and incomprehensible
landscape to the lay person'. In resolving which view of the scan was more
probably correct, one had 'to rely solely on the impressions created by the
various experts'. He referred to the evidence given by these experts and noted
that, notwithstanding his repeated questioning of one of them as to whether it
was part of the discipline of neuro-radiology to attempt to distinguish between
oedema and MS plaques, he had 'failed to get a satisfactory answer'. On
balance, he concluded that the MRI scan demonstrated oedema at the site of
the thoracic disc at D6/7. It necessarily followed that there must have been
compression of sufficient degree to cause oedema which in turn meant that
there had been a breach of the Blood Brain Barrier adjacent to the thoracic
disc D6/7.

On the question whether the acceleration of the plaintiff's multiple sclerosis
should be attributable to the fall, O'Neill stated:

> "There is undoubtedly a very strong temporal connection between the
> fall and the rapid development of MS symptoms thereafter throughout
> the rest of 1993. In the light of the breach of the BBB caused by the fall
> there is a plausible biological explanation of a connection between the
> fall and the plaintiff's very rapid decline. The question that arises is
> whether this rapid decline from March 1993 onwards is to be regarded
> as the coincidental natural progress of the disease, and unconnected to
> the fall.
>
> In the light of the effect of the thoracic disc in generating oedema
> associated with some degree of compression and the undoubted
> consequent breach of the BBB, and the onset or re-onset of a set of
> symptoms that rapidly progressed, it would seem to me that this
> coincidence is an unconvincing explanation.
>
> I have therefore come to the conclusion that as a matter of probability
> the fall resulting in the prolapsed thoracic disc did cause aggravation
> of the plaintiff's MS."

The next question related to the effect of the surgery on the plaintiff's condition.
O'Neill J. reviewed the evidence on this issue and stated:

"In the light of the very rapid development of very significant neurological symptoms so soon after her surgery, almost in a cascade, and having regard to the evidence I heard about the contra indication of surgery for patients with active MS, I am driven to the conclusion that it is probable that the symptoms of MS which the plaintiff undoubtedly developed in the aftermath of her surgery was an exacerbation of MS brought on by the surgery.

There is little doubt but that the decision to carry out the surgery notwithstanding the above contra indication was a reasonable one. At the time that that decision was made it was not clear whether it was the thoracic disc or the MS was causing the plaintiff's lower body symptoms. While the surgery carried with it the risk of making the MS worse, nevertheless the prospect of curing the plaintiff's near paraplegia at that point, by relieving the compression, was a real one and justified the surgery. It became clear, after the surgery that the real problem was the MS rather than the thoracic disc.

However, given that the decision to carry out the surgery was at the time that it was made, a reasonable and prudent one, the consequences of that surgery are inexorably connected back to the fall."

The final, and 'perhaps most difficult' question concerned the extent to which the fall and the surgery had exacerbated the plaintiff's condition. Some of the experts were reluctant to speculate on the time scale of the deterioration of the plaintiff's condition had these events not occurred. O'Neill J. concluded that the plaintiff would still have been walking at the time of trial, with the aid of a stick, that her bowel and bladder problems would have been much less severe but that she would have been likely to lose the ability to walk after a period of eight years from the onset of symptoms, 'so that she would have arrived at the stage she is now at, within ten years of first onset of symptoms'.

O'Neill J. calculated the damages on the basis of those projections. He awarded £200,000 by way of general damages 'for all of the disabilities and pain and discomfort and compromise of her independence that she has had to endure for the period in question, together with the shortening of her life expectancy'.

REMOTENESS OF DAMAGE

Contributory negligence   In *McEneaney v. Monaghan County Council*, High Court, July 26, 2001, O'Sullivan J. addressed the issue of remoteness of damage in the context of contributory negligence. It is well established in Irish law that a negligent defendant will have to compensate a plaintiff if the damage that occurred was of a type that was reasonably foreseeable: *Burke v. John Paul & Co ltd* [1967] I.R. 277, *Reeves v. Carthy* [1984] I.R. 348, McMahon &

Binchy, *op cit*, paras 3.20ff. In *McEneaney*, the plaintiff had been injured in a traffic accident caused by the first defendant's negligence. He had been travelling at an excessive speed. O'Sullivan J. referred to the principle stated above and commented:

> "If this applies in relation to allegations by a plaintiff against a defendant I cannot see why it does not apply the other way round. If I am correct in identifying an enhanced risk of serious consequences should an unforeseen accident occur as a *type* of damage for which an excessively speeding plaintiff must accept responsibility then the *extent* of that damage (namely the actual injuries suffered) must also be part of his responsibility. This is because his injury is of such a kind as the reasonable man should have foreseen, to use the test adopted by the Supreme Court in *Burke v. John Paul Co Ltd* [1967] I.R. 277 from *The Wagon Mound (No. 1)* [1961] A.C. 388."

Accordingly O'Sullivan J. reduced the plaintiff's damages by a third to take account of his contributory negligence in driving too fast.

This appears to be the first Irish decision in which the scope of foreseeability has been closely examined in the context of contributory negligence rather than negligence since the enactment of the Civil Liability Act 1961, section 34(2)(c) of which provides that:

> "[t]he plaintiff's failure to exercise reasonable care for his own protection shall not amount to contributory negligence in respect of the damage unless that damage results from the particular risk to which his conduct has exposed him..."

In the Supreme Court decision of *Moore v. Nolan* (1960) 94 I.L.T.R. 153, at 161, Kingsmill Moore J. gave an elaborate and convincing analysis of the relationship between the plaintiff's contributory negligence and the damage which he or she sustained. He articulated the principle which is now contained in section 34(2)(c). Of relevance to *McEneaney*, he went on to state:

> "I have said that to establish contributory negligence the plaintiff must be shown to have been guilty of a failure to take proper precautions for his own safety against the particular danger which eventuated. This statement perhaps requires elaboration. It does not mean that the particular form in which the danger manifested itself should actually have occurred to his mind. It is sufficient if it is a danger of a particular class whose occurrence he should anticipate and take reasonable precautions to guard against. Persons crossing a street must anticipate that the street may be used by any form of traffic which is legitimately entitled to be transversing it and danger from such traffic, whatever its

nature, is to be guarded against. No doubt a pedestrian ordinarily thinks in terms of motorcars, horse traffic, bicycles and other pedestrians. But if he were to run under the legs of an elephant belonging to a travelling circus which was being taken along the road he could not justify his failure to look out on the ground that a pedestrian is not expected to think in terms of elephants. An elephant is in the class of legitimate road users. On the other hand he would not be expected to look out for a helicopter making a forced descent. Whether he is bound to anticipate and take steps against the danger which eventuates on the ground that, though unusual, it is a danger of that particular class which he is bound to anticipate and guard against must usually be a question for the jury. It seems to me that the jury were entitled to say, and have said, that the danger of being hit by traffic disregarding the lights was not a danger of this class."

It is worth recalling that Kingsmill Moore J. was speaking at a time before the Privy Council, in *The Wagon Mound (No. 1)* [1961] A.C. 425 had rejected *Re Polemis and Furness Withy & Co Ltd* [1921] 3 K.B. 560 in favour of making liability in negligence depend on reasonable foreseeability. Kingsmill Moore J. was, moreover, prophetic in anticipating the analysis of the House of Lords in *Hughes v. Lord Advocate* [1963] A.C. 837 and of the Supreme Court itself in *Burke v. John Paul & Co Ltd* [1967] I.R. 277.

The same approach has found favour in Queensland: see *Hanly v. Berlin* [1975] Qd. R. 52, Trindade & Cane, *The Law of Torts in Australia* (3rd ed., Oxford University Press, Melbourne, 1999), 564, fn 11, Fleming, *The Law of Torts* (9th ed., Law Book Company, Sydney, 1998), 314–5. In the United States of America, there is some support for taking a more restrictive interpretation of what constitutes a kind of foreseeable damage in the case of contributory negligence than in that of negligence. Fleming, *op. cit.*, 315, fn 88, does not agree with this approach, going so far as to state:

"Although the effect of taking a more expansive view of a plaintiff's as opposed to a defendant's negligence is to limit recovery, this is no longer too punitive since apportionment."

It is true that American jurisdictions were far slower than in England or Ireland to move to apportionment regimes; nevertheless, even with the principles of the Civil Liability Act 1961 governing our law, an argument can be made against an overbroad application of the 'kind of injury' test when dealing with contributory negligence. There is little doubt that this formula was introduced in *Hughes* to temper the full pro-defendant effects of *The Wagon Mound (No. 1)*. It gives courts a flexibility to impose liability even where the accident or the injuries caused by it were not easy to characterise as foreseeable. Too stringent a foreseeability test might be considered to yield hardship on injured persons. This concern does not weigh so heavily when one is dealing with contributory negligence. Indeed, if an expansive application of the 'kind of injury' test were adopted, it could cause significant injustice, mitigated, but not removed, by the fact of apportionment.

The 'egg shell skull' principle   In *Mackey v. Iarnrod Irish/Irish Rail*, High Court, May 31, 2001, the working conditions to which the plaintiff employee was exposed by his employer exacerbated his pre-existent condition of asthma. The employer was found to have been negligent: see above, 582. Kinlen J. noted that, '[w]hile the doctors differ in language as to whether or not his asthma was caused by this exposure [to diesel fumes], it was clear that they all accept it was exacerbated …significantly.' Kinlen J. went on to observe that the plaintiff:

> "had an alcohol problem but apparently has it under control. He also smokes. Evidence is a little confused as to how much he smoked at the relevant time. He has given up the cigarettes on a number of occasions. Tobacco would certainly be a contributory cause for exacerbating asthma but since on the evidence (it is a matter of probability) his intake of tobacco was relatively small[,t]he overwhelming blame must be put on the occupational troubles and in the locomotive shed. The court has no evidence as to what proportion of the plaintiff's present disability would have occurred anyway because of his weak chest. In the absence of any evidence the court would assess it on the basis of a 50/50."

Accordingly Kinlen J. awarded the plaintiff only half the quantum of damages he sustained, both for loss of earnings and pain and suffering.

Kinlen J. made no reference to the issue of remoteness of damage and specifically the 'egg shell skull' principle. Under that principle, if a plaintiff sustains an exacerbated injury by reason of a particular pre-existent physical (or psychiatric) condition, the defendant will not be heard to complain that he or she should not have to compensate the plaintiff for this exacerbated injury on the basis of lack of reasonable foreseeability. Equally it is true that, where a plaintiff suffers from the foreseeable exacerbation of a pre-existent condition, the defendant should have to compensate him or her only for the exacerbatory component of the injury. Furthermore, if an injury is attributable to the defendant's negligence and the plaintiff's contributory negligence (by smoking, for example), the court should seek to assess their respective degrees of fault and make a proportionate reduction in the award. A careless failure to mitigate damage is characterised by section 34(2)(b) of the Civil Liability Act 1961 as contributory negligence to the extent that the damage is exacerbated. See McMahon & Binchy, *op. cit.*, paras. 20.24–20.33.

The Irish courts proceed on the express basis that fault 'is equated to blameworthiness and not to the potency of the causative facts moving from each side': *Kelly v. Jameson* Supreme Court, 1 March 1972, *per* Walsh J; see also *O'Sullivan v. Dwyer* [1971] I.R. 275. *Carroll v. Clare County Council* [1975] I.R. 275, *Carroll v. Clare County Council* [1975] I.R. 221. Nevertheless it is clear that in some cases it is necessary to make a causal severance. For example, it would seem wrong to make a proportionate reduction from the *total* award to take account of the plaintiff's failure to use a seat belt in a case where some of the plaintiff's injuries were not attributable in any way to that failure. Finnegan J. appreciated this in *Cassidy v. Clarke*, Doyle's *Personal Injury Judgements: Trinity & Michaelmas1999*, p. 183 (High Court, 1999): see McMahon & Binchy, *op. cit.*, 570, fn 93.

At all events, in *Mackey* Kinlen J. appears to have proceeded on the basis that, because it was not possible to identify what proportion of the plaintiff's disability would have occurred in any event because of his weak heart, a reduction of 50% was appropriate.

CONTRIBUTORY NEGLIGENCE

Failure to use seat belt   In *McEneaney v. Monaghan County Council*, High Court, July 26, 2001, O'Sullivan J. addressed the issue of how the defence of contributory negligence operates in relation to the failure by a plaintiff, injured in a traffic accident, to have used a seatbelt. That such a failure should be characterised in normal circumstances as contributory negligence is now beyond argument. What is less clear is the extent to which evidence as to a causal connection between this failure and the injuries actually sustained by the plaintiff should be investigated by the court.

In *Hamill v. Oliver* [1977] I.R. 73, the Supreme Court took the view that 'in most cases' no special evidence was required to prove that the wearing of the seat belt would have prevented or reduced the injuries the plaintiff actually sustained. This indulgent approach contrasts with the position in many other common law jurisdictions, which treat the causation issue as an important element of the defendant's case in favour of a reduction for contributory negligence. It should not be sufficient for the defendant to show that the plaintiff was careless in not wearing a seatbelt, any more than it is enough for a plaintiff who claims compensation for injury caused by the defendant's negligent driving to show merely that the defendant drove carelessly. Proof of a causal connection between the contributory negligence, or negligence, and the injury is a vital ingredient which cannot be presumed 'in most cases' unless there is an empirical basis for such presumption.

In *Sinnott v. Quinnsworth* [1984] I.L.R.M. 523, the majority of the Supreme Court also evinced a certain robustness as to the requirement of proof of a causal connection. It accepted as sufficient proof in the case evidence that, had the plaintiff been wearing a seat belt, the chances of his sustaining the injury which he suffered would have been reduced by about 25%. In *Conley v.*

Strain [1988] I.R. 628, Lynch held that a causal connection had been established on the basis of evidence by the plaintiff's surgeon that a person thrown out of a motor vehicle was thirty times more likely to suffer injuries than one who remained in the crashed vehicle, coupled with evidence that the plaintiff had been lying under his car after the accident.

In *McEneaney*, the plaintiff had been travelling at an excessive speed and had not used a seat belt. O'Sullivan J, after a review of earlier case-law, concluded:

> "firstly, that the prerequisite causation required by section 34(1) of the Civil Liability Act 1961 can be established, *inter alia*, by statistical proof of enhanced risk, and secondly, that in regard to causation no special evidence is required in an obvious case.
>
> To put the foregoing in another way, the law regards the accident in this context as sufficiently proximate to the injuries as to be capable of being, with little proof or persuasion, the *causa causans* thereof rather than merely the *causa sine qua non*.
>
> ..... [I]t seems to me that a driver of a car at 10 miles per hour in excess of the maximum national speed limit without appropriate excuse is guilty of a want of care for his own safety in that he thereby incurs an enhanced risk that the consequences of any unforeseeable accident will be worse by reason of this excess speed. Notwithstanding the absence of evidence comparable to the statistical evidence given to the Court in *Quinnsworth* and *Conley* it seems to me within the competence of a court to assign fault as between the plaintiff and the defendant in the circumstances of this case."

O'Sullivan J. held that the plaintiff's excessive speed constituted contributory negligence requiring a 33.3% reduction of the damages awarded to him but that his failure to use a seat belt should not reduce his damages further as expert evidence had been given that, as a matter of probability, the plaintiff had 'shot clean out of the back of his seat causing it to be flattened and through the rear windows and that a seat belt, if worn, would not have prevented that happening'. O'Sullivan J. observed:

> "In the absence of any other evidence on this topic, I cannot speculate and I hold that the first defendant has not discharged the onus on it to establish that the plaintiff contributed to his injury by not wearing a seat belt ...
>
> It was not suggested to [the medical witnesses] that the wearing of a seat belt would have affected the plaintiff's injury. In these circumstances there is no evidence before me which suggests that conclusion and accordingly I hold that the plaintiff was not guilty of contributory negligence on this count.

> It may be worth noting here that the difference in the context of the contributory negligence allegation in this case between the speed and safety-belt issues is that there was no evidence to rebut the inference that the plaintiff's excessive speed contributed to his injuries whereas there was evidence to rebut the inference that seat-belt could have reduced them."

This holding appears to place at least an evidential burden on the plaintiff to rebut an inference of causal connection. Perhaps it can best be understood in the context of the circumstances of the particular case. Although no doubt the facts of many accidents may be such as to support the Supreme Court's view that 'in most cases' proof of causal connection between the failure to use the seat belt and the injuries sustained will not be necessary, it would not seem desirable to translate this robust statement into a rebuttable presumption.

Occupiers' liability In *Sheehy v. The Devil's Glen Tours Equestrian Centre Ltd.*, High Court, December 10, 2001, Lavan J. acquitted of contributory negligence a woman who tripped on a door saddle, the metal top of which was about two inches above ground level. He invoked a spate of decisions relating to statutory duties owed to employees which stressed that a momentary act of inadvertence should not be regarded as contributory negligence. It is, of course, very important that the paternalistic values underlying regulation protecting employees should not be subverted by too easy a resort to the contributory negligence doctrine. Whether the translation of occupiers' liability from common law into statute should have the effect of constricting the scope of the contributory negligence defence may be debated.

Employers' liability In the section on employers' liability, earlier in this Chapter, above, 577, we analyse Kinlen J.'s decision in *Mackey v. Iarnród Éireann/Irish Rail*, High Court, May 31, 2001, holding that the plaintiff employee had not been guilty of contributory negligence in continuing to work in conditions that were dangerous to health.

LIABILITY FOR ANIMALS

In *Murray v. Millar*, Circuit Court, Roscommon, November 14, 2001, Judge McMahon imposed liability on the owners of a cow, which jumped out in front of the plaintiff's car as he was driving down a country road. He held that the *res ipsa loquitur* principle applied: see the *res ipsa loquitur* section of this chapter, above, 599.

INDUCING BREACH OF CONTRACT

In *Meridian Communications Ltd v. Eircell Ltd*, High Court, April 5, 2001, a claim of inducement to breach a contract failed. The defendant had sent a letter to its subscribers who wished to transfer to the plaintiff company. It was drafted as follows:

"Dear Customer,

Eircell has today received a request to transfer your mobile telephone service to Meridian Communications Limited.

Eircell shall of course process the transfer in accordance with this instruction. However, if you have not already committed yourself to a rental agreement with Meridian, we believe you should first be aware of the following. Meridian is in a position to offer you its service by virtue of a Volume Discount Agreement which it has with Eircell. This agreement is due to expire at the end of this year and will not be renewed. Consequently,

Meridian may not be able to continue providing its service to you on the terms and conditions which it may now be offering;

When you transfer your mobile phone service from Eircell to Meridian your mobile number is also transferred to Meridian. You may not be able to regain this number in the future;

If you have signed an agreement with Eircell in the last 12 months you should be aware that by terminating that agreement you will render yourself liable to a termination charge in accordance with the terms of the agreement.

Of course, if you have already contractually committed yourself to a rental agreement with Meridian, you are obliged to comply with the terms thereof and Eircell does not in any way invite you to do otherwise.

However, if you have not already entered into a rental agreement with Meridian and, having considered the above, you wish to continue your mobile service with Eircell, please complete the form below and fax it back to us ...

In the event that we do not receive the form below within 24 hours of our sending this letter to you we will proceed with the transfer of service ..."

O'Higgins J. held that the defendant had not induced breaches of contract by the subscribers, since the contents of the letter were true, accurate and they did not, in his view, go beyond 'what could be considered – at the very most – advice'. This view was fortified by the specific injunction in the body of the letter that, if the subscriber had already contractually committed himself or herself to a rental agreement with Meridian, the subscriber was obliged to comply with its terms and Eircell did not in any way invite him or her to do otherwise. O'Higgins J. observed:

> "The person to whom the letter is addressed is being told that he is obliged to honour his contractual commitment. That paragraph, in my view, constitutes an insurmountable barrier to the plaintiffs in their attempt to demonstrate that the letter constitutes an inducement to bring about a result directly opposite to the injunction addressed to the readers of that paragraph. The words of Decius Brutus in Act 2 Scene 1 of Shakespeare's *Julius Ceasar* are apposite. 'But when I tell him he hates flatterers, he says he does, being then most flattered'. I am not satisfied therefore that the process letter was an inducement to breach of contract.
>
> Even if the letter amounted to an inducement, it was not an inducement to *break* an contract but rather one to *terminate* it. The evidence established that there was no requirement for service of notice of termination as this had been waived in the industry."

O'Higgins J. also held that a conversation between a senior employee of an enterprise owned by the defendant and one of its employees who had been offered employment by the plaintiff, in which the senior employee had said that the plaintiff was 'a dodgy company' which would not be around in six months' time, did not constitute the tort of inducing a breach of contract as the employee had in fact taken up employment with the plaintiff. Moreover the statement had not been made with malice, the conversation had been solicited by this employee and had not been made in the course of the senior employer's employment.

O'Higgins J.'s holdings on all the key issues relating to the tort of inducing a breach of contract are clear and convincing. There have been many cases where the distinction between advice and inducement was far harder to draw on the facts: cf. McMahon & Binchy, *op. cit.*, paras 32.15-32.19.

In *Irish Sugar Ltd v. Parlon*, High Court, November 29, 2001, O'Donovan J. granted an interlocutory injunction against several defendants, including the Irish Farmers Association, in respect of alleged wrongdoing, including inducing breaches of contract between the plaintiff company and growers for the supply by them of sugar beet to the plaintiff. On the basis of the affidavit evidence, O'Donovan J. was persuaded, in accordance with the *Campus Oil* principles, that the plaintiff had established that there was a fair question to be decided at the trial of the action. He observed:

> "While the defendants protest that the alleged conduct on [their] part either did not happen at all, or cannot be given the sinister interpretation suggested by the plaintiff, I am left in no doubt but that, if the dispute is resolved in favour of the plaintiff, as it could well be, it will be open to the trial judge to consider whether or not such conduct constituted

conduct which induced the breaches of contract on the part of the growers of beet to which I have referred and/or an unlawful conspiracy on the part of the defendants or, indeed, an intentional interference by the defendants with the plaintiff's economic interests. For the purposes of adjudicating upon this application, it is neither necessary, nor desirable, that I should speculate upon how the trial judge might resolve these several issues."

Regarding the balance of convenience, O'Donovan J. considered that there was a high probability, not only that irreparable harm would be caused to the plaintiff in its production operation but that its seasonal workforce of two hundred workers would be deprived of their employment.

INTENTIONAL INTERFERENCE WITH ECONOMIC INTERESTS

In *Irish Sugar Ltd v. Parlon*, High Court, November 29, 2001, just considered in relation to claims for industry breach of contract, O'Donovan J. granted an interlocutory injunction in respect of a claim for intentional interference with economic interest, as well as the claims for other torts.

TRADE DISPUTES

In *Malincross v. Building and Allied Trade Union* High Court, November 30, 2001, McCracken J. granted an interlocutory injury against the continuation of picketing of the plaintiff's premises in respect of a dispute between the picketers and an employer who had been engaged in building work on the plaintiff's premises but, pursuant to its contract with the plaintiff, had ceased to do so. The picketing had commenced when the employer had been engaged in work on the site.

The defendants did not assert statutory justification for their actions on the basis that they constituted secondary picketing, under section 11(2) of the Industrial Relations Act 1990. Rather did they say that they were picketing at 'a place where their employer works or carries on business'. This phrase, they claimed, extended to situations where the employer had worked or carried on business in the past. McCracken J. admitted that, to his mind, this was 'a very strange construction of the present tense used in the section'. He noted that counsel for the defendants had referred him to the Dáil Debates of the legislation, which disclosed that an amendment had been moved to add the words 'or, at the commencement of the dispute, had normally worked or had normally carried on business'. This amendment had been withdrawn following a statement by the Minister for Labour that the situation was already covered

by the wording used, which the Minister called 'the historic present tense.'
McCracken J. observed:

> "While I do not think that the views of the Minister in a Dáil Debate
> should determine the construction of this section, nevertheless I think I
> can have regard to it in determining whether, at the hearing of this
> action, there is a fair question to be tried, as to the construction of the
> section. However, I have no doubt that the hearing of an interlocutory
> injunction is not the time to enter into a detailed discussion on grammar.
> I am satisfied, however, that there is a fair case to be tried as to the
> construction of section 11(1)."

The defendants also contended that, even if the employer had ceased to have
any function in relation to the site, nevertheless there had been a transfer of
undertaking from the employer to the plaintiff within the meaning of the
Directive 77/187/EEC as amended by Directive 98/50/EC. McCracken J.
acknowledged that this was 'possibly an arguable point that both were
successfully pursuing the same economic activity, namely the development of
a housing estate on the site', but it was in his view 'undoubtedly a matter for
the ultimate hearing of the action.'

The defendants argued that the court could not grant an interlocutory
injunction because they had complied with the requirements of section 19(2),
which provides:

> "Where a secret ballot has been held in accordance with the rules of a
> Trade Union as provided for in Section 14, the outcome of which or, in
> the case of an aggregation of ballots, the outcome of the aggregated
> ballots, favours a strike or other industrial action and the Trade Union
> before engaging in the strike or other industrial action gives notice of
> not less than one week to the employer concerned of its intention to do
> so, a court shall not grant an injunction restraining the strike or other
> industrial action where the respondent establishes a fair case that he
> was acting in contemplation or furtherance of a trade dispute."

McCracken J. was satisfied that the Union had held a secret ballot in accordance
with its rules, that those rules were in compliance with section 14 of the Act,
and that the Union had given notice of not less than one week to the employer
of its intention to take industrial action. He added:

> "I am also satisfied that the Union has established a fair case that it
> was, and I would emphasise that the sub-section uses the past tense,
> acting in contemplation or furtherance of a trade dispute, as there was
> clearly a trade dispute in existence at the time the ballot was held."

It seems, however, that the reference to the respondent's 'acting in contemplation or furtherance of a trade dispute' does not relate (or, at all events, relate exclusively) to the time the ballot was held but encompasses the time when the strike or other industrial action occurs. The ballot paper read as follows:

> "Subject: to engage in industrial action with P.P. O'Sullivan (Leinster) Ltd, including the placing of pickets on company site at Naul Road, Balbriggan."

This clearly authorized the original picketing; the question that concerned McCracken J. was whether it authorized picketing at the site after it ceased to be the company site of the employer. McCracken J. considered that the issue was almost identical to that which had arisen in *G & T. Crampton Ltd. v. Building & Allied Trade Union* [1998] 1 I.L.R.M. 430. He observed:

> "The sufficiency of the secret ballot is clearly a condition precedent to the right of the defendants to resist an interlocutory injunction under section 19(2). While the members of the Union clearly authorized strike action at the employers' premises, and therefore direct strike action against the employer, I think there is a serious issue as to whether that in itself is sufficient to justify strike action in relation to what were once the employers' premises but no longer remain so. The purpose of the Act would appear to ensure that, if the Union is entitled to the protection of section 19(2), then it must have the clear support of its members. I think there is a serious issue to be tried, but no more, as to whether the picketing of the plaintiff's premises once the defendant (*sic*) has left those premises is authorised by the ballot, and until that question has been determined, in my view the condition precedent to section 19(2) has not been established by the defendants."

Since there was a *bona fide* dispute as to whether the preconditions of section 19(2) had been complied with, the defendants were not entitled to rely upon that provision to prevent the grant of an interlocutory injunction.

Applying the *Campus Oil* test, McCracken J. found that the balance of convenience lay in favour of granting the interlocutory injunction. The plaintiff would suffer irreparable loss if it was refused since it would be unable to complete its contracts with twenty-eight purchasers to build houses for them. The loss of profits and reputation would be serious. The defendants had 'not demonstrated in any convincing manner just how th[e] trade dispute [with the employer] could be affected by picketing the plaintiff.' For a more detailed analysis of the decision, see Hilary Delany's Equity Chapter, above, 262.

INJURIOUS FALSEHOOD

In *Meridian Communications ltd v. Eircell Ltd*, High Court, April 5, 2001, O'Higgins J. held that the defendant company, which had written a letter to subscribers containing allegations about the plaintiff company, was not guilty of injurious falsehood since these statements were true and accurate. The terms of the letter are set out above, 620. O'Higgins J. also considered that the plaintiff had failed to prove malice:

> "Put at its highest, the plaintiff's case concerning the possible loss of the telephone number to the Meridian/Cellular 3 subscriber is that it was the invariable practice of the plaintiffs to restore the telephone number to the subscriber at the end of the contract. They argue that Eircell could have verified this by a simple enquiry. So indeed they could. However negligence does not constitute malice ..."

In the instant case, the plaintiffs had failed to demonstrate that the defendant had not an ongoing belief in the truth of the statement made in the process letter.

Another allegation of injurious falsehood was made by the plaintiff. This related to a conversation between a senior employee of an enterprise owned by the defendant and another employee who had been offered employment by the plaintiff. During this conversation the senior employee had said that the plaintiff was 'a dodgy company' which would not be around in six months' time.

O'Higgins J. acknowledged that the first part of the statement was clearly false and that the second part proved to be inaccurate. There was, however, no evidence of malice. Nor had there been damage as the employee to whom the statement was made had in fact taken up employment with the plaintiff.

The plaintiff argued that proof of special damage was not necessary in view of section 20(1) of the Defamation Act 1961, which provides:

> "In an action for slander of title, slander of goods or other malicious falsehood, it shall not be necessary to allege or prove special damage–
>
> (a) if the words upon which the action is founded are calculated to cause pecuniary damage to the plaintiff and are published in writing or other permanent form; or
>
> (b) if the said words are calculated to cause pecuniary damage to the plaintiff in respect of any office, profession, calling, trade or business held or carried out by him at the time of the publication."

O'Higgins J. held that section 20 did not assist the plaintiffs. Sub-section 1(a) clearly did not apply as the words had not been published in 'permanent form'.

Nor did sub-section (1)(b), as O'Higgins J. did 'not consider that the solicited advice given by [the senior employee] .... was calculated to cause pecuniary damage to [the plaintiff] in trade or business.'

Moreover, no liability could attach to the defendant for remarks made in private conversation by its employee in response to contact from the other employee. The senior employee had not been speaking as an employee of the plaintiff, but in a private capacity.

CONSPIRACY

In *Irish Sugar Ltd v. Parlon*, High Court, November 29, 2001, O'Donovan J. granted an interlocutory injunction in respect of a claim for conspiracy as well as claims for other torts. We note the decision in the section on inducing breach of contract, earlier in this Chapter, above, 621. In *McMullen v. Kennedy*, High Court, October 18, 2001, Ó Caoimh J. struck out proceedings for conspiracy on the basis that the plaintiff was 'seeking to litigate a fresh what ha[d] been previously litigated by him....'

In *Phelan v. Goodman*, High Court, September 11, 2001, Murphy J. held that the Supreme Court decision of *O'Neill v. Ryan* [1993] I.L.R.M. 557 was not a bar to a claim for conspiracy, *inter alia*, as it did not have a derivative character. Accordingly the claim was allowed to proceed.

MISFEASANCE OF PUBLIC OFFICE

In two recent decisions, the courts have emphasized that the absence of malice is fatal to a claim for misfeasance of public office. In *Glencar Exploration plc v. Mayo County Council* [2002] 1 I.L.R.M. 481, the facts of which we consider in more detail earlier in the Chapter, in the section on the duty of care, above, 562, the Supreme Court reiterated Finlay C.J.'s approval, in *Pine Valley Developments v. Minister for the Environment* [1987] I.R. 23, of the statement of the law by Wade, *Administrative Law* (5th ed. Oxford University Press, Oxford, 1982), p. 673, as follows:

> "The present position seems to be that administrative action which is *ultra vires* but not actionable merely as a breach of duty will found in action for damages in any of the following situations:
> If it involved the commission of a recognised tort, such as trespass, false imprisonment or negligence.
> If it is actuated by malice, e.g. a personal spite or a desire to injure for improper reasons.
> If the authority knows that it does not possess the power which it purports to exercise."

In *Glencar,* where the defendant county council had introduced a ban on mining in circumstances that rendered this act *ultra vires*, Kelly J. in the High Court found that it had not acted with malice and that this defeated the claim by the plaintiff mining company for damages for misfeasance of public office. The plaintiffs did not appeal this holding.

Both Keane C.J. and Fennelly J. emphasized that judicial review was the appropriate remedy for *ultra vires* acts that do not constitute misfeasance of public office or some other recognised tort, such as breach of statutory duty or negligence. The Chief Justice observed:

> "The remedy available to persons affected by the commission of an *ultra vires* act by a public authority is an order of *certiorari* or equivalent relief setting aside the impugned decision and not an action for damages, to allow which, in the case of public officials, would be contrary to the public policy for the reasons set out [in *Pine Valley*]."

In *An Blascaod Mór Teoranta v. Commissioners for Public Works* [2001] 1 I.L.R.M. 423, Budd J. held that the Minister for the Gaeltacht should not be held liable for the tort of misfeasance of public office for having introduced legislation relating to An Blascaod Mór which violated the plaintiffs' constitutional rights. He also held that in the circumstances of the case damages for infringement of constitutional rights should not be awarded: see below, 642. A clear bar was created by the Statute of Limitations 1957 since the claim must have accrued in 1989. A more fundamental objection was that the Minister as a member of the Oireachtas was not amenable to any court or authority other than the House itself in respect of any utterance in either House:

> "The need for freedom of debate in the Oireachtas and considerations stemming from the separation of powers give the background to this immunity. Furthermore Article 15.12 of the Constitution provides that utterances made in either House wherever published should be privileged. Article 15.13 operates so as to oust the jurisdiction of the courts over the Minister in respect of such utterances so that an utterance in either House of the Oireachtas is privileged and cannot form the subject matter of any form of legal proceeding."

There was no evidence that the Bill had been 'tainted by evasion of the normal departmental channels', although the Bill had been enacted with remarkable expedition. The plaintiffs had conceded that there had been no *mala fides* on the part of the members of the Oireachtas. Moreover, the ground for the claim of negligence against the Minister had not been laid.

DEFAMATION

Damages In *Annual Review of Irish Law 2000*, 456-9, we analysed the Supreme Court decision of *O'Brien v. Mirror Group Newspapers Ltd* [2001] 1 I.R.I., in which the court reaffirmed the approach it had adopted in *De Rossa v. Independent Newspapers* [1999] 4 I.R. 6 (*Annual Review of Irish Law 1999*, 518-23), while appearing nonetheless to modify certain aspects of that approach. The issue was revisited in *Hill v. Cork Examiner Publications Ltd*, Supreme Court, November 14, 2001. In *Hill*, the plaintiff, who was a prisoner serving a sentence for occasioning actual bodily harm, had been represented as being a sexual offender by the defendant's newspaper. The jury had awarded £60,000 damages. The defendant's appeal against (*inter alia*) quantum was dismissed.

Murphy J. (Murray and McGuinness JJ. concurring) gave an analysis of the subject which merits full quotation in order to see whether it is possible to discern any subtle further shifts of emphasis from *De Rossa*:

> "As to damages: in some cases it is possible to make a reasonably accurate estimate of the damages sustained by a plaintiff as a result of the wrongdoing of a defendant. Where a plaintiff is disabled as a result of the wrongdoing with the result that it can be anticipated with reasonable confidence that he would be unable to return to work at all or at any rate to resume employment at a particular level of remuneration for a period which can be ascertained with reasonable confidence the loss so sustained can be determined on the basis of mathematical – perhaps crude mathematical – principles. On the other hand it is difficult, if not impossible, to find any nexus between the pain, embarrassment or disfigurement suffered by a plaintiff and the sum of money which would be appropriate to compensate him for any such consequences of a wrongdoing. Judges in charging juries as to their responsibilities in determining damages or in performing the same task themselves can say or do little more than recall that damages are designed to compensate for the consequences of a wrongdoing and not to punish the wrongdoer. It will always be said – perhaps unhelpfully – that the sum awarded should be reasonable to the plaintiff and also reasonable to the defendant. ...[T]he extent to which a trial judge could and should give guidance as to an appropriate measure of damages was considered by this Court in *De Rossa v. Independent Newspapers* [1999] 4 I.R. 6 and again in *O'Brien v. Mirror Group Newspapers Ltd* [2001] 1 I.R.I. Whilst other jurisdictions have accepted the concept of such guidelines that concept has been rejected in this jurisdiction. Apart from any other considerations there would appear to be insuperable difficulties for any judge to assemble the appropriate body of information on which to base such guidelines."

Murphy J. went on to observe that 'a special status attaches to an award for damages for defamation as determined by a jury.' He referred to *Barrett v. Independent Newspapers* [1986] I.R. 13 where, said Murphy J., Finlay C.J. had pointed out that:

> "[t]he assessment by a jury of damages in a defamation action had an unusual and emphatic sanctity and an appellate court should be slow to interfere with such an assessment. However, the discretion of the jury in the assessment of damages was not limitless and the damages awarded must be fair and reasonable having regard to all of the circumstances and must not be disproportionate to the injuries suffered by the plaintiff and a necessity to vindicate the plaintiff in the eyes of the public."

(In fact, this is a verbation extract from the headnote to the report of *DeRossa*. Part of the quoted passage appears, in direct speech, in Finlay C.J.'s judgment in *Barrett*.)

In the instant case Barr J. had reminded the jury that 'the accused has a damaged character. He has pleaded guilty to a serious crime of violence in the course of an affray involving a number of people in which he has pleaded guilty to causing substantial personal injury to a member of An Garda Síochána. That is a serious offence.' Barr J. had gone on to instruct the jury that, if it found the plaintiff had been libelled he was 'entitled to damages but not to the extent which would be justified if he had himself a blameless character.' Barr J. had emphasised that there was 'no doubt about it that this case is not one where large damages are merited.'

On appeal, the defendant drew attention to the fact that any imputation that the plaintiff was a sex offender had been corrected by a notice or clarification published in its newspaper at the earliest practicable date. Murphy J. observed that:

> "[a]t the end of the day, this Court is left with the difficult task of determining whether an award of £60,000, for what was a fairly serious libel of a young man, albeit a young man with a somewhat flawed reputation, was disproportionate to the injury done to him in all the circumstances of the case ...
>
> There is no doubt that the sum of £60,000 awarded by the jury was a substantial sum. It may well be at the higher, or even the highest, of the figures in the range which would be appropriate to compensate a plaintiff for the wrongdoing which he has suffered. However I am not satisfied that the figure awarded is so disproportionate to the injury sustained by the plaintiff ... that it can or should be set aside by the court."

It is frankly difficult to see any movement away from *O'Brien* in Murphy J.'s analysis. Murphy J. went so far as to proffer a further, somewhat unconvincing rationale for rejecting the giving of guidelines to juries. It is scarcely the case that 'insuperable difficulties' would confront the trial judge seeking to assemble the appropriate information. Very few actions go to verdict, fewer still are appealed. Once this information had been assembled, it could be used and updated in later cases. One awaits the resolution of the *De Rossa* case at Strasbourg with some anticipation.

Evidence as to reputation and character   In *Hill v. Cork Examiner Publications Ltd*, Supreme Court, November 14, 2001, the issue of the scope of proof of bad reputation in defamation proceedings fell for consideration. The plaintiff was a prisoner serving a five year sentence (subject to review after eighteen months) for occasioning actual bodily harm contrary to section 47 of the Offences Against the Person Act 1861. This was his first prison sentence though he had other convictions. The defendant's newspaper published an article on the prison where the plaintiff was confined, including a photograph of his cell, under the headline which gave the impression that he was a sexual offender. The defendant in its defence asserted that the plaintiff was a man of worthless reputation, having been convicted of a number of offences. The jury found in the plaintiff's favour and awarded him £60,000 damages for the defamation.

The defendant's appeal to the Supreme Court took issue with the trial judge, Barr J.'s rulings as to the permissible scope of evidence of bad reputation that the defendant might adduce.

Prior to the trial, the defendant's solicitors gave notice to the plaintiff's solicitors of its intention to give evidence of his earlier convictions in mitigation of damages. As a result of that notice, a debate took place between counsel and certain rulings were made by Barr J. at the outset of the trial. It was accepted by both counsel that the *locus classicus* of Cave J.'s judgment in *Scott v. Samson* (1882) 8 Q.B.D. 491 correctly stated the law in relation to general evidence of bad reputation:

> "Damage, however, which he (the plaintiff) has sustained must depend almost entirely on the estimation in which he was previously held. He complained of an injury to his reputation and seeks to recover damage for that injury; and it seems most material that the jury who have to award those damages should know, if the fact is so, that he is man of no reputation. To deny this would, as is observed in Starkie, *Evidence*, be to decide that a man of the worst character is entitled to the same measure of damages with one of unsullied and unblemished reputation."

In the course of his discussion with counsel Barr J. summarised the position by stating that the plaintiff:

"has an admitted bad reputation relating to the offence of which he was serving a sentence at the time. That is a serious crime which the jury will be told about but I do not think it would be proper to go into the minutiae of that particular crime. It would mean investigating the entire of it and it would be bringing the jury down a *cul de sac* which would not really in the end help them very much. At the end of the day they know he has been convicted of a serious crime, that is all they require to know. I will certainly exclude all attempts to investigate the details of that particular crime."

When counsel on behalf of the defendant indicated his intention to put to the plaintiff the publicity which the offence had attracted, Barr J. commented as follows:

"You will be treading on delicate grounds but the way you put it just now.... it seemed to me to be acceptable but you are treading on delicate ground. [T]here is the risk of having the jury discharged it may be so it is only right to indicate that to you."

Barr J. went on to state expressly that the publicity attracted by the offence would have been well publicised in Cork and evidence of it would be unobjectionable. He observed that 'widespread publicity is fair enough because that relates to his reputation.'

In the Supreme Court Murphy J. (Murray and McGuinness JJ. concurring) was of the view that Barr J. in observations:

"made, as they were, at the commencement of the case and not directed to any specific application to tender any particular evidence or to rule on any question put in cross-examination [were] very helpful and entirely unobjectionable. Furthermore, the warning that a particular line of cross-examination might lead to the jury being discharged was not, in the context, a threat by the judge but a fair reminder by him to counsel of the delicate balance which the law requires to be preserved between giving evidence of general reputation and excluding the matters of specific misconduct (other than criminal convictions)."

Murphy J. observed that the problem had always been to distinguish between evidence of general bad reputation and evidence of specific conduct on which such reputation might be based. He referred to Lord Denning's statement in *Plato Films Ltd v. Speidel* [1961] 1 A.C. 1090 to the effect that:

"[i]n order to arrive at a man's character and reputation we should call those who know him and have had dealings with him; for they provide the only sound foundation on which to build... If it is evidence of good character, a witness of good standing is called, such as a clergyman, a schoolmaster, or an employer and is asked such questions as these: 'What are you? How long have you known him? Have you known him well? Have you had an opportunity of observing his conduct? What character has he borne during the time for honesty, morality or loyalty (according to the nature of the case)?' As far as you know, has he deserved that character? .... If it is evidence of bad character which is given (such as that of a man who is a reputed thief or a woman is a common prostitute), the evidence often takes the form of a police officer who knows him being called and saying: 'I know the defendant and have know him (or her) for some time. He is a well known pickpocket' or 'She is a common prostitute' or as the case may be."

Murphy J. endorsed the traditional approach, stating that:

"[i]n general, specific acts of misconduct are not admissible as proof of general bad reputation. Perhaps the primary reason for that restriction is that the allowance of such evidence would lead to innumerable subsidiary trials of collateral issues concerning the reputation of the plaintiff. It is clear that evidence of specific previous convictions is an exception to the rule. One justification for that exception is the clarity and certainty with which a conviction can be established.

It has to be said that the law on this subject is less than satisfactory. A pragmatic consideration, such as concern about lengthening trials with collateral matters, does not address the central issues of principle that arise. Moreover, the rationale – again a pragmatic one – for adducing evidence of previous convictions based on the clarity and certainty of such evidence is not totally convincing. If criminal convictions may be admitted, why not judgments in civil cases which involve findings of moral obloquy?

From the standpoint of principle, if it were possible without undue practical difficulty to adduce evidence of specific acts of the plaintiff which establish that he or she is a person of bad character, would it be just that this evidence should be admissible? A strong argument can be made that it would. There is an important difference between reputation and character. One person may have an excellent, but undeserved, reputation; another may be a person of excellent character but the victim of prejudice and thus of poor reputation. If a plaintiff's reputation is undeserved, it seems wrong that the defendant should be obliged to have to compensate that plaintiff for damage to it."

In Britain the Neill Committee, in its *Report on Practice and Procedure in Defamation*, published in 1991, proposed that it should be possible for defendants to rely on specific instances of misconduct on the plaintiff's part, for the purpose of mitigating damages rather than by way of defence, provided that the allegations related to the same sector of the plaintiff's life – for example business probity or conduct towards his or her family – and provided also that proper and specific notice was given in the defence. The Committee made this proposal because it considered that:

> "there is often a feeling of injustice or resentment on the part of the defendants when plaintiffs recover large damages from a jury which they would probably have been disinclined to award if they had been permitted to have a fuller picture of the plaintiff's conduct. It has been said that defendants would be less inclined to go for wide-ranging pleas of justification, sometimes based upon attaching imaginative or ingenious meanings to the words complained of, if it were open to them to bring the disreputable behaviour of the plaintiff before the court purely for the purpose of reducing damages."

The Defamation Bill 1995 included a provision on the issues recommended by the Neill Committee but did not survive the Committee stage in the House of Commons, being stigmatised as a "muckrakers' charter": *Winfield & Jolowicz on Tort* (15th ed, by W.V.H. Rogers, Sweet & Maxwell, London, 1998), 420. Plato thus continues to represent the law, though the English Court of Appeal in *Burstein v. Times Newspapers Ltd* [2001] W.L.R. 579 considered that it did "not exclude evidence of directly relevant background context."

Discharge of jury   In *Mangan v. Independent Newspapers Ltd*, Supreme Court, July 25, 2001, the Court addressed the circumstances in which a trial judge should discharge a jury in defamation proceedings.

The plaintiff had sued for libel. One of the defences was fair comment. Counsel for the defendants, in his address to the jury before going into evidence, had indicated what his view of the law of fair comment was. He had supported that view of the law by citing extracts from *Gatley on Libel* (described by Keane C.J. as 'the leading text book on the subject in these islands'). He also cited passages from the Consultation Paper published in 1991 by the Law Reform Commission dealing with the Civil Law of Defamation. The trial judge, Barr J, discharged the jury. He had:

> "no difficulty in accepting [the] submission that counsel for the defendant ought not to have selected text book extracts to the jury as an explanation for relevant legal principles. This is an undesirable way of explaining the law to a lay jury. Another possible objection is it opens up the possibility that the selected extracts that are relied upon may be incomplete and may therefore present an inaccurate picture. Subject to the right to quote from judgments or statutory provisions, the appropriate course for counsel in opening his client's case is to explain the law in

brief simple terms to the jury in his own words. In closing his case counsel may elaborate on the law in the light of the actual evidence. In defamation actions it seems to me that it may be unhelpful and potentially misleading for counsel in the course of the opening defence, or indeed the plaintiff's case, to dwell at length on difficult matters of law such as those which arise in connection with the defence of fair comment until the relevant evidence is before the jury.

However, the real difficulty, as I perceive it, as to matters that have emerged in this case is that counsel has opened the law relating to the defence of fair comment at length in advance of his client's evidence, and he has also criticized [counsel for the plaintiff] for not having done so in opening the case originally, thus implying that [counsel for the plaintiff]'s opening was unfair and misleading. For the reasons I have stated I do not accept that criticism. What emerges therefore is a situation that cannot be adequately put right and for that reason I am obliged to accede to [counsel for the plaintiff]'s application."

Barr J. awarded costs to the plaintiff.

The defendant's appeal to the Supreme Court was in form against the award of costs but in substance against Barr J.'s order discharging the jury.

Keane C.J. (Denham, Murphy, McGuinness and Geoghegan JJ. concurring) acknowledged that Barr J. was a very experienced trial judge, who had considerable relevant experience in his practice at the Bar. Moreover, considerable weight should be afforded to the exercise of discretion by a High Court judge. Nonetheless, the interests of justice required the Supreme Court to set aside the order for costs. The Chief Justice considered that the matter had been one that was to address, either at that stage or at a later stage, and when Barr J. indicated that there were difficulties in so doing, it was not clear what those difficulties were:

> "It would not be appropriate, having heard the submissions from counsel, to indulge in an elaborate argument and counter argument, hearing counsel fully as to these sometimes quite difficult aspects of the law of defamation and then make a ruling on them at that stage of the case. What would have been quite appropriate, and what was entirely within his power to do, was to remind the jury that they had heard a statement of the law advanced by counsel for the defendants, which counsel for the plaintiff were contending was incomplete and somewhat partial and that they should bear in mind the criticism advanced by counsel for the plaintiff when they proceeded to hear the evidence...."

In the circumstances, Barr J.'s decision to discharge the jury at that stage had been a disproportionate response to this situation:

"The discharge of a jury is a very serious matter in any case. It is a course which should not be undertaken unless there is no other way of dealing with a particular situation, because at the end of the day it is beneficial to neither of the parties in the case, it adds to the expense of the case, it prolongs its ultimate resolution and it is not conducive to the administration of justice."

Interrogatories   In the Chapter on Practice and Procedure, above, 475, we consider McCracken J's. decision in *Crofter Properties Ltd. v. Genport*, High Court, 30 November 2001.

Discovery   In the Evidence Chapter, above, 269, Declan McGrath analyses the Supreme Court decision in *McDonald v. Radio Telefís Eireann*, [2001] 1 I.R. 355.

Costs   In *Cooper-Flynn v. Radio Telefis Éireann*, High Court, April 5, 2001, Morris P. addressed the issue of costs in the context of defamation proceedings. The case, which attracted considerable public attention, involved an action for libel taken by the plaintiff, a Dáil Deputy, against the defendant, in which she claimed to have been libelled in a number of television and radio broadcasts in which it was said that she induced the third named defendant, Mr Howard, to evade his lawful obligations to pay tax by not availing himself of the tax amnesty. It was also alleged that she had induced others to make a particular investment in respect of which she had pointed to them the advantages which the investment had for tax evasion.

The plaintiff denied ever having spoken to Mr Howard and in particular denied ever making the statements which were attributed to her. Moreover she denied ever advising or encouraging other persons to make the investment for the purpose of evading tax.

The jury found that the defendants had not proved that the plaintiff had induced Mr Howard to evade his lawful obligation to pay tax, but that they had proved that she had advised or encouraged other identified persons to evade tax. The jury awarded 'Nil' damages. Order 99, rule 1 of the Rules of the Superior Court 1986 provides:

"Subject to the provisions of the Acts and any other Statutes relating to costs and except as otherwise provided by these Rules .... the costs of every action, question or issue tried by a jury shall follow the event unless the court, for special cause to be mentioned in the Order, shall otherwise direct."

Counsel for the plaintiff made two submissions which, he said, constituted 'special cause' within the meaning of the Rule.

The first was that a fundamental issue that developed during the hearing was whether the plaintiff had spoken the words alleged to Mr Howard. He submitted that the plaintiff's success on this issue should be treated as a 'special cause'.

Morris P. referred to *Roache v. Newsgroup Newspapers Limited* [1998] E.M.L.R. 161, where the plaintiff in a defamation action had obtained a favourable verdict but only obtained the same award of damages as the amount lodged in court. An issue arose as to whether he had in fact obtained 'something of value' by the favourable verdict. This test had been applied by the English Court of Appeal in *Reynolds v. Times Newspapers* [1998] 3 All E.R. 961.

In the instant case the issue which Morris P. had to consider was whether, by obtaining a finding from the jury that she had not induced Mr Howard to evade paying his lawful taxes, the plaintiff had obtained something of value. Morris P. considered that she had not:

> "It is beyond doubt that if this were the only issue in the case it would be of immeasurable value but, coupled with the finding of the jury that she had in fact advices and encouraged other [identified] persons ... to evade tax, the finding is in my view valueless and accordingly does not constitute 'special cause' for the purpose of the Rule."

Counsel for the plaintiff referred, secondly, to a variety of ways in which he said the defendants' conduct had been such as to bring the case within the definition of 'special cause'. Among other instances, he pointed out to what he alleged was the failure of the reporter to check on the story before he broadcast it and the fact that the reporter had targeted the plaintiff by advertising in the local paper, circulating in the area in which she did business.

Morris P. was, however, unable to identify anything in any of these criticisms referred to by the counsel (which might or might not be correct), which were of such a grievous nature as could cause him to depart from the general rule:

> "In my view all of these matters would be of extreme relevance if in fact the jury were to address the issue of damages but in this way in and in this way only are they of relevance. I accordingly reject counsel's submissions that there should be a departure from the general rule."

On the other hand, counsel on behalf of the first and second named defendants argued that the resolution of the matters in contention in relation to Mr. Howard in favour of the plaintiff was of no significance so long as the plaintiff's character had suffered no material damage. He submitted that the 'cause of action' only arose when defamatory matter was published causing damage to the plaintiff's character. He submitted that, since it had been found by the jury that prior to the commencement of the proceedings, the plaintiff's character was flawed, the resolution of the first question in her favour is irrelevant. Morris P. considered this to be a correct statement of the legal principles involved. Accordingly Morris P. entered judgment for the defendants awarding them costs against the plaintiff.

CONSTITUTIONAL TORTS

Collateral infringement In *Sinnott v. Minister for Education* Supreme Court, July 12, 2001, the important question of the possibility of what might be called collateral infringements of constitutional rights fell for consideration. The first plaintiff, a young man, with a condition of autism, sought damages and several other orders against the State on the basis of an alleged breach by the State of its constitutional duty to provide for primary education in relation to his particular circumstances under Article 42.4. Barr J. awarded him damages and made orders of general and specific characters against the State. He also awarded £55,000 damages to the second plaintiff, the young man's mother, for breach of her constitutional rights, negligence and breach of duty, on the basis that, in failing to discharge its constitutional duty to her son, the State had deprived the second plaintiff of her constitutional rights pursuant to Articles 40.1, 40.3.1° and 2° and 41.2.1° and 41.2.2°, 42.1 and 2, 3 and 4 of the Constitution.

The Supreme Court reversed Barr J. with regard to both plaintiffs' claims. We analyse the Court's decision on the first plaintiff's claim above. Here we consider the fate of the second plaintiff's claim.

Keane C.J. regarded the claim as 'wholly unsustainable'. He began his analysis with a 'slippery slope' argument:

"If Mrs. Sinnott is to be entitled to damages, it would follow inexorably that every member of a family in the constitutional sense would also be entitled to damages where another member of the family suffered personal injuries affording him or her a cause of action in tort, unless the injury was so trivial that the resultant anxiety caused to the other family members was transient and of such little moment as to justify its being disregarded. In every other case, from a moderate whiplash injury to the most mass quadriplegia, since the constitutional rights of the plaintiff to his or her bodily integrity would unquestionably have been violated, the other family members would be entitled to damages if they could plausibly assert that they suffered some degree of anxiety as a result of the person's injuries. That is plainly not the law."

The Chief Justice did not accept that the actions of the Minister of Education constituted a violation of the second plaintiff's right to choose the form of education appropriate to her child under Article 42:

"That again is a wholly unsustainable proposition. The parental right of choice as to the nature of the education which their children will receive is, of course, guaranteed by Article 42, but that was not what was being frustrated by the actions of the defendants in this case. It was the right of the [first] plaintiff to a form of primary education appropriate to his needs which was being denied and for that, as a result of the decision of the High Court, he was fully and properly compensated. Had the appropriate facilities which the [first] plaintiff required been available for him free of charge in a single institution in the Cork area capable of meeting his special needs, Mrs. Sinnott would have had no complaint either in law or in fact and there is not the slightest reason to suppose that she would have instituted proceedings on her own behalf against the defendants."

Expressing 'complete agreement' with the Chief Justice's analysis of the second plaintiff's claim, Geoghegan J. stated:

"[T]he only constitutional breach in respect of which the learned trial judge gave a reasoned judgment was a breach of the first part of Article 42.4. But even if an issue did properly arise under Article 40.1 it would be an equality issue involving Jamie Sinnott. Again, there is nothing in the written judgment explaining any reasons why there might have been infringements of Article 40.3.1° and 2° but, if there had been, it could only have been the constitutional rights of Jamie which would have been infringed and not of his mother. There is no doubt that in an appropriate case the mother might be able to claim breaches of constitutional duties towards her under Articles 41.2.1° and 42.2.2° as these are constitutional provisions directly dealing with the family, but it does not seem to me that any of the behaviour of the State disapproved of by the learned trial judge constituted an attack on the family. For the same reason it would not seem to me that Article 42.1.2° and 3° are in any way relevant to this case. Indeed, quite apart from the fact that no parental rights were being attacked contrary to those articles, the provisions of the articles themselves could not be relevant to the issues of the case. I therefore fail to understand how she can be held to have a right of action for infringement of any alleged constitutional rights."

Denham J. dissented. She held, first, that the second plaintiff had been a victim of a violation of Article 40.1:

"There is no question but that the treatment of Jamie by the State would not be as an able bodied child. However, he was entitled to be held equal – to be provided with free primary education. Similarly Mrs. Sinnott was entitled to be held equal before the law as a parent and a mother.

Mrs. Sinnott had duties in relation to all of her children – including those duties related to education. In her role as mother of Jamie, Mrs. Sinnott was subjected to discrimination as between herself and another mother of a child with no handicap and as between herself as mother to her other children and as mother to Jamie. Distinctions of themselves would not be invalid; indeed they would be valid in that the education of Jamie would follow a different pattern. But an absence of provision of free primary education for Jamie, which the State has conceded breached Jamie's rights, also discriminated against Mrs. Sinnott's duty and role, as opposed to that of the mother of a child of average intelligence, in a manner that was unjust and invidious. Thus Mrs. Sinnott's rights were breached and she was discriminated against invidiously."

The State was also liable to the second plaintiff for an infringement of Article 41. Denham J. observed:

"The rights recognised by Article 41 are those of the family and they may be protected by a member of the unit. The member *qua* member of the unit also has rights which he or she may defend. The parents have a duty to the children of the family which they may defend.

Thus Mrs. Sinnott has rights as part of the unit of the family and duties as a parent within that unit. If there is a breach by the State of a right of one of the members of the unit, as, for example, here the child Jamie, then because of the nature of the right breached this may have an impact on the family as a unit and the parent in the family. The negative impact on the family and Mrs. Sinnott of the breach by the State was fully documented by [Barr J.]."

Turning to Article 42, Denham J. held that again the State had breached its duty to the second plaintiff:

"Mrs. Sinnott had a constitutional right as part of the family and as mother in relation to her son's education. As a parent she had rights and duties. The duty included the education of Jamie. This duty was breached in that she could not afford private education and needed to rely on the constitutional right to have free primary education provided. This was not done. Thus her rights as a parent were breached. Mrs. Sinnott's rights under Article 42, and especially under Article 42.4, were breached. Indeed, as the case law over the last sixty years shows, most cases relating to children's education are brought by parents – not children – as a breach of their rights as well as the children's rights."

Finally, Denham J. referred to the second plaintiff's claim in negligence. She referred to two decisions involving 'nervous shock' claims by family members: to *Mullally v. Bus Éireann* [1992] I.L.R.M 722 and *Kelly v. Hennessy* [1995] 3 I.R. 253. In *Kelly* she had stated:

> "I am satisfied that a person with a close proximate relationship to an injured person, such as the plaintiff, who, while not a participant in an accident, hears of it very soon after and who visits the injured person as soon as is practicable, and who is exposed to serious injuries of the primary victims in such a way as to cause a psychiatric illness, then she becomes a secondary victim to the accident. In reaching these determinations it is necessary to review the accident and immediate aftermath in an *ex post facto* way to test the situation."

In the instant case, '[t]he nexus between Jamie and Mrs. Sinnott could not be closer'; nor had there been any appeal against the findings of fact of injury to the second plaintiff. Whether the State could 'breach with impunity the constitutional rights of a person and thereby injure a person in close proximity' was an issue that need not be determined in light of the breach of the second plaintiff's constitutional rights. Accordingly Denham J. made no decision in the issue of duty of care.

Some aspects of these judgments call for comment. First, the problem with the majority's analysis is its reluctance to accept the possibility that an infringement to a constitutional right may be indirect and consequential but no less real or worthy of compensation on that account. The jurisprudence on the vindication of rights under the Irish Constitution is still at a relatively early stage of development. The courts have generally been confronted with claims made by the most obvious holders of those rights. Yet the Constitution must be read in an integrated way. So, for example, the guarantee of equality given by Article 40.1 clearly vindicates the right a direct victim of invidious discrimination; perhaps less clearly but no less surely does it protect a person who, as a result of the discrimination of that direct victim, also suffers invidious discrimination. This is recognised by Denham J. in her dissenting judgment.

Just as wrongful conduct can have ripple effects extending the wrongful actor's liability to several claimants, so also can conduct that directly and patently infringes one person's constitutional rights also infringe the rights of others. Whether it will do so depends on the proximity of relationship between the various claimants, the foreseeability of the knock-on-effects and the values underlying the Constitution.

Articles 40.1, 40.3, and 41 and 42 cannot properly be understood in isolation: the Supreme Court itself gives a graphic example of the truth of this incontrovertible proposition in its judgment in *North Western Health Board v. W. and W.*, on November 8, 2001, which we discuss above. Citizens are not isolated rights-carriers whose fate does not depend on each other: they are part of a complex network of relationships based on mutuality of aspiration and dependency. If the State denies a child the right to primary education, the impact of that denial on those who love and care for the child is so foreseeable as to be beyond serious argument. If that impact has measurable effects on a parent in terms of extra financial burdens, inhibition of the discharge of the parental function and physical or psychiatric injury, the idea that the parent should have no entitlement to compensation seems mistaken.

So far as Article 40.1 is concerned, such the parent in such circumstances is surely treated unequally. The ties of family loyalty, love and obligation – which derive precisely from the values which the Constitution recognises and seeks to encourage in Articles 41 and 42 – almost inevitably mean that denying a child the right to education will place an unequal burden on his or her parent or parents. To treat the parent as some kind of stranger or opportunist seeking to make a parasitic claim seems directly opposed to these values. Even the common law, in both its criminal and civil manifestations, has recognised that affirmative obligations, which do not arise as between strangers, derive from parenthood. *Glencar*, in all its stringency, is scarcely seeking to contradict that tradition. Yet in *Sinnott* the Court appears unable to discern the inter-connectedness of family relationships.

Claims by family members under Article 41 have admittedly been problematic in a number of respects. There has been a judicial tendency to regard Article 41 as protecting the family as an institution rather than the individual family members, even where the damage allegedly done to them has been in the context of their membership of the family. In *H. v. Murphy & Sons Ltd* [1987] I.R. 621, Costello J. made a separate distinction. Where members of a family suffered damage by reason of an intentional attack on the family or other members of the family by the State or its agents, either through legislative or executive action, the courts should compensate them but where the damage was the consequence of negligence there should be no remedy. In the instant case, the policy of the State surely fell within the former category. The damage suffered by the first plaintiff was not some unfortunate and unintended side-effect of the State's conduct: it was exactly what the State intended should be his fate.

H. v. Murphy is a precedent contradicting the majority's view that the second plaintiff's claim was not sustainable because she was an indirect victim of infringement of another's constitutional rights. It is clear from Costello J.'s analysis that an intentional infringement of the constitutional rights of one family member in circumstances where this damages the entitlement of another family member to a constitutionally protected relationship with the primary victim generates liability to that other person.

Clearly the Chief Justice had in mind cases such as *H. v. Murphy* when he presented the 'slippery slope' argument that, if Mrs. Sinnott's claim were recognised it would 'follow inexorably' that all members of the family of a person tortiously injured who themselves suffering 'some degree of anxiety' as a result of those injuries would be entitled to compensation. One wonders whether such a consequence follows so inevitably. In *H. v. Murphy*, the plaintiffs' claim was not simply that they had suffered anxiety but rather that their relationship with their father, who had sustained brain damage in the accident, had been seriously interfered with. If a parent is no longer capable of discharging the function of parenting, that is a serious, not a trivial, loss, both from his or her standpoint and the standpoint of the children.

Of course the courts must be vigilant to ensure that the range of liability, whether at common law or under the Constitution, does not get out of control. That is why the 'control device' of the duty of care in negligence limits the entitlement of victims, even those who have undoubtedly been foreseeably injured by a defendant's carelessness, to recover damages for their loss. This explains the restrictions on claims for 'nervous shock', where a 'secondary' victim suffers psychiatric or psychological damage as a result of injury negligently inflicted on the 'primary' victim: see McMahon & Binchy, *op. cit.*, Chapter 17. It is interesting to note that with claims of this type, even in common law jurisdictions taking a particularly restrictive approach, the courts are very sympathetic to cases taken by close family relations of the primary victim. (Perhaps O'Neill J. was unduly cautious when he observed in *J.F. v. The Minister for Health*, High Court, November 9, 2001, that, '... in the law of tort ... only the direct victim of the tortious act can sue save, of course, for the well known exceptions of cases of nervous shock and claims for loss of *consortium* and *servitium*.")

Another factor should be kept in mind. A plaintiff whose claim in negligence is defeated by reason of the fact that the duty of care is so circumscribed as to place the claim outside its remit is not permitted to succeed by going through the formalistic process of recasting the claim as one for compensation for infringement of a constitutional right. Costello P. made this clear in *W. v. Ireland (No. 2)* [1997] 2 I.R. 141. There is no need to fear, therefore, that the limitations on the duty of care consciously sculpted by the courts at common law can be sidestepped by framing the claim in constitutional terms. (Butler J.'s ruling in *Kelly v. Minister for Agriculture, Food and Forestry*, High Court, May 1, 2001, which we consider below, 646, appears to take a more broad approach; we argue that it should not really be treated as going so far.) A claim for compensation for infringement of constitutional rights is subject to its own limits, as *H v. Murphy* makes plain. in the instant case, Mrs Sinnott's claim was far from the trivial assertion that she suffered 'anxiety': it was that, as a foreseeable result of the direct and knowing violation of the State's constitutional duty to her son, the State had also interfered with her constitutional rights to equality and her right as a member of a constitutionally protected family to discharge her constitutional duty to her son, without undue burden being placed upon her.

Claim for damages resulting from unconstitutional legislation   In *An Blascaod Mór Teoranta v. Commissioners for Public Works* [2001] 1 I.L.R.M.

423, Budd J. addressed the question whether the victims of the enactment of legislation which violated Article 40.1 of the Constitution were entitled to damages for the infringement of their right to equal treatment. The legislation in question – An Blascaod Mór National Historical Parks Act 1989 – had created two categories of landowner in relation to land on the Great Blasket, the distinction being based on whether the owner had been an ordinary resident on the island before November 17, 1953 or a relative of such a resident. Those who did not fall within this category were treated less beneficially than those who did. The Supreme Court ([2000] 1 I.L.R.M. 401) held that this distinction, based in essence on pedigree, had 'no place (outside the law of succession) in a democratic society committed to the principle of equality' and that it violated Article 40.1. The case returned to the High Court on the damages issue.

Budd J. held that damages should not be awarded for misfeasance in public office: see above, 627. As to whether damages could, or in the circumstances should, be awarded against the State for the effects of the enactment of the unconstitutional legislation, the issue was a novel one.

Analogies with the position under European Community and Union law, pressed by the plaintiffs, did not commend themselves to Budd J: the Irish Constitution had no specific provision comparable to Article 215 of the EC Treaty.

Eligibility for compensation for infringement of constitutional rights under the principles stated in *Meskell v. Coras Iompair Éireann* [1973] I.R. 121 was not based on strict liability:

> "The nature of the relationship between a citizen and the State is complicated by the obligations of the State which, through its organs or agents, must engage in such activities as policing, imprisoning and legislating. In the course of making laws, the legislature frequently has to take into account conflicting individual rights and the exigencies of the common good within a process involving balancing and adjusting the scope of rights. There is therefore little justification for a regime of strict liability for infringement of a constitutional right where such rights are competing and in conflict. In such circumstances *ubi ius, ibi remedium* is too simple a formula and strict liability would in many cases be too low and easy a threshold to reach."

The plaintiffs argued that there had been culpable negligence on the part of the Minister in either failing to seek, or in ignoring, legal opinion in respect of the constitutional validity of the pedigree classification. While Budd J. was 'sympathetic to the plaintiffs' suggestions on this aspect', he could not hold on balance that there had been 'adequate positive evidence of negligence'. Again he stressed the difficult balancing task facing the State where the protection of the right to private property had to be harmonized with the exigencies of the common good. If, according to *Pine Valley Developments*

Ltd v. Minister for the Environment [1987] I.R. 23 the Minister enjoyed a quasi-immunity in respect of administrative acts, it seemed to Budd J. that 'only in exceptional circumstances' could the State be made liable for damages in respect of invalid legislation, which involved such a balancing process.

Budd J. did not accept that Articles 15.4.2° and 34.3.2° should be interpreted as merely conferring on the courts the power to declare legislation invalid. He acknowledged that:

> "the courts have repeatedly given relief over and above a declaration of invalidity in appropriate cases in order to redress the actual disadvantage caused by the invalid law where it is practical to do so. For example, in *Murphy v. Attorney General* [1982] I.R. 241 the tax was repaid to the plaintiffs. Arguably this was necessary redress, permitted and justified as it was essential to give the court order practical effect by allowing relief to the plaintiff. In that case, it is also relevant that the loss was readily quantifiable and direct."

The central holding of Budd J.'s judgment needs to be quoted in full as it seems capable of a number of possible interpretations:

> "In the circumstances of this case, it seems to me that the plaintiffs have largely been vindicated by the declaration of invalidity of the 1989 Act. The informed public is aware of their stance and their vindication on the pronouncements of the Supreme Court as to the unjustified discrimination against them and the infringement of their property rights. While I do not accept that the Oireachtas has total immunity in respect of legislation, since the courts are specifically given the mandate to review legislation for repugnancy, nevertheless for public policy reasons, it seems to me that there must be considerable tolerance of the legislature particularly when it has to weigh in the balance conflicting rights.
>
> In the present case the legislature had to consider, among other matters, the preservation and demonstration of the culture of the Great Blasket ... Consideration had also to be given to the interests of those who had lived on the island and their relations as well as to the property rights of the existing landowners. It is clear that the legislature failed to strike a proper balance.
>
> There is no case in point to give a guideline where damage is alleged to flow from the actual invalid enactment. It seems to me that the appropriate redress in this type of case is a declaration of invalidity. In the circumstances of this case redress should not extend to damages. Having heard cursory evidence, I have concluded that there are a number of imponderables in respect of the heads of damage and that there is a lack of the type of direct causal link necessary. The plaintiffs have never been dispossessed of their property on the island and indeed the publicity

arising from the litigation may well have made the culture of the Great Blasket even more well known. Moreover it was argued on behalf of the plaintiffs that the literature emanating from the Blaskets was the monument to the culture of the Great Blasket and that the built structures were less important..

If the judiciary is to proceed resolutely but cautiously in relation to redress where a claim is brought in a recognised type of suit based on tort when an Act is found to be invalid, then the court should be all the more reticent where the claim is based on the effects of the actual enactment of an invalid Act.

My conclusion is therefore that under Articles 15.4.2° and 34.3.2° of the Constitution the court has jurisdiction to declare an Act invalid and to give necessary and appropriate redress only for such damage as is proved to have flowed directly from the effects of the invalidity without intervening imponderables and events."

Budd J. did, however, award costs to the plaintiffs in relation to the damages issue, bearing in mind, *inter alia*, that they could be excused for assuming that the Act had been aimed at them.

Budd J.'s analysis is open to at least three interpretations. The first is that, in cases where the legislature 'has to weigh in balance conflicting rights', an award of damages is not appropriate. This approach mirrors that adopted by the courts in relation to the duty of care, as is clear from decisions such as that of Blayney J. in *McMahon v. Ireland* [1988] I.L.R.M. 610 (analysed in *Annual Review of Irish Law 1987*, 322–4) and the Privy Council in *Yuen KunYeu v. Attorney General of Hong Kong* [1988] A.C. 175. It is understandable that similar 'public policy reasons' should affect the jurisprudence on damages for breaches of constitutional rights. In a case where the legislature introduced legislation which did not have this element of juggling with competing rights, the logic of this interpretation is that those affected by the legislation should not be denied a remedy in damages. Whether the juggling process may be considered to be present in relation to any particular statutory initiative is not easy to characterise, since in some respects all legislative strategies must take account, directly or indirectly, of potentially conflicting rights and interests.

The second interpretation of Budd J.'s analysis is that the task of awarding damages was too difficult since, it involved 'a number of imponderables' in relation to causation and quantification of damages; indeed, in part of the analysis, Budd J. indicates that the plaintiff's might have suffered no damage since they had 'largely been vindicated by the declaration of invalidity of the 1989 Act.' This rationale would not, of course, exclude the award of damages in other cases where the causal and damages issues were more ponderable.

The third interpretation is that judicial reticence might be appropriate in developing this novel area of law. While it is understandable that courts should be cautious lest they develop the law too radically in a way that does not withstand more considered reassessment, it seems hard on the victims of unconstitutional action by the State that they should not receive compensation on account of such a broad judicial concern. For further analysis of the decision, see Professor Yvonne Scannell's Chapter on Environmental Law, above, 248.

DAMAGES

Relationship between negligence and constitutional tort   In *Kelly v. Minister for Agriculture, Food and Forestry*, High Court, May 1, 2001, Butler J. took a broad view of the scope of the action for infringement of constitutional rights in circumstances where a duty of care in negligence might be considered inappropriate to impose. On a preliminary point of law, he held that a claim that the first defendant had been negligent in facilitating the plaintiff's prosecution for an offence of which he was completely innocent disclosed a good cause of action: see further above, 642. Butler J. went on to rule that, "[I]f it were the case that the alleged damage suffered by the plaintiff in this case could not be redressed in tort, he would have a cause of action for breach of his constitutional rights." On the case as pleaded, the plaintiff had, "at the very least, suffered an interference to his right to liberty". We suggest that this ruling should not be regarded as seeking to question Costello P.'s close reasoning in *W. v. Ireland (No. 2)* [1997] 2 I.R. 141, to the effect that where there are good reasons for not imposing a duty of care in negligence, a litigant can sidestep the barriers by reframing the claim in terms of infringement of a constitutional right. Butler J. was treating the plaintiff's claims for infringement of constitutional rights in isolation rather than in the specific context of a finding of the inappropriateness of imposing a duty of care, as was the position in *W. v. Ireland (No. 2)*.

Role of appellate court   An award of damages made in the High Court in tort litigation may be appealed by either party on the basis that the amount is too high or too low. What approach should the Supreme Court adopt in deciding whether to interfere with the High Court's award? In the Supreme Court decision of *Reddy v. Bates* [1983] I.R. 141, Griffin J. considered it:

> "well settled that this court cannot set aside the verdict of a jury on the grounds that the damages are excessive unless, adopting a view of the facts which is most favourable to the plaintiff, no reasonable proportion exists between the amount awarded and the circumstances of the case."

McCarthy J, dissenting, observed:

> "In order to warrant interference with an award of general damages, the disparity between the views of the individual members of this court

and each item of the award, however large it may be expressed in isolation, must be a significant percentage of that item of the award and, as a general rule, should not be less than 25 per cent. ... [T]his Court should be reluctant so to interfere and, in particular, ... it should avoid relatively petty paring from, or adding to, awards."

Reddy v. Bates was, of course, decided at a times when juries still determined personal injury awards in negligence litigation. Their role was abolished by the Courts Act 1988. In *Dunne v. Honeywell Controls Ltd,* Supreme Court, July 1, 1993 Blayney J. made it clear, however, that the approach of the courts to an appeal against the quantum of damages awarded remained the same as before1988 legislation with one 'slight qualification'. Because the findings of the High Court judge in regard to the injuries and the medical evidence were set out in detail in his or her judgment, the Supreme Court no longer had the task of adopting the view of the facts most favourable to the plaintiff.

In *Rossiter v. Dun Laoghaire Rathdown County Council* [2001] 3 I.R. 578, the issue was revisited. In 1997, the plaintiff, aged nine, received a serious injury to the right eye, resulting in almost total loss of vision. In the High Court Johnson J. awarded him £30,000 for loss of job opportunity and £90,000 general damages. The plaintiff appealed to the Supreme Court on the basis of the inadequacy of the £120,000 award.

Fennelly J. (Murphy and Geoghegan JJ. concurring) reasserted the "more or less unvarying test" of whether there was any reasonable proportionality between the High Court award and the amount that the Supreme Court would be inclined to give. He went on to observe:

"The test is one for application as a general principle, even if McCarthy J., in *Reddy v. Bates* .... suggested a possible rule of thumb, the need for at least a 25% discrepancy. That is no more than a highly pragmatic embodiment of his very proper counsel against '... relatively petty paring from or adding to awards.' In this respect, it seems to me that this Court is no longer bound by the special request due to a jury verdict. On the other hand, it is not a court of first instance. It should only interfere when it considers that there is an error in the award of damages which is so serious as to amount to an error of law. The test of proportionality seems to me to be an appropriate one, regardless – it need scarcely be said – of whether the complaint is one of excessive generosity or undue parsimony. It should, of course, be recalled that this test related only to the award of general damages, as explained by McCarthy J. in a further passage from the same judgment."

The plaintiff took issue with Johnson J.'s failure to break down the award into separate sums for past and future pain and suffering. In not doing so, his counsel alleged, Johnson J. failed to have sufficient regard to the several aspects of pain and suffering of the plaintiff up to the date of the trial. Fennelly J. responded by observing that this argument exemplified one of two of the schools of thought, which had debated the issue over many years. The contrary view, powerfully represented at one time, was that the division of an award – in particular, in an issue paper for a jury – tended to inflate awards. It seemed clear that it was in reaction to this second line of argument that the Supreme Court had introduced the corrective element described by Griffin J. in his judgment in *Reddy v. Bates* as follows:

> "In a case ... where damages are to be assessed under several headings, the jury, having added the various amounts awarded and having arrived at a total figure for damages, should consider the total sum (as should this Court on appeal) for the purpose of ascertaining whether the total sum is, in the circumstances of the case, fair compensation for the plaintiff for the injury suffered or whether it is out of all proportion to such circumstances."

Fennelly J. considered it:

> "not inappropriate to sound one note of warning about unduly literal reliance upon that passage. Griffin J. cited as the particular justification for having regard to the total sum the fact that 'notwithstanding the ravages of inflation, a very substantial income can be obtained from a large capital sum, while preserving the capital intact.' Circumstances change with the economic cycle. We now live, at least for a time, with comparatively stable prices and low interest rates. In reality, high interest rates usually mirror and compensate for the diminution in the value of money."

Fennelly J. explained that the reason for requiring the fact finder in the High Court to assess damages under separate headings was to facilitate the Supreme Court in the performance of its function as a court of appeal:

> "It is not designed to ensure that the Court awards to the plaintiff an adequate sum of damages under each heading. It has been pointed out in this Court that it is not required to compute damages under distinct headings when it assesses them on appeal. Where the damages are, as they are now, assessed by a judge sitting alone, it remains equally necessary that the Court be in a position to discern the findings of fact upon which damages have been assessed. It is, perhaps, not strictly necessary to assess them under separate heads, so long as the judge makes clear findings of fact, as the learned trial judge has done in this case. Nonetheless, it is likely, in many cases, to be of assistance to continue the practice. In deciding how to structure his assessment of

damages, it will be a matter for the trial judge to decide the extent to which separate heads are likely to be of assistance in the particular circumstances of the case."

One may wonder about the merits of the move away from assessment under seperate heads. If trial judges revert to awarding a global amount with no breakdown, this will complicate and lengthen the task of the Supreme Court in having to engage in some assessment of how much should have been awarded under each head. Griffin J.'s 'corrective element' in *Reddy v. Bates* cannot be grounded in reason, since it elevates judicial intuition over mathematical consistency: see McMahon & Binchy, *op. cit.*, para. 44–78. Dispensing with assessment under seperate heads would exacerbate that tendency.

Fennelly J. went on to consider the question of how to characterise the plaintiff's loss of job opportunities. A vocational rehabilitation consultant who had produced a report and given evidence on this aspect of the claim the plaintiff would suffer a reduction in options both in terms of the employment of which he would be capable, and the locations at which he could safely work. In particular, she would rule out working at an unprotected height, which would exclude many construction-related jobs. He could not operate forklifts or even work in areas where there was moving machinery.

Fennelly J. characterised the loss of job opportunities, which he described as 'the effects on future employment prospects', as falling within the category of general damages. In the instant case it was not possible, in view of the plaintiff's young age, to make a proper actuarial assessment of his likely loss of earnings. It had not been contested that the allocation of £90,000 for all of the plaintiff's pain and suffering, past and to come, 'was, though proper, on the lower side of what would have been permissible'. So far as guidance could be derived from earlier case law, Fennelly J. was persuaded that it was 'significantly less than what should be allowed in respect of the heading of pain and suffering alone'. As to the award of £30,000 for loss of job opportunities, Fennelly J. thought that there was 'a very real danger that [it] would, as a once and for all single payment, represent inadequate compensation for the plaintiff's lifetime disadvantages in employment.'

Adopting a global approach, Fennelly J. concluded that the award should be increased from £120,000 to £150,000, on the basis that it did not bear a reasonable proportion to the compensation to which the plaintiff was entitled.

Actuarial evidence In *McEneaney v. Monaghan County Council*, High Court, July 26, 2001, O'Sullivan J. gave an important judgment on how the discount rate should be calculated for the purposes of actuarial evidence. In determining a plaintiff's future loss, account must be taken of the estimated duration of that loss and the relevant interest rate used to translate the expected loss into a capital sum equivalent. The real rate of interest – that is, the nominal rate less the rate of inflation – has traditionally been taken by actuaries calculating these sums in Ireland at 4%. This was considered to be an appropriate value for the return which a prudent person might expect after inflation on a relatively risk-free portfolio in the early 1980s.

In *McEneaney*, where the plaintiff had a life expectancy of 39 years, O'Sullivan J. described as 'compelling' Lord Lloyd of Berwick's reasoning in *Wells v. Wells* [1998] 3 All E.R. 481, to the following effect:

> "The ordinary investor may be presumed to have enough to live on. He can meet his day-to-day requirements. If the equity market suffers a catastrophic fall, as it did in 1972, he has no immediate need to sell. He can abide his time, and wait until the equity market eventually recovers.
>
> The plaintiffs are not in the same happy position. They are not ordinary investors in the sense that they can wait for long term recovery, remembering that it was not until 1989 that equity prices regained their old pre-1972 level in real terms. For they need the income, and a portion of their capital, every year to meet their current cost of care. A plaintiff who invested the whole of his award in equities in 1972 would have found that their real value had fallen by 41% in 1973 and by a further 62% in 1974. The real value of the income on his equities had also fallen.
>
> So it does not follow that a prudent investment for the ordinary investor is a prudent investment for the plaintiffs. Equities may well prove the best long-term investment. But their volatility over the short term creates a serious risk. This risk was well understood by the experts. Indeed [one of them] conceded that if you are investing so as to meet a plaintiff's needs over a period of five years, or even ten years, it would be foolish to invest in equities. But that concession, properly made as it was on the evidence, is fatal to the defendant's case. For, as [another expert] pointed out in reply, every long period starts with a short period. If there is a substantial fall in equities in the first five or ten years, during which the plaintiff will have had to call on part of his capital to meet his needs, and will have had to realise that part of his capital in a depressed market, the depleted fund may never recover.
>
> While therefore I agree with the Court of Appeal that, in calculating the lump sum, courts are entitled to assume that the plaintiff will behave prudently, I do not agree that what is prudent for the ordinary investor is necessarily prudent for the plaintiff. Indeed the opposite may be the case. What the prudent plaintiff needs is an investment which will bring him the income he requires without the risks inherent in the equity market; which brings us back to the ILGS."

In *McEneaney*, O'Sullivan J., adopting this analysis, noted that, on the evidence there was no equivalent in Ireland of the ILGS. Accordingly he had to approach the assessment of the sum required to produce the appropriate annuity for the plaintiff over the following 39 years on the basis that it would yield 'a reasonably secure and reliable stream of annual funding (comprising income and capital)' and, to that end, that the investment of the award should be 'as risk free as reasonably possible in the absence of an equivalent of the ILGS in the UK.'

One economist had given to the effect that the actuarial discount should be 2%. Another had suggested a figure of 2.5% accepting a prudent element of equities investment. O'Sullivan J. considered that the appropriate rate for general calculation purposes should be 2.5%.

There had been uncontroverted evidence that the annual average rate of increase of medical and other costs was nearly 6% – 3% in excess of the general annual average rate of increase over the period since *Cooke v. Walsh* [1984] I.L.R.M. 208 had been decided. The expert evidence was to the effect that this was likely to continue to be the case. Accordingly, O'Sullivan J. proceeded on the basis of actuarial figures calculated on this premise.

Loss of earnings In *Pethe v. McDonagh*, Supreme Court, July 25, 2001, the Supreme Court affirmed O'Sullivan J.'s judgment in the High Court regarding the assessment of the plaintiff's loss of earnings. The plaintiff, the manager of a restaurant, with full responsibility for the running of the business, was injured in a traffic accident. His claim for loss of earnings raised an issue as to how they should be characterized. In the year 1995-6, he had received £11,500 as basic remuneration and over £8,000 by way of bonus. O'Sullivan J. rounded this total up to £20,000. The question arose as to whether this sum should be considered to represent the plaintiff's net income after deduction of tax. O'Sullivan J. held that it should.

It was the plaintiff himself in his capacity as manager of the business who paid all of the staff including himself. He gave evidence that the payments he made were 'net'. As he explained it, he did not handle the tax situation of any of the employees. That was a matter for the employer. It was, he said, the employer's duty to pay the tax.

The employer was not called as a witness by either party. However, the income tax forms known as P60s for the relevant years in respect of the plaintiff's earnings, signed apparently by the employer, were put in evidence. One of these showed the plaintiff's total earnings at £5,902 and tax deducted therefrom at £660.44.

On appeal to the Supreme Court, Murphy J. (McGuinness and Geoghegan JJ. concurring) considered it:

> "impossible to reconcile the gross earnings shown in that document with the evidence of [the plaintiff] as to his earnings: the gross figure is less than one half what appears to be his basic salary in that year. The document does appear to confirm, however, that [the employer] recognised that it was his responsibility to deduct tax and remit it to the Revenue authorities."

Murphy J. went on to observe:

> "As the person who had the day to day control of the business, including the payment of wages, [the plaintiff]'s position may have been equivocal and one might have anticipated that some debate would arise between him and his employer as to how the tax affairs of the business would be or had been dealt with. It is surprising that the P60 itself did not give rise to such debate and again it would seem extraordinary that the payment to a young man of very limited experience of a net remuneration of some £20,000 – amounting to approximately £35,000 gross – did not provoke envy from and discussion with the employer. On the other hand it must be recognised that insofar as the remuneration consisted of a bonus this was obviously calculated in such a way as to increase the profits of the employer and perhaps enhance the value of his asset. Above all, it is clear that an employee is entitled to assume that tax has been deducted or provided for by his employer. In my view the learned trial judge was correct in his conclusion that the payments made to and received by [the plaintiff] were net of tax. It may well be that the arrangement between the employer and his employee would have been reviewed at some future date. Certainly I would have been reluctant to accept that the earnings for the years 1993/4, 1994/5 and 1995/6 would have provided an appropriate basis on which to calculate the earning potential of the plaintiff in the restaurant business over any extended period. However that did not arise in the present case. The loss of earnings was confined to the period up to the date of the hearing and some months thereafter. In my view the appeal insofar as it challenges the award in relation to earnings should be rejected."

In *McDonnell v. Walsh*, High Court, March 1, 2001, Barr J. compensated the plaintiff for the loss of a range of social welfare entitlements which she would sustain as a result of the fact that the earnings from the damages awarded in the litigation would exceed £77.50. These entitlements consisted of her weekly disability benefit of £47, £5 fuel allowance, her entitlement to a medical car and the first ten days of in-patient hospital treatment *per annum*. Taking into account the *Reddy v. Bates* [1983] I.R. 141 principles, Barr J. calculated the capital value of the plaintiff's loss at £60,000. The plaintiff, who had always suffered from mild mental disorder sufficiently serious to prevent her from being employed, sustained a severe post-traumatic stress disorder in the accident, which would require in-patient psychiatric treatment for about three weeks every year for the rest of her life.

Special damages   The Health (Amendment) Act 1986 was designed to prevent the costs of medical care resulting from road accidents falling on the State to the relief of negligent drivers and their insurance companies. Section

2(1) requires health boards 'notwithstanding anything in the Health Acts 1947 to 1985', to 'make a charge upon the person who received or is entitled to receive ... damages or compensation in respect of ... in-patient services or out-patient services.' In *Crilly v. T & J. Farrington Ltd* [2002] 1 I.L.R.M. 161, [2001] 3 I.R. 251, the Supreme Court was called on to determine the nature of this charge and the basis of its computation. The subsection is singularly laconic. The Court held that it was not permissible to trawl through the Oireachtas Debates to seek to discern the Ministerial intent.

Denham J., with whose analysis of the issue Murphy, Murray, McGuinness and Fennelly JJ. concurred, noted that section 2 was a mandatory provision. It did not set out a specific method for calculating the charge, which might be complex as it could relate not only to past services but also to services to be given in the future. What was established under the statute was 'the basic policy for a pragmatic scheme.'

Section 55 of the Health Act 1970 was not an appropriate model for making a charge under section 2 of the 1986 Act since section 55 related to 'changes approved of or directed by the Minister': this convinced a specific scheme under Ministerial approval whereas section 2 required the health board to make a charge 'notwithstanding anything in the Health Acts 1947 to 1985.' The charge it made would have to be a reasonable one; it 'must not be arbitrary, unjust or partial.'

Denham J. approved of the system of making a charge known as the ADC, or Average Daily Cost. This was calculated by taking the hospital's total annual expenditure and dividing it by the number of bed days occupied in the year. The charge made by a hospital in a given year usually lagged behind the actual cost in that year because it was calculated on the basis of the preceding year's audited accounts. It excluded capital and capital appreciation costs. Denham J. regarded this as a transparent system of establishing the charge, which was reasonable and consistent. The Act did not require the charge to cover precisely the services given on an individualized basis. In an area where averaging was the norm, it would not be reasonable to interpret the section as requiring an individualized calculation, which would involve great expense in relation to road accident victims who represented 0.78% of users of hospital services.

General damages for pain and suffering   In *McEneaney v. Monaghan County Council*, High Court, July 26, 2001, O'Sullivan J. addressed the question of how the £150,000 sum for general damages prescribed by the Supreme Court in *Sinnott v. Quinnsworth Ltd* [1984] I.L.R.M. 523, should translate into the social and economic realities of 2001. The plaintiff, who was born in December 1972, was involved in an accident in February 1994 in which he received very serious injuries, involving paraplegia and certain psychiatric sequelae.

An economist gave evidence on behalf of the plaintiff, to the effect that the equivalent figure for the year 2000 using the CPI would be around £236,000.

A somewhat higher figure was produced by reference to the GDB deflator, a second measure of inflation, which included a wider range of goods than those in CPI, as well as taking account of housing costs.

In relation to the standard of living to which O'Higgins C.J. had referred on *Sinnott v. Quinnsworth,* in the absence of any specific criterion, the economist suggested several ways in which these changes could be measured. If a representative household's standard of living was the appropriate comparator, the average household consumption could be considered. If it was income level per head, average industrial earnings could be used. If the overall wealth of society was to be measured, reference could be made to the GNP per head. The GNP per head had increased by a multiple of 3.3 from 1984 to 1999, consumption per head had increased by 3.24 and average industrial earnings by 1.93. O'Sullivan J. observed:

> "These figures suggest that broadly speaking wealth or living standards measured in this way increased by a factor of 3 over the intervening period. Having regard to the increase suggested by the inflation figure (at some £235,000) and these figures (at something approaching £600,000) and given the fact that the Supreme Court was indicating a sum *in the region* of £150,000 it seems to me that a reasonable equivalent to the £150,000 for general damages in *Sinnott v. Quinnsworth Ltd.* in today's money would be £300,000.
>
> If I err in this figure I consider I do so on the side of conservatism, especially if I compare the income which £150,000 would have yielded in June 1984 (at say 10%) with that which £300,000 would yield (at 4%) some seventeen years later: I make this observation because O'Higgins C.J. had particular regard to the income which an award would yield in *Sinnott v. Quinnsworth.*
>
> I cannot accept, however, that a paraplegic no matter how aware he is of his condition or how long his life expectancy (and granted that the plaintiff's condition is extremely distressing to himself and his family, that he will be prone to disappointment, lack of fulfilment, depression and most likely further physical ailments together with the enormous loss of amenity and enjoyment of life that applies to any paraplegic) is in the same category as a quadriplegic. In the circumstances of the present case I would assess general damages having regard to the very large sums that must be awarded to the plaintiff under the headings of ascertainable loss of £75,000 for pain and suffering to date and £125,000 for pain and suffering in the future being amounts in both cases very considerably less than I would have assessed had I been considering them on their own."

Another case involving a huge award is *In re the Hepatitis Compensation Tribunal Act 1997; R.L. v. The Minister for Health and Children,* High Court,

April 6, 2001. O'Neill J. awarded the applicant £300,000 general damages for pain and suffering resulting from having been infected with Hepatitis C some time before 1983. The evidence was that he was likely to develop decompensation liver disease within five to ten years. This would require a liver transplant; in due course, should he survive that long, his transplanted liver would fail. At the time of the judgment, the applicant was thirty five years old. For the previous decade he had suffered profound fatigue.

In *Pethe v. McDonagh*, Supreme Court, July 25, 2001, the Supreme Court upheld an award of £85,000 general damages to date where the plaintiff, a young adult, had received serious injuries in a traffic accident, including a fractured femur, which resulted in a shortening of his leg by nearly two centimetres and affected his gait. The plaintiff had been trapped in his car for four hours before being cut free. A clinical neuro psychologist testified that the accident had impinged on his personality, leaving him no energy for life. The trial judge, O"Sullivan J. had also awarded £30,000 general damages for the future.

Murphy J. (McGuinness and Geoghegan JJ. concurring) considered that, while the amount awarded for general damages to date might be regarded as generous, it was not excessive. He noted that 'it could well be said that the figure awarded for general damages into the future is on the modest side.' Taking it 'in the round', he was satisfied that the award should be let stand.

In *Dunne v. Power Supermarkets Ltd t/a Quinnsworth*, Supreme Court, October 5, 2001 (*ex tempore*), the Supreme Court affirmed an award by Quirke J. of general damages of £30,000 for pain and suffering to date and a similar sum for future pain and suffering. The accident had exacerbated 'what can best be described as quite a significant back problem arising out of a previous accident': *per* Keane C.J., Murphy and Hardiman JJ. concurring. Keane J. noted the difficulty confronting Quirke J. in having to be careful not to compensate the plaintiff for so much of the damages as were not the defendant's responsibility. It was quite clear that there was evidence on which Quirke J. was entitled to find that there had been a significant deterioration in the plaintiff's condition following the accident. The amounts awarded by Quirke J. were not so disproportionate as to be disturbed on appeal.

In *Molloy v. Farrell*, December 11, 2001, Finnegan J. awarded £60,000 for pain and suffering to trial and £70,000 for future pain and suffering where the plaintiff, aged 37 at the time of the accident in 1996 sustained injuries to his neck, back and ankle, which led in turn to pain in his legs also. The injuries were so severe and lasting as to render him capable of only light work. He had also suffered from a depressive illness for a period after the accident. His tolerance of walking and standing had been significantly reduced.

In *Newell v. Bus Éireann/Irish Bus*, Supreme Court, July 10, 2001, the Supreme Court raised from £25,000 to £50,000 an award of general damages for future pain and suffering where the plaintiff, who had inhaled a large amount of smoke when a school bus went on fire, developed a condition akin to asthma which required her to inhale steroids at relatively high dosages twice a day. The prognosis, which Fennelly J. described as 'necessarily more in nature of a conjecture than any real evaluation of probability', was that the chances of her recovering from the condition was 'rather less than fifty per cent.' Fennelly J. (Denham J. and Hardiman JJ. concurring) considered that:

> "[t]he correct approach must be to take this element into account as amounting to a very real possibility that the plaintiff will continue to suffer from this condition all her life. An obvious consequence is that she will, on that hypothesis, have to follow a heavy daily drugs programme. Apart from the inconvenience of that course, it cannot be entirely devoid of risk and side effects. The plaintiff has also lost a significant element of enjoyment of life in no longer being able to pursue athletic pursuits. Her innate enjoyment of animals has been curtailed. There is some restriction of her employment possibilities consequent on the need to avoid inappropriate environments."

Fennelly J.'s willingness to characterise damages for the restriction of employment possibilities as general damages is echoed in his judgment in *Rossiter v. Dun Laoghaire Rathdown County Council*, Supreme Court, October 31, 2001, considered above, 647.

In *Cawley v. Foley*, Supreme Court, December 20, 2001, the Supreme Court reduced to £12,500 from £25,000 an award by Kinlen J. for general damages where the plaintiff driver sustained an injury when she had to brake suddenly to avoid a sink that fell from the defendant's vehicle. The injury included a pain in her neck, chest, shoulder and head, which interfered with her ability to do housework and made it painful when dressing. In view of the fact that it was 'obvious from his judgment that [Kinlen J.] did not attach great significance to any of her injuries' and had 'more or less rejected the chest injury', Geoghegan J. (Denham and Fennelly JJ. concurring) considered it appropriate to reduce the award for general damages by a half.

One often hears criticism about the law's delay in relation to personal injury litigation. In *McDonnell v. Walsh*, High Court, March 1, 2001, Barr J. engaged in the unusual strategy of ordering a three months' adjournment of proceedings, which were being heard three and a half years after the accident. He took this step 'in the interest of justice to both parties' because, in the light of a substantial conflict regarding the plaintiff's prognosis given by two psychiatrists, Barr J. considered it 'premature to arrive at any firm conclusion as to her probable future.' This highlights the difficulty involved in requiring courts, when awarding damages, to make a once–and–for–all award.

The plaintiff in this case had always suffered from mild mental disorder. The accidents occasioned a severe post-traumatic stress disorder, resulting in her having bouts of depression with suicidal tendencies. The psychotropic medication which she was required to take had the effect of promoting appetite, which in turn led to her becoming seriously overweight. The plaintiff's psychiatric condition would require in-patient treatment for about three weeks every year for the rest of her life. When the trial resumed after the adjournment, Barr J. awarded general damages of £60,000 to date and £80,000 for the future.

In *Rothwell v. Motor Insurers Bureau of Ireland*, High Court, July 6, 2001, McCracken J. awarded £30,000 general damages without assessing past and future damages separately where the plaintiff had sustained a dislocation in his shoulder region which resulted in a noticeable deformity of his right shoulder ... with a prominent bulge between his collar bone and his shoulder' of a permanent character. We have already noted the difficulties that can attach to awarding global awards rather than making awards under seperate heads. If only from the standpoint of easing the task of the Supreme Court on appeal, we would suggest that the courts cleave to the latter approach.

In *McCourt v. Dan Dooley Ltd*, High Court, June 25, 2001, O'Donovan J. awarded the plaintiff £15,000 general damages to date and £25,000 for future damages where the plaintiff sustained soft tissue injuries to her neck and back which were likely to cause some problems in the future

Exemplary damages In *Vesey v. Bus Éireann/Irish Bus*, Supreme Court, November 13, 2001, the interesting question fell for consideration as to whether the principles which warrant the awarding of exemplary damages can have, as it were, a mirror image which would make it appropriate to make a radical reduction in an award far below the level of due compensation, or even no award at all. The plaintiff had been involved in a traffic accident in which liability had not been denied. In his evidence as to the quantum of injuries and his loss of earnings, he led the trial judge to conclude that he had lied persistently. The trial judge nonetheless awarded him £35,000 for loss of earnings and £30,000 for pain and suffering.

The Supreme Court reduced these amounts to £7,500 and £15,000, respectively. As to the reverse analogy with exemplary damages, Hardiman J. (Denham and McGuinness JJ. concurring) said that he had considered the submission of counsel for the defence:

> "that the damages to which the court considers the plaintiff is entitled should be reduced or extinguished as a mark of the court's disapproval of the sustained dishonesty which characterised the plaintiff's prosecution of his claim. I am not satisfied that there is a direct analogy with an award of exemplary damages to mark the court's disapproval of the conduct of a defendant. Such exemplary damages are a graft upon the plaintiff's entitlement to compensatory damages and an award of damages of the latter sort is a condition of the award of exemplary damages."

Even if, contrary to his view, there was an inherent power to reduce damages in circumstances such as the instant case, Hardiman J. considered that 'it would not be appropriate to exercise it without warning in the circumstances of the present case.' Presumably Hardiman J. was envisaging a warning by the trial judge: there is no principle that an appellate court, which is entitled and indeed required to develop legal principles, has to relieve the litigants in a case before them of the prospect of their being affected, to their surprise, by the articulation in their case of a new legal principle. There may be some scope for the adaptation of a principle of 'prospective overruling' of a statute in a constitutional context but this scarcely carries over to the context of developing common law principles, even radically.

Hardiman J. noted with interest the established jurisprudence in the United States of America under which a court has power to dismiss an action for flagrant bad faith. cf. Papachristos, 'Comment, Inherent Power Found, Rule 11 Lost: Taking a Shortcut to Impose Sanctions in *Chambers v. Nasco*' (1993) 59 Brooklyn L. Rev. 1225.This power is exercised in such cases as where a litigant engages in dishonest conduct, obstructs the discovery process or otherwise seeks to perpetrate a fraud on the court. Hardiman J. observed that:

> "[t]he American context is of course rather different from that prevailing here: in particular the American courts usually lack the power to penalise conduct of the relevant sort by an appropriate order as to costs. But there is plainly a point where dishonesty in the prosecution of a claim can amount to an abuse of the judicial process as well as an attempt to impose upon the other party."

More generally, it is worth recalling Costello J.'s decision in *Dorene Ltd. v. Suedes (Ireland) Ltd* [1981] I.R. 312, in relation to the tort of malicious institution of civil proceedings. cf. McMahon & Binchy, *op. cit.*, paras 36.19–36.32. The House of Lords in *Gregory v. Portsmouth City Council* [2000] 1 A.C. 419, took a far narrower approach. It is not clear whether *Dorene* represents a useful precedent in cases of an inflated, as opposed to substantively unmeritorious, claim.

In its *Report on Aggravated, Exemplary and Restitutionary Damages* (LRC 60-2000), the Law Reform Commission, following a reference to it by the Attorney General, makes detailed proposals for reform. Its central approach is that the law should best be developed by the courts and that legislation should not interfere unduly with this process. Nonetheless it puts forward a range of recommendations on specific aspects of the subject.

After a comprehensive analysis of the existing law and of the arguments for and against the award of exemplary damages, the Commission recommends that the present common law position, which does not exclude the availability of exemplary damages from claims for damages for breach of constitutional rights or for any torts, should be retained: para. 1.65. It considers that the further development of the law regarding the availability of exemplary damages 'should be left to the courts, informed by the circumstances of each case': para. 1.64.

The Commission formally recommends, in para. 1.66, that the availability of exemplary damages should not be extended to cases of breach of contract. The reason for this is that the Commission considers that an extension of exemplary damages to contract cases 'would be at odds with the traditional concept of contract law as having an exclusively private law character': para 1.55. The Commission does not, however, recommend that exemplary damages for breach of contract should be *prohibited* by legislation: 'rather, any possible development of the law on this matter should be left to the courts where it can be judged on a case by case basis': para. 1.56. One possible *via media* is to countenance an award of exemplary damages for breach of contract where the breach is accompanied by an 'actimable wrong'. The Supreme Court of Canada is currently enthused by this solution: cf. *Whiten v. Pilot Insurance Co.* (2002) 170 D.L.R. (4th) 280.

In terms of the philosophy of exemplary damages, the Commission recommends that 'both the punitive and deterrent purposes of an award of exemplary damages should be recognised, but [that] the primary purpose of an award of exemplary damages should be the deterrence of conduct similar to the defendant's in the future': para. 1.67.

The Commission does not recommend that legislation be enacted to give effect to these recommendations. It notes the concern that was expressed during the consultative process that a legislative provision stating the wide availability of exemplary damages might lead to a flood of claims. There are perhaps two difficulties with this approach. First, on principle, if the intended legal position is that there should indeed continue to be an entitlement to an award of exemplary damages in a wide range of actions, citizens should not be deprived of knowledge of this fact out of fear that they may resort to the courts to assert their rights. Secondly, as a matter of practical reality, it is not easy to predict what effect proposals by the Commission will have on the development of the law by the courts. The Law Reform Commission Act 1975 envisages proposals for statutory reform. The Commission is, of course, perfectly entitled to elect to leave the law develop in the courts rather than make recommendations for statutory reform: that strategy often will be the more prudent and just one. Undoubtedly the Commission can express its preference for a particular direction in which the law might develop; what is less clear is the basis on which the judiciary might heed the prescription. Obviously the considered views of the Commission are deserving of the greatest respect from the courts. Under the present statutory position, however, there is a certain lack of clarity as to the nexus between the Commission's expressed preference for particular judicial developments and the execution of that preferred option by the courts. A purposive interpretation of the functions of the Commission under the legislation would allow, though not coerce, the courts to be guided by the Commission's recommendations for judicial development of the law.

The Commission goes on to recommend (para. 1.75) that legislation be enacted to the effect that exemplary damages should be awarded only where it has been established that the conduct of the defendant in the commission of a tort or breach of a constitutional right has been high-handed, insolent, vindictful or exhibiting a gross disregard for the rights of the plaintiff. The idea here is that the definition of the misconduct necessary to ground exemplary damages should be strict enough to confine exemplary damages to 'the most exceptional of cases' (para. 1.73), while not being so restrictive as to exclude completely the award of exemplary damages in any particular tort.

The approach favoured by the Commission would synthesise the criteria for awarding exemplary damages for torts and breach of constitutional rights. This would mean that the distinctive analysis of the circumstances in which an award for exemplary damages only be made for breach of constitutional rights, adopted by the Supreme Court in *Conway v. Irish National Teachers Organisation* [1991] 2 I.R. 305, would no longer apply. Whether the legislature has competence to achieve such a merger is theoretically a matter of debate but the recent judicial discomfort with the implications of *Meskell v. Coras Iompair Éireann* [1973] I.R. 121 suggests that it is most unlikely that this debate will find sympathy in the courts.

The Commission recommends (para. 1.78) that the term 'exemplary damages' should be adopted as the most appropriate term to describe an award of damages with both a deterrent and a punitive effect. The courts would continue their practice of separately identifying awards of compensatory, exemplary, aggravated and restitutionary damages: para. 1.79.

Turning to the factors affecting an award of exemplary damages, the Commission departs from a provisional recommendation, in its Consultation Paper, that the means of the defendant should be taken into account only on the application of the defendant to the court that the award of exemplary damages would impose undue hardship. It acknowledges that such an approach would not allow a court to impose a particularly large award where there is a particularly wealthy defendant who would be unscathed by an award which would normally be considered large. For this reason, it proposes in para 2.010 of the Report, that the court should be permitted by to take into account the means of the defendant in any case where it is assessing exemplary damages. It comments (para. 2.009):

> "Given that the focus of exemplary damages is the behaviour of the defendant, we see it as one of the advantages of an exemplary damages award that it can be calibrated to impose effective deterrence on either a poor or (more often) a rich defendant. Commercial strategies, which factor in the possibility of compensation to those they harm, or of fixed criminal penalties, are best undermined by exemplary damages. As the court noted in one recent US case [*Johansen v. Combustion Engineering Inc* (1999) 17 F. 3d 1320] a large exemplary damages award maybe the

only means by which the court can 'attract the attention' of a large corporate defendant. At the other end of the spectrum, care should be taken not to make an award, which would be so severe as to bankrupt a less wealthy defendant. It is therefore important that the wealth of the defendant should be taken into account so that a sum can be assessed which is appropriate to that defendant's means."

The Commission does not consider that the means of the plaintiff should be taken into account.

The Commission makes a convincing critique of the view favoured by some of the judges in *McIntyre v. Lewis* [1991] 1 I.R. 121, that exemplary damages should have a proportionate relationship with the amount awarded by way of compensatory damages. The Commission acknowledges that this principle is 'a useful means of preventing exorbitant awards' but considers it nonetheless to be 'a somewhat arbitrary limitation': para. 2.016. Clearly there can be cases involving little or no compensatory damage or injury but a very high element of oppression or vindictiveness. The Commission therefore does not make any recommendation as to a strict rule of proportion between the two categories of damage. It goes on, however, to recommend (para. 2.019) 'a general principle that exemplary damages should bear some reasonable relation to compensatory damages, taking into account the circumstances of the case and the public interest in deterring and expressing condemnation of the wrongdoing involved.' One may hope that such prudence will not translate into a judicial rule–of–thumb, prescribing a specific multiple of compensatory damages: cf. *Thompson v. Commissioner or the Police of the Metropolis* [1997] 2 All E.R. 762 (C.A.). There are other ways of ensuring that principles of proportionality and respect for constitutional rights are respected: cf. *Tolstoy–Miloslavsky v. United Kingdom*, 20 E.H.R.R. 442 (1995), *Cooper Industries Inc. v. Leatherman Tool Group Inc.* (2001) 532 U.S. 424, Madden, 'Renegade Conduct and Punitive Damages in Tort' (2002) 53 S. Carolina L. Rev. 1175.

The Commission gives a most thorough analysis of the options of 'split recovery', whereby part of an award of exemplary damages is diverted to the Exchequer or some other worthy public body. It regards this approach as being 'both defensible in principle and workable in practice'; nonetheless it does not recommend its adoption in view of the tiny number of cases in which exemplary damages are at present awarded and their relatively modest quantum. It acknowledges the possibility that there may in the future be a need to apportion exemplary damages as between the plaintiff and funds representing the public interest: para. 2.064.

Turning to the survival of actions and fatal accidents litigation, the Commission recommends that section 8 of the Civil Liability Act 1961, by which exemplary damages are available against the estate of a deceased wrongdoer. It acknowledges that this can result in punishment of the defendant's heirs and notes that the English Law Commission, in its *Report on Aggravated,*

Exemplary and Restitutionary Damages (Law Com No 247, 1997), paras. 5.276-8, came to a different conclusion. The Commission considers that the deterrent impact of exemplary damages on persons other than the deceased wrongdoer tilts the argument in favour of retention of section 8. Another aspect of the deterrence principle encourages the Commission to recommend that section 7(2) should be amended to permit the recovery of exemplary damages where a cause of action survives for the benefit of the estate of a deceased person: the fact that the exemplary damages will accrue to the plaintiff's estate rather than the plaintiff will not weaken the deterrent effects: para. 2.104. Similarly, the Commission recommends that section 49 of the Act be amended to permit the award of exemplary damages in fatal accident litigation. It regards the present exclusion as 'a result more of historical accident than of principle': para. 2.110.

Turning to the relationship between the criminal and civil law, the Commission notes the range of judicial authority in Australia (*Gray v. Motor Accident Commission,* 158 A.L.R. 485, New Zealand (*W. v. W.* [1999] 2 N.Z.L.R. 1 Privy Council) and England (*Archer v. Brown* [1985] 1 Q.B. 401, *AB v. South West Water Services Ltd* [1993] 1 All E.R. 609) hostile to awarding exemplary damages where the defendant has been convicted in criminal proceedings. It does not, however, follow their example though it proposes (para. 3.15) that in such cases such an award should be limited to 'exceptional circumstances'. The main argument against making awards of exemplary damages in these cases is that it involves double punishment but, if this is the true objection, one should simply scrap the category of exemplary damages. If they are to be available save in cases where the defendant has been convicted before the court in civil proceedings gives judgment, untold indefensible anomalies will arise as between defendants related to the accidents of the court calendar.

The Commission is in favour of the retention of the concept of aggravated damages in Irish law. It is conscious of the role that aggravated damages can play as a lightning conductor, diverting courts from too ready a tendency to award exemplary damages.

Section 14 of the Civil Liability Act 1961 protects concurrent wrongdoers from having punitive damages for the sins of one of them imposed on the other. The Commission proposes that section 14 be amended to have a similar protection for the innocent party from an award of aggravated damages. It presents (para. 5.28) the perfectly logical argument that:

> "[d]espite their compensatory nature, aggravated damages are grounded in the particular misconduct of a defendant, which has aggravated the loss to the plaintiff. Where the aggravation of the loss has been caused by the concurrent tortfeasor only, the allocation of this part of the damages should reflect his."

One suspects that, in practice, such a refinement would be more trouble than it is worth. The process of awarding damages is a good deal more intuitive and pragmatic than it may appear. The concept of aggravated damages is not easy to sever from the generic process of assessing the amount of compensatory damages; there is no clear line between the wrong, its effect on the plaintiff and the exacerbating factors resulting from the manner in which the defendant (or his or her legal representatives) conducted the defence to the plaintiff's claim.

Turning to the survival of actions, the Commission recommends that section 8 of the 1961 Act, by which aggravated damages are available against the estate of the deceased wrongdoer, be retained (para 5.32). On the premise that section 7 excludes an award of aggravated damages in survivor actions because it excludes damages for pain and suffering and in view of its proposed definition of aggravated damages (para 5.25) in terms of compensation to the plaintiff for added hurt, distress or insult, the Commission recommends that it should not be amended: para 5.34. The Commission recommends that aggravated damages be available in wrongful death actions: para. 5.36.

The Commission's recommendations on restitutionary damages, which are against legislation at this point, is welcomed by Eoin O'Dell in the Restitution Chapter of *Annual Review of Irish Law 2000*, 383. See further O'Dell's analysis in *Annual Review of Irish Law 1998*, 557-66. The Commission proposes (para 6.50) that section 8 of the Civil Liability Act 1961, by which restitutionary damages are available against the estate of the deceased wrongdoer, should be retained without amendment. It considers (para 6.52) that section 7(2) should be amended to permit the recovery of restitutionary damages where a cause of action survives for the benefit of the estate of a deceased person. Finally, it recommends (para 6.54) that restitutionary damages should be available in wrongful death cases.

Transport

AVIATION

Aviation Regulation Act 2001   The Aviation Regulation Act 2001 (No. 1) makes provision for the establishment of a body to be known as The Commission for Aviation Regulation and defines its functions; amends the Air Navigation and Transport Act 1973, the Irish Aviation Authority Act 1993, the Freedom of Information Act 1997, the Air Navigation and Transport (Amendment) Act 1998; operative on such day or days as the Minister may by order appoint.

The Aviation Regulation Act 2001 (Establishment Day) Order, 2001 (S.I. No. 47) made under the Aviation Regulation Act, 2001 (No. 1) section 3; provides for the initiation of the functions conferred on the Commission for Aviation Regulation; operative on February 27, 2001.

MARITIME

Passenger boats   The Licensing of Passenger Boats (Exemption) Regulations 2001 (S.I. No. 172) made under the Merchant Shipping Act 1992 (No. 2) section 14A; specify the classes of vessels which are exempted from the requirement to have a passenger boat licensed under section 14 of the Merchant Shopping Act 1992 and became operative on December 31, 2001.

Mechanically propelled pleasure craft   The Merchant Shipping (Mechanically Propelled Pleasure Craft) (Safety) Regulations 2001 (S.I. No. 284) made under the Merchant Shipping Act 1992 (No. 2) section 34; provide for regulations governing the safe use of mechanically propelled pleasure craft and became operative on July 1, 2001.

Investigation of marine casualties   The Merchant Shipping (Investigation of Marine Casualties) Act 2000 (Prescribed Classes of Vessels) Regulations 2001 (S.I. No. 285) made under the Merchant Shipping Act 1992 (No. 2) sections 35(1) and 36(1); prescribe personal watercraft and fast power craft for the purposes of the careless and dangerous navigation or operation provisions in the Merchant Shipping (Investigation of Marine Casualties) Act 2000 (No. 14) and became operative on July 1, 2001.

Safety surveys   The European Communities (A System of Mandatory Surveys for the Safe Operation of Regular Ro-Ro Ferries and High-Speed Passenger Craft Services) Regulations 2001 (S.I. No. 405) made under the European Communities Act 1972 (No. 27), section 3; give effect to Directive 1999/35 on a system of mandatory surveys for the safe operation of regular ro-ro ferry and high-speed passenger craft services and became operative on September 4, 2001.

Fishing boats   The Merchant Shipping (Registry, Lettering and Numbering of Fishing Boats) (Amendment) Regulations, 2001 (S.I. No. 411 of 2001) made under the Merchant Shipping Act 1894 (57 & 58 Vict. c.60); defines the "registered length" of a fishing boat and became operative on September 5, 2001.

Carriage of goods and passengers by sea   The European Communities (Statistics in Respect of Carriage of Goods And Passengers by Sea) Regulations 2001 (S.I. No. 501 of 2001) made under the European Communities Act 1972 (No. 27) section 3; oblige specified maritime transport operators and port authorities to provide information relating to goods loaded onto or unloaded from seagoing vessels and passengers who embarked onto or disembarked from seagoing vessels, required by Council Directive 95/64/EC of December 8, 1995 on statistical returns in respect of carriage of goods and passengers by sea and became operative on November 6, 2001.

ROAD TRAFFIC

Licensing of drivers   The European Communities (Licensing of Drivers) Regulations 2001 (S.I. No. 168 of 2001) made under the European Communities Act 1972 (No. 27) section 3; provide for the introduction of a driver theory test in accordance with the requirements of Council Directive 91/439/EEC on driving licences and became operative in April 25, 2001.

The Road Traffic (Licensing of Drivers) (Amendment) Regulations, 2001 (S.I. No. 169 of 2001) made under the Road Traffic Act 1961 (No. 24) sections 5, 23(2), 31, 33, 34, 35, 38(7) and 42; provide that all applications for first provisional licences made on or after June 11, 2001 must be accompanied by a theory test certificate; provides further that in the case of an application for a first provisional licence made in the period of April 25 to June 10, 2001 for the granting of a first provisional licence for a period of 90 days, and following the submission of a theory test certificate, for the balance of the normal period in respect of which such a provisional licence would be granted, without further change; provide that where a first provisional licence is granted on foot of an application made on or after April 25, 2001, that an application for a driving licence must be accompanied by a theory test certificate where such certificate has not already been submitted to a licensing authority. They became operative on April 25, 2001.

Licence fees   The Road Traffic (Licensing Of Drivers) (Amendment) (No. 2) Regulations 2001 (S.I. No. 516 of 2001) made under the Road Traffic Act 1961 (No. 24) sections 5 and 42; amend the fee payable for a provisional licence, a duplicate provisional licence, or a duplicate driving licence; amend the fee payable in respect of the furnishing of information by a licensing authority in relation to a provisional licence or driving licence, and the fee payable for a certificate of competency; amend the Road Traffic (Licensing of Drivers) Regulations 1999 (S.I. No. 352). They became operative January 1, 2002.

Road Traffic Act 1994   The Road Traffic Act 1994 (Part Iii) (Amendment) Regulations 2001 (S.I. No. 173 of 2001) made under the Road Traffic Act 1994 (No. 7) sections 3, 18, 19 and 22; amend the certificate to be issued by the Medical Bureau of Road Safety under section 19 of the RTA 1994 to provide to the certification of the presence of a drug or drugs and became operative on May 1, 2001.

National car test   The Road Traffic (National Car Test) (No. 2) Regulations 2001 (S.I. No. 298 of 2001) made under the Road Traffic Act 1961 (No. 24) sections 5, 11, 18 and 123; fix fees to be paid for a certificate of suitability or a test certificate for small public service vehicles and became operative on July 1, 2001.

CONSUMER INFORMATION

The European Communities (Consumer Information on Fuel Economy And CO_2 Emissions of New Passenger Cars) Regulations 2001 (S.I. No. 339 of 2001) made under the European Communities Act 1972 (No. 27) section 3; give effect to Council Directive 1999/94/EEC relating to the availability of consumer information on fuel economy and CO_2 emissions in respect of the marketing of new passenger cars. They became operative on August 24, 2001.

Certificates of conformity   The European Communities (Passenger Car Entry into Service) Regulations 2001 (S.I. No. 373 of 2001) made under the European Communities Act 1972 (No. 27) section 3; require that applications for the registration of certain new vehicles must include a short form of a certificate of conformity with specified E.U. Directives; prohibit the fitting of replacement catalysers unless they have been type approved. They became operative on August 1, 2001, except for Article 9, relating to manufacturers' and distributors' obligation to produce certificates of conformity, which will be operative on December 1, 2001.

The European Communities (Mechanically Propelled Vehicle Entry Into Service) Regulations, 2001 (S.I. No. 374 of 2001) made under the European Communities Act 1972 (No. 27) section 3; require that applications for the registration of certain new vehicles must include a short form of a certificate of conformity with specified E.U. Directives and became operative on October 1, 2001.

Compulsory third-party insurance The European Communities (Road Traffic) (Compulsory Insurance) (Amendment) Regulations 2001 (S.I. No. 463 of 2001) made under the European Communities Act 1972 (No. 27), section 3; give effect to provisions of the First Motor Insurance Directive (72/166) that extend certain reciprocal compulsory third-party motor insurance arrangements and that abolish random frontier and internal insurance checks on vehicles from certain designated territories and became operative on October 12, 2001.

Subject Index